LAW OF OBLIGATIONS

AND LEGAL REMEDIES

Cavendish
Publishing
Limited

LAW OF OBLIGATIONS AND LEGAL REMEDIES

Geoffrey Samuel,
MA, LLB, PhD (Cantab), Dr (Maastricht)
Reader in Law
Lancaster University
and
Jac Rinkes, Dr (Maastricht)
Senior Lecturer in Law
University of Limburg
(The Netherlands)

Cavendish
Publishing
Limited

First published in Great Britain 1996 by Cavendish Publishing Limited, The Glass House, Wharton Street, London WC1X 9PX.

Telephone: 0171-278 8000 Facsimile: 0171-278 8080

British Library Cataloguing in Publication Data

Samuel, Geoffrey

Law of Obligations and Legal Remedies

I. Title

344.2062

ISBN 1-85941-130-4

Printed and bound in Great Britain

PREFACE

This book is, in some respects, a re-orientated version of our monograph *Contractual and non–contractual obligations in English law* published by Ars Aequi Libri in the Netherlands in 1992 (published also in a student edition: *The English law of obligations in comparative context*, 1991). However, it is much more than a second edition of this work in that it has been extensively rewritten for the English market so as to develop topics, themes and ideas only briefly touched upon in 1992. Thus, remedies and certain procedural questions have been expanded to fill almost half the book and there are more focused chapters on history, method, theory and harmonisation. Much of the discussion of Dutch law will appear, at a later date, in a continental edition which will not only cover the European law of obligations but will maintain the 1992 objective of describing English law from the position of a jurist trained in the continental tradition. Yet, that said, the book maintains a comparative flavour: the English law of obligations and remedies is placed, as far as possible, in the structural context of the codes and there are continual references to the question, and problems, concerning harmonisation of private law within the European Union. On a more practical note, the book is designed to complement the Cavendish *Sourcebook on Obligations & Legal Remedies* published last year.

We are most grateful to Cavendish Publishing not just for their enthusiasm in respect to our vision of the law of obligations, but for the cheerful and helpful way they go about publishing. It is most refreshing. Thanks also to those friends, colleagues and family who have, as usual, proved so supportive. The footnotes will go some way in locating the influences on this book, but they are not definitive and we are thus conscious that there may be unjust omissions.

Finally we are sensitive to the (justified) calls by one or two colleagues for a new set of standards in comparative law and in legal epistemology (theory of knowledge). It would be idle to claim that this book meets these standards, yet we hope that those who use the book as a means of gaining knowledge of the English law of obligations will be sympathetic to the aim of pushing outwards from a survey of the source material towards something beyond the idea that legal knowledge consists of learning rules and principles.

Geoffrey Samuel
Lancaster University

Jac Rinkes
Rijksuniversiteit Limburg
May 1996

PREFACE

CONTENTS

PART I: THE LAW OF ACTIONS

TABLE OF CASES

A

C

D

E

H

I

J

M

N

R

S

T

U

V

W

X

Y

TABLE OF STATUTES

TABLE OF STATUTORY INSTRUMENTS

TABLE OF EU DIRECTIVES

ABBREVIATIONS AND REFERENCES

1 GENERAL ABBREVIATIONS

AC	Appeal cases (Third Series)
AJCL	American Journal of Comparative Law
All ER	All England Law Reports (Butterworths & Co)
App Cas	Appeal Cases (Second Series)
BGB	Bürgerliches Gesetzbuch
C	Code of Justinian
CA	Court of Appeal
CC	Code civil (France)
Ch	Chancery Division (Third Series)
Ch D	Chancery Division (Second Series)
CJQ	Civil Justice Quarterly
CLJ	Cambridge Law Journal
CLP	Current Legal Problems
CLR	Commonwealth Law Reports
COM	Commission Documents (EU)
D	Digest of Justinian
DS	Dalloz–Sirey
EC	European Community
ECR	European Case Reports
EG	Estates Gazette
EP	European Parliament
ER	English Reports
EU	European Union
Fs	Festschrift
G	Institutes of Gaius
HL	House of Lords
HR	Hoge Raad
ICLQ	International and Comparative Law Quarterly

IECL	International Encyclopedia of Comparative Law
IJSL	International Journal for the Semiotics of Law
J	Institutes of Justinian
JCP	Jurisclasseur Périodique
JLH	Journal of Legal History
KB	King's Bench (Third Series)
LJCP	Law Journal Common Pleas
LJ Ex	Law Journal Exchequer
LJQB	Law Journal Queen's Bench
Ll Rep	Lloyd's List Law Reports
LQR	Law Quarterly Review
LRCP	Common Pleas Cases (First Series)
LREq	Equity Cases (First Series)
LREx	Exchequer Cases (First Series)
LRHL	English and Irish Appeals (First Series)
LRQB	Queen's Bench Cases (First Series)
LS	Legal Studies
LT	Times Law Reports
MJ	Maastricht Journal of European and Comparative Law
MLR	Modern Law Review
NBW	Nieuw Burgerlijk Wetboek (Netherlands Civil Code)
NCPC	(French) Nouveau Code de Procédure Civile
NILQ	Northern Ireland Legal Quarterly
NJ	Nederlandse Jurisprudentie (Netherlands Law Report)
NJW	Neue Juristische Wochenschrift (Germany)
NLJ	New Law Journal
OJ	Official Journal (EC)
OJLS	Oxford Journal of Legal Studies
P	Probate Division (Third Series)
PC	Privy Council
PL	Public Law
PUF	Presses Universitaires de France
QB	Queen's Bench (Third Series)

QBD	Queen's Bench (Second Series)
RabelsZ	Zeitschrift für ausländisches und internationales Privatrecht
RIDC	Revue Internationale de Droit Comparé
RSC	Rules of Supreme Court
SLR	Statute Law Review
WLR	Weekly Law Reports
ZEuP	Zeitschrift für Europäisches Privatrecht

2 REFERENCE ABBREVIATIONS

Atiyah, *Rise and Fall*
PS Atiyah, *The Rise and Fall of Freedom of Contract* (Oxford, 1979)

Baker
JH Baker, *An Introduction to English Legal History* (Butterworths, 3rd edn, 1990)

Gordley
J Gordley, *The Philosophical Origins of Modern Contract Doctrine* (Oxford, 1991)

Harris & Tallon
D Harris & D Tallon (eds), *Contract Law Today: Anglo-French Comparisons* (Oxford, 1989)

Hartkamp et al
AS Hartkamp et al (eds), *Towards a European Civil Code* (Ars Aequi Libri, 1994)

Jolowicz, *Roman Foundations*
HF Jolowicz, *Roman Foundations of Modern Law* (Oxford, 1957)

Lawson, *Remedies*
FH Lawson, *Remedies of English Law* (Butterworths, 2nd edn, 1980)

Legrand (ed)
P Legrand jr (Sous la direction de), *Common law: d'un siècle l'autre* (Les Éditions Yvon Blais inc, 1992)

Malaurie & Aynès
P Malaurie & L Aynès, *Cours de droit civil: Les obligations* (Cujas, 5th edn, 1994)

Milsom
SFC Milsom, *Historical Foundations of the Common Law* (Butterworths, 2nd edn, 1981)

Ourliac & de Malafosse
P Ourliac & J de Malafosse, *Histoire du droit privé 1/Les Obligations* (Presses Universitaires de France, 2nd edn, 1969)

Rudden
B Rudden (ed), *A Source-book on French Law* (Oxford, 3rd edn, 1991)

Samuel, *Foundations*
G Samuel, *The Foundations of Legal Reasoning* (Maklu, 1994)

Samuel, *Sourcebook*
G Samuel, *Sourcebook on Obligations & Legal Remedies* (Cavendish, 1995)

Stein, *Institutions*
P Stein, *Legal Institutions: The Development of Dispute Settlement* (Butterworths, 1984)

Tettenborn, *Restitution*
A Tettenborn, *Law of Restitution* (Cavendish, 1993)

Treitel, *Remedies*
GH Treitel, *Remedies for Breach of Contract: A Comparative Account* (Oxford, 1988)

Von Mehren, *Formation*
A von Mehren, The Formation of Contracts, *International Encyclopedia of Comparative Law*, Volume VII, Chapter 9

Weir, *Casebook*
T Weir, *A Casebook on Tort* (Sweet & Maxwell, 7th edn, 1992)

Weir, *Common Law*
T Weir, The Common Law System, *International Encyclopedia of Comparative Law*, Volume II, Chapter 2, Part III

Weir, *Complex Liabilities*
T Weir, Complex Liabilities, *International Encyclopedia of Comparative Law*, Volume XI, Chapter 12

Zimmermann
R Zimmermann, *The Law of Obligations: Roman Foundations of the Civilian Tradition* (Juta & Co, 1990)

Zweigert & Kötz
K Zweigert & H Kötz, *An Introduction to Comparative Law* (Oxford, 2nd rev edn, 1992; trans T Weir)

PRELIMINARY REMARKS

The chapters which follow are not intended as an exhaustive and detailed description and analysis of the English law of contract, tort, restitution and remedies. Rather, they are an overview of these four areas in the context of a legal culture which, as a result of the European Union (EU), now embraces all of Europe. This is not to say that English law is merging its identity with the systems of its partners. In fact the survey which follows raises a number of questions about the viability of the common law adopting the Roman-inspired generic category of a 'law of obligations' (*cf* Ch 1). The purpose is to present a survey of English law that can at least connect with the thinking to be found in the continental civilian tradition with the aim of providing a means by which the two traditions can begin to understand each other's structural thinking and legal *mentalité*.[1] Harmonisation of private law, as desired by many European politicians and jurists, is of course another matter (see Ch 14). Yet fostering understanding between great legal traditions is intellectually beneficial provided that it is pursued with a critical spirit.

No doubt such a critical pursuit carries a risk since 'the comparatist will find himself irrevocably marginalised because he will no longer fully be of his own legal culture (while not fully being of the other legal cultures ...)'.[2] Yet in the case of the law of obligations this is a risk well worth taking; for not only is the term an import – one hesitates to say transplant – from a different legal culture, but it provides an excellent opportunity to investigate the question of what it is to have knowledge of the law of obligations. In other words, the law of obligations provides the opportunity 'to introduce distinction where there had been conformity, to foster differentiation where there had been homogeneity, to promote critique where there had been compliance, to show that what construction there is as law within a given culture is historically and epistemologically conditioned'.[3] Now this is not to claim that the chapters that follow will go anywhere near to achieving all of these intellectual objectives. The overriding objective is to provide an introductory overview to an English law of obligations and remedies. But there will be an attempt to connect with some of the larger theoretical questions that underpin comparative law even although this survey is not designed, on the whole (but *cf* Chs 1, 3, 14), as a work of comparative law. There will be an attempt to connect with theory, if only to stimulate students and lawyers to research beyond the chapters of this present work.

1 For a discussion of the common law and civil law *mentalités* see P Legrand, 'European Legal Systems are not Converging' (1996) 45 ICLQ 52.

2 P Legrand, *Comparatists-at-Law and the Contrarian Challenge* (Inaugural Lecture, University of Tilburg, 1995), p 45.

3 *Ibid*, p 47.

The theoretical questions become particularly important with respect to the EU encouragement for the harmonisation of private law (Chs 1, 14). No doubt this is a topic that in many respects lies outside the scope of a general survey of a particular area of positive private law. Nevertheless with regard to the law of obligations it is a question that is always in the background for several reasons. First, because English and continental lawyers both appear to subscribe to a law of contract whereby parties can create their own rights and duties, perhaps in the manner of private legislation (Chs 8–10).[4] A 'common law' of enforceable agreements looks a tempting possibility. Secondly, having established a European law of contractual obligations, all other compensation and debt claims falling outside of contract can be similarly subsumed under a common label of non-contractual obligations (Chs 11–13). Contractual and non-contractual obligations look like a common European legal language. Thirdly, the factual situations that underpin these contractual and non-contractual obligations are much the same throughout the market economies of the EU: commercial transactions, traffic and factory accidents, dangerous products, defective buildings and the like are to be found in France, Germany, Italy, the UK and so on. If there is one area fit for harmonisation it must, seemingly, be this section of private law motivated more by industrial and economic activity than by intellectual and cultural histories. In truth, the theoretical and epistemological (theory of knowledge) assumptions upon which ideas about harmonisation are based are much more complex and ambiguous than many comparatists seem to appreciate (Ch 14). No serious work on an aspect of legal knowledge should, these days, ignore such difficulties.

Indeed one good reason why such theoretical and epistemological issues should not be ignored is that of legal knowledge itself. What is it to have knowledge of the English law of obligations? It is easy to reply that it is a matter of learning rules and (or) principles. Yet the cases often tell a different story (see, eg Ch 1 § 7(a)). Legal classification, legal institutions and legal concepts (normative, quasi-normative and descriptive) seem, for example, to have roles that go beyond any structure of rules (Chs 1, 3, 14). And one must never ignore the way skilful lawyers and judges can reason from within the facts themselves.[5] Moreover, in the area of both contractual and non-contractual obligations the academic literature devoted to theoretical questions attaching to the various categories is now so voluminous that it can support a course in itself.[6] Accordingly, to gain any in-depth knowledge of the law of obligations it is necessary to go well beyond any propositional knowledge (regulations, rules and principles) and into methodology, theory and history. It has been said that, in science, 'the textbooks are the triumph of the anachronism and atrophy of knowledge'.[7] And even if law is not a science, any work on a particular area ought to strive to avoid such sterility.

4 CC art 1134; *Printing and Numerical Registering Co v Sampson* (1875) LR 19 Eq 462, 465. However, not all the codes see contract as a form of private legislation.

5 On this point see Samuel, *Sourcebook*, pp 81–88, 94–98.

6 See eg with respect to contract: HG Beale, WD Bishop & MP Furmston, *Contract: Cases and Materials* (Butterworths, 3rd edn, 1995) Chs 25–31.

7 See J-P Astolfi & M Develay, *La didactique des sciences* (PUF, 3rd edn, 1994), p 44.

In one very real way, the chapters that follow will go beyond a strict law of obligations. Part I will be devoted primarily to the Law of Actions, that is to say to remedies and certain procedural questions (Chs 2–6). The reason is simple: much of the English law of obligations has been fashioned at the level of the law of remedies and the remedy continues to play a fundamental role in developing and extending private law (see, eg Ch 4 § 1(b)).[8] Before the middle of the 19th century it might be said that all of English law was procedural and focused on the form of the action. Legal reasoning was a matter of matching one set of facts to a series of relatively fixed factual models to see if there was an analogous relationship (Ch 3). Now even if this is an historical exaggeration, the methods associated with the days of the forms of action (see Chs 1–3) remain very much in evidence with the result that the English law of obligations can on occasions appear as consisting of little more than a list of remedies (debt, damages, injunctions, rescission) together with a list of causes of action (trespass, nuisance, defamation, breach of contract).[9] Moreover, the absence of a clear distinction between substantive law and procedure – another hangover from the forms of action – means that important obligation questions find themselves on occasions being resolved as matters of procedure (Ch 2). The history of the common law has bequeathed a *mentalité* that ought never to be underestimated by the European lawyer (*cf* Ch 14).

8 Samuel, *Sourcebook*, pp 111–202.

9 On which see B Rudden, Torticles (1991–92) 6/7 *Tulane Civil Law Forum* 105.

CHAPTER ONE

GENERAL INTRODUCTION

The term 'law of obligations' is being used with increasing frequency in England to describe the law of contract, tort and restitution and as a term of convenience it presents few problems. However, as a term of art (or perhaps one should say science) its fundamental connection to the civil law tradition gives rise to a number of problems for anyone who might want to employ it as an analytical tool within the common law tradition: for in civilian (continental) legal thought the idea of a law of obligations goes well beyond a mere category. It represents a central part of a coherent system of legal thought which actually makes rational sense only when related to all the other parts of the system.[1] Accordingly, unless the system as a whole is understood in all its implications, some of the subtleties of the continental notion of a law of obligations can easily be missed.

1 THE NOTION OF A LAW OF OBLIGATIONS

The notion of a law of obligations goes back to Roman law where it was a category that consisted of what today one would call personal rights in respect of things (*iura in personam*). That is to say, it was a sub-category of the law of things, 'things' (*res*) in this respect being construed widely to include not only physical things, but intangible forms of property embracing even obligations, or legal duties, to act and to refrain from acting. The other sub-category in the law of things was, in Roman law, the law of property and this comprised what today one would call real rights (*iura in rem*). The law of obligations was thus partly defined by reference to the law of property. The Roman sources themselves reveal a lack of interest in developing any general theory of obligations; the jurists focused almost entirely on the various species falling within this area of law. In other words, they discussed only the various kinds of contracts, delicts (torts) and actions (remedies) that made up the generic category of the law of obligations. Indeed, they never fully distinguished between substantive obligations and procedural actions with the result that the actual Roman law of obligations seems more like a law of remedies.[2]

However, in later Roman law, the notion of an obligation was given a definition: 'An obligation is a legal bond (*vinculum iuris*) whereby we are constrained to do something according to the law of our state'.[3] The modern French definition retains this idea of a *vinculum iuris* in saying that an obligation is a legal bond binding the

1 See on the *corps législatif* laid down in the French *Code civil*: J Gordley, 'Myths of the French Civil Code' [1994] *American Journal of Comparative Law* 459.

2 The title in the *Digest* (D.44.7) devoted to obligations is entitled obligations and actions: *de obligationibus et actionibus*.

3 J 3.13pr.

creditor to the debtor.[4] It is a legal relationship uniting the creditor to the debtor.[5]

(a) Legal chain (*vinculum iuris*)

The most important aspect of an obligation is to be found in this idea of a legal bond. A right *in personam* is founded upon a legal relationship between person (*persona*) and person (*persona*) which, in turn, will entitle the right-holder to a personal action (*actio in personam*). The law of obligations is thus a category of law concerned with legal claims between individual legal subjects. A right *in rem*, in contrast, might be described as a legal bond between person (*persona*) and thing (*res*) which gives rise to a real action (*actio in rem*); thus the law of property is a category concerned with relations between people and things.[6] These relationships between people and things can vary depending on the number of persons who might have a relation with a particular thing; thus ownership, the most complete relationship with a piece of property, can be contrasted with possession, a notion that has part of its basis in fact.[7] With regard to the law of obligations, however, the notion of an obligation, despite its underdevelopment in terms of actual theory, was in Roman law a unique relation in itself: that is to say, although obligations had differing sources which could give rise to different types of obligations, the *vinculum iuris* between two persons was the formal 'mother' of all actions *in personam* (*obligatio mater actionis*).[8] The Romans endowed the idea of an obligation with a powerful metaphorical image.

This idea of a legal relation is still fundamental in civilian legal thinking and all of the civil codes are structured around the difference between real and personal rights. The New Dutch Civil Code, admittedly, now has a book devoted to patrimonial rights in general; but the concept of a single patrimony where real and personal rights are intermixed has its origin, also, in Roman law.[9] Obligational relations (*iura*) in Roman law were forms of intangible property (*res incorporales*).[10] Indeed, the recognition that property could be tangible (*res corporales*), that is to say could be touched (a cow, house etc) or intangible, existing only in law (for example, a debt), was one of the major contributions that Roman law has made to modern legal thought. For not only did it help turn the notion of a obligation from a legal chain into a legal right in the sense that all things became objects to be revindicated, but it facilitated the development of new

---

4 See generally J-L Gazzaniga, *Introduction historique au droit des obligations* (PUF, 1992), pp 19–20.

5 Malaurie & Aynès, para 1.

6 See generally A-M Patault, *Introduction historique au droit des biens* (PUF, 1989), pp 17–18, 84–85, 109–11.

7 P Ourliac & J de Malafosse, *Histoire du Droit privé: 2/Les Biens* (PUF, 2e.éd, 1971), pp 215–34. It is tempting to say that possession is always a question of fact, while ownership is a question of law. In reality possession is more complex since in ambiguous situations it is the court that has to decide if a person actually has, or had, possession: see M Bridge, *Personal Property Law* (Blackstone, 1993), pp 12–14.

8 A-J Boyé, '*Variations sur l'adage "Obligatio Mater Actionis"*', *Mélanges Le Bras* (Sirey, 1965) 815. And see D.44.7.41, 51, 53pr.

9 Ourliac & de Malafosse, *supra*, pp 60–68.

10 G.2.14.

kinds of commercial property without compromising the stability of ownership.[11]

In one of the first great textbooks of Roman law, the *Institutes of Gaius* (around 160 AD), obligations are said to have two main sources. They were founded either in contracts or in delicts.[12] The first category, contracts, consisted of a range of transactions such as sale, hire and loan where the common denominator was agreement (*conventio*) between two persons,[13] while the second category was founded on the notion of wrongs.[14] However, this twofold division of obligations proved unsatisfactory even for Gaius since it could not account for those obligations where one was under a duty to repay money in the absence of either agreement or wrong.[15] Thus, where P paid money to D under the mistaken impression that D was his creditor, D was under an obligational duty to repay P even if P could show neither a contractual nor a delictual obligation.[16] Later Roman lawyers developed two further categories, quasi-contracts and quasi-delicts, to rationalise these exceptional claims;[17] and although quasi-delict never, in the later civil law, really proved of much value in terms of an independent category,[18] quasi-contract achieved considerable independence in being associated with the common denominator of unjust enrichment.[19] Agreement, wrongs and unjust enrichment became the three principal sources of obligations and most of the modern codes think in terms of three categories associated with these sources: that is to say, they see obligations as arising from contract, delict and restitution.[20] Thus, the law of obligations can be sub-divided into these three subject areas.

(b) Obligations and actions

Despite the development of a substantive law of obligations, Roman law never lost sight of the means by which an obligation found expression at one and the same time

11 D.5.3.18.2.

12 G.3.88. 'Delicts' in civil law are more or less analogous to 'torts' in the common law.

13 D.2.14 1.3.

14 D.44.7.4 : *ex maleficio nascuntur obligationes.*

15 G.3.91; D.44.7.1pr, 5pr, 5.1. In his *Institutes* Gaius says that there is no contract because the payer is intending to discharge rather than form a contract.

16 G.3.91; D.44.7.5.3.

17 D.44.7.5.

18 Zimmermann, pp 19-20, 1126–35.

19 Zimmermann, pp 857–91. And see generally Unjustified Enrichment [1992] *Acta Juridica.*

20 The question whether Gaius' system of sources of obligations should be treated as a closed or open system has attracted much attention: *cf* M Kaser, '*Divisio Obligationum*', in P Stein & A Lewis (eds), *Studies in Justinian's Institutes in memory of JAC Thomas* (Sweet & Maxwell, 1983) 73. In continental law, the general concept is that obligations need a legal basis. Other sources have been identified, eg reasonableness and fairness, *fait accompli*, reliance, changes in *status quo* leading to just or unjust transfer of patrimonial assets etc. However, obligations based solely on such principles are generally unacceptable unless a legal basis also exists. Some inroads into this doctrine have been made in the area of pre-contractual liability (eg in Germany BGB § 242) or unjust enrichment (France). See also, eg the Italian CC art 1173; and according to the NBW bk 6 art 1 obligations can only arise from the law. See now *Kleinwort Benson Ltd v Glasgow CC* [1996] 2 WLR 655.

in law and in society. The law of things (property and obligations) was largely about the existence or non-existence of a legal action on behalf of one person against another person (or a thing). Is P entitled to an action against D for damage suffered by P when D sold him wine that turned out to be sour? Can a passer-by bring an action against a pruner for injury caused by falling branches? Can an owner of a cow bring an *actio in rem* against the thief of the cow even though the thief no longer possesses the animal? In order to decide if such actions were available within particular factual situations the Roman jurists had recourse to arguments, opinions, legal and factual relations, rules and principles that formed part of the law of obligations; yet at the same time they applied relations, rules and principles that attached to the remedy (*actio*) itself since law was not just about relations between people and people and things, but also about actions. Accordingly, in addition to a Law of Things, the *Institutes* of Gaius has a book devoted to the Law of Actions and in order to have a comprehensive knowledge of the law of obligations one must have also have knowledge of actions.[21]

Actions, as Jolowicz points out, do not form part of the civil codes in that they are no longer considered as part of substantive law (the law of rights).[22] They have been relegated to separate codes of procedure. Nevertheless, the law of actions is fundamental to our understanding of problem-solving in Roman law not only because there were separate actions for different kinds of transactions, wrongs and unjust enrichment situations, but also because the *actio* was one means by which factual situations were analysed. Roman jurists would often start out from situations where an *actio* might be available and, by gradually altering the factual situation, arrive at hypothetical situations where an action would not be available.[23] It was in this way that the professional jurists expanded and developed private law.

(c) Obligations, actions and reasoning

Take the following example from the delict of theft (a tort in Roman law). The jurist Ulpian (160–228 AD) asks who will have the action for theft if a letter he sends to another is intercepted before it arrives.[24] In order to answer this remedy question one must first ask, says the jurist, who did the letter belong to: was it the sender or the addressee? If the sender had given it to the slave of the addressee, then the latter would be the owner because he would acquire through the slave. And the same would be true if the letter was given to the addressee's agent, especially if the addressee had an interest (*interfuit*) in becoming the owner. On the other hand, if the sender had sent the letter on the understanding that it would be returned to him, then he would retain ownership. Having discussed these concrete situations, Ulpian returns to the question of who had the action. It is the person who had an interest in the letter not being

21 This is particularly true about property: although there are titles specifically devoted to acquiring and losing ownership and possession (D.41.1 & 2), one also has to look at the title dealing with the *actio in rem* (D.6.1) to get a full understanding of the mechanics of property law.

22 Jolowicz, *Roman Foundations*, pp 75–81. But *cf* NBW bk 3 arts 296 ff.

23 T Weir, 'Contracts in Roman and England' (1992) 66 *Tulane Law Review* 1615.

24 D.47.2.14.17.

stolen, that is to say the person who benefited from its contents. Does this mean that the messenger could bring the action? The jurist replies that he might well have an action since, if he was responsible for carrying it safely, he would have a personal interest in the letter being delivered. For example, if the messenger had expressly undertaken to look after the letter, or if he was to be paid for delivering it, he would be strictly responsible for the letter in the same way as an innkeeper or shipmaster; and as they had the action for theft, so should the messenger.

This example is revealing for a number of reasons. First, it shows how the law of delict (tort) is dependent upon other areas of the law such as the law of property and the law of contract. In order to decide who will have the action it is necessary to decide between which two persons there is a *vinculum iuris*, the legal obligation which will act as the 'mother' of the action; but in order to decide this, one must decide first who has the legal bond with the *res* (letter). The law of obligations is dependent upon the law of property. Ownership might, in its turn, be dependent, *inter alia*, on the law of persons (*status*): if the messenger is a slave the addressee will automatically acquire ownership; if he is not a slave, then possession might be acquired by the addressee since one can acquire possession through another person (*persona libera*). However, it transpires that it is not ownership as such which is the key: it is the person who has the interest. This latter notion is of particular importance in the law of actions because, on the whole, only persons with an interest are entitled to bring a legal claim.[25] Having used, then, the law of property as a means by which one can determine the interest, this notion of an interest can be used in turn as a means of bringing into play the law of contract (paid messenger) and the law of quasi-delict (strict liability of innkeeper and shipmaster). Liability under one obligation (contract, quasi-delict) becomes, via the notion of an interest, the reason for claiming under another (theft). A second reason, therefore, why the example is revealing is that it shows how reasoning, even when operating within the facts themselves, makes use of concepts such as property (ownership, possession) and interest that transcend the law of obligations itself.

A third reason why the example is revealing is that it indicates how obligations themselves interrelate, particularly when the facts disclose more than two legal parties. The question to be answered is whether sender or addressee has the *actio furti*, but the role and status of the messenger soon takes over as an important focal point. Not only might the status or obligation position of the messenger be important in deciding the remedy question as between sender and addressee, but the messenger himself becomes a party who might be entitled to sue. The action is one in delict (tort), yet the law of contract assumes an important role in the analysis of the facts. Did the messenger expressly undertake to keep the letter safe? One might note, in addition, how legal reasoning is a matter, not of applying pre-established legal rules as such, but of pushing outwards from the facts.[26] It is a question of starting with sender and addressee and working from them towards the third party. Of course, in doing this, the jurist was working within a highly structured model of legal relations between people (contract

25 See eg D.45.1.97.1; D 47.23.3.1.

26 *Cf* G Samuel, *Foundations*, pp 193–96.

and delict) and between people and things (ownership and possession) and this model could be seen to be one that contained a mass of rules. However, it was not rules as such that were employed as the main tools of analysis; far more important was the role of notions such as interest, possession and payment. And these notions are not really rules, any more perhaps than is the model upon which each *vinculum iuris* is founded. Legal chains, interests, damage, possession, fault and the like are focal points through which one moves from the world of fact to the world of law and vice versa. In other words, the law of obligations, in the context of actual problem-solving, is not a model of rules; it was, in Roman law at least, more a means of analysis. Law, then, might well be as much about the interpretation of facts as it is about the interpretation of written rules.[27]

(d) Obligations in the later civil law

The Roman law of obligations did not come to a halt with the end of the Roman world. From the 11th century onwards there was a revival of law studies in what were to be the first European universities and these law studies were based upon the rediscovered sources of Roman law (later to be called the *Corpus Iuris Civilis*).[28] The medieval jurists at first were content simply to comment upon (gloss) the Roman texts, but this glossing later took on a dynamic aspect as harmonisation of discordant texts was attempted and common denominators were induced out of the disparate Roman juristic writings to form the basis of general notions and principles. For example, the Roman jurists had never developed a law of contract let alone a general theory of obligations. They had been content with a list of specific types of contract (sale, hire, loan, stipulation and so on), observing only that all of these specific types had the common denominator of agreement (*conventio*)[29] and that there was a need for some abstract contracts to cover those situations which fell outside of the typical transaction.[30] It was the medieval Roman and canon lawyers, using *conventio* and the abstract contracts such as pacts and stipulations, who set in train the process of moving the law of contracts to a law of contract (from an inductive to a deductive approach).[31] By the 16th century the civilian jurists were talking in terms of a general theory of contract based on consent and this general notion of consensualism was developed into the modern theory of contract by the School of Natural Law. *Pacta sunt servanda* (agreements must be kept) became an axiom of Romanist legal thought.[32] In the *Code civil* this general theory of contract is given full expression in article 1134: 'contracts legally formed have force of legislation between those that have made them'.

The law of delicts was also subjected to an increasing systematisation by the later civil lawyers. In the Roman sources the law of delicts was, procedurally, little more

27 D.9.2.52.2.

28 See Jolowicz, *Roman Foundations*, pp 1–5; Stein, *Institutions*, pp 75–80.

29 D.2.14.1.3.

30 D.19.5.15.

31 Ourliac & de Malafosse, pp 84–89, 125–128; Zimmermann, pp 537–45, 561–69.

32 Zimmermann, pp 576–77.

than a law of actions in that there were a range of separate delicts and quasi-delicts dealing with particular types of harm.[33] Within these separate delicts, of which the most important was the action for wrongful damage based upon the *Lex Aquilia*, the Romans had again formulated some common denominators based upon wrongful behaviour. Moreover, they had also developed some elementary ideas with regard to blameworthiness (*culpa*), causation and damage.[34] However, they never developed a general theory of liability. Such a development was again achieved by the later civilian jurists using the notion of *culpa* and this idea of fault had the advantage not only of according with the prevailing moral ideals but of acting as a balance between freedom of action and the causing of harm.[35] Where an act caused damage, the loss would have to be borne by the victim except when there was fault; but if there was fault, then according to article 1382 of the *Code civil* the actor would have to make reparation. The general compensation claim based upon fault, causation and damage is one of the notable features of the French code. In the German Civil Code, by contrast, damage, causation and fault are not enough: the victim must show that a specific interest (life, body, health, freedom, property or other right) has also been invaded (§ 823).[36]

In addition to this general liability based upon *culpa*, some of the later civilian jurists never lost sight of a parallel idea to be found, seemingly, in the Roman law of delicts and quasi-delicts. This was the idea of liability without fault. Such strict liability took two broad forms: there was, first, the idea of a direct liability between plaintiff victim and defendant for harm done by some person or thing under the control of the defendant and, secondly, there was the idea of a vicarious responsibility whereby one person, the defendant, was held liable for a harmful act committed by another person. Accordingly, in Roman law, a contractor could be directly liable for damage done by himself or by those whom he employed to carry out the work.[37] Equally, an owner of a building was, more indirectly, strictly liable for damage done by things falling or thrown out on to a public place[38] and a *pater familias* was indirectly liable, up to the value of the slave or child, for damage caused by children and slaves in his power.[39] In fact these two ideas were never clearly separated in Roman law and so, for example, Gaius justifies the liability of an innkeeper for the theft by another of a guest's property on the basis of the innkeeper's own fault in employing bad men.[40]

This text is useful for another reason as well: for it indicates that the jurists had some difficulty with the whole idea of liability without fault and it is, accordingly, possible to see this field of non-contractual liability as dealing only with an evidential presumption of fault. In other words, there was no third principle as such concerned

33 See generally CF Kolbert, *Justinian: The Digest of Roman Law* (Penguin, 1979).

34 See generally FH Lawson, *Negligence in the Civil Law* (Oxford, 1950).

35 See generally Zimmermann, pp 1031–49.

36 Zimmermann, pp 1036–38.

37 D.19.2.25.7.

38 D 44.7.5.5. And see generally D.9.3.

39 See generally D.9.4.

40 D.44.7.5.6.

with liability for damage arising neither from a contract nor from *culpa*. Liability was simply based upon a presumption of fault. This difficulty was to plague the later civilians with the result that there are no paragraphs devoted as such to strict liability in the German Civil Code.[41] Even in France, which ended up with a general article in its Code imposing a liability for damage done by persons and things under the control of another (article 1384), the jurists were preoccupied with fault up until the 20th century.[42] It is only with the industrial and technological revolution that the French jurists escaped from the fault principle towards one based upon risk. *Ubi emolumentum ibi onus* (where there is profit there is also burden) became the basis of what is now called vicarious liability, that is to say the liability of an employer for harm caused by employees; and, with respect to things, ideas such as 'collective solidarity' based upon the widespread existence of insurance have come to displace liability for individual acts founded on fault.[43] Whatever the theoretical position may have been before the present century, there is now, thanks to the work of the modern French civilians, a powerful parallel principle of strict liability in the law of obligations for damage done by things.

The Roman jurists never developed, either, a general non-contractual unjust enrichment action. Instead they used a number of remedies to deal with debt claims that could not be rationalised under contract and these claims were subsequently classified by the Roman jurists under the heading quasi-contracts.[44] The two most important actions were the *condictio*, a free-standing *in personam* debt action that could be used in a range of restitution situations,[45] and the *actio negotiorum gestorum contraria* which was available to someone who had reasonably intervened in the affairs of another in the sole interests of that other.[46] However, in contrast to the situation concerning quasi-delicts, the Romans did hint at a general principle that might be said to underlie these non-contractual debt claims: no one should be allowed unjustly to enrich themselves at the expense of another.[47] This general principle was seized upon by the later civil lawyers[48] – in particular Hugo de Groot (Grotius)[49] – as the cause or principle underlying all of the quasi-contractual remedies with the result that it in some civilian systems it came to eclipse the specific remedies of Roman law. Thus, the German Civil Code states in § 812: 'A person who acquires something without any legal ground through an act performed by another or in any other manner at another's expense, is bound to render restitution'.[50] In this respect the German Code stands in

41 Zimmermann, pp 1124–26.

42 Gazzaniga, *op cit*, pp 261–63.

43 *Ibid*, pp 268–271.

44 J.3.27pr.

45 J.3.27.6; and see, eg, D.12.6 and D.12.7.

46 J.3.27.1.

47 D.12.6.14; D.50.17.206.

48 See generally DH van Zyl, 'The General Enrichment Action is Alive and Well', in *Unjust Enrichment* [1992] *Acta Juridica* 115.

49 Zimmermann, pp 885–86.

50 *Ibid*, p 891.

contrast to the *Code civil* which has no general enrichment action; it simply keeps the specific Roman quasi-contractual claims together with a range of other specific instances where an enrichment cannot be retained. However, the *Cour de cassation* has recognised unjust enrichment as a general principle of law outside of the Code,[51] and so a defendant who obtains an enrichment without a legitimate cause may have to make restitution to any person at whose expense the enrichment has been procured. The law of obligations in most of the civilian systems thus subdivides into three areas: the law of contract, the law of delict and the law of unjust enrichment.

2 THE ENGLISH LAW OF OBLIGATIONS

When one turns towards English law one encounters both similarity and difference. Certainly, as we have mentioned, the common lawyers are now beginning to talk in terms of a law of obligations.[52] Yet the civil lawyer who attempts to apply the symmetry of the codes to the case law and legislation of English law will have to proceed with care. For the history of English legal thought turns out to be quite different from that of the systems of the civil law tradition.[53]

(a) General remarks

One reason for this difference is, as we shall see (Ch 3 § 4), historical. As Lord Goff observed recently:

> The situation in common law countries, including of course England, is exceptional, in that the common law grew up within a procedural framework uninfluenced by Roman law. The law was categorised by reference to the forms of action, and it was not until the abolition of the forms of action by the Common Law Procedure Act 1852 (15 & 16 Vict c 76) that it became necessary to reclassify the law in substantive terms. The result was that common lawyers did at last separate our law of obligations into contract and tort, though in so doing they relegated quasi-contractual claims to the status of an appendix to the law of contract, thereby postponing by a century or so the development of a law of restitution. Even then, there was no systematic reconsideration of the problem of concurrent claims in contract and tort. We can see the courts rather grappling with unpromising material drawn from the old cases in which liability in negligence derived largely from categories based upon the status of the defendant. In a sense, we must not be surprised; for no significant law faculties were established at our universities until the late 19th century, and so until then there was no academic opinion available to guide or stimulate the judges ... [54]

The continental jurist who tries, then, to understand English law through the genera

---

51 Cass.req.15.6.1892; Dalloz.1892.1.596.

52 See eg A Tettenborn, *An Introduction to the Law of Obligations* (Butterworths, 1984); J Cooke & D Oughton, *Common Law of Obligations* (Butterworths, 2nd edn, 1993).

53 For a brief comparative history see RC van Caenegem, *Judges, Legislators and Professors: Chapters in European Legal History* (Cambridge, 1987).

54 *Henderson v Merrett Syndicates Ltd* [1995] 2 AC 145, 184.

and species framework of the *Institutes* of Justinian, which, as we have just briefly seen, has been a characteristic of the civil law from Gaius to the modern codes, will end up both encouraged and frustrated. The jurist will be encouraged both by the existence of the species of contract, tort (delict) and quasi-contract and by the use of the generic term law of obligations by some senior judges.[55] But the jurist will become very frustrated if an attempt is made to locate these species and the genus within a coherent and logical framework of rights conforming to the traditional pattern of *iura in rem* and *iura in personam* legal relationships. English law simply does not think in terms of rights (*les droits subjectifs*) nor does it really have a coherent notion of the distinction between rights and interests.[56] It is quite happy to use 'interest' where a continental lawyer would see rights, and 'rights' where it perhaps means interest (*cf* Ch 3 § 3).

There are a number of reasons why English law refuses to conform to the logic of the civil codes. First, and most obviously, because English private law has not been codified; it is, like French Administrative law, an area of case law. However, this is really only part of the problem. A more basic difficulty is that the common lawyer has historically thought more in terms of remedies rather than rights and the reason for this is that, unlike the civilian systems, the common law has never progressed to an axiomatic stage of legal science; that is to say, it has never thought of law as an abstract model of interrelating propositions capable of being applied deductively to any factual situation.[57] It remains rooted in an inductive stage[58] and, thus, even today, the nature of the claim can be of the utmost importance (*cf* Chs 4-6). In French Administrative law, in contrast, the case law is much less orientated in style towards facts and remedies; the jurisprudence is more concerned with the development of general principles capable of acting as an unwritten code. This is not to say that fact, argumentation and policy are not of equal importance in the French system.[59] The point to be stressed is that in England the judges are not that interested in expressing themselves in terms of general principle since they see their role as primarily deciding a dispute between two parties (*cf* Ch 3 § 2).[60]

A second reason is that there has never been a clear distinction in English law between actions *in rem* and *in personam*.[61] English judges have to some extent, like the old Roman jurists,[62] looked for their answers to legal problems in the circumstances of

---

55 See eg Lord Diplock in *Moschi v Lep Air Services Ltd* [1973] AC 331, 346.

56 G Samuel, '*Le Droit Subjectif* and English Law' [1987] CLJ 264; *ibid*, '*La notion d'intérêt en droit anglais*', in Ph Gérard, F Ost & M van de Kerchove (*sous direction de*), *Droit et intérêt*: volume 3 (Facultés Universitaires Saint-Louis, Bruxelles, 1990), pp 405–36.

57 Cf Zweigert & Kötz, pp 141–48.

58 G Samuel, '*Der Einfluss des Civil Law auf das englische Recht des 19 Jahrhunderts*', in R Schulze (ed), *Französisches Zivilrecht in Europa während des 19 Jahrhunderts* (Dunker & Humblot, 1994), pp 287–313.

59 Cf J Bell, 'English Law and French Law – Not So Different?' [1995] CLP 63; M Lasser, Judicial (Self-) Portraits: Judicial Discourse in the French Legal System' (1995) 104 Yale LJ 1325.

60 See eg Samuel, *Sourcebook*, p 68.

61 D.44.7.25.

62 Zimmermann, pp xi-xii.

the case (*in causa ius esse positum*)[63] viewed in the context of their own previous decisions (*stare decisis*).[64] But these previous decisions have been guided by a selection of remedies that have not been shaped by the Roman forms of action.[65] English lawyers traditionally thought more in terms of trespass and debt than in terms of a set of remedies which rigidly distinguished between real and personal relations and this has resulted in a system of remedies which at one and the same time uses ideas from the law of property and the law of obligations.[66]

A third reason is that the distinction between substantive law and legal procedure is not so clearly drawn in the English legal process as it is in the continental systems (*cf* Ch 2). Whether or not a plaintiff is entitled to a legal remedy can sometimes be influenced as much by the way a case has been presented – that is to say, it can turn on the presentation of evidence[67] and the nature of the action[68] – as by any pre-existing substantive legal relationship or legal rule (*cf* below § 7(a)). And thus in order to understand the functioning of the law of obligations in England it is always necessary to consider, at one and the same time, rules which in continental law would be separated into codes of rights and codes of procedure. English legal method, in other words, consists as much in knowing how to sue as in knowing what are the legal rights of the client.

(b) The development of a law of obligations

This procedural flavour to English law results from its historical attachment to the forms of action, an attachment that was severed formally only in the 19th century (Ch 3 § 4). The strict starting point, then, for the importation of a law of obligations category into English case law is no doubt the 19th century when, with the abolition of the forms of action, the judges looked to the civil law for inspiration (*cf* Ch 3 § 4(e)). However, the modern starting point is probably a statement by Lord Diplock in 1973: 'The law of contract', he said, 'is part of the law of obligations' and the 'English law of obligations is about their sources and the remedies which the court can grant to the obligee for a failure by the obligor to perform his obligations voluntarily'. Obligations which are performed require no intervention by a court, he continued, since they 'do not give rise to any cause of action'.[69] More recently, as we have seen, Lord Goff has observed that common lawyers separated 'our law of obligations into contract and tort' only after the abolition of the forms of action and, as a result, English law has given no systematic reconsideration to the problem of concurrent claims in contract and tort.

63 D.9.2.52.2.

64 See generally R Cross & J Harris, *Precedent in English Law* (Oxford, 4th edn, 1991).

65 G Samuel, '*System und Systemdenken – zu den Unterschieden zwischen kontinentaleuropäischem Recht und Common Law*' [3/1995] ZEuP 375.

66 Milsom, p 263.

67 See eg *Ward v Tesco Stores Ltd* [1976] 1 All ER 219.

68 See eg *Esso Petroleum Co Ltd v Southport Corporation* [1953] 3 WLR 773 (QBD); [1954] 2 QB 182 (CA); [1956] AC 218 (HL).

69 *Moschi v Lep Air Services Ltd* [1973] AC 331, 346.

This law of obligations analysis is both tempting and revealing. It is tempting in that it would be valuable in these days of European legal harmonisation[70] to think that English law accepts without hesitation the idea of an English law of obligations; for such an acceptance would have a number of advantages with respect not only to Europe but also to the internal architecture of the common law itself. It is revealing to the extent that the notion of an English 'law of obligations' is linked by Lord Diplock both to 'remedies' and to 'cause of action'. As we shall see (Chs 3, 14), neither the English law of remedies nor the law of causes of actions necessarily points in the direction of a law of obligations as it is understood in civil law systems.[71]

All the same there are a number of distinct advantages in thinking in terms of a 'law of obligations' as opposed to just 'contract' and 'tort'. For a start, the idea of an English law of obligations would act as a means of contextualising the teaching and practice of two areas of civil liability which do have common features. As Tony Weir observes, 'a tort suit is very like an action for damages for breach of contract' and it would seem that 'more and more breaches of contract simultaneously constitute torts as well'.[72] In addition, the adoption of a law of obligations category would bring the common law more into line with the mentality of the Romanist influenced systems of the continent and European Union (EU); and such a *rapprochement* of structure would no doubt be valuable in the quest for ever greater harmonisation between all the systems of the EC and, ultimately, for the development of a new *ius commune*.[73] Furthermore, the adoption of the 'law of obligations' as a generic category would facilitate the escape from the rigidity of the 'contract' and 'tort' dichotomy which has dominated civil liability in England for over a century and a quarter. As Lord Wright pointed out in 1943, 'any system of law is bound to provide remedies for cases of what has been called unjust enrichment or unjust benefit' and these 'remedies in English law are generically different from remedies in contract or in tort'.[74] A law of obligations category would, in other words, help match the English law of remedies with a substantive law of legal rights (*cf* Chs 4, 11).

---

70 On which see generally Hartkamp *et al*.

71 The term 'civil law', used to describe the legal systems of continental Europe, comes from the Roman law expression *ius civile* where it meant the particular law of the Roman state. This category of *ius civile* can be differentiated from the *ius naturale* (law of nature) and the *ius gentium* (law of nations): Samuel, *Foundations*, pp 40–42. For a general discussion of the continental systems see Zweigert & Kötz, pp 76–185.

72 Weir, *Casebook*, p 1.

73 The notion of a *ius commune* (common law) of Europe is no new idea; the expression, itself to be found in the Roman sources, essentially comes from the late Middle Ages where it meant the revived Roman law – and Roman law was 'common' to the universities of Europe – used in the courts alongside local and customary law. This European *ius commune* is of great importance historically to the law of obligations since it 'provided a sort of conceptual *lingua franca* for lawyers of different nations, enabling them to understand one another's formulations'; but this 'development, not having taken place in England, meant that English lawyers were excluded from this *lingua franca*; and the basis for the mutual sense of strangeness, as between the world of the English common law and that of what might be called the Romanesque civil law was laid': J M Kelly, *A Short History of Western Legal Theory* (Oxford, 1992), p 180. Many continental writers are thinking in terms of a new *ius commune*: see generally B de Witte & C Forder (eds), *The common law of Europe and the future of legal education* (Kluwer, 1992); Hartkamp *et al*.

74 *Fibrosa etc v Fairbairn* etc [1943] AC 32, 61; *cf Kleinwort Benson Ltd v Glasgow CC* [1996] 2 WLR 655.

The adoption of a law of obligations category is, however, not quite as straightforward as it might first appear. The bringing together of contract and tort under a single generic category raises a number of conceptual difficulties that remained relatively benign while civil liability was seen in terms only of two discrete categories. In particular, it will bring into focus certain areas of the law of tort which, once included within a law of obligations, will appear anomalous in that they will seem to be concerned with rights that are not obligational in the civil law sense of the term. The root of this problem is, as we have already indicated, to be found in the idea that in civilian legal thought the law of obligations is part of a coherent and rational structure which conceives the whole of law in terms of an institutional system (see Ch 3). Accordingly, a law of obligations in such a structure has meaning only in relation to other parts of the system.[75] In a sense it is a little like the concept of a number: a single number would have no meaning whatsoever in its own right since 'whole numbers do not exist in isolation and they were not discovered in just any order to be put together into a whole'; numbers appear as a sequence 'and this sequence has structural properties ... completely distinct from those of each number'.[76] Similarly, the institutional system of the civil law has a structural property, a corpus, quite distinct from the individual elements that make up the system and this has a direct bearing on the definition and the contents of a law of obligations.

This is not to suggest that the use of a continental category will necessarily lead to intellectual confusion or chaos within English private law. But it does have to be remembered that modern English law was, unlike the number system, to some extent discovered 'in just any order to be put together into a whole' in the middle of the nineteenth century (*cf* Ch 3 § 4). Consequently, there is not the same structural quality which attaches to contract and tort as a system. In addition, there are other historical and intellectual aspects of the common law tradition which differentiate it from the civilian tradition and these aspects can cause problems the moment they are forced into the kind of systematics attaching to a law of obligations. The point to be made, therefore, is that a law of obligations category will of itself have little impact or meaning unless it is accompanied by a conceptual re-evaluation of the whole of the common law. Indeed, if care is not taken, the adoption of an obligations category might even have some negative results. It might cause greater rather than less complexity in those areas where equity meets the common law, or where remedies meet rights or property meets obligations (see, eg Ch 4 § 5(d)).

(c) The desirability of a law of obligations

Perhaps the English private lawyer should go further and pose a more political question. Is it desirable that an institutional structure from one intellectual tradition be imposed upon a structure formed out of another, and perhaps rather different, tradition? This is a question that is beginning to concern those comparatists who value

75 Stein, *Institutions*, pp 126–29; Samuel *Foundations*, pp 171–82.

76 J Piaget, *Le structuralisme* (PUF, 9th edn, 1987), p 8.

polyjurality and pluralism (*cf* Ch 14).[77] Moreover, before any proper answer can be given to this question, time should be spent examining the habits of thought and the methods of the jurists from each tradition. However, one problem here is that we might know rather less than we think about the thought processes of lawyers. Certainly, as Strömholm has stated, legal historians possess a vast knowledge of the history of Roman law in respect of its concrete institutions and its rules; but 'they are less well-informed about the philosophical, theoretical and methodological ideas and principles adopted by the Roman lawyers'.[78] Strömholm, admittedly, was talking of Roman law and it could be argued that modern lawyers utilise methods that are well understood by legal theorists.[79] Yet there remains evidence that the lack of knowledge concerning the habits of thought of the Roman jurists applies equally to modern lawyers; thus, on the continent there is a debate as to whether legal reasoning is a matter of logic or argumentation[80] and a leading French law professor argues in a major, if underestimated, work that we know really rather little about what it is to have knowledge of law.[81] This latter view is receiving empirical support in the failure of artificial intelligence researchers to develop expert systems capable of reasoning like a lawyer.[82]

3 OBLIGATIONS AND LEGAL REASONING

The question, therefore, whether one system should adopt a structure from another tradition soon becomes submerged under more complex questions about theory and methods. This in turn impacts upon any work that sets out to describe and discuss the English law of obligations in that such a work will need to be aware not just that it is, by definition, entering the field of comparative law, but that the 'fundamental doctrines and principles', and the 'intellectual and practical skills needed to research the law [of obligations]', are themselves in question.[83] As the Law Society and the Council of Legal Education state, knowledge of a subject such as the law of obligations requires, in addition to the 'foundations of' contract, restitution and tort, a knowledge of how 'to apply the law to the facts' and 'to communicate the reasons' for decisions;[84] and so a

77 See eg P Legrand, 'European Legal Systems are not Converging' (1996) 45 *ICLQ* 52. And see T Weir, '*Die Sprachen des europäischen Rechts*' [3/1995] ZEuP 368.

78 S Strömholm, *A Short History of Legal Thinking in the West* (Norstedts, 1985), p 46.

79 See eg H Motulsky, *Principes d'une réalisation méthodique du droit privé* (Sirey, 1948); J Bell, *Policy Arguments in Judicial Decisions* (Oxford, 1983); R Alexy, *A Theory of Legal Argumentations* (Oxford, 1989; trans R Adler & N MacCormick); J Bengoetxea, *The Legal Reasoning of the European Court of Justice* (Oxford, 1993).

80 See generally J-L Bergel, *Théorie générale du droit* (Dalloz, 2nd edn, 1989), pp 261–86; M Stamatis, *Argumenter en droit: une théorie critique de l'argumentation juridique* (Publisud, 1995).

81 C Atias, *Épistémologie juridique* (PUF, 1985). And see also C Atias, *Épistémologie du droit* (PUF, 1994).

82 On the failure of artificial intelligence in general see: H Dreyfus, *What Computers Still Can't Do* (MIT, 1992). On the limitations of systems based on the theory that knowledge of laws to have knowledge of rules see: R Susskind, *Expert Systems in Law* (Oxford, 1987), pp 186–93. See also Samuel, *Foundations*; but *cf* J Bell (1995) LS 461.

83 The quotations are taken from the *Preliminary Notice to Law Schools Regarding Full-time Qualifying Law Degrees* issued jointly by the Law Society and the Council of Legal Education in July 1993.

84 *Ibid.*

work on the law of obligations will need to be comparative and theoretical as well as practical and analytical. It will need to be continually conscious of the methods of legal reasoning.

Here again Roman and civil law have an important role to play and not just in the way law is classified but also in respect of how these classifications have a direct influence on reasoning. For example, one might say, as we have mentioned, that the law of actions played an influential role in the way Roman jurists analysed and reasoned. In starting out from a particular factual situation and working towards a solution via the particular remedy the law might be said to be found in the facts themselves. Indeed, this was exactly how the Roman jurists and their medieval successors saw law as functioning: the law was not to be discovered in rules since these were simply brief *résumés* of what the law is.[85] Law arose out of the facts themselves (*ex facto ius oritur*).[86] All this may seem at first sight little more than rhetoric. Yet the methods of the Roman jurists do appear to be rather different from the interpretative techniques adopted by their modern civilian successors[87] and this has implications not just for the understanding of the law of obligations itself but for the difficult matter of harmonisation of private law in the context of the European Union (*cf* Ch 14). A system that emphasises facts and remedies may find itself thinking, as we have already suggested, in a way that is substantially different from one that functions via symmetrically structured codes whose propositions are seen as relating to facts by means of syllogistic reasoning (*cf* Chs 3, 14).

This difference of approach can reflect itself in the technique of problem-solving in the law of obligations. A system that functions at the level of fact is likely to make distinctions between different types of persons and different types of things. Thus, a ruling dealing with damage caused by a defective wall might not be relevant for damage inflicted by an old tree, even although both items can be described as 'things'. Equally, the hire of a supertanker could be treated quite differently than the sale of an orange. In a system that thinks in terms of abstract principles such distinctions might not always be so easily perceived; one is liable, so the *Code civil* informs its citizens in article 1384, for damage caused by a 'thing' under one's control. There is no logical reason why the notion of a thing in this proposition should not include both a wall and a tree. One difference, then, between a system that thinks in terms of facts and remedies and a system that thinks in terms of abstract principles is the difference between things and words (*cf* Ch 14).[88]

Now it has to be said that the differences of technique between the various legal systems of Europe turn out to be more complex and sometimes more contradictory than one might at first imagine.[89] Nevertheless, a system interested in solving problems

---

85 D.50.17.1.

86 P Stein & J Shand, *Legal Values in Western Society* (Edinburgh, 1974), pp 103–11.

87 See Samuel, *System und Systemdenken, op cit.*

88 G Samuel, '*Entre les mots et les choses: les raisonnements et les méthodes en tant que sources du droit*' [1995] RIDC 467.

89 J Bell, 'English Law and French Law', *op cit.*

at the level of fact, rather than through the application of a schematic set of propositions, is less likely to be concerned about high level abstract concepts such as the notion of an obligation. Roman law appeared to be different. But, as we have seen, higher level abstract conceptions played a vital role in supporting legal argumentation and analysis at the level of facts. In other words the schematic set of legal relations (*in rem* and *in personam*) played a practical role in the actual analysis of the facts themselves. Yet unless it can serve a practical end, it is unlikely that the concept of an obligation will have much relevance in the caselaw itself. One question, therefore, which must continually be faced when looking at the case law decisions is the question of the value of thinking in terms of a law of obligations. Is such a category really necessary?

4 OBLIGATIONS AND COMPARATIVE LEGAL METHOD

In fact some would argue (see Ch 14) that rigidly to distinguish between theory and practice, and between the comparative and the analytical, is misleading, particularly with respect to a work on the law of obligations. It is misleading because, as we have already seen, this is an area of private law that is common to the whole of Europe and has a history going back to the earliest days of Roman law. Consequently, it is simply unrealistic to think of the various analytical structures and ideas as belonging to a single nation state or single intellectual tradition. The modern law of obligations has been a melting pot of ideas coming from a variety of directions – from commerce and the *lex mercatoria*,[90] from academic traditions ranging from scholasticism to the *mos geometricus*[91] and from social facts embracing almost everything from bear pits to dangerous underpants.[92] And while the common law may well have been isolated from some of this, it would be very wrong to think that scholasticism, commerce and social fact have not injected into the common law ideas and methods which, when mixed with its own particular history, make it of relevance to anyone wishing to have knowledge of Western law.[93] Indeed, the importance of the common law's own contribution to legal methodology is increasingly being recognised by civil lawyers. The New Dutch Civil code (*Nieuw Nederlands Burgerlijk Wetboek*), for example, has specifically moved away from a *mos geometricus* view of law[94] towards one that is more in line with the English approach: it recognises the importance of judge-made law and reasoning by analogy and it sees legal development as being an interaction between legislator, judge and law professor.[95]

English law thus has its own contribution to make in any European law of obligations. But the comparative method goes much further than this: it reaches into

90 J Hilaire, *Introduction historique au droit commercial* (PUF, 1986).

91 JW Jones, *Historical Introduction to the Theory of Law* (Oxford, 1940), pp 1–78; and for the medieval period see H Berman, *Law and Revolution: The Formation of the Western Legal Tradition* (Harvard, 1983). See generally F Wieacker, *A History of Private Law in Europe* (Oxford, 1995; trans T Weir).

92 Lawson, *Negligence, op cit.*

93 Zimmermann, p xi.

94 On which see Zweigert & Kötz, p 146; Samuel, *Foundations*, pp 52–53.

95 AS Hartkamp, 'Civil code revision in the Netherlands' 1947–92, in P Haanappel & E Mackaay, *New Netherlands Civil Code* (Deventer, 1990).

legal method itself in that all legal analysis is to an extent an exercise in comparison. When lawyers argue, for example, over different tests of causation (Ch 7 § 4) they are offering different models for the categorisation of a factual situation and the role of the judge is to compare and to choose between competing models. What are the goals of legal comparison as a science? According to one leading comparative lawyer they are 'to know the differences existing between legal models and to contribute to knowledge of these models'; and it is only this comparative method which 'reveals to us certain details of the different models under consideration'.[96] Legal analysis and legal comparison of competing models are often one and the same exercise.

There is a further point that can be made with respect to tradition and methods. A comparison of the various approaches to problem-solving can often be revealing in respect of the specific categories used by lawyers within a generic classification and this is particularly true when it comes to the law of obligations. In English law, a court cannot normally intervene, as Lord Diplock pointed out, unless there exists a 'cause of action'. Now, as we shall see (Ch 3 § 4(d)), a 'cause of action' has been defined as a factual situation giving rise to a remedy. But just what kind of 'factual situation' will disclose a cause of action raises a question of method: is it a matter of matching the facts in issue with a set of model factual situations; of identifying 'rights' and 'duties'; or of drawing out of the case law or statutes a rule and to apply this rule to the factual situation? The view associated with the school of legal positivism – a school that sees law as a system of rules posited directly or indirectly by a ruler or ruling body – is that law is a matter of rule application. Yet how does the lawyer actually get from 'rule' to 'factual situation' to decision? And are 'rights' and 'duties' simply defined in terms of rules?

These questions become important in the law of obligations not only because areas like the law of tort, seemingly in contrast to the law of contract, appear devoid of many rules, but also because many of the actual rules turn out, in themselves, to be empty of content. It is easy enough to write down as a proposition that in order to succeed in the tort of negligence (*cf* Ch 12 § 3) a plaintiff must establish that the defendant owed a duty of care to the plaintiff, was in breach of the duty and the breach caused foreseeable damage, but what does any of this mean? The rule is devoid of meaning if taken on its own and will only begin to assume some meaning when placed in the context of the facts of cases.[97] So is it the facts and decision of cases that become the basis of the law of obligations? Is knowledge of law a matter of knowing a mass of cases? No doubt within these cases there are 'rules', but are these rules the same as those said to be the formal rules of the tort of negligence or are they more specific? And if they are more specific – for example, if the duty and foreseeability question are to be determined by a 'proximity' test – what is the relationship between the specific and the general rules?

In fact there are rules and rules. Some rules are capable of containing enough information in themselves to determine at least a provisional decision. Thus, a rule

96 S Sacco, *La comparaison juridique au service de la connaissance du droit* (Economica, 1991), pp 8, 10.

97 See eg *Marc Rich & Co v Bishop Rock Marine Co Ltd* [1996] 1 AC 211.

banning from a certain road motor vehicles with more than a certain engine capacity is relatively easy to apply since the rule as a proposition contains in itself most of the required information and, in addition, much of the information is mathematical. The rule can thus be applied by means of formal logic.[98] Other rules like the negligence rule are merely rhetorical devices designed to locate the information needed for a reasoning process elsewhere than in the rule itself.[99] Perhaps the information will be found in a more detailed sub-rule; and so for example there used to be a very clear rule in the tort of negligence that no duty of care was owed in respect of pure economic loss (Ch 13 § 9). Equally, the information might be located in a mass of case law out of which it is not easy, or even possible, to draw a single rule; in these circumstances legal reasoning is no longer a matter of rule application as such. It is more a matter of making analogies between factual situations (Ch 3 § 2). Even some apparently quite detailed rules can contain less information than might at first seem the case. Accordingly, the moment when a contract is concluded, although governed by quite detailed rules about offer and acceptance, can often depend upon a detailed examination of the factual circumstances.[100]

5 OBLIGATIONS AS A FORM OF LEGAL KNOWLEDGE

To know the law of obligations involves, then, two quite different kinds of knowledge. It involves, without doubt, a certain amount of what Gilbert Ryle[101] has called 'knowing that' knowledge (knowing that Paris is the capital of France, for example) (see Ch 3 § 1). Equally, the law of obligations has a 'knowing how' aspect (knowing how to ride a bike, for example). Accordingly, the student of the law of obligations must learn that the law of contract requires offer, acceptance, consideration and intention to create legal relations and all the relevant sub-rules attaching to these requirements (on which see Ch 9). In addition, however, the student must acquire the skill of knowing how to analyse a problem in order to see if there are any legal remedies available and this is not always a matter of applying logically-learned rules (see Chs 3, 14). Other reasoning techniques will be of importance. Just what these techniques might be raises, evidently, methodological questions and so one purpose of a work on the law of obligations will be to examine technique (see Ch 3 § 1). Yet the knowledge question goes beyond this into more speculative matters. How ought a judge to decide hard cases? This is a question that engages the legal philosopher as much as the black letter obligations lawyer.

No doubt a work on the law of obligations cannot afford to become too involved in speculative and abstract questions. Yet there are important philosophical issues attaching to the way some of the cases in the law of obligations are handled by the judges and these issues do need to be addressed at the level of the cases themselves. Ronald Dworkin has, for example, raised an important question about the reasoning in

98 *Cf* G-G Granger, *La raison* (PUF, 10th edn, 1993), pp 46–48.

99 See generally P Atiyah & R Summers, *Form and Substance in Anglo-American Law* (Oxford, 1987).

100 See eg *Blackpool & Fylde Aero Club Ltd v Blackpool BC* [1990] 1 WLR 1195.

101 G Ryle, *The Concept of Mind* (Penguin reprint, 1963), pp 26–60.

some major tort cases: was it right that the decisions were justified on grounds of policy or should they have been justified by reference to the plaintiffs' rights in turn determined via a structure of principles?[102] It may be that the views of a philosopher like Dworkin are too idealistic to act as the foundation of the law of contract and tort; however, it would probably be a mistake to think that there are no judges in the Court of Appeal or House of Lords who have not read, and been disturbed by, the writings of Dworkin.[103] Whatever the position, there is no doubting that legal reasoning is a subtle and complex process and so any work on the law of obligations ought to try to reflect these subtleties alongside the, seemingly, more mundane task of attempting to state the law. One way of doing this is to look at the law of obligations from a variety of approaches. The rules and principles will obviously be an important object of discussion. Equally, the 'knowing how' aspects must not be ignored and so there will be a need to look at legal problems and legal analysis from other viewpoints. The remedies available and how these relate to the other legal institutions of persons and property will provide other important, and solid, starting points (Chs 3–6). In addition, there are theoretical perspectives that must not be ignored (Chs 3, 14). The growth of new theories of liability has not been completely without influence in the English law of obligations, and there are now members of the judiciary who, not unreasonably, expect guidance as part of the price for recognising that the law faculties have a role to play in shaping the development of English – and indeed European – law.[104]

6 EUROPEAN UNION LAW

The development of a law of obligations must also be viewed within the rapidly increasing influence of EU law. In the area of product liability, product safety and unfair contract terms, EU law has provided new rules and concepts. Thus the directive on unfair contract terms is forcing common lawyers to think directly about the Romanist notion of good faith (*bona fides*).[105] On 26 May 1989 the European Parliament adopted a draft resolution regarding the development of a European private law[106] and, in this respect, the findings of the Lando Commission may well play an important role.[107] All this, of course, brings one back to the question of the practicalities and desirability of a uniform European private law. Nevertheless, it is

102 R Dworkin, *Taking Rights Seriously* (Duckworth, 1977), pp 82 ff. And see generally R Dworkin, *Law's Empire* (Fontana, 1986).

103 One might speculate about Lord Browne-Wilkinson's comment in *Airedale NHS Trust v Bland* [1993] AC 789, 884 that 'there will be no single "right" answer'. Was this an indirect reference to Dworkin's view of legal reasoning?

104 *Cf White v Jones* [1995] 2 AC 207.

105 See *Unfair Terms in Consumer Contracts Regulations 1994* (SI 1994/3159). See generally J Beatson & D Friedmann (eds), *Good Faith and Fault in Contract Law* (Oxford, 1995).

106 Pb EC C 158, p 400. And see Resolution 207.670/13 EP (1994).

107 See eg O Lando, 'European Contract Law' [1983] AJCL 653. And see Hartkamp *et al* 'The Lando Principles of European Contract Law and the Unidroit Principles of International Commercial Contracts' could indeed be influential: see, eg, KP Berger, '*Die Unidroit Prinzipien für Internationale Handelsverträge/ Indiz für ein autonomes Weltwirtschaftsrecht?*' [1995] *Zeitschrift für Vergleichende Rechtswissenschaft* 217.

inevitable that the EU and its legal system will always go some way in propelling legal systems towards a certain degree of harmonisation, if only at a metalevel, and thus, in the context of EU law, the notion of a law of obligations will always be important (*cf* Ch 14).

Whether the EU will encourage the emergence, or imposition, of a more systematic legal science remains uncertain. For the Union Treaty does not provide an explicit legal basis for structural community measures in the area of the law of obligations. And the necessity of such a development in the context of the convergence and divergence of the civil law and common law is open to question, even assuming that jurists succeeded in developing a truly European and transnational legal science (*Europäisierung der Rechtswissenschaft*).[108] Certainly, legal traditions should not be played off one against another since each has its own strengths and weaknesses and it is by no means certain, today, that the *scientia iuris* of the codes is intellectually superior to the *ars judicandi* of precedent (*cf* Ch 14). Consequently, the search should be for a more common *discours scientifique* which could act as the vehicle for EU law developments. In Germany, Coing has defended the need for a European legal science, arguing that the harmonising influence of EC (EU) law and of other international developments, important as it is, will not be sufficient to constitute a legal doctrine capable of solving all the problems that European lawyers will encounter in the future. According to Coing, European legal science is not an impossible dream since all the European legal systems are imbued with the same basic values of the European culture and, since the 19th century, have been subjected to similar developments in economic and commercial law. National private law is being influenced by uniform international private law, by EU law[109] and indirectly by the need to interpret national private law in conformity with EU law, whenever substantive EU rules are in issue.[110] In addition, contemporary problems such as consumer protection are common to all European legal systems. If nothing else, then, the EU legal system implies a role for comparative legal science, accepting of course that this science is itself not pre-determined by any particular legal culture.[111]

7 THEORY AND PRACTICE

Nevertheless the idea of a European legal science must not be exaggerated (*cf* Ch 14). And so perhaps these comparative and theoretical points, particularly the problem of differing mentalities between the civil and the common law, can be illustrated at a more practical level by reference to an English tort case and a French product liability decision. The English case reflects not only a methodology and procedure shaped by history, but a mentality which does not function at the level of abstract rules. In

108 H Coing, '*Europäisierung der Rechtswissenschaft*' [1990] *Neue Juristische Wochenschrift ss* 937–41. But *cf* R Schulze, '*Le droit privé commun européen*' [1995] RIDC 7.

109 See eg *Francovich and Bonifaci v Italy* [1991] ECR I-5357; *Brasserie du Pêcheur SA v Germany* [1996] 2 WLR 506.

110 See S Prechal, *Directives in European Community Law* (Oxford, 1995).

111 *Cf* P Legrand, *Comparatists-at-Law and the Contrarian Challenge* (Inaugural Lecture, University of Tilburg, 1995).

contrast, the French decision illustrates the interrelationship, at the general level, of the different categories of obligations (contract and delict) and the different kinds of liability which act as the basis for a compensation claim (fault and liability for things).

(a) English law

In *Esso Petroleum v Southport Corporation* a tanker owned by Esso ran aground in the Liverpool estuary and in order to stop the ship breaking up, which would have endangered the lives of the crew, the captain ordered the discharge of all the oil she was carrying. This oil ended up on Southport beach, causing serious pollution, and the Corporation spent much money in clearing up the mess. In an action for damages based on trespass, public and private nuisance and negligence of the captain (on which see Chs 12–13), the Corporation hoped to recoup its losses from Esso. However, the trial judge,[112] in a decision ultimately supported in the House of Lords,[113] found that the captain had not been negligent in discharging the oil; for 'if one seeks an analogy from traffic on land, it is well established that persons whose property adjoins the highway cannot complain of damage done by persons using the highway unless it is done negligently'.[114] The action for damages thus failed.

Now from a strictly common law point of view this decision has its own logic, as the approach of Denning LJ, who, as we shall see, supported the plaintiffs' claim in the Court of Appeal, clearly indicates. In order to determine if there is liability one goes through the various causes of action one after another to see if they fit the facts and if just one does, then, provided that the defendants cannot avail themselves of a defence, there will be liability.[115] Accordingly Denning LJ first discusses trespass to land, concluding that it does not lie since the damage was not caused directly by Esso: it was the wind that carried the oil towards Southport. He then moves on to private and to public nuisance holding that private nuisance did not lie because 'it did not involve the use by the defendants of any land, but only of a ship at sea'.[116] However, it was in his opinion a public nuisance to discharge oil into the sea in such circumstances that it was likely to be carried on to the beaches to the prejudice and discomfort of Her Majesty's subjects. It was an offence punishable by the common law and should any person suffer greater damage or inconvenience from the oil than the generality of the public, such a person would have an action to recover damages. Comparing nuisance with negligence, Denning LJ said that one of the principal differences was the burden of proof: once a public nuisance is proved and the defendant is shown to have caused it, then the legal burden is shifted on to the defendant to justify or excuse himself and, if he fails to do so, he is held liable. In an action for negligence, on the other hand, the

112 [1953] 3 WLR 773.

113 [1956] AC 218.

114 [1953] 3 WLR at p 777.

115 [1954] 2 QB at p 195.

116 [1954] 2 QB at p 196.

legal burden in most cases remains throughout on the plaintiff and, although the judge may gain much help from provisional presumptions like the doctrine of *res ipsa loquitur*, he must ask himself whether the legal burden is discharged. If the matter is left evenly in the balance in a negligence case, the plaintiff fails.

What is interesting from a legal method point of view about Denning LJ's use of public nuisance is how he uses the tort to expand the facts, so to speak. In public nuisance, said the appeal judge, the legal burden shifts to the defendant, and it is not sufficient for him to leave the matter in doubt; he must plead and prove a sufficient justification or excuse. And he continued:

> The defendants seek to justify themselves by saying that it was necessary for them to discharge the oil because their ship was in danger. She had been driven by rough seas on to the revetment wall, and it was necessary to discharge the oil in order to get her off. If she had not done so, lives might have been lost. This is, no doubt, true at that stage in the story, but the question is, how came she to get upon the wall? If it was her own fault, then her justification fails, because no one can avail himself of a necessity produced by his own default. Where does the legal burden rest in this respect? Must the Southport Corporation prove that the ship was at fault in getting on to the wall, or must the ship prove that she herself was not at fault? In my opinion the burden is on the ship. She does not justify herself in law by necessity alone, but only by unavoidable necessity, and the burden is on her to show it was unavoidable.[117]

What public nuisance has allowed the court to do here is to expand the facts so as to include not just the accident itself but the whole relationship between Esso and ship. The image here is not one of a dispute between two legal subjects involved in an accident; it is the much wider picture of a bond between *persona* (owner) and *res* (ship). This adds a whole new dimension to the facts since, as Denning LJ indicates, one does not look just at the act of discharging the oil; but at the whole activity of putting to sea a ship carrying a cargo capable of causing damage if it escapes. It is not so much a question of applying different rules as such, although the tort of public nuisance is different from the tort of negligence; it is a question of changing the dimension of the facts which in turn reveals a quite different image. It is no longer a question of an analogy with the act of driving a car.

In the House of Lords,[118] the only way to restore the original image of the traffic accident was through the law of procedure. Consequently, the plaintiffs were refused permission to plead a further cause of action based on the breach of a direct duty between Esso and Southport Corporation in respect of putting to sea an unseaworthy ship. According to Lord Radcliffe, the case had to be decided in accordance with the pleadings since the defendants were entitled to conduct the case and confine their evidence in reliance upon the particulars of the statement of claim which had been delivered by the plaintiffs. Such particulars, he continued, helped to define the issues and to indicate to the party who asked for them how much of the range of his possible evidence would be relevant and how much irrelevant to those issues. And if an

117 [1954] 2 QB at pp 197–98.

118 [1956] AC 218.

appellate court were to treat reliance upon them as pedantry or mere formalism, then Lord Radcliffe could not see what part they had to play in the English trial system.[119] In the House of Lords, then, the law lords contracted the facts by refusing to allow the plaintiffs to claim that Esso might owe a direct duty to Southport in respect of the control of its ship. As far as the law lords were concerned this was simply a case about the act of an employee of the defendants.

This ability to expand and contract factual situations is often central to the English law of obligations and indicates just how important it is for the common lawyer to be able to handle facts. Of course, one could analyse Denning LJ's approach by reference to a rule about liability for things: one is liable not only for damage caused by one's own act but also for damage caused by a thing under one's control.[120] Yet this was not the way the Court of Appeal approached the question of liability. The court did not abandon fault as such. What Denning LJ did was to decide the question of 'fault' through the manipulation of the causes of action and the rules of procedure so as to arrive, through a discussion of the facts themselves, at a similar conclusion as if one had applied, for example, article 1384 of the *Code civil.* Comparison with the civil law thus becomes possible even though a case like *Esso v Southport* uses notions such as trespass and nuisance which are completely alien to a civil lawyer. But such comparisons must be treated with great caution since English law is not operating through unstated abstract principles about liability for damage caused by a thing; it is in truth functioning through the comparison of images. The trial judge thus compared the accident at sea with the image of a road accident, while Denning LJ pushed the facts backward from the accident itself to an image of a heavily laden ship operating in rough seas. Even the House of Lords created an image of a hard-pressed defendant coming to court only to find that there is some 'new' allegation for which he is unprepared. One is, in other words, 'creating' rules out of different kinds of images, and this is why the facts of cases are always as important – perhaps more important – than any apparent principle to be found in the decision.

Indeed the whole idea of a decision, even of the House of Lords, standing as authority for some rule or principle independent of the material facts of the case has little meaning in the English common law. In *Spring v Guardian Assurance Plc*,[121] where the House of Lords decided that a former employee, financially damaged by a reference carelessly prepared by his former employer, was entitled to sue for damages in the tort of negligence (*cf* Ch 13 § 1), Lord Woolf finished his speech with the following warning:

> It only remains for me to underline what I anticipate is already clear, that is, that the views which I have expressed are confined to the class of case with which I am now dealing. Some of the statements I have made I appreciate could be applied to analogous situations. However, I do not intend to express any view either way as to what will be

119 Lord Radcliffe's views have been quoted with approval recently: *Barclays Bank Plc v Fairclough Building Ltd* [1995] QB 214, 231 *per* Beldam LJ.

120 CC art 1384.

121 [1995] 2 AC 296.

> the position in those analogous situations. I believe that they are better decided when, and if, a particular case comes before the court. This approach can lead to uncertainty which is undesirable. However, that undesirable consequence is in my view preferable to trying to anticipate the position in relation to other situations which are not the subject matter of this appeal ... [122]

(b) French law

When one turns to the French law reports one finds, not surprisingly, a range of factual situations very similar to those to be found in the United Kingdom cases. However, in form, the French decisions are of quite a different nature: judgments still reflect the *mos geometricus* idea that a code is an axiomatic set of propositions that can be applied syllogistically to any factual situation and thus such judgments are stylistically arranged as a series of premises seemingly leading to an inexorable conclusion (*cf* Ch 14). In substance, and usually behind the face of the actual law report, it is a quite different matter.[123] Nevertheless, even accepting the roles played by precedent, policy and interpretative discretion in French legal reasoning, there remains a very different mentality with respect to the representation of legal knowledge. French lawyers do not see legal propositions as trapped within factual situations nor do they adhere to the English view that the role of a supreme court is simply to decide particular cases between particular litigants (*cf* Ch 2 § 3). French lawyers talk, instead, of the '*règle qui se dégage des arrêts de justice*' which is '*aussi obligatoire que celle résultant de la loi*' (rules detaching themselves from cases and having the same obligatory force as statute).[124] This 'detached' view of law – that is to say, a view of legal knowledge detached from factual situations – has encouraged a much more 'geometric' vision of the institutional relationships between people and people, and people and things (*cf* Chs 3, 14), and, as a result the French jurists, including the judiciary, place emphasis on symmetry.

This symmetrical aspect is well brought out in the decision of the *Cour de cassation* (*chambre civile*) of 17 January 1995.[125] A small child was injured in the playground of a private school when a plastic hoop which she was using shattered. The parents brought an action for compensation against not only the manufacturer, the distributor and the reseller of the hoop but also the school. The *Cour d'appel* held the manufacturer and the distributor liable (the former having, however, to indemnify the latter in full), but dismissed the claims against the reseller and the school. Various motions against this decision of the appeal court were taken to the *Cour de cassation* and most of these motions were rejected. However, the supreme court quashed the decision dismissing the action against the school:

> See articles 1135 and 1147 *Code civil*. Whereas, contractually bound to ensure the safety of pupils placed in its hands, an educational establishment is liable in damages for damage caused not only by its fault but also by things that it supplies in the performance

122 *Ibid* at p 354.

123 J Bell, 'English Law and French Law', *op cit*; Lasser, *op cit*.

124 G Ripert, *Les forces créatrices du droit* (LGDJ, 1955), para 161.

125 DS.1995.350 note Jourdain.

> of its contractual obligation; – whereas, in order to avoid the liability of the Saint-Vincent-sur-Oust school, the decision states that it has not been shown that the accident was the consequence of a fault committed by this establishment in the performance of its contractual obligations; – whereas, in so deciding, the cour d'appel has violated the said texts.

These are the only reasons on the face of the judgment for holding the school liable and none of the reports drawn up and placed before the judges in advance of their decision were on this occasion printed with the report. In order to understand the background to the case the reader must, therefore, have recourse to the note written on this occasion by a university professor.[126]

What this note makes clear – and it must not be forgotten that academic writing is in theory a source of law in France[127] – is that the *Cour de cassation* is not just raising the intensity of the contractual obligation from the level of fault (*obligation de moyen*) to that of strict liability (*obligation de sécurité*), but doing this in part to reflect symmetries already existing in contractual and non-contractual liability (*la responsabilité extra-contractuelle*). With regard to the contractual symmetry, the French supreme court was, as the note writer points out,[128] purely and simply transposing to those cases where damage has been caused by the thing to third parties the *obligation de sécurité* that exists in a contract between the professional seller and buyer. The reason for doing this is to be found in the court's desire, first, to standardise the obligations of a professional seller to all consumers irrespective of their status as actual buyers or third parties and, secondly, to reflect the symmetry of EU law as expressed in the directive on defective products.[129] In other words the *obligation de sécurité* now transcends the contract and delict dichotomy to exist within a symmetrical relationship between seller, thing and victim defined by the law of obligations itself.[130] Symmetry also proves to be important with respect to the relationship between school and victim. This, again, was a contractual relationship. However, in holding curtly that an educational establishment is liable for damage caused not only by its fault but also by things supplied in the performance of the contractual obligation the *Cour de cassation* is extending into contract the symmetry to be found in delictual liability as expressed by article 1384 of the *Code civil*. As the note writer observes,[131] the court could simply have justified the liability of the school on the basis of the *obligation de sécurité*; but it preferred to go further and to base liability, not on the intensity of the contractual obligation as such, but on the institutional relationship between person and thing. This symmetry is more

126 Professor Patrice Jourdain, *Professeur agrégé*, Law faculty, University of Paris XII.

127 But *cf* A Tunc, '*La méthode du droit civil: analyse des conceptions françaises*' [1975] *RIDC* 817.

128 DS.1995 at p 352. The present analysis of the *Cour de cassation* decision draws heavily from Professor Jourdain's most thorough note.

129 Council Directive of 25 July 1985 No 85–474. France has not yet implemented the Product Liability Directive, and French case law tends to interpret the present law in conformity with the directive. In 1995 the French cabinet announced its intention to regulate developments in liability law via statute, including product liability.

130 *Cf* Y Lambert-Faivre, '*Fondement et régime de l'obligation de sécurité*', DS.1994.Chron.81 (quoted by Jourdain, *op cit*).

131 DS.1995 at p 354.

general than that of the contractual obligation for latent defects in the product in that it could in theory cover all things that do damage, provided such things were the active instruments of the harm. In seemingly going this far the *Cour de cassation* would appear to be moving towards a standardisation of the regimes of liability.

(c) Concluding remark

None of this is to suggest that such developments are impossible in the English common law world. In fact the recent decision of *White v Jones*[132] might well be seen as an example of the House of Lords extending a contractual warranty into the area of non-contractual obligations. Nevertheless, there is little interest in the symmetry of a law of obligations in common law thought, and the idea of an institutional relationship between person and thing finds little expression in the legal reasoning of judges who, as we have already mentioned, are more concerned with deciding particular factual disputes between particular parties.[133] The mentality of the English legal reasoner rarely rises above the particular nature of the person or thing in issue and so the mentality of the common lawyer is to think in terms of solicitors, occupiers, accountants, doctors, carriers and the like or in terms of animals, walls, trees, tools, lorries and so on. No doubt both French and English judges share the same values and policies – for example, with regard to the protection of the consumer – but the abstract structural thinking of the civilian jurist adds a particular kind of knowledge dimension to legal reasoning that is almost entirely absent from the mentality of the English judiciary. One need only look at a case like *Esso v Southport* to appreciate the difficulties of escaping from the details of the facts. This is not to say that the judiciary of one country is better or worse than the judiciary of another, nor is it to say that an abstract institutional model is always inapplicable in the common law. The point to be made is that the notion of a law of obligations, in the civil law, is always to be understood within the structural symmetries of the civilian legal mentality.

8 GENERAL THEORY OF OBLIGATIONS

Given the English pre-disposition to function at the level of facts, the idea of an abstract law of obligations may, then, seem almost irrelevant to common lawyers. Nevertheless, a law of obligations implies a general theory of obligations in much the same way as a law of contract implies a general theory of contract. The practical lawyer may be little interested of course;[134] but a general theory can still exert an important influence on the way certain kinds of issues and problems are handled. For example, if all obligations are reducible to fault, then all the various problems that arise in the law of obligations ought to be concerned with the behaviour of defendants. Equally, rules about differing limitation periods might seem to have less rationality once one thinks in terms of a generalised obligation. More important perhaps is legal education. A law of obligations

132 [1995] 2 AC 207.

133 Legrande, 'European Legal Systems', *op cit*.

134 See book review of G Samuel, *Sourcebook:* (1995) 145 NLJ 1452.

virtually dictates a rethinking of the traditional categories of private law and this in itself can change the content of these categories in ways that are not always easily perceivable. Thus, rules attaching to particular legal remedies or legal categories might become more generalised once these remedies and specific categories are seen within the general theory of obligations; and so, for example, the collateral contract (Ch 9 § 4) might give way to a more general idea of pre-contractual liability (Ch 10 § 2).[135] Indeed, unjust enrichment, a notion traditionally attaching largely to quasi-contract and equitable remedies (*cf* Ch 11 § 5), has indeed already achieved its independence in many law schools. It is now a subject in search of an independent normative criterion and this search has, in its turn, encouraged the courts to abandon traditional theories.[136] A general theory of obligations, in other words, can have important practical implications simply because the general theory exists as a concept.

135 *Cf Blackpool & Fylde Aero Club Ltd v Blackpool BC* [1990] 1 WLR 1195.

136 See *Lipkin Gorman v Karpnale* [1991] 2 AC 548.

PART I

THE LAW OF ACTIONS

CHAPTER TWO

PROCEDURAL AND SUBSTANTIVE QUESTIONS

One reason why a general theory of obligations is something that has little meaning for the common lawyer is that, as we have mentioned, the common lawyer is more used to thinking at the level of remedies and of specific causes of action. Of course, a remedies-orientated approach need not be incompatible with a law of obligations, as Roman law itself has shown (Ch 1); and the remedies and causes of action to be found in the common law can sometimes be related to ideas in the civil codes. But it has to be remembered that in terms of institutions the remedy and the cause of action can often act as a focal point for both substantive and procedural relations and rules and if these rules do not connect to a scientifically orientated model of real and personal relations, then it is unlikely that the remedies will conform to a rationalised model. For there is no science of remedies as such. In addition, the forms of action have left a legacy, as we have seen with the *Esso* case (Ch 1 § 7(a)), of procedural thinking that stretches beyond the conduct of the litigation itself and into the area of substantive rights. No work on the English law of obligations can ever ignore this legacy.

1 SUBSTANTIVE LAW AND PROCEDURE

When one turns towards the civil law systems one finds a distinction not only between rules of civil procedure and rules of substantive law but also, in the Germanic systems, between formal rules of civil procedure and substantive rules of civil procedure. Formal rules of civil procedure are rules concerned with the technical aspects of legal proceedings and with the execution and enforcement of judgments. Substantive rules of civil procedure are usually connected with the remedy itself, the competence to bring a claim before the courts and the rule *pas d'intérêt, pas d'action* (no interest, no action).[1] In civil law, even if rights can only become apparent through legal proceedings, this does not necessarily mean that such rights can only exist through remedies. In Netherlands law, for example, *rechtsmiddelen,* remedies against a judgment such as an appeal, form a closed system based on the doctrine *lites finiri oportet* and are found in a separate code of civil procedure. Certain rules concerning rights of action can be found in the civil code, for example general provisions concerning class actions, but on the whole civil codes lay down the subjective rights which will be enforced through the application of the provisions on rights of action to be found in the formal rules of civil procedure.

Common lawyers also make a distinction between civil procedure and substantive rules and between substantive principles and remedies. And so the rules governing, say, the launching of the civil action and the giving of evidence in court can be separated

1 This is a procedural rule that can be traced back to Roman law: see Zimmermann, pp 35–38, 935–36. It finds its modern expression in the NCPC art 31.

from the rules and principles of contract and tort. Equally, as we shall see (Ch 7), causation principles function both at a substantive level (did the defendant's act cause the plaintiff's damage?) and at the level of the remedy (did the defendant's act cause this particular head of damage?).[2] Nevertheless, when it comes to remedies this distinction can break down as a result of the legacy of the forms of action which themselves defined substantive ideas mainly through formal rules of procedure (*cf* Ch 3). Thus, as Sir Nicholas Browne-Wilkinson V-C pointed out in 1986, in English law, 'a man's legal rights are in fact those which are protected by a cause of action' and it 'is not in accordance ... with the principles of English law to analyse rights as being something separate from the remedy given to the individual'.[3] The analysis of the legal situation in *Esso v Southport* (Ch 1 § 7(a)) would also go far in confirming this observation – indeed, it seems that the plaintiff ultimately failed as a result of the intermixing of procedural and substantive notions. Remedies, then, can be seen as attracting their own rules and principles (*cf* Chs 4–6), but it is by no means always clear whether these rules and principles are procedural or substantive or, indeed, whether they belong to some intermediate category.

2 PUBLIC AND PRIVATE LAW REMEDIES

In addition to the distinction between procedure and substance, the civil law systems distinguish remedies in private law from remedies in penal and in administrative law. In France, for example, there is a rigid distinction between the remedies used against public bodies and those used against private and commercial defendants, and while this rigidity is not necessarily reflected in other civilian jurisdictions with quite the same enthusiasm, the status of the defendant is usually of importance. In fact, the question is often dealt with as a matter of judicial competence between the civil and administrative courts. In some contrast to this dichotomy, the criminal process can in France be used by the victim of a crime to obtain full compensation as if the victim were suing in the civil law courts.

(a) Civil and administrative process

In English law there is no formal distinction with respect to monetary remedies (debt and damages) between public (administrative) and private law: debt and damages actions based on contract or tort are *prima facie* available for and against public bodies in the same way as they are available in the private sector (Ch 8 § 4(c)). The only exception is in relation to the tort of defamation where the House of Lords has ruled that a public body, or at least a local authority, may not be able to bring proceedings in the same way as a private individual.[4] In short, there is no formal difference between *la responsabilité administrative* and *la responsabilité civile* or between administrative and private

2 See eg *Allied Maples Group Ltd v Simmons & Simmons* [1995] 1 WLR 1602.

3 *Kingdom of Spain v Christie, Manson & Woods Ltd* [1986] 1 WLR 1120, 1129.

4 *Derbyshire CC v Times Newspapers* [1993] AC 534.

contracts.[5] However, alongside the monetary remedies of debt and damages the common law also developed, from early days, a number of specific remedies, the prerogative writs, designed to deal with what today one would call judicial review;[6] and these administrative law remedies have always stood in contrast to the civil law claims for money.[7] The prerogative writs have now been amalgamated into a general remedy of judicial review[8] – a remedy governed by its own procedural process[9] – with the result that a 'private law' monetary remedy launched against a public body risks being struck out as an abuse of process if the court is of the view that the legal issue in question is one involving 'public' rather than 'private' rights.[10] This does not mean that a person who is, for example, owed a debt arising out of a public law relationship cannot bring a private law action in debt;[11] nor does it mean that an individual who suffers no special damage, and thus has no legitimate interest to bring an action in private law, has no remedy to vindicate the public interest. The common law refuses on the whole to erect a procedural or substantive frontier between the public and the private. But it does mean that there is now more of a formal awareness between actions against a public body and claims against a private or commercial enterprise and this awareness might well find expression when it comes to the interpretation of traditional principles (see Ch 13 § 3).

(b) Public and private interests

In fact, the dichotomy between the public and the private has always created certain difficulties in the English law of remedies. Where an individual has suffered special damage as a result of public action there has long been the possibility of a damages claim in the tort of, say, public nuisance, breach of statutory duty, trespass or negligence (*cf* Chs 12–13). Yet where an individual has suffered no such damage the common law has found it more difficult to protect class interests.[12] The main remedial possibility is the relator action whereby individuals or groups can commence an action usually for an injunction (Ch 5 § 4) via the office of the Attorney General;[13] but while this action can appear to be a kind of class action it has to be distinguished from a genuine class action in private law.[14] The nearest procedural process that English law has to the American class action is a representative action which is, in relation to the class action,

5 *In re Norway's Application* [1990] 1 AC 723.

6 Baker, pp 155–75.

7 Weir, *Common Law System*, paras 125–27; *X (Minors) v Bedfordshire County Council* [1995] 2 AC 633.

8 Supreme Court Act 1981 s 31.

9 RSC Ord 53.

10 *O'Reilly v Mackman* [1983] AC 237.

11 *Roy v Kensington and Chelsea Family Practitioner Committee* [1992] 1 AC 624.

12 *Cf* JA Jolowicz, 'Protection of Diffuse, Fragmented and Collective Interests in Civil Litigation: English Law' [1983] CLJ 222.

13 See *AG v PYA Quarries* [1957] 2 QB 169; *Gouriet v Union of Post Office Workers* [1978] AC 435.

14 See generally M Cappelletti, *The Judicial Process in Comparative Perspective* (Oxford, 1989), pp 25–28, 268–308.

quite limited in scope.[15] Furthermore, English law has not adopted the Netherlands and French idea of granting standing to certain bodies representing consumer class interests;[16] the nearest it gets to this institutional arrangement is to grant standing to particular public bodies or officers for the promotion and protection of certain class interests. Thus, a local authority has standing in respect of the protection of interests of the inhabitants of its area;[17] the Secretary of State has power to obtain injunctions and restitution orders for the protection of investors;[18] and the Director of Fair Trading has just been given new powers to obtain injunctions for the protection of consumers in respect of unfair terms in contracts.[19]

In one sense, then, it is possible to distinguish between public and private procedures, remedies and rights.[20] Moreover, there are a number of other procedural rules and remedies where the public and private distinction can be of relevance: for example, it may be that English law has not developed any general damages remedy for harm caused by maladministration,[21] but if a public official does commit any existing tort or other statutory wrong which a court considers amounts to a serious abuse the court has a common law power to award exemplary damages – that is to say, damages designed to punish rather than to compensate (Ch 6 § 5). Judicial review actions themselves are also useful in preventing a public body from utilising its private law rights and remedies in a way that would amount to an abuse of power. Thus, a local authority cannot exercise its property[22] or contractual[23] rights with the same freedom as a private person; equally, a private person cannot expect the breach of a public duty always to give rise to a right to damages in private law.[24] Much will depend upon the nature of the harm and the nature of the interest affected.[25]

Some remedies continue to cause classification problems. *Habeas corpus* is, these days, a public law remedy,[26] but in the last century it also had an important role in family (child custody) cases.[27] And many of the equitable remedies (injunction and

---

15 R Tur, 'Litigation and the Consumer Interest: The Class Action and Beyond' (1982) 2 LS 135.

16 Cappelletti, *supra*, pp 286–87.

17 Local Government Act 1972 s 222.

18 Financial Services Act 1986 s 6; *SIB v Pantell (No 2)* [1993] Ch 256.

19 Unfair Terms in Consumer Contracts Regulations 1994 (SI 1994/3159) reg 8. On 24 January 1996 the European Commission adopted a draft resolution for access-to-justice of consumers through their representatives, eg consumer organisations. The draft lays down limited options for consumer organisations to engage in cross-border procedures for the enforcement of substantive community law measures in specific areas (unfair terms, misleading advertisements): *Europe Agence*, 1996, 6671.

20 *Cf* Weir, *Common Law System*, paras 128–29.

21 *Dunlop v Woollahra Municipal Council* [1982] AC 158.

22 *Wheeler v Leicester CC* [1985] AC 1054.

23 *R v Lewisham LBC, ex p Shell* (UK) [1988] 1 All ER 938.

24 *Yuen Kun Yeu v AG of Hong Kong* [1988] AC 175; *X (Minors) v Bedfordshire County Council* [1995] 2 AC 633.

25 *Murphy v Brentwood DC* [1991] 1 AC 398.

26 *R v Secretary of State for the Home Office, ex p Cheblak* [1991] 1 WLR 890.

27 See, eg, *In re Alicia Race* (1857) 26 LJQB 169; *Ex p Ann Turner* (1872) 41 LJQB 142.

account for example) have a role in both public and private law.[28] Non-contractual debt claims for restitution can also give rise to specific public law problems. Where the state has obtained money pursuant to an *ultra vires* demand the inequality of the parties' positions is an important factor in giving to the citizen a right to the return of the money from the moment of payment, even although the money may have been paid under a mistake of law.[29] Other restitution claims such as salvage, although claims in private law, nevertheless have an important public interest dimension.[30]

(c) Civil and criminal process

The distinction between civil and criminal law proceedings is fundamental in both the civilian and the common law traditions. Nevertheless, the French model has a remedy which bridges the gap at the level of procedure: the victim of a crime can make use of the criminal process to obtain damages as if he or she was suing in the civil courts. This *action civile* is available to anyone who personally has suffered damage directly caused by the criminal act and it is exercised at the same moment as the *action publique*, that is to say the criminal prosecution.[31] The great advantage for plaintiffs, of course, is that they can make use of the evidence collected by the prosecuting authority and they can benefit from the more inquisitorial nature of the criminal proceedings. Obtaining damages can thus be more economic and rapid, especially in traffic accident cases.

In English law the relationship between damages actions and criminal prosecutions is, at the level of procedure, quite straightforward but at the level of fact it can give rise to conceptual problems.[32] A victim of a crime cannot use the criminal process itself to obtain damages, although the courts do have limited powers to make compensation orders.[33] However, the facts which constitute a crime may also constitute a tort (Ch 12 § 4), thus allowing the victim to use the civil courts to obtain compensation.[34] In addition to the law of tort there is also a statutory scheme of compensation for personal injury arising out of a crime[35] and the existence of this scheme may well have an indirect influence on the extent and nature of the duty owed in private law to individual citizens by certain government bodies.[36]

3 THE ROLE OF THE PARTIES AND THE JUDGE

Another important procedural distinction in all systems is to be found in the difference between the role of the court and the role of the parties. However, the position is

28 See eg Supreme Court Act 1981 s 31(2).

29 *Woolwich Building Society v Inland Revenue Commissioners* [1993] AC 70.

30 *The Powstaniec Wielkopolski* [1989] QB 279, 287.

31 *Code de Procédure Pénale* arts 1–5.

32 See eg *Black v Yates* [1992] QB 526.

33 Powers of Criminal Courts Act 1973 ss 35, 38.

34 See eg *Murphy v Culhane* [1977] QB 94; and note the Civil Evidence Act 1968 s 11, 13.

35 Criminal Justice Act 1988 ss 108–115.

36 *Hill v Chief Constable of West Yorkshire* [1988] QB 60 (CA); [1989] AC 53.

made more complicated in the common law tradition by the historical importance of a third institution (to use the term in its broad sense), in addition to the parties and the judge, namely the jury. Before the Judicature Acts 1873–75 there was a jury in nearly all cases, civil as well as criminal, and although it has now largely been removed from civil cases its imprint remains.

(a) Civil law model

Two principles of procedural law are particularly important in civil law. On the one hand there is the principle of the autonomy of the parties in legal proceedings which dictates that it is for the parties to decide the contents and scope of their litigation. On the other hand there is the rule that judges are not to be restricted in the application of the law, a rule which is expressed by the adage *ius curit novit.* This adage, which comes from the *ius commune* rather than Roman law itself,[37] was based on the fiction that judges were supposed to know the law and today gives expression to the idea that the parties need prove only the facts. The judge is the one who knows and applies the rules of law applicable to these proved facts. Thus, in principle, civilian judges are not bound by any qualification (categorisation) that the parties have given to the facts advanced, nor to any conclusions put forward by the parties with respect to the applicability of certain statutory provisions, although of course the actual decision of the judge or the court has to be supported by a valid qualification of the facts stated.

In French law, for example, the *Nouveau Code de Procédure Civile* article 12 lays down that the judge must decide a case in conformity with the rules of law that are applicable to it (*le juge tranche le litige conformément aux règles de droit qui lui sont applicable*) and that he must precisely categorise the facts without stopping at the legal categories put forward by the parties (*Il doit donner ou restituer leur exacte qualification aux faits et actes litigieux sans s'arrêter à la dénomination que les parties en auraient proposée*). Interestingly, the third section of article 12 stipulating that the judge could raise *ex officio* any question of law irrespective of those advanced by the parties (*le juge peut relever d'office les moyens de pur droit quel que soit le fondement juridique invoqué par les parties*) was annulled by the *Conseil d'État* on the ground that it contravened the principle of contradiction.[38] As far as facts are concerned, the French judge can take measures of his or her own accord (*d'office*) in order to advance the inquiry and he can ask the parties to provide further particulars. His decision must be based upon the facts advanced by the parties and if he does wish to invoke a different legal basis than those suggested by the parties he must, according to article 16 of the *Nouveau Code de Procédure Civile*, inform each party and invite them to respond. What has to be stressed with respect to all civilian systems is that the court is searching for the truth: accordingly both parties in civil legal proceedings are under a duty to adhere to the rules of good faith (*bona fides, Treu und Glauben*) and the judge him- or herself must be personally convinced of the facts stated. The parties and court are actively under a duty to establish the true facts.

37 M Kaser, *Das Römische Zivilprozessrecht* (München, 1960), p 17 f.

38 CE 12.10.1979; Dalloz 1979.606. And see JA Jolowicz, 'The Dilemmas of Civil Litigation' (1983) 18 *Israel Law Review* 161, 170–71; GH Samuel, *Ex Facto Ius Oritur* (1989) 8 CJQ 53.

(b) Common law model

In the common law model the role of the judge is much more passive than in continental systems.[39] It is for the parties to advance the facts and the law and, according to the House of Lords at any rate, it is the task of the court simply to decide particular cases between particular litigants.[40] There is no duty either to rationalise the law or to search for some independent truth.[41] Indeed, too many interruptions by a judge during the examination and cross-examination of the witnesses by the parties' lawyers will in itself be a ground for an appeal.[42] Furthermore it has been held by the House of Lords, as we have seen (Ch 1 § 7(a)), that a case ought to be decided in accordance with the pleadings; thus, a party may be prevented from raising new points of law at the trial or on appeal,[43] although the actual position is by no means clear in that, according to the procedural rules themselves, a party is supposed to plead only the facts and this suggests that the theoretical position in England is not so different from that of continental Europe.[44] The real problem for the comparatist is to be found in the comparison of trial with *le procès*. The notion of a trial is closely bound up with the institution of the jury and because jurors were, until the modern era, often illiterate the idea of written evidence and a *dossier* was impractical; instead the emphasis was on an oral process in which the jurors were directly exposed to the witnesses. The jury has now largely disappeared from private law,[45] but its spirit remains;[46] not only does the judge have to play two quite distinct roles – he must decide questions of fact (jury) and questions of law (judge)[47] – but substantive law itself must often be understood in terms of these two functions. The operation of precedent, for example, depends upon a clear distinction being maintained between the two separate roles of the trial judge and this point is sometimes poorly understood in the law of obligations.[48]

This last point can be illustrated by reference to *Bolton v Stone*[49] where the plaintiff was injured, while standing in the road outside her house, by a cricket ball hit out of a neighbouring cricket ground by a visiting batsman. The House of Lords denied the plaintiff damages on the basis that the cricket club had not been negligent. At first sight it might seem that this case sets a precedent: cricket clubs will not be liable for injury done to those outside of the ground unless the risk of injury is foreseeable. In truth,

39 Except perhaps in family law cases: see, eg, *In re G (A Minor)* [1994] 3 WLR 1211.

40 *Read v J Lyons & Co* [1947] AC 156, 175.

41 *Read v J Lyons & Co* [1947] AC 156, 175; *Air Canada v Secretary of State for Trade* [1983] 2 AC 394, 438.

42 *Jones v National Coal Board* [1957] 2 QB 55.

43 *Esso Petroleum Co Ltd v Southport Corporation* [1956] AC 218.

44 JA Jolowicz, in JA Jolowicz (*sous la direction de*), *Droit anglais* (Dalloz, 2e.éd, 1992), nos 133, 167; and see *Drane v Evangelou* [1978] 1 WLR 455.

45 *Ward v James* [1966] 1 QB 273.

46 Jolowicz, *supra* no 12.

47 *Ibid*, no 113.

48 See in particular *Qualcast (Wolverhampton) Ltd v Haynes* [1959] AC 743.

49 [1951] AC 850.

however, the decision, even although a decision of the House of Lords, sets no formal precedent whatsoever, save to restate the proposition that in order to succeed in a negligence claim the plaintiff must prove that the defendant behaved unreasonably. The House of Lords was deciding the question whether a defendant was in breach of his duty of care to the plaintiff and this was, and remains, a question of fact; formerly, therefore, this question would have been decided by the jury who, of course, did not give reasons for their decision. No doubt the case remains useful as a means of assessing what is and is not reasonable behaviour when it comes to remote but real risks. But no trial judge can ever be bound by the decision when deciding a breach of duty question since the question 'Did the defendant behave reasonably?' is a question of fact entirely dependent upon the circumstances of each individual case. Even foreseeability, so important to the causation (remoteness) question (Ch 7 § 4), is of no relevance to this case as such; for, as Lord Radcliffe specifically pointed out, the accident was foreseeable. '[B]ut the fact remains that,' said Lord Radcliffe, 'unless there has been something which a reasonable man would blame as falling beneath the standard of conduct that he would set for himself and require of his neighbour, there has been no breach of duty'.[50] Such a standard was typically for the jury.

Bolton v Stone does not mean that cases in which there is (or was) a jury can never act as important precedents. The point to be emphasised is that the jury's decision cannot in itself be a precedent. Accordingly, a judge's summing up to a jury before they retire to consider their verdict can contain statements of law which do have the capability of acting as precedents. For example, McNair J's explanation in *Bolam v Friern Hospital Management Committee*[51] of what is meant by 'negligence' in the context of professional skills has become a classic test in the area of medical negligence and has been used by the House of Lords on several occasions.[52] The summing up pointed out that the test for a breach of duty in situations involving a special skill is not the test of the conduct of the man on the top of the Clapham omnibus because such a person does not possess the special skill. It is 'the standard of the ordinary skilled man exercising and professing to have that special skill'. All that a doctor need exercise according to this legal test is 'the ordinary skill of an ordinary competent man exercising that particular art'.[53] In *Bolam* itself the jury returned to deliver a verdict in favour of the defendant, but the test would in theory have remained valid even if the jury had returned a verdict for the plaintiff.

4 BURDEN OF PROOF

One of the most important objectives of the continental model of civil procedure is to facilitate the search for the factual truth in order to realise the subjective rights of the parties. Now it might be argued that this objective can be achieved only by eliminating obstacles such as rigid rules for giving evidence, for distributing the burden of proof

50 At pp 868–69.

51 [1957] 2 All ER 118.

52 See eg *Whitehouse v Jordan* [1981] 1 WLR 246; *Sidaway v Bethlem Royal Hospital* [1985] AC 871.

53 [1957] 2 All ER at p 121.

between the parties and for allocating specific evidential value to certain facts. And so, certainly, *bona fides* may well play an important role in governing the relationship between the parties to litigation. Nevertheless, the objective of truth can in the end be achieved only by the proof of facts stated and the whole question of proof brings one back to the allocation of its burden. A compromise between fairness and rigidity is reached through the idea of inequality between parties which in turn can dictate the *onus probandi*; and such inequality can exist whenever one of the parties is a specialist or possesses specific knowledge as opposed to the other party who will not, therefore, be in a position to assess where the factual truth lies. Indeed when dealing with consumer protection, new rights for consumers, if they are to be effective, often require new procedural mechanisms and perhaps even a new approach to procedures;[54] for the complexity of legal rules can become a new source of imbalance.[55]

(a) Proof and substantive law

This whole question of burden of proof extends beyond the law of procedure as such since it is possible to argue that the introduction of strict liability (liability without fault) in the Roman law of obligations was motivated by a desire to help plaintiffs recover compensation in situations where proof of fault and causation might otherwise be impossible.[56] Thus, innkeepers and shipmasters were strictly liable for property lost while in their custody, and those occupying buildings adjacent to a public way were liable without proof of fault for injury caused to passers-by from things falling or thrown from the building.[57] Of course, such strict liability actions were also developed to protect certain class interests, such as the interest of people using public roads (*cf* Ch 12 §§ 4–5); but even though liability without fault has now the status of substantive principle and is to be found within the modern codes, the procedural advantages of such principles must never be underestimated. Having to prove fault is a major burden on any plaintiff wishing to use the legal system to obtain compensation for injury.[58] The introduction of liability without fault has the effect, therefore, of putting the burden of disproving liability on to the shoulders of the actor, or controller of a person or thing, who has caused the damage. Burden of proof acts as a bridge between procedure and substance.

---

54 M Cappelletti & B Garth, *Access to justice* (Alphen aan den Rijn, 1978), pp 49–50. The European Commission has identified access-to-justice as one of the main problem areas for consumers and it intends to take appropriate measures: *cf Europe Agence*, 1996, 6472, Green Paper on access-to-justice, *Third Action Programme Consumer Policy*, 1996–98, Europe Documents 1995, no 1960; draft directive on access-to-justice, *Europe Agence*, 1996, 6652/6667.

55 M Galanter, Afterword: 'Explaining Litigation', *Law and Society*, Winter, 1975, p 363.

56 See eg D. 9.3.2.

57 D.44.7.5.5-6. Gaius justified the liability of the innkeeper on the basis of fault in making use of bad people: D.44.7.5.6.

58 See eg *Whitehouse v Jordan* [1981] 1 WLR 246.

(b) *Res ipsa loquitur*

In English law the task of the court is only to do justice between the parties and there is no additional duty to search for some independent truth.[59] However, it would be idle to think that common lawyers are not aware of the problems of procedural inequality and access to justice and so the English law of obligations has fashioned various devices to aid plaintiffs with respect to the burden of proof. The most important of these devices, for an obligations lawyer, is the doctrine of *res ipsa loquitur*. In theory this doctrine of letting the facts (or thing which does damage) speak for themselves (itself) does not reverse the burden of proof as such; all that it does is to put an onus on the defendant to show that the accident and damage could have happened without any fault on his part.[60] Accordingly, when two patients, who had entered hospital as active persons for an operation, came out paralysed, Denning LJ observed that the facts did speak for themselves.[61] They certainly called for an explanation from the hospital authorities and if they had been unable to provide such an explanation the court would have been entitled to presume that the paralysis occurred as a result of the negligence of the hospital. However, in this case the authorities were able to provide an explanation – the accident happened as a result of invisible cracks in the anaesthetic ampoules the danger of which was unknown to the medical profession at that time – and once the accident was explained, no further question of *res ipsa loquitur* arose. The only question was whether, on the facts, the defendants were in breach of their duty of care (*cf Bolton v Stone*, above).

This analysis of *res ipsa loquitur* is, at any rate, the traditional view. However, there are cases which seem to go further and require of a defendant that he virtually prove that he was not negligent. Accordingly, in *Henderson v HE Jenkins & Co*[62] the House of Lords, by a bare majority, held that the owners of a lorry whose brakes had failed causing the death of the plaintiff's husband had not discharged the onus of proof on them in respect of the condition of the vehicle. The owners had proved that the brake pipe had been visually inspected and tested once a week according to Ministry of Transport recommendations; but a majority of the House of Lords said that they should have gone further. 'It was ... incumbent on the [owners], if they were to sustain their plea of latent defect undiscoverable by the exercise of ordinary care,' said Lord Donovan, 'to prove where the vehicle had been and what it had been carrying whilst in their service and in what conditions it had operated.'[63] More interesting in some ways is the case of *Ward v Tesco Stores*.[64] The plaintiff proved that while she was doing her shopping in one of the defendants' supermarkets she had slipped on some sticky substance, which turned out to be yoghurt, and that she had injured her ankle; moreover, some three weeks later, she had returned to the store to discover another

59 *Air Canada v Secretary of State for Trade* [1983] 2 AC 394, 438.

60 *The Kite* [1933] P 154.

61 *Roe v Minister of Health* [1954] 2 QB 66.

62 [1970] AC 282.

63 At p 300.

64 [1976] 1 WLR 810.

spillage which remained unattended for about a quarter of an hour. Were these facts advanced by the plaintiff enough to support her claim in negligence for damages? At the trial the defendants did not call any evidence as to when the supermarket had last been swept before the plaintiff's accident and as a result the trial judge decided that there was a *prima facie* case against the defendants. A majority of the Court of Appeal upheld this finding: 'the probabilities were that the spillage had been on the floor long enough for it to have been cleared up by a member of the staff'[65] and this spillage 'created a serious risk that customers would fall and injure themselves'.[66]

These two cases are no doubt reconcilable with the traditional theory of *res ipsa loquitur* in that the defendants in neither case did enough to rebut the onus of probability. Thus, if the defendants had been able to show that the accident would have happened irrespective of the existence of a proper and adequate system of checks and safety they would have escaped liability. Nevertheless, both decisions, in comparison with, say, *Bolton v Stone* (above), have moved quite some way away from the plaintiff having positively to prove that a defendant was acting unreasonably since all that was required of the plaintiff was to describe a series of events. As Ormrod LJ, the dissenting judge in *Ward v Tesco*, pointed out: the accident was described by the plaintiff but the crucial question of how long before the accident the yoghurt had been on the floor had been avoided.[67] The effect of this change in the onus of proof was to make the two defendants liable for injury done by things under their control. Whether such an onus of probability would be put on the owner of a private car whose brakes failed, or on the owner of a private house in which a visitor slipped, is another question; and one which makes the English law of obligations particularly complex since so much can depend upon the social and economic status of the parties and upon the particular facts of each case. One need only return to the *Esso* case (Ch 1 § 7(a)) to see how the intensity and level of duty in respect of damage done by things is as much dependent upon procedural as substantive ideas. In the civilian systems the dichotomy between fault and strict liability is, usually, clearly and abstractly stated as a matter of substantive obligational principle. In the common law, in contrast, much will depend on status, on the thing that does the damage and on how the case is pleaded.

5 QUESTIONS OF FACT AND QUESTIONS OF LAW

Facts are thus essential in the common law process and small variations of status or context can make all the difference. In *White v Jones*[68] for example the *ratio decidendi* does not, probably, extend beyond the facts of solicitor and beneficiary; equally, as we have seen, in *Spring v Guardian Assurance Plc*[69] Lord Woolf emphasised that the views which he expressed were confined to the class of case with which he was dealing and although he appreciated that these views could be applied to analogous situations, he

65 Lawton LJ at p 814.

66 Megaw LJ at p 816.

67 At pp 814–15.

68 [1995] 2 AC 207.

69 [1995] 2 AC 296, 354.

did not intend to express any opinion as to these situations, preferring to wait until a particular case was to come before the court. Rules, it would seem, remain firmly trapped within particular factual situations. Nevertheless, it is important to keep separate fact and law since the traditional distinction between questions of law and questions of fact is an essential and firmly established feature of the legal process in both civil and common law jurisdictions. Legal inquiries differ from factual inquiries because the former are governed by the need to find a decision based on normative (ought) criteria which will transcend the bare fact-finding inquiry.[70]

The distinction between fact and law is by no means an easy one since, as Jessel MR once pointed out, there is hardly any fact which does not contain some aspect which requires a knowledge of the law. 'If you state', he said, 'that a man is in possession of an estate of £10,000 a year, the notion of possession is a legal notion, and involves knowledge of law'.[71] It has been observed that the crucial issue is not what as a matter of theory ought to be classified as fact and as law, but what the law actually classifies as questions of fact and questions of law.[72] Accordingly, as we have seen, when it comes to the role of facts in continental legal reasoning they have, it would seem, little place save in matters regarding the distribution of the burden of proof. In truth the position is much more complex as some civilian judges now recognise. Legal decision-making is much less a matter of abstract codes and legal science and more a matter of interpreting the facts which takes place under the guise of qualification, value judgment and the interpretation of quasi normative notions such as damage and interest (*cf* Ch 6 § 1; Ch 3 § 3(c)).[73] Legal theory on the continent emphasises the abstract nature of legal reasoning in civil law cultures and this tends to underrate the importance of how facts are categorised and presented. In addition, the point that the French jurist Théodore Ivanier makes, is that judges tease *les faits inconnus* (hidden facts) from *les faits connus* (known facts) and this process is much more central than any recourse to the syllogism.[74] As far as Ivanier is concerned, the law may be rigid and abstract, but when it comes to interpretation one is working with a system of values right in the heart of concrete fact.[75] Nevertheless, the distinction remains of the utmost importance in continental civil procedure since many supreme courts – in particular *les cours de cassation* – can hear and decide only questions of law. Indeed, in French law, the trial court has a *pouvoir souverain* with respect to decisions of fact which cannot, in theory, be interfered with by the *Cour de cassation* (supreme court). However, if French trial judges venture beyond the world of fact and into the world of rule-making, they may find

70 JD Jackson, 'Questions of Fact and Questions of Law', in W Twining (ed), Facts in Law, *Archiv für Rechts- und Sozialphilosophie*, 1983, Beiheft nr 16, pp 85–87.

71 *Eaglesfield v Marquis of Londonderry* (1876) 4 Ch D 693, 703.

72 Jackson, *op cit*, p 87. And see F Rigaux, 'The Concept of Fact in Legal Science', in P Nerholt (ed), *Law, Interpretation and Reality* (Dordrecht/Boston/London, 1990), p 22 & 38 ff.

73 See eg T Ivanier, *L'interprétation des faits en droit* (LGDJ, 1988).

74 *Ibid*, pp 84–86.

75 *Ibid*, p 337.

their decisions being quashed for contravening article 5 of the *Code civil* which prohibits judges from usurping the function of the legislator.[76]

The distinction between questions of fact and questions of law is, as we have seen, of importance in English law as well as continental law. This is the result, however, not of any theory regarding the role of an appeal (*cassation*) court – the Court of Appeal and the House of Lords can in theory decide questions of fact as well as law.[77] It results from the need to distinguish between the roles of judge and jury. The jury may now have largely disappeared from the law of obligations (defamation and false imprisonment remain important exceptions),[78] but the fact and law dichotomy continues to be reflected not only in the procedural duties of the judge, but in the substantive law itself. Thus, causation in the law of obligations (Ch 7) is both a factual and a legal question, each question in turn being governed by a different test.[79] Equally, the question of vicarious liability, seemingly governed by a legal rule subdivided into three parts ((i) there must be a tort (ii) committed by a servant (iii) acting in the course of his employment) (*cf* Ch 12 § 6), is divisible into questions of law and questions of fact. Thus, the course of employment question is one that, ultimately, comes down to a question of fact which means that in former times it would have been decided by a jury and now requires an appeal court to examine, not the rule as such, but the evidence upon which the trial judge reached his or her decision.[80]

Where the dichotomy becomes difficult is when questions of causation become entangled with questions of burden of proof. D, an employer, fails to provide adequate washing facilities for his employees who have to work in a hot and dusty brick kiln; one of these employees, P, contracts dermatitis and brings an action against D for damages. P cannot prove one hundred per cent that the absence of the washing facilities was the cause of the dermatitis, but he can show that the hot and dusty kilns plus an absence of washing facilities significantly increases the risk of dermatitis. Ought his action for damages to succeed on these facts?[81] Much can depend upon how one views the facts. If the risk is seen as a specific fact proved by the plaintiff it is possible to use this as the basis for saying that D's breach of duty has caused specific damage, that is to say it has put P at risk of contracting dermatitis; risk, fault and damage thus become facts capable, when intermixed, of generating a normative duty. If, however, the risk is confined only to the question of proof, that is to say it is not used as an intermediary fact between the dermatitis and the absence of washing facilities, it is equally possible to hold that P has not proved that the absence of washing facilities has caused P's dermatitis. How facts are perceived in relation to notions such as risk and burden of proof not only becomes crucial to the way the case may be decided, but also goes far in

---

76 See eg Cass.crim 3.11.1955; Dalloz 1956.I.557 note Savatier.

77 *Viscount de L'Isle v Times Newspapers* [1988] 1 WLR 49, 62.

78 Supreme Court Act 1981 s 69.

79 See eg *McKew v Holland & Hannen & Cubits Ltd* [1969] 3 All ER 1621. And *cf The Wagon Mound (No 1)* [1961] AC 388.

80 *Keppel Bus Co Ltd v Sa'ad bin Ahmed* [1974] 2 All ER 700 (PC).

81 See *McGhee v National Coal Board* [1973] 1 WLR 1.

showing how quasi-normative notions such as risk, fault and damage act as vehicles for secreting normative legal principle within the factual question. Factual and legal questions thus become inextricably intermixed revealing in turn just how substantive law can both develop in the interstices of procedure[82] and arise out of fact (*ex facto ius oritur*).

6 LEGISLATION

A legal system that starts out from fact and procedure is, in the absence of a university tradition at least, unlikely to be structured in terms of the norms applicable, such norms being trapped, of course, within the concrete facts of each precedent. On the continent things are, traditionally, very different in that the codes deal only with abstract norms arranged according to the institutional system of persons, things and obligations (*cf* Ch 3 § 3(a)). In addition the codes have an important ideological role: they represent a system of morality, legality and political will (*lex, la loi*) rolled into one and even if they have encouraged a legalistic and positivistic approach in the past the codes provide clear rules and principles. They are seen as a form of *auctoritas* (authority). In fact few civilians believe today that codes act as axiomatic sources of private law, allowing the citizen to learn the law from legislation alone. Many of the abstract rules are simply empty of content. Legal practice and legal theory are just as important as sources of legal knowledge and, indeed, the civil law experience itself now indicates that statutory regulation is no obstacle to judicial lawmaking. From a comparative law viewpoint, differences in the theory of sources of law between common law and civil law are becoming more formal than real.[83] The civilian emphasis is shifting to the casuistics of case law while, so some say, the Anglo-American law is becoming more constructivist.[84]

Nevertheless, from the historical perspective one characteristic of the English law of obligations is clear: the structure is the work neither of any university nor of any reforming legislature. It is the work of law in practice – that is to say, the work of practitioners, of judges, and of those in the administrative bureaucracies.[85] From a procedural position, the role of the judges has been the key to the structure of the common law and their influence even today, particularly in the law of obligations, remains fundamental. However, in the 19th century the judge as source of law began to be usurped by a Parliament keen to haul the legal system into the age of industrial capitalism and to make the legal process more amenable to ideas which favoured a commercial rather than a feudal law.[86] As a result the written word increasingly replaced the *ratio decidendi* of precedent as the main source of law.[87] All the same, this

82 Sir H Maine, *Early Law and Custom* (John Murray, 1890), p 389.

83 M Vranken, 'Statutory Interpretation and Judicial Policy Making: Some Comparative Reflections' [1991] *Statute Law Review* 31.

84 J Esser, *Grundsatz und Norm* (Tübingen, 1974), p 223.

85 See generally RC van Caenegem, *Judges, Legislators and Professors* (Cambridge, 1987).

86 See generally M Lobban, *The Common Law and English Jurisprudence 1760-1850* (Oxford, 1991).

87 Atiyah, Rise and Fall pp 254–55, 506–68.

legislative revolution never directly interfered with the substantive structure of the law of obligations; indeed it did much to confirm the categories of 'contract', 'tort' and 'debt' by employing them in, typically, procedural statutes such as the County Courts Act[88] which gave rise, in turn, to interpretation problems demanding a conceptual (re)analysis of private law.[89]

But if statutes did not actually alter the basic conceptual structure of the law of obligations, they have certainly altered on occasions the substantive law. Thus, there are Acts which make alterations to rights by reversing a common law rule,[90] by introducing a new action for a new range of plaintiffs,[91] by establishing statutory defences to certain common law claims[92] and by giving the court more discretion in allocating responsibility or liability in certain situations.[93] And the way this kind of legislation operates can be similar to that of a new line of cases: the traditional conceptual ideas are usually retained but rearranged, added to or subtracted from in order to produce the desired results. Thus, to give a few examples, s 2(1) of the Misrepresentation Act 1967 restates, in effect, the tort of deceit, but withdraws the necessity of having to prove fault; the Occupiers' Liability Act 1957 states in s 2(1) that an 'occupier of premises owes the same duty, the "common duty of care", to all his visitors'; and the Torts (Interference With Goods) Act 1977 stipulates in s 2 not only that 'Detinue is abolished' but that an 'action lies in conversion for loss or destruction of goods which a bailee has allowed to happen in breach of his duty to his bailor ... '. Legislation is dependent on the pre-existence of case law and thus operates at the same conceptual and factual levels as the cases themselves. Indeed the pre-existing case law can sometimes prove to be relevant when it comes to the interpretation of such legislation. For example in *Merlin v British Nuclear Fuels Plc*[94] 'injury and damage' in s 12 of the Nuclear Installations Act 1965 was interpreted as not extending to pure economic harm since the common law tort of negligence had long distinguished between damage, injury and loss (*cf* Ch 13 § 9).

The results of this approach are twofold. First, the legislator cannot easily function at the level of principle: it can only function effectively via positive rules which the courts will enforce strictly within the limits of the language utilised. Thus, the courts could never use s 2(1) of the Animals Act 1971, which states that the keeper of a dangerous animal will be strictly liable for damage caused by the animal, as the basis for a general institutional liability for damage caused by dangerous things.[95] Indeed, they could not even extend by analogy s 3 of the 1971 Act to cover general damage done

88 See now County Courts Act 1984 s 15.

89 See eg *Bryant v Herbert* (1877) 3 CPD 389.

90 See eg Law Reform (Personal Injury) Act 1948 s 1(1).

91 See eg Fatal Accidents Act 1976.

92 See eg Civil Aviation Act 1982 s 76(1).

93 See eg Law Reform (Frustrated Contracts) Act 1943; Law Reform (Contributory Negligence) Act 1945; Civil Liability (Contribution) Act 1978.

94 [1990] 2 QB 557.

95 *Read v J Lyons & Co* [1947] AC 156.

by dogs since the words of the statute talk only of 'killing or injuring livestock'. Sometimes Parliament does try to work at more abstract levels by using the concept of 'duty', but this notion, as we have seen with the *Merlin* case, is usually trapped within fairly narrow factual situations. Statutes function within very defined factual boundaries.

Secondly, the legislator is not in a good position to try to give any shape to English law as a whole. In fact the structure of statutes themselves does not help in this respect, either, since sections in a single statute often meander between the legal worlds of fact, law, remedies and procedure and there is little regard for any schematic classification of rights. The sections of the Torts (Interference With Goods) Act 1977, for example, move from substantive law, to causes of action, to remedies, to procedure and back to substantive principle without any thought being given to overall structure of property and obligation duties. It is, of course, true that there is today a multitude of statutes establishing and regulating whole areas of economic life and a piece of legislation like the Sale of Goods Act 1979 does try to codify an area along continental lines.[96] But because of the lack of partnership between judge and draftsman, together with the general tradition of English lawyers to think about facts rather than principles, the courts often find themselves operating at a level which will not encourage the tackling of problems in any schematic or systematic way. Moreover, the use of opaque language in many statutes simply mitigates against rationalisation by placing legislation beyond the comprehension of many lawyers let alone ordinary citizens keen to grasp the structure and policy of any particular area.[97] Until 1965, the English legislator had never officially even considered a possible codification of English private law.[98]

It would, however, be a little unreasonable just to blame the legislator for the narrow and descriptive nature of legislative rules since part of the problem undoubtedly lies with the epistemological (theory of knowledge) development of English law itself. As will be seen (Ch 14), the tendency of the common law is to attach rules more to specific things, or classes of things, and to specific classes of people (occupiers, bailees, manufacturers etc), as opposed to any general notion of a legal institution in the sense of legal subject and legal object.[99] Consequently, one should not be surprised by a legislator which, in its own interest, perpetuates a particular scientific tradition. What is perhaps to be regretted is that English judges have not been able to escape from their own historical methodology when it comes to the interpretation of statutes. Yet this failure is, also, part of the descriptive tradition. English judges have never really been able to interpret statutes through the use of abstract institutions – that is to say, they have always treated, for example, an animal as an animal, rather than as a *res* capable of doing damage – and consequently the common law courts have not been able to develop the law via analogy with existing statutes. They have, in other words, been

96 Zimmermann, pp 336–37.

97 JA Clarence-Smith, 'Legislative Drafting: English and Continental' [1980] SLR 14; T Millett, 'A Comparison of British and French Legislative Drafting' [1986] SLR 130.

98 R van Caeneghem, *Geschiedkundige inleiding tot het privaatrecht* (Gent, 1985), p 176; *cf* Law Commission Act 1965.

99 G Samuel, '*Entre les mots et les choses*' [1995] RIDC 509.

rendered immobile when it comes to *lex* with the result that development of the law (*ius*, *le droit*) is often possible only in those areas where legislation has not intervened. There are exceptions of course – for example, in the area of remedies.[100] But, when invited to develop a liability for dangerous things by analogy with liability for dangerous animals, the House of Lords remarked that it was not its job 'to rationalise the law of England' and that '[a]rguments based on legal consistency are apt to mislead for the common law is a practical code adapted to deal with the manifold diversities of human life'.[101] Interpretation, then, is as much a prisoner of the past tradition as is the style and language of the statutory texts; and, as Bachelard might well have said of such a rationality, it is a science too close to the facts.[102]

7 PARTIES

Where legislation is particularly revealing, however, is in the way each statutory proposition is constructed around an institution, even if such institution is highly descriptive (*cf* Ch 3 § 3(a)). As Gaius insisted, law consists of persons, things and actions and these institutional focal points not only form the basis of all statutory rules, but also are capable of determining, to some extent, the way a section will be interpreted. Rules framed around things encourage the courts to focus only on the thing itself,[103] whereas rules attaching to persons emphasise the acts and behaviour of such persons.[104] In addition the Gaian scheme allows the interpreter to reflect upon the nature of legal subjects and legal objects in the context of the dichotomy between substantive and procedural rules. Thus, the Trade Union and Labour Relations (Consolidation) Act 1992 denies, as a matter of substantive law, that a trade union is a legal person (body corporate), but, as a matter of procedure, allows such an 'organisation' (s 1) to make contracts and to sue and be sued in its own name (s 10). Similarly the Law Reform (Miscellaneous Provisions) Act 1934, although refusing to resurrect a dead human as a legal person, nevertheless stipulates that certain causes of action shall survive against or for the benefit of his 'estate' (s 1). Equally, a child in the womb is not a legal person as such, but the Congenital Disabilities (Civil Liability) Act 1976, through the notions of 'damage' (s 1(1)) and 'parent' (s 1(3)), creates a situation whereby a tortfeasor can be liable to a child injured before birth.

These rules are clearly procedural, yet, more generally, they have fundamental implications for the substantive law of obligations. What 'rights' does a trade union, unborn baby or a dead person have? What if a member of a trade union commits a tort while acting for his union: can the victim sue the union for damages?[105] What if an employer libels a union: does a union have the right to bring proceedings for

100 See *Jaggard v Sawyer* [1995] 2 All ER 189.

101 Lord Macmillan in *Read v J Lyons & Co* [1947] AC 156, 175.

102 G Bachelard, *La formation de l'esprit scientifique* (Vrin, 1938), p 44.

103 *Frost v Aylesbury Dairy Co Ltd* [1905] 1 KB 608.

104 Supply of Goods and Services Act 1982 s 13.

105 *Cf* Trade Union and Labour Relations (Consolidation) Act 1992 ss 20–22.

defamation?[106] Can one owe a duty of care to an unborn child?[107] Or take the 'organisation' of the family. Does the law recognise that a family can sue or be sued in its own right? The general procedural rule is clear enough: only a living human being and a corporate legal person are treated as legal subjects as such. Thus if D contracts with Mr B to pay an annuity to Mr B until his death and thereafter to pay an annuity to Mrs B, the law will not treat Mr and Mrs B as a single *persona*; if Mrs B wishes to enforce the debt in the courts she must sue D either in her own capacity or via the estate of Mr B.[108] Equally, where a father makes a contract for himself and for his family, the family have no direct rights against the contractor.[109] At the level of procedure and remedies, however, the position can turn out to be more complex. Thus, family members who are not parties to a contract concluded by, say, a father might still find that the law of remedies recognises their 'legitimate interests' in the contract (*cf* Ch 4 § 2) and such a family interest might also be reflected in the quantum of damages awarded to a tort victim.[110] Furthermore statute has long given family members of a tort victim an independent claim against tortfeasors for financial losses arising out of the death of the victim.[111] Equally, the family member who suffers nervous shock from witnessing the death or injury of a loved one might well have an independent claim.[112]

Organisations can still cause conceptual problems even when they have full legal personality since a corporation can act only through living persons.[113] What, then, is the position if an employee of one company deliberately kills an employee of another company: can one company sue the other company for compensation? Will the employer of the killer be guilty of murder? Will the status of the killer be important – that is to say, will the company be liable if he is the managing director but not liable if he is the janitor? These may seem exotic questions, but they do contain very serious conceptual issues. Take two actual situations. A passenger on a bus is abused and insulted by the conductor and, having asked politely not to be abused, is assaulted and severely injured by the bus conductor: is the employer of the bus conductor, the operator of the bus, to be liable to the injured passenger? A patrolman working for a security company is sent by his employer to guard the plaintiffs' factory; instead of guarding the premises he deliberately starts a fire which leads to the destruction of the whole factory. Is the security company to be liable to the owner of the factory? In both situations it is possible to say that the plaintiff has been damaged by a member of an organisation, yet it is also possible to distinguish between organisation (one person) and human actor (another person) allowing the organisation to claim that the criminal act in

---

106 *EET&P Union v Times Newspapers Ltd* [1980] QB 585.

107 *Burton v Islington Health Authority* [1993] QB 204.

108 *Beswick v Beswick* [1968] AC 58.

109 *Jackson v Horizon Holidays* [1975] 1 WLR 1468.

110 *Pickett v British Rail Engineering Ltd* [1980] AC 126.

111 See now Fatal Accident Act 1976.

112 *McLoughlin v O'Brien* [1983] AC 410; *cf Alcock v Chief Constable of South Yorkshire* [1992] 1 AC 310.

113 *Tesco Supermarkets Ltd v Nattrass* [1972] AC 153; *Meridian Global Funds Management Asia Ltd v Securities Commission* [1995] 2 AC 500.

both situations was not its act. In what circumstances should the organisation be allowed to make such a claim?

In *Keppel Bus Co Ltd v Sa'ad bin Ahmad*[114] the Privy Council held that the bus company was not to be liable for the act of its conductor since it was outside the scope of his duties; but in *Photo Production v Securicor*[115] the House of Lords was not prepared to accept, as a matter of principle, that the act of the patrolman was not the act of the company. At one level this difference of liability is the result of a difference of interpretation of the substantive law principle of vicarious liability: an employer will be liable for torts committed by an employee acting in the course of his employment (see Ch 12 § 6(a)). In the *Keppel* case the Privy Council decided, on the evidence, that the conductor was acting outside the scope of his employment. Nevertheless, this analysis avoids the procedural nature of the problem. If as a matter of procedure an organisation is to have all the benefits of corporate personality, that is to say the group is to be treated as a unit capable of suing and owning property, why should it be able to escape the responsibilities attaching to such a unit? One answer, of course, is that the employer and the employee do have separate lives and thus it would be difficult, even as a matter of procedure, to say that the company should be liable for acts committed by an employee on his day off. Yet if one does make this distinction between two *personae*, it indicates the extent to which a procedural issue (who can sue and be sued) gives rise to substantive questions in the law of obligations. When is one person liable for acts committed by another person (Ch 12 § 6)? And what constitutes a 'person' for this purpose?

8 STATUS

Associated with the issue of personality is the question of status.[116] In Roman law slaves did not have legal personality because of their status as things (*res*), as opposed to persons (*personae*), and although slavery is, as a matter of law at any rate, not a feature of modern Western systems, the notion of status, as an aspect of the law of persons, can still be important in understanding how private law functions as a system. Legal situations can be predetermined simply as a result of a legal category into which a person can be classed. The most notorious uses of status in this century have been in Nazi Germany, where simply being Jewish meant fewer rights, and in South Africa, before the new constitution, where colour determined one's legal position. But today, in the EU countries, status is used in a more benign way, save perhaps over questions of citizenship where status is at the heart of immigration law. In private law status is used, for example, to distinguish consumers from professionals and commerçants from private citizens. Accordingly, in both common law and civil law systems, those individuals who contract as consumers might be subject to a different regime, for

114 [1974] 2 All ER 700.

115 [1980] AC 827.

116 See generally RH Graveson, *Status in the Common Law* (Athlone, 1953).

example in respect of exclusion clauses (*cf* Ch 10 § 4(c)),[117] than those who contract as professionals.

In fact status in a wide sense of the term can be found throughout the law of obligations. The Occupiers' Liability Acts 1957 and 1984, for example, talk in terms of duties owed by an 'occupier' towards a 'visitor' and a 'trespasser'; and whether or not a person falls into one of these categories could be seen as a question of status in that duties attach to the category itself and thus follow automatically from such a classification. Equally, the Employment Act 1989 in s 11 makes special provisions with regard to 'Sikhs' injured on construction sites while not wearing a safety helmet; and the Torts (Interference with Goods) Act 1977 extends the tort of conversion via the terms 'bailor' and 'bailee'. In the Sale of Goods Act 1979, and various other statutes, the duty to supply goods of satisfactory quality and reasonable fitness attaches only to those who supply 'in the course of a business' and such a requirement, if only indirectly, gives rise to a broad distinction between business and private sellers. In a narrow sense it may be that many of these supply of goods statutes are talking about capacity rather than status and thus merely because a person is a second-hand car salesman will not in itself prevent the salesman from transacting as a private person.

However, there are situations where the category can act as a status category in the full sense of the term. In *Stevenson v Beverley Bentinck*[118] the purchaser of a motor vehicle subsequently discovered, when a finance company seized the car, that the seller was not the owner of the vehicle. In an action for conversion and detinue against the finance company the purchaser claimed that he had obtained protection as an innocent purchaser by virtue of ss 27 and 29 of the Hire Purchase Act 1964; the finance company claimed, however, that the Act only applied to a 'private purchaser' which the plaintiff was not since he was a part-time car dealer. The Court of Appeal upheld the defence on the basis that the Act 'is concerned not with capacity, but only with status';[119] the plaintiff had the status of a 'trade or finance purchaser' and as a result he did not fall within the category of 'private purchaser' even if he had purchased the car in his private capacity. Ownership was denied to the plaintiff simply because of the category within which he found himself. A similar decision has been arrived at recently in respect of the right to possession (*ius possessionis*). In *Waverley BC v Fletcher*[120] the defendant found a medieval gold brooch while using a metal detector in a public park and the plaintiff council, which unknown to the defendant had a policy of prohibiting the use of metal detectors in parks, brought an action claiming the property. The Court of Appeal held that on these facts the council had the better possessory title since the defendant's behaviour in excavating the soil and removing property was an act of trespass. According to Auld LJ, 'the English law of ownership and possession, unlike that of Roman law, is not a system of identifying absolute entitlement but of priority of

117 See Unfair Contract Terms Act 1977 ss 3, 6, 12.

118 [1976] 1 WLR 483.

119 Roskill LJ at p 487.

120 [1995] 3 WLR 772.

entitlement';[121] in consequence the 'status' of the defendant as a 'trespasser' put him in a weaker position *vis-à-vis* the owner of the land in respect of a possessory title to the brooch. Status, it might be said, once again determined ownership.

At the level of case law the role of status, at least in the broad sense of the term, can be important in a range of obligation situations. The distinction between public and private bodies is of relevance not just in duty of care problems (Ch 13 § 3) but also in respect of pre-contractual rights and obligations. A public body simply does not have the same freedom of choice when it comes to decisions about with whom it will or will not contract.[122] And the distinction between consumers and commercial concerns is increasingly being reflected, if only implicitly, in the judgments of the House of Lords. On the whole it is probably easier for a plaintiff to obtain damages for pure financial loss in the tort of negligence if the plaintiff qualifies as a consumer[123] – although if the defendant is a public body things may well be different[124] – and in the area of contract law inequality of bargaining power between contractors has encouraged the courts to interpret contractual provisions in the context of the status of the parties.[125] These may not be strictly law of persons questions. Nevertheless, the notion of status can be useful in orientating the jurist away from the idea of an obligation existing as an abstract notion between two legal subjects and towards the idea that rights and duties also flow from the standing of the parties. Moreover, it must never be forgotten that some of the early rules of contract and tort were formulated within the law of persons rather than the law of obligations. Thus, the duties of a common carrier or an innkeeper largely predate the idea of a law of contract and tort in the common law;[126] and while these duties have now been redistributed amongst contract, tort and property (bailment) it is not always so easy to escape from the past. Carriage of goods can sometimes be complex because status and obligation are still capable of working in opposite directions[127] and family law, a central law of persons subject, can also seemingly function on occasions with concepts that are opposed to the procedural ideology of the law of obligations.

9 THE RIGHT TO SUE

Take for example the following problems. H contracts with D, a firm of builders, to replace the roof on the matrimonial home actually owned by W, H's wife; the work is done carelessly and when H goes to see his solicitor he is told that neither he nor his wife can sue D because H has suffered no damage, not being the owner of the house, and W has no contractual or tortious obligational link with D.

121 At p 781.

122 See eg Local Government Act 1988 s 17.

123 See eg *Smith v Eric Bush* [1990] 1 AC 831; *White v Jones* [1995] 2 AC 207.

124 *X (Minors) v Bedfordshire CC* [1995] 2 AC 633.

125 See eg *Photo Production Ltd v Securicor Transport Ltd* [1980] AC 827.

126 See eg *Forward v Pittard* (1785) 99 ER 953; *Liver Alkali Co v Johnson* (1875) LR 9 Ex 338; *Nugent v Smith* (1876) 1 CPD 423.

127 See eg *The Albazero* [1977] AC 774.

C consigns goods to B via D, a shipper, and the goods are lost at sea owing to the negligence of D. If property in the goods remained with C, but the risk of loss had passed via the contract of sale to B, it would appear that B, although the one to suffer loss as a result of the negligence, has no action at common law since he has neither a contractual relationship with D nor an action in tort because D owes a duty of care only to the person who has a property interest in the goods.[128] C, of course, can sue D, but as he has suffered no damage he will receive only nominal damages.[129] These problems can be approached from a law of persons, law of things and law of actions position.

From a law of persons position, the first problem could be easily solved by treating H and W as a single *persona*. Instead of saying that the contract was between H and D one might say that it was between the family and D: do not family lawyers talk of a matrimonial home instead of a house belonging to W? Of course, from a technical position, neither the law of procedure nor the law of persons is formally prepared to treat the family as a single unit as we have seen. Nevertheless, from a law of obligations position the House of Lords is not prepared to tolerate D being immune to liability: '[s]uch a result would ... be absurd and the answer is that the husband has suffered loss because he did not receive the bargain for which he had contracted with the ... builder and the measure of damages is the cost of securing the performance of that bargain by completing the roof repairs properly by [a] second builder'.[130] The second problem also raises a law of persons question if one thinks of rights attaching to 'consignors' or 'bailors'; one could, for example, allow C as 'bailor' to obtain the value of the lost goods which C would then hold either on trust for B or as money obtained on B's behalf.[131]

From a procedural position, one can say, with respect to the second problem, that although D is under an obligational (contract and tort) duty to look after the goods, the legal party who suffers the damage has no action in justice. Consequently, all that a law reformer need do to allow B to claim compensation for his loss is to pass a statute which vests in B 'all rights of suit under the contract of carriage as if he had been a party to that contract'.[132] The problem is largely solved at the law of actions (procedural) level. The reason for adopting this approach is to avoid a confrontation with the privity of contract rule whereby third party strangers to a contract can obtain neither rights nor duties from such an obligation (Ch 10 § 7).[133] Yet in *Beswick v Beswick*[134] Lord Denning MR said of this privity rule 'at bottom that is only a rule of procedure' in that it 'goes to the form of the remedy, not to the underlying right'. Again, then, law reformers have no need to function within the law of obligations itself

128 *The Aliakmon* [1986] AC 785; *cf* Carriage of Goods by Sea Act 1992 s 2(1).

129 *The Albazero* [1977] AC 774.

130 Lord Bridge in *Linden Gardens Ltd v Lenestra Sludge Disposals Ltd* [1994] AC 85, 97.

131 *The Winkfield* [1902] P 42.

132 Carriage of Goods by Sea Act 1992 s 2(1)(c).

133 *White v Jones* [1995] 2 AC 207.

134 [1966] Ch 538, 557.

if they wish to ameliorate the position of third parties; the whole problem could be treated as a question of procedure or remedies. In fact Lord Denning also suggested a law of things approach to the privity problem that presented itself in *Beswick*. A promise to pay a debt is, according to the Law of Property Act 1925, a form of property and once one is in the realm of *in rem* rights the problem of privity is again avoided. Admittedly the House of Lords refused to accept this analysis;[135] but in granting the estate the remedy of specific performance they avoided in practice the privity rule through recourse to the law of actions.

Problem-solving in the law of obligations is, accordingly, not just a question of applying rules from the law of obligations. The law of procedure, the law of persons and the law of remedies are equally important and this is why it is not particularly realistic to divide up the common law into scientifically arranged categories. Indeed even when there is a rationalised structure of obligations, as in Roman law, the rules of the law of obligations still cannot function in isolation from the other categories. As Oliver LJ once observed, 'many rules which are recognised as rules of substantive law could be classified merely as rules of practice'. And he continued: 'It may be that, in some jurisprudential theory, it is possible to classify as a legal right some claim which will not be enforced by the court, but on a practical level the existence of a right depends upon the existence of a remedy for its infringement.'[136] The English law of obligations is not, therefore, a subject that exists isolated from other areas of the law such as procedure and actions. It is a subject that is dependent upon them when it comes to the question of a right to sue. It is, of course, tempting to say that it is the role of a category like obligations to predict when such a right to sue will become a right to succeed. Yet it should be increasingly evident that English law does not always find it easy to distinguish between these two aspects of litigation. Did the plaintiff in *Esso v Southport* (Ch 1 § 7(a)) fail because the corporation had no right to succeed in the law of obligations or because the plaintiff had, in the situation before the House of Lords, no right to sue?

10 THE RIGHT NOT TO BE SUED

If one can talk of a right to sue, can one also talk of a right not to be sued? Two broad situations can be identified here. The first concerns the defendant who has what might be called a procedural answer to any action launched against him by a plaintiff with a prima facie claim. Defences such as limitation (Ch 13 § 5(b)), estoppel (Ch 5 § 1(c)), illegality (Ch 7 § 6(a); Ch 9 § 6(c)) and the like are all of procedural as well as substantive relevance and in theory should be dealt with just as much under the law of actions as under the law of things (property and obligations).[137] Indeed the defences of limitation and estoppel might be said to function only at the level of procedure.[138] The

135 [1968] AC 58.

136 *Techno-Impex v Geb van Weelde* [1981] QB 648, 672.

137 For a recent example of how limitation can raise issues of substantive law, see *Walker v South Manchester Health Authority* [1995] 1 WLR 1543.

138 See eg *D & C Builders Ltd v Rees* [1966] 2 QB 617.

second situation goes to the substance of the plaintiff's claim. What if it is evident from the facts as alleged by a plaintiff that they do not disclose a cause of action, that they do not show a good case in law?

Now, obviously, one would expect such a substantive situation to have been dealt with at an early stage by the plaintiff's lawyer who would, or should, have advised against litigation. Nevertheless, the logic of locating at a preliminary stage the right not to be sued is to create a situation whereby the law might never actually develop. If Mrs Donoghue had not insisted on suing the manufacturer for damages in respect of her claim that she was injured by a decomposed snail hidden in a bottle of ginger-beer, then presumably the tort of negligence would, at that moment in time, have not had a chance to develop (*cf* Ch 12 § 3(a)).[139] Indeed now that the House of Lords has openly recognised that it is no longer bound by its own decisions,[140] the idea that substantive law itself can always determine the right to sue or be sued has disappeared. Instead it has become a question of relative rights.

Where a defendant is faced with a claim in which the law seemingly appears to deny liability the defendant can apply to have the action struck out as an abuse of process on the ground that the facts, as alleged, disclose no cause of action.[141] Such striking out claims are, however, more than procedural processes since they can act as a forum for developing substantive law. Whether or not a manufacturer owed a duty of care to its consumers was, evidently, a major question of substantive law, but it was a question decided only in a striking out action – or at least as a Scottish preliminary procedural question about whether the case should go to trial.[142] In other words *Donoghue v Stevenson*[143] was not a case about whether there was actually a snail in the ginger-beer or whether the manufacturer was negligent (*cf* §§ 3–4 above). It was simply a case deciding a preliminary question of law on facts presumed, for the purposes of the striking out claim, to be true. Had the manufacturer not settled, a second process, the actual trial, would have been necessary in order to decide the questions of fact and any other questions of law left outstanding.[144]

No doubt it makes much sense to decide fundamental legal questions at a preliminary stage (particularly with regard to costs). Nevertheless, there are procedural and substantive repercussions arising out of this type of procedure. For a start it has to be remembered that the 'power to strike out is a draconian remedy which is only to be employed in clear and obvious cases'.[145] Consequently, when a plaintiff successfully

---

139 *Donoghue v Stevenson* [1932] AC 562.

140 Practice Statement (Judicial Precedent) [1966] 1 WLR 1234.

141 RSC Ord 18 r 19.

142 Sometimes cases might be decided as preliminary questions of law rather than as actual striking out claims: see eg *Marc Rich & Co v Bishop Rock Ltd* [1996] 1 AC 211. *Donoghue v Stevenson* was, of course, a Scottish case, but it was decided according to similar procedure: Sir JIH Jacob, *The Fabric of English Civil Justice* (Stevens, 1987), p 126.

143 [1932] AC 562.

144 These factual questions ought not to be underestimated: see eg *X (Minors) v Bedfordshire CC* [1995] 2 AC 633.

145 Neill LJ in *McDonald Corpn v Steel* [1995] 3 All ER 615, 623. See also *Kingdom of Spain v Christie, Mason & Woods Ltd* [1986] 1 WLR 1120.

resists such a procedural test case brought by the defendant it by no means indicates that the plaintiff has been successful in his substantive claim for, say, damages against the defendant. All it means is that the plaintiff might be able to get an action off the ground.[146] Furthermore there is a danger that the result of a striking out action might give a misleading picture of the litigation itself. In *Donoghue v Stevenson* and a range of other duty of care cases[147] it is sometimes tempting to say that the defendants were held liable in negligence to the plaintiffs. Such a statement would be quite untrue since these cases were all decided in effect on hypothetical facts. Strictly speaking, they were procedural disputes not touching on the factual question of negligence. Of course, from the viewpoint of precedent, such striking out actions might well be of fundamental importance to the substantive law of negligence and this is why such striking out claims take on importance. They provide major opportunities for the courts to expound and, if need be, to develop the law. All the same, it would be unwise to forget that the relationship between procedural and substantive rules of law is not easily divorced;[148] and thus the nature of the actual remedy pursued in any particular piece of litigation will always be of some importance when it comes to understanding any case law (jurisprudential) substantive rule. Moreover, pre-trial remedies such as striking out claims or interlocutory injunctions (Ch 4 § 1(b); Ch 5 § 4(b)) can raise fundamental questions of substantive law which, as will be seen, are not always best suited to such preliminary remedies.[149]

146 See eg *X (Minors) v Bedfordshire CC* [1995] 2 AC 633.

147 See eg *Home Office v Dorset Yacht Co* [1970] AC 1004; *X (Minors) v Bedfordshire CC* [1995] 2 AC 633.

148 JA Jolowicz, 'Procedural Questions', IECL, Vol XI, Chap 13, para 3.

149 See eg G Samuel (1983) 99 LQR 182.

CHAPTER THREE

THE INSTITUTIONAL BACKGROUND

The law of obligations, as Lord Diplock noted (Ch 1 § 2(b)), is closely interwoven both with remedies and with causes of action and this interrelationship raises a number of questions. To what extent is the idea of a law of obligations actually determined by the remedies that a court is able to grant? And how do these remedies relate to causes of action? In turn how do causes of action relate to specific legal categories within the law of obligations and how do these specific categories relate to the generic obligations category itself? These are questions that need to be discussed in more depth since they help locate the law of obligations within what might be called – or what civil lawyers call – an institutional structure.[1] Moreover, they are questions that are of importance to legal analysis and legal reasoning. In fact one could go further: the institutional structure is the key to an understanding of European legal thought in general in that it provides the link between what the Roman jurists called legal science (*scientia juris*) and what they understood as the art of deciding cases (*ars judicandi*).[2] Given that English law is, to an extent, in the process of adopting the language of Roman law – and not just in respect of a law of obligations, as we shall see – it might be valuable to examine the common law tradition in the context of *scientia iuris* and the *ars judicandi*. What is it to be knowledgeable in the common law?

1 LEGAL KNOWLEDGE

One of the objects of studying any aspect of law is to gain knowledge of what is being studied. This no doubt seems a simplistic and obvious remark, but students setting out on a law degree course are rarely asked to confront at an early stage what it is to have knowledge of law. Instead it is largely assumed that law consists of acquiring knowledge of rules. These rules are divided up into blocks and given labels like 'contract', 'criminal law', 'land law', 'public law' and so on. Some courses such as 'criminology' and 'jurisprudence' are clearly rather different, but often such courses are optional and so it would seem possible to acquire a degree in law simply by learning different blocks of rules. Yet the idea that cases can act as a source of rules is more complex than it might at first seem.[3]

(a) Law in context

Now many of the 'rule' courses do in fact consist of having to learn propositions which can be described as rules and or principles. Nevertheless, there are very few such

1 Stein, *Institutions*, pp 126–29.

2 The term *ars judicandi* is not Roman; what the Roman texts say is the art of what is good and fair (*ars boni et aequi*): D.1.1.1pr.

3 P Jestaz, '*La jurisprudence, ombre portée du contentieux*' DS 1989 Chron 149 (Rudden, pp 251–53).

courses where an arid learning of rules is considered sufficient. In addition to learning, or acquiring a familiarity with, formal rules and principles, a student is expected to have a good knowledge of the academic comment associated with the formal legal propositions. Many 'rule' courses would now expect students to be familiar with the social, economic and political contexts in which the rules operate and this contextual aspect to legal education has recently been endorsed by the Law Society and Council of Legal Education.[4]

Some traditional 'rule' courses might consist of few, if any, rules at all. Instead the course might take as its subject matter materials which emphasise the social, theoretical and (or) philosophical issues associated with the name of the course. Thus a 'tort' course might, on the one hand, concentrate on the formal sources of the legal rules said to make up that area (cases, statutes and academic comment); on the other hand it might focus only on the aims and philosophy of 'tort'.[5] This difference indicates that the sources of legal knowledge are variable. Knowledge of the law of tort (see Chs 12–13) might consist in knowing cases and statutes deemed by a textbook writer to fall within this category or it might consist in knowing a range of different views and theories on, say, accident compensation.[6] It is not at all inconceivable, therefore, that two students following two different tort courses might well be asked to read and digest quite different materials.

How can it be that two courses seemingly devoted to the same subject might in truth be providing quite different information? Several responses can be made here. First, the contents of a course can depend upon what the course organiser views as the 'source' of the relevant legal knowledge. Some teachers will be of the view that this matter is determined by what the law itself deems as formal sources (but how much of this has been determined by academic textbooks rather than by the judges or legislator?). Other teachers may take the view that the source of legal knowledge is not, and cannot be, just a matter for the law itself to decide. Indeed even lecturers who do take as their starting point the formal sources of law (cases and statutes), might nevertheless expect students to have a good knowledge of the academic literature (articles, textbooks, monographs) which, as far as English law is concerned at any rate, is not, or not yet, a formal source of law.

A second response is to focus on the notion of a category itself. The moment a course is defined in relation to a category such as 'tort', it becomes possible not only to interpret the notion and the word in several ways, but to treat the category itself as an

4 '[W]e recognise the validity of a variety of approaches to any subject – whether comparative, jurisprudential, historical, emphasising policy and reform, contextual teaching, interdisciplinary (for example, economic analysis of contract or tort) or clinical': *Preliminary Notice to Law Schools Regarding Full-time Qualifying Law Degrees* (issued jointly by the Law Society and the Council of Legal Education July 1993). See also The Lord Chancellor's Advisory Committee, *First Report on Legal Education* (ACLEC, 1996).

5 On which see the book review by T Weir [1992] CLJ 388.

6 P Legrand, '*Le droit des délits civils: pour quoi faire*', in Legrand (ed), 449. And see eg J Stapleton, *Product Liability* (Butterworths, 1994), Part 2 (Theory).

'object' to be studied. Now it may well be that, as a matter of history, tort as a category developed simply as an indirect response to the establishment of the category of 'contract' (see below § 4(f)). Any damages actions which could not be defined as contractual had to be tortious.[7] However, once established as an object of study, this object of tort can provoke questions whose answers will be forms of knowledge. Accordingly, in a celebrated article Professor Glanville Williams discussed, and raised questions about, the aims of the law of tort.[8] Are these aims deterrence, compensation or whatever? These questions having been raised, other academics responded with their own views and theories. Before long a substantial body of material had built up in the law journals and in books. Why should these papers and books not be just as valid objects of study in a tort course as cases and statutes?

A further response to the knowledge question with regard to particular courses is to highlight a difference mentioned by the philosopher Gilbert Ryle (Ch 1 § 5) that there are two kinds of knowledge. There is knowledge of how to do something such as riding a bike or driving a car – knowing how knowledge – and knowledge of things such as knowing that Paris is the capital of France. This dichotomy between knowing how and knowing that might be said to find expression in legal studies to the extent that one can distinguish between knowing that, for example, a court has power to award damages in lieu of specific performance and injunction[9] and knowing how to solve, in a reasoned way, a difficult litigation problem. Of course, it may be that the skill required to solve a tort, contract or restitution problem will require both of these forms of knowledge. Thus, a problem dealing with the escape of a dangerous animal which causes injury or damage will require a student to know the Animals Act 1971 and to appreciate how to apply to the factual situation particular sections of this statute. All the same, is this not a different skill than writing an essay about the latest compensation theories? Is not a special skill required to apply, say, s 2(2) of the 1971 Act to a situation where D's dog has bitten a child walking in the street?[10]

(b) Legal method

It should also be fairly clear, even at this stage, that to gain knowledge of any single area of law involves more than just the assimilation of a body of propositions which form the substance of the area being studied. The propositions to be studied will contain references and concepts that gain their meaning and definition outside of the actual area under consideration. Accordingly, to obtain a knowledge of, say, the law of contract (see Chs 8–10) will involve recourse to other bodies of knowledge about the English legal system. For example, the contract student will need to know about the doctrine of precedent in English law and about how judges go about interpreting written texts such as wills and statutes.[11] Law is not just about the assimilation of contract, tort and

7 *Bryant v Herbert* (1877) 3 CPD 389, 390–91.

8 'The Aims of the Law of Tort' (1951) 4 CLP 137.

9 Supreme Court Act 1981 s 50.

10 *Cf Curtis v Betts* [1990] 1 WLR 459.

11 See eg *Staffordshire AHA v South Staffs Waterworks* [1978] 1 WLR 1387.

other rules; it is also about their application to factual disputes and this will require some knowledge of linguistics and logic (*cf* Ch 14). In addition to these aspects of learning there is also the question of the effects of learning new areas on those areas of law that have already been studied and assimilated. To what extent will the study and acquisition of a knowledge of the law of tort affect existing knowledge about the law of contract? Will the study of jurisprudence – or indeed some non-legal subject like sociology or history – alter one's knowledge of an assimilated area? And, finally, will knowledge about knowledge affect the perception of a learned area of law? For example, if it transpires from the study of jurisprudence and philosophy that knowledge itself is not so much a matter of propositions (knowing that) but more an issue of knowing how, will this radically alter one's perception of a learned area of law such as the law of contract? Will it give rise to problems about seeing law as a mass of rules and principles (propositions)?

The point of raising these questions is, at this stage at least (*cf* Ch 14), simply to indicate that having knowledge of a particular area is by no means as simple as it might appear. And so to pose the question of what it is to have knowledge of the common law is fraught with difficulties from the very beginning. However, this need not necessarily be a negative starting point to the study of a particular area. In fact, rather the opposite in that it might encourage one to see the common law as a matter of layers: the assimilation (perhaps) of propositions (rules and principles) and sets of factual situations (cases) is the starting point, but, with continued study, this will turn out to be simply a first layer to be built upon by other layers.[12] These other layers will, hopefully, increase the depth of knowledge in the sense that the student of law will learn about the role and function of, say, certain legal concepts. Yet they should also affect the perception of the earlier layers. And the practical outcome of all of this will be, inter alia, not only a more sophisticated knowledge of the area to be studied in the context of a wider body, or bodies, of knowledge, but also a more informed approach to the solving of factual problems. For law is a subject to be both assimilated and applied.

2 METHODOLOGY

But is learning and applying rules the sum total of the learning experience in its formal sense? Here the experience gained from the study of any area of law should indicate that even if the rule is formally posed in a statute, the nature and ambiguity of language mean that the facts of life can still give rise to difficult application problems.

(a) Interpretation of rules

Take for example s 31(4) of the Factories Act 1961. This section provides that '[n]o plant, tank or vessel which contains ... any explosive ... shall be subjected ... to any operation involving the application of heat'. In one case a workman in a scrap yard was instructed by his employer to open an old safe, which unbeknown to either of them contained gelignite, with an oxyacetylene torch. Could the workman, severely injured

12 *Cf* C Atias, *Épistémologie du droit* (PUF, 1994), pp 66–77.

from the subsequent explosion, obtain compensation from his employer on the basis of the employer's breach of the 1961 Act? Only if such a safe was 'plant' or 'vessel', which a majority of the House of Lords decided it was not,[13] would damages be available in the tort of breach of statutory duty (*cf* Ch 12 § 4(a)). Parliament could 'have enacted that an oxyacetylene cutter is never to be used on a closed container unless the container has been emptied',[14] but as it had not used the more general term the legal analysis, it would seem, would have to stay at the level of specifics. Does this make the case one of applying a rule to facts or one of applying some kind of classificatory scheme which exists independently from rules and which operates at the level of – indeed within – the facts themselves? In other words, is one looking at a piece of equipment like a safe in order to determine its inherent nature (the essence of a safe) or is one attempting to analyse the normative (ought) content of s 31(4) of the Act? Each approach involves, perhaps, a different kind of knowledge. The former approach involves an analysis of things – what is a safe and how does it relate to other things in and around the workplace? – while the latter an analysis of words: what does the text mean?

If the rule is not to be found in a formal statute the problem of application becomes even more difficult. What is to be applied as the proposition of law? A rule induced out of a previous case (a proposition of language) or a rule plus the factual context of the previous case (propositions of language and fact)? For example, is a rule developed in respect of a bottle of ginger-beer applicable to a factual situation involving a pair of underpants?[15] Knowledge of law here involves not only skills as to legal rules, but skills as to arguing the similarities and the differences between objects in relation to the persons to whom these objects have, or had, contact. These arguments in turn will affect the granting or withholding of a particular legal remedy and, in its turn, this legal remedy will have helped define the particular legal problem that is in issue. Accordingly, if the remedy being sought is an action for damages arising out of an injury done to a person by a defective bottle of ginger-beer ('your thing hurt me'), this will ensure that the relationship between two persons is of the essence. What was the factual and legal connection between the supplier of the ginger-beer and its consumer? On the other hand if the remedy is one asserting possessory entitlement to a bottle of ginger-beer or to a pair of underpants ('these underpants are mine'), then the relationship between person and pants will be paramount.[16] What were the factual and legal connections between the claimant and the underpants?

(b) Application of rules

The traditional answer to this question is that the connection between claimant and thing (bottle of ginger-beer, underpants or whatever) is to be found in the rule of law.

13 *Haigh v Charles W Ireland* [1973] 3 All ER 1137.

14 Lord Kilbrandon at p 1151.

15 *Grant v Australian Knitting Mills Ltd* [1936] AC 85.

16 See eg *Houghland v RR Low (Luxury Coaches) Ltd* [1962] 1 QB 694.

Yet when the Romans observed that there were as many contracts (stipulations) about things as there were things themselves,[17] a question arose about legal knowledge: in order to appreciate how many different stipulations there may or not be in any particular contractual transaction, one would, seemingly, have to have as much knowledge about things (facts) as about words (law). Why, then, did knowledge of law become just a matter of rules? In many ways it was the law of actions that helped keep law close to the facts but, as we have already indicated, the question of what it is to have knowledge of a law of obligations in the common law presents difficulties owing to the burial of the forms of action (below § 4). In continental thinking legal actions are no longer determined by their form but by their causes, focused around a person's legal rights. These rights are, in turn, defined in systematised codes of legal propositions, applicable, according to traditional legal thinking, via syllogism.[18] Is this approach, with the abolition of the forms of action, also true of English law? Is legal knowledge in English law a matter of inducing a rule out of a precedent (*ratio decidendi*) or finding one in a statute and applying it logically to a set of facts?

(c) Logic and the common law

It is tempting to think that the position in English law is, in terms of knowledge, not that different from the position on the continent. It has, of course, been said that English law is a practical, rather than a logical, code and that, following Holmes, 'the life of the law has not been logic; it has been experience'.[19] But legal knowledge both on the continent and in the common law world is much more sophisticated than this crude logic-and-common sense dichotomy suggests. For a start, the civil law judge is not as logical as tradition seems to dictate;[20] precedent, interpretation and argumentation have central roles behind the scenes even if they do not appear on the face of the judgment. Also, this interpretation involves the facts as much as it does any code.[21] Furthermore, in English law, propositional logic would seem not to be entirely absent: thus, according to Lord Simon, a 'judicial decision will often be reached by a process of reasoning which can be reduced into a sort of complex syllogism, with the major premise consisting of a pre-existing rule of law (either statutory or judge-made) and with the minor premise consisting of the material facts of the case under immediate consideration. The conclusion is the decision of the case, which may or may not establish new law ...'[22] Similarly, in *Home Office v Dorset Yacht Co*[23] Lord Diplock

17 D.45.1.75.9; D.45.1.86.

18 P Orianne, *Apprendre le droit* (Labor, 1990), p 116; and see generally J-L Bergel, *Théorie générale du droit* (Dalloz, 2nd edn, 1989), pp 261–86. Indeed the role of the French *Cour de cassation* is based on the notion that legal reasoning is simply a matter of the syllogism: R Perrot, *Institutions judiciaires* (Montchrestien, 3rd edn, 1989), para 207 (Rudden, pp 273–74)

19 Quoted by Lord MacMillan in *Read v J Lyons & Co* [1947] AC 156, 157.

20 See eg M Lasser, Judicial (Self-)Portraits: Judicial Discourse in the French Legal System' (1995) 104 *Yale Law Journal* 1325; J Bell, 'English Law and French Law – Not so Different?' (1995) CLP 63.

21 T Ivainer, *L'interprétation des faits en droit* (LGDJ, 1988).

22 *FA & AB Ltd v Lupton* [1972] AC 634, 658–59 (HL).

23 [1970] AC 1004.

thought that legal analysis, in respect of duty of care in the tort of negligence at any rate, involved a two-stage approach: the method adopted at the first stage is analytical and inductive, while at the second stage it is analytical and deductive. Logic was not the whole story of course, since policy choices were involved in the initial selection of precedents to be analysed; consequently, the premise from which the deduction is made is not a true universal. Yet the process can again be seen as involving the syllogism and thus legal knowledge itself could be said to be a matter of pre-existing legal propositions and legal reasoning to be a matter of applying these propositions to facts (the application of existing law to the facts judicially ascertained).

Unlike on the continent, however, the 'pre-existing law' does not always exist in a purified form in that 'what constitutes binding precedent is the *ratio decidendi* of a case, and this is almost always to be ascertained by an analysis of the material facts of the case – that is, generally, those facts which the tribunal whose decision is in question itself holds, expressly or implicitly, to be material'.[24] English common law cannot, then, be seen as an organised system of legal propositions (major premises) existing in a metaphysical (or normative) world ready to be applied to sets of facts as they arrive. The propositions can often remain locked within the facts of previous cases. But does this mean that reasoning consists of matching one set of facts to another? Lord Simon thinks not: 'Frequently ... new law will appear only from subsequent comparison of, on the one hand, the material facts inherent in the major premise with, on the other, the material facts which constitute the minor premise. As a result of this comparison it will often be apparent that a rule has been extended by an analogy expressed or implied'.[25] The reasoning approach outlined here would appear to be a matter of both propositional logic (the vast majority of cases) and analogical reasoning (new law). Yet on closer examination of Lord Simon's speech it becomes clear that analogy applies more to the rule than to the isomorphic pattern of the facts. Thus a rule dealing with escaping water[26] can be extended by analogy to a situation of escaping electricity,[27] in turn electricity can act as the focus for some future analogy. Accordingly, in truth, it is not so much the rule, but a factual element around which the rule is framed that acts as the institution at the centre of the reasoning.

3 CONCEPTS AND CATEGORIES

Rules, therefore, do not attach directly to brute facts. They need focal points to which they can affix themselves and these focal points need, between them, their own structures of relations which have meaning both within the facts and within any legal discourse. Law needs to be able to function both within and without the facts. In other words, one has need of a knowledge model which at one and the same time encapsulates the discourse of law (cases, statutes, textbooks and the like) and analyses the facts of social reality.

---

24 Lord Simon, *op cit*.

25 Lord Simon, *op cit*.

26 *Rylands v Fletcher* (1866) LR 1 Ex 265; (1868) LR 3 HL 330.

27 *National Telephone Co v Baker* [1893] 2 Ch 186.

(a) Legal institutions

The starting point for this model is the legal institution. The notion of a legal institution is central to legal science on the continent and it is a notion that has its roots in Roman law. In civilian legal thought a legal institution is regarded as a social reality around which rules are framed;[28] and in Roman law there were three such institutions – persons (*personae*), things (*res*) and actions (*actiones*).[29] What this in effect means, as we have seen (Ch 1), is that all legal rules attach themselves to a person, to a thing or to a legal remedy. However, these institutions are not just legal concepts; they represent the meeting place between social fact and legal rationality and consequently they have a role not only in organising the law but also in organising the facts themselves (*cf* Ch 2 § 5). They are the means by which a raw set of facts is transformed into a legal scenario capable of receiving the application of a legal rule; and, in turn, the scenario plus rule can perhaps act as a precedent. Legal institutions are thus fundamental both to problem-solving and to legal reasoning. They are the vehicle both by which facts are categorised so that the law can be applied and by which the law itself is structured so as to render it capable of being applied in the first place.

This institutional analysis is primarily Roman rather than English in origin, but one of the effects of the abandonment of the forms in action in English law (see below § 4) was that Roman law categories were imported into English law and this had the effect of introducing, more clearly, legal institutions into English legal thought.[30] Thus, the parties (legal subjects), property (legal objects) and remedies (actions) are now the main starting points in analysing legal liability in the common law; and each of these institutions is capable of generating its own particular case law and sets of legal rules. Yet what is important to bear in mind is that the institutions are also fundamental to the analysis and categorisation of the facts themselves. They can go some way in actually determining the rules that find themselves being applied.[31]

(b) Legal categories

Legal institutions not only have a role in organising the facts, they are also, in the Roman tradition at least, a fundamental starting point for the organisation of the law. Accordingly, persons (*personae*), things (*res*) and actions (*actiones*) form the starting point of legal classification by giving rise to the general categories of the Law of Persons, Law of Things and Law of Actions. In the modern codes these actual Roman categories have been modified; the two sub-categories of the Law of Things – that is to say, the Law of Property and the Law of Obligations – have been elevated to a generic role,

---

28 J-L Bergel, *Théorie générale*, *op cit*, pp 177–91.

29 See generally Stein, *Institutions*, pp 125–29; Samuel, *Foundations*, pp 171–90.

30 See Stein, *Institutions*, p 125; G Samuel, 'Roman Law and Modern Capitalism' (1984) 4 LS 185.

31 See G Samuel, 'Epistemology and Legal Institutions' [1991] IJSL 309.

and the Law of Actions has now been relegated to separate procedural codes.[32] The rules that attach to the various institutions are thus classified within categories that reflect their institutional bias and it is, *inter alia*, via this bias that the categories themselves relate to the 'non-legal' (or social, for want of a better term) world.

In turn these general categories are subdivided into sub-categories. Thus, generally speaking, the Law of Obligations is sub-divided into contract, delict and (usually) unjust enrichment or quasi-contract (*cf* Chs 1, 8), while the Law of Property is usually separated into ownership, possession and rights over another's property. Each of these sub-categories contains highly detailed rules and provisions and so they, in turn, are subdivided into further categories. One arrives at the situation where legal knowledge itself can be seen as the contents of a number of particular categories: detailed provisions from statutes and cases become the subject matter of lectures and textbooks and these lectures and books become the means of defining the knowledge to be known. Law becomes a declarative subject, a set of detailed propositions within particularised categories. And it is at this stage that it is in danger of becoming dogmatic and positivistic.[33] It takes on the appearance of being a mass of propositions to be learned and applied logically.

Moreover, the relations between legal categories become important in that the categories appear to define the limits of the rules themselves. Thus, an action in tort might be refused simply on the basis that the facts fall within the law of contract.[34] This will not always be so. Indeed some of the most famous cases have in truth been cases where the courts have been able to establish new liabilities by switching categories.[35] But these exceptions often go far in proving the rule that legal categories form an essential part of legal science and legal rationalisation; they themselves become focal points of knowledge in that they act as a means of attracting theories – for example, the will theory of contract[36] – or policy implications (what is the function of the law of tort?). In turn these theories and policy implications can directly affect the contents of the categories. For instance, in a defamation case[37] raising the question of when exemplary damages could properly be awarded, Lord Wilberforce (dissenting) claimed that it 'cannot lightly be taken for granted, even as a matter of theory, that the purpose of the law of tort is compensation. ... As a matter of practice English law has not committed itself to any of these theories ...'. Now, despite what is being said here, the comment by Lord Wilberforce demonstrates clearly how the category itself can become a major influence on the actual rule it contains. The rules regarding exemplary damages – that is to say, damages awarded to punish the defendant (*cf* Ch 6 § 5) – were

---

32 HF Jolowicz, *Roman Foundations*, pp 61–81.

33 J-P Astolfi & M Develay, *La didactique des sciences* (PUF, 3rd edn, 1994), pp 44, 46.

34 See eg *Tai Hing Cotton Mill Ltd v Liu Chong Hing Bank Ltd* [1986] AC 80, 107; *cf Henderson v Merrett Syndicates Ltd* [1995] 2 AC 145.

35 See eg *Donoghue v Stevenson* [1932] AC 562; *Hedley Byrne & Co v Heller & Partners Ltd* [1964] AC 465.

36 On which see generally Gordley.

37 *Cassell & Co Ltd v Broome* [1972] AC 1027, 1114.

being attacked, *inter alia*, on the basis that punishment is not an aim that attaches to the category tort. The role of the law of tort, so it was argued, was to compensate and it should be left to the category of criminal law to punish. Legal categories thus become in themselves objects of knowledge. Tort claims are compared to contractual, quasi-contractual, equitable and proprietary actions; and differences between the various categories can have important effects on the rules applicable in the law of actions (remedies). Thus, the measure of damages might be different depending upon whether the action is founded in contract or in tort – for example, an expectation interest is not generally recoverable in tort, except in cases of fraud.[38]

Legal rules can sometimes be influenced by the introduction of new legal categories which highlight new interest groups. Thus, the development of labour and consumer law helped stimulate law reform by focusing attention on new classes of social interest groups and the new categories helped transform these interests into 'rights' and 'duties'. At one time these areas were governed by contract, tort and crime, but with the introduction of the new 'empirical' categories it became possible to talk about workers' and consumers' rights. What is interesting about these new categories is that, seemingly, they have developed independently from the Roman-based institutional system; they were categories that grew directly out of social reality, so to speak.

(c) Legal interests

What stimulated these new categories was the notion of a legal 'interest'. Now it is certainly true that consumer, worker and environmental interests are not to be found directly in traditional legal science. Yet the object of Roman legal science was – as is quite specifically stated in the *Digest* itself[39] – public and private interests (*utilitas*) and when this notion is associated with the Roman institution of the legal subject (*persona*) it can be seen that the recognition of new social realities in modern law does not require any new epistemological discourse as such. The recognition by the law of new interests is simply the application of a traditional scientific structure (*persona* and *utilitas*) to new social circumstances.

This is a fundamental aspect of legal method because not only does it illustrate the important interrelationship between legal institutions, legal categories and legal interests, but it also indicates how one moves from the world of social fact to the world of legal relations. The notions of *persona* and *utilitas* are acting as conduits from the social to the legal and once this transformation has taken place the factual situation is from then on subject to the rationality of the institutional model. And this rationality is not just a question of persons, things and actions; there is also a whole range of legal relations flowing between the three institutions. Thus, between the legal subject (*persona*) and legal object (*res*) there exist the property relations of ownership (*dominium*), possession and real rights (rights of way, mortgages, charges, liens and the like); and between two legal subjects there is the relationship of contractual and non-contractual

38 See eg *Swingcastle Ltd v Gibson* [1991] 2 AC 223.

39 D.1.1.1.2.

obligations. Between legal subject (*persona*) and legal action (*actio*) there is the relationship of 'legitimate interest' which can become quite crucial in those cases where the damage is more diffuse. For instance, in *AG v PYA Quarries Ltd*,[40] an action by the Attorney General (relator action) for an injunction against a quarry said to be causing a public nuisance, Denning LJ said:

> Take the blocking up of public highway or the non-repair of it. It may be a footpath little used except by one or two householders. Nevertheless, the obstruction affects everyone indiscriminately who may wish to walk along it. Take next a landowner who collects pestilential rubbish near a village ... The householders nearest to it suffer the most, but everyone in the neighbourhood suffers too. In such cases the Attorney General can take proceedings for an injunction to restrain the nuisance: and when he does so he acts in defence of the public right, not for any sectional interest ... But when the nuisance is so concentrated that only two or three property owners are affected by it ... then they ought to take proceedings on their own account to stop it and not expect the community to do it for them ...[41]

This litigation does of course involve one legal subject acting against another legal subject, but the main emphasis of the litigation is on the institution of the remedy (injunction) *vis-à-vis* the community interest affected. However, as is clear from Denning's comment, two interests are in play here: the public (community) interest and the private interest of each individual. These two interests can sometimes be crucial in deciding whether a remedy is to be available (*cf* Ch 4). Thus Lord Fraser in *Gouriet v Union of Post Office Workers*[42] said that the 'general rule is that a private person is only entitled to sue in respect of interference with a public right if either there is also interference with a private right of his or the interference with the public right will inflict special damage on him.'

Here we can see that the public and private interest have been transformed into 'rights' through the notion of 'damage' and this notion of damage is, in truth, simply an aspect of *utilitas*. Thus, in measure of damages cases lawyers often ask what interests are to be protected by an award of damages.[43] In this latter situation the interest question is one that functions in the law of actions, yet the moment one moves from interest (damage) to rights one is moving out of the law of actions and into the substantive law of civil liability and thus interest can become a means of creating new rights. Accordingly, Lord Denning MR in *Beswick v Beswick* said:

> The general rule undoubtedly is that 'no third person can sue, or be sued, on a contract to which he is not a party'; but at bottom that is only a rule of procedure. It goes to the form of remedy, not to the underlying right. Where a contract is made for the benefit of a third person who has a legitimate interest to enforce it, it can be enforced by the third party in the name of the contracting party or jointly with him or, if he refuses to join, by adding him as a defendant. In that sense, and it is a very real sense, the third person has a right arising by way of contract. He has an interest which will be protected by law

40 [1957] 2 QB 169.

41 *Ibid*, at p 191.

42 *Gouriet v Union of Post Office Workers* [1978] AC 435, 518.

43 See eg Fuller & Purdue, 'The Reliance Interest in Contract Damages' (1936) 46 Yale LJ 52.

> ... It is different when a third person has no legitimate interest, as when. ... he is seeking to rely, not on any right given to him by the contract, but on an exemption clause seeking to exempt himself from his just liability. He cannot set up an exemption clause in a contract to which he is not a party ...[44]

In this case Lord Denning was simply creating new law and not so much by inventing new rules as by adroitly manipulating the interrelationship between legal institutions (person and remedy), legal categories (procedure and substantive law) and legal concepts (interest and legal rights). He was, of course, overruled by the House of Lords,[45] but this should not detract from the techniques employed. It is English legal reasoning at its most revealing in that it shows that there is much more to legal technique than the syllogism.

(d) Legal rights

The movement from legal interest to legal right is easy enough to achieve at the level of rhetoric and language as Lord Denning (above) has so clearly illustrated. However, the two notions of right and interest are very different despite the fact that rights could be seen as legally protected social interests.[46] An interest, although undoubtedly a legal concept, is also a concept founded in other social science discourses and thus its definition is not dependent just on the structure of legal science. A right, on the other hand, is a construct of legal science: it takes its form from the relationship between *persona* and *res* and this is the reason why one always talks of a right to something.[47] In other words, a right is a legal concept that uses the conceptual structure of the property relationship between person and thing and applies it to other legal (and indeed political and social) relationships. Thus, performance under a contract can be seen as a *res* to which the other contracting party (*persona*) is entitled and this leads to a situation where one can talk in terms of a right arising from a contract.

In continental legal systems the notion of a right (*le droit subjectif*) is the fundamental concept of private law and its ascendancy led to the relegation of the law of actions to procedural codes. As HF Jolowicz has pointed out,[48] when the notion of a right 'became the leading conception in private law, there could be no doubt that the differences between types of action. ... were really differences of substantive right' and the 'modern codes of civil law therefore have no need for a special part on "Actions"'. The difference, then, between Roman law and modern civil law is that in the former entitlements in law were defined by the existence of a remedy (*ubi remedium ibi ius*), while in the latter they are defined without reference to the remedy (*ubi ius ibi remedium*). In modern civil law it is the civil codes which act as a source of rights, but

---

44 [1966] Ch 538, 557 CA.

45 [1968] AC 58.

46 F Ost, *Droit et intérêt*: volume 2: *entre droit et non-droit: l'intérêt* (Facultés Universitaires Saint-Louis, Brussels, 1990), pp 24–25.

47 G Samuel, 'Epistemology, Propaganda and Roman Law: Some Reflections on the History of the Subjective Right' (1989) 10 JHL 161.

48 *Roman Foundations*, p 81.

with respect to certain rights – formerly called 'natural rights' but today called 'human rights'[49] – they attach to each and every individual *qua* human being. These human rights – now the subject of their own 'code' or 'convention' – are, *prima facie* at least, inalienable which, in effect, makes the human being a source of law (leading to a contradiction with the positivist idea that the legislator is supreme).[50]

When one turns to English law there is no difficulty in distinguishing between 'law' and 'right' at the level of language and it is very common to see judges and lawyers use the term right as a means of describing, apparently, legal entitlements. Yet care must be taken before concluding that the notion of a right is a legal concept capable in itself of provoking a legal decision. In fact the position in the common law is little different from that of Roman law in that the maxim applicable is *ubi remedium ibi ius* (where there is a remedy there is a right). Thus, Sir Nicholas Browne-Wilkinson V-C in *Kingdom of Spain v Christie, Manson & Woods Ltd*[51] has observed:

> In the pragmatic way in which English law has developed, a man's legal rights are in fact those which are protected by a cause of action. It is not in accordance, as I understand it, with the principles of English law to analyse rights as being something separate from the remedy given to the individual ... In my judgment, in the ordinary case to establish a legal or equitable right you have to show that all the necessary elements of the cause of action are either present or threatened ...

The point being made here is that the notion of a right is not enough to generate a remedy: what has to be shown is that the facts themselves disclose a cause of action and only if such an action exists can one talk about the existence of a right. *Ubi remedium ibi ius.* This does have practical consequences in the law of civil liability. In *F v Wirral MBC*[52] two children were placed by their mother, who was suffering from depression, into local authority care. The mother claimed that she had agreed with the local authority that this should be a temporary arrangement and that the children would be returned when she recovered from her illness. The local authority subsequently assumed, in accordance with their statutory powers, parental rights over the children and refused to return them to the mother. The mother brought an action for damages against the local authority arguing, *inter alia*, that the unlawful interference with her parental rights should in itself give rise to a remedy. Her action was struck out by a judge as disclosing no reasonable cause of action and an appeal to the Court of Appeal failed. This case seems to confirm the observation of Browne-Wilkinson V-C that the notion of a right has no creative role in itself within the common law. It is a term that can be used simply to describe existing causes of action as revealed by precedent or statute. Indeed one reason why the mother failed in this case is that the relevant legislation covering local authority powers in respect of children stresses that the interests of the children are paramount. And so even if there was a right it would be displaced by the child's interests with the result that the term 'right' either is being used

49 See generally M Villey, *Le droit et les droits de l'homme* (PUF, 1983).

50 A-J Arnaud, *Pour une pensée juridique européenne* (PUF, 1991), pp 120–34.

51 [1986] 1 WLR 1120, 1129.

52 [1991] 2 WLR 1132 (CA).

to mean just a 'privilege' or is a term devoid of any real content.[53]

All the same the position is not quite as simple as it may appear. Certainly, a parent may not be able to claim a 'right' to a child, but what is the situation regarding actual property? Can an owner claim that he has a right to his chattels or his land? In this situation the law of tort is much more ambiguous because it will grant a damages remedy simply on the basis of an interference with a right to possession. Thus in *RH Willis & Son v British Car Auctions Ltd*,[54] a car owned by the plaintiffs was wrongfully sold, via the defendant auctioneers, by the person to whom it had been let on hire purchase. The owners brought an action for damages against the auctioneers and they were found liable despite the fact that they had acted in good faith. Lord Denning MR observed that:

> The common law has always ... protected the property rights of the true owner. It has enforced them strictly as against anyone who deals with the goods inconsistently with the dominium of the true owner. Even though the true owner may have been very negligent and the defendant may have acted in complete innocence, nevertheless the common law held him liable in conversion.[55]

In this kind of case cannot one talk in terms of rights? Indeed in all cases of strict liability it becomes more realistic to use the term 'right' because the plaintiff is entitled to damages simply on the basis of damage or interference. Thus, if the police, or anyone else, trespass, without lawful authority, on the person or property of another, an action for damages will often be available not only without the proof of a special damage but also without the proof of fault. This kind of remedy, as the House of Lords has indicated, is available to give expression to a constitutional right.[56] Much the same could be said about the tort of defamation: this is available, in the case of libel (written defamation), without proof of fault or damage and thus it is by no means idle to talk in terms of a right to reputation.

Interestingly in the *Willis* case Lord Denning went on to justify this situation by referring to insurance:

> The only way in which innocent acquirers or handlers have been able to protect themselves is by insurance. They insure themselves against their potential liability. This is the usual method nowadays. When men of business or professional men find themselves hit by the law with new and increasing liabilities, they take steps to insure themselves, so that the loss may not fall on one alone, but be spread among many. It is a factor of which we must take account.[57]

However, this kind of reasoning fails not only to disclose much about the nature of rights, it also begs the question about who ought to insure. Why should it be the

53 See *In re KD* [1988] AC 806.

54 [1978] 2 All ER 392 (CA).

55 *Ibid*, p 395.

56 *Morris v Beardmore* [1981] AC 446.

57 [1978] 2 All ER at pp 395–96.

auctioneers rather than the finance company who should insure? Is it not the finance company that is using ownership for its own benefit? If insurance is to be the key to understanding legal rights this can only be achieved via a policy theory of loss spreading. And, as we saw from Lord Wilberforce in the *Cassell* case, English law has committed itself to no such theory.[58]

(e) Legal duty

If English law has little or no theory with regard to rights, this could be because it has traditionally preferred to look at things from the defendant's, rather than the plaintiff's, point of view. That is to say, the key to 'right' might not to be found in the word right itself, but in the notion of 'duty' – a notion which could be seen simply as the correlative of a right.[59]

It is quite tempting to analyse all legal situations in respect of duty because it is a concept, like right, which transcends any particular legal category and thus can appear to act in itself as a means of provoking or denying a legal remedy. However, it is also a more subtle term than right because it does not import into any particular factual situation an all or nothing dichotomy: duty is not only a matter of relationship but also a matter of content. Thus, to say that A is under a duty to B to take reasonable care in situation X implies that A will not be liable if he, without fault, causes damage to B in situation X.[60] If on the other hand A is under a high, strict or absolute duty to B in situation X then this implies that A might be liable even in the absence of any fault on his part.[61]

The reason why duty is more subtle than right is that, despite the two being apparent correlatives, the term is derived not from *dominium* but from *obligatio*. In other words, duty implies the language of the law of obligations rather than the law of property, and this is why one talks about a duty to another (*in personam*) rather than a right to something (*in rem*). However, this does not mean that the institution of the legal object has no role to play. By attaching a rule to a legal object rather than to a legal subject the law can in effect create a high duty: accordingly the seller, and lender under a contract of hire, are under a strict duty with respect to the quality and fitness of the goods supplied simply because the focal point of the rule is the *res* and not the *persona*. And so, s 9(2) of the Supply of Goods and Services Act 1982 (as amended) stipulates: 'Where ... the bailor bails goods in the course of a business, there is ... an implied condition that the goods supplied under the contract are of satisfactory quality.' In a contract of service on the other hand the focal point is the legal subject and this has the effect of changing the level and content of the duty: in a contract for the supply of a service where the supplier is acting in the course of a business, there is an implied

58 See also J Stapelton, 'Tort, Insurance and Ideology' (1995) 58 MLR 820.

59 W Hohfeld, *Fundamantal Legal Conceptions* (Yale, 1919; reprint 1966).

60 See eg *Davie v New Merton Board Mills* [1959] AC 604.

61 See eg *Hyman v Nye* (1881) 6 QBD 685.

term that the supplier will carry out the service with reasonable care and skill.[62] The difference, as we have already suggested, between ss 9(2) and 13 is to be found in the institution around which the rule is formed: in s 9 the court need look no further than the chattel or product itself in order to arrive at the seller's duty. In s 13, however, the court must take account of the contractor's behaviour before it can decide if the supplier of the service is in breach of duty.

But what if the duty is more ambiguous? To illustrate this problem, the following examples should be compared. The Highways Act 1980 stipulates that 'the authority. .. are under a duty ... to maintain the highway'.[63] However, 'in an action against a highway authority in respect of damage resulting from their failure to maintain a highway ... it is a defence ... to prove that the authority had taken such care as in all the circumstances was reasonably required ... '.[64] According to the Water Act 1989, 'it shall be the duty of a water undertaker (a) when supplying water to any premises for domestic purposes to supply only water which is wholesome at the time of supply; and (b) so far as reasonably practical, to ensure ... that there is, in general, no deterioration in the quality of the water', whereas 'it shall be the duty of every local authority to take all such steps as they consider appropriate for keeping themselves informed about the wholesomeness and sufficiency of water supplies ... '.[65] According to the Factories Act 1961, ss 14 and 29(1), 'every dangerous part of any machinery ... shall be securely fenced ... ' and 'there shall, so far as is reasonably practicable, be provided and maintained safe means of access to every place at which any person has at any time to work, and every such place shall, so far as is reasonably practicable, be made and kept safe for any person working there.'

These examples illustrate that the content of the duty may have to be determined either by relating one section to another or by carefully scrutinising the language of the section in order to see if there is a qualification to the duty. If there is a qualification then the issue may well become one of proof: upon whom should the burden of proof fall when it comes to an expression such as 'reasonably practical'? This can, at one and the same time, raise a substantive and a procedural question.[66] For in breach of statutory duty cases the facts can give rise both to a criminal and to a civil law action and this begs a question as to what a plaintiff must allege against a defendant (*cf* Ch 12 § 4). One cannot normally be guilty of a crime simply by someone alleging that an event took place – normally there has to be some element of individual responsibility. Equally, one is not automatically entitled to damages simply because the defendant's act which led to the damage was unlawful.[67] Duty, in other words, has to be measured both against the right of a worker (or whomsoever) envisaged by the statute and against the rights of the person upon whom the duty is cast; and it is in this sense that one can

62 Supply of Goods and Services Act 1982 s 13.

63 Highways Act 1980 s 41.

64 Highways Act 1980 s 58.

65 Water Act 1989, s 52(1) and s 56(1).

66 See in particular *Nimmo v Alexander Cowan & Sons* [1968] AC 107.

67 *Lonrho Ltd v Shell Petroleum* [1982] AC 173.

talk about 'right' and 'duty' being correlative. That said, however, it must not be forgotten that the epistemological (theory of knowledge) basis of both concepts reflects a difference between the language of ownership and the language of obligations, and that is why civil liability issues are sometimes seen as arising from wrongs (breach of duty) and sometimes as arising from the interference with a right.

It is the flexibility that attaches to the concept of duty that makes it a central concept in civil liability cases: it allows the courts to bring into play a whole range of institutional, behavioural, damage and policy issues without, seemingly, abandoning the idea of a legal rule. Accordingly, before a person can obtain compensation from someone who has caused him damage he must normally show that the latter owed him a duty of care or was in breach of some other duty imposed by statute (breach of statutory duty) or arising out of some special responsibility such as an occupier's duty to passers-by[68] (see Ch 12 § 5). The term is also used in the analysis of three party situations where one person sues another in respect of an act done by a third party (non-delegable duty). 'Duty' thus acts not only to describe a particular relationship between two legal subjects ('A is under a duty to B') but also as a means of indicating the actual content of the obligation owed ('A is under a strict duty to B'); it is a term that appears to provoke in itself the right to a remedy. However, this appearance can sometimes be misleading in that the contents of certain duties may simply be the result of the intervention of particular types of remedy. Thus, the 'duty' to disclose in insurance contracts founded in the equitable remedy of rescission cannot in itself provoke a right to damages at common law; in order to obtain such damages for non-disclosure (in addition to an equitable remedy) a common law cause of action must be established.[69]

(f) Public and private law

The persons, things and actions structure was a model of private law: that is to say, it was a structure primarily concerned with the interests (*utilitates*) of private individuals. Roman law also recognised a category of public law (*ius publicum*) which was concerned with the interests of the state.[70] Now the idea of the state as an institution capable of supporting rights and duties is largely a post-Roman idea, but the Roman jurists went far in constructing a number of institutions which acted as the forerunners of the modern state. For example, the institution of the *fiscus* (treasury) was used by Roman lawyers as a public *persona* capable both of owning and contracting and of being endowed with privileges which allowed it to have a status and position in the institutional plan which was significantly different from that of private individuals.[71] Legal relations with the *fiscus* were, accordingly, of a special nature in that the

68 *Mint v Good* [1951] 1 KB 517.

69 *Banque Keyser Ullmann v Skandia Insurance* [1989] 3 WLR 25 (CA); [1991] AC 249.

70 D.1.1.1.1; and see J-L Mestre, *Introduction historique au droit administratif français* (PUF, 1985), pp 49–53.

71 Mestre, *supra*, pp. 106–08.

normative force which underpinned private legal relations – *dominium* and *obligatio* – were supplemented by an imperial power (*imperium*) that was later to become the basis of constitutional concepts such as sovereignty and state power (*imperium*, royal prerogative). In Roman law itself the *ius publicum* was in reality an area of non-law in that it was largely a category where administrative discretion rather than the rule of law held sway.[72]

All the same, what the Roman jurists did establish was a structural role for *imperium* within the private law plan; and so legal relations consisted of bonds not just between *personae* and *res*, but between *fiscus*, towns (*universitas*), magistrates and *personae* and *res*. Indeed there was even the germ of the modern judicial review remedy in the *actio popularis*: this was a remedy which, at the level of the law of actions, was more public than private, but at the level of the law of obligations was more private than public. The *actio popularis* in respect of *res deiectae vel effusae* (things thrown or falling from a building)[73] was quite close to the modern public law idea of administrative liability,[74] although, as in English law, it formed part of the private law of obligations.[75] Public and private law might be quite separate categories as a matter of legal theory, but as a matter of practice they were well integrated at the institutional level.[76]

(g) Comparative remarks: legal science and legal knowledge

Knowledge of law is not, then, just a matter of learning legal rules and applying them logically to factual situations. Knowledge of law also involves the appreciation of the systematic interrelation of legal institutions, legal categories, legal relations and legal concepts. In continental law these categories, institutions and concepts have, on the surface at least, been reduced to propositions arranged systematically in codes (following, for the greater part, the institutional system of Roman law) and it would thus appear that they can be consistently applied via the syllogism. In English law, however, although aspects of continental legal science have found their way into the reasoning discourse (particularly in the nineteenth century after the abolition of the forms of action) (see below § 4), the institutions, categories and concepts operate in a way that is much closer to the facts. They function as a means of categorising and arranging the facts so as to 'reveal' the existence of a legal remedy. Accordingly, in order to understand civil liability in English law it is necessary to focus on the role of institutions (legal subjects and legal objects), legal notions such as damage, interests, rights and duties and legal categories.

72 JW Jones, *Historical Introduction to the Theory of Law* (Oxford, 1940), pp 141–43.

73 D.9.3.1.

74 D.9.3.1.5.

75 D.44.7.5.5.

76 *Cf X (Minors) v Bedfordshire CC* [1995] 2 AC 633.

4 CIVILIAN AND ENGLISH LEGAL SCIENCE

English law, of course, is said to have developed in isolation of Roman law. Nevertheless, it is the dichotomy between remedies and rights which ironically brings Roman and English legal science quite close together.[77] The irony lies in the historical truism that although the common law developed as a system independently from the influence of the *Corpus Iuris Civilis*[78] – and thus English law does not belong to the *ius civile* tradition – it nevertheless seems to share many of the methodological characteristics of classical Roman law.

(a) Roman legal reasoning

As Tony Weir has reminded the legal community,[79] the Roman jurists were practical lawyers who reasoned by hypothetically varying 'the actual facts of the situations presented to them, and considered what the legal effect of such hypothetical variations would be'; as a result 'the *Digest* is full of cases, of actual situations that were presented to the jurists for advice'. Such a description could be applied equally to the *Weekly Law Reports* in that they, also, seem to be imbued both with the same casuistic technique and with a similar 'spirit'.[80] All the same, care must be taken when comparing English and Roman legal thought. For although the two systems share much in common at one level – in particular with regard to the casuistic methodology and the linking of substantive law to procedure – there are, from an historical point of view at any rate, profound differences between each system's law of actions.

(b) Forms of action

When one turns to the history of the common law the most striking feature of its law of actions is the absence, until relatively recent times, of any systematic interrelationship between persons, things and actions. Instead of a sharp division between obligations and property (*cf* Ch 1 § 1), the common law forms of action, the writs,[81] seemed to be both *in personam* and *in rem* in nature. Thus, the writ of debt was much closer, in the Roman sense of the term, to a proprietary claim than to an obligational one[82] with the result, for example, that an early sale of goods transaction could be said to belong to the

---

77 Zweigert & Kötz, pp 193–94.

78 The term *Corpus Iuris Civilis* is a post-Roman term applied to the codification of Roman laws by Justinian in 527–33AD. The *Corpus* consists of the *Institutes of Justinian* (an elementary manual), the *Digest* (a large collection of excerpts from the writings of jurists) and the *Code* (later imperial legislation). As Walter Ullmann has stated, the significance of this project can never be exaggerated since it was 'always regarded as the sum-total of Roman juristic wisdom': W Ullmann, *Medieval Political Theory* (Penguin, 1975), pp 46–47.

79 T Weir, 'Contracts in Rome and England' (1966) 66 *Tulane Law Review* 1615, 1616–17.

80 F Pringsheim, 'The Inner Relationship Between English and Roman Law' [1935] CLJ 347.

81 On the writ system and 'forms of action' see Baker, pp 63–83; RC van Caenegem, 'History of European Civil Procedure', *IECL*, Vol XVI, Chap 2, paras 22–23.

82 Milsom, pp 260–65.

law of property rather than to the law of contract.[83] An unpaid vendor would bring an action claiming the debt as his own, so to speak, while a purchaser would use the writ of detinue to enforce delivery.[84] Trespass, another key writ, did much of the same work as the Roman delictual claims; yet, equally, it covered areas that today would be seen as belonging to contract and (by a civilian) to property. Consequently, early 'contractual' claims were seen as trespasses – wrongs – rather than as the non-performance of a *obligatio* binding two persons. Indeed trespass went further than this: it had, and still has, an important role in protecting personality and possessory rights and this gave it a constitutional flavour as well.[85]

The history of the common law is, then, one of a tradition developing independently of the *Corpus Iuris Civilis* and this meant that, until *Blackstone*[86] at any rate, the classification scheme of the *Institutiones* found little reflection in what was basically a feudal customary tradition. There was little interest in a feudal society in the difference between *ius publicum* and *ius privatum*[87] or between property and obligations.[88] Legal thought, instead, preferred the distinction between real and personal property and this became more important than any between *res corporales* and *res incorporales*. Moreover, the basis of an English writ was a factual situation against which a potential plaintiff would compare the facts of his dispute; if the two factual situations matched, the plaintiff had, so to speak, a ticket to the Royal courts.[89] During the 13th century these writs became fixed with the result that the common law became in character a law of factual situations founded on the Register of Writs; and these writs were so closely tied up with the procedure and pleading that it is almost impossible to make many useful comparisons with either the law of persons and things, or the law of actions in the *Corpus Iuris*.[90] In fact so different was the writ system that in truth it seems that the early common law cannot be conceived at all in terms of a system of substantive ideas.[91] There was no abstract map of rules and thus 'there was no law of property, or of contract, or of tort'.[92]

---

83 Milsom, pp 265–66.

84 Baker, pp 433–34.

85 Well brought out by the 19th century case of *Cooper v Wandsworth Board of Works* (1863) 143 ER 414.

86 *Cf* J Cairns, Blackstone, 'An English Institutist: Legal Literature and the Rise of the Nation State' (1984) 4 OJLS 318.

87 See generally R van Caenegem, 'Government, Law and Society', in JH Burns (ed), *The Cambridge History of Medieval Political Thought c 350–c 1450* (Cambridge, 1988) 174.

88 A-M Patault, *Introduction historique au droit des biens* (PUF, 1989), p 22.

89 Milsom, p 36.

90 'In the 14th century there was no law of England, no body of rules complete in itself with known limits. ... [The] lawyer's business ... was procedural, to see that disputes were properly submitted to the appropriate deciding mechanism. The mechanism would declare that justice lay with the one side rather than the other': Milsom, p 83.

91 Milsom, p 43.

92 Baker, p 63.

(c) The teaching and practice of law

Another reason why the systematics of the common law, when viewed from the position of legal history, are so complex is that there was until the 20th century no university tradition in law. This is not to say that Roman law was never taught;[93] the point to be emphasised is that the common law was never subjected in the formative centuries to a universalised science that would lift it out of its factual categories of thought. It was a law of practice, created by the judges on an *ad hoc* basis, and 'the role of professors of law and of theoretical study – "legal science"– has in the course of the centuries been marginal.'[94] Transactions, as we have seen, were never analysed in the formative period in terms of an obligations and property dichotomy – it was more a matter of exchange – and accidents were seen as invasions of one's 'property' (including here one's body).[95] The descriptive nature of the forms of action kept thinking very close to the facts and very technical in a mechanical sense. As Milsom observes, 'the lawyer's business ... was procedural, to see that disputes were properly submitted to the appropriate deciding mechanism'.[96]

The main aim of these mechanisms was to settle disputes and, as such, systematics, in the sense of classification schemes, did not go beyond what was necessary.[97] Had there been a thriving academic community of philosophers and lawyers, integrated into the system and able to influence in a universalised way the remedies of the common law, the writ of debt might have been subsumed by the *condictio* rather than by the action of trespass, and detinue and trover might have been transformed into claims *in rem*. Equally, trespass itself, the most important of the old writs, might have become a general *actio in personam* based on *injuria* and *damnum*. But this kind of academic pressure did not, in England, start until the 19th century and by that time the *mentalité* of the common lawyer was too embedded in the mechanics of dispute settlement to think about law as a set of abstract structures capable of functioning in a world separated from that of social reality.[98]

(d) Abolition of the forms of action

Blackstone's Commentaries on the Laws of England (1765–70) form the most important landmark of 18th century continental influence on the common law. These commentaries were, quite simply, an analysis of English law along the lines of Justinian's Institutes.[99] As such they laid the foundation for conceiving of English law as

---

93 See eg De Zulueta & P Stein, *The Teaching of Roman Law in England Around 1200* (Selden Society, 1990).

94 R van Caenegem, *Judges, Legislators and Professors: Chapters in European Legal History* (Cambridge, 1987), p 53.

95 *Cf* D.9.2.13pr (*quoniam dominus membrorum suorum nemo videtur*).

96 Milsom, p 83.

97 *Ibid*, p 264.

98 M Lobban, *The Common Law and English Jurisprudence 1760–1850* (Oxford, 1991), pp 257–89.

99 Cairns, *op cit*.

a system of subjective rights rather than objective remedies and this made the common law more adaptable to the commercial reforms that Lord Mansfield was initiating during the same period.[100] By the 19th century the traditional forms of action were appearing increasingly unsuitable for the new industrial age, and there was pressure to move to a system of causes of action where it would be sufficient for a litigant simply to plead in his statement of claim the facts.[101] The change from a system of forms of action to a system of causes of action was not, however, achieved by means of a codification of rights. It was achieved by legislative action aimed at procedural reform. By no longer insisting that a procedural label – 'debt', 'trespass', 'case', 'nuisance' or whatever – had to be attached to the plaintiff's claim from the outset,[102] the way was open for an approach which looked to the substance of an action within a generalised procedural form. Facts were increasingly required to be categorised in terms of their cause rather than in terms of their form.

The basis of a cause, as opposed to a form, of action is to be found in the nature of the concepts used by jurists. In a system of forms of action the emphasis is on concepts geared to knowing how to sue rather than to knowing what is the law applicable to this particular factual situation (*cf* above § 1). In other words, the emphasis is more upon the pleadings and the way the case is presented than upon any inherent normative situation arising out of the facts themselves. Thus, in the early part of the 19th century, before the great procedural reforms, much of the law of obligations was simply 'haphazard'.[103] With the abolition of the forms of action the emphasis shifted to concepts reflecting a more normative system of legal thought. This, it must be said, did not entail an abandonment of the *ex facto ius oritur* approach, but it did involve the use of concepts such as fault, promise and damage which are, at one and the same time, both descriptive (is) and normative (ought).[104] Accordingly, although a cause of action, like the old form of action, might be 'used as a convenient and succinct description of a particular category of factual situation which entitles one person to obtain from the court a remedy against another person',[105] the concepts themselves belong to a system of knowledge that is rather different from that associated with the forms of action.

In fact the change created a number of difficulties. In particular, owing to there being no university tradition of legal rationalisation in England, categories from the continent had to be imported in order to give a semblance of organisation to a mass of case law which had been arranged around formal remedies.[106] The remedial categories of 'debt' and 'damages' found themselves replaced by the substantive categories of 'contract' and 'tort'. Yet such a transformation did not always work smoothly. Some debt actions, and many damages claims, could not be accommodated by 'contract'; and while the non-contractual damages actions could be put under the general rubric of

100 Atiyah, *Rise and Fall*, pp 120–24.

101 See G Wilson, *Cases and Materials on the English Legal System* (Sweet & Maxwell, 1973), pp 346–47.

102 Common Law Procedure Act 1852 s 3.

103 Lobban, *op cit*, pp 257–89.

104 P Dubouchet, *Sémiotique juridique: introduction à une science du droit* (PUF, 1990), pp 144–45.

105 *Letang v Cooper* [1965] 1 QB 232, 242–43.

106 Weir, *Complex Liabilities*, para 67.

'torts' (*cf* Chs 12–13), the non-contractual debt claims proved – and are still proving (*cf* Ch 11) – troublesome. Moreover, contract itself suffered from playing host to two quite different forms of action.[107] The action for damages founded upon breach of promise (*assumpsit*) was, historically, an action founded upon a wrong; the action for debt, on the other hand, was closer to – indeed it had once been one and the same as – the action for detinue and detinue was the nearest remedy that England had, until 1977 when it was abolished,[108] to an *actio in rem*. The action in debt, then, was one founded more upon a 'right' (*ius in re*) than a 'wrong' (*actio ex maleficio*). The modern English law of contract thus consists of both wrongs and rights and this can sometimes have an important bearing on the actual operation of the internal rules of contract law. Furthermore it gives rise to an important difference between a contractual liability action for damages and a debt action for a specific sum of money (*cf* Ch 4 § 5).

(e) Reception and non-reception of civil law

When, then, in the middle of the 19th century the forms of action were formally abolished[109] and the legal fraternity began to put its mind towards remedying the deplorable lack of legal education in England,[110] the judges and teachers turned to the civil law for help.[111] During a period of about 30 years from the 1850s until the end of 1870s English judgments began to move away from the procedural mechanism approach towards one that saw liability more in the language of a Romanist.[112] This was not a sudden shift of emphasis as such since the development of more substantive ideas, particular with respect to a law of contract, can be traced back into the

---

107 *Ibid*, para 8.

108 Torts (Interference with Goods) Act 1977 s 2(1).

109 Common Law Procedure Act 1852 s 3. '[The Common Law Procedure Acts] did not abolish forms of action in words. The Common Law Commissioners recommended that: but it was supposed that, if adopted, the law would be shaken to its foundations; so that all that could be done was to provide as far as possible that, though forms of actions remained, there never should be a question what was the form' *per* Bramwell LJ in *Bryant v Herbert* (1877) 3 CPD 389, 390.

110 P Stein, *Legal Evolution: The Story of an Idea* (Cambridge, 1980), pp 78–79.

111 See eg *Janson v Ralli* (1856) 25 LJQB 300, 309; *Blackmore v Bristol & Exeter Railway Co* (1858) 27 LJQB 167, 172; *Hall v Wright* (1858) 27 LJQB 345, 354; *Smeed v Foord* (1859) LJQB 178, 181–82; *Pinard v Klockman* (1863) 32 LJQB 82, 84; *Taylor v Caldwell* (1863) 32 LJQB 164; *Kemp v Halliday* (1865) 34 LJQB 233, 236, 237, 240; *Lloyd v Guibert* (1865) 35 LJQB 74; *British Columbia Saw-Mill Co v Nettleship* (1868) LR 3 CP 499, 508; *Banks v Goodfellow* (1870) 39 LJQB 237, 243 ff; *Notara v Henderson* (1872) 41 LJQB 158; *Searle v Laverick* (1874) LR 9 QB 122, 128–29; *Rouquette v Overmann* (1875) 44 LJQB 221, 232; *Mackenzie v Whiteworth* (1875) 44 LJ Ex 81, 84. In *Randall v Newsom* (1876) 45 LJQB 364 counsel cited *Pothier*, but the judges decided the case with reference only to English law. A range of introductory textbooks on the civil law also appeared just before, and during, this period: see eg G Bower, *Commentaries on the Modern Civil Law* (Stevens & Norton, 1848).

112 'I am aware that there may be causes of action for which a party may seek redress either in the form *ex contractu* or *ex delicto*; and there are instances in which advantages can be obtained in the procedure by suing in the form *ex delicto* instead of *ex contractu*' *per* Erle CJ in *Alton v Midland Railway* (1865) 34 LJCP 292, 296. '[S]ince the Common Law Procedure Act ... the form of action is out of the question. But I must say I have always understood that when a man pays more than he is bound to do by law ... he is entitled to recover the excess by *condictio indebiti*, or action for money had and received' *per* Willes J in *GWR v Sutton* (1869) LR 4 App Cas 226, 249.

eighteenth century;[113] indeed an appeal to legal maxims (*regulae iuris*) as a tool of reasoning was in evidence long before the great procedural changes of the 19th century.[114] Moreover, academic commentators such as Jeremy Bentham and John Austin acted as vehicles for the importation of the deductive and axiomatic systematics of the post-Enlightenment continental jurisprudence;[115] and while one must not over-emphasise the influence of these two writers on everyday case law, Austin's work on legal thought, which had been heavily influenced by the German Pandectists,[116] set the scene for the rise of the textbook era of English law which, in turn, was to provide the necessary conceptual basis for English legal reasoning in the century following the abolition of the forms of action.[117]

No doubt it would be a gross exaggeration to say that there was a reception of Roman law into the English common law in the second half of the 19th century. All the same, both the judges and the growing band of legal academics looked to the civil law for inspiration and, although this direct use of civilian material lasted only for a few decades until English law had built up its own sources of substantive rules, indirectly the continental influence has continued. Thus, English law has increasingly accepted the distinction between public and private law[118] and, in addition, the growing influence of EC (now EU) law is leading once again to a direct influx of civilian ideas. It could be that this influx is at least as strong as that experienced during the 1860s and, possibly, will prove much less transient.[119]

(f) Contract and tort

The key to the 19th century civilian influence is the law of contract (see Ch 8 § 5). For not only was the development of this branch of the law based indirectly, and on occasions directly, on the works of Grotius, Pufendorf, Domat and Pothier,[120] but once the category had established itself it forced lawyers and judges to think analytically about other areas of the law such as 'property' and 'tort'.[121] In other words the shift

113 Atiyah, *The Rise and Fall*, pp 139–216.

114 Lobban, *op cit*, pp 80–89.

115 *Ibid*, pp 223–56.

116 Stein, *Legal Evolution*, *op cit*, p 71. For a brief discussion of the German Pandectists see Zweigert & Kötz, pp 144–48.

117 Atiyah, *Rise and Fall*, pp 681–93.

118 *O'Reilly v Mackman* [1983] 2 AC 237.

119 X Lewis, '*L'européanisation du common law*', in Legrand (ed), p 275.

120 Gordley, pp 134–60; Zimmermann, pp 569–71.

121 See eg *Lee v Jones* (1864) 34 LJCP 131 where the Court of Exchequer Chamber (Bramwell B dissenting) used Roman law to establish a duty in respect of a non-contractual misrepresentation. Note also the use of *injuria* and *damnum* in *Wade v Tatton* (1856) 25 LJCP 240. With regard to physical damage Lord Blackburn said in 1877: 'Property adjoining to a spot on which the public have a right to carry on traffic is liable to be injured by that traffic ... [T]he owner of the injured property must bear his own loss, unless he can establish that some other person is in fault, and liable to make it good. And he does not establish this against a person merely by shewing that he is owner of the carriage or ship which did the mischief, for the owner incurs no liability merely because he is owner': *River Wear Commissioners v Adamson* (1877) 2 App Cas 743, 767; *cf* Lopes LJ in *Sadler v South Staffordshire & Birmingham District Steam Tramways Co* (1889) 23 QBD 17 for how this fault analysis related to the remedy of trespass.

from remedies and procedural mechanisms towards substantive ideas such as duties arising from promises compelled lawyers, however reluctantly, to be more abstract in their approach to problem-solving. Some of this is evident in the words of the judges themselves. For example, in *Bryant v Herbert*[122] Bramwell LJ was forced by the wording of the County Courts Act (which replaced the 'Debt and Damages' term used in an earlier statute with 'Action. ... founded on Contract, or ... founded on Tort') to consider what was meant by 'founded on contract' and 'founded on tort'.[123] 'One may observe', he said, 'there is no middle term; the statute supposes all actions are founded either on contract or on tort' and so 'that it is tort, if not contract, contract if not tort'.[124] Similarly, in *Pontifex v Midland Railway*,[125] Cockburn CJ said that in the days 'when there were forms of action, there would have been little difficulty in determining whether an action was founded on contract or tort, but now that the claim is made by a narration of facts, it does not always clearly appear to which class, contract or tort, the case properly belongs'.[126]

Interestingly Cockburn CJ sees part of the problem arising out of the procedural change which allowed the parties to an action to plead only the facts. Such a change had the effect of making judges look beyond the procedural mechanisms of the forms of action towards what became known as causes of action. Now to an extent these causes were, as we have seen, simply a new label for an old remedy allowing the courts to continue to determine the action through the use of the traditional method of comparing factual situation with factual situation.[127] But it was becoming increasingly difficult for the law of actions to support itself by its own bootstraps and legal practitioners and judges had to start thinking in terms of more general structures.

What made the task of producing a general model of liability along Romanist lines difficult was not only the strict dichotomy between contract and tort excluding, as Bramwell LJ observed, any middle term, but also the contents of contract and of tort themselves. If one returns to Cockburn CJ's words in *Pontifex*, he reveals that the category of tort includes 'intermeddling with property' and the facts of the case itself presented difficulties because 'there is undoubtedly an unauthorised intermeddling with property, but the act is connected with a contract originally entered into'.[128]

122 (1877) 3 CPD 389.

123 County Courts Acts Amendment 1867 s 5; *cf* County Courts Act 1846 s 58. Winfield commented: 'The influence of the County Court Acts on the division between contract and tort, whatever its practical success, has been unfortunate as a matter of science' (P Winfield, *The Province of the Law of Tort* (Cambridge, 1931), p 76).

124 At p 390. But contrast: 'Everyone who has studied the English law will know perfectly well that there is debateable ground between torts and contracts. There are what are called quasi-contracts and quasi-torts; and it is sometimes not easy to say whether a cause is founded on contract or on tort' *per* Lindley LJ in *Taylor v Manchester, Sheffield & Lincolnshire Railway Co* [1895] 1 QB 134, 138. (Lindley LJ wrote a work on the *Institutes of Justinian*.) For a general discussion of these cases see P Winfield, *op cit*, pp 40–91.

125 (1877) 3 QBD 23.

126 At p 26.

127 See eg *England v Cowley* (1873) LR 8 Ex 126.

128 (1877) 3 QBD at p 26.

Interference with possession, a property problem in Romanist legal science,[129] was, in the eyes of the common lawyer, a contract or tort problem since it involved either promise or trespass[130] and trespass was a form of action which had, along with debt, acted as the law of actions basis for the new law of 'actions founded on contract or on tort'.[131] The importing of a Romanist category like contract[132] was not undertaken, therefore, within a context of any general attempt to systematise private law at an abstract level. Instead it was a matter of inserting the idea through the linking of particular remedies with the notion of promise. The breach of a promise could give rise either to a 'trespass' (*assumpsit*) remedy in damages or to the 'proprietary' remedy of debt.[133] If there was no promise that could be breached but, nevertheless, there was an actionable remedy the logic of the new contract and tort classification system dictated that the substance of the claim must be either 'tort' or a matter for equity. There was no separate category to deal with property relations because the forms of action had never clearly distinguished ownership from possession; the remedies of trespass and detinue had been adequate enough to protect property – that is possessory – interests.[134]

To see the new categories of contract and tort as species of the law of obligations would thus be a mistake. The law of tort was, and indeed remains,[135] a category concerned as much with property relations – *dominium* and *possessio* – as *obligationes*, in the Roman sense; and the law of contract, the paradigm *vinculum iuris*, also turns out to be rather different in the English *mentalité*. Things may change, of course. But as Lord Goff recognised (above Ch 1 § 2(a)), much will depend on the interrelationship of doctrine (academic writing) with the perceptions of the judiciary.

---

129 But note: 'an action of *trover* ... rests on a right of property, wrongfully interfered with, at the peril of the person interfering with it, and whether the interference be for his own use or that of anybody else' *per* Lord O'Hagen in *Hollins v Fowler* (1875) LR 7 HL 757, 799.

130 See eg *Gibbs v Cruikshank* (1873) LR 8 CP 454, 459.

131 Note also the position with regard to detinue: 'notwithstanding to some purpose a common *detinue* is in form *ex contractu*, yet the gist of the action is the wrongful detention; and there is, therefore, no difficulty in holding that it falls within the words "alleged wrong" ... ' *per* Williams J in *Danby v Lamb* (1861) 31 LJCP 17, 19. An action in conversion (trover) or detinue 'is not a proceeding *in rem*: it is, to recover *prima facie* the value of the good' *per* Willes J in *Brinsmead v Harrison* (1871) LR 6 CP 584, 588. '[T]he action of detinue is technically an action founded on contract ... But ... where persons are sued in *detinue* for holding goods ... the real cause of action in fact is a wrongful act, and not a breach of contract, because it may arise and occur when there is no contract, and the remedy sought is not a remedy which arises upon a breach of contract' *per* Brett LJ in *Bryant v Herbert* (1877) 3 CPD 389, 392.

132 See AW Simpson, 'Innovation in Nineteenth Century Contract Law' (1975) 91 LQR 247.

133 'In the courts of common law the party who had earned wages might either sue for the wages as a debt and recover the amount, or bring an action of *assumpsit* and recover the same sum as damages for the breach of contract in not paying them' *per* Blackburn J in *Millett v Coleman* (1875) 44 LJQB 194, 201. In the early common law the writ of debt was originally more of a proprietary remedy than an obligational one (see Milsom, pp 260–65) and even today debt retains its property flavour (see eg *Lipkin Gorman v Karpnale* [1991] 2 AC 548).

134 Baker, pp 439–51. And see eg *Buckley v Gross* (1863) 32 LJQB 129.

135 See Torts (Interference with Goods) Act 1977 s 1.

CHAPTER FOUR

REMEDIES (1): INTRODUCTION

When one turns from the law of actions in civil law to remedies in the common law, one of the great differences often said to exist is that the former is more concerned with the specific performance of contracts while the latter sees such a remedy as exceptional.[1] The general common law principle in respect of the law of remedies is *omnis condemnatio pecuniaria*.[2] However, while there is no doubt some truth in this difference of approach, care must be taken since the principle is Roman in origin and in actual practice the distinction between specific performance and certain monetary claims is by no means clear cut. When a seller of goods claims in debt for the price of goods sold, is he claiming a monetary remedy or specific performance of the contract? This question can be important for the common lawyer since the distinctions between actions for monetary compensation, actions for an agreed price and actions for specific performance in equity are, institutionally speaking, quite separate kinds of claim.[3] Thus, while it is sometimes convenient to see civil liability claims primarily in terms of monetary actions, such an approach can also eclipse the operation of more structural ideas. English law sometimes expresses fundamental liability ideas through remedial differences and so before embarking on an analysis of the English law of obligations it might be helpful first to examine in some depth the English law of actions. For it must never be forgotten that the structure of English law owes much to the forms of action and, more generally, that actions are, in the legal plan, institutions.

1 INSTITUTIONS AND RULES

The notion of an institution has, as we have seen (Ch 3), a long history which stretches back to Roman law: legal rules can be framed around people (*personae*), around things (*res*) and around actions (*actiones*) and these are focal points which have an existence so to speak both for the sociologist and for the lawyer. People, things and courts (procedures) exist as physical and legal realities. English law, of course, is said to have developed free from the influence of Roman law, yet it is instructive to observe how it uses institutions in much the same way as the civilians.[4] Moreover, there is the added historical irony that in retaining an emphasis on the institution of the legal remedy (*actio*) – on damages, on debt, on injunction actions and the like – modern English law could be said to have more in common with classical Roman law than any modern civilian system now has despite its Roman roots.[5] Just as it is necessary in Roman law,

1 Treitel, *Remedies*, para 62.

2 Zimmermann, pp 770–82.

3 Treitel, *Remedies*, para 39.

4 See generally Samuel, *Foundations*, pp 191–207.

5 Zweigert & Kötz, pp 193–94.

in order to get a full picture of an area like the law of obligations, to study the law of actions (Book IV of Gaius) as well as the law of things (Book III), so it is necessary in English law to study the law of remedies as well as the principles of contract, tort and unjust enrichment.[6] One can often find in both systems rules which in form are remedial, but in substance are obligational.

(a) Framing legal rules

Even if one starts from the premise that knowledge of law is knowledge of rules – and for the purposes of European harmonisation one might, for historical reasons, have to start from this premise (but *cf* Ch 14) – a question arises as to how these rules should be framed. For, as we have emphasised, rules are sentence-like propositions and, like any sentence, can be framed around different subjects and objects. It is, for instance, possible to frame a rule around a person or around an object; equally, however, one can frame a rule around a legal remedy. Thus, the Supreme Court Act 1981 in s 37(1) stipulates that the 'High Court may by order (whether interlocutory or final) grant an injunction. ... in all cases where it appears to the court to be just and convenient to do so'. In this rule no mention is made of legal subjects or legal objects and, as a result, it is open to the literal interpretation that the court could issue a remedy whenever it wishes. Indeed this was just the interpretation once given to the section by Lord Denning.[7]

This difference of approach can have important implications at both a procedural and a substantive level. By framing the rule around the action the effect of s 37 of the 1981 Act is to give the remedy of an injunction an independent status free from, seemingly at least, substantive rules that attach to people generally. This independent status can, obviously, be achieved if the remedy is made the subject of the rule; but even where it is an object it can have the effect of determining the legal position of the subject of the rule. Accordingly, the Secretary of State is granted a considerable legal power of intervention in the financial sector by a provision which stipulates that he can apply for an injunction which will be granted if certain conditions are satisfied.[8] Equally, the Director of Fair Trading can now intervene by way of an injunction where a contractual party insists on using unreasonable exclusion clauses.[9] A legal person is thus given power in law simply by a rule that appears on the surface to be procedural. One important point about written legal rules is, then, that a legislator has a drafting technique at his disposal which he can use to implement, or help to implement, particular policies; the institutional framework around which a rule is drafted can in itself be used to achieve particular legal results.

6 See generally Lawson, *Remedies*.

7 See *Chief Constable of Kent v V* [1983] 1 QB 34.

8 Financial Services Act 1986 s 6.

9 Unfair Terms in Consumer Contracts Regulations 1994 reg 8(2).

(b) Injunction cases

Good examples in English law of this remedial approach to problems are provided by a number of injunction cases (cf Ch 5 § 4). In *Miller v Jackson*[10] the plaintiffs bought a newly constructed house that had been erected on a site close to a long established cricket ground. During the cricket season it became difficult for the plaintiffs to sit in their garden because of the danger of cricket balls being hit out of the ground; the club attempted to resolve the problem by erecting a high fence and offering to install unbreakable windows and a safety net, but the plaintiffs resorted to the legal remedy of an injunction (cf Ch 5 § 4(a)). That is to say, they sought a court order prohibiting the act complained of which, in this case, was the playing of cricket. An injunction was granted by the trial judge on the basis that the invasion of the plaintiffs' garden amounted to the tort of private nuisance; the fact that the cricket ground pre-dated the houses was no defence because legal precedent dictated that a defendant could not justify a nuisance by arguing that the plaintiff was the cause of his own misfortune in coming to live close to the defendant's activity.[11] In the Court of Appeal, however, the injunction was lifted as a result of the decision of two of the judges. Both Lord Denning MR and Cumming-Bruce LJ were of the view that an injunction should not issue, not because there was no nuisance as such (although Lord Denning himself was of the view that the club's activities should not be classed as a nuisance), but because an injunction was a discretionary remedy. Accordingly, even if the playing of cricket did amount to a nuisance – in other words, even if the plaintiffs' right was invaded – a court of equity could still refuse one of its remedies as a result of a rule of discretion attaching to the remedy itself.

This decision can be contrasted with another injunction case which, so to speak, shows the other side of the remedial coin. In *Gulf Oil (GB) Ltd v Page*[12] the defendants, petrol station owners in dispute with their suppliers, threatened to continue to fly an aeroplane over the racecourse at Cheltenham trailing a sign saying 'Gulf exposed in fundamental breach'. The plaintiffs sought an interlocutory, that is to say an emergency, injunction to stop further flights and their claim was granted by the Court of Appeal despite the fact that the statement on the sign was true and thus not capable of supporting an action in defamation. According to the Court of Appeal, there was an arguable case that the aerial display was part of a concerted plan to inflict deliberate damage and this was enough to grant interlocutory relief because, according to the court, the defendants at that time had no immediate interest of their own to protect.

It has to be admitted that both of these cases are, to some extent at least, controversial.[13] Yet much of this controversy arises out of the ambiguous relationship between rules defining rights and rules attaching to remedies. In the *Gulf Oil* case the court was, technically speaking at least, quite entitled to issue an interlocutory

10 [1977] QB 966.

11 *Sturges v Bridgman* (1879) 11 Ch D 852.

12 [1987] Ch 327.

13 See *Kennaway v Thompson* [1981] QB 88; *Femis Bank Ltd v Lazar* [1991] Ch 391.

injunction simply on the basis of rules attaching to the remedy of an interlocutory injunction itself; and these rules stipulate that such an injunction may be issued if the plaintiff can show that he, or more often it, has an arguable case and that on the balance of convenience such an injunction should issue.[14] No doubt a Court of Appeal more sensitive to the constitutional issue of free speech might have interpreted the injunction rules rather differently, but the fact remains that they were not formally bound to consider the substantive public and private rights attaching to the person of the defendant. They had the liberty of focusing just on the procedural principles attaching to the institution of the remedy; and these principles are relatively abstract.

2 REMEDIES AND INTERESTS

The *Miller* case is more problematic in that the tendency of the courts in this century is to issue an equitable remedy once a clear invasion, or threatened invasion, of the plaintiff's right has been established.[15] However, the area of nuisance (see Ch 12 § 5(b)) is such that a strict rights analysis is often unrealistic; what counts is a balancing of the various interests[16] and the notion of an interest is a notion that belongs more to the law of actions than to substantive law (cf Ch 3 § 3(c)). Indeed it is perhaps this notion of an interest that provides the link between rights and remedies in English law. In *Miller v Jackson* Lord Denning MR saw the problem as one of a contest between the interest of the public at large and the interest of the private individual; and, in deciding this contest, what became crucial was the nature of the remedy. Accordingly, in situations where the plaintiff was bringing an action in damages for compensation for physical damage the public interest would, Lord Denning assumed, play a different role than when it was a question of an injunction.[17] The injunction brought into play an element of judicial discretion and this discretion was in turn to be determined by the interests in play.

Such an analysis would appear valid for the *Gulf Oil* case as well. In a claim for damages the plaintiff would have to show more than an invasion of his commercial interest; he would have to establish a cause of action arising out of the defendant's act and (or) behaviour. However, in a claim for an interlocutory injunction the commercial interest itself becomes elevated into an element that can be used directly in the determination of dispute; once it is shown that there is an arguable case one of the factors that the court must then consider in the balance of convenience question is that of the commercial interests involved.[18] In the *Gulf Oil* case this interest question was crucial in that if the defendants had been held to have had an immediate interest of their own to protect the reasoning of the Court of Appeal appears to suggest that the injunction would not have issued. The plaintiffs would have been left only with a

14 *American Cyanamid v Ethicon Ltd* [1975] AC 396.

15 *Cf Mercedes Benz AG v Leiduck* [1995] 3 WLR 718 (PC).

16 *Gillingham BC v Medway Dock Co* [1993] QB 343.

17 [1977] QB at pp 981–82.

18 *American Cyanamid v Ethicon Ltd* [1975] AC 396, 409–10.

possible claim for damages in the tort of conspiracy which might or might not have succeeded depending, *inter alia*, on the hard evidence adduced.

All of this of course raises some fundamental questions about the actual relationship between rights and remedies. If remedies can operate independently of substantive legal rights, as defined by a cause of action, does this mean there are two systems of civil liability in operation, one focusing on the rights of people and the other on remedies and interests? Certainly, claims for money appear to fall into a different category from claims for injunctions and thus if the plaintiff in *Miller v Jackson* had been seeking compensation for physical injury to person or property there is little doubt on the evidence that the cricket club would have been liable.[19] Yet if that is the situation, if the cricket club would be liable in negligence or nuisance for injury done by one of their cricket balls, why is it that they were allowed to continue with an activity that was, in a sense, unlawful? Can it really be the legal situation that an occupier of property must live with a continuing risk of physical injury arising out of an activity which, even from the defendants' position, could cause foreseeable injury? One is getting very close to the idea that the plaintiffs were somehow consenting to the risk (cf Ch 13 § 5(a)), yet if such an argument were specifically to be pleaded by the defendant it could not, on existing authority, succeed.[20] The effect of the decision in *Miller v Jackson* is therefore to alter indirectly the plaintiffs established legal property rights and it did so without these rights themselves being fully argued and analysed by the court. The alteration took place entirely within the law of actions.

This indirect relationship between remedies and rights becomes even more difficult once it is remembered that, in English law at any rate, a person's rights are determined only by the existence of a cause of action and a cause of action, in turn, 'is simply a factual situation the existence of which entitles one person to obtain from the court a remedy against another person' (Ch 3 § 4(d)). The factual situation in *Miller v Jackson* revealed, via the conflicting interests, that the particular remedy of an injunction was not available given the actual complaint in issue (not being able to sit in one's garden) and thus it would seem to follow that the relationship between causes of action and legal remedies is not simply one of *ubi ius ibi remedium* (where there is a right there is a remedy). A cause of action is as much dependent on the nature of the complaint as it is upon a structure of pre-existing legal rights and duties and it is here that the role of a legal remedy can become crucial. For the remedy becomes an institutional means of describing and defining the harm in question and relating this harm to a wider structure of legal rights and duties which, themselves, have been gradually constructed out of various cases where the remedy was influential in shaping the outcome of the litigation.

At a conceptual level the key notion thus becomes, as *Miller* and *Gulf Oil* indicate, the notion of an interest in that this notion becomes something more than a mere descriptive term. When related to rules attaching to the institution of a remedy the notion of an interest becomes a quasi-normative concept – that is to say, a notion

19 See *Bolton v Stone* [1951] AC 850.

20 *Sturges v Bridgman* (1879) 11 Ch D 852.

capable of provoking a legal decision – and accordingly assumes a similar role to that of a right (*cf* Ch 3 § 3(d)). Between *ius* on the one hand and *remedium* on the other there is an intermediate zone where the dichotomies between substantive and procedural rules, between rights and interests and between facts and law become creatively confused (cf Ch 3 § 3(c)).

3 INTERESTS AND OBLIGATIONS

What, then, is the relationship between the notion of an interest and the law of obligations? The first point to be stressed is that the notion has rather specialised roles within the law of actions and these roles vary depending upon whether it is functioning as a descriptive ('is') or a normative ('ought') concept. As a descriptive notion it has a role in the law of damages of describing the particular heads of damage and thus acts as a means of objectivising harm in order that legal rules may be applied. For example, one can in the law of tort distinguish between physical and economic interests (Ch 13 § 9) and this in turn will facilitate the application of rules of remoteness of damage (see Ch 7 § 4).[21] In contract one can distinguish between reliance, expectation and restitutionary interests for the purposes of understanding the kind of compensatory objectives pursued by disappointed contractors.[22] It may be, of course, that these differences of interest are directly mirrored by different legal rights, and so for instance the kind of interest invaded has a direct relevance in the tort of negligence to the duty of care question.[23] However, it is not the notion of an interest which is directly provoking the outcome of the negligence problem in any case where the type of harm is in issue; it is the existence or non-existence of a duty of care.[24]

In relation to legal remedies the notion of an interest has another specific role: it acts as a means of relating the *actio* with the *persona*. That is to say, it can be used as a means of restricting access to particular legal remedies and so only those persons with an interest in the outcome of a legal claim will be allowed procedural access to the remedy. This principle is expressed in the civil law maxim *pas d'intérêt pas d'action* (Ch 2 § 1) and the principle itself finds expression in several European procedural codes. Thus, the French *Nouveau code de procédure civile*, in article 31, specifically states that those bringing or defending a claim must have a 'legitimate interest' in its success or failure before a party is allowed access to the *actio*. In English law, such a requirement is normally associated only with public law remedies where a plaintiff must have a 'sufficient interest' before he is allowed to bring a judicial review action.[25] However, the interest rule can also be found in certain private law remedies such as the admiralty *action in rem*[26] and in equity and property cases.[27]

---

21 See *Spartan Steel & Alloys Ltd v Martin & Co* [1973] 1 QB 27.

22 *Surrey CC v Bredero Homes Ltd* [1993] 1 WLR 1361, 1369.

23 See *Spartan Steel* above.

24 See eg *Marc Rich & Co v Bishop Rock Marine Co Ltd* [1996] 1 AC 211.

25 Supreme Court Act 1981 s 31(3).

26 *The Nordglimt* [1988] QB 183, 199–200.

27 See eg *Lall v Lall* [1965] 3 All ER 330.

The common factor between judicial review and admiralty claims to arrest ships is that they are more 'objective' rather than 'subjective' in nature. They are actions motivated more by the defendant's legal position than by the plaintiff's and so the remedy itself is not necessarily closely associated with any one particular plaintiff. In the law of obligations this difference between objective and subjective can become important in a number of situations. In the tort of public nuisance (Ch 12 § 4(b)) it is unlikely that an injunction could be obtained by anyone not having an interest in the matter any more than damages can be obtained in the absence of special damage.[28] However, what is the position of a person who is not a party to a contract but who has an interest in its performance? The general rule here, as we have seen (Ch 3 § 3(c)), is no third person can sue, or be sued, on a contract to which he is not a party; yet where 'a contract is made for the benefit of a third person who has a legitimate interest to enforce it, it can be enforced by the third party in the name of the contracting party'.[29] No doubt Lord Denning was overstating the legal principle, but the House of Lords certainly went on to allow a widow to use the remedy of specific performance (Ch 5 § 4(d)) to enforce a debt arising out of a contract in her favour made between a defendant and her late husband.[30]

This idea of a third party interest being protected independently of the substantive law of obligations by a legal remedy has also found expression in a damages action. In *Jackson v Horizon Holidays*[31] a father, in reliance upon statements made by a firm of travel agents over the telephone and in its brochure, booked a holiday for himself and his family. Many of the promised facilities were not available and when the father returned he brought an action for breach of contract against the travel agents. The judge thought that the father had had half a holiday and so awarded damages amounting to half the price paid together with an extra £500 for mental distress suffered by the father. The judge made the point that he could not award damages for the distress suffered by the family because they were not parties to the contract. The travel firm appealed in respect of these damages, but the Court of Appeal upheld them on the ground that, although £500 would be excessive in respect of the father himself, it was not an excessive figure for the distress suffered by the whole family. In other words, although the family had no rights under the contract because of the privity rule (Ch 10 § 7), the father could nevertheless obtain compensation in respect not only of his own interest but also the interest of his family.

This reasoning, but not the actual result of *Jackson*, has, it must be said, attracted criticism from the House of Lords.[32] Yet the case, even if somewhat extreme, does illustrate how the law of damages can exert its own independent force in the law of obligations simply as a result of the *actio* acting as an institutional focal point for rules and (or) for factual analysis. What the remedy cannot do, however, is to act

28 *Boyce v Paddington Borough Council* [1903] 1 Ch 109, 114.

29 Lord Denning MR in *Beswick v Beswick* [1956] Ch 538, 557.

30 *Beswick v Beswick* [1968] AC 58.

31 [1975] 1 WLR 1468.

32 See *Woodar Investment Development Ltd v Wimpy Construction UK Ltd* [1980] 1 WLR 277.

independently of other legal notions and concepts and this is why an 'interest', expressly or impliedly, assumes such an important role *vis-à-vis* the *actio*. When acting in conjunction with the remedy an interest can move from being a purely descriptive, or as one French writer puts it, quasi-normative,[33] concept to one that is fully normative and when it does this it is in effect moving from the world of the law of actions towards that of the law of obligations. The family's interest becomes a protected expectation and the expectation becomes one that is no longer an expectation of fact but one protected, even if indirectly, by an *obligatio*. No doubt this use of the language of Roman law might appear anachronistic, but it does serve the purpose of illustrating how reasoning in caselaw functions. And, as we shall see, how one gets from expectations to interests to obligations lies at the heart not just of the dialectical relationship between remedies and rights but also of the methodological relationship between fact and law.

4 CLASSIFICATION OF REMEDIES

A legal system that continues to make use of a law of actions as a means of describing and defining aspects of substantive liability needs to think about legal classification at the level both of substance and of procedure. No doubt in systems where actions have been relegated to separate codes of procedure the classification of remedies becomes less important in that it is the concept of a right which tends to act as the focal point of classification.[34] But even in codified systems the distinction between actions protecting ownership and remedies enforcing obligations remains an important structural support for the distinction between rights *in rem* and *in personam*. In the common law, which thinks more in terms of classifying causes of actions (*cf* Ch 3 § 4), the classification of various actions obviously retains a relevance. Yet in addition to classifying causes it has also to classify actions since, as we have already seen with respect to injunctions, the actual remedy in issue can have important repercussions upon how the substantive law is viewed.

(a) Methods of classification

There are a number of ways in which remedies can be classified. An historical classification would tend to look at the various forms of action and use the formalities between different kinds of claim as the basis for distinction. And so an historical approach to English remedies would require one to distinguish not only between, say, debt and trespass but also between debt and damages on the one hand and the equitable remedies on the other. An institutional classification scheme would tend towards differentiating actions involving relationships between people and things from those involving people and people. Thus, in Roman law the most important classification in private law was between *actiones in rem* and *actiones in personam*:[35] – the first type of

33 P Dubouchet, *Sémiotique juridique* (PUF, 1990), pp 144–45.

34 Jolowicz, *Roman Foundations*, p 81.

35 G.4.1.

action was used to assert ownership and associated rights (rights of way for example) while the second was used to express obligations to pay or convey (owing).[36] In English law the distinction between personal and proprietary remedies is of significance,[37] but it is not easy to use as the basis of a classification scheme since there are often no formal criteria upon which to fasten. A third scheme might base itself upon the consequences of liability. Under this scheme remedies would be classed in relation to the harm suffered by the plaintiff and so compensation claims would be distinguished from restitution actions[38] and orders to do or not to do would be differentiated from self-help and self-protection.

(b) Monetary and non-monetary remedies

Another *summa divisio* is one that distinguishes between monetary and non-monetary remedies. This is a scheme that does have much relevance in English law since it reflects, to some extent, the distinction between common law and equitable remedies. The distinction is not perfect since Chancery has the remedy of account if not damages;[39] and at common law there are powers to order specific restitution of property.[40] However, the distinction between monetary and non-monetary remedies is a useful one for the contract and tort lawyer in that a claim for specific performance or injunction may, as we have seen, bring into play different principles from those attaching to a claim for compensation. For example, the question whether a plaintiff is entitled to rescind a contract in equity for misrepresentation involves a quite different set of rules from those dealing with the question of whether the plaintiff is entitled to damages for misrepresentation.[41] Equally, an entitlement to damages for breach of contract cannot of itself give rise to an entitlement to an order in equity for rescission.[42] The various remedies can, in other words, dictate their own substantive rules.

(c) Forms of money claims

The distinction between monetary and non-monetary claims is not adequate in itself to reflect important institutional differences between remedies. And so although most monetary claims superficially look very much alike, differences of form can have important implications for legal analysis and legal reasoning. For example, a claim for an account of profits in equity is governed by a different set of principles than a claim for compensation at common law and it is, accordingly, quite possible that an account may lie in situations where an action for damages would fail.[43] Even within the common

36 G.4.2–3.

37 Staughton LJ in *Republic of Haiti v Duvalia* [1990] 1 QB 202, 213–14.

38 But *cf Friends' Provident Life Office v Hillier Parker May & Rowden* [1995] 4 All ER 260.

39 See *Jaggard v Sawyer* [1995] 2 All ER 189.

40 Torts (Interference with Goods) Act 1977 s 3.

41 *Banque Keyser Ullmann v Skandia Insurance* [1990] 1 QB 665 (CA); [1992] 2 AC 249 (HL).

42 *Leaf v International Galleries* [1950] 2 KB 86.

43 *English v Dedham Vale Properties* [1978] 1 All ER 382.

law the old distinction between trespass and debt has left its imprint on the modern law of obligations: an action for a specific sum of money is to be contrasted with a claim for compensation.

5 MONETARY REMEDIES

The distinction between trespass and debt has to some extent been eclipsed by the modern tendency to see all monetary claims as 'damages' actions.[44] This is dangerous because, however outdated the idea of a system of forms of action, such a system has the merit of emphasising the nature of the plaintiff's complaint and this in turn can help the jurist move from the world of fact to that of law. The distinction between debt and trespass, for example, was one way of expressing a difference between a claim for a right and a complaint for a wrong (*cf* Ch 3 § 3).

(a) Liquidated and unliquidated damages

In place of the distinction between different forms of action, there is now a procedural dichotomy between damages that are pre-determined before the trial – for example, an action for the price of goods sold[45] – and damages that are unascertained before the action and which the court itself will formally quantify during the trial itself. The former is known as liquidated damages and the latter as unliquidated. The distinction is important as a matter of substance because in a liquidated claim the approach will be all-or-nothing: either the defendant is liable for the specific sum or he is not.[46] In an unliquidated claim the action will also be all-or-nothing in respect of liability itself to pay damages, but a positive answer in the plaintiff's favour will not complete the process. The court will go on to determine what 'interests' will be compensated and these interests can themselves act as focal points for litigation. Thus, in *Jackson v Horizon Holidays* (§ 3 above) there was no dispute about the defendant's contractual liability to pay damages; what was disputed was whether the defendant was under a legal obligation to compensate for the mental distress interest of the family. Sometimes the compensation interest question can become intertwined with the liability question; and so in *Spartan Steel*[47] (Ch 6 § 3(a)) the economic loss question ended up by being both a damages and a liability issue, while in *The Albazero*[48] the award of nominal damages to a consignor of goods who had suffered no loss had the effect of maintaining the right but eclipsing the liability.

Accordingly, the distinction between liquidated and unliquidated damages goes beyond mere form. Actions for unliquidated damages are normally a means of obtaining monetary compensation for harm suffered by the plaintiff and, in addition to determining the liability question, the court must usually quantify the amount payable

---

44 See eg *Friends' Provident Life Office v Hillier Parker May & Rowden* [1995] 4 All ER 260.

45 Sale of Goods Act 1979 s 49.

46 See eg *Carlill v Carbolic Smoke Ball Co* [1893] 1 QB 256.

47 *Spartan Steel & Alloys Ltd v Martin & Co* [1973] 1 QB 27.

48 [1977] AC 774.

by reference to various heads of damage incurred by the plaintiff. Some of these heads may be disallowed as a result of rules attaching to the damages remedy itself and this means that, in addition to substantive works on the law of contract and tort, it is possible to write books on the law of damages.[49] Actions for liquidated damages do not, in contrast, usually involve the court in questions of 'interests'. Either a defendant is liable to pay the full amount or he is not and if he is liable the court is not in a position to dispute or adjust the sum payable since this would amount, in contract cases at least, to re-making the bargain. Furthermore in cases involving 'liquidated damages' clauses – that is to say, clauses fixing the amount payable for any breach of contract – equity might intervene to strike them down if they amount to a 'penalty'.[50] In such a case the liquidated sum will be ignored by the court and liability will be treated as if it is a claim for unliquidated damages. The distinction, therefore, between a liquidated and unliquidated claim in contract is often to be found in the distinction between breach of contract and performance of a contract. A liquidated claim often amounts to a claim for performance of an obligation to pay an agreed price,[51] whereas an unliquidated claim represents an action for compensation for damage incurred as a result of breach of contract (which, in a sense, is also a form of non-performance).

(b) Debt and damages

When viewed from the position of the form of the action, the distinction between a liquidated and an unliquidated claim can be described as a difference between an action for debt and action for damages.[52] '[A] debt', said Millett LJ recently, 'is a definite sum of money fixed by the agreement of the parties as payable by one party to the other in return for the performance of a specified obligation by the other party or on the occurrence of some specified event or condition; whereas damages may be claimed from a party who has broken his primary contractual obligation in some way other than by failure to pay such a debt'.[53] In the law of contract the distinction can be very important since, as we have just seen, a claim in debt is essentially an attempt to enforce performance of the primary obligation.[54] A damages claim in contract is one brought to obtain compensation for the breach of the primary obligation and thus the action is secondary to the contractual obligation itself.[55] A damages claim is brought not to compel performance, but to compensate for a non-performance (*cf* Ch 6). Accordingly:

49 See eg H Street, *Principles of the Law of Damages* (Sweet & Maxwell, 1962); A Ogus, *The Law of Damages* (Butterworths, 1973).

50 *Bridge v Campbell Discount Co Ltd* [1962] AC 600.

51 See eg *Interfoto Picture Library Ltd v Stiletto Visual Programmes Ltd* [1989] QB 443.

52 In fact a claim for liquidated damages and a claim for debt are not in theory identical; debt is a quite separate claim from damages: see, A Burrows, *Remedies for Torts and Breach of Contract* (Butterworths, 2nd edn, 1994), pp 322–23.

53 *Jervis v Harris* [1996] 2 WLR 220, 226.

54 A claim for liquidated damages is not, of course, a claim for the performance of a primary obligation.

55 *Photo Production Ltd v Securicor* [1980] AC 827, 848–49.

> The plaintiff who claims payment of a debt need not prove anything beyond the occurrence of the event or condition on the occurrence of which the debt became due. He need prove no loss; the rules as to remoteness of damage and mitigation of loss are irrelevant; and unless the event on which the payment is due is a breach of some other contractual obligation owed by the one party to the other the law on penalties does not apply to the agreed sum. It is not necessary that the amount of the debt should be ascertained at the date of the contract; it is sufficient if it is ascertainable when payment is due.[56]

The distinction between debt and damages is a formal one whose roots lie in the difference between property and obligations. A debt claim is historically closer to a 'proprietary' claim than to a claim for compensation and thus a plaintiff seeking such a liquidated sum of money is in effect claiming the money as an entitlement to the 'thing' (sum of money) itself (*cf* Ch 11 § 2). It is as if the plaintiff is asking the defendant to hand over property to which the plaintiff is entitled as of right.[57] As with a liquidated damages claim, an action in debt is an all-or-nothing claim: either the defendant is liable for the whole sum or he is not. However, there are some limited exceptions to this all-or-nothing rule. For example, a contractor who has rendered less than full performance may be allowed to claim his debt less a set-off for the work remaining to be done;[58] and in certain cases of supply of goods or services it may be for the court to fix the price payable.[59]

This distinction can be particularly useful when it comes to analysing some civil liability problems in that a number of transactional failures may involve both types of claim. For example, if H hires O's car for a week and returns it in a damaged state O might want to sue H both for the hire fee, if he has not paid in advance, and for the damage to the car. In this situation O will have two quite separate causes of action – one in debt for the hire fee and one in damages for the damage.[60] Even if it is possible for O to estimate very accurately the cost of repairing his vehicle, this will not turn his claim into one of debt; only if he was claiming the money as a result, say, of an indemnity clause in the contract in respect of 'expenses' incurred could the claim be conceived of as one in debt.[61]

The proprietary aspect to debt can sometimes become quite evident in the law of contract. In *White & Carter (Councils) Ltd v McGregor*[62] the defendant, after having agreed with the plaintiff that the latter should advertise the former's business on local authority litter bins, subsequently cancelled the agreement in breach of contract. The plaintiff refused to accept the cancellation, went ahead with the advertising, and then brought an action for the price of the service. The defendant argued that the plaintiff

---

56 Millett LJ in *Jervis v Harris* [1996] 2 WLR 220, 226.

57 See eg *Carlill v Carbolic Smoke Ball Co* [1893] 1 QB 256; but *cf Friends' Provident Life Office v Hillier Parker May & Rowden* [1995] 4 All ER 260.

58 *Hoenig v Isaacs* [1952] 2 All ER 176.

59 See eg Sale of Goods Act 1979 s 8.

60 *Overstone Ltd v Shipway* [1962] 1 WLR 117.

61 *Yorkshire Electricity Board v British Telecom* [1986] 1 WLR 1029; *Jervis v Harris* [1996] 2 WLR 220.

62 [1962] AC 413.

was not entitled to sue in debt for the price; his only remedy, it was claimed, was an action for damages for breach of contract and in such a claim the defendant was entitled to say that the plaintiff was under a duty to mitigate his damage (*cf* Ch 7 § 5(b)). The House of Lords, by a bare majority, gave judgment for the plaintiff. A contracting party faced with a breach of contract has an option: he can accept the breach and sue there and then for damages 'or he may if he chooses disregard or refuse to accept it and then the contract remains in full effect'.[63] On the facts of *White & Carter* the plaintiff had chosen the second option and this gave the plaintiff the right to claim the contract price; there was no question of mitigation since such a rule applied to a damages action and not to debt. The only restriction that might attach to the debt claim was one of abuse of the right to sue: 'if it can be shown that a person has no legitimate interest, financial or otherwise, in performing the contract rather than in claiming damages, he ought not to be allowed to saddle the other party with an additional burden with no benefit to himself'.[64] As Lord Denning subsequently pointed out, the plaintiff in this case was in effect asking the court specifically to enforce the contract; and the traditional view of equity is that specific performance should be refused where damages are an adequate remedy.[65]

(c) Debt and restitution

Debt, therefore, is like the claim for the return of a piece of property: the plaintiff is asking the court to restore, so to speak, to him what is rightfully 'his'. This restitutionary aspect to debt is also reflected in the fact that debt can have a wider role than just acting as a specific performance remedy in contract. It can also act as a remedial vehicle for the recovery of benefits which a defendant is not entitled to keep because he can show no good cause for the enrichment (*cf* Ch 11 § 2). Thus debt, or at least ***indebitatus assumpsit*** in its more developed form, 'was allowed in cases. ... where the plaintiff had intentionally paid money to the defendant, eg claims for money paid on a consideration that wholly failed and money paid under a mistake; cases where the plaintiff had been deceived into paying money, cases where money had been extorted from the plaintiff by threats or duress of goods' and 'cases where money had not been paid by the plaintiff at all but had been received from third persons'.[66] These quasi-contractual debt claims are, it must be said, not always easy to reconcile with the notion of liquidated damages.[67] Yet they nevertheless remain debt rather than damages claims because they are more proprietary in nature than an action for compensation.[68] Indeed the word debt can 'cover sums, whether liquidated or unliquidated, which a person is obliged to pay either under a contract, express or implied, or under a statute'; they 'would, therefore, cover a common claim on a "quantum meruit", or a statutory claim

---

63 Lord Reid at p 427.

64 *Ibid*, p 431.

65 *Attica Sea Carriers Corporation v Ferrostaal Poseidon* [1976] 1 Lloyd's Rep 250, 255.

66 Lord Atkin in *United Australia Ltd v Barclays Bank Ltd* [1941] AC 1, 26–27.

67 *Friends' Provident Life Office v Hillier Parker May & Rowden* [1995] 4 All ER 260, 273.

68 *Lipkin Gorman v Karpnale Ltd* [1991] 2 AC 548.

for a sum recoverable as a debt, for instance a claim for damages done to harbour works under s 74 of the Harbour, Docks, and Piers Clauses Act 1847'.[69]

(d) Tracing money

These quasi-contractual debt claims are no longer based on the fiction of an implied promise to repay. Indeed they seem to have moved from the law of obligations towards the law of property and the plaintiff is thus entitled to the debt, not so much because the defendant is under an obligation to pay (although the quasi-contractual debt claims are still actions *in personam*), but because the plaintiff has some kind of property interest or right in the debt itself.[70] A debt is a chose in action and a chose in action is a species of property.[71] This property approach to debt seems to arise not just from the nature of debt itself, but also from the idea that a plaintiff in a quasi-contractual debt claim – or at least in the action for money had and received (a species of non-contractual debt) (*cf* Ch 11 § 2(a)) – can trace his money into the patrimony of another.[72] Whether tracing at common law is a remedy separate from debt is open to some doubt, for it has been described as 'neither a cause of action nor a remedy', but something that 'serves an evidential purpose'.[73] Yet it does appear in form to be some kind of *actio ad rem* (if not *in rem*) since, although not it seems an actual proprietary remedy, it allows a chose in action to be claimed as a form of legal property.[74] Common law tracing and debt seem to have combined to take these quasi-contractual debt claims out of the area of the law of contract and into their own unjust enrichment or restitution category (*cf* Ch 11).

(e) Tracing and fiduciary relationship

Tracing in equity, in contrast to tracing at common law, is a proprietary remedy: it is a right *in rem* in the actual money in the patrimony of the defendant and, unlike tracing at common law, the plaintiff in equity is entitled to follow his money into a mixed fund where the fund itself will be charged (*cf* Ch 11 § 4).[75] Thus, money can be traced through various bank accounts and the proprietary claim will be defeated only if the defendant can show that he is a *bona fide* purchaser for value.[76] One major restriction is that there must be a fiduciary relationship which brings the equitable jurisdiction into play;[77] this is a relationship based on financial good faith and gives rise to a particular kind of equitable obligation which often has the effect of imposing duties beyond those

69 Brandon J in *The Aldora* [1975] QB 748, 751; but *cf Friends' Provident Life Office v Hillier Parker May & Rowden* [1995] 4 All ER 260, 273.

70 *Lipkin Gorman v Karpnale Ltd* [1991] 2 AC 548, 572–74.

71 Law of Property Act 1925 s 205(1)(xx).

72 *Lipkin Gorman v Karpnale Ltd* [1991] 2 AC 548.

73 Millet J in *Agip (Africa) Ltd v Jackson* [1990] Ch 265, 285.

74 *Lipkin Gorman v Karpnale Ltd* [1991] 2 AC 548, 572–74.

75 *Agip (Africa) Ltd v Jackson* [1990] Ch 265 (Millet J); [1991] Ch 547 (CA); but *cf* Millet LJ in *Boscawen v Bajwa* [1995] 4 All ER 769, 776.

76 *Agip, supra.*

77 *Agip, supra.*

recognised at common law. 'Fiduciary relations', said Fletcher Moulton LJ, 'are of many different types; they extend from the relation of myself to an errand boy who is bound to bring me back my change up to the most intimate and confidential relations which can possibly exist between one party and another where the one is wholly in the hands of the other because of his infinite trust in him'.[78] As the name suggests, fiduciary relationships usually involve, in addition to the *vinculum iuris* between two *personae*, some fund or other *res* which acts as the catalyst for the equitable intervention and, in the case of tracing, serves as an object for the *actio in rem*.

Tracing in equity was developed primarily to protect trust property, but it has a central role in the law of obligations in that it can be used as an unjust enrichment remedy (*cf* Ch 11). In one leading case[79] it was utilised to allow depositors to recover their money from a building society which had been carrying on an *ultra vires* banking business; an action in debt at common law (an action for money had and received) was unavailable since, at that time, such a debt claim was based on implied contract and the effect of the *ultra vires* activity was to make all contracts void. The problem in allowing tracing to function in this way is that it has the effect of turning ordinary creditors into privileged and secured creditors. For the plaintiff succeeds on the basis of owning rather than owing.

(f) *Persona et res*

In order to succeed, however, the plaintiff must be able to point to an actual *res* which forms the object of the tracing claim. In one recent case investors in a precious metal company were led to believe by misrepresentations that their money was secured by a stock of gold bullion of which they were the owners; when the company went bankrupt it was discovered that no bullion had actually been put aside and thus the goods which the investors thought they had purchased remained unascertained.[80] According to s 16 of the Sale of Goods Act 1979 where 'there is a contract for the sale of unascertained goods no property in the goods is transferred to the buyer unless and until the goods are ascertained'. Accordingly, there was no ascertained *res* to which the investors could lay claim. Obviously they had an *in personam* right against the company, but as Lord Mustill explained:

> ... Whilst it is convenient to speak of the customers 'getting their money back' this expression is misleading. Upon payment by the customers the purchase moneys became, and rescission or no rescission remained, the unencumbered property of the company. What the customers would recover on rescission would not be 'their' money, but an equivalent sum. Leaving aside for the moment the creation by the court of a new remedial proprietary right, to which totally different considerations would apply, the claimants would have to contend that in every case where a purchaser is misled into buying goods he is automatically entitled upon rescinding the contract to a proprietary right superior to those of all the vendor's other creditors, exercisable against the whole

78 *Re Coomber* [1911] 1 Ch 723, 728.

79 *Sinclair v Brougham* [1914] AC 398; but *cf Westdeutsche Landesbank v Islington LBC* [1996] 2 WLR 802.

80 *In re Goldcorp Exchange Ltd* [1995] 1 AC 74 (PC).

of the vendor's assets. It is not surprising that no authority could be cited for such an extreme proposition ... [81]

(g) Account

Equity has long recognised the idea that no one should unjustly enrich themselves at the expense of another and it has usually given expression to this old Roman principle[82] through tracing and through a selection of non-monetary remedies (see Ch 11). Tracing, however, is not the only device that can come to the aid of a person seeking restitution of a sum of money. Another equitable monetary remedy of great conceptual importance is equity's own special kind of debt claim called account. This remedy, which involves the taking of an account in order to ascertain what is owed, appears to be an alternative to common law damages and is available in situations where damages might not be an adequate remedy.[83] Thus, it may well be available in cases where a defendant has profited from a tort at the expense of the plaintiff and account may even lie in situations where the common law can offer no remedy at all (cf Ch 11 § 3(d)).

For example, in *English v Dedham Vale Properties*[84] an elderly couple agreed to sell their bungalow and four acres to a property company. Between the signing of the contract and the conveyance of the property, the property company, without informing the couple but using their name, applied for planning permission in respect of the four acres and when this was granted the value of the land increased substantially. After the conveyance the couple discovered what had happened and brought an action for damages based on misrepresentation (*cf* Ch 9 § 7; Ch 13 § 1) and an action for an account of profits in equity. Slade J held that the damages claim had to fail because the property company's behaviour did not actually amount to a misrepresentation; however, the claim for an account of the profit succeeded on the basis that there was a fiduciary relationship between the plaintiffs and defendants. The fiduciary relationship meant that the profit obtained by the property company could not in all conscience be retained and account was the remedy through which the equitable obligation was given expression.

Account is a most useful remedy to equity since it has long been accepted, perhaps wrongly,[85] that damages cannot be awarded in equity except in those situations where statute allows it to be substituted for a non-monetary remedy.[86] However, it is a remedy whose scope and function is by no means clearly defined in the modern case

81 *Ibid*, at pp 102–03.

82 D.50.17.206. See generally Zweigert & Kötz, pp 575–604.

83 *London, Chatham & Dover Ry Co v South Eastern Ry Co* [1892] 1 Ch 120, 140; *AG v Guardian Newspapers (No 2)* [1990] AC 109, 286; *Tang Man Sit v Capacious Investments Ltd* [1996] 1 All ER 193 (PC).

84 [1978] 1 All ER 382.

85 *Cf* PM McDermott, 'Jurisdiction of the Court of Chancery to Award Damages' (1992) 108 LQR 652.

86 *Jaggard v Sawyer* [1995] 2 All ER 189.

law. Does it lie only in cases of wrongful profit or could it also be available to restore a plaintiff to the position he should have been in if the defendant had not been in breach of a fiduciary duty? In *Cuckmere Brick Co v Mutual Finance Ltd*[87] a mortgagee, which had taken possession of mortgaged land, was held liable to the mortgagor when it carelessly sold the property well below its actual value. The sum awarded was the difference between the price actually obtained and the price that would have been obtained if the mortgagee had acted properly. Was this a damages or a debt claim? It was suggested by Salmon LJ in the Court of Appeal that this was just an ordinary damages action in negligence,[88] but this cannot have been correct since the loss was merely financial. Indeed, the Court of Appeal has more recently held that this kind of problem is not a common law claim.[89] Now if damages cannot be awarded in equity it would appear to follow that this action must be a species of account: equity, it might be said, can compensate a person damaged through the breach of a fiduciary duty by awarding an account of the loss incurred. The remedy, in other words, is restitutionary rather than compensatory. If this is so, then it might be a most useful monetary remedy in that it could operate alongside non-monetary remedies such as rescission in equity.[90] It might allow a person who has suffered loss to obtain recompense without having to prove a breach of a common law duty. The problem for the moment is that account remains an underdeveloped remedy in the modern law and its use has been overtaken by the common law action for money had and received (*cf* Ch 11).

6 SELF-HELP REMEDIES

Monetary remedies can be contrasted with non-monetary remedies (*cf* Ch 5). Thus, in addition to ordering a defendant to pay a debt or damages, a court, either as a result of a power conferred by history (usually traceable back to the royal power behind the Court of Chancery) or as a result of statute, also has power to make a range of orders. These non-statutory orders existed and exist as specific remedies, the most important of which is the injunction (Ch 5 § 4); and not only are they usually specifically pleaded by a plaintiff, but their form can still determine the outcome of a case. Thus, in *Leaf v International Galleries*[91] the plaintiff failed in his claim not because there was no breach of a legal obligation, but simply because he had brought an action only for rescission.

(a) Self-help as a legal remedy

In addition to these specific non-monetary remedies there are also remedies which do not require any court order whatsoever. A classic example is the refusal of a purchaser of goods or services to pay for what he or she has bought on the ground that the goods or the service are severely defective.[92] If the defect is serious enough the law of

87 [1971] Ch 949.

88 At p 966.

89 *Parker-Tweedale v Dunbar Bank Plc* [1991] Ch 12.

90 *Cf Banque Keyser Ullmann v Skandia Insurance* [1990] 1 QB 665 (CA); [1992] 2 AC 249 (HL).

91 [1950] 2 KB 86.

92 See eg *Vigers v Cook* [1919] 2 KB 475; *Bolton v Mahadeva* [1972] 1 WLR 1009.

contract has long granted what might be called the remedy of repudiation. Of course, the consumer who repudiates in such circumstances takes a risk: if the defect turns out not to be serious enough to justify the refusal to pay or to go on with the contract, then the consumer himself will be in breach of contract and might well be liable in damages to the supplier of goods or a service.[93] The principle is analogous to the other great self-help remedy of self-defence.

All Western legal systems have granted the right to individuals to protect themselves physically if they are attacked[94] and, in the English law of obligations, this right has an important constitutional status: a person whose liberty or property is unjustifiably invaded by another, including governmental agents, is entitled to use physical force to repel the attack.[95] Only if the force is unreasonable will the self-defender be liable.[96] Of course, the courts do not like to encourage citizens to take the law into their own hands and thus these self-help remedies tend to be quite narrowly construed.[97] Nevertheless, they form an important part of the English law of obligations, particularly since the exercise of self-help can often act as a factual source of litigation. P makes menacing gestures towards D and as a result D physically attacks P: if P sues D for trespass to the person, can D argue that he was entitled to use the self-help remedy of self-defence?[98] Troops arrive to carry out a search of P's house and a soldier is placed on guard at the front door to stop people entering or leaving: if P's wife uses physical force against the soldier in order to escape out of the house, will this be a legitimate act of self-defence?[99]

Self-help remedies are also available against property. In certain circumstances a person may be able to exercise against the goods of another a right of detention in order to encourage the owner of the goods to perform his legal obligation. Such a remedy is called a lien and is available, for example, to the repairer of a chattel in respect of work done on a thing for money consideration. A repairer's lien can thus be an important *in rem* remedy for an *in personam* contractual obligation.[100]Another self-help remedy exercisable against the (intangible) property of another is set-off (*compensatio*).[101] This is a remedy whereby the law allows one debt to extinguish, or partly extinguish, the other debt in a situation where two parties owe each other mutual debts. At common law the remedy is restricted to actual mutual debts, but in equity the remedy applies on a wider basis and can be used in cross-claims where the claims are so closely connected that it would be inequitable for one party to recover

93 See eg *Hong Kong Fir Shipping Co Ltd v Kawasaki Kishen Kaisha Ltd* [1962] 2 QB 26.

94 See in Roman law D.9.2.5pr.

95 For a recent English case, see *R v Self* [1992] 1 WLR 657.

96 *Revill v Newbery* [1996] 2 WLR 239. But *cf Murphy v Culhane* [1977] QB 94.

97 See eg *Burton v Winters* [1993] 1 WLR 1077.

98 *Cf Read v Coker* (1853) 138 ER 1437.

99 *Cf Murray v Ministry of Defence* [1988] 1 WLR 692 (HL).

100 *Tappenden v Artus* [1964] 2 QB 185. Note also the remedy of distress damage feasant: *Arthur v Anker* [1996] 2 WLR 602.

101 Zimmermann, pp 760–67.

without the cross-claim being taken into account.[102] Set-off is, of course, fundamental to banking transactions.

(b) Self-help as a means of pressure

These examples no doubt qualify as genuine remedies in that one person is directly reacting to a breach of obligation by the other party. Yet the idea of self-help has a more extended meaning as well. What if one party brings extra legal pressure on another party in order to make the latter perform his legal – or what is claimed by the first party to be his legal – obligation? Or what if one person digs holes on his land in order to bring pressure on his neighbour to act in a certain way? Or what if employees go on strike for better working conditions? All these acts of 'taking the law into one's own hands' could be seen as a kind of non-judicial 'remedy' and if they are held to be justified – that is to say, if the self-help act does not of itself amount to a breach of the law – then it becomes feasible to see such acts as a form of self-help remedy.[103] In fact whether or not the self-help action is justified often depends upon the way the problem is analysed and categorised within (or without) the law of obligations itself.

Take the example of the extra legal pressure brought by one contractual party on another. If such pressure results in actual damage on a contractual party the person suffering the damage may want to bring an action for damages, or for an injunction, based either on the contract or in tort; the question then becomes one of cause of action, breach, causation and the like.[104] Alternatively, if the pressure results in one party conferring a greater benefit than he originally agreed on the other party then the question may be one that raises questions of inequitable, as opposed say to tortious, behaviour.[105] In addition, the status of the parties can, from a remedies point of view, also be of importance. Thus, in *Bradford Corporation v Pickles*[106] the House of Lords held that a local authority, which suffered damage as a result of a neighbour deliberately digging holes on his own property with the intention of interfering with the corporation's water supply, had no claim in tort since the neighbour's act was a lawful act, however ill the motive might be. Yet if the parties had been reversed, that is to say, if it had been the corporation digging holes on its land in order to injure the citizen, there is little doubt that the citizen would, today, have had an action for judicial review.[107] Self-help in the wider sense can thus become simply a matter of wrongful acts that manifest themselves in various areas of the law of contract (duress, pre-contractual liability), tort (nuisance), restitution (undue influence) or remedies (exemplary damages).

---

102 *Eller v Grovecrest Investments Ltd* [1995] 2 WLR 278.

103 See *Arthur v Anker* [1996] 2 WLR 602.

104 See eg *Torquay Hotel Co v Cousins* [1969] 2 Ch 106.

105 See eg *D & C Builders Ltd v Rees* [1966] 2 QB 617; *CTN Cash and Carry Ltd v Gallaher Ltd* [1994] 4 All ER 714.

106 [1895] AC 587.

107 *Wheeler v Leicester County Council* [1985] AC 1054.

7 DECLARATION

Self-help can obviously give rise to risks on the part of the actor since the act might of itself give rise to litigation. One way of avoiding the risk is to seek the remedy of a declaration. This is a remedy, probably equitable in origin, whereby a court simply declares the rights of the parties without making any common law or equitable order. Thus in *Airedale NHS Trust v Bland*[108] a hospital authority sought a declaration from the courts as to whether it would be lawful for them to discontinue the life-support of a victim of the Hillsborough football ground disaster. Had the hospital simply switched off the machine they would have risked not just criminal proceedings for unlawful killing, but an action in tort by the estate of the victim. However, once the House of Lords had declared that the discontinuing of the life-support would not be unlawful any future public law or private law proceedings would be subject to an immediate striking out for abuse of the legal process on the ground of an absence of a cause of action. In effect, the remedy of a declaration becomes a means of objectively establishing the existence, or absence, of legal rights without damage as such being suffered by the plaintiff. Nevertheless, a plaintiff must have a legitimate interest in the proceedings and the facts themselves must not be hypothetical.[109]

8 COMPARATIVE REFLECTIONS

The idea of a law of remedies is something that is much more difficult to appreciate in the civilian systems. This does not mean that there are not different kinds of remedies in the civil law or that there is no distinction, say, between monetary and non-monetary claims. In fact the distinction between damages and specific (enforced) performance is important.[110] The point to be stressed is that remedies are always secondary in many civilian systems and for two reasons. First, the development of civil procedure in the civilian world was very different from the development in the common law world: procedural and remedial rules attached to the procedure of the court itself rather than to specific forms of action and this gave rise to a mentality whereby differences between types of claim and types of order were not fundamental.[111] In the common law world, in contrast, the writ defined both substantive and procedural rights and thus differences between the various types of writ stretched beyond both procedural and substantive rules as such to give rise to generically different types of claim.[112] Trespass and debt, for example, expressed fundamentally different ideas both at a conceptual (wrongs and property rights) and an institutional (claim for compensation and claim for a specific thing) level. Secondly, the whole point of a civil code is that it is supposed to define a person's legal position; the maxim is very much *ubi ius ibi remedium* (where there is a right there is a remedy) and

---

108 [1993] AC 789.

109 *In re S* [1995] 3 WLR 78.

110 See Treitel, *Remedies*, paras 38, 40.

111 RC van Caenegem, *History of European Civil Procedure*, IECL, Vol XVI, Ch 2, para 15.

112 *Ibid*, para 22.

the remedy thus tends to get eclipsed by the more important dichotomy between procedure and substantive law (*cf* Ch 2). Whether a remedy is to issue is, in traditional civilian thinking, a matter of inference from a code of axiomatic rights. The starting point is not the institutional difference between, say, a claim for damages and a demand for an injunction, but the *inexécution* (non-performance) of an obligation. The question thus becomes one of what the court can do in respect of the non-performance.

All the same, a remedies analysis remains useful in understanding certain aspects of the civilian legal mind. For a start, it has to be remembered that classical Roman law was, like the old common law, a law of actions as much as a law of rights and duties.[113] The distinction between real (*actio in rem*) and personal (*actio in personam*) remedies was fundamental[114] and this dichotomy between property and obligations remains a central characteristic of civilian legal thought. At the level of the action in justice, therefore, a distinction continues to be made between real and personal remedies. Again the Roman distinction between public and private law,[115] together with the idea of an *actio popularis*,[116] has resulted in the modern French distinction between a civil and a public action. *L'action civile*, in the context of the criminal process, allows the victim of a crime not only to claim damages in the criminal courts but to put into motion the public action if *le ministère public* has not already done so (*cf* Ch 2 § 2(c)).[117] Most important from a law of obligations point of view, however, is the distinction between enforced performance and damages: this dichotomy in many respects reflects the distinction between a claim for damages at common law and the seeking of an injunction or specific performance in equity; for, in French law at least, the power of the court to fix what is in effect a daily fine (*l'astreinte*) is similar to, in some ways at least, the power of an English court to fine for contempt.[118] In addition one can also distinguish between judicial and self-help remedies. Even though the maxim 'no one should take the law into his own hands' predominates in civil law, not only does each party to a bilateral contract have the right to suspend the performance of their obligations under a contract in situations where the other party is refusing to perform – the defence of *exceptio non adimpleti contractus*[119] – but a party can also repudiate the whole agreement where there is serious non-performance by the other party. In French law this latter remedy is not a self-help remedy since a party has in theory to go to court in order to obtain resolution, but it seems in practice that many contracts contain a clause allowing a party to repudiate unilaterally a contract for 'breach' (*la rupture*).[120] However, the exercise of such remedies in the civil law is doubtless subject to the

113 See generally Jolowicz, *Roman Foundations*, pp. 75–81.

114 See G.4.1; D.44.7.3pr.

115 Jolowicz, *Roman Foundations*, pp 49–53.

116 JAC Thomas, *Textbook of Roman Law* (North-Holland, 1976), pp 88–89.

117 *Cf Black v Yates* [1992] QB 526.

118 Malaurie & Aynès, p 583.

119 See eg Malaurie & Aynès, pp 401–06; NBW Bk 6 art 262.

120 Malaurie & Aynès, p 416.

doctrines of good faith and proportionality and, in turn, these ideas make useful points of comparison with English law.[121]

Some comparison at the level of remedies is therefore possible.[122] Nevertheless, the old Roman institutional scheme of persons, things and actions has been replaced in the modern codes by the persons, property and obligations structure and this change has eclipsed the *actio* as a formal focal point for substantive legal ideas. A law of obligations in the civil law embraces many of the substantive ideas once to be found in the Roman law of actions. Certainly, one can compare, say, damages in English and in French law; but in French law the actual principles of compensation are part of the substantive law of obligations rather than an aspect of the law of remedies (damages).[123] Instead of a law of damages, then, one talks of contractual and delictual liability (*la responsabilité contractuelle* and *la responsabilité délictuelle*) and it is this notion of liability (*responsabilité*) which acts as the meeting point of remedies and rights. As we shall see (Ch 6), liability in damages acts as a meeting point for remedies and rights in English law.

121 *Cf* eg *Hong Kong Fir Shipping Co Ltd v Kawasaki Kishen Kaisha Ltd* [1962] 2 QB 26.

122 On which see generally Treitel, *Remedies*.

123 CC arts 1146–55.

CHAPTER FIVE

REMEDIES (2): NON-MONETARY REMEDIES

Monetary remedies are largely creatures of the common law courts whereas the majority of the non-monetary remedies in the English law of obligations have been formulated in the Court of Chancery. One *summa divisio*, accordingly, is that between common law and equitable remedies. However, this division has implications that go far beyond the law of remedies in that a number of substantive areas of the law of obligations owe their existence to equitable remedies that have been able to exert influence directly or indirectly on rights at common law. One thinks of mistake in contract, which developed around the equitable remedies of rescission and rectification, or aspects of nuisance in tort associated with the remedy of an injunction. Non-monetary remedies have, then, their own particular place in the law of obligations. On some occasions they support existing rights (*ubi ius ibi remedium*), on other occasions they go further and act as vehicles for the development of new protected interests if not new rights (*ubi remedium ibi ius*).

1 COMMON LAW AND EQUITY

The fact that most non-monetary remedies are creatures of equity is important institutionally because it means that the remedies attract rules not just from the substantive law of things. They also attract principles from equity itself and this gives the law of equitable remedies an extra dimension. Thus, a party who seeks an equitable remedy may find himself debarred from relief, not because the remedy is inapplicable as such, but because the party claiming relief has not himself behaved equitably. They have not come to equity 'with clean hands'.[1] Equally, thanks to statute, a person entitled to equitable non-monetary relief may find that he has to accept damages instead; a court has a general power to give damages in lieu of an injunction or specific performance.[2] These extra dimensions to equitable remedies raise, in turn, a question about the interrelationship of rules underpinning the common law remedies of debt and damages and the principles arising out of equity. To what extent do the differences of rules indicate differences of remedy and to what extent do they simply reflect differences of mentality between Queen's Bench and Chancery?

(a) Discretionary remedies

If one returns to *Miller v Jackson* (Ch 4 § 1(b)) it is possible to argue that it is a decision which functions at the level of remedies rather than rights. The battle of interests arises out of the nature of the action – a claim for an injunction to stop the playing of cricket

1 See eg *D & C Builders v Rees* [1966] 2 QB 617.

2 Supreme Court Act 1981 s 50.

– and so, as Lord Denning indicated, quite different considerations might apply than if the claim had been one for damages. A monetary claim would not necessarily threaten the playing of cricket. However, in a case like *Solle v Butcher*[3] the reasoning goes beyond the nature of the equitable remedy of rescission to embrace principles which lie at the heart of equity itself. Ought a contractor to be able to take advantage of a mistake in order to make a profit for himself? At common law if the parties are agreed about the terms and about the subject matter a contract would be binding; equity, on the other hand, would 'set aside the contract whenever it was of opinion that it was unconscientious for the other party to avail himself of the legal advantage he had obtained'.[4] Chancery, in other words, does not like as a matter of principle either abuse of rights (*cf* Ch 12 § 3(c)) or unjustified enrichment (*cf* Ch 11 § 5).[5]

This attachment to principle means that equity can assert itself at two levels. At the level of principle it can modify the strictness of the common law by offering doctrines that are not in themselves confined to any particular category of substantive law.[6] Here, as Lord Scarman pointed out, one is not in a world 'of neat and tidy rules';[7] it is a world where conscience takes precedence and where definition is a poor instrument. Much will depend on the circumstances of each particular case. At the level of remedies, equity is able to intervene institutionally by offering a series of alternative *actiones* which, although more than capable of acting as vehicles for importing into litigation problems substantive principles, nevertheless go further and exert a direct influence on the way the facts themselves are perceived and organised.

In *Miller v Jackson*[8] (Ch 4 § 1(b)), for example, facts that were not normally relevant for the tort of nuisance assumed more importance when viewed from the position of the Court of Chancery. Cumming-Bruce LJ agreed with Geoffrey Lane LJ (the dissenting judge who thought that an injunction should have been issued) that the facts constituted a nuisance. But he went on to say:

> So on the facts of this case a court of equity must seek to strike a fair balance between the right of the plaintiffs to have quiet enjoyment of their house and garden. ... and the opportunity of the inhabitants of the village in which they live to continue to enjoy the manly sport which constitutes a summer recreation for adults and young persons, including one would hope and expect the plaintiffs' son. It is a relevant circumstance which a court of equity should take into account that the plaintiffs decided to buy a house which in June 1972 when completion took place was obviously on the boundary of a quite small cricket ground where cricket was played at weekends and sometimes on evenings during the working week. They selected a house with the benefit of the open space beside it ... [T]hey must have realised that it was the village cricket ground, and that balls would sometimes be knocked from the wicket into their garden, or even against the fabric of the house. If they did not realise it, they should have done. As it

3 [1950] 1 KB 671.

4 Denning LJ at p 692.

5 Weir, *Common Law System*, paras 93–96.

6 *Ibid*, para 89.

7 *National Westminster Bank Plc v Morgan* [1985] AC 686, 709.

8 [1977] QB 966.

> turns out, the female plaintiff has developed a somewhat obsessive attitude to the proximity of the cricket field and the cricketers who visit her to seek to recover their cricket balls. The evidence discloses a hostility which goes beyond what is reasonable, although as the learned judge found she is reasonable in her fear that if the family use the garden while a match is in progress they will run the risk of serious injury ... It is reasonable to decide that during matches the family must keep out of the garden. ... [9]

And he concluded:

> With all respect, in my view the learned judge ... does not appear to have had regard to the interest of the inhabitants of the village as a whole. Had he done so he would in my view have been led to the conclusion that the plaintiffs having accepted the benefit of the open space marching with their land should accept the restrictions on enjoyment of their garden which they may reasonably think necessary ... There are here special circumstances which should inhibit a court of equity from granting the injunction claimed ... [10]

(b) Damages in lieu

One way of balancing the public and private interest that can arise in cases like *Miller v Jackson* is for the court to use its discretionary power to award damages in lieu of an injunction or specific performance. The history of this procedural power has been summarised recently by Sir Thomas Bingham MR in *Jaggard v Sawyer*:[11]

> Historically, the remedy given by courts of common law was damages. These afforded retrospective compensation for past wrongs. If the wrongs were repeated or continued, a fresh action was needed. Courts of equity, in contrast, were able to give prospective relief by way of injunction or specific performance ... But these courts could not award damages. This anomaly was mitigated by the Common Law Procedure Act 1854 (17 & 18 Vict c 125), which gave courts of common law a limited power to grant equitable relief as well as damages. It was further mitigated by the Chancery Amendment Act 1858 (21 & 22 Vict c 27) ('Lord Cairns's Act') which gave the Court of Chancery the power to award damages ... This enabled the Chancery Court on appropriate facts to award damages for unlawful conduct in the past as well as an injunction to restrain unlawful conduct in the future. It also enabled the Chancery Court to award damages instead of granting an injunction to restrain unlawful conduct in the future. Such damages can only have been intended to compensate the plaintiff for future unlawful conduct the commission of which, in the absence of any injunction, the court must have contemplated as likely to occur. Despite the repeal of Lord Cairns's Act, it has never been doubted that the jurisdiction thereby conferred on the Court of Chancery is exercisable by the High Court and by county courts ... [12]

A similar power is to be found with respect to the equitable remedy of rescission in so far as it might be applicable in cases of non-fraudulent misrepresentation. According to

9 [1977] QB at pp 988–89.

10 *Ibid*, at p 989.

11 [1995] 1 WLR 269.

12 At pp 276-77.

s 2(2) of the Misrepresentation Act 1967 a court can refuse rescission in non-fraudulent misrepresentation cases and award damages in lieu 'if of opinion that it would be equitable to do so, having regard to the nature of the misrepresentation and the loss that would be caused by it if the contract were upheld, as well as to the loss that rescission would cause to the other party'. Equity may not have an original jurisdiction to award damages, but it has a considerable statutory one that operates through some of its non-monetary remedies.

(c) Estoppel

Another possible way of viewing the facts in *Miller v Jackson* is to say, following Cumming-Bruce LJ in particular, that the purchasers of the house were estopped from claiming a remedy for nuisance because they appreciated, or ought to have appreciated, at the time of buying the house that it was situated close to a cricket ground. Now estoppel was not specifically raised as such in the case, but Cumming-Bruce LJ, as we have just seen, hints at facts which go some way in suggesting that the plaintiffs acquiesced, if not consented, to the continuing of the cricket. In situations where such acquiesance or consent is proved, the Court of Chancery may well be prepared to intervene with its 'remedy' of estoppel. Whether estoppel deserves to be treated as an independent equitable remedy is open to doubt. In truth it is an equitable doctrine used to motivate certain equitable remedies such as injunction and rectification. Nevertheless, it is an area of Chancery relief that has attracted its own body of case law and is now of such practical importance that it needs to be distinguished from those substantive areas of law of obligations where it often finds expression.

Estoppel is a doctrine whereby a person (the representor) may be prevented by his statement or conduct from asserting or denying certain facts if the statement or conduct might cause loss to another (the representee) who has relied upon it. It is an equitable ground of relief that in some ways resembles the *exceptio* defence of Roman law whereby a plaintiff was prevented from continuing with an action by a procedural bar inserted by the magistrate.[13] As such it is in principle available only as a defence ('it is a shield not a sword') and cannot in theory create new substantive obligations. In practice, however, it can indirectly create not only *iura in personam* but *iura in rem* – for example, it can create a 'servitude'[14] – and, despite its procedural nature, it is a particularly useful doctrine in that its whole purpose can be to prevent a person from unreasonably exercising rights at common law (*cf* Ch 12 § 3(c)). Estoppel therefore is a useful device through which various fundamental principles of Western law can find expression. For example, it can be used not only to prevent, on occasions, unjust enrichment (*cf* Ch 11 § 5), but to give expression to principles such as *nemo auditur propriam turpitudinem allegans* (no one should be allowed to plead his own wrong) and *male enim nostro jure uti non debemus* (we ought not to use our rights abusively) (*cf* Ch 12

13 'An exception was a defence which did not deny the *prima facie* validity of the claim, but alleged some circumstance which nevertheless barred it': W Buckland, *A Text-book of Roman Law* (Cambridge, 3rd edn, revd by P Stein, 1966), p 653.

14 See eg *Crabb v Arun DC* [1976] Ch 179.

§ 3(c)). Thus, one who promises, in the absence of any consideration (*cf* Ch 9 § 3(f)), not to enforce his full contractual rights at common law might find himself estopped in equity from going back on his promise.[15]

There are a number of different kinds of estoppel. Estoppel by representation has a particular relevance to the law of contract in that it might, as has just been suggested, give legal force to some promises unsupported by consideration (*cf* Ch 9 § 3(f)); estoppel by negligence can have a relevance within the law of tort because it may raise questions on occasions as to whether a person who has been careless with his property ought to be allowed to enforce his property rights if this enforcement would cause damage to another[16] (*cf* Ch 13 § 8); and estoppel by acquiescence, or proprietary estoppel, has a relevance for the law of restitution in that an owner may legally be forced to give credit to one he has allowed to spend money on his property (*cf* Ch 11).[17] The fact that estoppel is a creature of equity in itself adds a further remedial dimension to the general law of obligations in that a court can take account of any behaviour by the representee; if the representee has acted in an abusive way he may be refused a remedy on the ground that it would not be 'inequitable' for the representor to enforce his full rights.[18]

(d) Equitable remedies and substantive law

The relationship between common law and equity is, then, not just a matter of differing rules within a law of obligations. Different remedies can impact directly on the perception of the facts themselves and how these facts are categorised and analysed. This provides great flexibility. Yet it also creates complexity in that it can become difficult to identify certain areas of the law of obligations with just one model of rules. Is there a doctrine of mistake in contract (*cf* Ch 9 § 8)? Are there special principles applicable to the award of damages in innocent misrepresentation problems? Is there a notion of pre-contractual liability (*cf* Ch 9 § 4)? Certainly, there is no established model of rules as such applicable to all factual situations disclosing mistake or *culpa in contrahendo*. However, there are plenty of cases where a remedy has been given on facts which could be said to fall within what a continental lawyer would see as mistake or as pre-contractual liability (*cf* Ch 10 § 2). How these cases are interpreted will often depend upon an understanding of the rules of both equity and the law of remedies and while these remedies will clearly have their place in the legal plan, they also have a distinctive influence on how the facts are conceived. In other words, the relationship between common law and equity, when it comes to interpreting cases, is a relationship which functions both within and without the facts and the means by which equity is able to function, so to speak, within the facts is through the institution of the equitable remedy.

15 *Central London Property Trust Ltd v High Trees House Ltd* [1947] 1 KB 130.

16 *Moorgate Mercantile Ltd v Twitchings* [1977] AC 890; *cf* Torts (Interference with Goods) Act 1977 s 11(1).

17 *Inwards v Baker* [1965] 2 QB 29.

18 *D & C Builders Ltd v Rees* [1966] 2 QB 617.

2 RECTIFICATION IN EQUITY

Take, for example, rectification in equity. This remedy is applicable where a written document wrongly records what was clearly agreed between two parties and is thus a most useful remedy for dealing with those contracts containing written errors (*cf* Ch 9 § 8(d)) which a court might not want to declare either void or voidable (*cf* Ch 9 § 6(a)). Nevertheless, for the relief to be available there must, in the absence of rectification, be some element of unjustified enrichment or abuse of right. Thus, in *Thomas Bates & Son v Wyndham's (Lingerie) Ltd*,[19] although the existence of 'sharp practice' by one of the parties to the contract was an open question,[20] the Court of Appeal ordered the rectification of a lease which did not record what had actually been agreed by the parties. Provided the conduct of the defendant was such as to make it inequitable that he should be allowed to object to rectification, the remedy would be available in cases of mistake. Knowledge of the error and silence on the part of a contractor likely to benefit from the mistake is, seemingly, enough.

In *Rose v Pim*[21] the Court of Appeal refused to rectify a written contract, which clearly misdescribed what the plaintiff expressly wanted to buy, on the ground that the relevant contract was part of a series of transactions. The 'parties to all outward appearances were agreed' and once 'they had done that, nothing in their minds could make the contract a nullity from the beginning, though it might, to be sure, be a ground in some circumstances for setting the contract aside in equity'.[22] In focusing upon errors in documents rather than in the mind equity is able to create a clear dichotomy between promise and intention in turn allowing the facts to take on an extra dimension of time. A written contract, even although it clearly does not express the intention of the parties, can stay valid and fully enforceable *vis-à-vis* the remedy of rectification simply because the document itself has become the basis for a series of multi-party institutional relationships which ought not to be upset. The reference point became the document rather than the contractors themselves and this document acted as a vehicle by which the institutional relationships between all the parties were assessed. 'It would not be fair to rectify one of the contracts', said Denning LJ in *Rose v Pim*, 'without rectifying all three, which is obviously impossible'.[23] Had the plaintiff sought damages the result may well have been different, as Denning LJ specifically recognised; for a damages claim would have attached to the promise (collateral warranty) and not to the document.[24] The remedy of rectification, in contrast, focused on the *res* (document) rather than the *personae* (intentions).

---

19 [1981] 1 WLR 505.

20 *Cf Riverplate Properties Ltd v Paul* [1975] Ch 133, 140.

21 [1953] 2 QB 450.

22 Denning LJ at p 460.

23 At p 462.

24 At pp 462–63.

3 RESCISSION IN EQUITY

Another, more important, equitable remedy that straddles the zone between contract and equity is the remedy of equitable rescission. This is a remedy designed to help a party who wishes to escape altogether from an obligation on the ground that enforcement of the obligation would be inequitable. Equity may, accordingly, order the rescission of a contract (or other transaction) entered into under fraud, duress, undue influence or mistake and it can set aside contracts which have been induced by statements (representations) which turn out to be untrue (*cf* Ch 9). It is a remedy which operates at the frontier of contract in that it is a means 'by which the unjust enrichment ... is prevented' and, 'though for historical and practical reasons [is] treated in books on the law of contract, is a straightforward remedy in restitution subject to limits which are characteristic of that branch of the law'.[25] This remedy must, however, be distinguished from other, seemingly similar, remedies such as declaration – whereby, for example, a contractor asks the court to declare that a contract is void[26] – or repudiation at common law. This latter remedy is a non-judicial self-help action where a contractor unilaterally repudiates a contract for serious breach, a course of action that does not require the intervention of the court.[27] Where equity does order rescission – and it retains a discretion to withhold relief where damages would be a more suitable claim[28] – it will only do so where *restitutio in integrum* is possible.[29]

There are, as *Rose v Pim* indicates, many occasions when a set of facts can disclose several institutional possibilities. D makes a misrepresentation (a false statement which induces a contract) (Ch 9 § 7) to P which results in P entering a contract with D and suffering financial loss. If P wants both to escape from the contract and to obtain compensation for his loss he will have to bring an action for rescission and an action for compensation. But what must P establish in order to succeed in both remedies? Can P simply allege that D is in breach of a duty in order to trigger both the non-monetary and the monetary claim? Or must P establish breaches of duty in equity (rescission) and at common law (damages)? In *Banque Keyser Ullmann v Skandia Insurance*[30] the Court of Appeal held that the existence of a breach of an equitable duty giving rise to rescission in equity was not enough in itself to act as the basis for a damages claim as well. In order to succeed in the monetary action the plaintiff must establish a cause of action in tort or contract. In some ways this decision may be seen as misleading in that there was no attempt to argue that the loss itself might have been subject to its own equitable

25 Robert Goff J in *Whittaker v Campbell* [1984] QB 318, 327.

26 *Barton v Armstrong* [1975] 2 All ER 465.

27 *Car & Universal Finance Co Ltd v Caldwell* [1965] 1 QB 525.

28 *Leaf v International Galleries Ltd* [1950] 2 KB 86.

29 But in order to achieve such restitution the court cannot make use of the remedy of damages in addition to rescission unless there is a separate right to damages at common law or under statute: *cf Jaggard v Sawyer* [1995] 2 All ER 189. However, it can, via the remedy of account, order that an indemnity be paid so as to prevent unjust enrichment: *Spence v Crawford* [1939] 3 All ER 271, 288–89.

30 [1990] 1 QB 665 (CA). The analysis by the Court of Appeal was not actually disputed in the House of Lords: [1992] 2 AC 249 (HL).

remedy such as account (*cf* Ch 4 § 5(g)). Ought not the representor to account to the representee for any losses arising out of the inequitable behaviour? All the same it would seem that duties are not defined just in terms of a relationship between two persons; a plaintiff must go further and establish a link between the *actio* and the defendant and it is this link that provides the normative force in the law of obligations. This decision should serve as a warning, therefore, to those tempted to think that English law thinks in terms of a law of obligations. Certainly, it is useful to have a general category into which one can place the common law and equitable claims; but this general category does not of itself provide a normative basis to the causes of action. The duties which provide such normative force are defined by categories (contract) or by causes of action (eg trespass, negligence, conversion) within categories (tort) and by remedies (rescission, injunctions etc) functioning, on the whole, at a low level of abstraction.

4 INJUNCTIONS AND SPECIFIC PERFORMANCE

One must not, for all that, exaggerate the position. Equitable remedies do not function in a legal world unrestrained by pre-existing rules and principles and so an injunction, perhaps the most important of the non-monetary private law remedies, is available only to protect against breaches, or threatened or feared breaches, of existing legal rights.[31] An injunction must in theory be related to a right and not a mere interest, although this distinction can become rather meaningless in the area of interlocutory (emergency) injunctions, and thus as far as the law of obligations is concerned, it is, seemingly, secondary to the rules and principles of contract and tort. Equally, the remedy of specific performance presupposes the existence of a contract, although, as we shall see, it may not be necessary that the plaintiff herself should have an enforceable contractual right.

(a) Injunctions

An injunction is a discretionary remedy derived from the equitable jurisdiction of the courts[32] and although it is normally cast in negative form there exists a positive form called a mandatory injunction. A negative injunction directs the person to whom it is addressed not to do something (for example, not to trespass on the applicant's land),[33] while a mandatory injunction requires that the person do something positive, such as removing a trespassing sign from the plaintiff's land.[34] Mandatory injunctions must be distinguished from other types of court orders[35] and from the equitable remedy of specific performance. However, in the area of the law of contract the distinction

31 *P v Liverpool Post Plc* [1991] 2 AC 370; *Mercedes Benz AG v Leiduck* [1996] 1 AC 284.

32 *Wookey v Wookey* [1991] 3 WLR 135.

33 *Anchor Brewhouse Developments v Berkley House* [1987] EG 173. See also *Law Debenture Corpn v Ural Caspian Ltd* [1993] 1 WLR 138, 144–45.

34 *Kelsen v Imperial Tobacco Co Ltd* [1957] 2 QB 334.

35 *In re P (Minors)* [1990] 1 WLR 613.

between mandatory injunction and specific performance is often difficult to perceive in substance and this is why both remedies tend, in contract, to be governed by the same principles.[36] Specific performance is, nevertheless, a quite separate remedy in form.[37]

Injunctions have a very significant role in the law of obligations. Injunctions can be used to prevent a contractor from breaching a contract[38] or indeed to enforce performance (where the remedy overlaps with specific performance). In the law of tort injunctions have an important role in areas such as nuisance[39] and the trade and business torts;[40] they can also be used to stop a person from profiting out of illegal behaviour[41] and perhaps out of certain kinds of invasions of privacy.[42] An injunction is also important in protecting property rights, although this is often achieved via such torts as trespass, nuisance and passing off; it can, for example, be used to order the removal of property from the plaintiff's land[43] or to stop a person from marketing a product under a name or design similar to that of the plaintiff's product.[44] A mandatory injunction may be available to force a possessor to deliver up goods belonging to the plaintiff (although now there is power for such an order under statute)[45] and in certain circumstances it might even protect a person's employment as if it were a kind of property right.[46] Injunctions, then, are remedies that respond not just to wrongs but also to rights and in this respect they are remedies that allow the court to move freely between property and obligations since equity tends to view all patrimonial rights as forms of property.[47]

(b) Interlocutory injunctions

Injunctions are, accordingly, creative remedies that can act as a means of turning certain kinds of patrimonial and economic rights into forms of property. If the court is prepared, for instance, to issue an injunction to stop an interference with a contractual right the *in personam* obligation becomes an *in rem* asset.[48] However, in these cases the plaintiff must usually show that the defendant is in breach of some existing tort or contract duty. But what if the plaintiff is seeking an emergency injunction in order to

36 *Mortimer v Beckett* [1920] 1 Ch 571; *Sky Petroleum Ltd v VIP Petroleum Ltd* [1974] 1 WLR 576.

37 Lawson, *Remedies*, pp 211–13.

38 *Warner Brothers Pictures Inc v Nelson* [1937] 1 KB 209.

39 *Kennaway v Thompson* [1981] QB 88; *cf Miller v Jackson* [1977] QB 966.

40 *Torquay Hotel Co v Cousins* [1969] 2 Ch 106; *Thomas v NUM* [1986] Ch 20.

41 *AG v Harris* [1961] 1 QB 74.

42 *Kaye v Robertson* [1991] FSR 62; *Khorasandijian v Bush* [1993] QB 727

43 *Kelsen v Imperial Tobacco Co Ltd* [1957] 2 QB 334.

44 *Erven Warnick BV v Townend & Sons* [1979] AC 731.

45 *Howard Perry v British Rail Board* [1980] 2 All ER 579; *cf* Torts (Interference with Goods) Act 1977 ss 3(2), 4.

46 *Nagle v Fielden* [1966] 2 QB 633; *Hill v CA Parsons & Co Ltd* [1972] Ch 305.

47 *Ex Parte Island Records* [1978] Ch 122.

48 *Torquay Hotel Co v Cousins* [1969] 2 Ch 106.

protect some interest that, to date, has not been the subject of litigation – that is to say, not formally protected as a right?

In *Gulf Oil v Page*, discussed earlier (Ch 4 § 1(b)), the Court of Appeal was prepared to issue an emergency (interlocutory) injunction on the basis that the defendant had no legitimate interest to protect and that the facts might disclose the tort of conspiracy. The court was, therefore, prepared to issue an effective remedy – the stopping of the defendants' self-help action – not on the basis that the defendants were in breach of any obligation or were invading any right of the plaintiffs, but on the basis that the plaintiffs' commercial interests should take precedence over the interests of the defendants. In fact the court was able to do this because special rules from the law of actions come into play when an injunction is interlocutory; such an injunction, temporary in kind, is an emergency remedy designed to prevent a *fait accompli* and as a result is only indirectly concerned with actual substantive rights and duties. The power to grant such an injunction is now to be found in statute;[49] but its existence predates the legislative confirmation[50] and the guidelines governing the issue of the remedy are to be found in Lord Diplock's judgment in the *American Cyanamid* case.[51] What a plaintiff has to show is that there is a serious question to be tried which if resolved in the plaintiff's favour could not be adequately compensated by the remedy of damages. If the plaintiff can pass these two hurdles, and provided also that the balance of convenience is in favour of the injunction being issued, he (or more usually, it) will be entitled to the emergency remedy, although, unless it is a public body,[52] it will have to give an undertaking in damages to the defendant that, should it transpire that the injunction was unjustified, any losses arising from the interlocutory relief will be compensated.[53]

Interlocutory injunctions are, then, remedies which can go far in laying the foundations for new 'rights' in that they are able to function in a world less restrained by substantive rules.[54] In commercial law they are, not surprisingly, of great importance since they seem to respond more easily to commercial interests and this response has, moreover, resulted in two new species of interlocutory injunction, both designed to deal with problems of property. The first, the *Mareva* injunction, takes its name from the case of *Mareva Compania Naviera v International Bulkcarriers*[55] which involved an application for an interlocutory injunction to prevent a defendant in a contractual claim from removing money out of the jurisdiction of the English courts. The Court of Appeal, in relatively short judgments, granted the remedy. 'If it appears that [a] debt is due and owing', said Lord Denning MR, 'and there is a danger that the debtor may dispose of his assets so as to defeat it before judgment, the court has jurisdiction in a

49 Supreme Court Act 1981 s 37.

50 *Mercedes Benz AG v Leiduck* [1996] 1 AC 284, 299.

51 *American Cyanamid Co v Ethicon* [1975] AC 396.

52 *Kirklees MBC v Wickes Building Supplies Ltd* [1993] AC 227.

53 See *Cheltenham & Gloucester Building Society v Ricketts* [1993] 1 WLR 1545.

54 On which see *Mercedes Benz AG v Leiduck* [1996] 1 AC 284 (PC).

55 [1980] 1 All ER 213.

proper case to grant an interlocutory judgment so as to prevent him of disposing of these assets'.[56] This case, barely reported at the time, not only has received statutory recognition,[57] but is now the basis for an established jurisprudence concerning the freezing of assets of a defendant and, for the obligation lawyer, its importance lies not just in its practical effects, but in the way that the law of things and the law of actions have become intertwined so as to produce an important shift towards pre-trial litigation.[58]

Given the nature of an interlocutory injunction this is, perhaps, inevitable. Nevertheless, the growth of powerful pre-trial remedies which impact on *in rem*, as well as *in personam*, relationships can have a distorting effect upon substantive rights and duties in that there is a tendency to elevate what are essentially empirical focal points (interests) to the level of substance (*cf* Ch 2). Pre-trial remedies by their very nature look to the immediate interests of the parties more than to the actual rights and duties in dispute and this in turn can benefit a powerful plaintiff in that his (or its) 'interest' can be used as a weapon against a defendant's 'right'. Thus, if care is not taken, the freezing of a defendant's assets through the use of a *Mareva* injunction can seriously interfere with ownership rights without the question of ownership ever being discussed.

This problem of interference with basic rights has become particularly acute with respect to the second species of new interlocutory injunction. 'Let me say at once', said Lord Denning MR in *Anton Piller KG v Manufacturing Processes Ltd*,[59] 'that no court in this land has any power to issue a search warrant to enter a man's house so as to see if there are papers or documents there which are of an incriminating nature'.[60] However, should a householder refuse to let the plaintiff's solicitors enter his premises under what has become known as an *Anton Piller* order he or she will be 'guilty of contempt of court'.[61] This *Anton Piller* order is a mandatory interlocutory injunction, acting *in personam* against the owner of premises, ordering him to allow an inspection of his premises; and the order was formulated as a pre-trial remedy to help owners of intellectual property gain evidence of infringements of their property rights. Having become quickly established as a pre-trial remedy capable of powerful intrusions into property rights and civil liberties, it soon became a tool of abuse with the result that the courts have had to have recourse to the EC (EU) principle of proportionality in order to try to limit its use.[62] The lower courts forgot, or seemed to forget, that this kind of

56 At p 215.

57 Supreme Court Act 1981 s 37(3)

58 *Mercedes Benz AG v Leiduck* [1996] 1 AC 284. With regard to the legal basis of the injunction, note the words of Lord Mustill (at p 299): 'After only a few years the development of a settled rationale was truncated by the enactment of s 37(3) of the Supreme Court Act 1981. This did not, as is sometimes said, turn the common law *Mareva* injunction into a statutory remedy, but it assumed that the remedy existed, and tacitly endorsed its validity.'

59 [1976] 1 All ER 779.

60 At p 782.

61 At p 783.

62 *Columbia Picture Industries Inc v Robinson* [1987] Ch 38; *Lock Plc v Beswick* [1989] 1 WLR 1268.

interlocutory injunction was at the 'absolute extremity of the court's powers'[63] and, like the *Mareva* injunction, represents an institutional meeting point between private remedies and constitutional rights.[64]

(c) Injunctions and public rights

Search warrants and the freezing of assets are clearly as much within the realm of public as private law and this should indicate just how difficult it is to relate an equitable remedy like an injunction to the established categories of law. Is a search warrant not a search warrant simply because it is called an interlocutory injunction? Is an order restricting the right to enjoy and to dispose of property not a constitutional infringement of a fundamental human right just because it is called a pre-trial commercial remedy? These kinds of question do not usually concern the English lawyer since there is little in the way of written constitutional rights and no formal definition of ownership. Indeed even the term 'right' has little meaning in English law (*cf* Ch 3 § 3(d)). Nevertheless, the idea of a law of obligations does require the drawing of some boundaries if the idea is to have any definition and it is here that the interlocutory injunction can give rise to difficulties. It may be that in theory both the *Mareva* and the *Anton Piller* injunctions act *in personam* and in a private law of actions capacity,[65] but the effect is *in rem*. That is to say, the two injunctions are in practice aimed as much at the *res* as at a *persona* and this property aspect in turn impinges upon public law. The private law of remedies thus cuts across any idea of a law of *in personam* obligations and *in rem* property rights.[66] In injunction cases it may be that principles of public law will need to be set alongside those of commercial law and this, of course, may impact upon commercial law itself in that in seeking to make use of certain equitable remedies such as the *Anton Piller* order a plaintiff might have to go far in satisfying principles more concerned with the exercise of power. Thus, principles such as natural justice and *audi alteram partem*[67] may well become of direct importance if the more traditional notions of commercial law such as good faith fail to satisfy the balance of power and conflict of interests.

If, or when, this happens equity itself could become a forum for an 'economic' law which brings together ideas from property, contract, tort, remedies and administrative law. And such a forum could be valuable in a European context in that it would not only act as a means of stressing to the civil lawyer the importance of remedies in commercial law but, in return, it would act as a means of introducing civilian ideas into the common law. By starting out from the remedy English law could reshape itself along lines that might be genuinely helpful to a *ius commune*. Whether this helpful reshaping will actually happen is quite another matter. Certainly, equity is a valuable

63 At p 784 *per* Ormrod LJ.

64 *Lock Plc v Beswick* [1989] 1 WLR 1268.

65 *Mercedes Benz AG v Leiduck* [1996] 1 AC 284.

66 *Cf Mercedes Benz AG v Leiduck* [1996] 1 AC 284.

67 See eg NCPC art 14.

forum for rethinking the traditional legal frontiers. But this rethinking can come up against serious *mentalité* problems: can one really 'own' one's voice as one injunction case came close to suggesting?[68] The civil lawyer is likely to be sceptical – not because the idea lacks institutional logic. After all if one can own an image[69] why not a voice? The scepticism is likely to arise from the mentality of the codes themselves which see property rights as embedded in the relationship between person and thing[70] and that in turn translates itself into a number of fundamental powers one of which is the right to dispose of the *res*.

(d) Specific performance

A mentality problem is also encountered when one turns from injunctions to the quite distinct – although often in substance similar – remedy of specific performance.[71] In continental legal thought the idea that an order instructing a recalcitrant contractor specifically to perform his obligation under a contract is an exceptional (that is equitable) remedy appears odd. In European legal systems it is damages that are in theory the exceptional remedy.[72] In truth there is much that is myth in the supposed difference.[73] For example, most contractual claims in the English lower courts are for debt, which of course is a common law form of specific performance (*cf* Ch 4 § 5), and on the continent compensation for non-performance of a contractual obligation is more widespread than principle might suggest.[74] All the same the existence of specific performance as an equitable remedy subject to its own rules and principles reveals much about English contract law (*cf* Ch 10). Failure to perform a contract is usually seen as a matter of breach of promise rather than non-performance of an obligation and as a result the emphasis tends to be on the damage as much as on the contractual relationship itself. Thus, only where damages are an inadequate remedy will specific performance be granted in equity.[75]

(e) Damages and specific performance

The relationship between damages and specific performance is more complex than it first might appear not only because the definition of 'inadequacy of damages' is itself difficult but also because specific performance, being an equitable remedy, is discretionary and subject to its own legal principles. Thus, it may be refused if a court thinks that it would cause hardship[76] or would lead, say, to an abuse of a contractual

68 *Ex p Island Records* [1978] Ch 122.

69 B Edelman, *Ownership of the Image* (RKP, 1979; trans E Kingdom).

70 A-M Patault, *Introduction historique au droit des biens* (PUF, 1989), pp 141 ff.

71 Treitel, *Remedies*, para 62.

72 *Ibid*, para 42.

73 *Ibid*, para 41.

74 *Ibid*, para 70.

75 *Ibid*, para 71; *Price v Strange* [1978] Ch 337, 360.

76 *Patel v Ali* [1984] Ch 283.

right or to unjustified enrichment (*cf* Ch 11). Furthermore equity does not like specifically to enforce certain kinds of contracts such as those for personal services; but this reluctance must be set against the willingness to issue an injunction to prevent a person from refusing to perform contractual services.[77] In addition there is a principle that equity will not grant specific performance if the court would have to supervise the enforcement to an unacceptable degree.[78]

What kind of contractual transaction will attract specific performance? In principle any contract of sale where the object of the transaction is unique and this will always apply to contracts for the sale of land – for each piece of land is considered unique. However, the remedy may well be available in sale of goods transactions if the buyer can show that the goods themselves are special and even everyday generic goods may become unique as a result of particular circumstances such as short supply.[79] In contracts for the supply of a service we have already said that equity does not like to force one person to work for another, but it might be asked whether the remedy could be developed in a creative way. For example, it is tempting to see it as a means of forcing employers to provide safety equipment or to encourage the provider of a service to fulfil all the terms of his obligation. No doubt a mandatory injunction could play the same role, but the advantage of specific performance is that it is a remedy more or less exclusive to contract and as such could influence the development of the law of obligations in ways that the remedy of damages cannot. It could, for instance, help shift the emphasis off the idea of breach of a promise and on to the idea of a failure to perform an obligation. This shift of emphasis may not always be desirable, yet on certain occasions it might add subtlety and flexibility to the law of remedies while at the same time influencing substantive law in a way that might be beneficial in terms of European harmonisation.[80] Specific performance as a remedy could, in other words, act as a medium through which a change of juridical mentality in respect of contract might be achieved and while this change of mentality might be of marginal importance to the English law of contract as a whole, it could perhaps facilitate a better understanding of a European law of obligations.

(f) Debt and specific performance

The creative potential of specific performance has already made itself felt in a problem involving the remedy of debt. In *Beswick v Beswick*[81] an elderly coal merchant transferred his small business to his nephew in return for a contractual promise that the latter would pay the coal merchant an annuity of £6.50 per week for the rest of his life and, thereafter, £5 per week to the coal merchant's widow. The nephew made the regular payments to the retired coal merchant, but after his death made only one

77 *Warner Brothers Pictures Inc v Nelson* [1937] 1 KB 209.

78 *Posner v Scott-Lewis* [1987] Ch 25.

79 *Sky Petroleum Ltd v VIP Petroleum Ltd* [1974] 1 WLR 576.

80 D Tallon, 'Breach of Contract and Reparation of Damage', in Hartkamp *et al*, pp 225–28.

81 [1968] AC 58.

payment to the widow; as a result, acting in her personal capacity and in the capacity as administratrix of the estate, she sought specific performance of the contract. In the Court of Appeal[82] the widow succeeded in both capacities: the promise to pay an annuity was a form of property (a *chose in action*) under the Law of Property Act 1925 and according to s 56(1) of this statute a person could take an immediate interest or benefit in the property even though the person might not be named as a party in the conveyance. The House of Lords, reversing in part, decided that the widow had no right to sue in her personal capacity. However, they were prepared to allow the estate to enforce the contract in equity on the basis that the common law remedy of damages was inadequate in that it would have awarded the estate only a nominal sum since the coal merchant had suffered no loss.

Admittedly this reasoning appears to confuse not only 'damage' and 'damages' (*cf* Ch 6 § 1) but also procedural and substantive rights. For it was not the inadequacy of the damages remedy which was the problem; it was the substantive rule of privity of contract which created the difficulty since the rule seems not to recognise a third party's 'loss' as a form of 'damage' capable of being directly remedied in contract (*cf* Ch 10 § 7). Nevertheless, the use of specific performance to enforce the payment of weekly debts is a helpful reminder of how equity, at the level of remedies, can give protection to an empirical interest which, if not protected, might well have resulted in contract becoming a means of unjustified enrichment which would have been to pervert its role in acting as a means of justified profit (*cf* Ch 11 § 5). As Lord Pearce observed, 'The appellant on his side has received the whole benefit of the contract and it is a matter of conscience for the court to see that he now performs his part of it'.[83]

(g) Remedies and the right to sue

Viewed from the position of substantive law, the decision in *Beswick* is rather intriguing. Is it in truth a law of persons case where the relevant *persona* is, unofficially, the family (*cf* Ch 2 § 7)? The courts have taken the view that the interests of a family member are not necessarily confined to immediate economic benefits of the individual plaintiff; they may embrace the well-being – that is to say, the interests – of spouses and children[84] and so it is not unreasonable to view *Beswick* as a case where the interest in issue was one attaching to the family rather than to the individual vendor of a business.[85] Alternatively, it might be asked whether *Beswick* is an example of the recognition of transferred loss. In the law of tort it has recently been re-affirmed that a disappointed beneficiary can sue the solicitors whose negligent performance of a contract with the testator to draw up a will caused the gift to fail.[86] Is *Beswick* not a situation involving a similar loss transferred from estate to third party? The main

82 [1966] Ch 538.

83 [1968] AC 58 at p 89.

84 See eg *Pickett v British Rail Engineering Ltd* [1980] AC 126.

85 *Cf Jackson v Horizon Holidays Ltd* [1975] 1 WLR 1468.

86 *White v Jones* [1995] 2 AC 207.

difficulty in using this analysis is that the House of Lords has specifically refused to recognise the German principle of transferred loss, thus making the institutional base to the specific performance remedy in *Beswick*, at least from a substantive law position, rather weak.[87] A third possibility is simply to say that the court was using the law of actions (equitable remedies) to enforce a substantive obligation (contract) between testator and nephew based on the notion of unjust enrichment. However, the difficulty here is that, in enforcing the obligation to avoid a 'loss' not actually suffered by the contractor himself (or itself), the law of actions was creating a new legal chain between widow and nephew based on the idea that the nephew ought not to be allowed to keep an enrichment for which there was no cause and which in turn caused loss to the widow. Unjust enrichment as an obligation thus came to displace the contractual rule that the debt was unenforceable by the widow. There may be no harm in doing this as a matter of what Lord Goff has called, in an analogous context, 'practical justice';[88] but it will evidently make it more difficult to talk about a law of obligations (contract, tort and restitution) as an area of law independent from the law of remedies (debt, damages and equitable remedies). Legal thinking will always need to function, at one and the same time, in several dimensions (*cf* Ch 14).[89]

5 SUBROGATION

There is a more general reason why *Beswick v Beswick* is an intriguing case: it concerns the whole problem of what might be called the institutional structure of law (*cf* Ch 3). This notion of an institutional structure is particularly important when it comes to understanding complex liabilities involving more than two parties. Traditional legal thought and analysis is governed by the paradigm that litigation, and thus legal disputes in general, are a matter between two parties each with an interest to protect.[90] It is a question of one person (*persona*) bringing a claim (*actio*) against, or having a legal relationship (*iuris vinculum*) with, another person (*persona*) and this formal structure is still to be found even in the codified systems where the formalities of a procedural system have been replaced by a model of rights.[91] In situations where ownership or property rights were in issue this bipolar structure was, in Roman thinking at least, preserved in the idea that one brought a claim (*actio*) against a thing (*res*);[92] if the necessary legal relationship was established in the thing (*dominium, ius in re*) this had the effect of implying rights (*iura in rem*) good against the world without upsetting the traditional institutional axis of a legal structure between two institutions.

87 *The Aliakmon* [1986] AC 785; *White v Jones* [1995] 2 AC 207, 264–66.

88 *White v Jones* [1995] 2 AC 207, 259, 264.

89 *Cf* Samuel, *Foundations*, pp 243–72.

90 See eg D.1.1.1.2; *R v Education Secretary, Ex p Avon CC* [1991] 1 QB 558, 561.

91 See eg *NCPC* art 31.

92 Thus, in early Roman law the thing itself, or part of it, had to be in court: G.4.16–17.

(a) Remedies and the individual legal subject

Another way of looking at all this is simply to say, as indeed we have already said, that Roman law was extremely individualistic in its approach to legal structures[93] and that this was particularly true when it came to what today we would call rights *in personam*. Thus, individualism became an essential feature of the institutional structure itself with the result that social interests – or more precisely the interests of particular classes – could be realised in the legal plan only through the manipulation of the individualistic institutions themselves. For example, it was through the manipulation of the institutions of *persona*, *res* and contract that the post-Glossators and early commercial lawyers were able to confer legal rights on corporate groups. The first great companies were, in institutional terms, individuals bound together via the Roman contract of *societas* and these loose groups were then given greater cohesion through the idea that it was the groups of individuals which controlled the common property (*res*); it was only a matter of time before the groups themselves became endowed with their own (individualistic) personalities and patrimonies.[94]

Yet even today the individualism of the institutional structure is able to assert itself when the occasion demands: a company may not itself be liable for certain acts or omissions of its employees even if these acts or omissions occur in the course of employment.[95] Contract, in other words, continues to exert its individualistic influence even in the world of corporate groups and this individualism is in turn preserved in the form and symmetry of the institutional structure of legal thought. Ever since Roman times lawyers have had a fundamental attachment to formalism and this formalism has generated its own kind of structural symmetry which itself can determine the norms to be applied. Contracts, for example, can only be discharged, or property alienated, by the same means as they are formed or acquired.[96]

(b) Personal and real subrogation

Structural symmetry and formalism are, then, an essential feature of Romanistic legal thought and it is within this formal structuralism that the remedy of subrogation can best be appreciated. Subrogation is an institutional device whereby one institution is substituted for another so as to enable the second institution to take the place of the first. It can involve either the institution of *persona* (personal subrogation) or the institution of the *res* (real subrogation); and so one person can be substituted for ('stand in the shoes of')[97] another person so as to be able to take advantage of the latter's relationship with – or, to use today's language, rights against – either a thing (*in rem*) or another person (*in personam*). Equally, one piece of property can be substituted for

93 Ourliac & de Malafosse, p 238.

94 J Hilaire, *Introduction historique au droit commercial* (PUF, 1986), pp 167–84.

95 See eg *Tesco Supermarkets Ltd v Nattrass* [1972] AC 153; *Seaboard Ltd v Secretary of State for Transport* [1994] 1 WLR 541.

96 D.50.17.153.

97 Lord Denning MR in *Morris v Ford Motor Co* [1973] 1 QB 792, 798.

another in a *patrimonium* or in a situation where the proprietary relationship will remain the same but the object itself is replaced.[98] Whether the actual device of subrogation is of Roman origin is not really of much relevance in itself since it is the Roman institutional structure which acts as the basis of the device: subrogation is simply a matter of allowing a third institution to gain access to an existing bipolar structure between two other institutions and thus subrogation was always implied by the institutional model of Roman law. It was a device waiting to be induced out of the *Corpus Iuris Civilis*.

It may be that the device was imported into English law through the Court of Chancery.[99] Certainly, it seems to be a remedy that at base is equitable since its primary function is to prevent unjustified enrichment[100] and so, according to Lord Diplock, subrogation is 'a convenient way of describing a transfer of rights from one person to another, without assignment or assent of the person from whom the rights are transferred and which takes place by operation of law in a whole variety of circumstances'.[101] It is 'an empirical remedy to prevent a particular kind of unjust enrichment'.[102] But, that said, in the one area where it has its main role there does seem to be little recognition that subrogation is a remedy more than a right. 'A policy of insurance', said Lord Templeman recently, 'is ... a contract of indemnity and by the doctrine of subrogation the insured person must pay back to the insurer' any sum received by way of damages up to the amount paid out by the insurance company so that the 'insured person will then have made neither a loss nor a profit'.[103] Thus, if D negligently damages O's yacht and O receives an indemnity in respect of the yacht from the I insurance company, I will be subrogated to any rights in contract or tort that O has against D.

Now this may seem a situation where subrogation is functioning so as to prevent O from making a profit at the expense of I. Yet the result of allowing I to sue D is that little account is taken of the principle of unjust enrichment *vis-à-vis* I and D. What if the yacht had been damaged by borstal boys who had escaped possibly because of negligence on behalf of prison officers: ought I to be able to sue D if D is a government department?[104] Why should the State carry the burden of such damage when an insurance company has actually been paid to bear the risk? Or what if D is a private commercial organisation itself covered by insurance: should its own insurance company, which might have had to pay out to I, be able to sue the negligent officers for their careless behaviour? Part of the problem is that the device of subrogation has become incorporated into contracts of insurance and thus it seems to have altered its status from restitution remedy to contractual right. However, another aspect of the

98 *Cf Aluminium Industrie Vaassen BV v Romalpa Aluminium Ltd* [1972] 2 All ER 552.

99 D Friedmann & N Cohen, 'Payment of Another's Debt', *IECL*, Vol X, Chap 10, para 19.

100 *Ibid*, para 20.

101 *Orakpo v Manson Investments* [1978] AC 95, 104.

102 *Ibid*.

103 *Lord Napier v Hunter* [1993] AC 713, 728.

104 *Cf Home Office v Dorset Yacht Co* [1970] AC 1004.

problem is the institutional structure itself. If prison officers are careless in the course of their employment, and this causes damage to a third party, that third party can sue the employer of the officers under the principle of vicarious liability which stipulates that an employer is liable for torts committed by an employee acting in the course of his employment (*cf* Ch 12 § 6(a)). What if some of these parties have insurance contracts? The individualism of the institutional model can assert itself in a way that works against the idea of subrogation as an equitable remedy.[105]

(c) Subrogation and personal injury claims

These problems have become particularly acute in the area of personal injury since many defendants in personal injury actions are legal (rather than natural) persons who are under a statutory duty to carry liability insurance. The institutional structure thus throws up a pattern of multiple debtors. The victim of an accident arising out of fault may have a claim in tort against the employer of the person who has carelessly caused the victim's injury and in turn the employer may have a claim in contract or under the Civil Liability (Contribution) Act 1978 against the actual employee who was at fault (*cf* Ch 13 § 6). If the employer is insured it is, of course, the insurance company who can take advantage of the employer's rights with the result that it is the person at fault, rather than the person who has the ability to pay, who must in theory bear the financial cost of the accident.[106] 'In the recourse action', as Tony Weir has pointed out, 'no account is taken of loss-spreading capacity, apportionment is generally on the basis of fault and the decision whom to sue is taken by an institution immune from humane considerations'.[107]

None of this was, or is, inevitable since the courts could have recognised the existence of the insurance company within the institutional model that underpins the law of obligations. They could, for example, have refused to recognise that a contract of employment contains an implied term (*cf* Ch 10 § 6) that the employee will exercise care and skill in the performance of his duties; they could have stipulated, instead, that only gross negligence or recklessness would amount to a breach of contract by the employee. Equally, they could allow an insurance company to use the remedy of subrogation only where there is unjustified enrichment and that where such a company has been paid to carry the risk that materialises it is hardly an unjustified enrichment if they have happily accepted premiums.[108] Yet all these possibilities were lost when a majority of the House of Lords in *Lister v Romford Ice & Cold Storage Co*[109] allowed an insurance company, subrogated to the contractual and contribution rights of an employer, to sue a careless employee for the amount it had paid out to a victim injured

---

105 Weir, *Complex Liabilities*, para 107.

106 D Friedmann & N Cohen, 'Adjustment Among Multiple Debtors', *IECL*, Vol X, Chap 11, paras 18, 20.

107 Weir, *Complex Liabilities*, para 107.

108 *Cf* P Cane, *Tort Law and Economic Interests* (Oxford, 1991), pp 450–51.

109 [1957] AC 555.

as a result of the employee's negligent act. 'As a general proposition', said Viscount Simonds, 'it has not ... been questioned for nearly 200 years that in determining the rights *inter se* of A and B the fact that one or other of them is insured is to be disregarded'.[110]

In Viscount Simonds' analysis the factual situation as viewed through the institutional model is simply one of an action between one contractor (employer) against another contractor (employee). In assessing the loss suffered by the plaintiff contractor, reference had of course to be made to the previous tort claim brought by the victim against the employer; but, strictly speaking, this claim together with the employer's contract with the insurance company is quite outside the relevant facts and law. This approach contrasts strongly with that of the dissenting judges in *Lister*, they emphasised the impossibility of divorcing the insurance contract and the original tort claim from the relevant institutional facts since liability insurance was compulsory under public law and the recourse action dependent upon the action by the injured victim. The relevant model of analysis, in other words, was not a *persona* versus *personam* structure but a more complex pattern consisting of a variety of institutions representing the lorry that did the injury (*res*), employees (*personae*), employer (*persona*), damages action (*actio*), the state (*respublica*), insurance company (*persona*), subrogation (*actio* or *ius*?) and debt claim (*actio*).

Perhaps a more socially realistic approach would have been to say that the level of an obligation is affected not only by the institutional pattern that comes into play – thus the hire of a *res* will always involve a different institutional model from the performance of a skill or the payment of a reward – but by the institutional context in which various transactions find themselves. Is it really realistic to assess motor insurance only in the context of insurer and insured when that insurance is part of a business context embracing employment, commercial and other transactions all of which impact upon each other? Certainly in *Morris v Ford Motor Co*[111] the context was all-important when it came to assessing the rights and remedies of a company which had indemnified an employer and then sought to recover the indemnity via subrogation from the employer's employee whose negligent act, which caused the victim's injury, had set the whole train of legal events in motion. As far as Lord Denning MR was concerned, when an employee made a mistake he was not expected to pay the damages personally because the risk of such injury was attendant on that work and should thus be borne by the employer. The contract of employment is fixed on that basis and thus if 'the servant is to bear the risk his wages ought to be increased to cover it'.[112] Moreover, the actual injury was, according to Lord Denning, probably covered by insurance and as the 'insurance company has received the premiums' they 'should bear the loss'.[113] The key to the liability question was not, therefore, some general principle about how one

110 At pp 576–77.

111 [1973] 1 QB 792.

112 At p 798.

113 At p 801.

isolated contractor should perform his duty *vis-à-vis* another isolated contractor; the relevant contract 'was operative in an industrial setting in which subrogation of the third party to the rights and remedies of the defendants against their employees would be unacceptable and unrealistic'.[114]

(d) Excluding subrogation through the law of remedies

The key to these cases is the exclusion of the right of subrogation either by implying a term into an indemnity contract that there should be no such right[115] or by arguing that there is no unjust enrichment. But what if the contract itself expressly grants the right? In this situation one cannot, evidently, use the implied term and the only answer, in the absence of legislation, is to formulate a rule or principle about unjustified enrichment which actually attaches to the remedy of subrogation itself. In other words subrogation has to become an institution (*actio*) within the model; and an institution which is subject to a *sui generis* obligations principle itself isolated from the contract which grants the remedy. This raises a theoretical question about the interrelation of obligations within the law of obligations. Yet once it is remembered that subrogation is an equitable remedy in English law the separation of subrogation from contract should present few difficulties since it is a fundamental characteristic of an equitable remedy that it is discretionary.[116] Just as a contract cannot stipulate when a court is to grant specific performance or an injunction, so a contract ought not to be able to demand when a contractor is to be entitled as of right to subrogation. Now it may be that insurance companies would not like this. But it is in their longer term interests that the institutional model adapts itself to a liability structure that recognises the existence of insurance companies and insurance contracts: for how else can employers, property owners, car drivers and the like sensibly adjust their own contracts and commercial arrangements if the institutional models, and the rules and principles that such models dictate, are completely out of synchronisation with social and economic reality?[117] Indeed the taking out of insurance could become an obligation itself within the institutional model of the law of obligations[118] and this is surely to the benefit of the insurance industry. Moreover, insurance companies, which have to date escaped from the direct effect of the Unfair Contract Terms Act 1977[119] (*cf* Ch 10 § 4) are benefiting from the statute indirectly in that the reasonableness provision allows commercial parties to use exclusion clauses to place risks. Is this not more stabilising than the destabilising tendencies encouraged by subrogation?

114 James LJ at p 815.

115 See also *Mark Rowlands Ltd v Berni Inns Ltd* [1986] QB 211; *Norwich City Council v Harvey* [1989] 1 WLR 828.

116 See Lord Denning MR in *Morris v Ford Motor Co* [1973] 1 QB 792, 800–01.

117 *Cf* Cane, *op cit*, p 459.

118 See eg *Lamb v Camden LBC* [1981] QB 625.

119 See s 1(2) and Sch 1.

(e) Subrogation and legal reasoning

Perhaps this last point can be developed through a discussion of *Photo Production Ltd v Securicor.*[120] The owners of a factory contracted with a security company for the latter to provide a visiting patrolman to keep a check on the former's premises; unfortunately, the patrolman turned out to be something of an arsonist and he succeeded in burning the factory down. Now from the position of the law of obligations it is clear, if one adopts a *Lister* approach, that the person who should pay for a new factory is the patrolman since he was the one who culpably caused the loss. However, from the position of social reality there would seem to be little point in suing such an asset-less person and thus the alternative was to sue his employer either in tort on the basis of vicarious liability (Ch 12 § 6(a)) or in contract on the basis that the security company was in breach of what it had promised to do. When the factory owner – or in truth its insurance company – did this they were met with defences based on an exclusion clause (*cf* Ch 10 § 4) which stipulated that the security company was not to 'be responsible for any injurious act or default by any employee of the company unless such act or default could have been foreseen and avoided by the exercise of due diligence on the part of the company as his employer' nor was it to be responsible for 'any loss suffered by the customer through ... fire ... except insofar as such loss is solely attributable to the negligence of the company's employees acting within the course of their employment'. The security company claimed, not surprisingly, that the patrolman had not been acting in the course of his employment when he set fire to the building. This was rather an ingenious argument since a contractual obligation is normally seen as a non-delegable duty.[121] Yet in the context of the case in hand it was based on the contractual obligation itself which the defence no doubt thought imported tort vicarious liability rules into contract relationship. In fact the House of Lords refused to accept that the patrolman had been acting outside the course of his employment and specifically rejected this aspect of the defence. However, they were prepared to give general effect to the exclusion clause and the House gave judgment for the defendants.

When one looks at the speeches it becomes quite clear that this is not a decision based upon the institutional structure of one isolated contractor suing another. It is a decision about which insurance company should carry the risk of this fire and the focal point of the decision is, in essence, neither fault nor promise. Thus, Lord Wilberforce refers to the risk assumed by Securicor as being a modest one[122] and Lord Diplock talks of the 'misfortune risk'.[123] Indeed Lord Salmon thought that 'any businessman entering into this contract should have no doubt as to the real meaning of [the exclusion] clause and would have made his insurance arrangements accordingly'.[124] The institutional

---

120 [1980] AC 827.

121 See eg *Riverstone Meat Co Pty Ltd v Lancashire Shipping Co Ltd* [1961] AC 807.

122 [1980] AC at p 846.

123 At p 851.

124 At p 852.

approach underpinning the reasoning in this case is, in other words, very different from the one that underpinned Viscount Simonds' speech in *Lister v Romford Ice*. In *Photo Production* the relevant institutional model used to arrive at a decision consisted, not of a *persona* versus *personam* structure, but a model that encapsulated a factory (*res*) and five *personae* of which two were insurance companies. And the pattern of this model gave rise to a quite different question: instead of asking whose fault or breach of promise caused the harm, the House of Lords asked who should bear the risk of this fire loss. No doubt this risk question reflects a different social and perhaps even moral outlook. Yet the epistemological (theory of knowledge) foundation of such a question is rooted in the actual institutional model itself. The moment that one replaces the image of two isolated contractors, or simple victim and tortfeasor, with an image of a building as the object of two insurance contracts the basis of liability itself has to change. It is simply no longer feasible to assess responsibility in terms of individual behaviour.

(f) Concluding remark: subrogation and other remedies

Subrogation thus becomes a means of expanding the institutional model to embrace people and (or) things beyond the bipolar structure of traditional litigation. Subrogation, however, is not the only equitable remedy to do this: when subrogation fixes upon a *res* in the hands of a third party it exhibits certain similarities with the remedy of tracing (Ch 4 § 5(d); Ch 11 § 4) and thus, on occasions, it may be that the two will be relevant in the same set of facts.[125] Nevertheless, both of these equitable notions are remedies (in a wide if not the narrow sense)[126] rather than causes of action and their purpose is to protect equitable property interests arising out of fiduciary relationships and trusts. They are said to be applicable only according to 'well-settled principles and in defined circumstances' where it would be 'unconscionable for the defendant to deny the proprietary interest claimed by the plaintiff'.[127] But such principles must be treated with a certain caution since equity looks to unconscionable enrichment more than to well-settled rules and thus tends to function institutionally. The strength of remedies such as subrogation and tracing is that they work within the institutional model of persons, things and actions so as to effect assignments of property or personal relations in situations where the common law is immobile. In *Beswick v Beswick* the House of Lords seemed to suggest that specific performance could perform such an institutional role as well. The law of equitable remedies thus tells the jurist much about the structure of litigation and about the manipulation of institutions within an environment that might be described as a classic form of methodological individualism.

125 *Boscawen v Bajwa* [1995] 4 All ER 769.

126 Cf Millett LJ in *Boscawen v Bajwa* [1995] 4 All ER 769, 776.

127 Millett LJ in *Boscawen v Bajwa* [1995] 4 All ER at p 777.

CHAPTER SIX

REMEDIES (3): DAMAGES

Damages are said to be 'the remedy of most general application at the present day, and they remain the prime remedy in actions for breach of contract and tort'.[1] Even if this observation does underestimate the importance of debt claims in contract,[2] damages merit particular attention since they are the remedy designed to compensate for damage, injury and loss. Unlike debt, whose formal nature tends to eclipse questions of damage and causation, damages must be quantified by the court and the question of quantum not only can be complex but can raise fundamental substantive issues about damage and obligations themselves.

1 DAMAGE AND DAMAGES

The rules and principles of the law of damages are evidently closely interrelated with the whole question of what amounts to damage. Yet it is important to stress at the outset that damages and damage remain different notions: damages are, on the whole, the monetary compensation that a court awards to compensate a plaintiff for damage suffered; damage, however, is often both a constituent of liability and a generic term for a variety of interests invaded. To refuse an action in the law of obligations on the basis of no damage is no doubt often to say that there is, in the eyes of the law, nothing to compensate.[3] Yet to award damages of a certain amount is not necessarily to hold that this amount equals the actual damage suffered by the plaintiff. There may well be a gap between damage and damages which has the effect either of leaving certain kinds of harm – certain 'interests' (*cf* Ch 4 § 3) – uncompensated for reasons of, for example, legal policy[4] or of 'overcompensating' a plaintiff through an award of a sum which appears to bear little or no relation to the actual harm suffered.[5]

In fact the gap between damage and damages results not just from a dichotomy between compensatory and non-compensatory damages. It also results from the distinction between compensation and restitution.[6] Some damages actions are designed to act as restitutionary claims more than compensation actions and thus they are not necessarily related in a direct sense to the plaintiff's loss. For example, the torts designed to protect property rights may end up by giving the plaintiff more than his apparent loss since these torts also have a restitutionary role in that they are designed both to

1 Lord Hailsham in *Cassell & Co v Broome* [1972] AC 1027, 1070.

2 Over 90% of contractual claims are in debt: T Weir, '*Droit des contrats*', in JA Jolowicz (ed), *Droit anglais* (Dalloz, 2nd edn, 1992), no 193.

3 See eg *Lazenby Garages Ltd v Wright* [1976] 1 WLR 459.

4 See eg *Spartan Steel & Alloys Ltd v Martin & Co (Contractors) Ltd* [1973] QB 27.

5 *Cf Sutcliffe v Pressdram Ltd* [1991] 1 QB 153.

6 *Cf Friends' Provident Life Office v Hillier Parker May & Rowden* [1995] 4 All ER 260.

compensate and to stop a defendant from profiting from his invasion of another's property.[7] No doubt it is possible to turn many restitutionary claims into compensation actions by reinterpreting the notion of 'loss' to include an 'expectation' interest (*cf* § 4(b) below),[8] but on the whole the distinction between compensation and restitution remains an important frontier in the law of remedies. Leaving aside the property torts and exemplary damages (§ 5 below), unless the plaintiff can point to damage it will be difficult to succeed in a compensation claim.[9] Restitution actions, in other words, usually have to be founded in debt or account (Ch 11) which are remedies designed to extract benefits, although, as we shall see, the restitution interest is an interest that is protected by contractual and property damages.

The relationship between damage and damages is particularly intense when it comes to the problem of limiting the defendant's liability. Many litigation problems that arise in the law of damages focus on the quantum and on the extent of damage to be compensated and while this problem can often be conceptualised through the notion of protected 'interests' (see below § 3), the courts traditionally approach the question in terms of cause and consequence. Starting out from the idea that the 'law cannot take account of everything that follows from a wrongful act', the courts divide up harm into a series of consequences and, having done this, it then becomes possible to assign some of these consequences to independent causes.[10] Is this particular item of harm caused by the defendant's breach of contract or tortious wrong? Sometimes the notion of causation is directly used, but on a broader level the topic itself has been broken down into a series of devices and techniques each attracting, seemingly, its own rules and principles (see Ch 7). Thus, there are separate principles concerning factual causation (question of fact), remoteness of damage (question of law), contributory negligence, mitigation of damage, illegal behaviour and so on.[11] And all of these different devices and principles usually warrant separate chapters or sections in the textbooks. In total, however, they are all concerned with the single question of connecting the damage in question with the breach of the obligation.

2 COMPENSATION ACTIONS

Damages claims thus have two aspects: they have a substantive aspect which is to be found in the law of obligations and a remedial aspect which is to be found in the law of remedies. In addition, such claims have to be distinguished from other types of action such as a claim for debt or an injunction (*cf* Chs 4–5). These distinctions, in turn, can be reflected, as we have just seen, in the dichotomy between compensation and restitution claims (*cf* Ch 11).

---

7 *Strand Electric and Engineering Co Ltd v Brisford Entertainments Ltd* [1952] 2 QB 246.

8 *Cf Friends' Provident Life Office v Hillier Parker May & Rowden* [1995] 4 All ER 260.

9 *Stoke-on-Trent CC v W & J Wass Ltd* [1988] 1 WLR 1406; *Surrey CC v Bredero Homes Ltd* [1993] 1 WLR 1361.

10 *The Liesbosch* [1933] AC 449.

11 *Cf The Borag* [1981] 1 WLR 274.

(a) Compensation and restitution

A restitution claim, although capable of being related to a loss suffered by another, is concerned primarily with a benefit in the defendant's patrimony, whereas a compensation claim 'relates to damage and engenders special problems in the case of damage which is not commensurate to any equivalent, such as non-pecuniary harm'.[12] Often, of course, it is unrealistic to separate liability from remedy in that notions such as remoteness of damage can function at both levels – indeed this is one important reason why any work on the English law of obligations needs to include the law of remedies within its scope. Yet an ability to separate the remedy from issues of liability can on occasions be important since, for example, compensation and restitution respond to differing normative and policy ideas.

Take once again the decision of *Lister v Romford Ice & Cold Storage Co* (Ch 5 § 5(c)). The strict logic exercised by the fault principle could have been avoided if the legal analysis had distinguished between the compensation and the recourse action.[13] The first was a claim in damages for the injury suffered by the victim and this was rightly governed by principles from the law of tort; the second claim, made by the insurance company against the employee, was in effect one of debt and subrogation and this ought to have been governed by principles of unjust enrichment. In one sense, of course, it was. But the unjust enrichment was in turn governed by the fault principle in that it was thought to be unjust that one person should pay for the wrongful act committed by another.[14] If, in contrast, the unjust enrichment had been viewed from the position of an insurance company as a direct party, rather than from the position of the employer, then the enrichment picture would have changed: it soon would have become evident that one was shifting a risk from the party that had contracted to bear it onto the shoulders of the person who in factual (if not legal) truth had not. No doubt simply to distinguish between damages and debt and between tort and unjust enrichment will not of itself avoid the kind of policy contradictions to be found in *Lister*, for the debt claims for contribution between wrongdoers continue to be governed by the fault principle.[15] But if it is appreciated that the remedy has an active role in determining liability, and that different remedies are capable of bringing into play different principles, it becomes easier to analyse multi-party problems within a number of different institutional models (*cf* Chs 3, 14). It might seem just in one model to make the person at fault pay, but in another model – one, for example, where the insurance company is treated for what it is rather than as an individual person with the same status as a human worker – a different pattern of justice could well emerge. In other words, the law of persons, the law of obligations and the law of actions can combine and recombine in a variety of different patterns, each pattern disclosing a different picture of justice.

---

12 H Stoll, 'Consequences of Liability: Remedies', *IECL*, Vol XI, Chap 8, para 9.

13 But *cf Friends' Provident Life Office v Hillier Parker May & Rowden* [1995] 4 All ER 260.

14 Weir, *Complex Liabilities*, paras 77, 106.

15 Civil Liability (Contribution) Act 1978 ss 1, 6(1); *Friends' Provident Life Office v Hillier Parker May & Rowden* [1995] 4 All ER 260.

In fact if one poses the question whether the insurance company as plaintiff in *Lister* had suffered 'damage' the answer can appear ambiguous.[16] Certainly, they had suffered a financial 'loss' in the sense that they had been legally obliged to make a payment to a victim whose injuries had been caused by the negligent act of a fellow employee. Yet not only is such a loss ambiguous in the sense that the maturing of such a risk could well be seen as simply an expense for which they had received premiums, but the idea of loss itself is something that is not always seen as a form of damage (*cf* Ch 13 § 9). English law traditionally distinguishes between 'damage', 'injury' and 'loss'[17] and the law of tort has long taken the view that, with regard to certain causes of action (in particular negligence), pure financial loss is an imperfectly protected interest.[18] It would have been quite proper, therefore, to hold that the insurance company ought not have been able to use subrogation, an equitable remedy in substance, on the basis that it was being used to subvert the policy of the law of tort.

(b) Loss transfer

The real problem behind complex liability cases such as *Lister* is that of transferring losses. The law of tort envisages a transfer from the victim suffering damage either to the wrongdoer who has caused the damage or, more often, to the employer of the wrongdoer (vicarious liability) (Ch 12 § 6). The law of contract may, in turn, transfer this loss from wrongdoer or employer to insurance company; and the law of restitution re-transfers this loss, via subrogation, back to wrongdoer (*cf* Ch 13 § 6). The assumption all the time is that the law of obligations functions only at the level of two individuals (Ch 5 § 5(a)). This individualism is inherent in the Gaian institutional model, as we have seen, and probably cannot be purged from the system without threatening the whole model of private law itself. Nevertheless, it is this individualism that lies at the heart of many legal problems, particularly when the law of persons dictates that a corporate legal person has the same status as an individual human.

D carelessly injures V, but V's employer, his own insurance company and a disaster appeal fund, all pay V a sum of money that more than makes up for V's harm in terms of existing legal rules of compensation. Has V suffered damage? At a social level it is possible to say that V's needs have been met, but at an individual level there are still losses that could become the object of litigation.[19] Assuming that V's injuries are attributable to a tortfeasor, why should the latter be allowed to take advantage of the kindness of others? 'It would', according to Lord Reid, 'be revolting to the ordinary man's sense of justice, and therefore contrary to public policy, that the sufferer should have his damages reduced so that he would gain nothing from the benevolence of his friends or relations or of the public at large, and that the only gainer would be the

16 See *Friends' Provident Life Office v Hillier Parker May & Rowden* [1995] 4 All ER 260.

17 See *Everard v Kendall* (1870) LR 5 CP 428; *Smith v Brown* (1871) LR 6 QB 729; *Seale v Laverick* (1874) LR 9 QB 122, 131. And see more recently *Merlin v British Nuclear Fuels Plc* [1990] 2 QB 557.

18 See eg *Spartan Steel & Alloys Ltd v Martin & Co (Contractors) Ltd* [1973] QB 27.

19 See eg *Hussain v New Taplow Paper Mills* [1988] AC 514.

wrongdoer'.[20] If, however, the amount paid by the employer to V was to qualify as sick pay the justice position would, it seems, change. 'It positively offends my sense of justice', said Lord Bridge, 'that a plaintiff, who has certainly paid no insurance premiums as such, should receive full wages during a period of incapacity to work from two different sources, his employer and the tortfeasor'.[21] If the employer is a separate party from the tortfeasor, is it just that the latter should benefit at the expense of the former? If one imagines that both employer and tortfeasor are individual human beings, then clearly the fault principle dictates that it is the tortfeasor who should ultimately bear the loss. Yet once one views the employer as a large organisation capable of taking out group insurance as a running expense, it has to be said that the justice picture changes. One is no longer comparing like with like whatever the law of persons might dictate (a point now recognised by the law of contract) (Ch 8 § 5). Or what if the State has provided benefits: should the State be able to claim these benefits from V or from the tortfeasor?[22] Again if one sees the State as a person with the same interests, rights and duties as each individual citizen, it is possible to construct a system whereby losses are transferred from, say, the NHS onto the tortfeasor's insurance company. But ought the State (or whatever relevant public body) to be viewed in this way? Could it not be said that the State or various public bodies represent the community? And what are the responsibilities of the community towards those injured even by the (statistically foreseeable) fault of others (*cf* Ch 13 § 3)?

(c) The law of obligations and the law of damages

Many of these types of question raise issues of substantive law and thus will be founded in the legal relations flowing between all of the parties involved.[23] But some issues belong only to the law of damages. In the abstract example above, if it comes to assessing damages in court the question whether insurance money and gifts are to be taken into account is a question that goes to the remedy (law of damages) rather than to liability;[24] whether or not one party can claim contribution or an indemnity from another person goes to the question of liability.[25] The point to be stressed at this stage is that compensation claims involve two different focal points. First, there is the focal point of the damage itself: what actual harm has V suffered as a result of D's wrong? This question raises an issue about the nature of damage and, as such, is likely to be a problem involving the actual obligation (duty) of the tortfeasor towards the person claiming compensation.[26] Secondly, there is the focal point of the boundary of the harm. Liability for some damage having been admitted, should the tortfeasor be liable

20 *Parry v Cleaver* [1970] AC 1, 14.

21 *Hussain v New Taplow Paper Mills* [1988] AC 514, 532.

22 Administration of Justice Act 1982 s 5; Social Security Administration Act 1992 s 82.

23 On which see eg *London Drugs v Kuehne & Nagel International* (1993) 97 DLR 4th 261.

24 Insurance money and gifts are not taken into account: *Hussain v New Taplow Paper Mills* [1988] AC 514.

25 See eg *Receiver for Metropolitan Police District v Croydon Corporation* [1957] 2 QB 154.

26 See eg *Best v Samuel Fox & Co Ltd* [1952] AC 716.

for the extra damage (for example, mental distress) of the victim?[27] This is not to say, of course, that there are no cases which, at one and the same time, involve both focal points. However, if a court decides to award only nominal damages it is, in theory, making the point that in terms of legal relations the plaintiff might well have a legal right *vis-à-vis* the defendant.[28]

(d) Envisaging the damage

Compensation actions do, then, involve rules and principles. But, and this is where the notion of damage becomes important, they go beyond the language of propositions to embrace sets of structural relations between parties and the 'things' that they claim of value. With regard to the latter, much will depend, in hard cases, on whether or not they are capable of being 'seen'. Accordingly, when the plaintiff in *Lazenby Garages v Wright*[29] asked the court to award damages it was also inviting the judges to envisage the world in a particular way. The defendant had contracted to buy a second-hand BMW car, but later returned the vehicle saying that he no longer wished to continue with the transaction. The plaintiff sellers subsequently sold the BMW for more than they had contracted to sell it to the defendant, yet they still claimed that the defendant's breach of contract caused them a loss of profit since it resulted in one less sale. Lord Denning MR, supported by the other members of the Court of Appeal, refused to see the facts in this way; for him, each second-hand car was a unique item and in selling this particular item for more than the original contract price they had profited rather than lost as a result of the defendant's breach of contract. Had he seen all the second-hand cars as a class, no doubt he would have accepted the plaintiff's argument that he had lost a profit on a sale. However, in seeing the world in terms of individual vehicles, each with its own character, he was able to conclude that 'they clearly suffered no damage at all'.

3 DAMAGES AND INTERESTS

The key mediating concept between damage and damages is, as we have seen (Ch 3 § 3(c); Ch 4 §§ 2–3), the notion of an interest. This idea of reducing damage to interests goes back to Roman law where the jurists first distinguished between two types of losses: there was, in addition to physical damage to person or property, the loss consequent upon this damage (*damnum emergens*) which, in the case of say injury to a slave, would include medical expenses incurred and loss of value of the slave. A separate loss or interest was the failure to make a gain (*lucrum cessans*) resulting from the defendant's wrong.[30] The *Code civil* has retained this distinction: 'The damages payable

27 See eg *Attia v British Gas Plc* [1988] QB 304.

28 See eg *The Albazero* [1977] AC 774.

29 [1976] 1 WLR 459.

30 Lawson, *Negligence*, 59–63.

to the creditor are, in general, the loss that he has suffered and the gain of which he has been deprived ...'.[31]

(a) Consequential damages (*damnum emergens*)

English law has not formally adopted the distinction between consequential loss and failure to gain – as we shall see, it prefers to think in terms of protected interests. But the distinction can certainly be found in substance within the case law. Perhaps the best example is provided by the decision of *Spartan Steel & Alloys v Martin & Co*.[32] The defendants were digging up the road when they carelessly damaged a cable which supplied electricity to the plaintiffs' factory and as a result power to the factory was cut off for 14 hours. During this period the plaintiffs' furnaces were unable to function and they subsequently brought an action claiming damages under three heads. They claimed: (i) for physical damage to metal which was in the furnace at the time of the power cut; (ii) for the loss of profit on the metal so ruined; and (iii) for the loss of profit on four other 'melts' they could have carried out if the factory had not been shut down for 14 hours. A majority of the Court of Appeal held that the plaintiffs were entitled to damages only under (i) and (ii); the third head was economic loss independent of the actual physical damage suffered as a result of the negligent act. According to Lord Denning MR such economic loss was, as a matter of policy, not recoverable either because there was no duty of care in respect of head (iii) or because the loss was too remote.

Spartan, of course, was an action in tort. What if the defendants had been working under contract with the plaintiffs and had carelessly cut the cable while digging on the plaintiffs' land? In *Victoria Laundry (Windsor) Ltd v Newman Industries Ltd*[33] the plaintiffs, keen to expand their laundry and dyeing business, contracted to purchase a larger capacity boiler from the defendants. Delivery of the boiler was delayed owing to a breach of contract by the defendants and the plaintiffs brought an action for damages claiming compensation: (i) for loss of profits in respect of new customers they could have accommodated if the new boiler had arrived on time; and (ii) for loss of profit of £262 per week in respect of certain lucrative dyeing contracts with the government. The Court of Appeal held that although the defendants did not have knowledge of the specific contracts under head (ii), the plaintiffs were not 'precluded from recovering some general (and perhaps conjectural) sum for the loss of business in respect of dyeing contracts to be reasonably expected, any more than in respect of laundering contracts to be reasonably expected'.[34] If this reasoning is applied to *Spartan* it would seem that the pure economic loss rule would not come into play as such since contract is about profits and expectations; in other words, the typical damage arising in a breach of

31 Art 1149. See generally Treitel, *Remedies*, paras 84, 89.

32 [1973] QB 27.

33 [1949] 2 KB 528.

34 Asquith LJ delivering the judgment of the court at p 543.

contract case is economic loss. Nevertheless in *Hadley v Baxendale*,[35] where delivery of a mill shaft was delayed in breach of contract, the plaintiffs, owners of a flour mill, claimed damages both for the value of the mill shaft and the loss of profits arising from the delay; the Court of Exchequer held that the loss of profits were not recoverable since they did not flow naturally from the breach. In order to recover such profits the defendant would need to have had knowledge of the special circumstances arising from the delay. If this reasoning is applied to *Spartan* it is possible that the consequential damages would stop with the *res* itself (metal in the machines) unless it could be proved that the defendants had special knowledge of the circumstances, which of course they might well have been deemed to have.

Clearly the civilian distinction between *damnum emergens* and *lucrum cessans* can be used to analyse the result of these cases. Nevertheless, the actual analytical notion used is not so much that of the protected interest *per se*, but one that is relational in the sense that it focuses on causation.[36] The loss of profits might be deemed too remote from the negligent act and thus, as a question of law, seen as not being caused by the breach of obligation (Ch 7 § 4). This approach is evident in cases involving damage other than economic loss. In *Attia v British Gas Plc*[37] the defendant contractors negligently started a fire while working in the plaintiff's house and the plaintiff, when returning home, suffered nervous shock on seeing smoke pouring out of her house and watching the building burn for several hours. Was this nervous shock consequential damage flowing from the negligent act? The Court of Appeal rejected the idea that as a matter of legal analysis the defendants could not be liable for this kind of damage since it was obvious that the contractors owed the plaintiff a duty of care. The real question was whether the damage was too remote and, as far as the appeal judges were concerned, there was no reason in principle why damages for nervous shock should not be recovered on the facts of the case. In other words, nervous shock is a protected interest, even if subject to more stringent rules than other types of personal injury.

(b) Personal injury

Personal injury does in itself raise difficulties when it comes to the assessment of damages and the nature of these difficulties is threefold. First, there is the problem of assessability: how does one compensate in money very serious personal injury? One possible response to this question is to leave the assessment to a jury, but this just results in a second problem, that of randomness and unpredictability. As Lord Diplock once pointed out,[38] if all claims for personal injury damages were to reach the courts the civil justice system would break down; what prevents this breakdown are settlements. But if such settlements are to be encouraged there must exist some reasonable degree of predictability about the sums likely to be paid in respect of particular injuries and in

35 (1854) 156 ER 145.

36 *Cf* Treitel, *Remedies*, para 136.

37 [1988] QB 304.

38 *Wright v British Railways Board* [1983] 2 AC 773, 776–77.

order to achieve such predictability the courts have adopted a tariff system. This means that the empirical basis for the assessment of damages for the actual physical injury to a person – the non-pecuniary loss as it is called[39] – is not so much the injury itself as the scale set by the judges and, in particular, by the Court of Appeal.[40] Secondly, pecuniary losses up to the date of the trial are, evidently, easier to assess; but with regard to future economic losses the situation is rendered particularly difficult by the general rule that any judgment for damages must be for one lump sum. There is, as Lord Scarman observed, only one certainty in all of this and that is that 'the future will prove the award to be either too high or too low'.[41]

The third difficulty with regard to the personal injury interest is the nature of personal injury itself. Certainly broken bones and lesions are easily identifiable. But what about mental injury? Now from an interest point of view, the main subdivision within the category of personal injury is between economic and non-economic losses. With regard to this latter interest, the courts are concerned with pain, suffering and loss of amenities of life and one objective here is to compensate for mental anguish.[42] But what if the injured person is rendered permanently unconscious by the accident? Two separate issues are raised here. First, there is the mental anguish, or perhaps lack of it, with respect to the injured person him or herself; the issue here is whether an unconscious victim should receive damages for this non-pecuniary harm or whether he or she should be treated as if they were dead. A majority of the House of Lords has rejected the death analogy and held that damages should be awarded even if the victim is unaware of the loss.[43] However, they have held recently that it is not necessarily in the best interests of such a victim that he be kept alive by artificial means.[44] Secondly, there is the family (*cf* Ch 2 § 7). Should the mental anguish of members of the victim's family be compensated in some way? As far as civil liability is concerned such dependants are owed no duty of care at common law[45] – under statute they have a claim for their economic losses only if the victim is killed[46] – but their interest may be recognised, to some extent, in the award of damages made to the victim.[47] Of course, those dependants who actually witness the accident or its immediate aftermath may have an independent claim for their own nervous shock damage,[48] but this form of damage is quite independent from the mental anguish at seeing loved ones reduced to helpless victims. The interest problem is institutional in that the interests of the family members of the victim are only imperfectly protected as far as the law of obligations is

39 Royal Commission on Civil Liability and Compensation for Personal Injury (Cmnd 7054-I, 1978), paras 359–98 (Pearson Report); Law Commission Consultation Paper No 140 (1995).

40 *Wright v British Railways Board* [1983] 2 AC 773, 784–85.

41 *Lim Poh Choo v Camden Area Health Authority* [1980] AC 174, 183.

42 *West v Shepherd* [1964] AC 326, 349.

43 *West v Shepherd* [1964] AC 326.

44 *Airedale NHS Trust v Bland* [1993] AC 789.

45 *Best v Samuel Fox & Co Ltd* [1952] AC 716.

46 Fatal Accidents Act 1976.

47 *Pickett v British Rail Engineering* [1980] AC 136.

48 *McLoughlin v O'Brien* [1983] AC 410.

concerned. Lord Reid has suggested that more might be done for them[49] and the law of actions may help on occasions.

(c) Mental distress

One example of where the law of actions has helped a member of the family is *Jackson v Horizon Holidays* (Ch 4 § 3). Moreover, this case involved an interest – mental distress – that in itself was, and indeed remains, only imperfectly protected. The general rule, at first sight, seems clear enough: the law of tort, as we have mentioned, recognises the mental anguish consequent upon personal injury as a head of damages (non-pecuniary loss) and it also accepts nervous shock as a form of damage for which damages in certain circumstances may be available.[50] However, when it comes to lesser forms of mental damage much will depend upon the cause of action in play since, as far as the tort of negligence is concerned, this type of distress is not recognised as giving rise to a duty of care.[51] Clearly, the large damages awarded in defamation cases are designed to remedy mental rather than physical damage[52] and no doubt the same could be said for the amounts awarded in false imprisonment and malicious prosecution actions.[53] In addition statute specifically recognises bereavement as a form of damage suffered by those very close to the dead victim (parents, spouses and children), although the amount awarded is a fixed sum thus making the claim look more like one in debt rather damages.[54] It is also possible to see exemplary damages (below § 5) as protecting the mental distress interest in practice; but in law it has of course to be emphasised that such damages are specifically non-compensatory and thus will bear no formal relationship with any protected interest as such. Damages in nuisance can also compensate for mental distress caused by noise and smell,[55] yet the actual interest protected is a proprietary rather than a personal interest, although one recent case involving harassment by telephone suggests a shift of emphasis.[56]

In contract the general rule again seems clear: 'A contract-breaker is not in general liable for any distress, frustration, anxiety, displeasure, vexation, tension or aggravation which his breach of contract may cause to the innocent party'. However, as Bingham LJ (as he then was) went on to point out, 'the rule is not absolute'. And so where 'the very object of a contract is to provide pleasure, relaxation, peace of mind or freedom from molestation, damages will be awarded if the fruit of the contract is not provided or if the contrary result is procured instead.'[57] Thus, damages for mental distress can be

49 *West v Shepherd* [1964] AC 326, 342.

50 See generally *Alcock v Chief Constable of South Yorkshire* [1992] 1 AC 310.

51 See *Best v Samuel Fox & Co Ltd* [1952] AC 716.

52 Law Commission Consultation Paper No 140 (1995) paras 4.88–4.89.

53 Weir, *Casebook*, p 381. See also *The Guardian* 27 April 1996, p 1 (£302,000).

54 Fatal Accidents Act 1976 s 1A.

55 *Bone v Seale* [1975] 1 All ER 787.

56 *Khorasandijian v Bush* [1993] QB 727.

57 *Watts v Morrow* [1991] 1 WLR 1421, 1445.

awarded in cases where package holidays do not live up to promises made in the brochure[58] and mental distress damages have been awarded against a firm of solicitors which failed through incompetence to obtain an injunction to stop the plaintiff being molested by an off-duty policeman.[59] The position, however, is not quite so simple as it seems since damages can be awarded in contract for inconvenience and discomfort and the mental suffering directly related to such damage. How is such harm to be measured as against a defendant who has not done what he has promised to do? Is it to be measured in terms of the mental interest or the expectation interest (*cf* below §§ 4–5) protected by contract?

This point arose in *Ruxley Electronics Ltd v Forsyth*[60] where the plaintiff had contracted with the defendants to have a swimming pool built in his garden. The contract specified that the pool was to have a maximum depth of 7ft 6in, but when constructed the plaintiff discovered that the deepest point was only 6ft 9in. The trial judge found as a fact that the pool was perfectly safe to dive into and that there was no decrease in the actual value of the pool: ought, then, the plaintiff to be able to recover the full cost of demolishing the pool and having one built that conformed to the contract (£21,560) or must he be satisfied with damages for loss of pleasure and amenity (£2,500)? The trial judge awarded £2,500; a majority of the Court of Appeal replaced this award with the full £21,560, holding that this was the 'only way in which his interest [could] be served';[61] and the House of Lords restored the amount awarded by the trial judge on the basis that the contractual objective had been substantially achieved and that it would be unreasonable to award the cost of reinstatement on these particular facts. According to Lord Lloyd, the analogy to be applied was the package holiday contract: the plaintiff's damage in *Ruxley* was not damage that attached to the swimming pool as such – he had received a perfectly good pool – but damage that was a form of mental distress. He had lost the pleasure of having a 7ft 6in swimming pool and he should be compensated only for that damage.

(d) Proprietary interests

This question of reinstatement is a more general problem in the law of damages. Take several examples. D carelessly burns down P's factory: can P claim the cost of rebuilding his factory or can he claim only the difference of value in respect of the land and building before and after the fire? According to the Court of Appeal the appropriate measure will depend upon a number of factors.[62] If P has an on-going business the reinstatement interest might be appropriate, but if P is a property investment company then things may be different. D negligently writes off P's much loved car: can P claim the cost of rebuilding the car or can he claim only the market

58 *Jarvis v Swans Tours Ltd* [1973] 1 QB 233.

59 *Heywood v Wellers* [1976] QB 446.

60 [1995] 3 WLR 118.

61 [1994] 1 WLR 650, 660 *per* Mann LJ.

62 *Dodd Properties (Kent) Ltd v Canterbury CC* [1980] 1 All ER 928, 938.

value? According to the Court of Appeal the car owner must behave like a reasonable businessman and such a person would not, it seems, incur the cost of rebuilding the vehicle.[63] D carelessly causes the destruction of P's second-hand industrial carpet grip purchased for £12,000: if no second-hand grip is available, can P claim the cost of a new grip at £62,000? It would seem that P can claim the £62,000.[64] The situation becomes even more complex if the thing damaged or destroyed is a profit earning chattel in that the plaintiff will want to claim, as has been seen with the *Spartan Steel* case, not only the value of the thing destroyed but also the consequential damages and perhaps even the failure to gain (*cf* below § 4(b)). Accordingly, in *The Liesbosch*[65] the owners of a dredger bought for £4,000, and negligently sunk by the defendants, put in a claim for £23,500 (they were awarded around £11,000), while in *The Mediana*[66] the owners of a lightship, sunk by the defendants, successfully put in a claim for the hire of a replacement lightship even though they themselves had such a replacement in reserve. Equally, the owners of a Rolls-Royce wrongfully detained by the defendants managed to obtain twice the value of the vehicle as a result of a claim for consequential damages.[67]

When it comes to property damage the general rule is always the same: the basic principle governing the measure of damages where the defendant's tort or breach of contract has caused physical damage to the plaintiff's real or personal property is *restitutio in integrum*. But in practice things are much more complex, both because certain items of property are difficult to value, and because the loss of a thing involves interests over and above the physical value of the thing itself. In commercial law the relationship between the value of tangible (chattels, land and buildings) and intangible (contracts) property makes the assessment of 'damage' often a matter of limiting liability through the rules of causation and remoteness. Yet as the *Ruxley* case shows, much also depends on how one interprets the interests in play.

(e) Mental and proprietary interests

Real property can entail mental interests as well. In *Attia v British Gas*, as we have seen, the plaintiff was entitled in principle to claim for nervous shock in addition to the damage to her building and chattels and in *Miller v Jackson* (Ch 4 § 1(b)) the problem was not so much the physical damage caused by the cricket balls as the interference with the use and enjoyment of property. The danger of cricket balls prevented the owners of the house from using their garden on days when a match was in progress and this can be seen as an invasion of their right of ownership. Similar types of damage are suffered by those who have to endure, as a result of a neighbour's activities, unpleasant

63 *Darbishire v Warran* [1963] 1 WLR 1067.

64 *Dominion Mosaics & Tile Ltd v Trafalgar Trucking Co Ltd* [1990] 2 All ER 246.

65 [1933] AC 449.

66 [1900] AC 113.

67 *Hillesden Securities Ltd v Ryjack Ltd* [1983] 1 WLR 959.

smells,[68] irritating noise[69] or even offensive activities.[70] Many of these cases involve interlocutory injunctions rather than damages (Ch 5 § 4(b)) and thus it is difficult to assess the mental interests in terms of money. However, in *Bone v Seale*[71] Scarman LJ seemed prepared to go some way in drawing an analogy between non-pecuniary personal injury litigation and mental distress attaching to property interests. This gives rise to a question about the extent to which the mental element can be detached from the property interest.

Take the following example. P goes to live with her parents and while there receives unwanted and abusive telephone calls from her ex-boyfriend D: can P sue D for damages in respect of the mental distress caused by the harassment? Now there is little doubt that if P had a property interest in the house where the calls were being received she would have an action in private nuisance, if they were coming from private land, or perhaps public nuisance if coming from a public call box. But if P has no property interest, can she still claim damages? It may be that P will now have a claim in nuisance, not so much on the basis that her property interest is being invaded, but simply because 'it is ridiculous if in this present age the law is that the making of deliberately harassing and pestering telephone calls to a person is only actionable in the civil courts if the recipient of the calls happens to have the freehold or a leasehold proprietary interest in the premises in which he or she has received the calls'.[72] The key to this legal development is, perhaps, not the application of a principle or a change in the rules of private nuisance. It is a matter of the court pushing outward from what was once a proprietary interest towards an independent mental interest and this is one reason why the whole notion of an interest within the law of damages can play such a creative role in the law of obligations (*cf* Ch 4 § 3).

4 ECONOMIC INTERESTS

All interests are in theory capable of being reduced to economic interests of one kind or another and even mental injury has its price.[73] The law of tort (*cf* Ch 8 § 3(d)), then, might be said to be protecting three major interests reflected in the distinctions between injury, damage and loss; and in turn these major interests can be sub-divided into the 'good things in life, such as liberty, bodily integrity, land, possessions, reputation, wealth, privacy, dignity, perhaps even life itself'.[74] It might not of course protect these interests equally, but at a very general level tort might be said to be concerned with a plaintiff's restoration interest. Damages in tort attempt to restore the balance after a wrongful invasion of a protected interest.

68 See eg *Halsey v Esso Petroleum* [1961] 2 All ER 145.

69 See eg *Kennaway v Thompson* [1981] QB 88.

70 See eg *Thompson-Schwab v Costaki* [1956] 1 All ER 652.

71 [1975] 1 All ER 787.

72 Dillon LJ in *Khorasandijian v Bush* [1993] QB at p 734.

73 P Cane, *Tort Law and Economic Interests* (Oxford, 1991), p 8.

74 Weir, *Casebook*, p 4.

(a) Damages in contract

When one turns to the law of contract, however, the role of damages might be said to be different in that contract's main function is to secure a result rather than to protect an existing interest as such. Yet even this result can be reduced to an interest as Steyn LJ, adopting a celebrated American analysis,[75] has shown:

> An award of compensation for breach of contract serves to protect three separate interests. The starting principle is that the aggrieved party ought to be compensated for loss of his positive or expectation interests. In other words, the object is to put the aggrieved party in the same financial position as if the contract had been fully performed. But the law also protects the negative interest of the aggrieved party. If the aggrieved party is unable to establish the value of a loss of bargain he may seek compensation in respect of his reliance losses. The object of such an award is to compensate the aggrieved party for expenses incurred and losses suffered in reliance on the contract. These two complementary principles share one feature. Both are pure compensatory principles ... [76]

And Steyn LJ continued:

> There is, however, a third principle which protects the aggrieved party's restitutionary interest. The object of such an award is not to compensate the plaintiff for a loss, but to deprive the defendant of the benefit he gained by the breach of contract. The classic illustration is a claim for the return of goods sold and delivered where the buyer has repudiated his obligation to pay the price. It is not traditional to describe a claim for restitution following a breach of contract as damages. What matters is that a coherent law of obligations must inevitably extend its protection to cover certain restitutionary interests ... [77]

One reason why such a claim in restitution is not seen as a claim in damages is that it is usually a claim in debt (Ch 4 § 5). One can then pose the question: what interests does a debt claim protect?

(b) Expectation interest (*lucrum cessans*)

In *White & Carter (Councils) Ltd v McGregor*,[78] as we have seen (Ch 4 § 5(b)), the plaintiff succeeded in obtaining full performance of the contract by framing his action in debt rather than damages. In other words, the plaintiff obtained a specific sum of money seemingly unrelated to any damage suffered. However, one way of turning this claim into a form of 'damage' is to say that the plaintiff was obtaining compensation for his failure to gain an expectation (*lucrum cessans*): that is to say, he was obtaining from the court a remedy protecting his expectation interest.[79] In tort, as the *Spartan Steel* case

75 L Fuller & W Purdue, 'The Reliance Interest in Contract Damages' (1936) 46 *Yale LJ* 52.

76 *Surrey CC v Bredero Homes Ltd* [1993] 1 WLR 1361, 1369.

77 *Ibid.*

78 [1962] AC 413.

79 *Cf* Treitel, *Remedies* paras 82, 84.

illustrated, the courts are reluctant to award compensation for a lost expectation, except perhaps in those situations where tort is in effect playing a contractual role and thus protecting a contractual interest;[80] for the role of tort is, as we have mentioned, to protect the restoration interest which encourages it to think in terms of *damnum emergens* rather than *lucrum cessans*. Contract, in contrast, is different. Contract is forward-looking and when it comes to awarding compensation the aim is to put the injured party in the position he would have been in had the contract been performed. In one sense, then, *White & Carter* is no different in principle from a damages claim in contract: the plaintiff was being awarded his profit.

Yet if a contractor, by suing in debt, is entitled to have his expectation interest satisfied, does this mean that had the plaintiff actually sued in damages he would have received the same sum of money? One immediate difficulty here is the damages rule that a plaintiff cannot claim compensation for losses that he could reasonably have avoided; this mitigation rule, now seen as a question of causation (Ch 7 § 5(b)), is, of course, bypassed if one sues in debt or claims specific performance in equity. All the same, there are cases where contractors have sued in damages and recovered a sum equivalent to what might have been obtained in debt. For example, in *Damon Compania Naviera SA v Hapag-Lloyd International SA*[81] a majority of the Court of Appeal allowed the seller of a ship to recover more than the loss of bargain when the prospective buyer of the ship failed, in breach of a collateral contract, to sign a memorandum of agreement which contained a clause stipulating that a 10% deposit was to be paid on the signing of the memorandum. The majority allowed the plaintiff to recover the 10% as damages. According to Fox LJ the plaintiff was 'entitled to be placed in the same position as if the contractual obligation had been performed' and 'if the obligation had been performed, Hapag-Lloyd could have sued Damon in debt for the amount of the deposit'.[82] In a dissenting judgment Goff LJ made the point that to quantify the damages by reference to the deposit was to assess the damages on the basis that the contract would not be performed by the defendants: 'the inability of Hapag-Lloyd to obtain the protection of the deposit ... flows from their contracting on such terms that the deposit was not payable forthwith upon the making of the contract'.[83] In other words, the cause of the loss of expectation ought to be located, not in the facts of breach, but in the location of the actual debt clause and that, at the factual level, the expectation interest ought to be measured by reference to full performance of the sale of ship contract. Measured in these terms, the only expectation that the plaintiff had in *Damon* was the loss of the bargain on the sale itself and in this situation the normal measure of damages 'is of course the difference between the contract and market prices for the goods'.[84]

80 See eg *White v Jones* [1995] 2 AC 207.

81 [1985] 1 WLR 435.

82 At p 449.

83 At pp 456–57.

84 Goff LJ at p 456.

What makes *Damon* so difficult is that the expectation interest varies according to the legal scheme of intelligibility that one applies to the facts. Take once again the recent decision of *Ruxley Electronics v Forsyth*.[85] The defendants, in breach of contract, did not construct the swimming pool specified in the contract: how are these facts to be interpreted in terms of the expectation interest supposedly protected by the law of contractual damages? To hold that the plaintiff got his expectation – that is to say, that he received a perfectly reasonable and safe pool – requires that one views the object of the contract in a way that involves splitting the interest of the plaintiff contractor into two separate interests, one interpreting the *res* (swimming pool), the other the *persona* (the contractor's state of mind). Mr Forsyth received his *res* expectation since the defendants supplied an objectively reasonable swimming pool and thus there could be no question of damages attaching to the *res*; there was, with regard to the pool, no damage. What Mr Forsyth did not receive was the mental satisfaction of having a pool of a certain depth and this expectation, referred to as the 'consumer surplus' by Lord Mustill, was incapable of precise valuation because it represented a personal, subjective and non-monetary gain.[86] In other words, since the decision of *Jarvis v Swans Tours*, which specifically recognised for the first time mental distress as a valid head of damages in contract, the whole idea of expectation interest has become a category which can no longer be determined simply by reference to the contractual obligations.

Does this approach affect in any way how a case such as *Damon* should be analysed? The majority in this case analysed the 10% deposit clause as defining the expectation itself; yet arguably this failure to gain the 10% was, in terms of damage and the law of damages, not the expectation interest because such an interest cannot of itself be defined by a contractual clause, particularly given that there is no rule at common law that clauses have to be reasonable.[87] Interests are factual, and *Ruxley* appears to be dictating that it is to the facts and not to the contract that one must look in order to determine the benefit that has been lost. As with *Lazenby Garages* (above § 2(d)) it is often a question of how one views the world.

(c) Reliance interest

On occasions it may not be possible to determine any expectation interest. For example, in *Blackpool & Fylde Aero Club Ltd v Blackpool BC*[88] the Court of Appeal held that the plaintiff tenderers, whose tender had negligently been rejected by the defendants, were entitled in principle to damages for breach of a collateral contract between tenderer and invitor. Now it is inconceivable that the plaintiffs could obtain damages on the basis of an expectation that they would have been awarded the contract even if their tender had been properly considered; consequently, any award would have to be based upon a different interest. One such interest might be the loss of a

85 [1995] 3 WLR 118.

86 At p 127; and see Harris, Ogus & Phillips, 'The Consumer Surplus' (1979) 95 LQR 581.

87 But cf Unfair Terms in Consumer Contracts Regulations 1994 regs 3–4.

88 [1990] 1 WLR 1195.

chance.[89] Alternatively, it is in circumstances like these that the reliance interest can come into play and this interest will represent what losses the plaintiff has incurred, including those incurred before the actual contract was secured, as a result of relying upon the plaintiffs' promise.[90] In the context of the law of obligations in general, reliance interest becomes a part of the restoration interest: the object of the award of damages is to put the plaintiff in the position he would have been in if the plaintiff had not committed the breach of obligation.

If, however, the reliance interest is simply part of the restoration interest a question arises over the relationship between expectation and reliance. What if D fails to pay a debt to P when it legally becomes due and as a result P has to borrow money at a high rate of interest so as to be able to proceed with other contracts he has made in reliance on the debt being paid on time? The technical difficulty here is that the common law gives a direct remedy in respect of the specific sum itself – an action in debt – but has not traditionally allowed interest to be added by the creditor for late payment.[91] To have allowed such interest would have been in effect to fashion a new remedy at common law. But can this interest rule be used to defeat an action in damages for loss caused through the non-payment of a debt? In *Wadsworth v Lydall*[92] the Court of Appeal held that a damages claim could in principle be available against a debtor who failed to pay a debt on the due date. What the creditor has to do is to plead and prove that he has suffered special damage as a result of the debtor's failure to pay and that such damage is of a kind that the debtor should have contemplated under the remoteness principle (Ch 7 § 4). This kind of claim is protecting both the expectation (debt) and the reliance (damages) interest. But what if a debtor maliciously refuses to pay a debt: can this give rise to a damages claim in tort? If so, and the debtor is a public body, would this entitle the creditor to claim exemplary damages under the principle of abuse of public power (below § 5(a))?

(d) Restitution interest

This reference to exemplary damages leads one to the third interest said to be protected by damages in contract. Damages can sometimes be awarded in situations where the law wishes to emphasise that 'tort does not pay'.[93] In such a situation damages are being awarded not so much to compensate the plaintiff – although there may be an element which compensates the mental distress caused by a defendant's outrageous behaviour – but to deprive the defendant of an unjust benefit. Here, then, the object of the damages is not damage (*damnum*) but benefit (*lucrum*). The action is designed to stop a person retaining an illegal, or inequitable, profit.

---

89 *Chaplin v Hicks* [1911] 2 KB 786; *Allied Maples Group Ltd v Simmons & Simmons* [1995] 1 WLR 1602.

90 See eg *Anglia TV v Reed* [1972] 1 QB 60.

91 *London, Chatham & Dover Ry v South Eastern Ry* [1893] AC 429; but *cf* Supreme Court Act 1981 s 35A. See now *Westdeutsche Lundesbank v Islington* LBC [1996] 2 WLR 802 (HL).

92 [1981] 1 WLR 598.

93 See eg *Cassell & Co v Broome* [1972] AC 1027.

In such cases there must obviously be a plaintiff and the interest that might be said to be protected is the restitution interest. Now in situations where the defendant's profit has been obtained at the plaintiff's expense there is no conceptual problem; one can point to the symmetry of defendant's profit and plaintiff's loss. But where the profit has not actually resulted in any identifiable loss in a plaintiff a problem arises in that it is difficult to see what individual interest is being protected. The policy, of course, is straight-forward enough – people ought not to profit from their own wrongs. Yet the individualistic nature of the legal reasoning model (*cf* Ch 5 § 5(a)) implies that only those with an interest to protect should be allowed to sue in private law. Thus, in *Stoke-on-Trent CC v W & J Wass Ltd*[94] a local authority unsuccessfully sued a market trader, who had been illegally trading on the authority's land, for damages in trespass; and in *Surrey CC v Bredero Homes Ltd*[95] a local authority was awarded only nominal damages, this time for breach of contract, from a builder who in breach of planning permission built more houses on a plot of land than he had agreed to build. In both cases the local authority was held to have suffered no loss. The general legal position was set out by Dillon LJ in the *Surrey* case:

> The starting point ... in my judgment is that the remedy at common law for a breach of contract is an award of damages, and damages at common law are intended to compensate the victim for his loss, not to transfer to the victim if he has suffered no loss the benefit which the wrongdoer has gained by his breach of contract ...[96]

And he later continued:

> ... Every student is taught that the basis of assessing damages for breach of contract is the rule in *Hadley v Baxendale* (1854) 9 Ex 341, which is wholly concerned with the losses which can be compensated by damages. Such damages may, in an appropriate case, cover profit which the injured plaintiff has lost, but they do not cover an award, to a plaintiff who has himself suffered no loss, of the profit which the defendant has gained for himself by his breach of contract.[97]

In the field of tort, said Dillon LJ, there are areas where the law is different and the plaintiff can recover in respect of the defendant's profit:

> Thus, in the field of trespass it is well established that if one person has, without leave of another, been using that other's land for his own purposes he ought to pay for such user [*sic*]. Thus, even if he had done no actual harm to the land he was charged for the user of the land ... The same principle was applied to patent infringement ... The infringer was ordered to pay by way of damages a royalty for every infringing article because the infringement damaged the plaintiff's property right, that is to say, his patent monopoly. So in a case of detinue the defendant was ordered to pay a hire for chattels he had detained: *Strand Electric and Engineering Co Ltd v Brisford Entertainments Ltd* [1952] 2 QB 246 ...[98]

94 [1988] 1 WLR 1406.

95 [1993] 1 WLR 1361.

96 At p 1364.

97 At p 1365.

98 *Ibid.*

And with regard to the facts of the case before him Dillon LJ concluded:

> As I see it, therefore, there never was in the present case, even before the writ was issued, any possibility of the court granting an injunction ... The plaintiffs' only possible claim from the outset was for damages only, damages at common law. The plaintiffs have suffered no damage. Therefore on basic principles, as damages are awarded to compensate loss, the damages must be merely nominal.[99]

The difficulty with these cases is, of course, that the defendant is left with his profit earned in breach of the law. In tort there is the theoretical possibility of exemplary damages founded on the principle that tort must not pay; but this possibility does not exist at all in contract since exemplary damages cannot be awarded in contract.[100] Another possibility is for a local authority to seek an injunction to stop, say, illegal trading[101] and then to ask the court to use its statutory power to award damages in equity.[102] Again, however, one wonders if damages will be forthcoming if the plaintiff cannot point to any loss. It is true that a local authority is empowered to seek an injunction on behalf of the interests of the local community,[103] yet it is difficult to see the courts thinking in terms of the profit being held on trust, or on behalf of, the community.[104] And what if the local authority is in no position to sue in terms of a cause of action? The point to be recognised is that damages are not the appropriate remedy for an unjust enrichment claim. The appropriate remedy is either debt or account (Ch 4 § 5; Ch 11).

5 NON-COMPENSATORY DAMAGES

Exemplary, or punitive, damages are the exception to the general rule that damages are awarded to compensate for damage. Yet from time to time their role can be important in areas such as trespass where behaviour on the one hand and damage suffered on the other seem out of proportion.[105] If a trader or builder deliberately and consistently flouts the law for his own benefit, is private law to remain impotent? No doubt with the extension of damage into the area of mental distress the need for recourse to punitive damages will become less pressing; yet there remain areas where certain kinds of harm do not qualify as damage in the common law. In *Constantine v Imperial Hotels*[106] a West Indian cricketer was refused accommodation in one of the defendants' hotels on the ground of his colour; he obtained only nominal damages even though the hotel was in breach of its duty of common innkeepers and that this breach had caused much humiliation and distress (not to mention invasion of a constitutional right). Such

99 At p 1368.

100 *Addis v Gramophone Co Ltd* [1909] AC 488.

101 See eg *AG v Harris* [1961] 1 QB 74.

102 See *Jaggard v Sawyer* [1995] 2 All ER 189.

103 Local Government Act 1972 s 222.

104 *Cf* G Samuel, 'Consumer Rights and the Law of Restitution' (1987) 38 NILQ 328.

105 See eg *Drane v Evangelou* [1978] 2 All ER 437.

106 [1944] KB 693.

mental distress does not in itself appear to be damage for the purposes of the common law of damages.

(a) Abuse of power

Admittedly, if this case arose today and the defendants had been a public body, the defendants might well have found themselves having to pay non-compensatory damages. Exemplary damages are designed to punish a defendant who has behaved outrageously. Thus, in *Bradford CC v Arora*[107] the Court of Appeal restored an award of £1,000 exemplary damages made by an Industrial Tribunal to a woman who had been discriminated against contrary to the Sex Discrimination Act 1975 and the Race Relations Act 1976. This decision would not, however, benefit anyone in the position of the plaintiff in the *Constantine* case because the defendant hotel was a private body; exemplary damages, so declared Lord Devlin in 1964, are awarded, in the absence of statutory power, only where there has been oppressive, arbitrary or unconstitutional behaviour by a servant of the government or where the defendant's conduct was calculated to make him a profit and such profit might exceed any compensatory damages payable.[108]

On a closer examination of the two heads under which exemplary damages can be awarded, a more complex picture emerges than might at first be imagined. Punitive damages awarded against the State for oppressive behaviour may in form appear non-compensatory, but in substance can be linked to the invasion of what might be said to constitutional rights. Is not the plaintiff in *Bradford* in effect being compensated for the mental distress arising from governmental abuse of power? No doubt the aim of the award of exemplary damages goes beyond the plaintiff's individual interests and into the public interest of deterring certain kinds of behaviour. But do not all awards of damages based on wrongs have this public interest aspect? At all events, the importance of Lord Devlin's first category goes well beyond the mere form of a compensation award; it recognises as a matter of substance that those in power ought not to abuse that power and any payment to a victim can hardly be seen as a windfall even if it is awarded on top of compensatory damages. This is not to say that such damages do not cause problems when related to awards made in, for example, personal injury cases.[109] For there is no proper way of assessing invasions of constitutional rights just from the position of the plaintiff; much will depend also on the behaviour of the public body. The more relevant question is whether such damages should lie only against public bodies. Was not the plaintiff in *Constantine* just as deserving a victim as the plaintiff in *Bradford*? One answer is that they both suffered serious invasions of their constitutional rights and thus their claims were both of a public law nature. This gives rise to a question concerning substantive law. Ought there to be a tort of abusively invading the

107 [1991] 2 QB 507.

108 *Rookes v Barnard* [1964] AC 1129, 1221–33.

109 Law Commission Consultation Paper No 140 (1995) paras 4.88–4.89.

constitutional rights of a citizen? There are few precedents for such a general tort; yet, as we have seen (above § 3(e)), there are certain kinds of invasions (damage) not covered by an existing cause of action which are in need of a remedy.

(b) Unjust enrichment

The second of Lord Devlin's categories is equally problematic in that while the idea that it is necessary to teach a wrongdoer that tort does not pay is understandable, such a principle not only is restricted to tort but can give a plaintiff a windfall in that it is not matched to any loss. Lord Devlin talked of profiting through 'a cynical disregard for a plaintiff's rights', and while it is no doubt true that there may be cases where the mental distress caused by such disregard warrants compensation, it has to be asked whether an amount awarded in, say, a defamation case under this heading is healthy when the award is compared to those made in personal injury cases.[110] All the same, there are cases where a defendant can profit from his wrong at the expense of the plaintiff. In *Drane v Evangelou*[111] a landlord evicted a tenant in an outrageous manner and the Court of Appeal upheld an award of £1,000 exemplary damages based on Lord Devlin's second category. In getting rid of the tenant in the way that he did, the landlord was aiming to increase the profits from his property. This is a generous interpretation since the substance of the behaviour was abuse of private (ownership) power by a landlord and if the latter had been a public servant the award would have fallen into the first category. The gymnastics in moving from public law to enrichment can appear awkward, yet it does illustrate how the law of actions can fill the gaps left by substantive law.[112]

(c) Nominal damages

One finds a similar situation with nominal damages. These damages are, in a way, the reverse of exemplary damages in that they are symbolic amounts indicating that although the plaintiff has suffered an invasion of a right he has not incurred any recognised damage. Thus, in *The Albazero*[113] a consignor of a cargo of oil who tried to recover its value from the person whose breach of contract caused its loss was held to be entitled only to nominal damages since, no longer having a proprietary interest in the oil, he had suffered no loss. To have allowed the plaintiff to recover the full value would have resulted in an unjustified enrichment since the plaintiff would have received, or have been entitled to receive, the price of the oil from the person to whom he had transferred his title. This lack of damage can, then, be a matter of actual fact (or at least proof of damage), as in cases like *The Albazero* and *Lazenby Garages v Wright* (above § 2(d)), or more a matter of law – that is to say, the damage is not recognised by the law of actions and obligations – as in the *Constantine* case. In the

110 *Cf Cassell & Co v Broome* [1972] AC 1027; *Sutcliffe v Pressdram Ltd* [1991] 1 QB 153.
111 [1978] 2 All ER 437.
112 *Cf Chapman v Honig* [1963] 2 QB 502.
113 [1977] AC 774.

latter situation one can genuinely talk of nominal damages as a form of non-compensatory damages in that the plaintiff's undoubted harm (mental distress) was met with an award of damages that in form was not in any way meant to compensate for the harm caused.

6 DAMAGES AND BEHAVIOUR

Exemplary damages are extra damages awarded as a result of a defendant's bad behaviour and such damages lead to the more general question of the link between the nature of the behaviour and the quantum of damages. Do bad people pay more? Clearly, when viewed from the position of punitive damages, the answer is that they may do provided the action is not one for breach of contract.[114] But what if the defendant in *Ruxley Electronics v Forsyth* (above § 4(b)) had deliberately built a shallower pool in order to save £6,000 in costs: would the plaintiff still have been entitled only to the £2,500 damages for the mental distress? Strictly speaking, the object of an award of damages for any breach of contract is to compensate only for the damage suffered; accordingly, the loss of amenity (mental distress) would in theory be the same whether the defendant accidentally or deliberately failed to perform the contract as stipulated. All the same, there are cases where the courts have been more generous.

In *Doyle v Olby (Ironmongers) Ltd*[115] the plaintiff was induced by a series of fraudulent misrepresentations (Ch 9 §§ 7(b), 9) to buy the defendant's ironmongers business and, having been landed with the business, the plaintiff decided to attempt to run it successfully. This attempt turned out to be economically disastrous with the result that the plaintiff was put to much extra expense. The plaintiff brought an action for damages against the seller claiming compensation (i) for the losses in making good the actual misrepresentations and (ii) for the losses incurred in trying to run the business. The trial judge held that he was entitled to compensation only under head (i), but the Court of Appeal said this approach was wrong; the plaintiff was entitled to be indemnified under both heads. Lord Denning MR explained that had this been an action for damages for breach of contract the amount recoverable would have been an amount to put the plaintiff in the position he would have been in if the promises made by the defendant had been performed. However, this was not a claim in contract but one in the tort of deceit involving fraud. In this situation, said Lord Denning, the plaintiff was to be compensated for all his losses flowing from the bad behaviour since damages 'for fraud and conspiracy are assessed differently from damages for breach of contract'.[116]

Several points emerge from the *Doyle* case. If the plaintiff's action had been founded on a contractual obligation it might have resulted in a different definition of damage than the one actually employed. Does this mean that the measure of damages

---

114 *Addis v Gramophone Co Ltd* [1909] AC 488.

115 [1969] 2 QB 158.

116 At p 166.

in contract and tort compensation claims can be different? The answer to this question can be complex because not only can it depend upon the type of harm suffered – personal injury and property damage will probably attract the same rules,[117] whereas economic loss gives rise to a range of differently defined interests – but the contract and tort dichotomy can itself be influenced by the actual behaviour of the defendant in as much as the existence or non-existence of fault can allow a plaintiff the choice of suing in tort or in contract.[118] If the defendant in *Doyle* had been negligent rather than fraudulent would the plaintiff have recovered all of his losses? And if there had been some cut-off point, would this cut-off point in tort be the same as the one in contract? These questions evidently involve definitions of damage in turn leading to questions about protected economic interests. Yet is *Doyle* saying that where a defendant has behaved fraudulently he might find himself liable for more than just the expectation interest? Or was Lord Denning just distinguishing on the facts between the reliance and the expectation interests? Indeed, do these labels really have any meaning when it comes to assessing losses flowing from tort?

More difficult again is the fiction of fraud used in s 2(1) of the Misrepresentation Act 1967. Ought this section to attract the *Doyle* measure? According to the Court of Appeal it will[119] and so it may be that a victim of a misrepresentation can recover everything that flows from the tort.[120] Yet the point to emerge from cases such as *Doyle* is that the problem of damage and damages is not one that can easily be analysed in terms of *damnum emergens* and *lucrum cessans*, or, alternatively, reliance and expectation interests, since the losses often involve falls in valuation and the loss of good money after bad. Viewed from the position of a restoration interest the question becomes one of limiting liability and here the central notion is causation.

---

117 *Parsons (Livestock) Ltd v Uttley Ingham & Co* [1978] QB 791.

118 *Henderson v Merrett Syndicates Ltd* [1995] 2 AC 145.

119 *Royscot Trust Ltd v Rogerson* [1991] 3 All ER 294.

120 *Naughton v O'Callaghan* [1990] 3 All ER 191.

CHAPTER SEVEN

CAUSATION

Many litigation problems that arise in the law of damages focus on the quantum and on the extent of the 'damage' to be compensated and conceptually this kind of problem, as has been seen (Ch 6), can be rationalised through the notion of a recognised and protected interest. Yet the courts themselves rarely use this language, save perhaps under the guise of 'policy'. Instead the courts prefer to approach the problem of assessing the extent of damage from the starting point that the law cannot take account of everything that follows from a wrongful act and this leads to the practice of dividing up harm into a series of consequences flowing from the wrongful act.[1] This having been done, it becomes possible to assign some of these consequences to an independent cause. Thus, the language of damage limitation is, on the whole, one of cause.[2] Sometimes the notion of cause is used directly, but on a more general level the topic itself has been broken down into a series of devices and techniques each attracting, seemingly, its own principles and rules. Thus, in addition to factual causation itself, there are rules regarding remoteness of damage, contributory negligence, loss of a chance, mitigation of damage, illegal behaviour, consent and so on. And all of these different devices and principles warrant separate chapters in the textbooks. In total, however, they are all concerned with the single question of connecting the damage to the breach of obligation.

1 ROLE OF FAULT

If one had to identify a single normative principle in the whole of the law of obligations it would undoubtedly be that of fault. In civil law countries both breach of contract – or, more accurately, non-performance (*inexécution*) of a contract – and liability in tort (delict and quasi-delict) are *prima facie* based upon fault and even the long-standing exceptions to the fault principle, such as liability for damage done by things, were often justified by reference to some idea of wrongdoing.[3] In civilian contract law fault has played a central role primarily because problems of contractual liability are seen as a failure in performance;[4] a contractor who does not carry out his contractual obligations must pay damages or justify the absence of performance by pointing to some event which cannot be blamed on him.[5] This does not mean that there is never contractual liability without fault (strict liability, to use the common law term) in civil law systems (see Ch 1 § 7(b); Ch 10 § 8(a)); the point to be emphasised is

1 *The Liesbosch* (*The Edison*) [1933] AC 449, 460.

2 *Cf Allied Maples Group Ltd v Simmons & Simmons* [1995] 1 WLR 1602.

3 Malaurie & Aynès, no 181. Roman law: D.44.7.5.

4 Treitel, *Remedies*, para 9.

5 See eg CC art 1147–48.

that 'civil law systems start with the theory that fault is a requirement for the availability of contractual remedies'.[6]

The common law, at first sight, appears to take a very different approach in that liability in contract is said to be strict.[7] But this is a very misleading proposition, as statute now makes clear. In contracts where the institutional focal point is a *res* – typically, a contract for the sale or hire of goods – liability attaches to the *res* rather than to the *persona* and as a result the courts have held that where the goods turn out to be defective, liability is strict.[8] In contracts for the provision of a service, however, the promissory obligation is one of care and skill; consequently, a contractor wanting to obtain damages for damage arising out of the performance of a contract must prove fault.[9] Indeed this fault requirement can play a role even in remedies other than damages. In *Vigers v Cook*[10] an undertaker sued a customer in debt for the price of a service carried out in respect of the defendant's dead son. The customer refused to pay because the coffin had started to leak during the service and had had to be taken outside of the church. The Court of Appeal refused to allow the undertaker to succeed in his claim since 'the onus was on the plaintiff to establish that it was not in that state owing to no default on his part'.[11] In other words, the contractor failed to obtain performance by the other party – payment of the price of the service – because he was not able to show that he had himself performed his side of the contract. Performance and fault had become intertwined not only with the substantive obligation in contract, but also with the procedural requirement of proof.

The starting point for an action for damages founded on a breach of a non-contractual obligation (see Ch 12) is often related to a greater or lesser extent to fault. The tort of negligence evidently requires carelessness,[12] while the tort of deceit requires proof of fraud.[13] And an absence of fault even in respect of some of the strict liability torts can on occasions act as a defence to a claim for compensation.[14] An action in restitution may be determined in relation to the behaviour of the parties and so, for example, a voluntary payment which enriches another may be irrecoverable; equally, good faith change of position by a defendant can now act as a defence.[15] Estoppel by negligence also plays an important role across private law.[16] In the law of procedure and remedies fault can be important inasmuch as some kinds of behaviour may amount to an abuse of process and, as we have seen, the measure of damages may be affected by

6 Treitel, *Remedies*, para 9.

7 *Raineri v Miles* [1981] AC 1050, 1086.

8 See eg Sale of Goods Act 1979 s 14; *Frost v Aylesbury Dairy Co Ltd* [1905] 1 KB 608.

9 Supply of Goods and Services Act 1982 s 13.

10 [1919] 2 KB 475.

11 Bankes LJ at p 482.

12 On which see *Bolton v Stone* [1951] AC 850; *Qualcast (Wolverhampton) Ltd v Haynes* [1959] AC 743.

13 *Derry v Peek* (1889) 14 App Cas 337.

14 See eg *Cambridge Water Co v Eastern Leather Plc* [1994] 2 AC 264.

15 *Lipkin Gorman v Karpnale* [1991] 2 AC 548.

16 See eg *Entores v Miles Far East Corporation* [1955] 2 QB 327, 333.

the seriousness of the defendant's – or indeed the plaintiff's – behaviour (see Ch 6). Thus, even if there remain pockets of genuine strict liability, fault pervades the law of obligations.

Where the relationship between fault and obligation is particularly important is with regard to the whole question of causation. As Tony Weir reminds us, 'cause' and 'blame' are not synonymous,[17] but with respect to the law of remedies the interrelationship between the two plays a fundamental role in determining not just the availability of a remedy but also the extent of liability.[18] This is not to say that a plaintiff in a claim for extensive damages must always show fault with respect to all or some of the heads claimed. For example, this is not the case with regard to a claim for damage and loss under s 14 of the Sale of Goods Act 1979. Yet fault, if excluded from the front door, may re-enter through the back and so the absence of fault can play a negative role. Accordingly, a defendant is not normally to be liable for all the losses flowing from a breach of obligation; however, the presence of unreasonable behaviour by one or other of the parties can impact on questions of liability and extent of liability. A good example is provided by *Lamb v Camden LBC*.[19] Owing to the negligence of the local authority the foundations of the plaintiff's house were damaged and as a result the plaintiff moved all her furniture out intending to leave the premises empty until rebuilding work had been completed. While it was empty squatters moved in and caused further damage to the property. Was the local authority to be liable for this further damage? The Court of Appeal held that this second damage was too remote. Now according to Lord Denning MR it was the plaintiff 'herself who paved the way for the squatters by moving out all her furniture and leaving the house unoccupied and unfurnished'.[20] Moreover, this was, on the 'broader grounds of policy', the kind of loss that should have been borne by the house insurance rather than by the local authority; and if the plaintiff had not taken out insurance 'that is her misfortune'.[21] In other words, the plaintiff was at fault in failing to insure what normally should be insured by private houseowners.

This idea that an owner might be under a duty to insure becomes particularly relevant in cases where liability can exist in the absence of a direct fault: for in these kinds of cases the normative idea often becomes that of risk rather than behaviour and risk is a central concept in insurance. In *Photo Production v Securicor*[22] the question of fault, strict liability and risk came face to face when the insurance company of a factory owner, whose factory had been burned down by an employee of Securicor, sued the insurance company of Securicor in respect of the loss (see Ch 5 § 5). As is usual in these subrogation cases, the legal issues were fought out on the basis of the rights flowing between factory owner and security company and in this particular case one of

17 Weir, *Casebook*, p 9.

18 Treitel, *Remedies*, para 123.

19 [1981] QB 625.

20 At p 637.

21 At p 637–38.

22 [1980] AC 827.

the central questions was whether Securicor, who had contracted to guard the factory, could rely upon an exclusion clause attempting to put the risk of its employees' behaviour on to its customers. Viewed from the position of a traditional law of obligations, Securicor's (or at least its insurance company's) argument looks outrageous – they had, after all, promised to protect the plaintiff's factory but ended up doing quite the opposite. However, viewed from the position of insurance and risk the picture very quickly changes in that causation becomes secondary. Instead of asking who caused the loss, one asks who should take the risk for this kind of loss; and once this question is posed the actual cause of the fire appears secondary, in that such events can be triggered by a whole range of possible causes, none of which actually matters as far as the immediate parties are concerned. What the plaintiff owner wants is security against the risk of fire, howsoever caused, and what the defendant wants is a reasonable limitation of potential liability in relation to the price charged. Behaviour in this kind of situation would, it seems, be a matter only for the criminal law.

Nevertheless, there are occasions when fault can be of some relevance even with respect to risk. In *George Mitchell (Chesterhall) Ltd v Finney Lock Seeds Ltd*[23] the seller of Dutch Winter cabbage seed tried to rely upon a limitation clause when the seed proved of inferior quality and caused extensive loss to its buyer. The House of Lords held that the clause was not 'fair and reasonable' under the Unfair Contract Terms Act 1977 and gave judgment for the plaintiff in respect of his full loss. Lord Bridge went through a whole range of factors which weighed the scales in favour of the plaintiff farmer, but added, finally, that the supply of the wrong seeds was due to the negligence of the defendant's sister company. This factor, as Lord Bridge made clear, was simply one of many and was not in any way the determining factor as such. But the existence of fault still played an indirect normative role: it helped the court to decide where the risk should lie when the normal strict liability of s 14 of the Sale of Goods Act had been modified by a clause which tried to place the risk of any damage on to the buyer rather than the seller. Fault, so to speak, had re-entered through the back door.

2 LIMITING DAMAGES

The clause in *George Mitchell* attempted to limit the amount of damages payable to the buyer to a strict restitution interest, that is to say to the cost of the seeds. Such clauses are a common feature in the law of contract and their effectiveness, now largely governed by statute and by regulations, depends not just upon the interpretation of the clause itself, but on the context in which the clause is to operate (*cf* Ch 10 § 4). But what if there is no such limitation clause specifically written into the contract? Given that a defendant in breach of an obligation is not to be liable for all losses flowing from the wrongful act – some might be assigned to independent causes – how will a court go about deciding what consequences will be attributable to the wrongful act and what consequences will not? In certain circumstances this problem can be resolved by reference to protected interests (Ch 6 § 3). But even here the specific notion used is

23 [1983] 2 AC 803.

causation: certain heads of damage will not be recoverable because they are too remote in causal terms from the breach of obligation.

(a) Actionability

The rules of causation cannot, however, be looked at in isolation since they tend to function at a range of different levels. First, certain causal rules are to be found at the level of actionability itself: a cause of action may well be dependent upon the way the damage has occurred and if it arrives in a manner not envisaged by the action itself there may simply be no breach of obligation. For example, liability is incurred in the tort of trespass only if the defendant has directly caused the plaintiff harm; if the damage is indirect then the defendant may well escape liability, not on the ground that he has not caused the plaintiff harm as such, but on the basis that he is not guilty of trespass.[24] Accordingly, the question of actionability and causation can lead to an all-or-nothing approach. In *The Majfrid*[25] the defendants moved the plaintiffs' barge so as to be able to moor their own and, in its new position, the plaintiffs' barge was unforeseeably damaged; the defendant was held liable in trespass for all the damage arising. This situation can be compared to that in *Harnett v Bond*[26] where the plaintiff managed to get leave from a mental hospital in which he had been confined and went to the offices of the Commissioners of Lunacy in order to try to convince them that he was sane. The defendant at the Commissioners came to the opposite conclusion and detained the plaintiff in one of the offices for several hours until a proper examination by a doctor could be carried out. The doctor who examined the plaintiff decided he was insane and the plaintiff was reconfined in mental hospitals for a further nine years until he managed to escape and was found to be perfectly sane. Was the defendant in locking the plaintiff in a room for several hours to be liable for the nine years' imprisonment in mental institutions? The House of Lords held that the nine years' imprisonment was not something that could be attributed to the defendant's act since it did not directly result from the act.

In the tort of trespass the causal requirement is a formal condition of actionability, whereas in the tort of negligence the actionability question is subsumed under the broader requirement of duty of care (*cf* Ch 12 § 3(a)). Certain kinds of damage can be excluded at the actionability level in negligence by holding that the defendant owed no duty of care in respect of harm such as nervous shock and pure economic loss (Ch 13 § 9). A case like *Spartan Steel* (Ch 6 § 3(a)) can therefore be analysed either as a remoteness of damage or as a duty problem; the defendant owed no duty of care in respect of the *lucrum cessans* head. In many ways the different methods of analysis are simply matters of form. Nevertheless, different formal approaches to the problem of causation can involve different tests. In *Harnett v Bond* the question was whether the

24 *Scott v Shepherd* (1773) 96 ER 525. And see eg *Harnet v Bond* [1925] AC 669; but *cf Wilkinson v Downton* [1897] 2 QB 57.

25 [1942] P 145.

26 [1925] AC 669.

defendant was the direct cause of the plaintiff's damage, while in *Spartan Steel* the formal test of remoteness was that of foreseeability. This dichotomy between directness and foreseeability – between an objective and, seemingly, a subjective approach – pervades the whole of the law of obligations and remedies and at the level of actionability the dichotomy can often manifest itself through a confusion of the two notions. For example, in *Vacwell Engineering Ltd v BDH Chemicals Ltd*[27] the defendants argued that a lethal explosion which caused extensive damage was not foreseeable and that in consequence they should not be liable for the havoc that occurred from their breach of contract in failing to put adequate warnings on bottles of chemicals likely to explode if mixed with water. The judge responded by holding that the large explosion was 'the direct result of the supply of boron tribromide without an adequate warning label' and that taking all the circumstances into account 'the explosion was reasonably foreseeable'.[28] The mere fact that the extent of the damage was unforeseeable did not render it too remote in law.

(b) The nature of the damage

The difference of course between *Harnett*, *Spartan Steel* and *Vacwell* is one of types of harm as much as one of types of liability. In *Harnett* there is a clearly distinguishable borderline between the few hours' imprisonment in the office and the nine years incarceration in institutions and it is difficult to hold, as a matter of actual fact, that the defendant was the cause of the nine years. Similarly, in *Spartan Steel* the well established distinction between 'damage' and 'loss' (Ch 6 § 3(a); Ch 13 § 9), or even between *damnum emergens* and *lucrum cessans*, invites a cut-off at the level of substantive law. *Vacwell*, however, is different. Here there was a sudden single event which resulted from the breach of contract and in this situation all that the court could in effect do was to hold either that the defendant was not liable for the explosion – something that would be most difficult given the case law surrounding damages for breach of a sale of goods contract[29] – or that he was liable for the explosion and all its consequences. It must be emphasised, therefore, that while the formal concepts and tests used to decide complex causation problems are of great importance, one must never ignore the damage itself. Does the harm that has occurred, from its nature, invite a cut-off point or is it of a type that simply does not lend itself to any sub-division into discrete parts? Analysing damage and liability is no doubt a matter of rules, principles and concepts, but these rules, principles and concepts often arise out of the facts themselves, and thus damage limitation requires an understanding of damage itself and of the factual context in which it occurs. This may seem a trite observation, yet the notion of 'foreseeability' is a legal proposition that has little connection with reality.

27 [1971] 1 QB 88.

28 Rees J at p 106.

29 *Cf Re Polemis* [1921] 3 KB 560.

(c) The nature of the act

In addition to difficulties over the nature of the damage, causal problems can also arise out of the nature of the act. In the old common law it was said that 'not doing is no trespass' and this distinction between misfeasance and nonfeasance continues to find expression in the modern tort of negligence.[30] A naval rating gets very drunk on a base where alcohol is extremely cheap and discipline perhaps not quite what it should be: if the rating dies from an excess of alcohol one evening will the naval authorities be liable to his widow? *Prima facie* the authorities will not be liable since even if they were negligent in disciplinary supervision the cause of the rating's death was his own act; only when the authorities physically take the rating into custody or hospital will they become in a causal sense responsible.[31]

Sometimes the indirectness of the negligent act becomes a more subtle factor. In *Marc Rich & Co v Bishop Rock Ltd*[32] the owners of a cargo lost at sea when a ship sank brought an action against the firm of ship surveyors who had negligently passed the vessel as being seaworthy; a majority of the House of Lords dismissed the action for damages on the basis of an absence of a duty of care. One factor that helped point to an absence of the duty of care was the way the physical loss had been inflicted: if the surveyors 'had carelessly dropped a lighted cigarette into a cargo hold known to contain a combustible cargo, thereby causing an explosion and the loss of the vessel and cargo, the assertion that the classification society was in breach of a duty of care might have been a strong one', said Lord Steyn.[33] However, on the facts before them, there was no direct infliction of physical damage. That did not conclude the question, but it did 'introduce the right perspective on one aspect of this case'.[34]

3 FACTUAL CAUSATION

The second level, after actionability, at which causation functions is the level of fact. It is a general requirement of the law of obligations that the defendant's tort or breach of contract is the cause of the plaintiff's harm and if there is no, or insufficient, causal link then the defendant cannot be liable, however bad his breach of obligation. The paradigm case is *Barnett v Chelsea & Kensington Hospital Management Committee.*[35] A doctor working in an out-patients' department was careless in failing to treat a patient who arrived at the hospital complaining of stomach pains; the patient subsequently died from poisoning but the hospital was held not liable since, even if he had been given the best treatment available, he would have died anyway. The negligence of the doctor was not the factual cause of the death of the patient.

30 Baker, p 380.

31 *Barrett v Ministry of Defence* [1995] 1 WLR 1217.

32 [1996] 1 AC 211.

33 At p 237.

34 *Ibid.*

35 [1969] 1 QB 428.

(a) Burden of proof

Barnett is, it must be said, a rather exceptional case in that the causal question seems quite clear cut. The evidence, presumably, was more or less uncontroversial. On the whole, however, causation cases are much more problematic because it is often very difficult to make a scientific decision about factual causation (as any reader of science fiction would no doubt appreciate). What if the medical evidence had been disputed in the *Barnett* case? What if the plaintiff had been able to produce expert witnesses claiming that the out-patient's life had a 5% chance of being saved if treatment had promptly been given? In the past the jury would have decided the factual causation question without giving reasons; today it is the judge who must play the role of the jury and this can have the effect, given that judges give reasons for their decisions, of injecting into this area of factual causation a conceptual aspect. Accordingly, the area has become subject to its own specific notions such as 'but for', 'reasonableness' and '*novus actus interveniens*' and these notions must be carefully distinguished from those used to decide questions of remoteness (legal causation).[36]

What if the evidence is equally balanced between plaintiff and defendant? As a matter of principle in the law of actions the defendant ought to win in such a situation on the basis that the plaintiff has not proved his case. To succeed a plaintiff must prove that the defendant's breach of obligation caused his or her damage and establishing such proof of cause can, needless to say, be extremely difficult. In areas such as medical negligence proof often depends upon a battle between each side's expert witnesses. Indeed the same is true with respect to nuclear power or the effects on health of electricity; establishing cause and connection is often no more than asserting a probability possibly dependent in turn upon statistical patterns. Admittedly, the role of the court is not to search for scientific truths as Viscount Simon LC once pointed out;[37] but areas of causation involving actual science do often come down to scientific debates within the context of the trial and this can prove extremely costly and time-consuming. As a result lawyers have sometimes attempted to develop alternative strategies and tactical devices to help plaintiffs faced with complex causation issues.

(b) Loss of a chance

One strategy that has met with some limited success is to extend the notion of 'damage' itself.[38] Take the facts of *Barnett* and imagine that the balance of evidence is equally weighted between plaintiff and defendant; that is to say, the plaintiff can produce experts who claim that had the patient received prompt treatment his life might have been saved, while the defendant can produce experts denying this. Could the plaintiff argue that on these facts there was damage inasmuch as the failure to treat had deprived the out-patient of a chance to survive? Two decisions can appear helpful in these

36 *McKew v Holland & Hannen & Cubitts* [1969] 3 All ER 1621.

37 *Hickman v Peacey* [1945] AC 304, 318.

38 See generally T Weir, '*La notion de dommage en responsabilité civile*', in Legrand (ed), pp 1–55.

circumstances. The first is the contract case of *Chaplin v Hicks*[39] where the defendants' breach of contract had prevented the plaintiff from taking part in the final stage of a beauty competition. The Court of Appeal rejected the defendants' contention that the plaintiff's loss was incapable of being assessed and thus too remote; the very object of the contract was to give the plaintiff a chance of being selected as winner and while this was not a 'right' that could be sold in the market place 'a jury might well take the view that such a right, if it could have been transferred, would have been of such a value that ... a good price could be obtained for it'.[40]

The second case is *McGhee v National Coal Board*.[41] The plaintiff was employed in the defendants' hot and dusty brick kiln, where no washing facilities had been provided, and having contracted dermatitis the plaintiff brought an action for damages against the employer for breach of a duty of care in failing to provide the washing facilities. The plaintiff could not prove one hundred percent that the dermatitis was caused by the absence of washing facilities, but the evidence indicated that on the balance of probabilities there was cause and connection. The House of Lords held that the damages claim could succeed on the ground that although the plaintiff had not proved that the breach of duty had caused the actual damage he had shown that the breach had created a sufficient risk of damage. Policy and justice then dictated that the creator of the risk should carry the burden of this risk of damage. This decision is similar to *Chaplin v Hicks* in that it gives concrete form to what is an intangible kind of harm: the plaintiff had been deprived of an opportunity to avoid getting dermatitis. There was no absolute certainty that the washing facilities would have prevented the disease any more than there was an absolute certainty that the plaintiff in *Chaplin* would have won the competition. Yet both plaintiffs had been deprived of an intangible 'right'.

At the time *McGhee* was seen as an important change of direction with regard to proof and causation in personal injury litigation.[42] However, its success was, it would seem, relatively short-lived. In *Wilsher v Essex Area Health Authority*[43] Lord Bridge said that '*McGhee v National Coal Board* laid down no new principle whatsoever'; quite the contrary, he went on to say, since 'it affirmed the principle that the onus of proving causation lies on the pursuer or plaintiff' and all that the majority in *McGhee* had done was to conclude 'that it was a legitimate inference of fact that the defendants' negligence had materially contributed to the pursuer's injury'.[44] *Wilsher*, it must be said, was a medical negligence case rather than an employers' liability problem and although in form the two situations are governed by the same duty of care principle (*cf* Ch 12 § 3(a)), in substance medical cases attract special policy considerations.[45] In

39 [1911] 2 KB 786.

40 Vaughan Williams LJ at p 793.

41 [1973] 1 WLR 1.

42 See eg EJ Weinrib, 'A Step Foward in Factual Causation' (1975) 38 MLR 518.

43 [1988] AC 1074.

44 At p 1090.

45 See eg *Sidaway v Governors of Bethlem Royal Hospital* [1985] AC 871, 887.

Wilsher the evidence indicated that there was only a probability that a baby's blindness had been caused by the negligent excess of oxygen given at birth and while it could be said that the negligence had increased the risk of blindness, it does not necessarily follow as a matter of policy that this is a risk that ought to be borne by the hospital. Employers are usually in business for profit and thus it is easier to put the burden of risk on their insurance companies. But can the same be said for hospitals operating within the ever-tightening constraints of the NHS?

Loss of a chance problems can, accordingly, be approached from two angles. They can be seen as remedy cases giving rise to questions of quantification of damages or they can be seen as substantive law problems presenting factual causation difficulties. Or, put another way, the causal rules with respect to the loss of a chance can operate at two different levels, factual causation and damages. Where is the line to be drawn between these two approaches? According to Millett LJ, in a recent Court of Appeal case, a plaintiff who sues in negligence must establish duty, breach and loss resulting from the breach. Furthermore, with respect to the loss requirement, the plaintiff 'must also identify some head of loss which is alleged to have resulted from the breach and, if it is not of a kind which would naturally result from the breach, establish a causal link between the breach and the loss'. Only having done this, 'is he entitled to have the loss quantified'.[46] Stuart-Smith LJ, in the same case, made a similar point: 'in my judgment, [a] plaintiff must prove as a matter of causation that he has a real or substantial chance as opposed to a speculative one' and if 'he succeeds in doing so, the evaluation of the chance is part of the assessment of the *quantum* of damage'.[47] The case itself concerned an action for damages in negligence brought by a take-over company against a firm of solicitors who had drafted a take-over agreement which failed to protect the plaintiffs from certain contingent claims that might and did eventuate from leases originally held by the vendor group of companies. The plaintiffs claimed that if the solicitors had properly advised them about the possibility of contingent claims, a warranty could probably have been obtained from the vendors in respect of the liabilities. The plaintiffs, in other words, were claiming that the solicitors' omission had deprived them of a chance to protect themselves against financial loss. Basing themselves on, *inter alia*, the decision in *Chaplin v Hicks* a majority of the Court of Appeal held that the plaintiffs were entitled as a matter of principle to succeed. The loss was not too speculative and there was ample evidence that but for the solicitors' negligence the plaintiffs would have obtained a warranty protecting them against the contingent liability. Millett LJ, dissenting, was unconvinced: the lost chance was 'a matter of pure speculation' and no 'case has gone so far as to allow damages in such a situation'; to allow damages in such a situation would be wrong.[48]

46 *Allied Maples Group Ltd v Simmons & Simmons* [1995] 1 WLR 1602, 1622.

47 *Ibid*, at p 1614.

48 *Ibid*, p 1625.

(c) Tangible damage and intangible loss

Wilsher v Essex Area Health Authority had been preceded by another medical negligence case in which Lord Bridge commented on the loss of a chance argument. In *Hotson v East Berkshire Health Authority*[49] the young plaintiff had fallen out of a tree and was rushed to hospital where the staff failed to diagnose a serious hip injury which had a 75% chance of causing permanent disability. The correct diagnosis was made five days later, but by that time the disability factor had risen to 100%. Could the plaintiff claim compensation for the loss of 25% chance of making a full recovery? The trial judge and the Court of Appeal thought that he could, but the House of Lords allowed an appeal on the basis that this was a straightforward factual causation case where the plaintiff had failed to prove that the disability was caused by the defendants' negligence. Even if the correct diagnosis had been made on the first visit to the hospital the plaintiff may still have ended up disabled. 'There is a superficially attractive analogy between the principle applied in such cases as *Chaplin v Hicks*. ... and the principle of awarding damages for the lost chance of avoiding personal injury,' said Lord Bridge. But he went on to conclude that 'there are formidable difficulties in the way of accepting the analogy.'[50]

The difficulty with a medical case like *Hotson* is really twofold. First, it is difficult to convince the House of Lords that the loss of a chance is a real loss in the damage sense of the term; for although it is a question of fact, such facts are dependent not only upon how the judges see the world (*cf* Ch 6 § 2(d)) but also upon the testimony of doctors. 'Clearly medical evidence will be of the utmost importance,' observed Lord Scarman in another medical case, 'in determining whether such a risk is material.'[51] Secondly, it is difficult to convince the House of Lords that the relationship of doctor and patient is analogous to other professional relationships such as solicitor and client. The 'relationship between doctor and patient is a very special one', to quote Lord Scarman again, where the patient is 'putting his health and life in the doctor's hands'.[52] And although Lord Scarman was also at pains to stress that in all matters of civil wrongs the courts are concerned only with legal principle, when 'policy problems emerge they are best left to the legislature'.[53] The relationships between doctor and patient, and between solicitor and client, afford no basis for comparison since the latter is of a fiduciary character and the former of a life and death nature.

Given this lack of an analogy one should not be surprised if the notion of 'loss' is perceived rather differently in the two situations and this means that causation is not just a matter of linking act and harm. In *Hotson* the harm was the personal injury damage and this had to be related in causal terms with the breach of duty. In *Bell v Peter*

49 [1987] AC 750.

50 At p 782.

51 *Sidaway v Governors of Bethlem Royal Hospital* [1985] AC 871, 889.

52 At p 884.

53 At p 887.

Browne & Co[54] the damage was different. The plaintiff had gone to a firm of solicitors following the breakdown of his marriage so as to find out what might be done with the family home. It was agreed that the house would be transferred to the wife, that it would not be sold in the immediate future, and that when it was eventually sold, the plaintiff would receive one sixth of the proceeds. The house was transferred, but the solicitors failed to protect the plaintiff's one sixth interest with the result that when it was sold some eight years later the plaintiff got nothing because the wife had spent all the proceeds. When the plaintiff sued the solicitors, the firm claimed that the action was time-barred under the Limitation Act because the damage, which was the basis of the cause of action in tort, had started to run as soon as the solicitors had failed in their duty. The Court of Appeal upheld the solicitors' defence on the basis that the plaintiff had suffered loss when he transferred the house to his wife. It might have been only a nominal loss at that time, but it was nevertheless real and the plaintiff could have sued the solicitors for what was in effect the loss of a chance. After six years the plaintiff lost the right to sue and the solicitors' defence had to succeed.[55]

One of the problems with this type of case is that contractual damage is being transferred to the law of tort and thus one can understand why one of the judges was tempted by the *non-cumul* rule of French law.[56] All the same, it is not difficult to see why the court was prepared to countenance such a transfer: in tort there is usually no liability for pure economic loss (Ch 13 § 9) and if a plaintiff thus wishes to use tort as a means of getting around the limitation period – where for contract time starts to run from the breach[57] – he ought in justice to be judged according to its own general outlook. Yet perhaps a more fundamental reason for the decision in *Bell v Peter Browne*, although it must be stressed that this is not explicitly stated, is that the court did not want to hold the solicitors liable for an out of limit breach of duty where the loss had actually been caused by the wife's act. There is a tendency in the law of obligations to be reluctant to make one person liable for acts committed by another, save in those specific situations where the law is designed to do just that (*cf* Ch 12 § 6); and this reluctance perhaps manifested itself in the willingness to allow the solicitors the benefit of the limitation.

(d) *Novus actus interveniens*

Normally the courts use the doctrine of a new intervening act (*novus actus interveniens*) to isolate one person from a wrongful act committed by another person. Thus, if A negligently injures B and B's condition is made much worse as a result of a further accident involving the ambulance taking B to hospital, A will not normally be liable for this further damage. The 'chain of causation' is said to be broken by a new intervening

54 [1990] 2 QB 495.

55 See now Limitation Act 1980 s 2.

56 Mustill LJ at p 511.

57 Limitation Act 1980 s 5.

act.[58] However, in just what circumstances a defendant will be relieved from any extra damage – or indeed from liability itself – by a *novus actus* is by no means always an easy question. If D1 wrongfully injures P and this creates a condition which makes any injury or damage caused subsequently by D2 much worse than it would have otherwise been, will D1 be liable for this extra damage? Will D2 be liable for all the damage on the basis that a defendant must 'take his victim as he finds him'? If D wrongfully causes P's ship to be delayed and the ship is later sunk in a storm, will D be liable for the loss of the ship if it can be shown that but for the delay the ship would not have been caught in the storm? Much depends on how lawyers decide to view the facts: if the whole event from beginning to end is seen as a continuing event it is much easier to establish cause and connection between original wrongdoer and final damage. If, on the other hand, the situation is compartmentalised into separate events then it becomes possible to apportion harm to independent causes.

Thus, in *Baker v Willoughby*[59] the defendant negligently caused an injury to the plaintiff's leg which subsequently had to be amputated when the leg received a further injury as a result of a shooting by robbers. Was the defendant to be liable for the loss of the leg? The House of Lords thought that the defendant should be so liable: the 'loss' suffered by the plaintiff was the same whether he had a stiff leg or an amputated leg and so the second injury did not obliterate the loss caused by the first accident. The supervening event did not reduce the plaintiff's loss and he 'should not have less damages through being worse off than might have been expected'.[60] The loss in this case was not so much a loss in the economic sense as one flowing from personal injury, and so the approach of the House of Lords is perhaps understandable – although it is by no means clear if *Baker* would be decided the same way today.[61] Would the analysis have been the same if the damage had been property damage rather than personal injury? In *Carlogie SS v Royal Norwegian Government*[62] the defendants carelessly damaged the plaintiffs' ship with the result that the vessel needed long-term repairs which could only be carried out on the other side of the Atlantic. While crossing the Atlantic the ship suffered further damage in a storm which in turn meant that the repairs took much longer than they would have done if the boat had not encountered the storm. Were the defendants to be liable for loss of profits arising from these further repairs? The House of Lords thought that they would not be so liable since the second damage obliterated the first.

In both of these examples the *novus actus* resulted from external factors. However, the new intervening act can also come from the plaintiff himself and in this situation the same test is applied: was the intervention 'reasonable' in the circumstances? Now in interpreting 'reasonable' in this factual sense care must be taken to assess the act in the context of all the surrounding circumstances; consequently, an act which might at first

58 See *The Oropesa* [1943] P 32.

59 [1970] AC 467.

60 Lord Pearson at p 495.

61 *Cf Jobling v Associated Dairies Ltd* [1982] AC 794.

62 [1952] AC 292.

sight appear unreasonable could be deemed reasonable in the circumstances of an emergency.[63] Indeed even an objectively 'unreasonable' act like suicide can be deemed 'reasonable' in the context of factual causation.[64] All the same, a person who takes risks when he has suffered, say, a leg injury might find that such action is deemed unreasonable with the result that any extra damage flowing from this unreasonable act cannot be attributed to the defendant who wrongfully caused the original leg injury.[65] It may seem odd that a disabled plaintiff who fails to take proper care of himself can be deemed 'unreasonable' while a person who deliberately causes further injury or death to himself can be deemed to have acted 'reasonably'. Yet it has to be remembered that the judge in these circumstances is assuming the role of a jury and thus is entitled, as a matter of procedure, to take each case on its own facts.[66] Often judges will cite previous cases, but assessing factual causation and reasonableness is not a matter of precedent as such. No doubt judges should be sensitive to the policy factors inherent in the case law, but factual causation is very dependent upon how one analyses and views the facts.

4 REMOTENESS OF DAMAGE

Causation did not end with the jury verdict since the judges reserved for themselves the power to deny liability, or a head of liability, on the ground that the defendant's wrong was not the legal cause of the plaintiff's harm. The third level at which causation can operate, then, is the level of law.

(a) Fact and law

At this level the court is holding as a matter of law that the defendant was not the cause of the plaintiff's harm and the metaphor adopted is that of 'remoteness'. The law can disregard some heads of damage, or indeed the whole of the harm suffered by the plaintiff, on the basis that it is too remote from the breach of obligation. In contrast to factual causation, remoteness ought in principle to be governed by precedent in that it is a question of law: thus, the emphasis is not so much on the causal link itself between breach and harm as on the nature of the interest protected (Ch 6 § 3) and the policy factors attaching to certain kinds of liability. Nevertheless, precedent is not always of help at the level of factual analysis given the infinite complexities of the topic in question and so what counts is the legal test applicable. Such a test is governed by precedent, but can vary depending on the cause of action in issue and the nature of the damage suffered by the victim.

---

63 *The Oropesa* [1943] P 32.

64 *Pigney v Pointers Transport Ltd* [1957] 1 WLR 1121.

65 *McKew v Holland & Hannen & Cubitts* [1969] 3 All ER 1621.

66 *Qualcast (Wolverhampton) Ltd v Haynes* [1959] AC 743.

(b) Directness test

The general test of liability in the 19th century is still to be found in ss 50 and 51 of the Sale of Goods Act 1979: 'The measure of damages is the estimated loss directly and naturally resulting, in the ordinary course of events, from the ... breach of contract ... ' This test was also applied in the law of tort up until 1961, and so, for example, where the defendants carelessly set fire to some grass cuttings and the fire spread to the plaintiff's cottage, destroying it, the defendant was held liable for this damage on the ground that it directly flowed from the wrongful act.[67] Again in *Re Polemis*[68] the Court of Appeal held that charterers of a ship were liable for its destruction when one of their employees negligently let slip a plank which fell into the hold causing a spark which ignited petrol vapour. The total destruction of the vessel was not to have been anticipated from the mere falling of a plank, but the loss directly flowed from the negligent act and thus the damage was not too remote.

In both of these examples the harm was physical and the directness principle no doubt worked well enough. Indeed in the case of the charterers an analogy can be made with bailment: a hirer (bailee) is normally responsible for the *res* hired unless he can prove that the destruction occurred without fault on his part.[69] But what if the owner of the cottage or the ship were to claim, in addition to the physical damage (*damnum emergens*), loss of profits (*lucrum cessans*)? Is this loss of profits the direct result of the defendants' wrongful act?

(c) Contemplation test

In order to cope with these kind of *lucrum cessans* problems the 19th century courts developed, or at least borrowed from French law,[70] the test that the loss of profits must have been in the contemplation of the party in breach of contract. In *Hadley v Baxendale*[71] a bailor of a mill shaft sued the bailee, a carrier, for the value of the shaft plus lost profits when the mill shaft was delayed in transit causing a prolonged stoppage of the mill. In refusing the lost profits, the Court of Exchequer laid down the rule that damages for breach of contract should be those 'either arising naturally, ie according to the usual course of things, from such breach of contract itself, or such as may reasonably be supposed to have been in the contemplation of both parties, at the time they made the contract'.[72] Several points arise from this decision. First, is there one rule or two?[73] The judgment of Alderson B seems to indicate that damages may be awarded on the basis that they arise naturally from the breach and this suggests that he was preserving the directness test. However, another interpretation might be that he was subjecting the

67 *Smith v London & South Western Ry* (1870) LR 6 CP 14.

68 [1921] 3 KB 560.

69 Weir, *Casebook*, pp 208–09.

70 CC art 1150.

71 (1854) 156 ER 145.

72 Alderson B at p 151.

73 Treitel, *Remedies*, para 131.

directness rule to the contemplation test. Thus, to go back to the facts of *Re Polemis*, could the defendant charterers have claimed that the destruction of the whole ship was not to be contemplated? In fact such an argument appears to have made little headway with the Court of Appeal and in *Vacwell Engineering v BDH Chemicals* (above § 2(a)) the idea that the damage was unforeseeable counted for little. The effect of Alderson B's rule seems to be, then, that the directness rule applied to *damnum emergens* while the contemplation test was concerned with *lucrum cessans*.

Nevertheless, there remain difficult cases. In *Parsons (Livestock) Ltd v Uttley Ingham & Co*[74] the sellers of a pig food hopper failed to remove, when erecting the hopper on the plaintiff's land, some sticky tape holding closed a ventilator at the top of the hopper and the lack of ventilation caused the pig food nuts to go mouldy. The mouldy nuts in turn caused a rare illness in the pigs which devastated the plaintiff's herd. Were the sellers of the hopper to be contractually liable for the death of the pigs? A majority of the Court of Appeal thought that they should be so liable since there was a 'serious possibility of injury and even death among the pigs'. However, Lord Denning MR, who differed to some extent from the other two judges, was of the view that liability should be restricted to the *damnum emergens*. More confusing still was the view of the trial judge, perhaps misconstrued by the majority in the Court of Appeal, who appeared to be basing liability on the directness test as laid down in the Sale of Goods Act. If *Parsons* does nothing else, it at least shows that it would be dangerous to dismiss the facts of the old directness cases.

(d) Foreseeability test

Lord Denning MR in *Parsons* also thought that the test of liability should, in cases of physical damage to property, be governed by the foreseeability rather than the contemplation test. This leads to a second point to arise out of the judgment in *Hadley v Baxendale*: what is meant by 'contemplation' and what is the relationship of such a notion with another term used in the law of obligations, that of 'foreseeability'? The question is important not just because the directness test in the law of tort has been replaced, as a result of the Privy Council decision in *The Wagon Mound (No 1)*,[75] by the foreseeability test, but also because the relationship between directness, contemplation and foreseeability can depend upon the specific factual nature of the problem. In *Parsons v Uttley Ingham* the decision seems to suggest that in respect of the dead pigs the difference between the three tests can depend upon both the obligational relationship between the parties and the interest in play. In fact the problem is intertwined with the question of factual causation and contributory negligence. If the seller should have contemplated that mouldy nuts might possibly make pigs seriously ill, why was the plaintiff pig farmer not deemed the cause of his own damage given that he continued to feed the mouldy nuts to his pigs? One answer no doubt is that the buyers were

74 [1978] QB 791.

75 [1961] AC 388.

relying on the skill of the sellers and thus the emphasis on directness and contemplation. If one views the problem in terms of foreseeability it raises an awkward question about the behaviour of the plaintiff.

In fact a similar problem lies at the heart of *The Wagon Mound (No 1)*. The defendants had carelessly allowed bunker oil to escape into Sydney harbour and this oil drifted under the plaintiffs' wharf where welding operations were being carried out. The plaintiff halted operations in order to seek expert advice as to whether such oil was a fire risk; having been assured that there was not a fire risk, the plaintiff continued the welding and this caused the oil to catch fire which in turn led to the destruction of the wharf. The plaintiffs brought an action in negligence against the defendants claiming that the damage to their wharf was the direct result of the spillage of oil, but the Privy Council, overruling the directness test, held the defendants not liable on the ground that the damage was unforeseeable. It might seem odd that such damage was deemed unforeseeable, yet the plaintiffs were in an awkward position: if they pleaded that the fire was foreseeable, then they themselves should not have continued with the welding. Remoteness thus became eclipsed by factual causation. In *Parsons* contributory negligence had no role since the claim was based in contract (cf § 5(a) below); the defendants had promised a result.[76] Yet, had the foreseeability approach been emphasised, it might have led the judge to see the facts in a way that might not have been advantageous to the plaintiff farmer.

The problem therefore in trying to compare contemplation with foreseeability is that one ends up comparing two different obligations. According to Lord Reid in *The Heron II*[77] the foreseeability test in tort is much wider than the contemplation test in contract: 'The defendant will be liable [in tort] for any type of damage which is reasonably foreseeable as liable to happen even in the most unusual case.' But if the defendant is not to be liable in *The Wagon Mound* (foreseeability test) but is to be liable in *Parsons* (contemplation test) one can legitimately ask what Lord Reid was trying to say. Indeed it is difficult not to sympathise with Lord Denning MR in *Parsons* that the key factor ought not to be the nature of the obligation but the type of damage. One applies the same test (foreseeability) to physical damage cases irrespective of the obligation broken.[78] In truth both judges have a point. The difficulty with contract is that it involves the expectation interest and this can raise special problems which, in theory, do not arise in tort – or at least in the tort of negligence – since there seems to be no duty of care in respect of pure economic loss.[79] Accordingly, the role of remoteness in the law of contract is one of limiting liability; the remoteness rule of *Hadley v Baxendale* is, as in French law, simply an implied limitation clause that takes effect in all contract cases[80] and is a rule primarily designed to deal with problems of *lucrum cessans*. The foreseeability principle, in contrast, is a remoteness rule designed to

76 *Barclays Bank Plc v Fairclough Building Ltd* [1995] QB 214.

77 [1969] 1 AC 350.

78 [1978] QB at pp 801–04.

79 *Spartan Steel & Alloys Ltd v Martin & Co* [1973] QB 27.

80 Weir, *Casebook*, p 209.

handle problems of *damnum emergens*; its purpose is to establish a link between breach of duty and damage, and once the link is established, its role, in physical damage cases, is then to delimit the extent of the restoration interest. Thus, in tort, a defendant must 'take his victim as he finds him', a rule that seems to echo the old directness test[81] but in truth is more a means of linking the tort with the restoration interest in personal injury cases. In contract a defendant may indeed be directly liable for physical damage in terms of the restoration interest as *Vacwell Engineering* and *Parsons* indicate. But where the contemplation rule has its specific role is in limiting claims for lost profits which can so easily be slipped in under the expectation interest. Put another way, remoteness of damage cannot be divorced from the question of protected interests (cf Ch 6 § 3).

(e) Typical damage

Tony Weir suggests that the directness, contemplation and foreseeability tests are not comprehensive enough to cover certain kinds of physical damage problems. He adds a further test called the typical damage test.[82] This test results from the decision in *Hughes v Lord Advocate*[83] where a small boy was badly injured while playing with one of the defendant's paraffin lamps used to guard an open manhole in the street. The injury did not arise from fire as such but from an explosion caused when the lamp fell into the manhole, and the defendants resisted liability by arguing that, although injury by burning was foreseeable, injury by explosion was not. The House of Lords, in refusing to accept this argument, seemed to be holding that the damage was typical enough to establish cause and connection in law; the accident was caused by a known source of danger and a distinction drawn between burning and explosion was too fine to warrant acceptance. It might seem, then, that such an approach involves a mixture of the directness and the foreseeability tests: if the defendant could have foreseen some kind of damage then he will be liable for all the direct damage that actually flows from the wrongful act, at least where the damage is physical. Where the harm is economic loss the defendant will not necessarily be liable under the directness principle; he will only be liable for the typical losses that flow from the wrong.[84]

In fact the position is more complicated since, once again, it involves how one views the world (*cf* Ch 6 § 2(d)). If explosion and fire are seen as quite separate events then it is possible to attach separate causal chains to the two events with the result that one event might be foreseeable and the other unforeseeable. If, on the other hand, fire and explosion are lumped together as a single, universal event, then only one causal chain need come into play; if the 'fire-explosion' event is foreseeable the defendant will be liable whether the damage is actually caused by a fire or by an explosion. Take another example. D negligently allows his farm to become infested with rats and this is obviously a source of danger for his visitors and employees; however, P, an employee,

81 See eg *Robinson v Post Office* [1974] 1 WLR 1176.

82 Weir, *Casebook*, p 10.

83 [1963] AC 837.

84 Treitel, *Remedies*, para 130.

contracts a rare and unforeseeable disease from rats' urine (Weil's disease). Can P recover damages from D? It has successfully been argued that the damage is unforeseeable, thus rendering D not liable.[85] But this decision seems extraordinarily unjust given that the damage suffered is directly linked to the source of the danger. If the judge had asked whether rats present health problems and whether the plaintiff had suffered a health problem caused by rats it is difficult to see how the defendant could have escaped liability. The point of the typical damage test is, then, to deal with these kinds of problems: the test invites the court to look at the damage that actually occurs, and not at the way it occurs, and if this damage as a whole can be linked to the breach of duty then there will be sufficient cause in law.

5 CAUSATION AND DAMAGES

The tests considered so far apply, on the whole, at the level of substantive law rather than at the level of the law of actions (remedies). However, there is a fourth level at which causation can function and that is the level of damages as a remedy. Here liability is not being denied as such, but the damages themselves might be reduced on the basis that the defendant was not the cause of this part of the damage. In other words, either the plaintiff or some third party or event might be deemed to be the cause of part of the damage suffered by the plaintiff.

(a) Contributory negligence

Where a plaintiff has partly caused his own damage a court now has power to apportion damages between plaintiff and defendant. Thus, if the defendant is 60% to blame and the plaintiff 40% to blame for the plaintiff's damage the court can reduce the defendant's (fully assessed) damages by 40% under the Law Reform (Contributory Negligence) Act 1945. Before this statutory intervention contributory negligence was a matter of factual causation (above § 3) and this meant that in situations where the plaintiff had suffered damage partly as a result of his own fault the court could treat this fault as a *novus actus interveniens* isolating the defendant from any liability whatsoever. In other words, the plaintiff's own negligence broke the chain of causation. By the end of the Second World War this approach was seen as unjust in that it could be used to shift the risk of industrial accidents off the employer and on to the worker. The effect of the 1945 Act is to move contributory negligence from the level of factual causation to the level of the law of remedies and this usually means that a plaintiff who himself has been at fault will at least receive something. Nevertheless, the Act does not prevent a court from continuing to treat a contributory negligence problem as one of factual causation: thus, in one case it was held that an employer would not be liable to the wife of an employee killed while not wearing a safety belt because the evidence showed that even if the employer had not been in breach of his duty to supply belts the employee would not have worn one.[86] Indeed in contract cases contributory negligence continues to be

85 *Tremain v Pike* [1969] 3 All ER 1303.

86 *McWilliams v Sir William Arroll* [1962] 1 WLR 295.

treated as a problem of factual causation in that the 1945 Act applies exclusively to tort;[87] only if the facts disclose, in addition to a breach of contract, a cause of action in tort will the Act be applicable.[88]

This all-or-nothing approach is evident in a number of contract cases. In *Parsons v Uttley Ingham* (above § 4(c)) the court could not, it seems, have applied the 1945 Act as this was a claim based on breach of s 14 of the Sale of Goods Act. If an action had been founded in negligence as well, there seems no reason in principle why the damages should not have been apportioned; but it does not follow that all breaches of s 14 amount to carelessness, and it may be that the failure to remove the sticky tape, while rendering the hopper itself unfit, did not amount to behaviour that could be deemed negligent.[89] Similarly, in *Ingham v Emes*[90] the plaintiff was denied compensation on the ground of her own failure to disclose to a hairdresser that a product which the hairdresser used, and which caused the plaintiff to suffer dermatitis, had once before caused her problems. As Denning LJ observed, 'This looks like a plea of contributory negligence, or a plea that Mrs Ingham was the author of her own misfortune' but 'that has never been pleaded or found'.[91] However, he arrived at the same result through an interpretation of the implied term of reasonable fitness itself: the customer, in failing to disclose, did not make known to the hairdresser the particular purpose for which the product was required (cf Ch 8 § 5(f); Ch 10 § 6).

(b) Mitigation

Unreasonable behaviour by a plaintiff can also bring into play another, quite separate, damages rule also designed to deal with problems of causation. A plaintiff cannot saddle a defendant with losses that the plaintiff himself could have avoided. Thus, to give the classic example, if D dismisses P in breach of contract P is under a 'duty' to search for a new job in order, so to speak, to cut down his loss. Indeed this rule used to be analysed in terms of a 'duty to mitigate', but such an approach gave the impression that a failure to mitigate would amount to a legal wrong. In fact, as Sir John Donaldson pointed out, a plaintiff 'is completely free to act as he judges to be in his best interests'; what he cannot do is to try to claim that his act, or failure to act, is necessarily a consequence of the defendant's original breach of duty.[92] The question, once again, is that of reasonableness.

Just what amounts to unreasonable behaviour is not always an easy or uncontroversial matter. In *Darbishire v Warran*[93] the Court of Appeal held that a

87 See eg *Quinn v Burch Brothers* [1966] 2 QB 370.

88 See generally *Barclays Bank Plc v Fairclough Building Ltd* [1995] QB 214.

89 See eg *Doughty v Turner Manufacturing Co* [1964] 1 QB 518. And see also *Barclays Bank Plc v Fairclough Building Ltd* [1995] QB 214.

90 [1955] 2 QB 366.

91 At p 374.

92 *The Solholt* [1983] 1 Lloyd's Rep 605, 608.

93 [1963] 1 WLR 1067.

plaintiff was not entitled to claim the full cost of having his vintage car repaired after it had been seriously damaged in a collision caused by the defendant's negligence. The claim was unreasonable because he could have purchased a similar vehicle on the open market at a price which was less than the repair bill. 'The question', said Pearson LJ, 'has to be considered from the point of view of a businessman.' The case has come in for criticism on the basis that a private individual ought not to be subjected to a reasonable businessman test,[94] but it now seems in line with the attitude displayed by the House of Lords in *Ruxley Electronics v Forsyth* (Ch 6 § 4(b)). The courts will not compensate what they consider idiosyncratic heads of damage, although one might ask whether the plaintiff in *Darbishire* might now be able to claim for mental distress. Or, put another way, the consumer, as a price for special status, is to be subject to the laws of economics. Just how far these laws of economics will be taken is not entirely clear; in one recent case a judge commented that the question of mitigation is not to be answered solely in terms of the commercial optimum, for it would be a grey world indeed if such were to be the case.[95]

6 CAUSATION AND UNLAWFUL BEHAVIOUR

The rule of mitigation dictates that a plaintiff must behave reasonably. But what if the plaintiff's behaviour is not just unreasonable in a private law sense, but unlawful in the criminal law sense? P and D embark upon a bank robbery and P is badly injured as a result of D's negligent driving of the getaway car: can P sue D for damages? P supplies D with an unlawful drug and D refuses to pay: can P claim either the price in debt or the drugs in restitution? P consents to being physically tortured by D: can P later claim damages in trespass? These kinds of problem raise two broad legal issues: to what extent does, first, unlawful behaviour and, secondly, consent, break the chain of causation between wrongful act and damage? A third question, which really goes to the remedy, is the extent to which one can use the law of property to avoid delicate questions of behaviour in the law of obligations.

(a) Illegality

Illegality can affect a plaintiff's claim in a number of ways. It may bring into play the principle *ex turpi causa non oritur actio* (no action arises out of an illegal cause) which in turn may be seen as part of the more general principle that 'no one should be allowed to take advantage of his own wrong'. Thus, where a gang of bank robbers engage in a robbery and one of them is injured as a result of the careless driving of the getaway driver, the injured robber will probably not have an action against the driver.[96] But what if one of the robbers viciously assaults another in an argument over the stolen money? Again the unlawful nature of the whole enterprise may well act as a bar to any action.[97] But much may depend upon the nature of the illegality and the surrounding

94 Weir, *Casebook*, p 642.

95 Rougier J in *Thomas v Countryside Council for Wales* [1994] 4 All ER 853, 859.

96 *Ashton v Turner* [1981] QB 137

97 *Murphy v Culhane* [1977] QB 94.

circumstances: if the unlawful behaviour is only incidental to the plaintiff's cause of action the court may ignore the illegality. Accordingly, one test is whether the action arises directly out of the illegal cause. In *Pitts v Hunt*[98] two youths, plaintiff and defendant, were riding a motor cycle in a highly dangerous manner with the result that it collided with a car injuring the plaintiff. The defendant, the driver of the bike, had no licence or insurance and was drunk while at the controls; the plaintiff, his passenger, had not only also been drunk but had actively encouraged the dangerous driving. The Court of Appeal held that the passenger was not entitled to recover damages from the driver. Would the result have been the same if the passenger, although having knowledge of the absence of licence and insurance, had nevertheless pleaded with the driver to go carefully?

The *ex turpi* principle also applies in contract. Thus, where the owners of a coach hired to a prostitute sued for the hire fees the court held that they could not succeed since they knew that the coach was to be used for immoral purposes.[99] This case is not quite so straightforward as it might at first seem since a contract to hire a coach is, unlike, say, a contract to have someone killed or even a contract to supply an illegal drug, *per se* a legal transaction; it became illegal in law because of the knowledge of both parties. But what if the owners of the coach had been completely unaware of the hirer's motives? The problem then becomes one of illegal performance by one or by both parties and the emphasis shifts from the law of obligations to the law of remedies.[100] Can the contract be enforced? Much will depend upon the knowledge of the plaintiff pursuing a remedy. P contracts with D, a road haulier, for D to carry P's property from Leeds to London and en route there is an accident caused by the negligence of D: what is the position if (i) D had put all of P's property on one lorry, thus overloading it in contravention of statute; or (ii) D did not have a licence to carry goods belonging to other people? If P has no knowledge of the illegality he can probably sue D for damages;[101] however, if P acquiesced in the overloading he will be denied a remedy in damages.[102] What if P only discovered the illegality after the performance of the contract: can he refuse to pay the freight fee? In this situation much will depend upon how the court interprets the relevant statute: did Parliament intend to prohibit this kind of contract or did it intend only to impose a penalty for infringement? In the case of the overloading it may be that the D could claim in debt if he delivered the goods without damage to London, provided the court drew an analogy with carriage by sea.[103] But much will depend upon the circumstances, the statute, the nature of the illegality and the knowledge of the parties. And so it may be that the court would take the view that the object of the statute was road safety and

98 [1991] QB 24.

99 *Pearce v Brooks* (1866) LR 1 Ex 213.

100 See eg *Marles v Philip Trant & Sons Ltd* [1954] 1 QB 29.

101 *Archbolds (Freightage) Ltd v S Spanglett Ltd* [1961] 1 QB 374.

102 *Ashmore, Benson, Pease & Co Ltd v A V Dawson Ltd* [1973] 1 WLR 828.

103 *St John Shipping Corporation v Joseph Rank Ltd* [1957] 1 QB 267.

that this policy would dictate the prohibition of any contract that compromised such a policy.

(b) Proprietary claims

Illegal contracts also give rise to problems in the law of restitution as the freight example above suggests. P delivers goods to D under a hire purchase contract that turns out to be illegal. P supplies a prohibited drug to D and D refuses to pay. Can P reclaim his property in these situations? The main problem facing P is another maxim that is attached to illegal contracts: *in pari delicto portior est conditio possidentis* (where parties are equally in the wrong the possessor is in the stronger position). Like the *ex turpi causa* principle, this second maxim would appear to deny any claim in restitution where the parties both have knowledge of the illegality and thus it is unlikely that the unpaid supplier of illegal drugs would be allowed to bring an action. Nevertheless, the supplier of machinery under an illegal contract may have a claim in the law of property (or more specifically the tort of conversion) (Ch 13 § 8(a)) if he can rest his cause of action on his *in rem* relationship with the property rather than upon the illegal *in personam* contract. And such a claim, which will be technically for damages for conversion, may not be thwarted by the defendant's selling of the machines.[104] In other words, the plaintiff may be able to trace his property or its proceeds at common law (Ch 11 § 4(b)).

More generously, the House of Lords has allowed one person to recover a house which had been transferred to another person as part of a social security fraud. The transferor was able to rely upon a resulting trust arising from the transfer rather than upon the illegal contract.[105] If the plaintiff is able to base the action upon a right *in rem*, rather than upon the contractual obligation *in personam*, that is enough to allow recovery.[106] Viewed from the position of causation, one can say that the illegal behaviour is not causally linked to the nature of the institutional relationship in issue: ownership, unlike obligation, is a matter of legal right independent of the merits of the owner's behaviour.[107] And only in exceptional cases will restitution be denied.[108]

(c) Consent

A third maxim which can prevent a plaintiff from recovering in an action based on the law of obligations is *volenti non fit injuria* (consent to injury is no injury). Such a maxim overlaps with illegality inasmuch as unlawful behaviour might be deemed a species of consent,[109] but, evidently, it is much wider in scope. Consent to damage, or to a risk

104 *Bowmakers Ltd v Barnet Instruments Ltd* [1945] KB 65.

105 *Tinsley v Milligan* [1994] 1 AC 340. See also *Tribe v Tribe* [1995] 3 WLR 913.

106 *Tinsley v Milligan* [1994] 1 AC 340, 370.

107 Thus, contributory negligence is no defence to an action in conversion or intentional trespass to goods: Torts (Interference with Goods Act) 1977 s 11(1).

108 *Tribe v Tribe* [1995] 3 WLR 913.

109 *Murphy v Culhane* [1977] QB 94.

of damage, will prevent one party from transferring to another party via the law of obligations harm that falls within the risk.[110] In contract consent usually takes the form of a written clause in the contract itself and thus the problem is often one of interpretation (Ch 8 § 5(f)) and exclusion clauses (Ch 10 § 4).[111] However, it may also be imported into contract via, for example, consideration[112] or equitable estoppel.[113] The law of restitution makes use of estoppel as well,[114] but consent is the idea behind the notion of a voluntary payer; one who consents to a payment may well be denied recovery on the basis that he has volunteered the payment[115] and a similar principle may well apply where a person confers benefits in kind without any antecedent request.[116] In tort consent and *volenti* are specific defences to claims for damages and such defences can be viewed as species of causation in that they link the risk of damage with the plaintiff's behaviour as opposed to the defendant's.[117] Thus, a surgeon is not liable in trespass to a patient if the patient has expressly or impliedly consented to the treatment.[118]

The problem of course is what amounts to consent and whether such consent can be vitiated by misrepresentation and by non-disclosure. Indeed there is the further problem of the person who, for reasons of incapacity or unconsciousness, cannot give or withhold consent. There is no doubt that a woman's consent to sexual intercourse will be vitiated by fraud and thus she will have an action for trespass;[119] equally, the doctor who performs a circumcision instead of a tonsillectomy will be open to a claim for damages in trespass.[120] However, where things go wrong in hospitals the courts prefer that the claim is handled in negligence rather than in the tort of trespass since it is deemed that the patient has generally consented to treatment.[121] And where a patient is unconscious, or has refused consent, the appropriate remedy is, according to the Court of Appeal in *Re T*,[122] an action by the doctor for a declaration that the treatment is lawful. Such a claim will consider the problem in terms of the 'patient's best interest' which, where a patient has seemingly refused consent, will be considered, in turn, within the context of the 'conflict between two interests, that of the patient and that of the society in which he lives'.[123] The right of the individual to refuse treatment is

110 See eg Occupiers' Liability Act 1957 s 2(5).

111 But cf Unfair Contract Terms Act 1977 s 2.

112 See eg *Williams v Roffey Brothers & Nicholls (Contractors) Ltd* [1991] 1 QB 1.

113 See eg *Central London Property Trust Ltd v High Trees House Ltd* [1947] KB 130.

114 *United Overseas Bank Ltd v Jiwani* [1977] 1 All ER 733.

115 See on this point the dissenting judgments in *Woolwich Building Society v IRC* [1993] AC 70.

116 See eg *Sumpter v Hedges* [1898] 1 QB 673.

117 *Morris v Murray* [1991] 2 QB 6. Note however that the *volenti* doctrine cannot apply to the passenger of a drunk driver: Road Traffic Act 1988 s 149(3).

118 See eg *Chatterton v Gerson* [1981] QB 432. See also *Arthur v Anker* [1996] 2 WLR 602.

119 *Chatterton v Gerson* [1981] QB 432, 442.

120 *Chatterton v Gerson* [1981] QB 432, 443.

121 *Sidaway v Governors of the Bethlem Royal Hospital* [1985] AC 871.

122 [1992] 3 WLR 782.

123 Lord Donaldson MR at p 796.

paramount, but in case of doubt – for example, in respect of the patient's capacity to decide – the public interest of preserving life will take precedence. Moreover, the courts will not treat this kind of problem in terms of an exclusion clause, and so even if the patient has signed a form absolving the hospital from liability this may well not protect them; there is an overwhelming obligation on doctors and hospitals to save lives and if they fail in this obligation it could leave them open to an action by the estate.[124]

(d) Necessity

Where a patient is in no position to consent it may be that a doctor will be able to resist liability in trespass on the basis of necessity (*cf* Ch 13 § 5(c)). Again the better remedy will be an action for a declaration before any operation is carried out, but where a person trespasses upon another in order to save the latter's life the actor will have committed no wrong. This point was reaffirmed by the House of Lords in the case of *In re F (Mental Patient: Sterilisation)*[125] where a hospital had sought a declaration that they could carry out a sterilisation on a 36 year old woman with a mental capacity of a five year old child. In granting the declaration reference was made to the principle of necessitous intervention in general.[126]

Now what is important in respect of this general principle of intervention is that it reveals several problems with respect to liability. First, there is the question of whether the intervenor is exposing himself to an action by his act of intervention; the test seems to be framed around the best interests of the individual whose consent cannot in the circumstances be sought.[127] In the case of personal injury and health the best interests test is understandable enough. But what if the intervention is with respect to the interests of another? D removes one of P's kidneys to save the life of a child. This kind of problem has arisen with respect to property and financial damage, and it is one of the issues at the heart of *Esso v Southport Corporation* (Ch 1 § 7(a)). How can it be negligent to do an act calculated to save lives? This problem arose again in *Rigby v Chief Constable of Northamptonshire*[128] where the police recaptured a dangerous criminal who had taken refuge in the plaintiff's gun shop only at the cost of destroying the building. The police fired CS gas into the shop and this started a fire, but when sued for damages by the owner of the shop the police raised the defence of necessity. As it happened, the judge was able to find that the police had been negligent and thus the plaintiff (or his insurance company) got his damages. But what if there had been no negligence? In this situation the judge held that the defence of necessity would be available as a defence to trespass and to an action under the rule of *Rylands v Fletcher* (Ch 12 § 2(a)). The public interest would, it seems, take precedence over the private interest.[129]

124 Lord Donaldson at p 798.

125 [1990] 2 AC 1.

126 See Lord Goff at pp 74–75.

127 *Airedale NHS Trust v Bland* [1993] AC 789.

128 [1985] 1 WLR 1242.

129 *Cf Miller v Jackson* [1977] QB 966.

A second question with respect to necessitous intervention is whether the intervenor can be accused of deliberately exposing himself to, and thus consenting to, the risk of injury. Where a rescuer intervenes to save lives this *volenti* argument has been unequivocally rejected on grounds of policy[130] and thus the defendant whose breach of obligation created the dangerous situation will be deemed to have foreseen that a rescuer might intervene.[131] Indeed such an intervention will not preclude a claim for nervous shock.[132] But what about the person who intervenes to save property? There is some evidence that the courts will not be so generous.[133] Nevertheless, much might depend upon the circumstances. If a person attempts to save the PhD thesis of his student neighbour from a fire caused by the defendant's negligence and is injured in the attempt it may be that the courts will not reject the rescuer's claim for damages.[134]

In these rescue cases the plaintiff was claiming damages for harm suffered. But a third problem with respect to intervention focuses on the remedy of debt: can an intervenor who expends money and time in protecting another's interest claim this expense as a non-contractual debt? In civil law such a claim has been known since Roman times;[135] but common lawyers have been more reluctant. Where there is a pre-existing relationship between the parties the intervenor may well have a claim for expenses as an agent of necessity[136] and such a right may even be one of the elements of bailment (Ch 8 § 3(c)).[137] But there is no general doctrine of *negotiorum gestio* (management of another's affairs) in English law and even the existence of an emergency will not in itself give rise to a debt claim. As Lord Goff observed in the case of *In re F*, 'officious intervention cannot be justified by the principle of necessity'.[138] Much will always depend upon the interests in play.

7 CAUSATION AND NON-MONETARY REMEDIES

Most of the causation problems encountered in the private law of actions and obligations involve the remedy of damages. This is because causation is primarily concerned with linking harm and reparation and the most common remedy for repairing damage is damages. Even the declaration cases are usually about the possibility of liability in trespass. Nevertheless, important causal questions can be found in non-monetary cases as well. For example in *Redgrave v Hurd*[139] the purchaser of a solicitor's practice sought rescission in equity (Ch 5 § 3) of the contract of purchase on the

130 *Baker v Hopkins* [1959] 1 WLR 966.

131 *Haynes v Harwood* [1935] 1 KB 146.

132 *Chadwick v British Railways Board* [1967] 1 WLR 912.

133 *Cutler v United Dairies* [1933] 2 KB 297.

134 *Cf Attia v British Gas* [1988] QB 304, 320.

135 See generally D.3.5; CC art 1375.

136 *GNR v Swaffield* (1874) LR 9 Ex 132.

137 *The Winson* [1983] AC 939.

138 [1990] 2 AC at p 76.

139 (1881) 20 Ch D 1.

ground that the seller had misrepresented the income; the seller insisted that the contract be performed on the ground that the purchaser was the cause of his own loss in not examining the books before agreeing to buy. The Court of Appeal held that the law would infer that the misrepresentation was the cause of the purchaser entering the contract and they granted rescission. In contrast it could be said that the reason why the majority of the Court of Appeal refused an injunction against the cricket club in *Miller v Jackson* (Ch 4 § 1(b)) was, in part, because the plaintiffs were the cause of their own mental distress: the plaintiffs 'must have realised that it was the village cricket ground, and that balls would sometimes be knocked from the wicket into their garden'; and if 'they did not realise it, they should have done.'[140]

Specific performance (along with, of course, damages and declaration) can also raise causal questions. If one party refuses to perform a contract on the basis that an external event has so frustrated the commercial basis of the transaction that the parties are freed from their obligation, the other party, if he wishes to enforce the obligation, will have to show, for example, that the frustrating event was self-induced (Ch 10 § 8(f)). This is a question of causation and fault.[141] Equally, a party wishing to enforce a promise will have to show that such a promise is either supported by consideration given in return for that promise – in other words, that there is a connection between the consideration moving from both parties – or has acted as the basis upon which the party has relied to his detriment so as to form an estoppel. Again these kinds of problem can raise cause and connection issues. Such issues may not always be clear since they are hidden behind other notions such as 'self-induced' frustration and 'past consideration'. But from the position of factual analysis legal problem-solving across the law of obligations is often, *inter alia*, a matter of linking behaviour with result.

140 [1977] QB 966, 989 *per* Cumming-Bruce LJ.

141 See eg *The Super Servant Two* [1990] 1 Lloyd's Rep 1.

PART II

THE LAW OF OBLIGATIONS

CHAPTER EIGHT

INTRODUCTION TO CONTRACTUAL AND NON-CONTRACTUAL OBLIGATIONS

The previous chapters have, on the whole, attempted to examine private law from the position of – to use Roman terminology – the law of actions: for one starting point of legal thinking, owing to the historical legacy of the forms of action (Ch 3 § 4), has been the institution of the remedy. Can the plaintiff obtain an injunction to stop the defendants' cricket balls from landing in the plaintiff's garden? Can the plaintiff obtain the cost of a new swimming pool from a defendant contractor who has failed to produce the product specifically requested by the plaintiff? Nevertheless, there has since the abolition of the forms of action (if not before) been another aspect to English law. Actions cannot support themselves but need to be founded upon a cause; and once it is appreciated that the role of actions was simply indirectly to give expression to these causes the easier it becomes to see that it is the substantive foundation of the action and not its form that makes up the object of legal knowledge. *Obligatio mater actionis*, said the medieval Roman lawyers (obligations are the mother of actions);[1] and the maternal categories that acted as the basis for these obligations were, by Justinian's time, the categories of contract, quasi-contract, delict and quasi-delict.[2] These categories, or most of them, will act as the framework for the second half of this book.

1 OBLIGATIONS AS A CATEGORY

The civil codes do not as between themselves take an identical approach towards the law of obligations. The *Code civil* for example sees obligations as an extension of the law of property,[3] whereas the German BGB rigidly distinguishes personal relations (obligations) from real relations (property).[4] In the New Dutch Code the classification is rather different again. Book three of the Dutch code deals with patrimonial rights in general and thus actually mixes both property and obligations, although, having done this, the code continues to insist on the distinction between real and personal rights.[5] No doubt it might be claimed by some that one code is more true to Roman law than another, but this would be false; all of the different approaches have some basis in the *Institutiones* of Gaius or Justinian and the idea that an obligation is a form of property is specifically Roman.[6] Moreover, it has to be emphasised that the Romans themselves

1 A-J Boyé, '*Variations sur l'adage "Obligatio Mater Actionis"*' in *Mélanges Le Bras* (Sirey, 1965), pp 815–33.

2 J.3.13.2.

3 Thus, Book III of the French Code is entitled *Des différentes manières dont on acquiert la propriété*. See generally Jolowicz, *Foundations*, p 75.

4 Jolowicz, *supra*.

5 NBW Bk 5 art 1; Bk 6 art 1. Bk 3 art 1 states: 'Property is comprised of all things and of all patrimonial rights.'

6 G. 2.14.

did not think in terms of rights even if they started to separate obligations from actions. The modern codes take their classification structure from a Roman pattern that was largely defined by the existence of different types of action; thus, the Romans did not distinguish as such real rights from personal rights. They distinguished between *actiones in rem* and *actiones in personam*.[7]

What the Romans did, but the modern codes do not really do, is to define an obligation. Justinian said that an obligation was a *vinculum iuris* (a legal chain) binding two parties to perform something according to the laws of the state.[8] This metaphorical idea has been retained by the modern civil law. Thus, French law talks of an obligation as *un lien de droit*[9] uniting two legal subjects *à donner, à faire ou à ne pas faire quelque chose*[10] while Dutch law tends to see it as a statutory and patrimonial relationship between two or more persons giving rise on the one hand to a right and on the other to a duty.[11] In fact the New Dutch Code does not give a definition of an obligation; but legal doctrine describes it as a patrimonial relationship between two or more persons on the basis of which one person is entitled to a prestation *vis-à-vis* the other person, and the other is obliged to perform his prestation. 'Obligation' should not be confused with 'legal duty' (cf Ch 3 § 3(e)), although the precise distinction between them remains unclear.

In all civil law systems the parties are referred to as creditor (right) and debtor (duty), these terms having a much wider definition than in English law; and the object of an obligation is the right of performance.[12] This notion of performance is important from a legal object point of view since it is something that must be distinguished from a physical asset that may form the object of a contract. Accordingly, if S contracts to sell B a cow, but fails to perform the contract of sale, the obligational right of B is to the performance of the contract rather than to a direct right in the cow itself. That is to say, the object focuses on the verb *dare* (*donner*, to give) and not on the physical object of the cow.[13] Of course, matters become complicated when the contract itself acts as a conveyance of title to the cow in that the buyer might well gain a property as well as an obligational right. All the same, it is a fundamental characteristic of the civil law to keep these two kinds of right separate. Ownership attaches to the thing (*res*) itself and there is little room for nuance. However, the parties to an obligation are under a duty to act reasonably and fairly in Dutch law[14] and in French law contracts (*conventions*) must be performed in good faith.[15] Just what these terms mean has given rise to

7 But *cf* P Stein, 'The Development of the Institutional System', in PG Stein & ADE Lewis (eds), *Studies in Justinian's Institutes in memory of JAC Thomas* (Sweet & Maxwell, 1983), pp 151–63.

8 J.3.13pr.

9 See eg Malaurie & Aynès, no 1.

10 CC art 1101.

11 NBW Bk 3 art 1; Bk 6 art 1.

12 Ourliac & de Malafosse, p 16.

13 See eg NBW Bk 3 art 296.

14 NBW Bk 6 art 2.

15 CC art 1134.

difficulties since Roman times but there is no doubt that the doctrine of *bona fides* is another distinguishing characteristic of the civil law.[16] Obligations, then, are strictly binding, but the iron chain (*vinculum iuris*) they constitute is enclosed in the velvet cover of a certain moral responsibility.

Obligations are usually legally enforceable and thus are closely associated with the formal sources of law. However, there are some obligations which are not and the most important of these, recognised originally in Roman law,[17] is the *obligatio naturalis* (natural obligation). Accordingly, in addition to the *vinculum iuris*, there is in civil law a *vinculum aequitatis.*[18] Such an obligation may arise to prevent the recovery of a payment made in circumstances where the law will not recognise an enforceable obligation as such but will recognise, indirectly, a moral or social obligation.[19] Equally, a natural obligation may exist in certain social relationships where the law, while not recognising a right, may recognise a duty. Thus, in Roman law a natural obligation was held to exist in certain situations where the legal obligation was unenforceable or had never come into existence because of some procedural or structural problem with the law.[20] In the later civil law, under the influence of the canonists, this notion of a natural obligation evolved and developed and in modern French law it is now closely associated with moral duties and individual conscience; the *vinculum aequitatis* thus became a vehicle for incorporating moral obligations into the positive law. It has been suggested that gambling debts, unenforceable in French law, might now be founded on a natural obligation and while such an analysis is not without its problems[21] it does illustrate the kind of situation where a natural obligation might be relevant. To put it briefly, a natural obligation may prevent an enrichment without legal cause from becoming an unjustified enrichment.

Although, as we have seen (Ch 1), the term 'law of obligations' is being used with increasing frequency in English law[22] it can never have quite the same meaning for common lawyers as it does for the continental jurist. There are two main reasons for this *décalage*. First, in the continental systems the law of obligations is part of a complete logical system of private law (Ch 1); in England such a logical system is, despite *Blackstone's* use of the Roman institutional scheme, largely absent (Ch 3). The English lawyer has traditionally thought only in terms of autonomous legal categories like contract, tort, real property, family law and so on.[23] Secondly, the continental systems, following Justinian, have always had an abstract notion of a *vinculum juris,* that is to say a legal chain binding two persons,[24] pre-existing any legal action or sanction; in England

16 See most recently Quebec CC art 1375.

17 Zimmermann, pp 7–10.

18 D.46.3.95.4

19 See NBW Bk 6 art 3.

20 Ourliac & de Malafosse, pp 203–07.

21 Malaurie & Aynès, no 1131.

22 See eg Zimmermann; A Tettenborn, *An Introduction to the Law of Obligations* (Butterworths, 1984); J Cooke & D Oughton, *Common Law of Obligations* (Butterworths, 2nd edn, 1993).

23 Stein, *Institutions*, pp 125–29.

24 *Ibid*, p 184.

there has, historically at least, rarely been any notion of an abstract *in personam* obligation pre-existing a legal remedy. English law has, instead, usually started out from the idea of an invasion of an interest and it is the invasion rather than the relationship which has triggered liability. Moreover, the mechanisms of liability were not founded upon substantive relationships; the forms of action acted as the main focal point and these were institutions which at one and the same time described the right, the remedy and the procedure applicable. Only in the area of debt has there been some firm idea of a pre-existing relationship and even this relationship was both more proprietary than obligational and more transactional than abstract.[25] There has, historically, never been a law of obligations in the common law. What there was, and to some extent there still is, was a 'law of liability' and a 'law of remedies'.[26] Put another way, common lawyers never developed the notion of a law of obligations as a technique in itself designed to achieve, efficiently, certain ends.[27]

The abolition of the forms of action gave English lawyers the opportunity to reconsider these forms of liability and to some extent ideas from civil law were imported into English law.[28] Thus, liability became a matter of actions founded on contract and actions founded on tort (cf Ch 3 § 4).[29] This development has, without doubt, allowed English law to fashion some notion of an *obligatio* in that actions are said to have causes and these causes have been interpreted in terms of 'duties' *ex contractu* and *ex delicto*.[30] Thus, in 1870 Kelley CB observed that acts and facts do not of themselves constitute a cause of action; to 'make up a cause of action ... it is necessary to import the preceding contract'.[31] And in tort there had to be either a wrong 'or breach of some positive duty'.[32] Indeed there is even an attempt to link the action for money had and received (Ch 11 § 2(a)) with the Roman *condictio indebiti*, suggesting in turn the third obligations category of quasi-contract.[33] Yet even though it is possible to talk of contractual and tortious 'duties' this notion of a duty does not have the same structural significance as the civilian *obligatio*. For a start, duty is not linked, as we have seen, to any pre-existing logical model of rights; it arises in an empirical fashion out of particular factual situations or as a result of specific pieces of legislation. Furthermore there is no abstract *vinculum iuris* that applies generally within the law of tort; as Lord Griffiths said in 1993, if one invites a lady to one's house 'one would naturally think of a duty to take care that the house is safe but would one really be thinking of a duty not

---

25 Milsom, p 263.

26 R David & D Pugsley, *Les Contrats en Droit Anglais* (LGDJ, 2nd edn, 1985) no 72.

27 *Cf* J-L Gazzaniga, *Introduction historique au droit des obligations* (PUF, 1992), pp 95–101.

28 Gordley, pp 134–60.

29 *Bryant v Herbert* (1877) 3 CPD 389.

30 See eg *Alton v Midland Ry* (1865) 34 LJCP 292, 296; *Taylor v Manchester, Sheffield & Lincolnshire Ry* [1895] 1 QB 134, 138.

31 *Durham v Spence* (1870) LR 6 Ex 46, 50.

32 Willes J in *Gautret v Egerton* (1867) LR 2 CP 371, 375.

33 Willes J in *GWR v Sutton* (1869) LR 4 App Cas 226, 249; *cf* Lindley LJ in *Taylor v Manchester, Sheffield & Lincolnshire Ry* [1895] 1 QB 134, 138.

to rape her?'.[34] Of course, things may change. But whether one century of academic law has the capacity to overcome many centuries of forms of action thinking is debatable;[35] for the development of a law of obligations in the continental sense of the term within English law will, as has already been suggested (Chs 1 and 3), require a rethinking of the English law of property (*cf* Ch 13 § 8).

2 CONTENT OF AN OBLIGATION

All the same, once one has shifted the emphasis from the idea of a *vinculum iuris* to a law of liability and remedies it does become possible, with the help of the notion of a duty, to work back from the liability and remedy to some kind of pre-existing relationship. Or, at least, it becomes possible to do this in contract problems and in a number of tort situations. Thus, with regard to damage caused carelessly the common law has deliberately used the idea of a pre-existing relationship – the duty of care relationship – as the basis for extending the implied duty of care contractual term[36] to non-contractual situations.[37] It is not, therefore, the causing of damage which triggers liability, although damage and cause remain essential ingredients; it is the breach of a pre-existing duty of care that acts as the cause of the action (Ch 12 § 3(a)). A similar analysis can be applied to the tort of breach of statutory duty (Ch 12 § 4(a)). It is not so much the damage which is the basis for the action as the breach of a pre-existing duty imposed by the statute in relation, often, to some specific place or thing. If the duty exists there will be liability, but if it does not exist can be no liability, however unfair this may seem in relation to, say, employers' liability in general.[38]

Duty must not, however, be confused with obligation in the technical sense of each term. In civil law the notion of an obligation primarily expresses a legal bond and once it exists it simply becomes a matter of determining whether the obligation has been performed not. Non-performance, unless it can be justified, is the starting point of liability. In the common law breach of duty is a more complex notion in that the term duty is meaningless in the abstract; whether or not a person is in breach of a duty will depend upon the intensity of the duty itself. As Lord Griffiths indicated, there are some kinds of behaviour which are so disreputable that it is worthless even conceptualising the invasion of the interest in terms of a pre-existing duty. Yet there are many other situations where the behaviour itself can be measured only in terms of a pre-existing duty. Thus, whether or not the owner of a coach let out on hire is to be responsible for a latent defect which causes injury is dependent upon the nature of the duty attaching to those who hire out goods.[39] If the duty attaches to the thing itself – that is to say, if the thing hired out must be reasonably fit for its purpose[40] – then the duty is effectively

34 *Stubbings v Webb* [1993] AC 498, 508.

35 *Cf* Lord Goff in *Henderson v Merrett Syndicates Ltd* [1995] 2 AC 145, 184–85.

36 See now Supply of Goods and Services Act 1982 s 13.

37 *Donoghue v Stevenson* [1932] AC 562.

38 *Haigh v Charles Ireland Ltd* [1974] 1 WLR 43; *cf Knowles v Liverpool CC* [1993] 1 WLR 1428.

39 *Hyman v Nye* (1881) 6 QBD 685.

40 See now Supply of Goods and Services Act 1982 s 9.

a high one in the sense that the owner will be liable even if the thing is unfit through no fault of his.[41] One talks in these cases of the owner's duty to supply goods of a particular standard and such a duty finds its normative foundation in the contractual promise; it is an implied term (*cf* Ch 10 § 6) of the contract of hire or sale that the goods are reasonably fit for their purpose and of satisfactory quality. In tort duties are often not so high because the normative foundation has to be located elsewhere than in the promise; such a foundation is usually located in the behaviour of the defendant, but this foundation mitigates against the idea of strict duties since the law would appear to be demanding the impossible.[42]

In some factual situations, it must be said, the notion of duty can eclipse its legal source category in that the court will pay little regard to whether the action is contractual or tortious.[43] In other cases, however, the source of the duty can be crucial.[44] Accordingly, in determining questions of liability, it can matter not only whether the duty relationship actually existed between defendant and plaintiff (*cf* Ch 12 § 3(a)), but whether this duty arose out of statute, when it is the words of the statute which will determine the level of duty,[45] or out of factual circumstances when it will be promise, fault, intention to injure or intention to act which will determine the intensity of the duty. Indeed, in the absence of a logical and scientific structure of private law it is these factual circumstances that can determine at one and the same time both the legal source of the duty (contract or tort) and the level of diligence required. The question, then, whether a defendant has promised a result (strict liability) or is merely under a duty to take reasonable care (fault) is not a question that is determined by the idea of a pre-existing obligation (*vinculum iuris*) as such. It is a question to be determined by the level of duty itself which, in turn, can be achieved by reference to the legal source – for example, the court holds that the duty is contractual rather than tortious[46] – or, if there already exists a definite contractual relationship, by the nature of the contract and the kind of term implied. As we have seen, in a contract for the supply of goods the level of duty is normally high in that liability is determined with reference to the objective quality of the goods themselves. With regard to a contract for the provision of a service the duty is normally only to take reasonable care. In turn this choice as to the level, although now largely enshrined in statute, was originally governed by notions of risk, loss-spreading or some other socio-economic policy which the judges thought the law should reflect.[47] When it comes to tort, the level of duty question may be governed either by the nature of the cause of action (for

41 *Frost v Aylesbury Dairy Co Ltd* [1905] 1 KB 608.

42 *Readhead v Midland Ry* (1869) LR 4 QB 379.

43 *Midland Bank Trust Co Ltd v Hett, Stubbs & Kemp* [1978] 3 All ER 571, 595; *Henderson v Merrett Syndicates Ltd* [1995] 2 AC 145.

44 *Davie v New Merton Board Mills Ltd* [1959] AC 604; *cf* Employers' Liability (Defective Equipment) Act 1969.

45 Compare, for example, s 4 with s 13 of the Supply of Goods and Services Act 1982.

46 *Lockett v A & M Charles Ltd* [1938] 4 All ER 170.

47 See eg *Hyman v Nye* (1881) 6 QBD 685; *Young & Marten Ltd v McManus Childs Ltd* [1969] 1 AC 454.

example, public nuisance or defamation) or by the burden of proof doctrine of *res ipsa loquitur*, although these devices may be hidden within the facts themselves.[48] Thus, a high duty is owed at common law by an occupier, and perhaps a landlord, of premises adjoining the highway to persons on the highway and this high duty can be expressed through the tort of public nuisance or by a shifting, or partial shifting at least, of the burden of proof in the tort of negligence.[49] English law does not easily think in terms of an obligation in respect of the control of things (*cf* Ch 12 § 5), but it can reach the same result on occasions by the manipulation of the facts which give rise to the duty.[50]

3 SUBJECTIVE ACTS AND OBJECTIVE FACTS

One fundamental distinction made by civil lawyers is that between subjective legal acts, such as making a will or a contract, and objective facts such as the happening of some event (for example, accident and damage) over which legal subjects have little or no control. Legal facts will include any fact which creates a legal effect and so such facts can be caused by human acts; equally, they can be quite separate, relatively speaking, from human acts and will thus include birth, death, age, the passing of time and the like. Human acts can be either subjective juridical acts, that is to say the legal effect is created by the will (*volonté*) of a person, or objective in the sense that the legal effect is independent of *volonté*. Thus, the creation of a work of art, science or literature is an objective legal fact in that, although it is subjective to the creator, it is independent of any intention to create a legal act as such.

(a) Legal acts and legal facts

The emphasis on factual circumstances in the common law system, and the formal distinction between a law of contract and a law of tort,[51] might suggest at first sight that English law also makes a distinction similar to continental law between the legal act and the legal fact.[52] And to some extent it does distinguish between acts intended to have legal effects, external events and voluntary acts that are not intended in themselves to have legal effects. But on closer examination it will be found that the division between legal ('juridical') acts and legal facts is largely unhelpful simply because it is unable to reflect with any consistency the difference between contractual and tortious situations in the common law. As we shall see (below § 5(c)), the basis of contract in English law is promise rather than agreement and this has led the courts to concentrate upon objective statements, that is to say upon the promise as an objective fact, as much as upon any notion of *volonté*. Whether or not a person is liable in contract can depend just as much upon the existence of objective facts as upon any specific intention to be

48 See eg *Esso Petroleum Co Ltd v Southport Corporation* [1953] 3 WLR 773 (QBD); [1954] 2 QB 182 (CA); [1956] AC 218 (HL); *Ward v Tesco Stores Ltd* [1976] 1 WLR 810.

49 *Mint v Good* [1951] 1 KB 517.

50 See in particular the judgment of Denning LJ in *Esso v Southport* [1954] 2 QB 182 (cf [1956] AC 218).

51 *Bryant v Herbert* (1877) 3 CPD 389; County Courts Act 1984 s 15(1).

52 See eg J Dupichot, *Le droit des obligations* (PUF, 4e.éd, 1993).

bound. Thus, if one person makes to another a statement capable of being construed as a promise and this promise fulfils all the objective requirements of an enforceable contract, then the fact that there was no intention to perform a legal (juridical) act is irrelevant.[53] Indeed the existence of an objective relationship close to a contractual one (legal fact) can even be a reason in itself for making a statement (representation) by one party a legal fact capable of giving rise to a tortious duty of care.[54] The English law of obligations is, in other words, more interested in the objective than the subjective.[55]

The question, then, whether the duty is contractual or tortious – or even equitable (*cf* Ch 4 § 5(e), (g)) – is a question that cannot be answered by reference to a dichotomy between subjective intention and objective events. The duty relationship, particularly in damages actions (as opposed to debt), is often determined objectively by the circumstances themselves, including perhaps the policy requirements (for example, certainty) of commercial law (*cf* below § 4). If the legal act has any relevance at all it is usually only at the level of linguistic interpretation – what did the parties mean by this or that word?[56] – or at the level of the effect of a contractual term such as, for example, a clause giving a defence to an action for failure to take reasonable care – did the parties mean to exclude liability for this loss?[57] And so whatever the source of the legal action one is continually forced back to the objective factual circumstances of the relationship of the parties, often in the context of the requirements of commerce rather than in the context of the subjective intentions of the parties as interpreted by the judge.

(b) Contract or contracts

This emphasis on factual circumstances gives rise to another characteristic in the area of contract: the rules applicable tend to be determined, at least in part, by the nature of the transaction in issue. Thus, the hire of a supertanker will attract one set of rules and attitudes,[58] while the sale of a kettle will attract another, perhaps rather different, set of propositions. Instead of thinking in terms of a law of contract one might, instead, think of a law of contracts. Indeed a fundamental characteristic of the Roman law of obligations was that liability for transactions was a matter of predetermined contractual categories – sale, hire, loan and the like[59] – and traces of this mentality are still to be found in the civil codes which, in addition to the articles dedicated to a general theory of contract, have sections dealing with the specific contracts inherited from Rome.[60]

---

53 See eg *Carlill v Carbolic Smoke Ball Co* [1893] 1 QB 256; *Blackpool & Fylde Aero Club Ltd v Blackpool BC* [1990] 1 WLR 1195.

54 *Hedley Byrne & Co Ltd v Heller & Partners* [1964] AC 465.

55 This is well brought out in *Blackpool & Fylde Aero Club Ltd v Blackpool BC* [1990] 1 WLR 1195.

56 *Cf L Schuler AG v Wickman Machine Tools Sales Ltd* [1974] AC 235.

57 *Cf George Mitchell (Chesterhall) Ltd v Finney Lock Seeds Ltd* [1983] 2 AC 803.

58 *Cf The Chikuma* [1981] 1 WLR 314.

59 T Weir, 'Contracts in Rome and England' (1992) 66 *Tulane Law Review* 1615.

60 Theoretically, the specific contracts are species of the general law of contract: See eg NBW Bk 6 art 213. General rules of contract apply except when statute provides specific rules for particular kinds of contract.

In fact, at the theoretical level, English law has specifically rejected the Roman analysis preferring instead to approach all transactions via a general theory of parol contracts (as indeed in modern civilian contract theory). Thus, specific contracts such as sale, hire, insurance, employment and the like are all species of a general law of contract.[61] The reason for this singular approach is to be found in history: the modern contractual action grew out of two main forms of action and the first form, debt, got swallowed up by the second form, *assumpsit*, at the beginning of the 17th century.[62] The general principle since that time is that contract is founded upon breach of promise sanctioned, at common law, either by a debt claim where the breach consists of a failure to pay what one has promised (*cf* Ch 4 § 5(b)) or by a damages action where one party has suffered damage as a result of the other party's breach (*cf* Ch 6). The debt and damages distinction is thus a characteristic, strictly speaking, of a law of actions rather than a law of obligations.[63]

All the same, it should be evident from the survival of debt and damages as conceptually separate causes of action[64] that the idea of an all-embracing general theory of contract is in need of qualification. Despite the existence of a general part to the English law of contract, the reality is that the rules governing many transactions are to be found in books on specific contracts. Thus, sale of goods, agency, insurance, hire purchase, partnership, charterparties (hire of ships) and various other types of contract have all attracted their own special pieces of legislation and their own textbooks. Indeed some areas of contract have now become almost separated from the law of obligations and form part of new classification categories such as labour and consumer law; and even the 'innominate' contracts tend to fall within identifiable patterns of factual transactions. Carriage of goods, for example, can be contrasted with sale transactions in shops and supermarkets and family arrangements can be compared with the hire of boats, cars and bicycles; equally, the purchase of a car can be contrasted with the sale of a house or the buying of a package holiday. Indeed some transactions transcend the category of contract itself with the result that new sub-categories such as professional and product liability are appearing within the law of obligations.

(c) Bailment

One reason why carriage of goods contracts tend to generate their own particular rules is to be found in the dichotomy between obligations and property.[65] Carriage of goods involves, in addition to any contract rights and duties, the legal relationship of bailment. This relationship arises out of any situation where one person (the bailor) transfers to another person (the bailee) the possession, but not the ownership, in a piece of moveable property (a chattel). In the absence of any specific contract the bailee owes to

61 *Ashington Piggeries Ltd v Christopher Hill Ltd* [1972] AC 441, 501–02.

62 *Slade's Case* (1602) 76 ER 1074.

63 *Photo Production Ltd v Securicor Transport Ltd* [1980] AC 827, 848–49.

64 *Overstone Ltd v Shipway* [1962] 1 WLR 117; *Jervis v Harris* [1996] 2 WLR 220.

65 See eg *The Albazero* [1977] AC 774.

the bailor a strict duty of care with regard to the chattel bailed and this duty can be discharged only by the bailee producing the goods to the bailor on demand or by the bailee proving that the goods were lost without any fault on his part.[66] In return, the bailor owes a duty to reimburse the bailee – in a commercial bailment at least – for any expenses incurred in the upkeep of the goods.[67]

Bailment thus has a central role to play in commercial and consumer law given that many business transactions involve the transfer of possession of goods. The hire of a car and the cleaning of a jacket both involve the transfer of possession in a chattel and while the duties and rights are normally contained within an accompanying contract the bailment may prove important when third parties become involved. In *Morris v C W Martin & Sons*[68] the owner of a mink stole sent it to a firm of cleaners for cleaning; this firm, with the owner's consent, sent it on to the defendants to clean. The employee of the defendants who was supposed to clean the stole stole it instead. The owner brought an action for its value against the defendants and the question arose as to whether the defendants, as a legal person, should be held liable for a criminal act committed by their employee, another legal subject in the eyes of the law. In holding the defendants liable, Diplock LJ specifically referred to the duties of bailor and bailee and pointed out that one 'of the common law duties owed by a bailee of goods to his bailor is not to convert them, ie not to do intentionally in relation to the goods an act inconsistent with the bailor's right of property therein.'[69] This duty, he said, is additional to the other common law duty of a bailee for reward to take reasonable care of his bailor's goods. If the bailee in the present case had been a natural person and had converted the plaintiff's stole by stealing it himself, no one would have argued that he was not liable to her for its loss. However, as Diplock LJ observed, the defendant bailees were a corporate person and they could not perform their duties to the plaintiff to take reasonable care of the fur and not to convert it otherwise than vicariously by natural persons acting as their servants or agents. 'Why', he asked, 'should they not be vicariously liable for this breach of their duty by the vicar whom they had chosen to perform it?'[70] Had the duty simply been a contractual duty the position would have been much more difficult since the contract between the first firm of cleaners (the bailees) and the defendants (the sub-bailees) contained a clause limiting the liability of the defendants. Equally, had the relationship been just a tortious one it is arguable that the courts would not have made one person liable for a criminal act committed by another person.[71] However, the moment one can establish a bailment the relationship and duty structure becomes subtly modified.

This relationship of bailment looks at first sight, then, similar to a real contract – that is to say, a (Roman law) contract having its origin in the transfer of a thing – and

66 *Mitchell v Ealing* LBC [1979] QB 1.

67 *The Winson* [1982] AC 939.

68 [1966] 1 QB 716.

69 At p 732.

70 At p 733.

71 *Smith v Littlewoods Organisation Ltd* [1987] AC 241.

no doubt the whole notion was originally influenced by Roman law.[72] Nevertheless, it must be stressed that although bailment is often closely associated with contract and with tort – the bailee might, for example, try to limit or exclude via a contractual term liability for loss and damage (*cf* Ch 10 § 4)[73] and the bailor's actual remedy is now the tort of conversion (*cf* Ch 13 § 8(a))[74] – the legal relationship itself belongs to the law of property rather than to the law of obligations.[75] Consequently, before liability can arise there must be the required mental element for possession.[76] Moreover, although the bailor's remedy is a claim for damages in tort, the law of damages itself reflects the property nature of the relationship by granting an action for the full value of the chattel lost,[77] save perhaps where this would lead to unjustified enrichment.[78]In other words, the original remedy in respect of a bailment, an action in detinue (now abolished in form and incorporated in substance within conversion),[79] was akin to an action *in rem*.[80]

(d) Tort or torts

In contrast to the law of contract and the law of bailment, the law of torts has its historical roots in a number of old writs – trespass, trover (conversion), nuisance and the action on the case – and this historical diversity of separate legal actions, each attracting its own procedural rules, has traditionally made it more difficult to see any unitary idea underlying the subject.[81] It is only with the development of negligence as an independent tort (*cf* Ch 12 § 3(a)) – a development that cuts across the old forms of action because it is a substantive normative idea rather than a remedial procedural category – that lawyers began to be able to think along the lines of a law of tort rather than torts. Yet even with the rapid expansion of negligence in this century, it remains difficult to perceive a common theoretical basis for a law of tort because the subject still finds itself having to perform a range of different functions. Non-contractual damages actions are used by the common law to protect personal, proprietary and economic interests on the one hand, and constitutional, property and personal rights on the other.[82] Moreover, correlative to these interests and rights are a range of duties differing in both extent and intensity; sometimes liability focuses on individual acts (*cf* Ch 12 § 3), where one searches for fault; at other times one looks only at the invasion

72 *Coggs v Bernard* (1703) 92 ER 107.

73 See eg *Levinson v Patent Steam Carpet Cleaning Co Ltd* [1978] QB 69.

74 Torts (Interference with Goods) Act 1977 s 2.

75 *Building and Civil Engineering Holidays Scheme Management Ltd v Post Office* [1966] 1 QB 247, 261.

76 *Ashby v Tolhurst* [1937] 2 KB 242.

77 *The Winkfield* [1902] P 42.

78 *Wickham Holdings Ltd v Brook House Motors Ltd* [1967] 1 WLR 295.

79 Torts (Interference with Goods) Act 1977 s 2.

80 *IBL Ltd v Coussens* [1991] 2 All ER 133, 137.

81 See generally B Rudden, 'Torticles' (1991–92) 6–7 *Tulane Civil Law Forum* 110.

82 Weir, *Casebook*, pp 14–15; *cf* P Cane, *Tort Law and Economic Interests* (Oxford, 1991).

of the plaintiff's right, as in the torts of defamation and trespass, or even the invasion of an interest, as in some of the economic torts cases. Liability for things (*cf* Ch 12 § 5) is recognised by statute if not by the common law itself;[83] but there is no general doctrine of strict liability that one can contrast with liability based upon fault (*cf* Ch 12 § 2). Much depends upon the cause of action in play[84] and the role of various control devices such as foreseeability.[85] Indeed, as we have seen (Ch 4), liability can be determined as much by the law of actions as by any reference to a law of non-contractual obligations and this has resulted in a situation where injunction cases have to be distinguished from compensation actions.[86]

The problem therefore with the notion of a law of tort is that such a category, in trying to protect so many different kinds of interests, simply ends up as a category with little internal unity. Some areas, such as private nuisance (Ch 12 § 5(b)) and breach of statutory duty (Ch 12 § 4(a)), are increasingly being treated as a species of fault liability;[87] other areas, such as defamation (Ch 13 § 1(b)) and conversion (Ch 13 § 8(a)), seem closer to the law of property than to the law of obligations.[88] Thus, it is difficult to describe these non-contractual damages actions as being founded upon 'wrongs' since some of them are clearly motivated by the idea of an interference with proprietary rights. One can call such interferences 'wrongs' in themselves,[89]but all this will do is to mask the fact that the law of tort(s) is a category that contains aspects of administrative, constitutional and property law.[90] In truth the law of torts bears witness to the fact that it can never be an obligations category in the sense of being a category that stands in contrast to a law of property category.

4 OBLIGATIONS AND EXTERNAL CLASSIFICATIONS

The categorisation of obligations works, so to speak, in two directions. First, one can talk about the sub-divisions operating within the law of obligations: that is to say, the sub-divisions into contract, tort and restitution (common law) or into contract, quasi-contract, delict and quasi-delict (French law). Secondly, one can talk about classifications which might be said to operate from outside the obligations category itself. Thus, the distinctions between the law of actions and the law of things (Roman law), or between public and private law (civil law), might be said to be classifications which function at a higher level than the law of obligations, and this raises the question of how these higher categories might affect the sub-categories within the law of

83 See eg Animals Act 1971.

84 See eg *Spring v Guardian Assurance Plc* [1995] 2 AC 296, 334, 351.

85 See eg *Leakey v National Trust* [1980] QB 485

86 See eg *Cambridge Water Co v Eastern Leather Plc* [1994] 2 AC 264.

87 See *Leakey* and *Cambridge Water* above.

88 Cane, *op cit*, p 105. Thus, damages awarded in defamation cases used to bear no relation to those awarded in personal injury or property damage cases (*Sutcliffe v Pressdram Ltd* [1991] 1 QB 153); the situation may now be changing: *John v MGN Ltd* [1996] 2 All ER 35.

89 *Cf* Torts (Interference with Goods) Act 1977 s 1.

90 See eg *Hussien v Chong Fook Kam* [1970] AC 942 (PC); *R v Chief Constable of Devon and Cornwall, ex p Central Electricity Generating Board* [1982] QB 458.

obligations. Thus, in French law the distinction between public and private law affects the law of obligations in a fundamental way, as we have already seen (*cf* Ch 2 § 2): *la responsabilité civile* must be distinguished from *la responsabilité administrative* – the former is governed by the *Code civil* while the latter is a product only of *la jurisprudence* of the *Conseil d'État* – and private agreements must be distinguished from administrative contracts. Equally, the distinction between civil and commercial law has exercised an important influence in the later history of the civil law.[91]

(a) Civil and commercial law

In Roman law itself the distinction between a business or commercial law on the one hand and a non-commercial or 'private' law on the other hand had little or no meaning other than in a very general sense in respect to certain types of property.[92] However, during the later life of Western law a distinction began to emerge between the law attaching to particular territories (customary, royal and Roman law) and the *lex mercatoria*, this latter system developing around the mercantile community of the late Middle Ages and functioning wherever trading fairs were held. It was a body of law that transcended the local systems and was thus truly universal in nature.[93] Nevertheless, it took ideas from all the various types of law, including the rediscovered Roman law, and fashioned these ideas for its own ends. Thus, for example, it was the law merchant that developed corporate personality and negotiable instruments using institutions from civil and from customary law. During the 17th century commercial law was seen in the France of Louis XIV as an aspect of public law and this helped consolidate a dichotomy that is still to be found in post-Revolutionary French law: the *Code civil* and the *Code de commerce* remain independent, in theory, one from the other.[94]

In England, however, the law merchant was said to have been captured for the common law by Lord Mansfield, but the reality is more complex. It would probably be more accurate to say that the common law was captured by the law merchant[95] with the result that the English law of obligations, or at least the law of contract, is the starting point for a commercial rather than a private law (in the French sense). The law exists to meet the reasonable expectations of businessmen rather than the desires of the private citizen.[96]

The traditional answer, then, to the question whether English law distinguishes between civil and commercial matters is to say that the distinction is ignored because the *lex mercatoria* was absorbed into the common law in the 17th and 18th centuries.[97]

91 See generally D Tallon, 'Civil and Commercial Law', *IECL* Vol VIII, Chap 2.

92 *Cf* Ourliac & de Malafosse, pp 45–46.

93 J Hilaire, *Introduction historique au droit commercial* (PUF, 1986), pp 39–43.

94 Tallon, *op cit*, paras 63–75. Dutch law has abandoned the distinction.

95 FH Lawson, *A Common Lawyer Looks at the Civil Law* (Ann Arbor, 1953), p 90.

96 See eg *Darbishire v Warran* [1963] 1 WLR 1067.

97 Tallon, *op cit*, paras 98–100.

Nevertheless, this absence of a distinction is often more a matter of form rather than practice in that in substance the courts and the legislature often do make distinctions between, on the one hand, commercial and business relationships and, on the other hand, private relationships. For example, commercial bailments are distinguished from non-commercial;[98] goods supplied in the course of a business attract different rules from goods supplied privately;[99] trade and finance purchasers are treated differently from private purchasers;[100] business liability is, for exclusion clause purposes, to be separated from non-business liability;[101] and the distinction between business and social contexts can be of vital importance in claims for financial loss arising out of careless statements.[102] The importance of these cases and statutes is that they show that at a factual level the dichotomy between civil and commercial (or business) law can be of relevance to the English law of obligations. Indeed, even at the procedural level the distinction has relevance to the extent that 'commercial actions' can be put into a special Commercial Court where they will be dealt with by a procedure more suited to the needs of the mercantile community.[103] Accordingly, if one asks whether the division between civil and commercial law exists as a formal category of legal rationalisation, the response of the judges will be to say that the only meaningful external distinction in English law is the one between civil and criminal proceedings.[104] But if one asks whether the commercial factual situation can be distinguished from the private relationship as a matter of argumentation and reasoning the response will have to be more reserved. Commercial law is a category that can play a role in the analysis of facts even if it has no place in the grand plan of English law.

Perhaps a more relevant dichotomy for common lawyers is a distinction between commercial law and public law. Traditionally, as we have said, neither of these categories has had any formal role in the common law, but with respect to local authorities there seems now to be a difference of attitude with respect to commercial and non-commercial plaintiffs. For example, a local authority must take care when negotiating contracts with commercial bodies not to cause loss through careless behaviour to those who invest time and money in preparing tenders. If they do cause such loss they may well be open to an action for damages on the ground, perhaps, that the public body must have some regard for the commercial expectations (interests) of the local business community.[105] Equally, the local business which wrongfully profits at the expense of the local authority may find itself immune from any restitution claims on the basis that it has caused no damage to any private individual.[106] In contrast public

98 *The Winson* [1982] AC 939.

99 See eg Sale of Goods Act 1979 s 14.

100 See *Stevenson v Beverley Bentinck Ltd* [1976] 2 All ER 606.

101 Unfair Contract Terms Act 1977 s 1(3).

102 *Hedley Byrne & Co v Heller & Partners Ltd* [1964] AC 465.

103 Supreme Court Act 1981 s 6; RSC Ord 72.

104 *In re Norway's Application* [1990] 1 AC 723.

105 *Blackpool & Fylde Aero Club Ltd v Blackpool BC* [1990] 1 WLR 1195.

106 *Surrey CC v Bredero Homes Ltd* [1993] 1 WLR 1361.

policy considerations may prevent damages claims from being brought by individuals against local authorities in situations where the local authority is acting in its capacity as guardian of the public interest. Thus, it may be difficult to bring a compensation action against a local authority in respect of a failure to prevent child abuse, or the failure to diagnose special educational needs, even though the authority may have been grossly negligent.[107] To the French lawyer this distinction may seem a curious one: why should the patrimony of the *commerçant* be given preference over the bodily integrity of the citizen? Several responses can be offered – mental damage has, for example, always caused difficulty for the courts – but the main problem is one of an absence of concepts for handling administrative liability and the kinds of damage it can cause. The 'breach of a public law right', as Lord Browne-Wilkinson reminded lawyers, 'by itself gives rise to no claim for damages'. If an injured citizen wants damages such a claim 'must be based on a private law cause of action'.[108] And these causes of action have, on the whole, been fashioned in the context of a commercial rather than political environment. It is largely a question of mentality.[109]

(b) Commercial and consumer law

The needs of commerce have, all the same, had to adapt to the growth and influence of an interest group which, at one and the same time, has given a new impetus to the traditional civil and commercial distinction as well as bringing it into question. This new interest group is that of the consumer. Perhaps the most obvious influence of consumer pressure has been felt in regard to the principle of freedom of contract (below § 5(e)) with the result that some areas of contract, where there had been frequent abuse of consumer interests, are now controlled by statute. Yet the influence of this class extends back at least a century where it can be seen to have been a determining factor in establishing a manufacturer's duty in respect of advertising[110] and the quality of products.[111] And this influence continues to be felt within the case law. The courts are now more willing to look at the status of the parties in certain kinds of contract and tort cases and to decide liability in terms of a policy which distinguishes the consumer from the commercial relationship. Thus, in principle the law of tort cannot, in commercial relationships, be used as a means of extending the law of contract;[112] but if the relationship is one involving loss to a consumer, and the insurance position is such that the consumer ought to be protected against this type of harm, then the courts may allow the tort of negligence to be used to extend what is in essence a contractual situation.[113]

107 *X (Minors) v Bedfordshire CC* [1995] 2 AC 633.

108 *Ibid* at p 730.

109 P Legrand, 'European Legal Systems are not Converging' (1996) 45 ICLQ 52.

110 *Carlill v Carbolic Smoke Ball Co* [1893] 1 QB 256.

111 *Donoghue v Stevenson* [1932] AC 562.

112 *Tai Hing Cotton Mill Ltd v Liu Chong Hing Bank Ltd* [1986] AC 80, 107.

113 *Smith v Eric Bush* [1990] 1 AC 831.

The modern European jurist ought accordingly to be thinking of contract in terms of commercial and consumer transactions rather than in terms of a division between a business and a private sphere.[114] This does not mean that there will not be cases where the courts might be asked to consider, say, family arrangements in the context of the rules of contract. Yet status as an issue in the law of obligations is increasingly concerning itself with the standing of particular classes *vis-à-vis* the supply of goods and services[115] and this has resulted in a significant decrease in what might be called areas of non-commerce. Private life, in other words, has become commercialised inasmuch as holidays,[116] home life[117] and house moves[118] are all now areas where the law of obligations has had to assume a role. This is not to say that such areas of non-commercial life were traditionally excluded from the law of obligations – contract, nuisance, trespass and the like always had their relevance. The point to be stressed is that the rise of the consumer has done much to incorporate such private areas into what might more generally be called economic law.[119] Leisure and privacy are now commodities, or legal objects, which determine, in turn, their own class of legal subjects. In the codified systems this development has, on the whole, been formally recognised; but it may be asked whether this is a development which will, in the long run, endanger the consistency of private law codification in that the notion of an economic law undermines the older distinction between public and private law.

(c) Public and private law

This distinction between public and private law is another division which causes rationalisation problems for the common lawyer.[120] It is a distinction which goes back to Roman law – Ulpian states at the beginning of the *Digest* that the *ius publicum* is concerned with the interests of the state, while the *ius privatum* deals with the private interests of individuals[121] – and it reflected an important difference between *imperium* and *dominium*, a difference still entrenched in modern Western political thought. *Imperium* represented the power (*pouvoir*) of command, nowadays described as sovereignty, which attached to the emperor and state; *dominium*, in contrast, was the power that each individual had as a result of private right (*ius*) and private property (*droit*). With the growth of the nation state after the late Middle Ages the notion of a *ius publicum* became an important means not only of constructing constitutional doctrines – often in truth using institutions from Roman private law[122] – but also of formulating a

114 Quebec CC art 1384.

115 See eg *Stevenson v Beverley Bentinck Ltd* [1976] 2 All ER 606.

116 *Jackson v Horizon Holidays Ltd* [1975] 1 WLR 1468.

117 *Ruxley Electronics Ltd v Forsyth* [1995] 3 WLR 118.

118 *Smith v Eric Bush* [1990] 1 AC 831; *Pitt v PHH Asset Management Ltd* [1994] 1 WLR 327.

119 A Jacquemin & G Schrans, *Le droit économique* (PUF, 3e.éd, 1982).

120 *X (Minors) v Bedfordshire CC* [1995] 2 AC 633.

121 D.1.1.1.2; Jolowicz, *Roman Foundations*, pp 49–53.

122 See generally B Tierney, *Religion, Law, and the Growth of Constitutional Thought 1150–1650* (Cambridge, 1982); J Canning, *The Political Thought of Baldus de Ubaldis* (Cambridge, 1987).

juridical political structure within which administrative and private legal relations could function without theoretical contradiction. Moreover, in France, a country where the notion of a central state became particularly pronounced in the seventeenth and eighteenth centuries, the dichotomy was used after the Revolution as a means of limiting the political power of the judiciary; private law stopped at the doors of government with the result that the administration and all its officials were, in an official capacity, sheltered from the *Code civil.* This area of non-law was subsequently filled by an extraordinarily rich case law from what became an administrative court, the *Conseil d'État,*[123] and today this institution is at the pinnacle of a whole structure of administrative courts and administrative appeal courts. Public law in France is a separate system of law from private law.

The dichotomy between public and private law is a general characteristic of all civil law systems.[124] However, in many civilian countries it is not so pronounced as it is in France and so in the Netherlands, for example, public bodies can use private law to attain some of their (public) goals. Equally, certain private bodies can use private or public law to protect class interests.[125] What public law does in general is to limit the right of public bodies to act as private citizens: if these public law rules do not provide a solution for a decision as to whether the relevant remedy is public or private the Netherlands supreme court (the *Hoge Raad*) has held that the private law remedy, if used, must not infringe on the public law applicable. This will involve an examination of the nature and the goals of the relevant public law and an important additional factor is whether similar results would have been attainable both in private law and in public law.[126] In principle, then, the use of private law by public bodies is acceptable because the open structure of private law, the New Dutch Civil Code, is sensitive to the safeguards that public law – especially administrative law – offers to the citizen.[127] Moreover, public and private law have nowadays become so entangled in areas such as environmental and construction law – not to mention tort actions against public bodies – that the distinction itself is becoming rather unrealistic. That said, it has to be emphasised that most civil lawyers, while no longer perhaps subscribing to the rigid French model, continue to believe that private law cannot replace the function of public law. Thus, administrative law is a system that generates its own particular principles – for example, *le principe d'égalité des citoyens devant les charges publiques* – which have meaning only within a context where the State or government body is a party.[128]

The public and private distinction causes problems for the common lawyer for both historical and conceptual reasons. Feudalism, the system in which the common

123 For a legal history of French administrative law see J-L Mestre, *Introduction historique au droit administratif français* (PUF, 1985).

124 Stein, *Institutions*, p 122.

125 NBW Bk 3 art 305a.

126 *De Staat der Nederlanden v Windmill*, NJ 1991 nr 393.

127 M Kobussen, *De vrijheid van de overheid* (Zwolle, 1991), Chs 3 & 4.

128 G Samuel, 'What is it to Have Knowledge of a European Public Law', in B De Witte & C Forder (eds), *The Common Law of Europe and the Future of Legal Education* (Kluwer, 1992) 171.

law developed, did not distinguish between *imperium* and *dominium* – indeed it used ownership as the basis of royal power[129] – and the forms of action were in theory a set of public law remedies.[130] Accordingly, an action in trespass was a public law remedy which protected what today would be seen as public law and private rights;[131] and even a seemingly public law remedy such as *habeas corpus* once had an important role in private (family) law (*cf* Ch 2 § 2(b)). Equally, government bodies had the right to use the common law to protect their interests either as against other public bodies[132] or as against individual citizens.[133] Moreover, in the 19th century the refusal to distinguish between public and private bodies in the eyes of the law was seen, politically, as a strength rather than a weakness in that it meant that all legal subjects were governed by the same (common) law and that government institutions and officials could claim no special status and protection from the law of the land.[134] Consequently, the modern law of obligations is in theory applicable to both public and private bodies alike.

However, as with the distinction between civil and commercial law, the position is not as simple as it first seems. At the general level it is certainly true to say that there is no distinction between private liability in tort and administrative liability in public law; commercial enterprises and governmental organs, together with private citizens and public officials, are equally subject to the same law of tort. Indeed some of the most important developments in the area of negligence have resulted from litigation involving central[135] and local government bodies.[136] Equally, in the law of contract, no formal distinction is made, at common law at least,[137] between private contracts and administrative contracts.[138] Thus, a local authority has the same commercial rights as any business enterprise.[139] Yet at a substantive level the courts now recognise that public bodies can present special problems for the law of tort (*cf* Ch 13 § 3) and that in contract there may be occasions when the public interest will affect the normal rules of contract[140]or indeed exclude it altogether.[141] Thus, gas, water and electricity are supplied pursuant to a statutory duty rather than a private law contract since the

---

129 RC van Caenegem, *An Historical Introduction to Western Constitutional Law* (Cambridge, 1995), pp 77–78.

130 R David & X Blanc-Jouvan, *Le droit anglais* (PUF, 7th edn, 1994), p 8.

131 See eg *Cooper v Wandsworth Board of Works* (1863) 143 ER 414.

132 For a modern example, see *Minister for Housing and Local Government v Sharp* [1970] 2 QB 223.

133 For a modern, but now discredited, example see *Bognor Regis UDC v Campion* [1972] 2 QB 169; *cf Derbyshire CC v The Times* [1993] AC 534.

134 Van Caenegem, *op cit*, pp 198–99.

135 See eg *Home Office v Dorset Yacht Co* [1970] AC 1004; *Yuen Kun Yeu v AG of Hong Kong* [1988] AC 175.

136 See eg *Murphy v Brentwood DC* [1991] 1 AC 398.

137 But *cf* Local Government Act 1988 s 17.

138 See eg *Blackpool & Fylde Aero Club Ltd v Blackpool BC* [1990] 1 WLR 1195.

139 See eg *Davis Contractors Ltd v Fareham UDC* [1956] AC 696; *William Sindall Plc v Cambridgeshire CC* [1994] 1 WLR 1016.

140 See eg *Staffordshire Area Health Authority v South Staffordshire Waterworks Co* [1978] 3 All ER 769.

141 See *Roy v Kensington & Chelsea Family Practitioner Committee* [1992] 1 AC 624.

relationship is not one founded upon negotiation.[142] Indeed the courts have even held that the public benefit aspect of gas, water and electricity is a reason for restricting the liability of what were then public bodies,[143] a use of public law that stands in contrast to the jurisprudence of the *Conseil d'État*.[144]

The reality seems to be, therefore, that although 'the common law does not – or at any rate not yet – recognise any clear distinction between public and private law', it is a distinction that 'is beginning to be recognised' in England.[145] Just what substantive consequences will flow from a recognition of the division is by no means clear as yet. In the area of tort it does not seem to be acting, as in France, as a means of extending liability without fault and this has the consequence that, in the absence of fault, the public interest will take precedence over the private when it comes to damage caused in pursuit of *le bien public*.[146]Indeed the cases suggest that public law will act as an excuse for restricting duties of care in respect of governmental organs that cause damage to citizens.[147] However, it may be that public bodies, in turn, will not be so free to use private law remedies to suppress some constitutional liberties.[148] In contract public law has the effect of preventing public bodies from being able to exercise private rights with the same degree of freedom as private persons; and so a refusal to contract without giving reasons will, for example, amount to an abuse of power.[149] Indeed a careless disregard for the commercial interests of local businesses tendering for public works contracts could lead to a claim for damages.[150] In addition, as we have seen, the courts may well take account of the public interest when it comes to the interpretation of contracts involving public bodies as parties.[151]

These exceptions to the normal principles of the law of obligations do not, however, form a coherent system of public law and thus it remains difficult to see how the division might function as an aspect of the law of obligations itself. What the dichotomy can do is to operate at the level of fact in distinguishing the public interest from the private within particular sets of factual situations. For example, it may be that a public body has to be more sensitive to the interests of those with whom it contracts or impacts upon and these interests will, in turn, help determine the way the various 'private' rights and duties are interpreted.[152] Equally, the public body may be able to

142 *Norweb v Dixon* [1995] 1 WLR 636.

143 *Dunne v North Western Gas Board* [1964] 2 QB 806.

144 *Cf* L Neville-Brown & J Bell, *French Administrative Law* (Oxford, 4th ed, 1993), p 184.

145 *In re Norway's Application* [1987] QB 433, 475 *per* Kerr LJ.

146 See eg *Rigby v Chief Constable of Northamptonshire* [1985] 1 WLR 1242; *X (Minors) v Bedfordshire CC* [1995] 2 AC 633.

147 See eg *Yuen Kun Yeu v Att-Gen of Hong Kong* [1988] AC 175; *X (Minors) v Bedfordshire CC* [1995] 2 AC 633.

148 *Derbyshire CC v Times Newspapers* [1993] AC 534.

149 *R v Lewisham LBC, ex p Shell (UK) Ltd* [1988] 1 All ER 938.

150 *Blackpool & Fylde Aero Club Ltd v Blackpool BC* [1990] 1 WLR 1195.

151 *Staffordshire Area Health Authority v South Staffordshire Waterworks Co* [1978] 3 All ER 769.

152 See eg *Blackpool & Fylde Aero Club Ltd v Blackpool BC* [1990] 1 WLR 1195.

take greater advantage of, say, the economic loss rule of negligence when it comes to defending actions for damages brought by irate citizens (*cf* Ch 13 § 9). What the division seems incapable of doing, as yet, is to act as the foundation for a discrete set of principles defining an administrative liability in contract, tort or restitution.

(d) Law of persons and law of things

The traditional refusal formally to distinguish between public and private litigants is in many ways part of a more general English habit of paying little regard to the need for a rational law of persons.[153] And this lack of a rationalised law of persons has in turn meant that there is no clearly defined notion of patrimony.[154] This is not to say that English law does not on occasions think in terms of status and capacity;[155] nor is it to say that it has no notion of the legal person.[156] Nor, also, is it to say that the common law does not hold the legal subject's tangible and intangible (corporeal and incorporeal) property responsible for his obligations.[157] The point to be made is that as the common law has no real tradition of a system of rights classified along the lines of Justinian's *Institutes*, it has not worked out a rational scheme of legal relationships between legal subjects and legal objects.[158] *Persona* and *patrimonium* have little independent existence outside of the standard categories of law or rules of procedure. The best one can say is that most of the problems concerning the law of persons likely to arise in the English law of obligations are handled either as integral parts of contract and tort or as issues to be dealt with at the level of the law of procedure.[159]

This lack of a rational structure underlying the law of persons is mirrored in the law of things by the lack of any theory concerning patrimony in the French sense of the term or *vermogen* in the Netherlands Civil Code. Instead the common lawyer thinks either of property – debts and the like being a form of intangible property (choses in action) – or of actions, the latter being assignable only if they can be described as commercial assets.[160] In fact one advantage in eschewing the continental notion of patrimony is that English law has no difficulty in conceiving of an independent 'patrimony': the trust in England does much of the work that the legal person plus patrimony does in the continental legal systems. Thus, one reason why English law can seemingly defy the classification system of Justinian's *Institutes* is because equity has been happy to turn legal objects – a patrimony – into what is in effect a legal subject: it is the trust itself that is often seen as being entitled to certain legal remedies like tracing (*cf* Ch 4 § 5(d)).[161]

153 But *cf* RH Graveson, *Status in the Common Law* (Athlone, 1953).

154 *Cf* B Nicholas, *French Law of Contract* (Oxford, 2nd edn, 1992), pp 29–30.

155 See eg *Stevenson v Beverley Bentinck Ltd* [1976] 2 All ER 606.

156 See *Tesco Supermarkets Ltd v Nattrass* [1972] AC 153.

157 County Courts Act 1984 s 85(1).

158 A Heldrich & A Steiner, 'Legal Personality', *IECL* Vol IV, Chap 2, Part 1, para 1.

159 See eg Trade Union and Labour Relations (Consolidation) Act 1992 ss 10, 12.

160 Weir, *Complex Liabilities*, para 42.

161 FH Lawson, *Selected Essays:* Volume I (North-Holland, 1977), p 60.

However, one area where English law does make use of a concept quite close to the notion of patrimony is the law of succession as it affects, *inter alia*, the law of obligations.[162] When a person dies all 'causes of action' subsisting for the benefit of, or against, the deceased will survive for the benefit of his or her 'estate'.[163] In the context of the law of obligations 'estate' takes the place of the deceased legal subject and acts as a kind of *corpus ex distantibus* in both the law of persons (*universitas personarum*) and the law of things (*universitas bonorum*) sense (*cf* Ch 2 § 8). It can, as a result, motivate a damages action on behalf of a victim killed by the defendant's tort or breach of contract, thus helping to ensure that the family receive compensation.[164] Sometimes, indeed, it can even motivate an equitable remedy like specific performance (*cf* Ch 5 § 4(d)) so as to ensure that a family member continues to receive an annuity or some other debt.[165] All the same the continued existence of a *persona* can also be the cause of problems within the law of obligations. Thus, if D contracts with C to confer a benefit upon P, the death of C will not alter the *vinculum iuris* structure between D and C from a law of obligations position; however, it might well have repercussions from a law of actions (remedies) position since C as an 'estate' might be rendered incapable of suffering certain kinds of loss. In *Beswick v Beswick*[166] the House of Lords, as we have seen (Ch 5 § 4(f)), had recourse to equity to get around this problem and in *White v Jones*[167] they used the law of tort. But the structural difficulty behind these cases is just as much a law of persons problem as a problem within the law of things in that obligation and loss (*res*) are being determined in accordance with a structure of persons (*personae*) that does not always conform to social reality. In cases like *Jackson v Horizon Holidays* (Ch 4 § 3) it is the family rather than the individual which is the real plaintiff (*cf* Ch 2 § 7).

5 CONTRACTUAL OBLIGATIONS

Persons and things cannot always be divorced even in the most scientific of systems since the law of obligations is dependent upon subjective aspects of the legal subject: intention, for example, is fundamental both to contract and to tort. Indeed in the civilian systems the whole modern idea of contract is based upon the will (*volonté*, *Willenserklärung*) of two legal subjects.[168] Civilian private law is premised on the fundamental right of self-determination and so the exercise of a right or the coming into existence of a *juris vinculum* is, then, left to the initiative and the free choice of the parties (the principle of autonomy).[169]

162 Heldrich & Steiner, *op cit*, paras 5, 12.

163 Law Reform (Miscellaneous Provisions) Act 1934 s 1.

164 On which see *Pickett v British Rail Engineering Ltd* [1980] AC 136.

165 *Beswick v Beswick* [1968] AC 58.

166 [1968] AC 58.

167 [1995] 2 AC 207.

168 Gordley, pp 162–64.

169 Von Mehren, *Formation*, paras 6, 31.

(a) Contract in civil law

Contract in civil law is governed by three principles. First, contracts are generally concluded by communion of the wills of the parties.[170] Secondly, once concluded, the parties are subject to rules attaching to the notion of contract itself; thus, a contract is binding upon the parties and has not only the legal effects intended by the parties, but also the effects based on statute, usage or the demands of good faith taking into account the nature of the contract.[171] The third principle is freedom of contract: parties should be free, within the limits of public law and public order, to make whatever contracts they wish, even if unreasonable to the outside observer.[172] These three principles form part of the general theory of contract but the existence of such a general theory does not preclude the recognition of several types of contracts such as mixed, nominated and non-nominated contracts. Consequently, following Roman law, the various civil codes denominate different types of contracts such as sale, hire and deposit.[173] Further distinctions are, for instance, contracts *ex consensu* and *ex re*, contracts for which formalities are statutory and contracts governed by ordinary principle and bilateral and unilateral contracts (*cf* below § 5(d)).[174] Principal contracts can be distinguished from auxiliary contracts, of which the *pactum de contrahendo* (*Vorvertrag*, *avant-contrat*, collateral contract) is a good example. Unilateral acts with intended legal effect created by the expression of will towards another person can be distinguished from contracts, and for the validity of such acts (for instance, an offer) it is often required that the declaration made to another, specifically determined, person must have reached that person. The distinction between these acts and contracts is difficult, but is an important aspect of civilian thinking.[175]

All civilian contracts are governed by the principle of *bona fides* which in Roman law meant commercial honesty, that is to say a kind of compromise between the pursuit of individual profit and dishonesty.[176] The notion reflected the idea that consensual contracts were mutually supportive relationships through which one could profit (including the gaining of an advantage over another)[177] but only to the extent that this was just. *Bona fides quae in contractibus exigitur aequitatem summam desiderat* (the good faith required in contracts is the need for the highest equity).[178] To quote an English judge:

> In many civil law systems, and perhaps in most legal systems outside the common law world, the law of obligations recognises and enforces an overriding principle that in

170 *Ibid*, para 6; Quebec CC art 1386. See generally G Rouhette, 'The Obligatory Force of Contract in French Law', in Harris & Tallon, pp 38–67. And see NBW Bk 6 art 217.

171 Von Mehren, *Formation*, paras 65–69; CC art 1135; Quebec CC art 1434; NBW Bk 6 art 248.

172 Zweigert & Kötz, pp 354–56.

173 See eg Malaurie & Aynès, pp 169–72.

174 See CC arts 1102–03; Quebec CC art 1380.

175 NBW Bk 6 arts 217–25; Bk 3 art 37.

176 Ourliac et De Malafosse, p 41.

177 D.4.4.16.4; D.19.2.22.3.

178 D.16.3.31pr.

> making and carrying out contracts parties should act in good faith. This does not simply mean that they should not deceive each other, a principle which any legal system must recognise; its effect is perhaps most aptly conveyed by such metaphorical colloquialisms as 'playing fair', 'coming clean' or 'putting one's cards face upwards on the table'. It is in essence a principle of fair and open dealing.[179]

Until recently the good faith provision to be found in article 1134 of the Code civil was, in contrast to some other civil law systems, of rather marginal importance; it never acted as a vehicle for setting aside unreasonable contracts since the autonomy of wills was always paramount. Today, however, it is a principle *en expansion*. Parties to a contract must adopt a behaviour which will inspire the confidence to be expected from a *iuris vinculum* based upon the exchange of assents.[180] As a result those who abuse their contractual – or indeed pre-contractual[181] – position run the risk of falling foul of article 1134. And this new role of good faith is shifting contract theory away from autonomy of wills (intention) towards ideas of confidence and contractual justice (reliance).[182]

A uniform definition of contract – leaving aside the question whether contract is dead or *en renaissance*[183] – is, not surprisingly then, almost impossible to determine. However, depending on the background of the jurist, an historical approach is probably one of the best ways of grasping the notion both at the abstract and at the transaction levels since the formal foundations are to be found in Roman law whilst the theoretical bases are post-Roman. In other words the notion of contract is absorbed by its long historical development.[184] Moreover, such an historical development encapsulates not just the writings and texts on contract(s); the law of persons, property and actions, together with non-contractual obligations, have also influenced the development of *la responsabilité contractuelle* and thus cannot be fully left out of account.

For the formalists, the notion of contract offered either by the Codes or the Restatement 2nd of the law on contracts (USA) is a sufficient starting point. Thus, a contract is either an agreement legally formed which has force of statute between those that have made the contract (French CC) or a promise or a set of promises for the breach of which the law will give a remedy (Restatement). These formalist definitions must never be underestimated in that they continue to determine the internal structure of contractual obligations. Nevertheless, they say little about the empirical basis of the subject and, consequently, economists and sociologists tend to take rather different views.

For the law and economics theorist, contracts are agreements concluding economic operations at the lowest transaction costs possible; in other words, contract in a free

179 Bingham LJ in *Interfoto Picture Library Ltd v Stiletto Visual Programmes Ltd* [1989] QB 433, 439.

180 Malaurie & Aynès, pp 342–43.

181 Von Mehren, *Formation*, para 123.

182 Malaurie & Aynès, p 332; Von Mehren, *Formation*, para 16.

183 *Cf* G Alpa, '*L'Avenir du contrat: aperçu d'une recherche bibliographique*' [1985] RIDC 7.

184 Von Mehren, *Formation*, paras 5–8; and see generally Gordley.

market is a means by which resources can be allowed to gravitate toward their most valuable uses.[185] Sociologists regard contract as one of the many types of agreements people can enter into, albeit that contracts are not strictly essential to make the market work. Thus, because the notions of contract vary fundamentally, contract should not be defined or at least only be defined in the traditional way so that the definition can change according to the circumstances.[186] In Netherlands law, contract (*overeenkomst*) is defined as an act realised through the consensus and interdependent will of two or more persons, with due observance of possible statutory formalities, created with intended legal effect for the benefit of one party or for the reciprocal benefit and to the charge of both (all) parties concerned.[187] The new Quebec Civil Code retains the traditional definition: 'A contract is an agreement of wills by which one or several persons obligate themselves to one or several other persons to perform a prestation'.[188] However, it goes some way in accommodating contemporary economic and social theory in recognising that contracts may be sub-divided into various different types, including contracts of adhesion, where the terms have not been negotiated but imposed by one of the parties,[189] and consumer contracts.[190] The point to be emphasised about contemporary civilian contract theory is that contracts are agreements based both on intention and, in varying degrees, on factual reality.

(b) Contract in English law

We have already mentioned that the common law thinks in terms of a general principle of contract as a result of a single form of action (*assumpsit*) establishing itself at the end of the 16th century to deal with loss and damage (including the failure to pay a debt) arising from undertakings (above § 3(b)). This single form of action, as we shall see (below § 5(c)), was based on the notion of promise, and it is this notion of promise which ultimately allowed English lawyers to escape from the procedural technicalities of the forms of action and to think in terms of a general law of contract.[191] By the late 19th century this form of action had become the basis of a general theory of contracting with the result that even pragmatic English judges began to see contract as an obligation created by a communion of wills.[192] Alongside this development of a general theory of contract, there also developed the notion of contractual freedom: 'If

185 Kronman & Posner, *Economics of Contract Law* (Little Brown, 1979), p 1; extracted in HG Beale, WD Bishop & MP Furmston, *Contract: Cases and Materials* (Butterworths, 3rd edn, 1995), p 71.

186 See eg Von Mehren, *Formation*, paras 19–22.

187 NBW Bk 6 art 213-1: 'a contract in the sense of [title 5 Book 6] is a multilateral juridical act whereby one or more parties assume an obligation towards one or more other parties' (trans Haanappel & Mackaay). The draft for 6: 213–1 was translated in 1977 as follows: 'a contract within the meaning of this chapter is a multilateral juristic act by which one or more parties enter into an obligation with one or more others.'

188 Art 1378.

189 Art 1379.

190 Art 1384.

191 Atiyah, *Rise and Fall*, p 215.

192 *Ibid*, p 407.

there is one thing which more than another public policy requires it is that men of full age and competent understanding shall have the utmost liberty of contracting, and that their contracts when entered into freely and voluntarily shall be held sacred and shall be enforced by Courts of Justice.'[193]

This judicial statement bears a very close policy relationship with French law,[194] yet care must be taken before concluding that the common law has a law of enforceable agreements (*les conventions*). In reality *assumpsit*, the remedy upon which the modern English law of contract is constructed, was an action founded originally upon wrong and, later, upon breach of undertaking and these are ideas quite different from agreement.[195] Consequently, the historical emphasis in English contract law cannot be likened to the one to be found in Roman legal scholarship. It may be that English lawyers were influenced by Roman legal scholarship during the 19th century,[196] but if Roman concepts are to be emphasised in this respect it is *pollicitatio* rather than *conventio* that forms the basis of the modern contractual obligation.[197] Moreover, the transactional contexts within which undertakings are made are capable of having, as we have seen (above § 3(b)), an important bearing on the substance of the promises to be enforced. Accordingly, before looking at the actual requirements for an enforceable parol contract – an enforceable promise – it will be necessary to say something about contractual promises themselves and their classification (*cf* Ch 10 § 3).

(c) Promise and agreement

English judges and academics state from time to time that the English law of contract is about enforceable agreements[198] and it has to be said at once that there is a certain truth in this view.[199] Thus, most English commercial contract documents superficially look little different from the commercial agreements to be found anywhere in Europe, and even the legislator in the United Kingdom occasionally uses the language of agreement.[200] Yet a strict legal analysis of English contract law will reveal, as we have already indicated, that it is not the notion of convention but the notion of *pollicitatio* or *promissum* that forms the focal point of liability; the English contractor is liable in damages at common law for breach of promise rather than non-performance of an agreement.[201]

---

193 *Printing and Numerical Registering Co v Sampson* (1875) LR 19 Eq 462, 465.

194 French CC art 1134: '*les conventions légalement formées tiennent lien de loi à ceux qui les ont faites. Elles ne peuvent être révoquées que de leur consentement mutuel, ou pour les causes que la loi autorise. Elles doivent être exécutées de bonne foi.*'

195 Milsom, pp 317, 355–56.

196 Zimmermann, pp 569–71.

197 Zimmermann, pp 572–73.

198 See eg GH Treitel, *An outline of the law of contract* (Butterworths, 5th edn, 1995), pp 2–3.

199 See eg Law of Property (Miscellaneous Provisions) Act 1989 s 2(1); Timeshare Act 1992 s 1(4). And see C Fried, *Contract as Promise* (Harvard UP, 1981), pp 14–17.

200 See eg Law Reform (Miscellaneous Provisions) Act 1970 ss 1–3.

201 Zweigert & Kötz, p 353.

In fact a close look at the 19th century cases reveals that the English law of contract was, in its formative days at least, founded on two ideas. First, there was a general principle that 'if a man has made a deliberate statement, and another has acted upon it, he cannot be at liberty to deny the truth of the statement'.[202] Secondly, there was the principle that any contractual promise was *prima facie* actionable even if it lacked an object and a cause in the French law sense of these terms.[203] Accordingly, if a person was contractually to promise that it would rain the next day he would be liable not only on the basis that he ought not to be allowed to go back on his word[204] but also on the basis that he had assumed a risk and must bear the consequences.[205] These two ideas give rise to a law of contract in England which is really very much more objective in its foundation than the French model which is founded on the subjective notion of consent.

Of course the law of contract has matured conceptually since the mid-19th century – and it must not be forgotten that some 19th century English judges were, as we have already said, influenced by the *Institutes* of Justinian and the writings of Pothier and von Savigny.[206] Yet the promise aspect of contract is still to be found alive and well in the common law. Thus, it remains possible that a contractor who has relied upon a contractual promise can obtain damages for breach of promise even if the object of the obligation is non-existent,[207] and only a decade ago an attempt by one English appeal judge to found contract upon agreement rather than upon an exchange of promises was quashed by the House of Lords.[208] The standard definition of an English contract remains 'a promise or set of promises which the law will enforce',[209] and it is only in the notion of 'consensus' that the English lawyer comes anywhere near to the idea of subjective agreement (*cf* Ch 9 § 2(e)).

202 Baron Bramwell in *McCance v L & N W Ry* (1861) 31 LJ Exch 65, 71.

203 It is a fundamental principle of French law that a contract must have an object and a cause: see CC art 1108. Such an object and cause form important 'empirical' focal points around which the abstract idea of consent can affix itself: see CC art 1126 and CC art 1131. In English law such focal points are unnecessary because the idea of promise includes within itself object (*quid debetur*? What is owing?) and cause (*cur debetur*? Why is it owing?); one cannot make a promise in the abstract whereas one can make abstract legal connections based on consent: Ourliac & De Malafosse, p 157. See generally Nicholas, French *Law of Contract*, *op cit*, pp 114–28.

204 *Canham v Barry* (1855) 24 LJCP 100, 106.

205 *Hall v Wright* (1860) 29 LJQB 43, 46.

206 See Atiyah, *Rise and Fall*, pp 405–08; and see *Hall*, *supra*, pp 46–47.

207 *McRae v Commonwealth Disposals Commission* (1951) 84 CLR 377 (damages awarded in contract for the sale of a non-existent ship).

208 *Gibson v Manchester City Council* [1979] 1 WLR 294. Lord Diplock said (p 297): 'I can see no reason in the instant case for departing from the conventional approach of looking at the handful of documents relied on as constituting the contract sued on and seeing whether on their true construction there is to be found in them a contractual offer by the council to sell the house to Mr Gibson and an acceptance of that offer by Mr Gibson.'

209 See eg Lord Diplock in *Ashington Piggeries Ltd v C Hill Ltd* [1972] AC 441, 501.

(d) Types of contract

The principle of a general law of contract covering all transactions (*cf* above § 3(b)) means that there is no theoretical distinction in English law between general and special contracts; and the lack of a formal distinction between public and private law and between civil and commercial law means that administrative and commercial contracts are in form indistinguishable from ordinary private contracts. All the same, we have seen that this general principle of contract must be treated with some caution in practice and so when it comes to the question of, for example, implied terms (*cf* Ch 10 § 6) the courts can find themselves looking at types of contractual transaction in order to determine, for example, the level of duty (*cf* Ch 10 § 8). Legislation also distinguishes between different types of contract as we have seen (above § 3(b)).

One French distinction that is, seemingly, used by English law is the distinction between unilateral and bilateral contracts.[210] Indeed the terms *synallagmatique*, bilateral and unilateral have been specifically referred to by the English Court of Appeal.[211] However, while there are similarities between the French and English approaches – for example, the promisee in a unilateral contract is under no obligation to the promisor – there are also important differences.[212] In the common law the distinction is founded in the requirement of consideration (*cf* Ch 9 § 3), not in the type of obligation, and this means that most English unilateral contracts consist of a promise in return for an act, the promise becoming operative only if the act is performed. In other words, an English unilateral contract is one in which only one party makes a promise in consideration for something other than a return promise. In fact a promise to make a gift cannot be a contract under the general common law principle of contract law (unless it is under seal)[213] because there is no consideration for the promise and English law does not recognise any specific category of real contracts. Most 'real contract' problems in England fall either within the category of bailment – which, as we have seen, has its own special rules (above § 3(c)) – or within the category of loan, which is governed by the contract principle that there is an implied promise to repay.[214]

(e) Freedom of contract

The emphasis upon promise rather than agreement has meant that English law has not developed a general theory of will (*volonté*) or consent as such. Nevertheless, it had, by the late 19th century, developed, as we have seen, a theory of freedom of contract, and so there is a general principle that 'parties to contracts have freedom of choice not only as to what each will mutually promise to do but also as to what each is willing to accept

210 *Cf* CC arts 1102–03.

211 *UDT v Eagle Aircraft Services Ltd* [1968] 1 WLR 74, 82.

212 Treitel, *Remedies*, paras 189–93.

213 Law of Property (Miscellaneous Provisions) Act 1989 s 1.

214 *Slade's Case* (1602) 76 ER 1074. The consideration for the implied promise to repay is the creditor's 'promise' to convey the money to the debtor.

as the consequences of the performance or non-performance of those promises so far as those consequences affect any other party to the contract.'[215]

In the 20th century consumer society, this general principle was to give rise in England to many of the same problems that standard form contracts produced on the continent.[216] In particular, the widespread use of exclusion clauses was adopted as a means by which vendors could put the risk of poor quality, even dangerous, goods on to the buyer.[217] And although the courts created a number of devices to combat these kinds of abusive clauses (*cf* Ch 10 § 4),[218] it was only when the legislature intervened that the problems for consumers were generally eased.[219] In commercial contracts freedom of contract remains the general principle, but the rationalisation of this freedom tends to be based less and less upon notions of individualism and *laissez-faire* and more and more upon questions of risk, insurance and commercial certainty.[220] Accordingly, while it is true to say that there is a general feeling in the courts that it is not the role of the judges to 'police the fairness of every commercial contract by reference to moral principles',[221] this reluctance is no longer rooted in liberal individualism as such. It is more a matter of economic and social interests and thus England, it would seem, has passed out of the Age of Principle into the Age of Pragmatism.[222]

(f) Interpretation of contracts

The idea of freedom of contract expresses to some extent the view that contract is based upon subjective consent: the court will enforce what the parties themselves have subjectively constructed. And, as we shall see, the English judges have talked of the need for *consensus ad idem* before there can be a binding contract (Ch 9 § 2(e)). But, because of the emphasis on objective promise rather than subjective agreement, the notion of contract is interpreted in a particular way by common lawyers in that the court rarely looks at the actual subjective intention of the contracting parties. In contrast to the position in French law, where one has to search for the common intention of the parties rather than relying upon the literal sense of the written terms,[223] English law looks only at their outward actions and construes contractual liability from their objective behaviour. This point has been recently re-emphasised by Lord Steyn:[224]

215 *Per* Lord Diplock in *Ashington Piggeries Ltd v C Hill Ltd* [1972] AC 441, 501.

216 Zweigert & Kötz, pp 354–68.

217 *Cf* eg *Karsales (Harrow) Ltd v Wallis* [1956] 1 WLR 936.

218 See eg *Webster v Higgin* [1948] 2 All ER 127.

219 Unfair Contract Terms Act 1977; and see now Unfair Terms in Consumer Contracts Regulations 1994.

220 *Photo Production Ltd v Securicor Transport Ltd* [1980] AC 827.

221 *Banque Keyser Ullmann v Skandia (UK) Insurance* [1990] 1 QB 665, 802.

222 Atiyah, *Rise and Fall*, p 649 ff.

223 CC art 1156.

224 *Genossenschaftsbank v Burnhope* [1995] 1 WLR 1580, 1587.

> It is true the objective of the construction of a contract is to give effect to the intention of the parties. But our law of construction is based on an objective theory. The methodology is not to probe the real intentions of the parties but to ascertain the contextual meaning of the relevant contractual language. Intention is determined by reference to expressed rather than actual intention. The question therefore resolves itself in a search for the meaning of language in its contractual setting.

And he continued:

> That does not mean that the purpose of a contractual provision is not important. The commercial or business object of a provision, objectively ascertained, may be highly relevant: see *Prenn v Simmonds* [1971] 1 WLR 1381, 1385B, *per* Lord Wilberforce; *Reardon Smith Line Ltd v Yngvar Hansen-Tangen (trading as HE Hansen-Tangen)* [1976] 1 WLR 989, 996, *per* Lord Wilberforce. But the court must not try to divine the purpose of the contract by speculating about the real intention of the parties. It may only be inferred from the language used by the parties, judged against the objective contextual background. It is therefore wrong to speculate about the actual intention of the parties in this case ...

This strictly objective approach to interpretation is adopted for reasons of commercial policy: businessmen need to know what are their contractual rights and duties so that they can plan and act accordingly. Consequently, as Lord Bridge has asserted, the ideal at which the courts should aim in interpreting contractual clauses is to produce a result which will lead to confident and clear answers from lawyers advising contractual parties. The aim is to avoid long and expensive litigation 'in the belief that victory depends on winning the sympathy of the court'.[225] Whether, of course, the objective approach achieves this commercial law ideal is another question. But it does have the effect of granting to contractual parties the power to legislate privately as between themselves, at least where the parties are *commerçants* in the business of looking after their own interests[226] The approach thus goes far in seemingly fulfilling the empirical objective to be found in the French law of contract. The approach is a *stricti iuris* approach to the *iuris vinculum* as expressed in the language of the texts which indeed has the 'force of legislation' as between the parties.

However, unlike the continental systems, the English common law has no general doctrine of *bona fides*. All it has are specific doctrines which apply to certain kinds of contract (for example insurance, which are contracts *uberrimae fidei*)[227] and certain kinds of relationship – for example, fiduciary relationships (*cf* Ch 4 § 5(e)) – and thus it 'has, characteristically, committed itself to no such overriding principle [of *bona fides*] but has developed piecemeal solutions in response to demonstrated problems of unfairness'.[228] Accordingly, the fact that one party negotiating a contract is aware that the other party is labouring under an error will not, at common law, mean that any subsequent

225 *The Chikuma* [1981] 1 WLR 314, 322.

226 *The General Capinpin* [1991] 1 Lloyds's Rep 1, 9.

227 The principle of *uberrimae fidei* can actually come close to contradicting the principle of *bona fides*: see eg *Lambert v Co-operative Insurance Society Ltd* [1975] 2 Lloyd's Rep 485.

228 Bingham LJ in *Interfoto Picture Library Ltd v Stiletto Ltd* [1989] QB 433, 439.

contract will be a nullity if the former has not corrected the latter's mistake (*cf* Ch 9 § 8). In other words, there is no general duty of disclosure because there is no general theory of consensuality; what matters is an objective view of promise.

However, there are ways in which the courts can inject into contracts doctrines about good faith, error and the like.[229] Given that the basis of contractual liability is the promise, the way the courts analyse any one contract is as a bundle of different promissory obligations (*cf* Ch 10 § 3) and while some of these obligations will arise from the express intentions of the parties others will have to be implied (*cf* Ch 10 § 6). It is this concept of the implied promissory obligation – the implied term – that is the means by which both the courts and the legislator can inject into contracts a whole range of doctrines, principles and rules.[230] In practice this results in much interpretation taking place at the level of some objective contractor such as the 'commercial man' or the 'reasonable man' – a role to be assumed by the judge(s)[231] – who, within the context of the class of transaction in question (sale, hire or whatever), acts as the source of the implied term. And sometimes, as has been the case with the doctrine of frustration (*cf* Ch 10 § 8(f)), this objective contractor can become completely divorced from the implied term to find himself a direct source of a contractual rule which will then exist as a matter of objective law.[232] English law thus arrives at the situation where it does have the means to interpret promises. As Bingham LJ expressed it:

> The tendency of the English authorities has, I think, been to look at the nature of the transaction in question and the character of the parties to it; to consider what notice the party alleged to be bound was given of the particular condition said to bind him; and to resolve whether in all the circumstances it is fair to hold him bound by the condition in question. This may yield a result not very different from the civil law principle of good faith, at any rate so far as the formation of the contract is concerned.[233]

Where contracts have been reduced to writing the general rule is that the court can look only at the written document. The parties cannot adduce parol evidence to vary or to add promises to those set out in the document. However, not only is this rule subject to many exceptions and evasions – so many in fact that the Law Commission concluded that the rule no longer existed[234] – but linguistic interpretation of the written promises themselves can give rise to teasing problems. For example, promises labelled as 'conditions' are said to be so fundamental that, if broken, the innocent contractor can repudiate the contract (*cf* Ch 10 § 3(c)); but merely because a term is described as a condition in the document does not settle the matter because in the English language the word condition has many meanings.[235] And so even at the level

229 Von Mehren, *Formation*, para 83.

230 See eg *The Moorcock* (1889) 14 PD 64; Sale of Goods Act 1979 ss 12–15; Supply of Goods and Services Act 1982; Landlord and Tenant Act 1985 s 8; Housing Act 1988 s 16.

231 See eg *Staffs Area Health Authority v South Staffs Waterworks Co* [1978] 3 All ER 769.

232 See *Davis Contractors Ltd v Fareham UDC* [1956] AC 696, 728–29.

233 *Interfoto Picture Library Ltd v Stiletto Ltd* [1989] QB 433, 445.

234 Law Commission Report (cmnd 9700, 1986).

235 *Schuler v Wickman Machine Tools* [1974] AC 235.

of linguistic interpretation the objective contractor – that is, the judge playing the role of the reasonable or commercial man – may have to make an appearance before the court can decide how to construe any particular contract. Indeed the 'business common sense' of such an objective commercial man is likely to trump 'a literalist argument devoid of any redeeming commercial sense'.[236]

Interpretation of contracts is, then, primarily a matter of linguistic interpretation of written promises in the case of written contracts – and here the approach of the courts is to look at the final document rather than the negotiations which preceded it[237] – or of the formulation of implied promises if such promises are necessary to give the contract 'business efficacy'.[238] If there is one overriding or general principle it is that the courts will not 'give the words a meaning that would defeat the clear intention of the parties as revealed by the rest of the relevant evidence of the agreement'.[239] However, that said, it must not be forgotten that many contractual problems find themselves before the court via the institution of the remedy rather than the right; accordingly, interpretation problems can sometimes be found behind estoppel, rescission and rectification (*cf* Ch 5 §§ 2–3) cases and these remedies are on occasions capable of importing their own rules and principles into the problem. For example, it is possible to argue that in a rescission for breach case – that is to say, in a case where the court is being asked to interpret a term in order to see if the breach of it will give rise to a right to repudiate the whole contract – the court may well want to apply, implicitly, some notion of proportionality: is it reasonable to allow a contracting party to use this particular self-help remedy given the breach in question?[240] One might add that when the courts are having to interpret an exclusion clause they will make use of a number of specific interpretation techniques (*cf* Ch 10 § 4(b)): for example, they will interpret such a clause strictly as against the party attempting to rely on it (*contra proferentem*).

6 PROVINCE OF THE LAW OF CONTRACT

Once remedies bring their own rules into the area of contract this raises a question about the scope and province of the law of contract itself. Does one have to have a knowledge of all the remedies before one can safely attempt to answer a 'contract' problem? And what about the law of non-contractual debt and damages actions: will these have a role to play in the province of contract?[241] There is no doubt that in certain areas of contract a knowledge of the law of tort and the principles of equity is essential. Thus, in the area of misrepresentation (*cf* Ch 9 § 7), the availability of damages and rescission may well be governed by non-contractual principles with the result that a plaintiff damaged by a statement made in the course of contractual negotiations could

236 *Genossenschaftsbank v Burnhope* [1995] 1 WLR 1580, 1589.

237 *Prenn v Simmonds* [1971] 1 WLR 1381.

238 *Liverpool CC v Irwin* [1977] AC 239.

239 *Amalgamated Investment & Property Co v Texas Commerce International Bank Ltd* [1982] QB 84, 125.

240 See eg *Hong Kong Fir Shipping Co Ltd v Kawasaki Kishen Kaisha Ltd* [1962] 2 QB 26; *Vaswani v Italian Motors (Sales and Services) Ltd* [1996] 1 WLR 270 (PC).

241 *Cf Kleinwort Benson Ltd v Glasgow CC* [1996] 2 WLR 655.

possibly receive damages in tort.[242] Equally, a non-contractual debt claim (*cf* Ch 11 § 2) might be available at common law[243] or in equity[244] founded on principles of restitution and unjust enrichment (*cf* Ch 11 § 5). The law of contract cannot, therefore, be fully understood from a practical point of view without a knowledge of the torts of negligence and deceit, of the law of quasi-contract, of some of the general principles surrounding equitable remedies and, as we have seen, of aspects of the law of property (*cf* above § 3(c); Ch 13 § 8).

That said, however, it must be added that there has been something of a regression in recent years associated with the reluctance both to award damages in negligence for pure economic loss (*cf* Ch 13 § 9) and to allow the intervention of equity to undermine the security of transactions. Where there is a commercial relationship governed by a contract it would seem that there is now much less scope for actions in the tort of negligence,[245] and legislative intervention in the field of consumer protection has led to the view that further restriction upon the principle of freedom of contract (*cf* above § 5(e)) is a matter for Parliament rather than the courts.[246] In truth the position is complex because the interrelation of contract, equity and tort is itself complex and the exclusion from contract either of the law of tort or of equitable doctrines will always be an unrealistic exercise in some respects.[247] If the damage is physical the law of tort will have something of a role even if this role is, in the end, subsumed by a contract apportioning risks via an exclusion clause;[248] if it is financial, and results from reliance, the role of the law of tort will largely be dependent on the aims of the two categories as viewed through the status of one or more of the parties. When a consumer is involved the tort of negligence may well come to the aid of the law of contract where, for example, this latter category is unable to found a damages action simply on the basis of a technicality[249] or where a contracting party has clearly assumed a duty beyond the contract.[250] And while the equitable jurisdiction to grant relief does not formally distinguish between consumer and commercial contracts the 'fact of an unequal bargain will, of course, be a relevant feature in some cases of undue influence even if it can never become an appropriate basis of principle of an equitable doctrine ... of relief against inequality of bargaining power'.[251]

In the civil codes the province of the law of contract seems clear: contractual situations are those factual situations that fall within the contractual obligations section

242 *Box v Midland Bank Ltd* [1979] 2 Lloyd's Rep 391.

243 *British Steel Corporation v Cleveland Bridge & Engineering Co Ltd* [1984] 1 All ER 504.

244 *English v Dedham Vale Properties Ltd* [1978] 1 WLR 93.

245 *Tai Hing Cotton Mill Ltd v Liu Chong Hing Bank Ltd* [1986] AC 80, 107; *Marc Rich & Co v Bishop Rock Ltd* [1996] 1 AC 211.

246 *National Westminster Bank v Morgan* [1985] AC 686, 708.

247 *Henderson v Merrett Syndicates Ltd* [1995] 2 AC 145.

248 See eg *Photo Production Ltd v Securicor* [1980] AC 827. But *cf Marc Rich & Co v Bishop Rock Ltd* [1996] 1 AC 211.

249 See eg *Smith v Eric Bush* [1990] 1 AC 831; *White v Jones* [1995] 2 AC 207.

250 See eg *Al-Kandari v J R Brown & Co* [1988] QB 665; *White v Jones* [1995] 2 AC 207.

251 Lord Scarman in *National Westminster, supra*, at p 708.

of the code. In practice facts can sometimes be more elusive and the court will find itself having on occasions to interpret the facts in order to see if they fall within the scope of the contractual provisions.[252] For example, in one French case[253] a consumer in a supermarket was injured by an exploding bottle of lemonade just as she was about to hand it to the check-out cashier: were these facts that fell within the contractual provisions of the code or were they facts to be determined by the non-contractual obligations provisions? This kind of situation involves the application of those rules dealing with the formation of contract – in French law the test being the existence of an agreement based 'on the exchange of consents, the meeting of two wills'[254] – and thus, in the strict sense, the province of the law of contract is determined simply by reference to rules dealing with the making of contracts.

Nevertheless, while it is 'deceptively easy to describe the heartland of contract ... its borders are very hard to map save by the use of *a priori* assumptions'[255] and thus some of the more difficult areas of the law of obligations are just those areas where contract seems to have stopped short of incursion. These areas are described by expressions such as 'pre-contractual obligations' (*cf* Ch 9 § 4) or 'post-contractual situations' and while they are often covered in textbooks dealing with the law of contract, the actual rules in play may well be code provisions from quasi-delict or unjust enrichment. In other words, the civilian jurist is continually aware that the province of the law of contract is always to be appreciated within the wider context of the province of a law of obligations. In turn the law of obligations results only from the code[256] and thus it is the code as a whole that will, in the end, determine how factual situations are to be qualified and interpreted. In English law such systematics are not perceivable since contract, tort and restitution are discrete categories not subject to higher norms arising from the system. Nevertheless, the law of actions can on occasions stand outside these three substantive categories so as to provide a counterpoint. Accordingly, one can sometimes start out from a 'right to damages' or a 'right to an account' and work from there towards an obligations category – contract, tort or even equity – in which the remedy can be anchored; and when this happens the effect on the relevant category itself can sometimes be to modify the province of the particular category.[257] This is one important reason why, in English law, no work on the law of obligations can ignore the law of remedies (*cf* Chs 4–6).

---

252 See eg Von Mehren, *Formation*, para 29.

253 Cass civ 20.10.1964; DS.1965.62. Discussed in more depth in Samuel, *Foundations*, pp 138 ff.

254 C Jauffret-Spinosi, 'The Domain of Contract', in Harris & Tallon, p 114.

255 B Rudden, 'The Domain of Contract', in Harris & Tallon, p 89.

256 NBW Bk 6 art 1.

257 See eg *Blackpool and Fylde Aero Club Ltd v Blackpool BC* [1990] 1 WLR 1195.

CHAPTER NINE

THE FORMATION OF A CONTRACT

The province of the law of contract is determined at the level of positive law by rules dealing with the formation of a contract. Thus, in French law in order for there to be a binding contract between two legal subjects the *Code civil* states in article 1108 that four conditions are essential: there must be consent, capacity, object and cause. Each of these requirements is, in turn, given its own more specific rules and these rules have in their turn become the basis of a mass of case law and doctrine. Equally, in English law, there are specific requirements for a binding contract and these requirements can be stated as essential conditions. Thus, in order for there to be a contract there must be offer and acceptance, consideration and an intention to create legal relations. As with French law, these conditions have attracted much case law which has resulted in a mass of more detailed rules; these rules in turn have attracted much academic writing.

Capacity, one might observe, is not an essential condition since it is theoretically possible for a contract to be created in England even by an incapable, although such a contract is liable to be set aside. Accordingly, in addition to rules about the formation of contracts, common lawyers have separate rules concerning vitiating factors such as incapacity, misrepresentation, mistake, illegality and the like. In French law such 'vitiating factors' are to be found within the rules of formation themselves.

1 THE ESSENTIAL REQUIREMENTS OF A CONTRACT

The reason why continental lawyers do not often distinguish between formation and vitiating factors is to be found in the overriding principle that the formation of a contract rests upon capacity, communion of the wills of the parties and valid formation of the *volonté*. Sometimes formalities are required. Every natural person has the capacity to perform a juridical act to the extent that the law does not provide differently but minors and people under guardianship do not have the capacity to perform the act necessary for a contract and contracts with persons lacking the capacity mentioned may be annulled. A unilateral juridical act of a person lacking capacity is void;[1] and in general, a juridical act of such a person is voidable. Communion of the wills is, then, an essential part of civilian contract law.[2]

Viewed from the position of logic, the *vices du consentement* make rational sense. However, in commercial practice the position is by no means as simple since a subjective approach to contract creates difficulty in situations where *volonté*, declaration and reliance diverge. Could a contract be valid, for example, if there was no *volonté* corresponding to the declaration? The protection of other persons acting in good faith on the assumption of a certain declaration or in reliance on the existence of a specific

1 See eg Quebec CC art 161.

2 See eg Quebec CC arts 1385–86.

juris vinculum raises further problems. In all of the civil law systems the legislators and the courts have had to develop solutions that act as a compromise between the subjective and the objective and thus one can find approaches allowing all the circumstances to be taken into account when judging formation cases, especially the nature of the act, the special expertise (or the absence thereof) of the parties, the duties to inform the other party or to inquire into the intention, and the various interests concerned.[3]

English law, which bases contract upon promise rather than agreement (Ch 8 § 5(c)), escapes these consent problems and is thus able to concentrate on objective factors. The three broad requirements – offer and acceptance, consideration and an intention to create legal relations – are all that is required to establish a promissory obligation at common law, although certain types of contract sometimes attract further formal or evidentiary requirements. In particular, contracts for the disposition of land or an interest in land must be in writing,[4] and various consumer credit contracts must be in a required form.[5] However, a failure to comply with such statutory requirements usually makes a contract unenforceable rather than non-existent (*cf* below § 6(a)).

2 OFFER AND ACCEPTANCE

In the civil law systems agreement is evidenced by offer and acceptance. In French law this requirement is not to be found in the *Code civil* as such, but it has been developed by the case law as the means for determining agreement. Other codes are more explicit. Accordingly, the New Dutch Civil Code states simply in Book 6 article 217(1) that: 'A contract is formed by an offer and its acceptance'. More interesting from a traditional civilian (French model) perspective is the new Quebec Civil Code which states in article 1386: 'The exchange of consents is accomplished by the express or tacit manifestation of the will of a person to accept an offer to contract made to him by another person.' Offer and acceptance for most of the codified systems act as the means by which will and consent are manifested.

In English law offer and acceptance is also an essential condition and it functions in much the same way as it does on the continent, although the actual results may differ on occasions.[6] However, instead of it acting as the manifestation of consent, offer and acceptance is a complete legal requirement in itself; that is to say, it is as much a question of law as fact and so it is quite possible for the supreme court (the House of Lords) to be called upon to decide questions which, in France, if not in other continental jurisdictions such as the Netherlands, would belong only to the trial judge.[7] The reason for this difference is to be found in the source of contract law. As we have seen, the foundation in the common law is promise rather than agreement and this has

3 See JBM Vranken, *Mededelings – informatie- en onderzoeksplichten in het verbintenissenrecht* (Zwolle, 1989).

4 Law of Property (Miscellaneous Provisions) Act 1989 s 2(1).

5 See Consumer Credit Act 1974 s 60.

6 See eg Rudden, pp 310–12.

7 See eg *Gibson v Manchester City Council* [1979] 1 WLR 294.

resulted in contract formation rules which generally function at a lower level of abstraction than in jurisdictions where contract is founded directly upon *volonté*.

All the same teasing conceptual problems can still arise. What is the position if A makes a promise to B that he, A, will compensate C if he damages C's property in certain circumstances? Will there be a contract between A and C? Much will depend upon the view taken of the context. If the promise is made in the context of an association in which all three parties are involved, then the court may decide that there are contractual relations flowing between A and C thus allowing C to sue A in contract if A was to damage C's property.[8] However, if the court takes an atomistic approach there is the possibility that no contractual relations will be established between A and C and this will then give rise to privity problems (*cf* Ch 10 § 7). It is easy enough to say that the common law of contract is based on an exchange of promises via offer and acceptance, but, as we shall see, something more is required (*cf* § 2(e) below) and it is with this 'something more', said to lie in the notion of 'intention',[9] that problems arise as to the exact basis of English contract law.

(a) Offer and invitation to treat

In many ways the whole dichotomy between law and fact is unreal in this area of English contract law and this is particularly true with regard to the distinction between an offer and an invitation to treat (*invitatio ad offerendum*). In this area of law one has to think in terms of rules emerging from particular fact situations (*ex facto ius oritur*).[10] Many of these fact situations are similar to both continental and English law but the practical approaches taken by the two systems can differ considerably. In an English supermarket, for example, goods on display shelves constitute only an invitation to treat – the consumer makes the offer to the cashier[11] – and this means that if, before payment, there is an accident in the supermarket arising from a defective product the problem will be one for the law of tort rather than contract.[12]

It might be tempting to conclude from this that the emphasis in English law is usually on the consumer, as opposed to the supplier, when it comes to the making of contractual offers. Certainly, it is true that the courts do not usually treat advertisements and displays in shop windows as constituting offers.[13] Nevertheless, an offer for a reward in return for an act, if specific enough, can constitute an offer to the public at large; consequently, a company which stated, by way of a newspaper advertisement, that £100 would be paid to anyone who caught influenza after having used their medical product for two weeks was held liable in debt to a consumer who caught the

---

8 *Clarke v Dunraven* [1897] AC 59.

9 *The Hannah Blumenthal* [1983] 1 AC 854, 915–16.

10 See generally G Samuel, '*Ex Facto Ius Oritur*' (1989) 8 *CJQ* 53.

11 *Pharmaceutical Society of GB v Boots* [1953] 1 QB 401.

12 *Ward v Tesco Stores Ltd* [1976] 1 All ER 219.

13 *Fisher v Bell* [1961] 1 QB 394.

illness and claimed that there was a (unilateral) contract between herself and the company.[14]

(b) Counter-offers

When one moves from consumer to commercial law the problem of identifying contractual offers often takes a different contextual form. The problem usually becomes one of distinguishing between offers and counter-offers. This is because businesses tend to use standard forms of offers and acceptances. Here the law is simple enough – a counter-offer destroys the original offer and so the original offer cannot thereafter be accepted – but the facts can be complex because standard form offers and acceptances can often contain conflicting clauses when compared in detail. For example, in one case the sellers of a machine brought an action in debt against the buyers for a sum in excess of the original sale price. The sellers argued that they were entitled to this extra sum because of a price variation clause in their original written offer of sale. However, the buyers said the contract was governed by their written acceptance form which did not contain a price variation clause and which contained a tear-off acknowledgment slip which the plaintiffs had returned.[15] The Court of Appeal held that the sellers were not entitled to recover the extra sum because the contract was based upon the buyer's, rather than the seller's, written terms. The delivery and acceptance of the machine prevented there being no contract and so the question came down to a battle of forms.

In these battle of forms situations the courts are faced with a dilemma as to whether to take an obligational (logical) or a commercial (flexible) approach (*cf* below § 3(d)). The tendency these days is to take the commercial law approach, if only because the parties have usually acted upon the basis that there was a contract; and this means that the doctrine of counter-offer is often less a method of establishing *consensus ad idem* (*cf* § 2(e) below) and more a tool of contractual interpretation (*cf* Ch 8 § 5(f)). Indeed, were it otherwise, 'there would be many important mercantile contracts which would, no doubt to the consternation of the parties, be nullities.'[16]

(c) Termination of offer

A counter-offer is, of course, not the only way an offer can be terminated. Besides lapse (after a stipulated or reasonable time), an offer may be revoked by the offeror at any time before acceptance, the only requirement being that the revocation be communicated, from any source, to the offeree.[17] Indeed because of the requirement at common law that all enforceable promises be supported by consideration (below § 3), an offeror can in principle revoke at any time even when he has promised to keep an offer open for a stipulated period. This could be problematical. However, in practice a

14 *Carlill v Carbolic Smoke Ball Co* [1893] 1 QB 256.

15 *Butler Machine Tool Co Ltd v Ex-Cell-O Corporation* [1979] 1 WLR 401.

16 Megaw J in *Trollope & Colls Ltd v Atomic Power Constructions Ltd* [1962] 3 All ER 1035, 1040.

17 *Dickinson v Dodds* (1876) 2 Ch D 463.

court will not allow an offeror to revoke until the offeree, once he has embarked upon performance, has had a reasonable chance to complete,[18] and it may be that equity, via, for example, estoppel (Ch 5 § 1(c)), would not allow a contractor to abuse his common law rights in such circumstances (*cf* Ch 12 § 3(c)). Moreover, an offeror who has allowed another to expend money or work upon the offeror's property might be liable in the law of restitution if not in contract.[19]

(d) Acceptance

In unilateral contracts, as we have seen (Ch 8 § 5(d)), it is the performance or conduct which amounts to the acceptance of the offer and there is often no need to communicate actual acceptance because the offeror is deemed to have dispensed with the requirement.[20] In bilateral contracts an offer must be specifically accepted by the offeree, but there are several exceptions to this rule, one being that conduct might, on occasions, amount to acceptance.[21]

A more curious exception to the communication of acceptance rule is where a contract is concluded by post. Provided that it is reasonable to use the post as a means of acceptance, the rule formulated in the last century is that an offer is accepted at the moment the letter of acceptance is posted.[22] Whether this rule has much of a future is now in some doubt,[23] but modern means of communication can still present problems with regard to the receipt of an acceptance. If, for example, a telex message of acceptance fails to be recorded then there will be no contract unless the offeree can show that the offeror was at fault in some way; and, if fault can be shown, the reason why the acceptance will be effective is that the offeror will be estopped (*cf* Ch 5 § 1(c)) from denying the existence of a contract.[24] 'No universal rule can cover all such cases', said Lord Wilberforce, 'they must be resolved by reference to the intentions of the parties, by sound business practice and in some cases by a judgment where the risks should lie.'[25]

(e) *Consensus ad idem*

The idea that a person may be estopped from denying the existence of a contract indicates, again, how English law is closely attached to remedies and to objective promises. Nevertheless, there has to be some element of subjectivity before an exchange of promises can constitute a binding contract. Accordingly, if two promises

---

18 *Daulia Ltd v Four Millbank Nominees* [1978] Ch 231.

19 *British Steel Corporation v Cleveland Bridge and Engineering Co Ltd* [1984] 1 All ER 504.

20 *Carlill v Carbolic Smoke Ball Co* [1893] 1 QB 256.

21 *Brogden v Metropolitan Ry* (1877) 2 App Cas 666.

22 *Household Fire Insurance Co v Grant* (1879) LR 4 Ex D 216.

23 *Holwell Securities Ltd v Hughes* [1974] 1 WLR 155.

24 *Entores Ltd v Miles Far East Corporation* [1955] 2 QB 327, 333.

25 *Brinkibon Ltd v Stahag Stahl* [1983] 2 AC 34, 42.

happen by chance to cross in the post as cross-offers this will not constitute a contract despite the fact that there is objective accord; equally, there will not be a contract if the offeree has not outwardly exhibited his intention to be bound. Silence cannot amount to acceptance.[26] Indeed the offeror who tries to impose chattels upon a silent offeree may find himself the unwilling distributor of free gifts.[27]

What has to be shown is that there is objective evidence of an apparently subjective *consensus ad idem*.[28] If the offeree objectively appears to have knowledge of, and be accepting, the offeror's promise then the promise will be binding:[29] 'what is necessary is that the intention of each as it has been communicated to and understood by the other (even though that which has been communicated does not represent the actual state of mind of the communicator) should coincide.'[30] But if specific evidence is introduced to show that the motivation of the 'accepting' act has no causal connection whatsoever with the offeror's promise then the result might be different. It seems that the offeree must go to the length of showing that he knew of the offer and that he acted in reliance on it.[31] What if there is *consensus ad idem* but no offer and acceptance? In principle there can be no contract because one looks to the facts to see if they constitute a contract and not to the subjective intention of one or both parties.[32] Yet on rare occasions the courts have been prepared to view the relations between persons engaged in a common venture as contractual; these exceptional cases thus tend to involve problems arising from groups and, as such, the starting point is not the individual promise at the basis of the dispute itself but the more general promise to become part of a corporation, *societas* or association.[33]

The question whether there is a general principle of English law that injurious reliance on what another person has done can be a source of legal rights against him is potentially of great importance for the development of English law[34] and so it may be valuable to recall one of the main conceptual distinctions to be found in continental legal systems. This is the basic distinction between contract and delict (tort), the former category implying not just the freedom of parties to enter into a contract but the strict boundary between being bound and not being bound to a contract. The fundamental difference between contract and tort is, on the one hand, the voluntary act by which one person binds himself to another by entering into a contract and, on the other hand, the creation of a bond (legal relation) between persons only because the law so stipulates (tort). In some civilian systems this rigid distinction is beginning to break down; accordingly, expectations, reliance, the intention to create legal relations, norms

---

26 *The Leonidas D* [1985] 2 All ER 796, 805.

27 Unsolicited Goods and Services Act 1971.

28 *The Hannah Blumenthal* [1983] 1 AC 854, 915.

29 *Ibid*, pp 915–16.

30 *Ibid* p 915 *per* Lord Diplock.

31 *Taylor v Allon* [1966] 1 QB 304.

32 *Gibson v Manchester City Council* [1979] 1 WLR 294.

33 *Clarke v Dunraven* [1897] AC 59.

34 *Cf* PS Atiyah, 'The Hannah Blumenthal and Classical Contract Law' (1986) 102 LQR 363.

of proper legal behaviour and legal policies are in themselves capable of acting as a basis for legal relations. In the absence of agreement or consideration, or any of the requirements for a valid contract, or in the presence of a breach of form, obligations and remedies based on reliance are beginning to occupy the centre ground between contract, delict and unjust enrichment.[35]

In English law, with its objective approach to contractual liability and its emphasis on remedies, the problem of reliance has never had to face the same conceptual problems. Consequently there is 'a general principle of English law that injurious reliance on what another person did may be a source of legal rights against him'.[36] Such a principle encompasses both equity (estoppel) and common law and, as such, possibly adds up to more than just the sum of the parts of offer, acceptance and estoppel; it probably includes, for example, the common law doctrine of waiver of rights.[37] None of this undermines as such the requirement of *consensus* in contractual obligations. As we have just seen, even in the civil law systems the absence of *consensus* does not mean that the law of obligations has no role in a factual situation where a party has suffered harm as a result of reliance upon another's words or acts. One just moves into the area of non-contractual obligations. The common law, with its more objective view of a contract, has always been able to use contract itself in certain situations which would have given problems to a continental contract lawyer. Accordingly, in the *Blackpool* case from 1990 the Court of Appeal held a local authority liable to an invitee for carelessly failing to consider the invitee's properly submitted tender.[38] It is fairly clear that the authority had not willingly consented to be contractually liable at this stage of the tendering process; yet this did not inhibit the judges from finding a collateral contract. If the invitee submits 'a conforming tender before the deadline', said Bingham LJ, [39] 'he is entitled, not as a matter of expectation but of contractual right, to be sure that his tender will after the deadline be opened and considered.' If the law was otherwise, it would 'be defective'.

(f) Certainty

Even if there is both offer and acceptance and *consensus ad idem* a transactional relationship can still fail contractually because the promises themselves remain too vague or because the factual basis of the alleged contract is too abstract. Accordingly, and despite the *Blackpool* case, a 'contract to contract' will not be an enforceable contract because it is too uncertain to have any binding force; and in such a situation there is a general principle that where there is a fundamental matter left undecided and to be the subject of negotiation there is no contract.[40]

35 Von Mehren, *Formation*, para 15.

36 *The Hannah Blumenthal* [1983] 1 AC 854, 916 *per* Lord Diplock.

37 *Charles Rickards Ltd v Oppenheim* [1950] 1 KB 616.

38 *Blackpool & Fylde Aero Club Ltd v Blackpool BC* [1990] 1 WLR 1195.

39 At p 1202.

40 *Courtney v Tolaini* [1975] 1 All ER 716, 720; *Walford v Miles* [1992] 2 AC 128.

However, merely because an agreement to negotiate is not a contract, it does not always follow that there is no contract when an agreement contains a provision that some important matter, such as the price, is left to be agreed. In fact it is a matter of general principle in English law – in contrast to Roman and French law – that a sale of goods contract can exist without a price having been agreed.[41] Much will depend upon the circumstances of the case. Thus, in some situations a failure to agree upon a price can be fatal, while in other situations – particularly where the principle *certum est quod certum reddi* (what can be rendered certain is certain) is applicable or where the parties have actually conveyed property – the contract can be binding.[42] No doubt the distinction between civil and commercial relationships (*cf* Ch 8 § 4(a)) will, once again, be of relevance to the court's interpretation of the facts.[43]

3 CONSIDERATION

The dichotomy between civil and commercial law might be said to be at the philosophical root of the second major requirement of English contract law. Only those promises that have been bargained for will be enforceable under the general principle of contract. Consequently, with the exception of a promise made under a formal written document (a hangover from the ancient writ of covenant),[44] a mere gratuitous promise cannot amount to a contractual obligation. In other words, there is no notion in English law of a contract *à titre gratuit* (where 'one party obligates himself to the other for the benefit of the latter without obtaining any advantage in return').[45] However, what amounts to a 'gratuitous' promise, particularly within a commercial relationship, is by no means an easy question.

(a) Definition of consideration

The notion of bargain is translated into contract law via the essential requirement of consideration. For the continental lawyer this notion of consideration is difficult because the basis of contract in the codes is *pacta sunt servanda* and this imports into the law of obligations a moral dimension.[46] English contract law, on the other hand, is, as David and Pugsley point out, an economic rather than a moral law (*un droit économique, non une morale transplantée sur le terrain du droit*).[47] Both parties must accordingly have an economic interest in the contract and although this interest is a requirement which goes to the formation, rather than to the actual performance of the contract, the notion of consideration sometimes finds itself being used to assess whether there has been

41 Sale of Goods Act 1979 s 8. The same applies to a contract for the supply of a service: Supply of Goods and Services Act 1982 s 15. And see NBW Bk 7 art 4.

42 *Sudbrook Trading Estate Ltd v Eggleton* [1983] 1 AC 444.

43 See eg *Hillas & Co v Arcos Ltd* (1932) 147 LT 503.

44 Law of Property (Miscellaneous Provisions) Act 1989 s 1. In making such formal and 'gratuitous' promises so much easier to execute, this statute could have an interesting future.

45 Quebec CC art 1381.

46 Harris & Tallon, p 386. See generally Zimmermann, pp 537–79.

47 R David & D Pugsley, *Les Contrats en Droit Anglais* (LGDJ, 2nd edn, 1985), para 130.

performance.[48] This is unfortunate because the actual definition of consideration is 'the price for which the promise of the other is bought'; and it may consist of an act, a forbearance or a promise made or given by the promisee.[49]

In a typical bilateral contract such as sale, the consideration consists of the exchange of promises, not the actual conveyances; in a typical unilateral contract the consideration is the act performed or the forbearance made. Thus, if D promises a reward of £50 to anyone who returns D's lost cat Tibbins, P can only claim the debt once he has performed the act of returning Tibbins to D.[50] However, the mere exchange of consideration is not itself enough: there must be a sufficient connection between the consideration moving from each of the parties. If, therefore, one person does a gratuitous act or service for another and the latter subsequently promises a reward or payment for this service the promise will not be supported by consideration because the original act or service was not connected with the subsequent promise to pay. The consideration is said to be past consideration. In order for the promise to be enforceable by the promisee in such circumstances the original act would have had to be performed as a result of a prior request by the promisor and in the expectation by the promisee of some reward.[51]

Consideration is associated with the very definition of contract in English law. Nevertheless, the civil law systems have been able to develop an adequate law of contract without consideration and so when discussing harmonisation of civil law, the abolition of the doctrine of consideration is, it would seem, one possible option.[52] This would imply, however, the need for legislation both to validate all contracts where there is genuine agreement and to provide for various types of essential unilateral promises, in order to avoid uncertainty in the law and this would, in theory, involve a major reform of the English law of contract.[53] In this respect, the development of the equitable doctrine of promissory (quasi) estoppel protecting promisees who have been led to act differently from how they would otherwise have done (change of position) is one possibility;[54] another option is simply to use writing and signature.[55]

(b) Sufficiency of consideration

The problem of past consideration in English law is really an aspect of a more general question: what amounts to sufficient consideration in English contract law? The general rule here is that consideration must be 'sufficient' – that is to say, real – but it need not be 'adequate'. It will be sufficient only if it is of some real value in an objective sense

48 See eg *Rowland v Divall* [1923] 2 KB 500.

49 *Dunlop v Selfridge* [1915] AC 847, 855.

50 *Carlill v Carbolic Smoke Ball Co* [1893] 1 QB 256.

51 *Pau On v Lau Yiu Long* [1980] AC 614, 629–30.

52 See H McGregor, *Contract Code* (Giuffrè, 1993).

53 But cf Law of Property (Miscellaneous Provisions) Act 1989 s 1.

54 See eg *Crabb v Arun DC* [1976] Ch 179.

55 Law of Property (Miscellaneous Provisions) Act 1989 s 1.

and so a promise in return for 'love and affection' would probably not be an enforceable contractual promise. Yet once there is sufficient consideration the fact that it is out of all economic proportion to the other party's consideration is irrelevant; one can promise to convey a valuable painting in return for a nominal sum of money, or indeed three sweet wrappers, and this, in principle, would be a binding contract.[56] It may be, however, that inadequate consideration would be evidence of an unconscionable bargain and thus subject to the attention of equity (*cf* Ch 11 § 3). Alternatively, a low price in a sale of goods contract may affect the expectation interest of the purchaser in certain consumer and commercial contracts.[57]

One particular problem that can arise in the area of sufficiency of consideration concerns a promise in return for some performance which the promisee is already under an existing public or private duty to perform. Here there are two possible approaches: a legal approach which focuses strictly on the actual existence or non-existence of a duty in law; or an empirical approach which investigates whether the promisor actually received a benefit in practice. The tendency of the courts in recent years has been to favour the latter approach for reasons both of 'commercial reality' (see below § 3(d)) and of developments in the area of economic duress (*cf* Ch 11 § 3(c)). English contract law still insists on consideration, but 'the courts nowadays should be more ready to find its existence so as to reflect the intention of the parties to the contract where the bargaining powers are not unequal and where the finding of consideration reflects the true intention of the parties.'[58]

(c) Third parties

The existence of sufficient consideration, even if adequate, will be of no use if it does not move from the promisee. This rule is often said to be at the base of the principle of privity of contract (*cf* Ch 10 § 7) whereby only those persons who are parties to the contract can sue or be sued on it. But the privity principle itself has a more complex history[59] and has been extended beyond its original scope, as a result of the consideration rule, to prohibit any third party from taking the benefit of a clause in a contract between two others. Thus, where a third party is sued in the tort of negligence (*cf* Ch 12 § 3(a); Ch 13 § 1) for damage carelessly caused to property forming the subject matter of a contract between two others, the third party cannot, in principle, claim the protection of any exclusion clause in the contract even if the clause specifically purports to cover the third party.[60]

(d) Commercial reality

However, the English courts are recognising that multi-party commercial transactions

56 *Chappell & Co v Nestle Ltd* [1960] AC 87.

57 See Sale of Goods Act 1979 s 14(2A).

58 Russell LJ in *Williams v Roffey Brothers* [1991] 1 QB 1, 18.

59 See V Palmer, *The Paths to Privity* (Austin & Winfield, 1992).

60 *Scruttons Ltd v Midland Silicones Ltd* [1962] AC 446.

must be treated with a certain flexibility. Admittedly, the problems of the privity and consideration rules could, anyway, often be avoided by recourse to other remedial or substantive doctrines such as bailment (*cf* Ch 8 § 3(c)),[61] estoppel (Ch 5 § 1(c)) or even, perhaps, the defence of consent in tort (*volenti non fit injuria*) (Ch 13 § 5(a)). And so hardships created in the commercial world by English contract law ought not to be exaggerated. Yet the main difficulty with regard to consideration is that it has always attached itself to the promise rather than to the bargain as a whole and this atomistic approach to the analysis of transactions can cause particular problems in international trade and commerce agreements; for there is always the danger that one particular promise may turn out, in isolation, to be devoid of consideration.

The courts, in recognising this difficulty, have recently suggested that it may be unreal to describe one set of promises as a *nudum pactum* in a complex commercial transaction. And so what they have done is to have recourse to the distinction between civil and commercial relationships (*cf* Ch 8 § 4(a)) to make the point that 'commercial reality' may dictate that 'a practical approach' be injected into the law of contract when it comes to contracts 'of a commercial character'.[62] They have, in other words, taken a more universalist view of the notion of bargain in certain kinds of commercial dealings.[63] All the same, the consideration rule has not been abandoned: an atomistic approach to promises can still be useful, for example, in preventing unjust enrichment in situations where a promise has been extracted under economic duress.[64]

(e) Public policy

In fact the cases where the rules of consideration have been applied to deprive a promise of its legal force may well, on closer examination, be 'cases in which public policy has been held to invalidate the consideration'.[65] This suggests that the problem of consideration must be looked at not just in the context of the dichotomy between commercial and non-commercial relationships, although public policy can be of relevance to 'commercial reality'; it must be looked at in the context of the distinction between public and private law (*cf* Ch 8 § 4(c)) as well. Consideration is a useful device for defining the boundaries between public and private obligations, particularly where a public organ such as the police finds itself performing services for the private sector.[66] And in understanding how the common law approaches questions of sufficiency of consideration it is as important to look at the nature of any pre-existing legal or factual relationships as it is to look at the economic value of the alleged consideration itself.

61 But *cf Morris v C W Martin & Sons Ltd* [1966] 1 QB 716.

62 *The Eurymedon* [1975] AC 154, 167 *per* Lord Wilberforce.

63 See most recently *Darlington BC v Wiltshier Northern Ltd* [1995] 1 WLR 68.

64 *D & C Builders v Rees* [1966] 2 QB 617.

65 *Pau On v Lau Yiu Long* [1980] AC 614, 633.

66 See eg *Glasbrook Bros Ltd v Glamorgan CC* [1925] AC 270.

(f) Estoppel and abuse of contractual rights

The fact that a gratuitous promise is unenforceable in the law of contract does not mean that such a promise is without legal effect. If a promisee relies to his detriment upon such a promise it may be that equity, through its doctrine of estoppel (*cf* Ch 5 § 1(c)), will prevent the promisor from going back upon her statement.[67] For example, a promise made by a creditor to a debtor to accept a lesser sum than the legal debt is not, in principle, binding at common law because of a lack of consideration.[68] Yet a creditor who makes such a promise, provided the debtor relies and acts upon it, might be estopped in equity from going back upon his statement.[69] In other words, equity may prevent a creditor in a contractual relationship from abusing his right at common law (*cf* Ch 12 § 3(c)) where it would be 'unconscionable in all the circumstances' for him to do so.[70] Whether the doctrine of estoppel will be available to enforce a promise to pay a larger debt than the one originally agreed is open to question since estoppel is supposed to operate as a shield rather than a sword. However, it has recently been faintly suggested, *obiter,* that the defence of estoppel might be available to preclude a contractor from denying that his promise to pay is legally binding.[71]

4 PRE-CONTRACTUAL LIABILITY

Remedies like estoppel can also be used to solve problems of pre-contractual liability. The offeror who carelessly fails to maintain his telex machine might find himself estopped from denying a contractual relationship with an acceptor whose acceptance was not actually received by the offeror because of the defective telex machine. And this in effect means that the offeror might be liable in damages for what a German lawyer would call *culpa in contrahendo* (fault in contracting).[72] This doctrine of pre-contractual liability is based on the idea that parties negotiating a contract owe to each other certain minimum duties founded either in contract itself (for example, the doctrine of good faith) or in the law of delict (tort).[73] In French and Dutch law a party who breaks off pre-contractual negotiations without good reason may, accordingly, find himself liable in damages.[74]

The doctrine of *culpa in contrahendo* has spread to a number of civil law systems with the result that it is becoming a general principle of the civilian law of obligations that parties in negotiation have to have a certain regard for each other's interests. However, when English law was invited to adopt such a principle in *Walford v Miles*[75] Lord Ackner responded:

---

67 *Crabb v Arun DC* [1976] Ch 179.

68 *Foakes v Beer* (1884) 9 App Cas 605.

69 *Central London Property Trust Ltd v High Trees House Ltd* [1947] 1 KB 130.

70 *Amalgamated Inv & Property Co v Texas Commerce Int Bank* [1981] 1 All ER 923, 937.

71 *Williams v Roffey Brothers* [1991] 1 QB 1, 13, 17–18.

72 Von Mehren, *Formation,* paras 23–29; Atiyah, Harris & Tallon, pp 29–30.

73 See eg J Ghestin, 'The Pre-contractual Obligation to Disclose Information', in Harris & Tallon, pp 151–66; Von Mehren, *Formation*, paras 27–29.

74 Von Mehren, *Formation*, para 29; Malaurie & Aynès, no 875.

75 [1992] 2 AC 128.

> ... [T]he concept of a duty to carry on negotiations in good faith is inherently repugnant to the adversarial position of the parties when involved in negotiations. Each party to the negotiations is entitled to pursue his (or her) own interest, so long as he avoids making misrepresentations. To advance that interest he must be entitled, if he thinks it appropriate, to threaten to withdraw from further negotiations or to withdraw in fact, in the hope that the opposite party may seek to reopen the negotiations by offering him improved terms. [Counsel for the plaintiffs], of course, accepts that the agreement upon which he relies does not contain a duty to complete the negotiations. But that still leaves the vital question – how is a vendor ever to know that he is entitled to withdraw from further negotiations? How is the court to police such an 'agreement'? A duty to negotiate in good faith is as unworkable in practice as it is inherently inconsistent with the position of a negotiating party. It is here that the uncertainty lies. In my judgment, while negotiations are in existence either party is entitled to withdraw from those negotiations, at any time and for any reason. There can be thus no obligation to continue to negotiate until there is a 'proper reason' to withdraw ... [76]

In truth English law, as we have seen with estoppel, is more complex. If one party invites another with whom he is negotiating a contract actually to start work before a formal contract is signed it may well be that a non-contractual debt claim will be available in restitution.[77] Equally, a damages action might be available to any negotiator who suffers damage as a result of another's fraudulent or negligent misrepresentation (see § 7). Another way of achieving liability in respect of bad faith or negligence in the conduct of pre-contractual negotiations is via the concept of a collateral contract (*pactum de contrahendo*). In this situation a statement is regarded as a contractual promise by treating the entering into the main contract as consideration for the enforceability of the collateral statement.[78] This notion of the collateral contract – *pactum de contrahendo* – is particularly useful in turning pre-contractual expectations into actual contractual obligations; however, the court will probably only be prepared to do this in rare cases where both parties had a clear commercial interest in the proper conduct of pre-contractual negotiations and where one party had acted in bad faith, amounting to abuse of power or of its (pre-contractual) rights, leading to wasted expenditure on the part of the other party.[79]

If the party acting in bad faith is a public rather than a private body then the rules of administrative law may also come into play. Thus, a local authority does not have the right at public law to exercise private law rights in an unreasonable way.[80] This public law liability for abuse of rights brings one back to the question about the duties of private bodies: is there a duty to negotiate in good faith? As we have seen, it would appear that there is no such duty – indeed a contracting party is not even under an obligation to correct a mistake on behalf of the other party.[81] And even where there

---

76 At p 138.

77 *British Steel Corporation v Cleveland Bridge & Engineering Co Ltd* [1984] 1 All ER 504.

78 See eg *Carlill v Carbolic Smoke Ball Co* [1893] 1 QB 256.

79 *Blackpool Aero Club v Blackpool BC* [1990] 1 WLR 1195; *cf Walford v Miles* [1992] 2 AC 128.

80 *Wheeler v Leicester CC* [1985] AC 1054; *R v Lewisham LBC, Ex p Shell UK* [1988] 1 All ER 938; Local Government Act 1988 s 17.

81 *Smith v Hughes* (1871) LR 6 QB 597.

might be a specific duty of good faith it does not automatically follow that breach of this duty will in itself give rise to a claim in damages; accordingly, a duty to disclose which attaches to contracts of insurance gives rise only to the equitable remedy of rescission.[82] If a party wishes to obtain damages then it would have to be shown that the silence amounted to a negligent misstatement giving rise to a liability in tort (*cf* Ch 13 § 1(a)) or in contract. Of course, once a fiduciary relationship (*cf* Ch 4 § 5(e)) is established between the negotiating parties it might well be possible for one of the parties to bring an action for account when there has been a breach of this duty; and it must not be forgotten that the common law might allow a non-contractual restitution claim in a situation where one party has expended money at another's request.[83] In short, pre-contractual liability can be a matter for the law of contract, tort, unjust enrichment, equity or administrative law depending on the circumstances of each case.

5 INTENTION TO CREATE LEGAL RELATIONS

The distinctions between civil and commercial law and between *ius publicum* and *ius privatum* emerge once again in the third essential requirement for the validity of an English contract. The parties to a contract must intend the promise or promises to be legally binding. Accordingly, if a clause is inserted into an agreement specifically stating that the promises are not intended to have legal effect, then the promises will in principle be unenforceable for a lack of an intention to create legal relations.[84]

The civil and commercial distinction is of relevance to this essential condition because in many transactions the parties do not actually put their minds to the question of whether they are entering a legal relationship. The question of an intention to create legal relations has, accordingly, to be determined from the context out of which the promise arises.[85] The traditional approach is that in social and family relations there is a prima facie presumption that no legal relations were intended, whereas if the transaction took place in the context of business relations the court will be very hesitant before allowing either party to claim that no legal transaction was intended.[86] All the same, if the commercial relationship is outweighed by other considerations things may be different; and one such consideration is a business relationship involving the public rather than the private bond. Thus, the supply of energy (gas, electricity) is pursuant to a statutory and not a contractual duty;[87] and industrial relations agreements are usually regarded at common law as being matters of public policy outside the private law.[88] One practical use, then, of the requirement of an intention to create legal relations is

82 *Banque Keyser Ullman v Skandia (UK) Insurance* [1990] 1 QB 665; [1991] AC 249.

83 *BSC v Cleveland Bridge & Engineering Co Ltd* [1984] 1 All ER 504.

84 *Jones v Vernons Pools Ltd* [1938] 2 All ER 626.

85 See eg *Albert v Motor Insurers' Bureau* [1972] AC 301; *Blackpool Areo Club v Blackpool BC* [1990] 1 WLR 1195.

86 *Esso Petroleum Ltd v Commissioners of Custom and Excise* [1976] 1 All ER 117, 120, 121.

87 This remains true even although the public utilities have now been privatised: *Norweb v Dixon* [1995] 1 WLR 636.

88 *Ford Motor Co Ltd v AUEF* [1969] 2 All ER 481.

that it can be used to recategorise problems out of private law and into the field of *ius publicum*, labour law or perhaps quasi-contract.

6 VITIATING FACTORS

In civil law systems, because contract is based upon consent, invalid or defective formation of the *volonté* can bring about the annulment of a contract. The *vices du consentement* are classified as error, duress and fraud; and a contract concluded under the influence of error, the most important of the *vices du consentement* according to Pothier, can be annulled since *non videntur qui errant consentir.*[89] The theory, then, is simple enough: there cannot be true consent and agreement where the *volonté* has been affected by the existence of mistake or where one person has used threats, underhand tricks or deceit to secure the contract.

In English law the historical emphasis upon promise rather than consensual agreement and will (*volonté*) has resulted in the question of contracts defective in formation being treated in a piecemeal fashion. Both common law and equity have developed their own separate doctrines and remedies to deal with mistake, duress and fraud, and this piecemeal approach has given rise to distinctions which are unknown in some of the continental systems. For example, in the area of mistake, an important distinction is made between non-contractual statements (representations) and contractual promises (terms); and this distinction in turn is related to the objectivity and sanctity of promises. Once an objective enforceable promise has been established the law often prefers to look, not at the institution of the contract itself in order to see if it is non-existent, but at the surrounding circumstances in order to see if relief can be granted. Accordingly, the emphasis is more often (but not always) on voidability rather than voidness.

The underdeveloped notion of the law of persons (*cf* Ch 2 § 8) in the common law is also of importance here because it has led to the topic of incapacity being treated as a vitiating factor and not as an essential requirement of a valid contract.[90] Accordingly, a contract with a minor or a drunkard is *prima facie* valid. Here again one can see that the focal point is not subjective agreement, but objective promise. English law starts from the assumption that promises supported by consideration are enforceable; one only looks into problems of consent and the capacity of a legal subject as something which may undermine the established contract.[91]

(a) Void, voidable and unenforceable contracts

The piecemeal approach of the common law to problems that the continental jurist would see as defects of consent has resulted in some important conceptual distinctions. A contract may be defective in such a way that, in truth, there was no contract at all (void); in these situations to talk of a 'void contract' is something of a contradiction in

89 Pothier, *Traité des obligations* (1761), no 17. And see eg the NBW Bk 6 art 228.

90 See *Hart v O'Connor* [1985] AC 1000. But *cf Kleinwort Benson Ltd v Glasgow CC* [1996] 2 WLR 655.

91 Except when a legal person has no actual power to contract: see *Kleinwort Benson, supra.*

terms since there never was a contract,[92] save, perhaps, in those situations where the voidness results from a condition precedent (Ch 10 § 3(d)). Alternatively, a contract may be valid but the defect gives one or other of the parties the right to rescind (voidable). Here one is really talking about the equitable remedy of rescission (Ch 5 § 3). However, some contracts may be neither void nor voidable but, because of some defect of form or some principle of public policy, unenforceable in the courts. These unenforceable contracts are of a different class from either void or voidable contracts.

A 'void contract', although often used by lawyers, is, then, a contradiction in terms: there never was a contract in the eyes of the law, even though the parties may have believed that they had entered a contract. Such voidness may result either from the absence of some essential condition such as a valid acceptance or possibly from a rule of public policy[93] and thus void contracts are questions for the common law. They are questions of substantive contract law (offer and acceptance, implied condition precedent).[94] Contracts that are voidable for some defect are, in contrast, mainly problems for equity; they tend to be questions located in the law of actions or remedies. This is because the common law could offer only monetary remedies and it was the Court of Chancery that supplied the more flexible methods of intervention. This intervention at the remedial level in turn encouraged a more subtle approach towards both the formation of substantive equitable doctrines of intervention and the analysis of facts.

An unenforceable contract is, in theory, valid at law and it is only at the level of procedure that the law intervenes for want of form, proof or public policy. Accordingly, an unenforceable contract can still have substantive legal effects and this means that there may well be situations where it is of importance to distinguish between a void and an unenforceable contract. For example, an unenforceable contract may be able to effect a conveyance of moveable property, at least if there is physical delivery,[95] whereas a void contract cannot.[96] It must be said, however, that the judges themselves have not always been that precise in the distinction between void, voidable and unenforceable contracts, particularly in the area of illegality.

(b) Incapacity

Incapacity in the common law of contract differs from problems of capacity in continental law in two main ways. First, it is not really part of any general theory of the law of persons primarily because the common law has not worked out any such theory (*cf* Ch 2 §§ 7–8). Legal personality, for example, is a somewhat restricted concept

92 *Kleinwort Benson Ltd v Glasgow CC* [1996] 2 WLR 655, 663.

93 Where contracts are 'void' for public policy reasons it is often difficult to know whether they are really void or just unenforceable: *Bennett v Bennett* [1952] 1 KB 249, 260; *Shell UK Ltd v Lostock Garages Ltd* [1977] 1 All ER 481, 488–89.

94 See eg *Financings Ltd v Stimson* [1962] 1 WLR 1184.

95 *Singh v Ali* [1960] AC 167.

96 *Cunday v Lindsay* (1878) 3 App Cas 459.

applied mainly to public or commercial organisations and, as such, the associated problems of contractual capacity belong more to public or to company law.[97] Secondly, capacity is not an essential requirement for the validity of a contract and this means that a contract with a person of unsound mind will *prima facie* be valid and only voidable in equity if equitable fraud can be shown.[98]

The same is true for a contract with a minor – that is, a person under the age of 18 years – except that the contract is either fully valid (for example, a contract for the sale of necessary goods[99] or a beneficial contract of employment) or voidable or unenforceable as against the minor. And even if a contract is voidable or unenforceable against a minor, the law of restitution (*cf* Ch 11) has now been given a statutory role. A court may, if it is 'just and equitable' to do so, require a person who was a minor when the contract was made to transfer to the other contractor any 'property' acquired under the contract or any property representing it.[100]

(c) Illegality

The problem of whether certain contracts are void, voidable or enforceable is to be found in a more acute form in contracts that are deemed illegal. Part of this difficulty may be due to the fact that English contract law, because it focuses upon promise rather than agreement (*cf* Ch 8 § 5(c)), does not use any concept such as illegal cause; it can therefore be very difficult to find within a transaction tainted with illegality any firm focal point around which can be made a decision as to whether or not a remedy should be available. English law, instead, distinguishes between contracts illegal *per se* (for example, a contract to murder), contracts illegal in motive (for example, a contract to hire a vehicle for prostitution) and contracts illegal by statute (for example, a contractor fails to have a proper licence as required by public law) (*cf* Ch 7 § 6).

The general principle of English law is that if the illegality arises out of public morality or public policy – that is, contracts illegal at common law – the contract will be unenforceable if not void: *ex turpi causa non oritur actio* (an immoral cause gives rise to no action).[101] And if both parties are equally in the wrong the court will give no effect to the contract or allow any remedy whatsoever: *in pari delicto potior est conditio possidentis* (where both parties are equally in the wrong, the position of the possessor is stronger).[102] However, if the parties are not *in pari delicto*, or the contract is illegal only because of the motive of one of the parties, the court might be prepared to entertain an

97 HW Goldschmidt, *English Law from the Foreign Standpoint* (Pitman, 1937), pp 168–72. Note, however, that an *ultra vires* contract will be void: *Kleinwort Benson Ltd v Glasgow CC* [1996] 2 WLR 655.

98 *Hart v O'Connor* [1985] AC 1000 PC; *Kleinwort Benson Ltd v Glasgow CC* [1996] 2 WLR 655, 672.

99 Sale of Goods Act 1979 s 3.

100 Minors' Contracts Act 1987 s 3.

101 *Euro-Diam Ltd v Bathurst* [1990] QB 1.

102 *Taylor v Chester* (1869) LR 4 QB 309.

action in tort,[103] in restitution[104] or via a collateral contract.[105] But much depends upon the circumstances of the case and the degree of innocence with regard to the person seeking enforcement or some other remedy,[106] and in this context the maxim *nemo auditur propriam turpitudinem allegans* (no one alleging his own wrong is to be heard) can be of relevance.[107]

When a contract is illegal as a result of statute the position becomes even more complex because the courts make a distinction between illegal activities and illegal contracts; that is to say, they will interpret the legislation to see if it was the intention of Parliament to make any contract arising out of the illegal activity also illegal.[108] For example, it is in breach of statute to overload any lorry or ship, but the question as to whether any contract of carriage will be illegal and unenforceable will depend upon the aims of the statute in question, the degree of culpability of both parties and the public interest in making any such contracts illegal.[109] In addition, a contracting party to an illegal contract may be able to rely on his or her property rights, thus avoiding the illegality of the obligation (*cf* Ch 7 § 6(b)).

(d) Contracts void by public policy

There are certain classes of contract which, although not illegal as such, are said to be 'void' for reasons of public policy. The most important of these contracts are contracts in restraint of trade and these are usually dealt with in depth in competition law rather than in a general work on contract.[110] But it is worth mentioning in a general survey of the law of obligations that the restraint of trade doctrine might now be available as a means for avoiding some oppressive standard form contracts where the bargaining power of the parties has not been equal.[111] An unconscionable bargain between economically unequal parties may, in some circumstances, be against the public interest and void, 'void' here probably meaning unenforceable.[112]

7 MISREPRESENTATION

Error, duress and fraud are, as we have seen, the three most important *vices du consentement* in the civil law systems. They all affect the formation of the agreement and they all undermine the formation at the subjective level. English law, thinking in terms of promises rather than agreement, has to approach the problem in a different way:

---

103 *Bowmakers Ltd v Barnet Instruments Ltd* [1945] KB 65.

104 *Kiriri Cotton Co Ltd v Dewani* [1960] AC 192.

105 *Strongman v Sincock* [1955] 2 QB 525.

106 See eg *Euro-Diam Ltd v Bathurst* [1990] QB 1; *Howard v Shiristar Ltd* [1990] 1 WLR 1292.

107 See eg *Ashmore, Benson, Pease & Co Ltd v A V Dawson Ltd* [1973] 1 WLR 828.

108 *St John Shipping Corp v Rank* [1957] 1 QB 267; *Archbolds (Freightage) Ltd v Spanglett Ltd* [1961] 1 QB 374.

109 *Ashmore, Benson, Pease & Co Ltd v A V Dawson Ltd* [1973] 1 WLR 828.

110 See generally *Esso Petroleum Ltd v Harper's Garage* [1968] AC 269.

111 *Schroeder Music Publishing Co Ltd v Macaulay* [1974] 1 WLR 1308.

112 *Bennett v Bennett* [1952] 1 KB 249, 260; *Shell UK Ltd v Lostock Garages Ltd* [1977] 1 All ER 481, 488–89. But *cf Kleinwort Benson Ltd v Glasgow CC* [1996] 2 WLR 655.

instead of looking at the subjective minds of the parties the emphasis is on the facts and on the law of remedies. Accordingly, the problem of error is seen as a matter of circumstance. Contract lawyers in a commercial and a consumer environment are often faced with the problem of having to analyse contractual liability within a mass of negotiating statements motivated by the legitimate self-interest of the parties. Many of these statements can be ignored by the law as being non-specific advertising 'puffs'; other, more specific statements, may not end up as part of any formal contract. Nevertheless, statements made before contract can affect the beliefs and assumptions, if not the will (*volonté*), of one or both parties.

(a) Contractual and pre-contractual promises

English law, in analysing all negotiations leading to the completion of a contract, focuses on the statements themselves more than on the actual contractual intention of the parties. Promises made to induce a contractual bargain (representations) are distinguished from promises (terms or warranties) that go to make up the bargain itself.[113] However, representations made to induce a contract, although conceptually separate from the contract itself, are not without legal consequence if untrue (misrepresentations), provided that the representee has relied and acted upon them. In equity a misrepresentation may give rise to the remedy of rescission[114] (*cf* Ch 5 § 3) – although if the representee delays, or third parties gain property rights in the subject matter, the remedy may be refused.[115] And at law, if a representor cannot prove that the representation was made without negligence, a misrepresentation can form the basis of an action in tort.[116] Before 1967 such a damages action could be founded only in the tort of deceit, where fraud had to be proved,[117] or, after 1964, in the tort of negligence where carelessness had to be shown[118] (*cf* Ch 12 § 3(a)). The new statutory action continues to use the tort of deceit, but with the requirement of fraud removed and replaced by a presumption of negligence.[119]

(b) Types of misrepresentation

As a result of these differing remedies for pre-contractual statements it has traditionally been necessary to distinguish between three kinds of misrepresentation. The first is fraudulent where the untrue statement was deliberately or recklessly made; the second is negligent where the untrue statement was made without due care; and the third is innocent misrepresentation where the untrue statement was made in good faith and on

113 *Dick Bentley Productions Ltd v Harold Smith (Motors) Ltd* [1965] 1 WLR 623.

114 *Redgrave v Hurd* (1881) 20 Ch D 1.

115 *Leaf v International Galleries* [1950] 2 KB 86.

116 Misrepresentation Act 1967 s 2(1).

117 *Derry v Peek* (1889) 14 App Cas 337.

118 *Hedley Byrne & Co v Heller & Partners* [1964] AC 465.

119 *Howard Marine & Dredging Co v Ogden & Son (Excavations) Ltd* [1978] QB 574.

reasonable grounds. In principle, innocent misrepresentation is incapable of giving rise to an action for damages at common law unless the representation can be deemed a collateral contract[120] (see below); but equity now has the statutory power to award damages in lieu of rescission for misrepresentation[121] and so it may be that damages are now, in practice, generally available for all types of misrepresentation. Damages in lieu of rescission cannot, however, be awarded in cases of fraudulent misrepresentation.

(c) Definition of misrepresentation

It has already been suggested that not all statements made to induce a contract can be treated as statements having legal effects. A mere advertising puff does not, to put it another way, amount to a 'misrepresentation' in law. The statement must be of a particular kind in order to amount to a misrepresentation and the starting point is the definition of a misrepresentation itself. A misrepresentation is an untrue statement of existing fact which induces the representee to enter into a contract with the representor and to suffer loss in consequence. As a result of this definition neither a statement of opinion[122] nor a statement of law[123] can in theory amount to a misrepresentation, but in practice the court will look closely at 'opinions' to see if they do amount to statements of fact.[124] The definition also excludes statements of future intention and silence. The former is excluded on the questionable ground that a promise to do something in the future cannot be said to have been true or false at the time when it was made;[125] and the latter is subject to exceptions – indeed contracts of insurance, contracts *uberrimae fidei*, actually impose a positive duty of disclosure,[126] although this non-disclosure will not necessarily found a damages (as opposed to a rescission) action.[127] Non-disclosure may, however, give rise to an action in restitution (*cf* Ch 11 §§ 2(a), 3(d)) if a party to a fiduciary relationship (*cf* Ch 4 § 5(e)) gains an unjustified profit as a result of the silence.[128]

(d) Collateral warranties

The limited power of the courts to award damages for non-fraudulent misrepresentation before the expansion of the law of tort into the field of negligent misstatement (*cf* Ch 13 § 1) led the courts sometimes to take a more generous view of what amounted to a contractual promise. The courts were sometimes prepared either to incorporate a representation into the main contract as a term or to treat a

---

120 *Heilbut, Symons & Co v Buckleton* [1913] AC 30.

121 Misrepresentation Act 1967 s 2(2).

122 *Bisset v Wilkinson* [1927] AC 177 (PC).

123 *Eaglesfield v Marquis of Londonderry* (1876) 4 Ch D 693, 708.

124 *Esso Petroleum v Mardon* [1976] QB 801.

125 *R v Sunair Holidays Ltd* [1973] 2 All ER 1233, 1236.

126 See eg *Lambert v Co-operative Insurance Society* [1975] 2 Lloyd's Rep 485.

127 *Banque Keyser Ullmann v Skandia Insurance Ltd* [1990] 1 QB 665.

128 *English v Dedham Vale Properties Ltd* [1978] 1 WLR 93.

misrepresentation as forming a separate contract collateral to the main one, the consideration for such a collateral contract being found in the entering of the main contract (a burden). Whether or not a representation amounts to a collateral warranty or a collateral contract depends upon a number of factors: for example, the courts will look at the time the statement was made[129] or the status and expertise of the representor.[130] Thus, a representation by a car dealer (as opposed to a private vendor) about the condition or mileage of a car subsequently sold to the representee by the representor might well amount to a contractual term.[131]

Once the court had incorporated a representation into a contract the right to rescind in equity for misrepresentation was lost on the ground that the statement was logically under the control of the substantive doctrine of contract itself. Thus, rescission would become a matter of the status of the term broken (*cf* Ch 10 § 3). This bar has now been removed,[132] but this means that a party to a contract can rescind the contract for the breach of a relatively minor term if such a term started its life as a representation (*cf* Ch 10 § 3(e)). Whether the courts would actually treat the contract as voidable in these circumstances is uncertain now that they have power to award damages in lieu of rescission.[133]

The concept of a collateral contract (*pactum de contrahendo*), besides being useful in getting around the parol evidence rule (*cf* Ch 8 § 5(f)), is also a useful device for giving damages at common law for innocent misrepresentations. It can turn an 'expectation' induced by a misrepresentation into a legal 'right'.[134] Furthermore the collateral contract has also shown itself useful in three-party situations where the representation does not come from the contractor (for example, a retailer) but from a third party (for example, a manufacturer). Thus, an advertisement by a manufacturer which makes specific promises to the public at large could form the basis for not only an action in debt[135] but one in damages if loss results from reliance upon the statements.[136]

(e) Concurrence

With the expansion of the tort of negligence into the area of misstatement these three party situations can become legally quite complex in that the rules and remedies of contract, tort and equity (estoppel) often exist side-by-side. In some factual situations the rule of non-concurrence used to operate, particularly in the area of professional liability; however, in contrast to French law, there is now no formal rule that tort

129 *Hopkins v Tanqueray* (1854) 139 ER 369.

130 *Esso Petroleum v Mardon* [1976] QB 801.

131 *Dick Bentley Productions Ltd v Harold Smith (Motors) Ltd* [1965] 1 WLR 623.

132 Misrepresentation Act 1967 s 1.

133 Section 2(2).

134 *Blackpool & Fylde Aero Club v Blackpool BC* [1990] 1 WLR 1195.

135 *Carlill v Carbolic Smoke Ball Co* [1893] 1 QB 256.

136 *Wells (Merstham) Ltd v Buckland Sand & Silica Ltd* [1965] 2 QB 170.

actions will be excluded when there is a contractual relationship.[137] Certainly, in the field of commercial law contractual duties are capable of excluding tort duties, even in three party situations;[138] but in the area of misrepresentation the idea of non-concurrence can often be rather unrealistic since the established rights and remedies straddle the boundaries of contract, tort and equity. A misleading statement can, at one and the same time, lead to a number of causes of action and a number of different remedies. Moreover, the idea that a breach of contract can, as against a third party, amount to a tort[139] and that a tort can affect the doctrine of estoppel[140] is established in the case law. All the same the courts still claim to be keen to uphold the boundaries between the various causes of action[141] and this can effect the scope and application of remedies particularly in the area of misrepresentation.[142]

8 MISTAKE

Misrepresentation, although not actually part of the law of contract itself, nevertheless does much of the same kind of work that the doctrine of error does in the continental legal systems. Thus, an error induced by a misrepresentation coming from one of the parties will in principle make a common law contract voidable in equity even if the aggrieved party is guilty of contributory negligence.[143] However, the other side of the coin is that if there is an error but no misrepresentation then, bearing in mind that silence is prima facie no misrepresentation, the promises will be valid and enforceable; for there is no mechanism by which the subjective intentions of the parties can affect the objectivity of the promises. Consequently, the general principle at common law is that a contract is neither void nor voidable simply as a result of the existence of an error.[144]

(a) Consensus and error

In fact, as one might expect, the position is not quite as simple in practice as the general principle suggests.[145] A fundamental mistake with regard to the subject matter of the contract (*error in corpore*), to the nature of the legal transaction (*error in negotio*), to the recording of an agreement (*error in verbis*) or to the identity of one of the contracting parties (*error in persona*) might result in the court holding that there never was consensus *ad idem* (*cf* above § 2(e)). In other words, the mistake will make a contract void because of the failure of an essential condition of validity. Thus, in a sale agreement, if one party

---

137 *Henderson v Merrett Syndicates Ltd* [1995] 2 AC 145. *Cf Bell v Peter Browne & Co* [1990] 2 QB 495.

138 See eg *Pacific Associates Inc v Baxter* [1990] 1 QB 993; *Marc Rich & Co v Bishop Rock Ltd* [1996] 1 AC 211.

139 *White v Jones* [1995] 2 AC 207.

140 *D & C Builders v Rees* [1966] 2 QB 617.

141 *China & South Sea Bank Ltd v Tan* [1990] 1 AC 536, 543–44.

142 *Banque Keyser Ullmann v Skandia Insurance Ltd* [1990] 1 QB 665 (CA).

143 *Redgrave v Hurd* (1881) 20 Ch D 1.

144 *Bell v Lever Brothers* [1932] AC 161.

145 Zimmermann, p 619.

had in mind one object and the other party had in mind quite a different object then the contract might well be void for lack of *consensus*.[146]

(b) Implied condition precedent

Alternatively, a court might hold that the contract is void for the failure of an implied condition precedent upon which the whole contract is founded. Here the court is using a device well known to civil lawyers,[147] and so if two parties make a contract of sale or hire of a thing which, unknown to them, has perished the contract will be 'void'[148] on the basis that it was an implied condition precedent (*cf* Ch 10 § 3(d)) of the contract that the goods remained in existence or in substantially the same condition.[149]

However, the courts are not overready to imply such terms into a contract.[150] For example, if a buyer appears objectively to agree to the actual promises of the seller the fact that the buyer may be labouring under some mistake will not in itself be grounds for setting the contract aside. Indeed even if the seller was aware that the buyer was labouring under an error the seller is under no duty at common law to speak out, for there is no general doctrine of *bona fides* in English contract law.[151] Furthermore the emphasis upon promise rather than agreement (*cf* Ch 8 § 5(c)) means that it is theoretically possible to have *consensus ad idem* and a binding contract even if both parties are in error as to the actual existence of the subject matter.[152] Consequently, much will depend upon the nature of the promises themselves and the practices of commerce, the question often being as to whether or not the promise(s) contained an implication or guarantee as to the existence or generic quality of the subject matter.[153]

(c) Contracts voidable in equity

If the general principle of the common law seems unduly strict, recent developments in equity suggest that English law is becoming more sensitive to situations where the abuse of a contractual right gives rise to an unjustified enrichment. If a contract is subject to a mistake and the mistake is of such a type that the enforcement of the bargain would in all conscience turn a justified means of enrichment into an unjustified one then equity might be prepared, in the last resort, to allow its remedy of rescission (*cf* Ch 5 § 3) to be used to set the contract aside on terms stipulated by the court.[154] Such rescission will, however, be available only where the mistake was fundamental

146 *Raffles v Wichelhaus* (1864) 159 ER 375.

147 Zimmermann, pp 716–18, 743–47.

148 Sale of Goods Act 1979 s 6.

149 *Financings Ltd v Stimson* [1962] 3 All ER 386; *Associated Japanese Bank v Credit du Nord* [1989] 1 WLR 255.

150 *Associated Japanese Bank*, above, pp 268–69.

151 *Smith v Hughes* (1871) LR 6 QB 597.

152 *McRae v Commonwealth Disposals Commission* (1951) 84 CLR 377.

153 *William Sindall Plc v Cambridgeshire County Council* [1994] 1 WLR 1016.

154 *Solle v Butcher* [1950] 1 KB 671.

and common to both parties;[155] and it is highly unlikely that it will be available to set aside the 'good bargain' in that it is one of the principles of commercial law that one person should be allowed to take advantage of another's miscalculation or mistake with regard to the value of the subject matter of the contract.[156] Equity will not protect a person from his own imprudence, save in cases where this imprudence is outweighed by fraud or sharp practice on the part of the other party.[157]

(d) Rectification and refusal of specific performance (*error in verbis*)

Equity can also provide relief for mistake by granting rectification of a written contract containing an error (*cf* Ch 5 § 2).[158] Here of course equity is simply following the common law in upholding what in truth was promised. Once again the court will have to strike a balance between the legitimate objectives of commerce and the dictates of conscience, and it will often look for some inequitable behaviour – for example, silence as to the error on the part of the person benefiting from the mistake – which can be used as a focal point for turning the good bargain into an unconscionable transaction.[159] Alternatively, equity can prevent a person profiting from a mistake in a contract by refusing, as a matter of discretion, to grant specific performance of a contract containing an error (*cf* Ch 5 § 4(d)).

(e) *Error in corpore*

At one level, then, error is largely a matter of remedies and defective formation rather than a question of substantive legal rules attracting their own chapter in the textbooks. Accordingly, if a contractor wishes to escape from a contract on the basis of a mistake as to the quality of the thing sold or on the basis of the existence or non-existence of some fact that, had it been known at the time of the contract, would have affected one party's consent to contract, then the contractor must show that the quality or fact either forms part of the offer and acceptance process or amounts to a condition upon which the whole obligation depends. This is by no means an easy task. For example, it is unlikely that the junk shop owner who unknowingly sells a priceless picture would be able to have the contract of sale set aside on the basis that he consented only to sell a near worthless painting; the risk is on the seller and there is no general duty on the buyer to tell the seller that the painting is valuable.[160] Equally, the employer who pays an employee a sum of money to determine a contract of employment will not be able to claim restitution of the sum if it transpires that there had been grounds for discharging the contract of employment for breach.[161] Only where the whole subject

155 *William Sindall Plc v Cambridgeshire County Council* [1994] 1 WLR 1016.

156 *Riverplate Properties Ltd v Paul* [1975] Ch 133.

157 *Redgrave v Hurd* (1881) 20 Ch D 1.

158 *Roberts & Co v Leicestershire CC* [1961] Ch 555.

159 *Thomas Bates & Son Ltd v Wyndham's (Lingerie) Ltd* [1981] 1 All ER 1077, 1086.

160 *Smith v Hughes* (1871) LR 6 QB 597; *Bell v Lever Brothers* [1932] AC 161.

161 *Bell v Lever Brothers* [1932] AC 161.

matter of the contract turns out to be non-existent will there be a basis for saying that there was no offer and acceptance[162] or that there is an implied condition precedent.[163] In theory, the equitable remedy of rescission might be available on these facts, thus giving rise to the possibility of making the contract voidable, but it is unlikely that Chancery will be ready to compromise the security of transactions. There will probably have to be some kind of unconscionable behaviour on the part of a contractor before equity will intervene on the ground of mistake as to the quality of a thing sold or mistake arising from the silence of a contractor.

(f) *Error in persona*

The principle governing mistake of identity (*error in persona*) has already been mentioned as being a problem of offer and acceptance. Yet because many of the cases in this area have a common factual pattern and raise a particular property problem they need to be looked at on their own. The common factual pattern takes the form of a three-party situation where the seller of a chattel is misled by a buyer's misrepresentation into believing that he is dealing with someone quite different from the person standing before him and as a result the seller hands over the goods either on credit or against a cheque which later turns out to be worthless. In such circumstances the contract is voidable either for misrepresentation (rescission in equity) or for breach (repudiation); but by the time the seller discovers the true situation the rogue buyer has usually sold the goods to a *bona fide* purchaser.[164] The mistake of identity cases thus involve, at the level of the remedy, an action in tort for revindication of property or its value (see Ch 13 § 8(a)) and, at the level of substance, a claim by the original seller that the original contract of sale was void for mistake (thus preventing the passing of title).

What makes these cases so difficult in England is that the common law has no equivalent to the French principle that *en fait de meubles, la possession vaut titre* (in the case of moveable property possession is equivalent to title).[165] Instead a number of principles of law oppose each other in an attempt to settle a dispute between two innocent parties. The first principle, from the law of property, is *nemo dat quod non habet* (no one can give a better title than he himself has); the second principle, from the law of contract, is 'that if you propose to make a contract with A, then B cannot substitute himself for A without your consent and to your disadvantage';[166] and the third principle, from equity, is 'that whenever one of two persons must suffer by the acts of a third, he who has enabled such third person to occasion the loss must sustain it.'[167] If the court wishes to give expression to the first two principles then the mistake of

162 *Financings Ltd v Stimson* [1962] 1 WLR 1184.

163 *Associated Japanese Bank v Credit du Nord* [1989] 1 WLR 255.

164 But see *Car & Universal Finance Co v Caldwell* [1965] 1 QB 525.

165 CC art 2279. What it has is Sale of Goods Act 1979 s 23. *Caldwell*, above, shows the limits of this section.

166 *Boulton v Jones* (1857) 157 ER 232.

167 *Lickbarrow v Mason* (1787) 100 ER 35, 39.

identity will make the contract void and thus incapable of effecting a conveyance.[168] If the court wishes to give expression to the last principle then it will arrive at the conclusion that the mistake made the contract voidable, the seller being deemed to have made the contract with the actual person standing before him.[169]

What principle a court may wish to give expression to in these mistake of identity cases in turn can depend upon a number of factors. The court may, for example, pay particular regard to the status of the parties on the ground that the business salesman is usually protected by insurance;[170] and so not just insurance but the private and commercial law dichotomy (*cf* Ch 8 § 4(a)) could be of relevance in this area of mistake in that it might help determine the route to be followed in allocating the risks and losses of commerce in a consumer society. Nevertheless, it has to be emphasised that mistake of identity is unlikely to be treated these days as a reason for declaring a contract void; there is a strong presumption in supply of goods and services cases that contractors contract with the person before them and that identity (*intuitious personae*) is of little importance.[171]

(g) *Error in negotio*

A similar property and principle problem can arise when a party misrepresents the nature of the contract or document to the other party. In this situation the contract will be voidable for misrepresentation or breach, but when it comes to the question of whether it is void as a result of the representee's plea of *non est factum meum* (this is not my document) the courts have reached something of a compromise. The contract will be void only if the representee signed, without any negligence on his or her part, a contract which was radically different from the document that the signer believed it to be.[172] Particular emphasis, then, is put not just on the nature and contents of the contractual document, but upon the maxim *quod quis ex culpa sua damnum fecit, non intelligitus damnum sentire* (whoever is damaged as a result of his own fault is deemed not to suffer damage) in order to protect third party rights (*cf* Ch 7). However, if the third party should have been put on guard then equity may intervene to set aside any charge or security transaction.[173]

(h) Mistake: concluding remarks

The general principle that promises are *prima facie* enforceable as a valid contract even if they have been arrived at on the basis of a mistake is subject to so many exceptions that the exceptions are now becoming the rule. This development may or may not be desirable in terms of contractual justice, but the piecemeal approach of English law to

---

168 *Ingram v Little* [1961] 1 QB 31.

169 *Lewis v Averay* [1972] 1 QB 198.

170 *RH Willis & Son v British Car Auctions Ltd* [1978] 1 WLR 438, 442.

171 *Lewis v Averay* [1972] 1 QB 198.

172 *Gallie v Lee* [1971] AC 1004.

173 *Avon Finance Co Ltd v Bridger* [1985] 2 All ER 281.

the problem of mistake has resulted in a confused legal situation. At the level of contractual rights there is no separate doctrine of mistake as such, only doctrines about formation and terms which may be applicable to factual situations involving mistakes. At the level of remedies, on the other hand, the Court of Chancery has taken a more subtle approach and might be prepared to allow one of its remedies to be used so as to prevent unjustified enrichment or abuse of a contractual right. Nevertheless, in one contract case involving contractual mistake one judge thought that the contract was void at common law, another judge thought that it was voidable in equity, and the third judge thought that the contract was valid.[174] The confusion between these legal judgments reflects only the confusion of the law itself.

9 FRAUD

When one turns from mistake to fraud it would be misleading to say that English law is equally confused. Nevertheless, as Robert Goff LJ (as he then was) pointed out in an *obiter dictum*, 'There is ... no general principle of law that fraud vitiates consent.'[175] And he later elaborated:

> What is the effect of fraud? Fraud is, in relation to a contract, a fraudulent misrepresentation by one party which induces the other to enter into a contract or apparent contract with the representor. Apart from the innocent party's right to recover damages for the tort of deceit, the effect of the fraud is simply to give the innocent party the right, subject to certain limits, to rescind the contract. These rights are similar to (though not identical with) the rights of a party who has been induced to enter into a contract by an innocent, as opposed to a fraudulent, misrepresentation, though there the right to recover damages derives from statute, and the limits to rescission are somewhat more severe. It is plain, however, that in this context fraud does not 'vitiate consent', any more than an innocent misrepresentation 'vitiates consent'. Looked at realistically, a misrepresentation, whether fraudulent or innocent, induces a party to enter into a contract in circumstances where it may be unjust that the representor should be permitted to retain the benefit (the chose in action) so acquired by him. The remedy of rescission, by which the unjust enrichment of the representor is prevented, though for historical and practical reasons treated in books on the law of contract, is a straightforward remedy in restitution subject to limits which are characteristic of that branch of the law.[176]

In equity the notion of fraud is wider than at common law in that certain kinds of behaviour not involving *dolus malus* (serious fraud) can amount to 'constructive fraud' for the purposes of equitable remedies; but in these equity cases, as one might expect, the emphasis is often less on the substantive law of contract and more on the law of actions. Accordingly, one should not be surprised if the boundaries between mistake, fraud and duress (undue influence) become, at the level of remedies, rather indistinct.[177]

174 *Magee v Pennine Insurance Co* [1969] 2 QB 507.

175 *Whittaker v Campbell* [1984] QB 318, 326.

176 *Ibid*, p 327.

177 See eg *Avon Finance Co Ltd v Bridger* [1985] 2 All ER 281.

10 DURESS

Duress to the person, like fraud, will probably make a contract voidable rather than void, both at common law and in equity.[178] But, as with fraud, equity has traditionally taken a much wider view of the notion of duress and includes within its scope not only certain relationships between the parties which raise a presumption of undue influence but certain kinds of commercial pressure said to constitute 'economic duress' which vitiate the consent of the victim, making the contract 'not a voluntary act'.[179]

Undue influence is a form of equitable duress that arises either out of certain relationships which raise its presumption – and this aspect of equitable duress is usually tied up with fiduciary (*cf* Ch 4 § 5(e)), family or guardianship relationships (presumed undue influence) – or out of its proof in any individual case (actual undue influence).[180] It is an extended form of *metus reverentialis* and is based on the idea of an abuse of personal influence.[181] In recent years the commercial transaction has increasingly been brought within its scope – indeed undue influence and economic duress are the main ways by which equity now tackles the 'unconscionable' bargain, there being no independent doctrine of unconscionability or inequality of bargaining power either in equity or at common law.[182] But this does not mean that equity will necessarily set aside any transaction involving an inexperienced consumer or indeed any person subjected to undue influence. The court will look to see if the stronger contracting party abused his position *vis-à-vis* the weaker consumer, for example by not advocating that the latter seek independent legal advice before signing some important legal document.[183] In situations involving third parties – where, say, a husband procures through undue influence the signature of his wife to a document charging the family home to a bank (the third party) – the charge contract will be voidable in equity (equitable remedy of rescission) if the husband acted as the agent of the third party[184] or if the third party had actual or constructive notice.[185]

11 RESTITUTION PROBLEMS

Once a contract is set aside on the ground of mistake, incapacity, duress or whatever, restitution problems can arise if property or money has been conveyed under the defective transaction: for the contractual obligation is often no longer around to adjust the parties' rights and duties. In the case of infants, restitution is now available under

178 Much will depend on the actual nature of the duress: extreme duress could presumably make any extracted promise quite meaningless and thus void in the eyes of the law, although in turn this could depend on the definition of *vis absoluta*: Zimmermann, pp 660–62.

179 *Pau On v Lau Yiu Long* [1980] AC 614, 636; the duress does not have to amount to a tort: *Dimskal Shipping Co v IWTF* [1992] 2 AC 152.

180 *Barclays Bank Plc v O'Brien* [1994] 1 AC 180.

181 *Morley v Loughnan* [1893] 1 Ch 736.

182 *National Westminster Bank Plc v Morgan* [1985] AC 686.

183 *Ibid.*

184 See eg *Avon Finance Co Ltd v Bridger* [1985] 2 All ER 281.

185 *Barclays Bank Plc v O'Brien* [1994] 1 AC 180; *Kleinwort Benson Ltd v Glasgow CC* [1996] 2 WLR 655, 671–72.

statute (above § 6(b)), and in a range of other situations the quasi-contractual remedy of money had and received might be available to prevent one party from unjustly enriching himself at the expense of another (*cf* Ch 11 § 2(a)). Thus, at common law money paid under a defective contract will be recoverable if there has been a 'total failure of consideration',[186] unless the defect in the contract arose as a result of illegality (*cf* above § 6(c)) or the defendant is able to establish a change of position.[187] One might add that money paid under a mistake of law was, *prima facie*, not recoverable since ignorance of the law is seen as no excuse; however, it is unlikely that this rule retains its full force today.[188]

Illegal contracts, as we have seen (and see Ch 7 § 6), pose special problems. However, if an owner is able to trace money or property transferred under the illegal contract – that is, if he is able to rely on his right *in rem* rather than on the contractual right *in personam* (*cf* Ch 7 § 6(b)) – then restitution might be available,[189] although it may be that an illegal contract, not being void as such, can act as a valid conveyance.[190] Gaming contracts also present restitutionary problems in that the courts do not like to use the law of restitution to enforce indirectly contracts which are illegal or void for public policy reasons.[191] However, if stolen money is used for gambling, the gambling club is bound to reimburse the victim for the stolen money received and retained by the club provided that the club has been 'unjustly enriched'.[192] This does not mean, of course, that a gambler himself can recover his lost bets on the basis of a failure of consideration: for he has relied upon the casino to honour the wager – he has in law given money to the casino, trusting that the casino will fulfil the obligation binding in honour upon it and pay him if he wins his bet.[193] Restitution, when the contract has disappeared, remains largely a question of remedies more than specific rights

12 CONCLUDING REMARKS

In comparison with the civil law, the formation of contracts in the common law is governed by a set of attitudes and concepts rather different from those to be found in the codes. This does not mean that the practical results will always be so different. Yet it has to be recognised that English contract law responds to a different theoretical underpinning. By way of a concluding summary, then, it might be useful simply to quote, once again, the words of Robert Goff LJ:

> [T]here is, in our opinion, no general principle of law that fraud vitiates consent. Let us consider this proposition first with reference to the law of contract. In English law every valid contract presupposes an offer by one party which has been accepted by the offeree.

186 *Rover International Ltd v Canon Films Ltd* [1989] 1 WLR 912; *Kleinwort Benson Ltd v Glasgow CC* [1996] 2 WLR 655, 671–72.

187 *Avon CC v Howlett* [1983] 1 WLR 605; *Lipkin Gorman v Karpnale Ltd* [1991] 2 AC 548.

188 *R v Tower Hamlets LBC, Ex p Chetnik Ltd* [1988] AC 858, 874–77, 882.

189 *Bowmakers Ltd v Barnet Instruments Ltd* [1945] KB 65; *Amar Singh v Kulubya* [1964] AC 142; *Lipkin Gorman v Karpnale Ltd* [1991] 2 AC 548, 572–74.

190 *Singh v Ali* [1960] AC 167.

191 *Orakpo v Manson Investments Ltd* [1978] AC 95; *Lipkin Gorman v Karpnale Ltd* [1991] 2 AC 548.

192 *Lipkin Gorman v Karpnale Ltd* [1991] 2 AC 548.

193 *Ibid*, at p 577.

> Plainly there can be no such acceptance unless offer and acceptance correspond, so the offer can only be accepted by the offeree, the acceptance must relate to the same subject matter as the offer and must also be, in all material respects, in the same terms as the offer. But the test whether there has been correspondence between offer and acceptance is not subjective but objective. If there is objective agreement, there may be a binding contract, even if in his mind one party or another has not consented to it, a principle recently affirmed by the Court of Appeal in *Centrovincial Estates plc v Merchant Investors Assurance Co Ltd* (1983) *Times*, 8 March. Furthermore putting on one side such matters as the ancient doctrine of non est factum and relief from mistake in equity, there is no principle of English law that any contract may be 'avoided', ie not come into existence, by reason simply of a mistake, whether a mistake of one or both parties. The question is simply whether objective agreement has been reached and, if so, on what terms. If objective agreement has been reached, in the sense we have described, then the parties will be bound, unless on a true construction the agreement was subject to a condition precedent, express or implied, failure of which has in the event prevented a contract from coming into existence.[194]

These words can be compared with those to be found in the French model as expressed in the new Quebec Civil Code:

> 1385. A contract is formed by the sole exchange of consents between persons having capacity to contract ...
>
> 1400. Error vitiates consent of the parties or one of them where it relates to the nature of the contract, the object of the prestation or anything that was essential in determining that consent.
>
> 1401. Error on the part of one party induced by fraud committed by the other party or with his knowledge vitiates consent whenever, but for that error, the party would not have contracted, or would have contracted on different terms.

No doubt the two approaches will arrive at similar results on many occasions, but they are testimony to two very different mentalities (*cf* Ch 14).

194 *Whittaker v Campbell* [1984] QB 318, 326–27.

CHAPTER TEN

NON-PERFORMANCE OF A CONTRACTUAL OBLIGATION

To move from the formation of a contractual obligation to its non-performance is to move, so to speak, from one extreme to another inasmuch as such a move might appear to overlook the scope and contents of the contractual obligation itself. However, it may be argued that questions of analysis and interpretation of contractual obligations usually arise only when there has been a failure of performance; consequently, it is not unreasonable to view problems of interpretation, effects and contents of contractual obligations from the position of what a French lawyer would call *inexécution*.[1] Now in English law, because contractual obligations are based upon promise rather than agreement (Ch 8 § 5(c)), the overwhelming tendency is to talk in terms of a breach of contract (*la rupture*) and not non-performance (*inexécution*). Nevertheless, the idea non-performance can become relevant when one wishes to talk generally of contractual expectations failing to materialise; for such failures can occur even when there has been no breach of promise. Moreover, the distinction between breach and non-performance can sometimes be relevant in relation to the law of actions (contractual remedies).

1 CONTRACTUAL REMEDIES AND CONTRACTUAL RIGHTS

Contractual rights and duties can, rationally speaking, be said to exist in their own abstract world, and independently of any particular factual situation, the moment a contractual obligation comes into existence.[2] In reality, however, such rights and duties usually have practical meaning only in relation to a set of particular facts. Consequently, when things go wrong for a contracting party the starting point for an analysis ought to be the harm, or potential harm, arising out of the relationship. This may well lead on to questions of interpretation of the contract[3] and (or) to an analysis of the facts in relation to both the law of remedies and the law of contractual obligations.[4]

For example, P hires a ship from D for 12 months at a time when prices are high; several months later, when prices have plunged, P wishes to escape from the hire contract (charterparty) and hire another ship at a much lower price. If there is a vague clause perhaps giving a party the right to determine the hire at will and if P uses this term to determine the contract, then D will be the one suffering loss of hire. If D sues P for compensation, the court may well be involved in an exercise of contractual interpretation (*cf* Ch 8 § 5(f)). Did the clause give P the right to determine the charterparty at will? If it did, then D's damages claim will fail; if it did not, D may well

1 See eg CC art 1142.

2 See eg CC art 1134.

3 See eg CC art 1156.

4 See eg CC art 1142.

have a claim for breach of contract. In the absence of any specific clause in the contract allowing P to determine the hire at will, P will have to search amongst the facts for a reason to determine the obligation. If the ship is, strictly speaking, unseaworthy, can P repudiate the contract for D's failure to provide a seaworthy ship? This will require an analysis not just of the rights and remedies of contract, but of the facts themselves to see if the ship was indeed unseaworthy. This kind of problem, so common in commercial law,[5] evidently involves the contents and interpretation of a contractual obligation. However, such an exercise has arisen largely as a result of a perceived failure of performance of the contractual obligation.

Other quite different examples could be given. P contracts with D for D to build a system for pumping and storing molten plasticine; the wrong kind of pipe is specified in the plans, prepared by D and agreed by P, and when the system is built and put into operation the pipe fails causing a huge fire which destroys the whole of P's factory. Can P claim damages for a new factory from D?[6] Can D claim that P was under a contractual duty to stop him using the wrong pipe at the planning stage? What if the contract contains a clause excluding liability for fire 'howsoever caused'? Or what if the contract contains a clause obliging P to take out fire insurance in respect of the new system? Alternatively, does P have to pay for the work done by D in building the system? Again this kind of problem could be classified under the nature, contents and interpretation of contractual obligations; yet the problem has arisen in the context of a devastating fire causing much loss of property, if not personal injury. Problems of the effects of contractual obligations can also arise when third parties are involved. What if P had sold the factory to T before D had finished the plasticine system: can T sue D for the damage caused by the fire? Or take a different problem. H transfers his business to D in consideration of a promise by D that he will pay an annuity to H's wife, W, for the rest of her life; after H's death D refuses to pay anything to W. Does W have a right to the annuity? Does H's estate have the right to have the business re-transferred back? Or is D under no duty to pay anyone to whom he has made no actual promise? It is in the context of an apparent failure of the contract (damage or loss of expectation) that interpretation problems find themselves before the courts and, once before the court, it is the remedy being pursued that often holds the key to the obligation problem in issue (*cf* Ch 5 § 4(e)).

2 BREACH OF A PRE-CONTRACTUAL OBLIGATION

When dealing with failures of contractual expectation the tendency, evidently, is to think of the obligation only from the moment of its formation. Thus, if P is injured in D's supermarket by an exploding bottle of lemonade before P has entered into any contract to buy the lemonade, the logical conclusion would appear to be that D cannot be in breach of any contractual obligation. But what if P had entered the supermarket only because D had tempted passers-by with offers of healthy and delicious lemonade at cheap prices? Might it be possible to talk of a pre-contractual liability?

5 For a paradigm case see *Hong Kong Fir Shipping Co Ltd v Kawasaki Kisen Kaisha Ltd* [1962] 2 QB 26.

6 *Cf Harbutts Plasticine Ltd v Wayne Tank and Pump Co Ltd* [1970] 1 QB 447.

The notion of pre-contractual liability as a subject in itself has an important place in civil law systems, as we have seen (Ch 9 § 4). It is particularly important with regard to pre-contractual negotiations which may have important consequences in, for example, Netherlands law. Not only can contracts come into existence without a formal agreement or any other explicit offer and acceptance, but pre-contractual negotiations may also influence the legal relationship of the parties once a contract exists. In the famous case *Baris v Riezenkamp*,[7] the *Hoge Raad* held that parties, when negotiating a contract, enter into a special legal relationship governed by the rules of reasonableness and fairness; these rules stipulate that the parties have to allow for their conduct to be assessed by the justified interests of the other party. These rules of reasonableness and fairness can mean that a party is not free to end the negotiations and is, therefore, given the circumstances, obliged to continue the negotiations (by order of the court). If a party stops the negotiations at a certain advanced stage, an obligation to compensate the damage of the other party may exist.[8] The source of the obligations arising from pre-contractual negotiations can be delict, a collateral contract (*pactum de contrahendo*), reliance or, possibly, the (unwritten) rules of reasonableness and fairness.[9] In French law the principle of good faith has been extended to cover pre-contractual situations in certain cases.[10]

In English law, as we have seen, if one attempts to isolate pre-contractual liability as a subject in itself several problems arise. First, the causes of action underpinning such liability are widely dispersed and this mitigates against the development of any general principle. Secondly, the pre-contractual stage has been largely commandeered by the doctrine of misrepresentation (Ch 9 § 7); the development of some new principle might thus be seen to undermine well established rules and principles now enshrined even in statute. Thirdly, English law still appears hostile to any doctrine of good faith at the pre-contractual stage. In *Walford v Miles*[11] Lord Ackner, as we have seen (Ch 9 § 4), said that 'the concept of a duty to carry on negotiations in good faith is inherently repugnant to the adversarial position of the parties when involved in negotiations.' For each contractual 'party to the negotiations is entitled to pursue his (or her) own interest, so long as he avoids making misrepresentations.' Accordingly, 'to advance that interest he must be entitled, if he thinks it appropriate, to threaten to withdraw from further negotiations.' Whether, of course, English law will remain committed to this position is another question. But for the moment the situation with regard to pre-contractual liability remains typical: in order to obtain damages for loss one must establish a cause of action either in contract or in tort. And in order to establish a contract one must establish promise, consideration and intention to create legal relations.

---

7 NJ 1958, 67. See also NJ 1983, 723; NJ 1988, 1017; NJ 1991, 647.

8 Von Mehren, *Formation*, paras 26–29.

9 See eg EA Farnsworth, 'Negotiation of Contracts and Precontractual liability: General Report', in: *Conflits et Harmonisation* (Fribourg, 1990).

10 Von Mehren, *Formation*, para 29.

11 [1992] 2 AC 128.

3 CONTENTS OF A CONTRACT

If the English law of contract is founded upon promises and not some abstract *iuris vinculum* then the nature and contents of the English contractual obligation are likely to be expressed as a bundle of promises and not as a single obligation containing various rights and duties. Yet while this is largely the conceptual position, care must be taken in analysing the bundle of promises that make up the contract. For the courts not only distinguish between the status of the promises themselves but sometimes distil out of the bundle a single, fundamental promise or term upon which the whole contract exists. Thus, in a contract for the sale of a car the promise by the seller to convey title is so fundamental that if it is broken there will be a 'total failure of consideration', allowing the buyer to recover as a debt the whole of the sale price.[12] All the same, it is doubtful if the breach of such a fundamental term will actually destroy the contract itself,[13] and so as a matter of common law principle any express term or clause will, despite the breach, remain in existence and *prima facie* valid.

(a) Comparative considerations

In civil law determining the contents and scope of a contract is closely related to the interpretation of contracts (*cf* Ch 8 § 5(f)). When interpreting a contract, the judges are not restrained by the words used by the parties, but must search for what was their common intention when they made the contract.[14] They must try to establish the meaning of the declarations of the parties and the subsequent legal effects thereof. In Dutch law the interpretation is, furthermore, based on the rules of reasonableness and fairness.[15] Contracts are binding upon the parties, but the nature of the contract, statute, usage and the rules of reasonableness and fairness can supplement the contract and these latter may be considered as a separate source of contractual obligations.[16] Civil law systems also offer, in varying degrees, protection against abusive and (or) unreasonable clauses. In addition, countries like France and the Netherlands give the *ius agendi* and *ius standi* to, for instance, consumer organisations in their battle against unfair contract terms.

Whether or not English law will ever go so far as to alter the law of persons so as to give standing to consumer groups is an interesting question not only because of its traditional hostility to such procedural innovations (although EU law may prove important on this), but also because of the epistemological (theory of legal knowledge) questions such a change might provoke. Would the law of obligations have to think in terms of class interests and what would be the effect of a formal recognition of these interests on the existing model of contract and tort?[17] In fact what English law has

---

12 *Rowland v Divall* [1923] 2 KB 500.

13 *Photo Production Ltd v Securicor* [1980] AC 827, 844, 850.

14 CC art 1156.

15 NBW Bk 6 art 2(2).

16 NBW Bk 6 art 248.

17 *Cf* JA Jolowicz, 'Protection of Diffuse, Fragmented and Collective Interests' in Civil Litigation: English Law [1983] CLJ 222.

recently done is to use public law to protect consumer interests in respect of onerous clauses in contracts: the Director of Fair Trading has just been given power to use the remedy of an injunction against those who persist in using unfair contract terms.[18] In private law itself the Unfair Contract Terms Act 1977 continues to give power to the judges to strike down as unreasonable certain promises that fulfil the definition of 'exemption clause' and this general power in effect means that the scope to interpret contracts has been considerable widened. Indeed, with respect to exclusion clauses in consumer contracts, there is, as a result of an EU directive,[19] now a requirement of good faith,[20] which allows the courts, *inter alia*, to have regard to the strength of the bargaining positions of the parties, to any inducements to the consumer and to the extent to which the seller or supplier 'has dealt fairly and equitably with the consumer'[21] One difficulty, however, is distinguishing between ordinary 'terms' and 'exclusion clauses'.[22]

(b) Terms and their classification

When one looks at a transaction as a whole we have already seen that promises made in the course of negotiations and bargain can fall into one or other of two general categories: those outside of the contractual bargain are classed as representations while those inside are classed as contractual terms (*cf* Ch 9 § 7(a)). These contractual terms are in turn classified into various types. Traditionally, those that are fundamental to the whole contractual obligation are called 'conditions' and those that are merely accessory are called 'warranties'.[23] However, when these two different classes of term are put into the context of an actual breach of contract the classification can sometimes prove inadequate in that it is not always practical to use the status of terms as a means of determining whether the breach is serious enough to allow an innocent party to repudiate the whole of the contract. Moreover, there is an added difficulty that the word condition itself has a number of meanings depending upon the context within which it is used.[24] Accordingly, other categories of term have appeared alongside the traditional conditions and warranties.

(c) Conditions

The common law, like the Romanist systems, has had to face the problem that some breaches of contract are so serious that they should allow the injured party to treat the

---

18 Unfair Terms in Consumer Contracts Regulations 1994 reg 8.

19 Council Directive of 5 April 1993 (93/13/EEC: L 95/29) art 3(1).

20 Unfair Terms in Consumer Contracts Regulations 1994 reg 4(1).

21 Unfair Terms in Consumer Contracts Regulations 1994 Sch 2.

22 *Cf* Unfair Contract Terms Act 1977 s 13; Unfair Terms in Consumer Contracts Regulations 1994 Sch 3.

23 Sale of Goods Act 1979 s 11(3). Note that 'condition' comes from the latin word *condicio* and thus has an important relationship with the civilian learning on conditions: Zimmermann, p 743.

24 See Zimmermann, p 743 note 184; Treitel, *Remedies*, paras 194–200.

whole obligation as being at an end.[25] Yet the question as to which breaches should give rise to the right to repudiate the contract[26] and which breaches should give rise only to a right to damages has been rendered rather complicated in the common law by the fact not only that has it been dealt with at two levels – at the level of breach and the level of terms – but that the repudiation is a 'self-help' remedy (*cf* Ch 4 § 6). A contractor who wishes to repudiate a contract for serious breach does not have to go to court to obtain the rescission.

The traditional approach of the common law towards this self-help right to repudiate for a serious breach was to look at the nature of the term broken. If the breach involved a promise that could be described as an implied condition precedent to the whole contract then the obligation would be destroyed as a result of the operation of this rule.[27] The approach, in other words, was not that different from the one adopted in dealing with mistake at common law (*cf* Ch 9 § 8(b)).[28] However, in the course of time the precedent aspect became lost and the notion of condition took on a rather different meaning: it became a way of describing the status of a fundamental term of the contract which, if broken, would give rise to the right of repudiation.[29] This is the meaning adopted in contracts for the sale of goods[30] and is a meaning in theory applicable to all contracts.[31]

The question whether a term is a condition or not depends either on the intention of the parties[32] or, if the parties are silent on the matter, on whether the term is one that is 'so essential to [the] very nature [of the contract] that [its] non-performance may fairly be considered by the other party as a substantial failure to perform the contract at all'.[33] In some types of transaction the courts will determine the status of the term with reference to commercial usage and the like; in some other types of transaction – in particular, supply of goods – the status of the most important terms are implied into the contract by statute.[34] And this statutory approach to implied conditions has now been extended to other kinds of consumer contracts.[35] All the same, it must be borne in mind that many actual cases dealing with the status of terms involve the question of whether an innocent party was correct in repudiating the contract for breach: thus, in

25 Zweigert & Kötz, p 547.

26 It is necessary to use the term 'repudiate' rather than 'rescind' as otherwise there might be confusion with the equitable remedy of rescission: for rescinding a contract for serious breach is a common law remedy which has no conceptual relation whatsoever with the equitable remedy of the same name. See Treitel, *Remedies*, para 188.

27 Zimmermann, p 803.

28 Note also that conditions precedent are civil law devices: Zimmermann, pp 717–47. And see eg Quebec CC arts 1497–1517.

29 Treitel, *Remedies*, para 198.

30 Sale of Goods Act 1979 s 11.

31 Treitel, *Remedies*, para 198.

32 *Bunge Corporation v Tradax Export* [1981] 1 WLR 711 (HL).

33 *Wallis, Son & Wells v Pratt & Haynes* [1910] 2 KB 1003, 1012; see also *Trans Trust SPRL v Danubian Trading Co Ltd* [1952] 2 QB 297 and eg *The Alecos M* [1991] 1 Lloyd's Rep 120.

34 Sale of Goods Act 1979 ss 12–15; Supply of Goods and Services Act 1982.

35 Supply of Goods and Services Act 1982.

interpreting the terms, the court may well look at the nature and effects of the breach itself, even if the parties themselves have used the word condition.[36] In other words, they may weigh the remedy (self-help repudiation), in terms of proportionality, against the actual breach.

(d) Conditions precedent

The complexities surrounding the meaning of condition are made worse by the survival of the original notion of condition precedent.[37] As in French[38] or Netherlands law,[39] an English contract can be subject either to a condition precedent (*condition suspensive*) or to a condition subsequent (*condition résolutoire*) and so a promise to pay a debt can be made to be dependent upon the promisee catching influenza[40] or the validity of a contractual bargain can be made to be dependent upon the subject matter of the contract remaining in existence[41] (*cf* Ch 9 § 8(b)). True conditions subsequent are actually hard to find in the English case law, and so most of these kinds of conditions are referred to as conditions precedent. The point, however, that needs to be stressed is that a 'condition' in English law has both a linguistic meaning (nature of a promise) and an institutional meaning (operative factor in contractual obligations).

(e) Warranties

Warranty, like condition, has a number of different meanings. As we have seen, the name can be applied to a contractual promise in general and when used in this sense it acts as a generic term within which a condition is merely a species.[42] This general meaning is of use in the area of misrepresentation when it can be of importance to distinguish between contractual promises (warranties) and mere representations (*cf* Ch 9 § 7(a)). To add to the confusion, however, the term warranty has a special meaning in insurance law: here it 'is a term whose breach discharges the insurer from liability even if the breach is unconnected with the loss'.[43] In addition to these meanings, the word

36 And note the reverse: 'a stipulation may be a condition, though called a warranty in the contract' *per* Sale of Goods Act 1979 s 11(3).

37 One might say that the common law uses 'condition' to refer either to an event or to a term of the contract: see Treitel, *Remedies*, para 195.

38 *Cf* CC art 1168: '*l'obligation est conditionnelle lorsqu'on la fait dépendre d'un événement futur et incertain, soit en la suspendant jusqu'à ce que l'événement arrive, soit en la résiliant, selon que l'événement arrivera ou n'arrivera pas,*' And CC art 1181: '*l'obligation contractée sous une condition suspensive est celle qui dépend d'un événement futur et incertain, ou d'un événement actuellement arrivé, mais encore inconnu des parties*.'

39 NBW Bk 6 arts 21–26.

40 *Carlill v Carbolic Smoke Ball Co* [1893] 1 QB 256.

41 *Financings Ltd v Stimson* [1962] 1 WLR 1184.

42 Zimmermann, p 803: 'Every contractual term, express or implied, is in law a "warranty", and breach of a warranty entitles the innocent party to claim damages. If, however, the term which has been broken is not only a warranty but also a "condition", the innocent party has the option of withdrawing from the contract.' See also Treitel, *Remedies*, para 198.

43 *Euro-Diam Ltd v Bathurst* [1988] 2 All ER 23, 33 CA. See also Marine Insurance Act 1906 s 33(3).

warranty can also be used to describe a particular type of contractual term which, if broken, will give rise only to an action for damages;[44] in this context it is used to contrast an ancillary term with a condition. A breach of warranty, unless it started life as a representation, will not therefore give rise to a right to repudiate the contract.

(f) Innominate terms

The conditions and warranties dichotomy no doubt works well enough for some kinds of contract – or, at least, for some kinds of contractual stipulations. For, so it is said, it has the great merit of providing certainty in commercial law.[45] However, when applied to some other types of contract, or some other contractual stipulations, it can cause logical problems in that once there has been a breach of any term which formally has the status of a condition it must follow that the innocent party has the right to repudiate the whole of the contract and to claim damages for the loss of the whole bargain.[46] This could mean that repudiation might be available for what in reality was just a minor breach of contract.[47]

In recognising this logical problem the Court of Appeal decided that a breach of condition might not always give rise to a right to repudiate the contract.[48] It held that with regard to some kinds of contract, or at least with regard to some kinds of contractual promises, reliance upon the condition and warranty dichotomy was no longer to be the only method of determining the right to repudiate for breach; regard was also to be had, in certain circumstances, to the gravity of the breach itself. However, the House of Lords has reaffirmed that in commercial contracts the intention of the parties is paramount. If the parties to a mercantile contract have made it clear that the breach of a particular stipulation is to give rise to a right to repudiate then the courts should not be reluctant to class such a stipulation as a condition; for the gravity of the breach approach in commercial transactions, where the parties are entitled to know their rights at once, is often unsuitable.[49]

It would seem, then, that there is now no complete dichotomy between conditions and warranties. There is also a third class of term, the 'innominate term', breach of which will give rise to a right to repudiate only if the parties have impliedly agreed that this is what should happen given the nature and consequences of the breach.[50] Of

44 Sale of Goods Act 1979 ss 11(3), 61(1).

45 *Bunge Corporation v Tradax Export* [1981] 1 WLR 711, 715, 720, 725, 729.

46 *Cf Lombard Plc v Butterworth* [1987] QB 527.

47 'My Lords, it is beyond question that there are many cases in the books where terms, the breach of which do not deprive the innocent party of substantially the whole of the benefit which he was intended to receive from the contract, were nonetheless held to be conditions any breach of which entitled the innocent party to rescind,' *per* Lord Roskill in *Bunge Corpn*, above, at p 724.

48 *Hong Kong Fir Shipping Co Ltd v Kawasaki Kisen Kaisha Ltd* [1962] 2 QB 26.

49 *Bunge Corporation v Tradax SA* [1981] 1 WLR 711, 716, 725.

50 'A condition is a term, the failure to perform which entitles the other party to treat the contract as at an end. A warranty is a term, breach of which sounds in damages but does not terminate, or entitle the other party to terminate, the contract. An innominate or intermediate term is one, the effect of non-performance of which the parties expressly or (as is more usual) impliedly agree will depend upon the nature and the consequences of breach,' *per* Lord Scarman in *Bunge Corpn,* above , at p 717.

course, whether or not the parties were clear as to the repudiation issue is itself a difficult contractual interpretation problem,[51] but unless the wording is very clear, the approach of the court is likely to be one of interpreting the language of the contractual document (*cf* Ch 8 § 5(f)) in the context both of any breach[52] and of any established commercial usage.

(g) Fundamental terms

The innominate term has not been the only development to cause problems for the traditional conditions and warranties dichotomy: the 'fundamental term' has given rise to confusion as well. At one time it seemed that the fundamental term was a promise even more fundamental than a condition,[53] and so if it was broken this would give rise to a fundamental breach.[54] The effect of such a fundamental breach was, according to the Court of Appeal,[55] not only to give the innocent party the right to repudiate the contract but, on such repudiation, to sweep away the whole of the primary contractual obligation taking with it any exclusion clauses (see below § 4). This fundamental breach doctrine has now been abolished by the House of Lords[56] with the result that there is less reason to distinguish conceptually between conditions and fundamental terms. The only reason for making the distinction is to separate from conditions those terms which, if broken, would deprive the other party of substantially the whole benefit of the contract. In other words, the distinction might serve to distinguish defective performance from effective non-performance.

(h) Express terms or clauses

The concept of a fundamental term was a device employed to tackle the widespread use in standard form contracts of clauses designed to exclude or limit the liability of a contractor (see below § 4). These clauses came in many forms.[57] They might exclude altogether the liability of a party for breach of some or all of the terms of the contract; they might limit the amount payable in damages for a breach of contract; or they might

51 'It is by construing a contract (which can be done as soon as the contract is made) that one decides whether a term is, either expressly or by necessary implication, a condition, and not by considering the gravity of the breach of that term (which cannot be done until the breach is imminent or has occurred). The latter process is not an aid to construing the contract, but indicates whether rescission or merely damages is the proper remedy for a breach for which the innocent party might be recompensed in one way or the other according to its gravity,' *per* Lord Lowry in *Bunge Corpn, supra*, at p 719.

52 See Lord Scarman in *Bunge Corpn* at p 717.

53 '[A fundamental term] must be something ... narrower than a condition of the contract ... It is ... something which underlies the whole contract so that, if it is not complied with, the performance becomes something totally different from that which the contract contemplates,' *per* Devlin J in *Smeaton Hanscomb v Sassoon I Setty* [1953] 2 All ER 1471, 1473.

54 *Sze Hai Tong Bank Ltd v Rambler Cycle Co Ltd* [1959] AC 576.

55 *Harbutts Plasticine Ltd v Wayne Tank and Pump Co Ltd* [1970] 1 QB 447.

56 *Photo Production Ltd v Securicor* [1980] AC 827.

57 *Cf* Unfair Contract Terms Act 1977 s 13.

require a contractor to indemnify (in debt) a party in breach of contract who has had to pay damages (below § 5). Furthermore, as in French law,[58] an English contract might also contain a clause requiring a party in breach, or on termination of the agreement, to pay a fixed sum (in debt) by way of compensation (see below § 5). These penalty clauses, unlike the other stipulations, have however attracted the attention of equity.[59] All of these different kinds of express terms and clauses have attracted their own case law and doctrine and thus should be treated separately.

4 EXCLUSION AND LIMITATION CLAUSES

The area of exclusion and limitation clauses was, until 1978, one of the most conceptually complex areas of English contract law. The reason for this complexity lay primarily in the conflict between two principles of contractual justice: on the one hand the courts were keen to uphold the principle of freedom of contract (*cf* Ch 8 § 5(e)); on the other hand they wished on many occasions to give relief to consumers oppressed by powerful contractual corporations who, from a monopoly or quasi-monopoly position, were relying upon exclusion clauses in standard-form contracts to the point of abuse.[60]

(a) Level of operation

A second reason for the complexity once to be found in this area of law lay in a divergence of approach towards the level of operation of exclusion clauses. Some judges and academics[61] took the view that such clauses defined the actual contractual obligation itself; other judges were of the opinion that such clauses operated only in respect of the remedy. According to this latter view, an exclusion clause gave protection only on a secondary level for breach of an obligation on the primary level. Today the approach adopted by the House of Lords would seem to be the former: in commercial contracts where the parties are of equal economic strength and the risks are ones that can be covered by insurance an exclusion clause would seem to be – or certainly capable of being – part of the definition of the primary contractual 'duty'.[62] This view has now been reflected in statutory regulations.[63]

(b) Interpretation of exclusion clauses

Another reason, perhaps, for the complexity surrounding the problems posed by exclusion clauses is that neither the common law courts nor the Court of Chancery developed a general doctrine of abuse of rights (*cf* Ch 12 § 3(c)) or good faith (*cf* Ch 8 § 5(a)). Consequently, consumer transactions were always to be treated, at common law,

---

58 CC art 1152.

59 See Treitel, *Remedies*, para 179.

60 *George Mitchell (Chesterhall) Ltd v Finney Lock Seeds Ltd* [1983] QB 284, 297.

61 B Coote, *Exception Clauses* (Sweet & Maxwell, 1964), pp 1–18.

62 *Photo Production v Securicor* [1980] AC 827, 843, 851.

63 Unfair Terms in Consumer Contracts Regulations 1994 reg 3.

on the same level as commercial contracts. This meant that the courts, in order to combat the abusive use of standard-form contracts by contractors in a powerful economic position, had to develop a number of rather artificial rules of interpretation.[64]

In order for a clause to be effective at common law it must have been properly incorporated into the contract;[65] its language must cover both the actual event or breach that has occurred and the actual party attempting to rely upon the clause;[66] and in cases of ambiguity the clause must be read *contra proferentem*.[67] It seems, also, that if there is a very serious breach of contract – the breach of a fundamental term (see above) or a fundamental breach – the clause will specifically have to cover the breach and the damage that has occurred. For there is a rule of construction that an exclusion clause or similar provision should not be interpreted as covering a fundamental breach of contract.[68] Put another way, 'the agreement must retain the legal characteristics of a contract'.[69]

(c) Statutory protection and the consumer

Many of the abuse problems associated with standard-form contracts have been alleviated by statutory intervention aimed at protecting the consumer.[70] Thus, in consumer sale of goods and hire purchase contracts the statutory implied terms as to title, fitness for purpose and quality cannot now be excluded,[71] and in many other consumer transactions an exclusion clause will be effective at best only if it is 'fair and reasonable'.[72] This fair and reasonable provision also applies to any clause attempting to exclude any liability or any remedy available for misrepresentation, and it is unlikely that businesses will be able to have recourse to any collateral contracts to evade liability for their defective products.[73]

In interpreting 'fair and reasonable' under the Unfair Contract Terms Act 1977 the courts will no doubt look at the circumstances of each case.[74] Yet the Act is, primarily,

---

64 *George Mitchell (Chesterhall) Ltd v Finney Lock Seeds Ltd* [1983] QB 284, 297; [1983] 2 AC 803, 812-813.

65 *Thornton v Shoe Lane Parking Ltd* [1971] 2 QB 163.

66 See eg *Hollier v Rambler Motors Ltd* [1972] 2 QB 71.

67 Ambiguous clauses are to be construed against the party putting them forward: see Zweigert & Kötz, p 358. This ambiguity rule is an example of a very old (ie Roman) interpretation principle being adapted to deal with a modern problem: on which see Zimmermann, pp 639–42.

68 *Suisse Atlantique etc v Rotterdamsche etc* [1967] 1 AC 361.

69 *Photo Production*, *supra*, at p 850.

70 *George Mitchell (Chesterhall) Ltd v Finney Lock Seeds Ltd* [1983] QB 284, 296–99; [1983] 2 AC 803, 812–13; Zweigert & Kötz, pp 359–64.

71 Unfair Contract Terms Act 1977 s 6.

72 Sections 2(2), 3, 11.

73 Sections 5, 10.

74 Section 11. In the case of a contract term the contemplated circumstances are at the time of the making of the contract (s 11(1)); in the case of a general notice the circumstances are at the time of liability (s 11(3)). With regard to supply of goods contracts the Act sets out certain guidelines in the Schedule. Note also that the burden of proof is on the person claiming reasonableness (s 11(5)).

a piece of legislation designed to protect the consumer and so the courts are likely now to distinguish between the commercial and the consumer factual situation.[75] In the latter situation an attempt to exclude negligence, especially by a professional institution in a powerful economic position, will no doubt be treated with scepticism, especially where the institution can spread the loss via insurance and the loss itself is not open-ended.[76]

In addition to the 1977 legislation, the legislature has again intervened in order to give expression to the EU Council Directive of 5 April 1993 on unfair terms in consumer contracts.[77] The Unfair Terms in Consumer Contracts Regulations 1994[78] differ from the 1977 Act in that they apply exclusively to consumer contracts and decree simply that an unfair term shall not be binding upon the consumer[79] in situations where such a term has not been individually negotiated in a contract between seller or supplier and a consumer.[80] Following the directive, they prohibit any clause that, 'contrary to the requirement of good faith, causes a significant imbalance in the parties' rights and obligations arising under the contract, to the detriment of the consumer'.[81] Power is also given to the Director of Fair Trading to seek an injunction (*cf* Ch 5 § 4) to prevent a contractor continuing to use unfair exclusion clauses in contracts.[82] What is particularly striking about this new regulation is that it formally introduces into the English law of contractual obligations the notion of good faith, something traditionally said to be absent, as a matter of form if not substance,[83] from the English contract. As far as the (delegated) legislation itself is concerned, this requirement of good faith is, inter alia, a matter of the strength of the bargaining position of the parties, the existence of inducements to the consumer, whether the goods are the result of a special order and the extent to which the seller or supplier has dealt 'fairly and equitably' with the consumer.[84] Yet one might ask if the courts will use this legislation as the starting point for a more general application of the requirement of good faith: is it possible that it might become a notion implied in all consumer contracts? No doubt the role of good faith in pre-contractual situations will remain ambiguous.

(d) Commercial contracts

The effect of the legislative intervention on behalf of the consumer has, then, been to create not just a distinction between the business and the purely private transaction but

75 *Thompson v T Lohan (Plant) Ltd* [1987] 1 WLR 649.

76 *Smith v Eric Bush* [1990] 1 AC 831.

77 93/13/EEC: L 95/29.

78 SI 1994/ 3159.

79 Reg 5.

80 Reg 3(1).

81 Reg 4(1).

82 Reg 8.

83 *Cf Interfoto Picture Library Ltd v Stiletto Visual Programmes Ltd* [1989] QB 433, 439, 445.

84 Reg 4(3), Sched 2.

between the consumer and the commercial contract.[85] This has had the beneficial effect of sweeping away some of the conceptual confusion surrounding exclusion clauses and freedom of contract: for 'in commercial matters generally, when the parties are not of unequal bargaining power, and when risks are normally borne by insurance, not only is the case for judicial intervention undemonstrated, but there is everything to be said ... for leaving the parties free to apportion the risks as they think fit'.[86] However, in introducing the notion of good faith into English law the legislator might just be heralding a new approach to English contract law.

Moreover, it must not be forgotten that some of the provisions of the Unfair Contract Terms Act 1977 stretch beyond the consumer contract. Liability arising from negligence, whether it is a question of contractual or tortious liability, is to be treated differently from general contractual liability. Accordingly, negligence liability can be excluded in cases of property and financial loss only if the exclusion clause or notice is reasonable,[87] and in cases of personal injury or death no exclusion clause or notice will be effective.[88] In sale of goods and hire purchase commercial contracts liability arising from failure to pass good title, or to provide quiet possession, cannot be excluded,[89] and liability arising from breach of description or a failure to provide goods that are reasonably fit for their purpose or of satisfactory quality will be excluded only if such a clause is 'fair and reasonable'.[90] Furthermore, the reasonableness provision applicable to liability in contract applies not just to situations where one party 'deals as consumer' but where one of them deals 'on the other's written standard terms of business'.[91] Accordingly, the reasonableness provision has an extensive role to play in commercial, as well as consumer, law.

It has to be added, however, that there are a number of contracts which fall outside the 1977 legislation. At the general level the 1977 Act applies only to 'business liability' obligations,[92] although this will include a professional activity and the activities of any public department,[93] and at the specific level the Act, or parts of the Act, will not apply to certain contracts like insurance or to contracts involving the creation or transfer of real or intellectual property interests or rights.[94] It is, then, a technical piece of legislation that highlights the dangers of putting too much emphasis on the theory that English law thinks just in terms of a single principle of contract and not in terms of specific contracts (*cf* Ch 8 § 3(b)). Legislation, if not the case law, seems often to operate at the level of a law of contracts.

85 Unfair Contract Terms Act 1977 ss 1(3), 12.

86 *Photo Production*, *supra*, p 843.

87 Section 2(2).

88 Section 2(1).

89 Section 6(1).

90 Section 6(3).

91 Section 3(1).

92 Section 1(3).

93 Section 14.

94 Section 1(2) and Schedule 1.

5 DEBT CLAUSES

Exclusion and limitation clauses are express terms that are negative in effect inasmuch as they usually protect a contractor from all or part of a claim for damages. A contractual clause can, however, be positive in effect: it can put one contractor under a liability to pay a specific sum of money to the other party on the happening of some event.

(a) Indemnity clause

The first main type of debt term is an indemnity clause. This is a clause whereby one party agrees to indemnify the other for a liability incurred and it is positive in effect in that its operation will involve a contracting party being put under a legal duty to pay to another party a specific sum of money. In other words, an indemnity clause creates a right to a debt on the happening of some event, the liability which creates the indemnity right.[95] As a result, the indemnity provision is a conditional obligation. Despite the different function relative to an exclusion or limitation clause, and despite the fact that an indemnity provision need not involve a breach of contract, the approach of the courts is nevertheless the same towards an indemnity clause as it is towards an exclusion clause; and this means that if such a clause is to be effective it must be very clearly worded, especially if the indemnity debt claim arises out of the claimant's own negligence.[96] In commercial contracts these clauses are usually inserted to locate insurance risks,[97] but if they occur in consumer contracts as an indirect means of protecting the business party against the consequences of its own negligence or breach of contract they will be effective, according to the 1977 legislation, only if they are reasonable.[98] According to the 1994 regulations such clauses will probably be ineffective against a consumer. Reasonableness and effectiveness will, once again, depend *inter alia* on the status of the parties.[99]

(b) Penalty clause

A penalty clause is similar to an indemnity clause inasmuch as it puts one contracting party under a debt liability to the other on the occurrence of some event, but the difference is that a penalty clause comes into operation only where there has been a breach by the debtor.[100] And so, as in French law,[101] the penalty clause in an English contract can just be a means by which a person who has broken a contract is put under a debt liability to the other party in place of a liability in unliquidated damages.[102]

---

95 See eg *British Crane Hire Corpn v Ipswich Plant Hire Ltd* [1975] QB 303; Civil Liability (Contribution) Act 1978 s 1(1).

96 *Smith v South Wales Switchgear Ltd* [1978] 1 WLR 165.

97 *Thompson v T Lohan (Plant) Ltd* [1987] 1 WLR 649.

98 Unfair Contract Terms Act 1977 s 4.

99 See eg *Thompson v T Lohan (Plant) Ltd* [1987] 1 WLR 649, 656–57.

100 Treitel, *Remedies*, paras 165–66.

101 CC arts 1152, 1226.

102 Treitel, *Remedies*, para 167.

Provided that such a clause is a genuine pre-estimate of the damage – not always an easy question – it will at common law be effective. But if such a clause is not a genuine pre-estimate and is excessive equity will intervene to relieve the person in breach from liability in debt, the creditor in such a situation being allowed to sue only in damages for the actual loss.[103] This equitable relief is, however, available only for debt clauses that come into operation on the debtor's breach of contract.[104] Consequently, a penalty clause must be carefully distinguished from termination, price and damages clauses.[105] If a party legally terminates, rather than breaks, a contract it is quite possible that the equitable doctrine against penalties has no place; and if on a serious breach the innocent party elects to keep the contract alive a subsequent claim for the contract price will not be treated as a penalty or an abuse of a right unless the creditor has no 'legitimate interest' whatsoever in performing the contract.[106]As against a consumer, a penalty clause will be ineffective where it amounts to an unfair term.[107]

Care must also be taken to distinguish a penalty clause from a condition (above § 3(c)). If a contract contains a clause which expressly turns a relatively minor breach of contract into a breach of condition this will have the effect of allowing the innocent party to recover damages for the whole loss of the bargain; yet such a clause is not a penalty and so will not be subject to the equitable doctrine against penalties.[108] Whether, then, equity can gain entry to the problem of payments to be made when a contract is terminated can depend both on the drafting of the contract and on how the courts choose to interpret the facts, the law and the contractual document. This question of interpretation might well be dependent, also, upon the nature of the contract; charterparties are, for example, interpreted differently from consumer contracts,[109] the latter often being subject to various statutory provisions as well.[110]

6 IMPLIED TERMS

Penalties, exclusion clauses and the like are clauses written into contracts as express terms, or perhaps incorporated by way of dealing.[111] But a contract can also contain a great many promises which are implied and these implied terms are classified in the same way as any other contractual term (*cf* above § 3).

The theoretical starting point of the implied term is the presumed intention of the contractual parties. The law will not, in theory at least, make, or remake, a contract for the parties, but it will imply into any existing contract such terms as are necessary to give 'the transaction such efficacy as both parties must have intended that at all events it

103 *Dunlop Pneumatic Tyre Co Ltd v New Garage & Motor Co Ltd* [1915] AC 79.

104 *Bridge v Campbell Discount Co Ltd* [1962] AC 600; *ECGD v Universal Oil Products* [1983] 1 WLR 399.

105 Treitel, *Remedies*, para 166.

106 *White & Carter (Councils) Ltd v McGregor* [1962] AC 413.

107 Unfair Terms in Consumer Contracts Regulations 1994 reg 4, Sch 3.

108 *Lombard Plc v Butterworth* [1987] QB 527.

109 See eg *The General Capinpin* [1991] 1 Lloyd's Rep 1, 9.

110 See now Unfair Terms in Consumer Contracts Regulations 1994.

111 *British Crane Hire Corpn v Ipswich Plant Hire Ltd* [1975] QB 303.

should have.'[112] This means that the court will interpret a contractual obligation in such a way as either to make it conform, in the case of mercantile transactions where the parties are silent as to the point in issue, to established commercial usage or custom, or to give it efficacy when, without the implied term, the contract would simply not work.

The courts will not, however, imply a term into a contract unless in all the circumstances it is reasonable to do so and this imports into this area of contract a certain objectivity. The implied term is a means by which the court can grant compensation claims on the basis of a range of different relationships. But this notion of reasonableness is a condition, not a reason in itself, for implying a term and so the courts have stopped short of admitting that they will imply a term merely because it is reasonable to do so.[113] Accordingly, in order to appreciate the way an implied term operates it is necessary to treat the doctrine either as a means of contractual interpretation or as a kind of supplementary law. Terms are implied directly on the basis of an intention imputed to the parties in order to make the contract workable in particular circumstances or indirectly via the notion of particular contractual transactions – sale, hire, insurance and so on – within which certain general obligations have been established by mercantile usage or custom.[114]

The idea of the implied term acting as a form of supplementary law is reinforced by statute.[115] Certain pieces of legislation dealing with particular types of transaction specifically imply terms into contracts involving the relevant transaction;[116] and in the case of some of these transactions – in particular, sale and supply of goods – the parties are no longer free to depart from some of these implied terms by an express term.[117] Thus, the concept of an implied term, for some transactions, has become a vehicle for the imposition of imperative laws – a form of *ius cogens*.[118]

7 PRIVITY OF CONTRACT

One of the major distinctions between contractual and tortious liability is to be found in the relative effect of a contract. In English law, as in classical Roman law,[119] a contract cannot in principle confer upon a third party either any contractual obligations or any contractual rights because it is a general rule of English law that consideration must move from the promisee (*cf* Ch 9 § 3(c)).[120] In principle the only common law

112 *The Moorcock* (1889) 14 PD 64.

113 *Liverpool City Council v Irwin* [1977] AC 239.

114 *Young & Martin Ltd v McManus Childs Ltd* [1969] 1 AC 454.

115 The reverse is also true in certain circumstances: that is to say, the courts will refuse to imply a term because of the absence of legislation; see eg *Reid v Rush & Tompkins Plc* [1990] 1 WLR 212.

116 See eg Sale of Goods Act 1979 ss 12–15; Supply of Goods and Services Act 1982.

117 Unfair Contract Terms Act 1977 ss 6–7.

118 *Euro-Diam Ltd v Bathurst* [1987] 2 All ER 113, 119.

119 Zimmermann, pp 34–40 (*Alteri stipulari nemo potest*: D.45.1.38.17); Zweigert & Kötz, pp 488–502.

120 The history of privity of contract is complex and is not based on the history of a single doctrine: see generally V Palmer, *The Paths to Privity* (Austin & Winfield, 1992).

(*in personam*) obligation that a contractual party might owe to a third party is a duty of care arising in the law of tort[121] and the only right that a third party can obtain from the contract is a right attaching to property.[122] This rule is known as the doctrine of privity of contract and, despite criticism,[123] it remains a valid principle of English contract law.[124]

All the same there are a range of important exceptions to the privity doctrine which curtail its application. Certain obligations and rights can be conveyed to third parties via the law of property and although this conveyance will not extend *per se* to debts,[125] despite their property status, the doctrine of assignment allows for the transfer of contractual rights from a creditor to a third party.[126] The device of agency allows an agent to contract on behalf of a principal;[127] and both statute and the common law have abrogated the doctrine of privity with regard to certain mercantile transactions involving banking and insurance.[128] Moreover, the institution of the trust – where one person (trustee) holds as owner property for the enjoyment of another person (beneficiary) – can be used to grant equitable rights directly upon third parties in respect of a fund of property established as a result of an agreement between others.[129]

Developments in the law of remedies have also outflanked the privity doctrine in a number of situations. Thus, contractors who cause damage may find themselves liable in damages to third parties in a number of different ways. The third party might be deemed to be a contractual party and thus the contractor could be liable for breach of a contractual term;[130] the third party might indirectly be able to obtain compensation through an award of damages to the actual contractor;[131] or the third party might be able to obtain damages in the tort of negligence either for breach of a duty 'falling only just short of a direct contractual relationship'[132] or for a breach of a contractual duty which injures a foreseeable and proximate third party in respect of a quantifiable and

---

121 *White v Jones* [1995] 2 AC 207.

122 Law of Property Act 1925 ss 47(1), 56(1); and see *Beswick v Beswick* [1966] Ch 538 (CA), revsd [1968] AC 58.

123 For the later developments in civil law, and how the rule was finally overcome, see: Zimmermann, pp 41–45; Zweigert & Kötz, pp 488–96. Lord Denning adopted, *inter alia*, the 'interest' strategy in his attempt to avoid the privity rule in *Beswick v Beswick* [1966] Ch 538, 557 (CA).

124 *Beswick v Beswick* [1968] AC 58.

125 *Beswick*, *supra*.

126 Law of Property Act 1925 s 136. See generally Zweigert & Kötz, pp 471–87. The *ius commune* developed assignment by analogy with the transfer of a corporeal thing: does this make assignment part of the law of property rather than the law of obligations?

127 For the general background in civil and common law see: Zimmermann, pp 45–58; Zweigert & Kötz, pp 459–70.

128 See eg Marine Insurance Act 1906 s 14(2); Road Traffic Act 1988 s 148(7); *Hepburn v A Tomlinson (Hauliers) Ltd* [1966] 1 QB 21 (CA); [1966] AC 451. But *cf Bradley v Eagle Star Insurance* [1989] AC 957; *In re Workvale Ltd* [1991] 1 WLR 294.

129 For an excellent description and discussion of the concept of a trust see: K Gray, *Elements of Land Law* (Butterworths, 2nd edn, 1993), pp 34–50.

130 *Lockett v A & M Charles Ltd* [1938] 4 All ER 170.

131 *Jackson v Horizon Holidays Ltd* [1975] 1 WLR 1468.

132 *Junior Books Ltd v Veitchi Co Ltd* [1983] AC 520.

particular loss.[133] Indeed, if the third party is particularly close to the contractor (family relationship or assignee), it may be possible for the third party to obtain damages directly for breach of the contract simply on the basis that it would be unreasonable and unjust to refuse the remedy.[134]

If the problem is one of debt rather than damages it may be that a third party will, on occasions, be able to have recourse to the equitable remedy of specific performance to enforce the claim.[135] And if the difficulty is one involving the benefit of an exclusion clause the third party might be able to look to estoppel (*cf* Ch 5 § 1(c)) or commercial reality (*cf* Ch 9 § 3(d)) in order to avoid the privity doctrine.[136] In truth it may be that a third party can obtain no direct rights from a contract to which he is not a party, but this does not mean that the third party will have no legal or equitable remedies if he suffers an injury arising from a breach of contract between two other persons.

8 DISCHARGING CONTRACTUAL OBLIGATIONS

Privity of contract raises a number of quite separate issues. For example, there is the question of the effect of a contractual obligation on a third party: can a third party gain contractual rights from a contract between two others? Furthermore, there is the question of non-performance. What is the position if a contractor fails to perform his obligation and this has damaging effects on a third party? Both of these questions raise the issue of the effects of a contractual obligation and, in turn, the effects of a contract relate directly to the law of remedies. The law of actions can, however, only respond to the existence or non-existence of a private law obligation. What if such an obligation has ceased to exist? Or what if a promise cannot be performed as a result of a change of circumstances? What if the party in default can show an absence of fault?

(a) General and comparative considerations

In French law a contractual obligation (*iuris vinculum*) once formed has the force of legislation between the two parties that have made it.[137] To escape from such a binding chain the obligation has to be dissolved or transmitted; and to dissolve an obligation requires the same symmetrical formality as its formation.[138] The normal way in which such a contractual obligation is extinguished is either by performance – *solvere dicimus eum, qui fecit quod facere promisit* (we say untie when someone has done what they promised to do)[139] – or by mutual agreement.[140] However, if a contract ends as a

133 *White v Jones* [1995] 2 AC 207.

134 *Darlington BC v Wiltshier Northern Ltd* [1995] 1 WLR 68.

135 *Beswick v Beswick* [1968] AC 58.

136 *Norwich CC v Harvey* [1989] 1 WLR 828.

137 CC art 1134.

138 D.50.17.153.

139 D.50.16.176.

140 D.2.14.7.6.

result of a vitiating factor such as fraud (see Ch 9 § 9) the obligation will, it seems, vanish as a legal entity.[141] Until performance or new agreement, contracts are, then, binding upon the parties and so unilateral repudiation and interference by judges are in principle impossible; only if the parties themselves have agreed within or without the contract that an event would discharge the obligation will the contract dissolve before performance.

Non performance (*inexécution*) will in principle give rise to contractual remedies, of which the most important are specific performance, damages and repudiation. However, if the non-performance arises for reasons other than the fault of the debtor (the non-performer) there is a general principle in the civil law that the debtor is not liable in damages.[142] This general principle is ambiguous in France since every failure in the performance of an obligation obliges the debtor to repair the damage which the creditor suffers therefrom.[143] Thus, a contractor can be strictly liable (liable without fault) in situations where he is said to have guaranteed a result (*obligation de résultat*) or where he is in breach of an *obligation de securité* (*cf* Ch 1 § 7(b)). However, if the non-performance involves an *obligation de moyen* then the debtor can be liable only if the non-performance is due to his fault. All the same, fault is a general concept in civilian contract law[144] and thus a debtor can in principle avoid damages if he can show that the non-performance is the result of a cause outside of his control (*une cause étrangère*).[145] Where a contractor is in serious default, the other party has the right to set aside the contract in whole or in part, unless the failure, given its special nature or minor importance, does not justify the setting aside of the contract.[146] In French law the contract can in principle be set aside only by a court order, but this rule can, it seems, be avoided by inclusion in the contract of a specific term allowing a party to repudiate for non-performance.[147]

When one turns to English law one sees that the binding nature of the English contractual promise has its original historical roots in three rather different forms of action and these differences of form have left their mark on the modern law. In the old writs of covenant and debt the emphasis was on the binding nature of the promise undertaken[148] and in the modern law there is a survival of this approach in that courts are still reluctant to relieve a party who has specifically bound himself to complete a certain act[149] or to pay a specific sum.[150] In these *stricti iuris* 'covenant' and 'debt' transactions the approach is all or nothing: either the contractor has performed the act

141 CC art 1234.

142 See eg Swiss Code of Obligations arts 97, 99; CC art 1147.

143 CC art 1142; Malaurie & Aynès, no 814.

144 Treitel, *Remedies*, paras 8–37.

145 CC art 1147; Swiss Code of Obligations art 97.

146 Malaurie & Aynès, pp 407–22.

147 *Ibid*, no 749.

148 *Paradine v Jane* (1647) 82 ER 897.

149 *Bolton v Mahadeva* [1972] 1 WLR 1009.

150 *White & Carter (Councils) Ltd v McGregor* [1962] AC 413.

or, unless he is to be relieved by some external event, he has not. There is no half-way house in these kinds of cases and equity will intervene only where there has been abuse or unjustified enrichment.

In the contractual liability cases, on the other hand, the historical action of *assumpsit* – a form of trespass – asserts itself by locating the point of emphasis in the damage as much as in the undertaking. The plaintiff will have to show that the damage or loss that is being claimed is caused by the defendant's contractual liability.[151] If the damage is caused by the plaintiff's own failure to mitigate his loss,[152] or is caused by an external event rather than by the defendant's own voluntary act,[153] the courts are likely to attribute the cause of the loss, or parts of it, to events beyond the contract. In these situations, then, the emphasis may well be on 'liability' both in a causal and in a behavioural (*culpa*) sense.[154] All the same much can depend upon the interpretation of the contractual promise, the way the case is pleaded and the burden of proof. If there is a contractual relationship between the parties any loss suffered by one party will, probably, *prima facie* be attributable to the other party's breach of contract[155] and so if a contractual party wishes to escape liability in damages, or indeed to claim in debt for the price of a service rendered, he will have to show that any damage suffered by the other contractual party is not the result of a breach of a term of the contract.[156]

(b) Non-performance and the nature of the claim

That said it must be remembered that it is a general rule of pleading that in damages cases arising out of fault it is for the party alleging fault to prove it. Accordingly, if the subject matter of a contract is destroyed for some unexplained reason it would seem that the question of liability might simply be one of burden of proof.[157] Take the case of the hiring out of a chattel by O (owner) to H (hirer): if the chattel explodes and is destroyed for some unexplained reason several quite different questions can arise. Can O sue H in damages arguing that H is in breach of his obligation towards the chattel?[158] And if so, for how much? Can O sue H in debt for the hire fee if H refuses to pay anything because of the loss of the chattel hired?[159] Can H sue O for damages for any physical injury he might have suffered as a result of the explosion?[160] Can H sue O for his economic losses resulting from the loss of use of the chattel?[161] Each of

151 *Quinn v Burch Brothers* [1966] 2 QB 370.

152 *The Solholt* [1983] 1 Lloyd's Rep 605.

153 *Taylor v Caldwell* (1863) 122 ER 309.

154 Treitel, *Remedies*, paras 10, 32; and see Supply of Goods and Services Act 1982 s 13.

155 *Reed v Dean* [1949] 1 KB 188; Treitel, *Remedies*, para 19. But *cf Joseph Constantine SS Ltd v Imperial Smelting Corporation* [1942] AC 154.

156 *Vigers v Cook* [1919] 2 KB 475.

157 Treitel, *Remedies*, para 12.

158 *Re Polemis* [1921] 3 KB 560.

159 *Vigers v Cook* [1919] 2 KB 475. See also *The Eugenia* [1964] 2 QB 226.

160 *Reed v Dean* [1949] 1 KB 188.

161 *Joseph Constantine SS Ltd v Imperial Smelting Corporation* [1942] AC 154.

these questions, it might be said, arises out of the same contractual relationship, but the way that they are answered may depend on issues which reach beyond the contractual bond itself because the common law has never devoted much attention to the role of fault in contractual liability.[162] It has on the whole preferred to start from the nature of the remedy pursued and to deal with difficult causal problems by reference to notions which function at this level, for example burden of proof, defences, remoteness of damage and the like.

One starting point, then, for discharge of contractual obligations is often to be found in the distinction between debt and damages (*cf* Ch 4 § 5(b)) which, in turn, may well be related to the unilateral and bilateral dichotomy (Ch 8 § 5(d)). In a bilateral contract non-performance will usually be seen as a breach of contract and the legal action will focus around the issue of liability in damages;[163] in a unilateral contract non-performance by the promisee will often be seen as a failure to provide consideration and the legal claim will centre upon liability for debt. Today most commercial contracts are bilateral but aspects of the unilateral approach can still attach to the way the problem is analysed;[164] incomplete or different performance by a potential creditor could free the potential debtor from the promise to pay simply because the potential creditor has not furnished the required consideration.[165] Many cases involving liability for defective or incomplete performance should, as already suggested, be approached both from a substantive and from a remedial point of view. Under what circumstances will a contractor be relieved from having to pay rent, a price or some other contractual sum? Under what circumstances can a contractor refuse to go on with performance of his obligations under the agreement? Or under what circumstances can a contractor claim compensatory damages for damage caused by an accident or other event which has interrupted the contractual transaction?

(c) Discharge by performance

The general rule as to the entitlement to a contractual debt is governed first of all by the doctrine of performance. A creditor is entitled to the contract price only when he has completed his part of the bargain and only if his performance is exactly in accordance with the contract;[166] an incomplete performance will entitle the creditor to nothing at all under the contract.[167]

This performance rule may seem unduly strict but it is subject to a number of exceptions. The rule will apply only to entire contracts and so in certain transactions the liability to pay the entire price will be apportioned into smaller debts payable on the completion of certain stages of performance.[168] The courts have also formulated the

162 Treitel, *Remedies*, para 10.

163 *Ibid*, para 109.

164 *Ibid*, para 233.

165 *The Liddesdale* [1900] AC 190. But *cf Ruxley Electronics Ltd v Forsyth* [1996] 1 AC 344.

166 *The Liddesdale* [1900] AC 190.

167 *Bolton v Mahadeva* [1972] 1 WLR 1009.

168 Treitel, *Remedies*, para 233.

doctrine of substantial performance. In this situation the court adheres to the principle that fulfilment of every promise or term is not necessarily a condition precedent for the payment of a lump sum price; if the performance of the contract could be said to be complete but defective then the court will, provided the defects are minor, allow recovery of the debt subject to a set-off for the cost of the defects.[169] If the defects are serious, however, the strict rule will apply.[170]

(d) Discharge by breach

A plaintiff who complains that a party has not rendered complete performance is, if the contract is bilateral, in effect claiming that there has been a breach of an implied term – an implied condition precedent (above § 3(d)) – that the work will be completed.[171] A debtor who refuses to pay for incomplete performance can, therefore, be seen as a contractor who is effectively repudiating the agreement for breach of a condition (above § 3(c)); and such a repudiation is, as we have seen, a matter of general principle if the breach is either a breach of condition or is in itself grave enough to 'go to the root of the contract'.[172]

Yet it is important to stress that it is not the breach itself which discharges the obligation but the election by the innocent party to bring the primary obligations under the contract to an end.[173] This point is of importance in cases of 'anticipatory breach' where a party declares that he will not perform, or behaves in such a way as to disable himself from performing, the contract.[174] In this situation the innocent party has a choice. He can either repudiate the contract at once and sue in damages for his loss – that is to say, he can rely upon the 'secondary obligation on the part of the contract breaker ... to pay monetary compensation for the loss'[175] – or keep the contract alive, perform his promises and then sue in debt for the full contract price provided that performance is possible without the co-operation of the party in breach.[176] Only if such a debt claim were to amount to a very clear abuse of a contractual right would the court think about preventing the innocent party from recovering the price, although one judge has expressed his dislike for such an action in debt on the ground that it amounts to a form of specific performance of a contract (*cf* Ch 5 § 4) in circumstances where damages 'would be an adequate remedy'.[177]

What breaches will entitle an aggrieved, or innocent, party to repudiate the contract? There are, as we have seen (above § 3), two approaches to this problem. The

169 *Hoenig v Isaacs* [1952] 2 All ER 176; applied in *Williams v Roffey Brothers Ltd* [1991] 1 QB 1. See also *Ruxley Electronics Ltd v Forsyth* [1996] 1 AC 344.

170 *Bolton v Mahadeva* [1972] 1 WLR 1009.

171 *Hoenig v Isaacs, op cit*, at pp 180–82; Treitel, *Remedies*, para 257.

172 *Decro-Wall v Practitioners in Marketing Ltd* [1971] 2 All ER 216.

173 Treitel, *Remedies*, para 280.

174 *Ibid*, para 279.

175 Lord Diplock in *Photo Production Ltd v Securicor* [1980] AC 827, 849.

176 *White & Carter (Councils) Ltd v McGregor* [1962] AC 413.

177 Lord Denning in *Attica Sea Carriers Corpn v Ferrostaal* [1976] 1 Lloyd's Rep 250, 255.

court can look at the status of the term broken and, if it was a condition, give the innocent party the right to repudiate.[178] The problem with this approach, however, is that it may give the innocent party the right to terminate for what is in truth a relatively minor breach.[179] The other approach is to look at the breach itself and to decide whether such a breach goes to the root of the contract.[180]The problem here is that it may allow a party to repudiate a contract for the breach of a relatively minor term.[181] No doubt this latter approach appears more sensible given that it is a general feature of the law of obligations both to measure liability against the degree of harm and of default[182] and to try to prevent situations where one party might be able to enrich themselves from the abuse of a contractual right.[183] Yet the doctrine of freedom of contract (*cf* Ch 8 § 5(e)) would appear to dictate that it should be left to the parties to decide upon the status of terms[184] and so the whole question of discharge by breach might also have to be viewed in the context of a dichotomy between commercial and consumer law.

(e) Discharge by agreement

It must be said, of course, that in many commercial and business relationships an innocent party might elect to keep the contract alive for reasons other than a desire to extract the full debt. An innocent party might, for example, decide to keep the contract alive and accept a different performance from the other party or to abandon completely both the primary and the secondary obligations under the contract. In other words, the parties to a contract may expressly or impliedly agree to discharge or vary the original contract.

Such a discharge or variation presents few problems when the contract to be discharged or varied is still executory on both sides – that is, when neither party has performed his promise(s) under the bargain. For the new pact will generate its own consideration and the agreement will be seen as a new contract replacing an old one. Problems arise when a contract is varied or discharged after one of the parties has executed his part of the bargain because the new pact will lack the necessary consideration to make it enforceable at common law (*cf* Ch 9 § 3). Thus, the creditor who agrees to accept a lesser sum than the contractually stipulated debt can, if he has performed his side of the bargain, disregard this subsequent agreement as a *nudum pactum* and sue for the full debt (*cf* Ch 9 § 3(f)). Equally, the contractor who subsequently promises to pay more than the originally agreed price can, in theory if not in practice,[185] claim there is no consideration to support the second promise.

178 Treitel, *Remedies*, para 267.

179 *The Hansa Nord* [1976] QB 44; Treitel, *Remedies*, paras 259, 264.

180 Treitel, *Remedies*, paras 260, 264.

181 *Aerial Advertising Co v Batchelors Peas Ltd* [1938] 2 All ER 788.

182 Treitel, *Remedies*, para 268.

183 *Ibid*, para 267 (p 363).

184 *Bunge Corpn v Tradax Export* [1981] 1 WLR 711.

185 *Williams v Roffey Brothers Ltd* [1991] 1 QB 1.

Nevertheless, as we have seen, the position is by no means as simple as the common law at first suggests because a promise unsupported by consideration, although in principle a *nudum pactum*, is not necessarily without legal effect (*cf* Ch 9 § 3(f)). The doctrine of estoppel (*cf* Ch 5 § 1(c)) may well prevent a promisor going back on his bare promise and this equitable doctrine has, in the area of discharge and variation of contracts, been given added support by the common law doctrine of waiver.[186]This latter doctrine is founded in the election right given to an innocent party faced with a serious breach of contract: if the innocent party elects to waive his right to repudiate the contract for breach of condition this election will act as 'a kind of estoppel'[187] and he will be forced from then on to rely upon his remedy of damages for breach of warranty (*cf* above § 3(e)).

When estoppel and waiver are taken together it seems that an agreement to discharge or to vary an existing, but partly executed, contract will be effective in law to the extent that the promisor in the second pact will be prevented from going back on his promise if the promisee has relied upon the promise and it would be inequitable to allow him to enforce his strict contractual rights. Whether this doctrine has its foundation in common law or in equity is not entirely clear;[188] what is clear is that an existing substantive contractual obligation can, in strict contractual theory, be replaced only by a second contract supported by consideration. Consequently, when a partly executed contractual obligation is varied or discharged for the benefit of just one of the parties any legal consequences attaching to this new pact belong, not so much to the substantive law of contractual rights, but more to the law of actions or remedies. English law, in other words, has not worked out a coherent doctrine of discharge of an obligation by consent.

(f) Discharge by frustration

One of the dangers that threatens the innocent party who elects to keep a contract alive after a serious breach is the danger that some later event (*casus*) may supervene to discharge the contractual obligation, freeing the party in breach from any potential liability.[189] Such a supervening event which leads to impossibility of performance is known as the doctrine of frustration and, in English law, it plays a similar role to that played by *cause etrangère* and *force majeure* in French law.[190]

However, the doctrine of frustration differs in its approach to contractual liability from the continental doctrine of *force majeure* in that frustration is, in theory, less a question of contractual liability and more a question of the frustration of the bargain

186 Treitel, *Remedies*, para 290.

187 *Charles Rickards Ltd v Oppenheim* [1950] 1 KB 616; see also Sale of Goods Act 1979 s 11(2).

188 *W J Alan & Co Ltd v El Nasr Export & Import Co* [1972] 2 QB 189, 212–13.

189 See eg *Avery v Bowden* (1855) 119 ER 647; *Bank Line Ltd v Arthur Capel & Co* [1919] AC 435.

190 See CC art 1148: '*Il n'y a lieu à aucuns dommages et intérêts lorsque, par suite d'une force majeure ou d'un cas fortuit, le débiteur a été empêché de donner ou de faire ce à quoi il était obligé, ou a fait ce qui lui était interdit.*'

itself. The approach is to focus upon the object of the economic transaction and not upon the party claiming impossibility of performance. It may be that a party claiming frustration of the venture will have to go some way in showing that the alleged frustrating event is not due to any fault on his part.[191] And even then it must be remembered that it is an axiom of English contract law 'that, in relation to claims for damages for breach of contract, it is, in general, immaterial why the defendant failed to fulfil his obligation, and certainly no defence to plead that he had done his best'.[192] But if the intervening event is held to be a frustration of the contract the doctrine operates to set the venture aside rather than to relieve performance of one of the parties. Indeed the doctrine of frustration was, and still is to some extent, much closer to a 'vitiating factor' and this was once reflected in the idea that frustration, like mistake (*cf* Ch 9 § 8(b)), was dependent upon an implied condition precedent concerning the continued existence of the subject matter of the contract,[193] later extended to the commercial substance of the bargain.[194]

Today the subjective implied term theory has been discarded and replaced by the objective 'reasonable man' hypothesis. It is the court, acting as the reasonable man, which discharges the contract on the basis that the frustrating event would make performance of the promise radically different from that originally undertaken: *non haec in foedera veni*.[195] All the same, the doctrine of frustration is applied only within very narrow limits.[196] Thus, if the frustrating event is 'self-induced' – that is, it arises from the fault, default or deliberate act of one of the parties[197] – the venture will be discharged but the person who induced the *casus* will remain contractually liable to the other party.[198] And a mere increase in expense[199] will not be enough to set the venture aside unless, perhaps, the increase is so astronomical as to give rise to a 'fundamentally different situation'.[200] Also, if there is an express clause in the contract which specifically covers the *casus* this will prevent the doctrine of frustration from applying, save where the intervening event is illegality arising, say, from the outbreak of war.[201]

In debt cases arising from the hire of property difficult problems can arise where the supervening event frustrates the purpose for which the property was to be used. In

191 *The Hannah Blumenthal* [1983] 1 AC 854, 882 (CA); *Maritime National Fish Ltd v Ocean Trawlers Ltd* [1935] AC 524; but *cf Joseph Constantine SS Ltd v Imperial Smelting Corporation* [1942] AC 154; *Shepherd & Co Ltd v Jerrom* [1987] QB 301.

192 Lord Edmund-Davies in *Raineri v Miles* [1981] AC 1050, 1086. And see Treitel, *Remedies*, para 10.

193 *Taylor v Caldwell* (1863) 122 ER 309.

194 *Jackson v Union Marine Insurance Co Ltd* (1874) LR 10 CP 125.

195 *Davis Contractors Ltd v Fareham UDC* [1956] AC 696.

196 See eg Treitel, *Remedies*, para 18.

197 *Maritime National Fish Ltd v Ocean Trawlers Ltd* [1935] AC 524.

198 *Shepherd & Co Ltd v Jerrom* [1987] QB 301, 325–27.

199 The doctrine of *imprévision*: Zweigert & Kötz, pp 563–66; Isabelle de Lamberterie, Harris & Tallon, pp 228–34.

200 *The Eugenia* [1964] 2 QB 226, 240. But see *Staffs Health Authority v S Staffs Waterworks* [1978] 1 WLR 1387; and the NBW Bk 6 arts 258 and 260 (*imprévision*).

201 J Bell, The Effect of Changes in Circumstances on Long-term Contracts, Harris & Tallon, p 208.

these situations the courts have to distinguish between contractual venture (the 'foundation of the contract') and motive and this can often be a difficult question of fact, and law,[202] depending on the circumstances of each particular case.[203] However, the House of Lords has indicated[204] that when it comes to applying the doctrine of frustration it is not a matter of reasoning by analogy, involving the massive citation of previous cases, but the application of Lord Radcliffe's 'radically different' test.[205]

All the same it can still be important to distinguish between various classes of contract because in cases where a contractor is claiming in debt much can turn on the 'consideration' furnished in respect of the debt. Did the debtor contract for a specific thing or did he contract for a chance to make a profit which has not materialised? Or, put another way, upon whom should fall the risk when expectations fail to materialise because of some unforeseen event? Leases present particular difficulties here because a debtor can rent land for a particular commercial purpose. If that purpose is frustrated by some supervening event does that also frustrate the lease? One old case made the point that there are profit and loss risks attached to land and the court refused to relieve the debtor from liability to pay the rent because, in effect, the owner of the property had performed his side of the bargain.[206] This decision was later seen as denying completely any doctrine of frustration in English contract law.[207] Yet leases can still appear immune in practice, if not in theory, from the doctrine of frustration and this is simply because in this class of case the risks attach to the property rather than to the obligation.[208] There is, it might be said, no total failure of consideration and consequently the contractual promise remains in existence.[209]

9 NON-PERFORMANCE AND THE LAW OF REMEDIES

This idea of a total failure of consideration, although unfortunate in the way it misleadingly appears to involve an essential formation condition (*cf* Ch 9 § 3), nevertheless goes far in expressing the idea of a failure of expectation. Two problems immediately arise. First, to what extent can a contractor, whose expectations have totally failed to materialise, recover any benefits that he has conferred on the other party? This is a problem for the law of restitution (*cf* Ch 11). Secondly, to what extent can a contractor recover compensation for the loss of expectation? This is a problem for the law of damages (*cf* Ch 6).

---

202 *The Nema* [1982] AC 724.

203 *Krell v Henry* [1903] 2 KB 740.

204 *The Nema* [1982] AC 724.

205 *Davis Contractors Ltd v Fareham UDC* [1956] AC 696, 729.

206 *Paradine v Jane* (1647) 82 ER 897.

207 J Cooke & D Oughton, *Common Law of Obligations* (Butterworths, 2nd edn, 1993), p 364.

208 *National Carriers Ltd v Panalpina (Northern) Ltd* [1981] AC 675; and see also *Amalgamated Investment & Property Co v John Walker & Sons* [1976] 3 All ER 509.

209 Zweigert & Kötz, pp 555–57.

(a) Restitution and discharge of contract

The notion of a total failure of consideration is an important concept in handling the very difficult restitution problems that can arise when contracts are discharged. As a general principle an action in quasi-contract (*cf* Ch 11 § 2) is available only when the contract itself has been completely discharged; and such discharge will take effect only if there has been a total failure of consideration.[210] If there has been no such failure then the contract will remain in existence, although this may prove just as advantageous for any plaintiff in that a damages action for breach is usually as good as, if not better, than any debt claim in restitution.[211]

These restitution problems were at one time particularly acute with regard to frustrated contracts because, in the absence of a total failure of consideration, the rule at common law was that the loss was to lie where it fell.[212] And even if there had been a total failure of consideration allowing one party to recover a payment made before frustration, there were no means by which the other party could recover an indemnity for any expenses incurred unless, perhaps, some tangible benefit had been bestowed.[213] Some of these 'all-or-nothing' defects with regard to frustrated contracts have been remedied by the Law Reform (Frustrated Contracts) Act 1943. If money has been paid, or has become payable, before the frustration the payer can recover the sums paid, or will cease to be liable for the sums payable, except in so far as the court can allow the payee to deduct, or to claim for out of money due, any expenses incurred in the performance of the contract.[214] And if one party has obtained under the contract a 'valuable benefit' as a result of anything done by the other party before frustration, the person receiving the benefit can be made by the court to pay for such a benefit received.[215] The principle upon which the court operates in ordering these deductions or claims with regard to expenses and benefits is the equitable principle of unjust enrichment; the court orders a deduction or an indemnity where it is just in the circumstances of the case to do so. Yet the use of this principle of restitution or unjust enrichment also has its disadvantages in that, in looking to the defendant's benefit rather than to the plaintiff's loss, the words 'valuable benefit' will be interpreted, not by reference to things done or to money expended by the plaintiff, but by reference to the benefit itself. If the defendant has received no actual or real benefit he will not be liable under the statute.[216]

It must also be observed that the 1943 statute applies only when a contract has been discharged through frustration and so where a contract has been discharged for breach

---

210 *Rover International Ltd v Canon Films Ltd* [1989] 1 WLR 912.

211 See *Yeoman Credit Ltd v Apps* [1962] 2 QB 508.

212 *Chandler v Webster* [1904] 1 KB 493.

213 *Fibrosa v Fairbairn* [1943] AC 32.

214 Law Reform (Frustrated Contracts) Act 1943 s 1(2).

215 Section 1(3).

216 *BP Exploration (Libya) Ltd v Hunt (No 2)* [1979] 1 WLR 783; [1983] 2 AC 352; *Gamerco SA v ICM/Fair Warning (Agency) Ltd* [1995] 1 WLR 1226.

the rules of common law are applicable. One of these rules, as we have seen, stipulates that a party who fails to render complete performance is in principle entitled to nothing. But this strict rule may not be applicable if it can be shown that the innocent party to a breach expressly or impliedly agreed to accept a partial performance;[217] and it may be that a party who has received a large advance payment would not be entitled to keep the whole amount if such a deposit amounted to a penalty (*cf* above § 5(b)). Furthermore, statute allows the court to order restitution of advance payments in certain kinds of transaction, for example in consumer hire purchase and consumer hire contracts.[218]

Sometimes it is tempting to think that there is a general principle of unjust enrichment which will come into play in all situations where a contract has been discharged.[219] Yet if there is such a principle it is not one that *per se* will give rise to any restitutionary remedy in this area of the law (*cf* Ch 11 § 5). In unjust enrichment problems arising out of a breach of contract the rules applicable will be the rules that attach to any restitution remedy existing in the law of actions; but these law of actions rules will in turn be subject to any policy considerations that attach to the law of contract.

(b) Breach of contract and damages

When a contract is discharged for breach we have already seen that the distinction between debt and damages can be of relevance because the remedy of debt is, in truth, a kind of specific performance of the contract (*cf* above § 8(d)). It is a remedy that grows directly out of the primary contractual obligation itself.[220] A damages claim, in contrast, does not arise out of the primary contractual obligation; it is a 'secondary obligation ... to pay monetary compensation to the other party for the loss sustained by him in consequence of the breach'.[221] This difference gives rise to some teasing questions.

First, what if a failure to pay a contractual debt causes loss to the creditor over and above the amount of the debt itself? Can the creditor sue the debtor both at the primary (debt) and the secondary (damages) levels? As the two remedies are also separate causes of action (*cf* Ch 4 § 5(b)), it would appear that a compensation claim can be mounted, although the loss would specifically have to be proved as 'special damage' and not be too remote.[222] One might add that interest on a debt, irrecoverable at common law, can now under statute be awarded at the discretion of the court.[223]

217 *Sumpter v Hedges* [1898] 1 QB 673.

218 Consumer Credit Act 1974 ss 100, 132.

219 *Stockloser v Johnson* [1954] 1 QB 476, 492.

220 *Moschi v Lep Air Services Ltd* [1973] AC 331, 346–47; Treitel, *Remedies*, para 39.

221 Lord Diplock in *Photo Production Ltd v Securicor* [1980] AC 827, 849.

222 *Wadsworth v Lydall* [1981] 1 WLR 598.

223 Supreme Court Act 1981 s 35A; *cf Westdeutsche Landesbank v Islington LBC* [1996] 2 WLR 802.

A second question concerns the nature of the interest protected by debt and damages actions. If an award of money at common law is, in general, to compensate a contracting party for breach of promise, what kind of interest does a debt claim protect? And is the interest protected by a debt claim one that will be protected by an award of damages as well? The standard response here is to say that a successful debt claim is protecting a contractor's 'expectation interest'[224] and that this is an interest which an award of damages will also seek to protect in contract.[225] In other words, a monetary remedy for breach of contract will compensate both consequential losses (*damnum emergens*) and failure to make gains (*lucrum cessans*).[226] The problem, however, is that in fact this is not always true of a damages action because, unlike debt, it is subject not only to questions of definition of loss but also to the rules of causation and remoteness (*cf* Ch 7). In truth the expectation interest may well find itself excluded, perhaps because of difficulties of proof of damage[227] or causation,[228] leaving the plaintiff either to his reliance[229] or to his restitutionary[230] interests.

A third question arises out of the nature of the interests themselves. Will a monetary award protect only the economic interests of the contractor or will it extend to the more intangible losses? Here the position is quite complex because although an award of damages will go well beyond the immediate economic loss in personal injury and physical damage cases – for the damages rules here are the same as in tort[231] – the courts are often reluctant to compensate for mental distress and disappointment.[232] For example, they will compensate for the loss of a chance to win a competition[233] and they will give damages for mental distress in a certain kind of contract case, namely where the object of the contract is to provide peace of mind and freedom from distress.[234] Yet on the whole contract, being a creature of commercial law, finds itself protecting interests which are usually solidly economic and its damages rules, in commercial law itself, thus tend to be quite generous in terms of *lucrum cessans*,[235] at least when compared with tort,[236] and quite strict in terms of certain *damnum emergens* interests. A breach of contract must disclose actual economic loss before a plaintiff can

224 *Fuller & Perdue* (1936) 46 Yale LJ 52; Treitel, *Remedies*, para 82; *Surrey CC v Bredero Homes Ltd* [1993] 1 WLR 1361, 1369.

225 *Damon Compania Naviera v Hapag-Lloyd International* [1985] 1 WLR 435.

226 Treitel, *Remedies*, para 84; *cf* CC art 1149. For the historical background see Zimmermann, pp 826–33.

227 *Ruxley Electronics Ltd v Forsyth* [1995] 3 WLR 118 (HL).

228 See generally Treitel, *Remedies*, paras 93–98.

229 See eg *Anglia TV v Reed* [1972] 1 QB 60.

230 See eg *Farnworth Finance Facilities Ltd v Attryde* [1970] 1 WLR 1053.

231 *Parsons v Uttley Ingham & Co* [1978] QB 791; Treitel, *Remedies*, para 86.

232 *Addis v Gramophone Co* [1909] AC 488.

233 *Chaplin v Hicks* [1911] 2 KB 786. See also *Allied Maples Group Ltd v Simmons & Simmons* [1995] 1 WLR 1602.

234 *Jarvis v Swan's Tours* [1973] QB 233; *Watts v Morrow* [1991] 1 WLR 1421, 1445.

235 *Victoria Laundry (Windsor) Ltd v Newman Industries Ltd* [1949] 2 KB 528.

236 *Spartan Steel & Alloys Ltd v Martin & Co* [1973] 1 QB 27; *Swingcastle Ltd v Gibson* [1991] 2 AC 223.

recover substantial damages.[237] If there is no physical loss or economic loss as such, then a contractor will be awarded damages for mental distress only if he or she is a consumer and, as such, has not received what he or she had bargained for.[238]

237 *Lazenby Garages Ltd v Wright* [1976] 1 WLR 459; *C & P Haulage v Middleton* [1983] 1 WLR 1461.
238 See *Ruxley Electronics Ltd v Forsyth* [1995] 3 WLR 118.

CHAPTER ELEVEN

NON-CONTRACTUAL OBLIGATIONS: DEBT AND EQUITABLE ACTIONS

When one moves from contractual to non-contractual obligations one is moving, broadly speaking, from obligations founded upon a juridical act to obligations founded upon juridical facts. The key facts which give rise to such obligations are damage and enrichment. Accordingly the *Code civil* states in article 1382 that: 'Any act whatsoever by a person which causes damage to another obliges the person by whose fault it has occurred to repair it.' Damage is not in itself enough to trigger liability, but it is the starting point for the law of delict and quasi-delict. The French code, it must be said, has no such general action in respect of enrichment. However, a French professor once suggested that the following principle be adopted into French law: 'Any act whatsoever by a person which causes an enrichment to another gives rise to a right on behalf of the person by whose act the enrichment has been procured to recover it.' And the French *Cour de cassation* has recognised unjust enrichment as a general principle of law. Moreover, the Swiss Code of Obligations states in article 62 that: 'Anyone who, without legitimate cause, is enriched at the expense of another, must make restitution.'[1] Wrongful damage and wrongful enrichment, using wrongful in a broad sense, are, then, facts which form the basis in civil law systems for two categories of *in personam* obligational rights and duties that exist alongside the category of contract.

1 DEVELOPMENTS BEYOND CONTRACT

Lord Haldane said in 1914 that 'broadly speaking, so far as proceedings *in personam* are concerned, the common law of England really recognises (unlike the Roman law) only actions of two classes, those founded on contract and those founded on tort.'[2] This twofold division of the law of obligations would, in fact, cause little surprise to a Roman lawyer since the history of the classical and post-classical Roman law is beset with conceptual difficulties not dissimilar to those experienced by the modern common law. The inadequacies of the contract and delict (tort) dichotomy were recognised at almost the same moment as they were originally proposed.[3]

(a) Non-contractual debt claims

In particular, the dichotomy left little place for the non-contractual debt claims of the kind arising out of, for example, mistake. P pays a sum of money to D thinking that D is C: upon what obligational basis can P recover the sum paid in error given that D has committed no wrong and that no contract exists between P and D? A debt remedy (the *condictio*) certainly existed in Roman law, but how was it to be classified at a substantive

1 See also NBW Bk 6 art 212(1).

2 *Sinclair v Brougham* [1914] AC 398, 415; *cf Westdeutsche Landesbank v Islington LBC* [1996] 2 WLR 802.

3 Zimmermann, pp 14–15.

level? Subsequent Roman jurists developed the category of quasi-contract to accommodate these *in personam* debt actions which could be based neither on agreement nor on wrongs and this categorisation exercise was completed when the late medieval and Renaissance civilians brought together various *in personam* remedies, the category of quasi-contract and the principle, to be found in Roman law, that no one should be unjustly enriched at the expense of another.[4] Modern civil lawyers, to a greater or lesser extent, all now recognise that the law of obligations consists of a threefold subdivision of contract, quasi-contract (French model) or restitution (German model), and delict.[5]

In general, in most of the civil law systems, in addition to delict and contract, *negotiorum gestio*, *solutio indebiti* and unjustified enrichment exist as sources of obligations. *Negotiorum gestio* consists in intervening intentionally and on reasonable grounds in order to safeguard another person's interests without any authority derived from a juristic act or a specific statutory (legal) relationship.[6] *Solutio indebiti*, performance in the absence of any obligation to perform, gives the right to reclaim money paid or to force the other party to undo any enrichment as a result of any performance by the other party.[7] More generally, anyone who has been unjustifiably enriched at the expense of another is obliged, as far as is reasonable, to compensate the other's loss to the extent of his enrichment.[8]

When one turns to English law the position appears to be, as we have seen, that there are only two categories within the law of obligations.[9] This lack of any general substantive principle of restitution is indicative of the dominating role that contract has exerted on the English law of obligations for well over a century now. What developments there had been in quasi-contract at the dawn of the industrial revolution were quickly restricted by the theory that quasi-contracts were implied contracts based upon the fiction of an implied promise.[10] And even if such a fiction has now been abandoned, the relationship of the parties can still remain a pre-condition for restitution. Thus, the nearest that English law can get to a doctrine of *negotiorum gestio* is to allow a debt claim for necessary expenses to arise out of the relationship of agency or bailment.[11]

(b) Non-contractual damages actions

In tort, also, the dominating role of contract was given support by the 19th century empirical reality that most accidents happened on the railways or in the workplace.[12] A

4 Stein, *Institutions*, p 205.

5 Zimmermann, pp 1–31. But *cf* NBW Bk 6. And see *Kleinwort Benson Ltd v Glasgow CC* [1996] 2 WLR 655.

6 CC arts 1372–75.

7 CC arts 1376–77.

8 See eg Swiss Code of Obligations art 62.

9 See also County Courts Act 1984 s 15(1). But *cf Kleinwort Benson, supra*.

10 Zimmermann, pp 22–24.

11 *The Winson* [1982] AC 939.

12 Atiyah, *Rise and Fall*, pp 501–05.

great many damages claims could thus be decided on the basis of an implied term within a contractual relationship. It was only with the growth of road accidents that the 'contractual' duty of care was transferred from the implied term to the tort of trespass.[13] In the 20th century the development was taken a stage further when consumer protection problems finally stimulated the courts into giving legal independence to the 'implied duty of care'.[14] All the same, the separation has never been a complete one; the scope and contents of the independent duty of care can, on occasions, still be dependent, if not actually upon the existence of a contractual relationship, then upon a relationship that is 'near to' or 'equivalent to' contract.[15]

Yet the rapid growth of the tort of negligence in this century (*cf* Ch 12 § 3(a)) ought not to be allowed to obscure the fact that its history in many ways predates that of the category of contract: for the idea of promissory liability is, in England, a relatively recent phenomenon associated with the decline and abolition of the forms of action (*cf* Ch 3 § 4).[16] In the early era of the common law most compensation actions were 'tortious' in the sense that they were, directly or indirectly, founded on trespass or nuisance; and those actions that were not – debt and detinue, for example – were more proprietary than obligational.[17] Before the 19th century English lawyers thought more in terms of trespass and debt than contract and tort and this older dichotomy, emphasising as it does the remedy rather than the right, is still a characteristic of the modern common law (*cf* Ch 4 § 5(b)). Accordingly, it remains difficult to talk of a law of unjust enrichment in England since most such claims tend to be classified either within the existing categories of contract and tort or under the heading of equity and remedies.

(c) Debt and unjust enrichment

When viewed from the position of the law of actions, the distinction between debt and damages is not only fundamental to the English law of remedies but is a distinction that can also act as a good guide when it comes to the classification of non-contractual obligations. For the distinction between debt and damages reflects in English law, just as it did in Roman law, a difference between unjust loss and unjust benefit. The action of debt, like the Roman *condictio*, can be used to claim money in situations where a defendant has obtained a benefit which it would be unjust for him to retain.[18] The action for damages, although it can be used to prevent unjust enrichment, has been fashioned mainly to deal with problems of compensation, and so is more suitable for dealing with problems of loss and injury. Non-contractual debt actions might, then, be

13 *Holmes v Mather* (1875) LR 10 EX 261.

14 *Donoghue v Stevenson* [1932] AC 562.

15 *Junior Books Ltd v Veitchi Co Ltd* [1983] AC 520; *Smith v Eric Bush* [1990] 1 AC 831.

16 Milsom, p 355.

17 Note how debt continues to be proprietary in nature; it is still something that can be 'owned': *Lipkin Gorman v Karpnale Ltd* [1991] 2 AC 548, 573–74.

18 *United Australia Ltd v Barclays Bank Ltd* [1941] AC 1, 26–27; *Fibrosa etc v Fairbairn etc* [1943] AC 32, 61–64; *Lipkin, supra*, pp 572–74.

said to form the basis of quasi-contract, while non-contractual damages might be seen as the basis of delictual liability – that is to say, the law of tort.

2 NON-CONTRACTUAL DEBT ACTIONS (QUASI-CONTRACT)

The idea that some debt claims can be justified by reference neither to the law of tort nor to the law of contract has exercised the minds of the modern common lawyers as much as it once exercised the minds of Roman and civilian jurists. Traditionally, many of these debt claims have been rationalised either as implied or fictitious contracts[19] or as 'empirical' remedies in the law of actions.[20] Today the tendency is to agree with Lord Wright and to see such claims as falling 'within a third category of the common law which has been called quasi-contract or restitution'[21] – although a complete separation from contract or the law of actions has, perhaps, not yet fully been achieved.[22] These non-contractual debt claims developed in form from the old action of *indebitatus assumpsit* and in substance from the equitable action of account (*cf* Ch 4 § 5(g)); and in the modern law they take several forms depending upon the nature of the benefit conferred upon the defendant (see below § 3(d)). But it has to be stressed that this is an area of the English law of obligations that is somewhat underdeveloped[23] in that quasi-contract remains closely tied to the forms of action. Moreover, the position is complicated by the remedy of tracing at common law (*cf* Ch 4 § 5(d)). This remedy, *in rem* in nature, appears to attach itself to the *in personam* debt claim of money had and received.

(a) Action for money had and received

The first form of quasi-contractual claim, an action for money had and received, is an action which quite closely resembled, indeed may even have taken its 19th century motivation, from the old Roman *condictio*. It is thus available for the return of money paid under a mistake of fact, under compulsion or under a transaction whose consideration has wholly failed (*cf* Ch 9 § 11; Ch 10 § 9). Thus, where a bank mistakenly credits a customer's account for a second time the bank can, in principle, recover such an amount via an action for money had and received.[24]

Furthermore, the action for money had and received is available in situations where the defendant has received money from a third party of which account ought to be made to the plaintiff,[25] and where the defendant has profited at the plaintiff's expense

19 Zimmermann, pp 22–24.

20 *Orakpo v Manson Investments Ltd* [1978] AC 95, 104.

21 *Fibrosa v Fairbairn* [1943] AC 32, 61; *Lipkin Gorman v Karpnale Ltd* [1991] 2 AC 548, 572.

22 But cf *Westdeutsche Landesbank v Islington LBC* [1996] 2 WLR 802, 833.

23 For an excellent survey from the position of unjust enrichment see Zweigert & Kötz, pp 590–600.

24 *United Overseas Bank v Jiwani* [1977] 1 All ER 733.

25 This kind of claim is akin to a tracing (*in rem*) action and thus is not based on the notion of a 'wrong': *Lipkin Gorman v Karpnale Ltd* [1991] 2 AC 548, 572–73.

through the commission of an unlawful act. In this latter situation the action for money had and received might be a useful alternative to a damages claim for breach of statutory duty (*cf* Ch 12 § 4(a)) where the defendant has made a profit from his crime,[26] although it is likely that the equitable remedy of account (*cf* Ch 4 § 5(g)) will now be more relevant.[27]

An action for money had and received is, then, likely to be the main claim in situations where a plaintiff has transferred, directly or indirectly, to a defendant a sum of money which in all the circumstances it would be unjust for the defendant to keep. This notion of 'unjust' does not necessarily imply a wrong on behalf of the defendant and thus a casino has been held liable to a firm of solicitors for money embezzled by a partner and lost at the casino's gambling tables (*cf* Ch 14 § 3(e)).[28] Equally, the bank that puts money into a customer's account in error can use the claim to recover the amount.[29] Nevertheless, an action for money had and received will also be available to deal with situations where a defendant has enriched himself through his own wrong; thus, the person who extorts money from a plaintiff through duress or fraud will be liable to make restitution and this will extend to public bodies that demand money when they have no statutory power to do so.[30] An action will also be available in situations where money is paid under an ineffective transaction or where the consideration has totally failed (*cf* Ch 10 § 9(a)). Thus, if B buys a car from S that subsequently turns out to have been stolen with the result that B has to return the car to its true owner, B will have an action for money had and received against S for the return of the purchase price.[31]

However, not all wrongful profits will be open to abstraction. The trader who trades without a local authority licence will not necessarily have to disgorge his profits to the council[32] nor will the builder who builds more houses than he should in breach of planning permission.[33] The difficulty encountered in these situations is that the defendant has not enriched himself at the expense of the local authority as such; and thus not only has the council not suffered damage, hence the difficulty of claiming damages for breach of contract, but there is no sum of money in the defendant's patrimony that could be said to have been extracted from the plaintiff's patrimony. The only 'person' who might be said to be the loser is the community as a whole and such a group is not recognised as a legal person capable of vindicating its rights directly in the law of actions. No doubt it could be argued that the local authority represents the interests of the community in a range of situations where the public interest is in issue;[34] but when it comes to unjust profiteering it is difficult to link the defendant's

26 *Reading v AG* [1951] AC 507.

27 *AG v Guardian Newspapers (No 2)* [1990] AC 109.

28 *Lipkin Gorman v Karpnale Ltd* [1991] 2 AC 548.

29 *United Overseas Bank v Jiwani* [1977] 1 All ER 733.

30 *Woolwich Equitable Building Society v IRC* [1993] AC 70; *Westdeutsche Landesbank v Islington LBC* [1996] 2 WLR 802.

31 *Rowland v Divall* [1923] 2 KB 500.

32 *Stoke-on-Trent CC v W & J Wass Ltd* [1988] 1 WLR 1406.

33 *Surrey County Council v Bredero Homes Ltd* [1993] 1 WLR 1361.

34 Local Government Act 1972 s 222.

gain to any specifically identifiable loss on behalf of an identifiable legal person. Accordingly, if the law is to be criticised, it is not so much the law of restitution that is wanting but the law of persons.

(b) Action for money paid

The second form of quasi-contractual debt claim is available in cases where the defendant has received a benefit by reason of money paid by the plaintiff to a third party. This claim is useful in situations where the plaintiff has paid money on the defendant's behalf in circumstances of necessity and thus it can resemble the Roman action of *negotiorum gestio* which allowed the good neighbour who unofficiously intervened to protect the property of another to recover his expenses.[35] However, in contrast to *negotiorum gestio* the action for money paid is probably available only in situations where there is some pre-existing relationship between the parties such as agency or bailment and thus the existence of a factual emergency will not *per se* be enough to give rise to quasi-contractual liability.[36]

The action for money paid is also available in situations where the plaintiff has been compelled by law to pay money on behalf of another. Thus, if O stores goods in P's bonded warehouse O will, *prima facie*, be liable to reimburse P for any duties that P might be forced to pay in respect of the goods.[37] Whether or not this liability will be incurred in situations where the compulsion is moral rather than legal is a more difficult question. In *Owen v Tate* Scarman LJ said that if 'without an antecedent request a person assumes an obligation or makes a payment for the benefit of another, the law will, as a general rule, refuse him a right of indemnity.' However, if the person 'can show that in the particular circumstances of the case there was some necessity for the obligation to be assumed, then the law will grant him a right of reimbursement if in all the circumstances it is just and reasonable to do so.'[38]

(c) *Quantum meruit*

The third form of debt claim is available, together with its sister *quantum valebat*, to recover money for services or for property supplied to the defendant. However, it must be remembered that it is an established principle of English law that the mere rendering of services or property to another is not enough, in itself, to give rise to restitutionary liability since 'liabilities are not to be forced upon people behind their backs'.[39] Accordingly, in a *quantum meruit* or *valebat* action the plaintiff must normally show that the defendant expressly or impliedly requested, or at least he freely accepted, the services or goods in question.[40] If such services or goods were rendered pursuant to a

35 Zimmermann, pp 433–50.

36 *The Winson* [1982] AC 939; *In re F* [1990] 2 AC 1.

37 *Brook's Wharf & Bull Wharf Ltd v Goodman Brothers* [1937] 1 KB 534.

38 [1975] 2 All ER 129, 135.

39 *Falcke v Scottish Imperial Insurance Co* (1886) 34 Ch D 234, 248.

40 *Sumpter v Hedges* [1898] 1 QB 673.

contract incompletely performed then it is unlikely that the courts would allow a quasi-contractual claim unless there is evidence that the defendant had agreed to accept incomplete performance (*cf* Ch 10 §§ 8(d), 9(a)). But where services have been rendered under a void contract the court will in principle allow a quasi-contractual action for their value[41] provided that the principle of restitution takes account of any policy considerations which underlie the rule that makes the contract void, illegal or unenforceable (*cf* Ch 9 § 6). The courts are not prepared indirectly to enforce certain contracts that statute has made illegal or void.[42]

One exception to the general principle of services performed without prior request is maritime salvage. One who saves another's ship or cargo is entitled to reward from the owners of the ship or cargo. This is a true restitution claim inasmuch as the entitlement is measured in terms of the property saved and thus the salvor who fails to save the defendant's ship is entitled to nothing since the defendant has not been enriched by the salvor's (intervenor's) act. Equally, the debt claim by the salvor in respect of any cargo saved cannot exceed the value of the property saved. It is, in other words, a debt claim based upon a *quantum meruit.*[43] However, in practice it may be that most of the law of salvage is a matter of contractual rather than non-contractual obligations.[44]

(d) Defences to restitution

Given that most of these non-contractual debt claims have their foundation in the law of actions rather than in some rationalised structure of restitutionary rights,[45] it has not been that easy to develop a coherent set of defences to such claims. Furthermore, the vagueness of the whole area ('unjust' enrichment) has also meant that defences have tended to become swallowed up by the discretionary nature of the 'right' itself. However, developments are now taking place in English law. A plaintiff who, in full knowledge of a possible ground on which to contest liability, nevertheless pays a claimed debt in consequence of a deliberate decision not to contest the claim can be met with the defence of voluntary payment should he ever wish to claim restitution.[46] And a defendant who can show that he has changed his position as a result of the payment – for example, he has given the money to a charity – now has a substantive defence provided he can show that he was neither a wrongdoer nor one who has paid in bad faith.[47] It must be stressed, however, that merely showing that the money received has been paid to some third party will not of itself amount to the defence of change of position.[48]

41 *Craven-Ellis v Canons Ltd* [1936] 2 KB 403.

42 *Orakpo v Manson Investments Ltd* [1978] AC 95.

43 *The Aldora* [1975] QB 748.

44 Tettenborn, *Restitution*, para 8–17.

45 But see generally P Birks, *An introduction to the law of Restitution* (Oxford, revised edn, 1989).

46 *R v Tower Hamlets LBC, Ex p Chetnik Ltd* [1988] AC 858, 880–81, 882–83.

47 *Lipkin Gorman v Karpnale Ltd* [1991] 2 AC 548.

48 *Lipkin Gorman v Karpnale Ltd* [1991] 2 AC 548, 580.

3 EQUITABLE REMEDIES

In addition to the quasi-contractual debt claims, equity has available a number of remedies that can be used to prevent unjust enrichment (*cf* Ch 5). Indeed, along with abuse of rights, it might be said that the idea of unjust enrichment (see below § 5) is one of the great motivating principles of Chancery. Thus, each time equity intervenes in the area of contractual obligations it could be said that it is preventing a means of justified enrichment being turned into, because of, say, mistake or misrepresentation, a vehicle of unjustified enrichment. Such intervention can be positive or negative in operation. It is positive when equity grants a remedy such as rectification, rescission or injunction (*cf* Ch 5); it is negative when it refuses to grant, for example, specific performance or injunction. In other words, equity can simply refuse to order the performance of a contract and this will have the effect of forcing the contractor demanding performance to sue for damages at common law; and if such a contractor cannot show damage, or is deemed to be the cause of his own loss, the common law court, again perhaps reflecting the principle of unjust enrichment, will award only nominal damages.[49]

(a) Misrepresentation and mistake

Equity has long permitted a representee to rescind a contract entered into as a result of a misrepresentation by the other contracting party (*cf* Ch 9 § 7) and this right to rescind has been extended in more recent times to mistake (*cf* Ch 9 § 8(c)).[50] As Robert Goff LJ pointed out, the remedy of rescission is more restitutionary than contractual in that, at common law, a promise is objectively binding even if it has been made on the basis of misrepresentation, mistake or other vitiating factor; the contract is voidable in equity on the basis that the enrichment by a contractual party would be rendered unjust as a result of the vitiating factor.[51] There are limits to the remedy. Thus, where restitution has in substance become impossible or where third parties have gained rights in the subject matter the remedy will be refused;[52] delay is also likely to act as a bar.[53] In cases of non-fraudulent misrepresentation a court may now refuse rescission and give damages in lieu.[54]

The remedy of rescission can be accompanied by other forms of equitable relief. Accordingly, a court can attach terms to the action[55] and it can give restitutionary monetary relief so as to ensure there is no unjustified enrichment after a contract has been set aside. This latter relief, not being damages, is probably an order in account (*cf*

49 See eg *The Albazero* [1977] AC 774.

50 *Solle v Butcher* [1950] 1 KB 671.

51 *Whittaker v Campbell* [1984] QB 318, 327.

52 GH Treitel, *The Law of Contract* (Sweet & Maxwell, 9th edn, 1995), pp 349–56.

53 *Leaf v International Galleries* [1950] 2 KB 86.

54 Misrepresentation Act 1967 s 2(2).

55 *Solle v Butcher* [1950] 1 KB 671.

Ch 4 § 5(g)).[56] Presumably, once a contract is rescinded, an action for money had and received would also be a possibility.

Just what kind of mistakes will make a contract voidable in equity is by no means an easy question. There is no doubt that the doctrine of error is wider than at common law, but the mistake must still be fundamental and common to both parties.[57] Traditionally, it must also be a mistake of fact rather than law since ignorance of the law is said to be no excuse. However, not only is the distinction sometimes difficult to operate,[58] but the rule itself is now in some doubt.[59] The guiding principle is probably that of unjust enrichment: the person seeking rescission must be able to show that enforcement of the contract would give rise to a situation where one party will be unfairly profiting at the other party's expense. All the same, the courts will not ignore the question of commercial risk. Merely because one party's expectations do not materialise as a result of some fact unknown to the parties at the time of the contract is not a reason in itself to set aside a contract in equity; the mistake must undermine the commercial basis of the contract.[60]

(b) Duress and undue influence

The equitable remedy of rescission will also be available in situations where a contractor has entered into a contract under duress or undue influence, this latter notion being a form of equitable duress (Ch 9 § 10). Thus, where a contractor uses threats of violence to secure the signing of a contract, the contract itself will be voidable.[61] Equally, where the relationship between the parties is one of undue influence the Court of Chancery will not enforce this transaction. The circumstances in which rescission for undue influence might be available have been reviewed recently in *Barclays Bank Plc v O'Brien* and the legal position has been set out by Lord Browne-Wilkinson:[62]

> A person who has been induced to enter into a transaction by the undue influence of another ('the wrongdoer') is entitled to set that transaction aside as against the wrongdoer. Such undue influence is either actual or presumed. In *Bank of Credit and Commerce International SA v Aboody* [1990] 1 QB 923, 953, the Court of Appeal helpfully adopted the following classification.
>
> Class 1: Actual undue influence
>
> In these cases it is necessary for the claimant to prove affirmatively that the wrongdoer exerted undue influence on the complainant to enter into the particular transaction which is impugned.

---

56 *Spence v Crawford* [1939] 3 All ER 271.

57 *William Sindall Plc v Cambridgeshire CC* [1994] 1 WLR 1016.

58 See eg *Solle v Butcher* [1950] 1 KB 671.

59 Tettenborn, *Restitution*, paras 3-23, 3-24.

60 *William Sindall Plc v Cambridgeshire CC* [1994] 1 WLR 1016.

61 *Cf Barton v Armstrong* [1976] AC 104 where the Privy Council used the term 'void' when they probably meant 'voidable' given the analogy with rescission for misrepresentation.

62 [1994] 1 AC 180, 189–90.

> Class 2: Presumed undue influence
>
> In these cases the complainant only has to show, in the first instance, that there was a relationship of trust and confidence between the complainant and the wrongdoer of such a nature that it is fair to presume that the wrongdoer abused that relationship in procuring the complainant to enter into the impugned transaction. In Class 2 cases therefore there is no need to produce evidence that actual undue influence was exerted in relation to the particular transaction impugned: once a confidential relationship has been proved, the burden then shifts to the wrongdoer to prove that the complainant entered into the impugned transaction freely, for example by showing that the complainant had independent advice. Such a confidential relationship can be established in two ways, *viz*:
>
> Class 2(A)
>
> Certain relationships (for example solicitor and client, medical advisor and patient) as a matter of law raise the presumption that undue influence has been exercised.
>
> Class 2(B)
>
> Even if there is no relationship falling within Class 2(A), if the complainant proves the de facto existence of a relationship under which the complainant generally reposed trust and confidence in the wrongdoer, the existence of such relationship raises the presumption of undue influence. In a Class 2(B) case therefore, in the absence of evidence disproving undue influence, the complainant will succeed in setting aside the impugned transaction merely by proof that the complainant reposed trust and confidence in the wrongdoer without having to prove that the wrongdoer exerted actual undue influence or otherwise abused such trust and confidence in relation to the particular transaction impugned.

Undue influence is now the leading non-statutory device that the court has in its armoury to deal with problems of unconscionable bargains since it can no longer rely directly upon inequality of the bargaining power.[63] Unjust enrichment, in other words, continues to stay outside of the transactional substance of the contractual relationship in that the equitable remedies fasten on to the forms of contracting more than on to the adequacy of consideration. Nevertheless, the scope of this equitable doctrine has been expanded in recent years to cover commercial relationships and it is a useful device in situations beyond the reach of the exclusion clause legislation (*cf* Ch 10 § 4). Certain comparative law questions remain, however. Will undue influence be available to set aside contracts where there has been a manifest abuse of contractual rights? Or, indeed, an absence of good faith? Is there a general principle behind all of the equitable remedies to guard against unjust enrichment, even if the rules governing each remedy are reluctant to contradict, at the formal level, the common law rules of contract? Some might welcome such a development. Yet care must be taken since the policy questions are complex as a difference of opinion between the Court of Appeal and House of Lords indicates.

In the undue influence case of *Barclays Bank Plc v O'Brien* the judges had to decide if a mortgage contract with a bank could be avoided in favour of a wife whose

63 *National Westminster Bank plc v Morgan* [1985] AC 686.

signature to the mortgage document had been obtained by misrepresentation and undue influence on the part of her husband. In the Court of Appeal Scott LJ considered what he believed to be the policy in issue:

> These authorities seem to me to leave the developing law, if not at the crossroads, at least at the junction of two diverging roads ...[64]

And he later concluded:

> The choice between the two roads cannot, in my opinion, be made simply by reference to binding authority. Binding authority can be found to justify either. The choice should, I think, be a matter of policy. Ought the law to treat married women who provide security for their husband's debts, and others in an analogous position, as requiring special protection? The position of married women today, both generally and *vis-à-vis* their husbands is very different from what it was ... But ... in the culturally and ethnically mixed community in which we live, the degree of emancipation of women is uneven.[65]

In the House of Lords Lord Browne-Wilkinson responded to this policy approach by highlighting the dangers of appeals to policy as a form of (legal) reasoning:

> On the other hand, it is important to keep a sense of balance in approaching these cases. It is easy to allow sympathy for the wife who is threatened with the loss of her home at the suit of a rich bank to obscure an important public interest *viz*, the need to ensure that the wealth currently tied up in the matrimonial home does not become economically sterile. If the rights secured to wives by the law renders vulnerable loans granted on the security of matrimonial homes, institutions will be unwilling to accept such security, thereby reducing the flow of loan capital to business enterprises. It is therefore essential that a law designed to protect the vulnerable does not render the matrimonial home unacceptable as security to financial institutions.[66]

The sheer impreciseness of some equitable principles endows areas of unjust enrichment with an ambiguity since these remedies are operating within a commercial context where enrichment itself is the legitimate goal. This, no doubt, is one reason why policy arguments suddenly seem more relevant. Yet the nature of contract is that it is a means of securing an enrichment within a commercial and consumer context where exploitation, using the term in a relatively benign way (if such a thing be possible), is of the essence. Thus, notions of unconscionability, if introduced into contract itself, are likely to relate to contractual rules only in ways that give rise to contradiction.

(c) Economic duress

Some of this contradiction is to be found with the doctrine of economic duress which has now become an independent form of pressure which may attract rescission. It

64 [1993] QB 109, 137.

65 *Ibid*, at p 139.

66 [1994] 1 AC 180, 188.

would appear that such duress does not necessarily have to amount to behaviour that would give rise to a tort or some other legal wrong ('lawful act duress') and thus a contract secured by the threat of a strike might be voidable even if the strike would not have been illegal.[67] The test seems to be a mixture of good faith and morally or socially unacceptable behaviour; and so where one party brings pressure on another to enter into a contract the party claiming rescission on the basis of economic duress will, in commercial law at least (*cf* Ch 8 § 4(a)), have to show, *inter alia*, unreasonableness in respect of the economic pressure exerted and an absence of commercial belief in the contractual claim secured by the pressure.[68] The temptation is to think in terms of the reasonable businessman, but this can be misleading since there are times when such a notion is a contradiction in terms. What English law appears to have done in recognising economic duress as a basis for equitable intervention is to move another step closer to a requirement of good faith at the pre-contractual stage. A party may have the right to threaten to withdraw from contractual negotiations without having to take account of the other party's interests; but he, she or it does not have the right to make any other threats where such threats will force the other party to jeopardise his interests in a way that contravenes the general freedom to contract (*cf* Ch 8 § 5(e)).

(d) Account of profits

There will be occasions when the equitable remedy of rescission will not be sufficient to prevent unjust enrichment. What is needed is a monetary remedy. However, equity does not appear to have any inherent jurisdiction to award damages[69] and thus it cannot restore an enrichment through the protection of the restitutionary interest by means of a compensation claim as such. What it has are procedural remedies which can be used to extract unjustified profits or receipts of money. Indeed the remedy of account (*cf* Ch 4 § 5(g)) has been specifically described as an equitable debt claim and it is of use in situations where the parties are in a fiduciary relationship.[70] It may also be available as an alternative to an action for money had and received where one person has profited from a wrong at the expense of another.[71]

The action of account has been adopted by statute as a means of preventing unjust enrichment in several situations. For example, a person who converts goods may be liable in tort to more than one plaintiff since conversion is based on a possessory title rather than actual ownership and liability is measured in terms of the value of the goods converted (Ch 13 § 8(a)). The converter might accordingly be liable first to the finder of goods converted and then to the true owner.[72] In order to prevent unjust enrichment statute decrees that a 'claimant is liable to account over to the other person

67 *The Evia Luck* [1992] 2 AC 152.

68 *CTN Cash and Carry Ltd v Gallaher Ltd* [1994] 4 All ER 714.

69 *Jaggard v Sawyer* [1995] 1 WLR 269.

70 *English v Dedham Vale Properties* [1978] 1 All ER 382.

71 *AG v Guardian Newspapers (No 2)* [1990] 1 AC 109, 286.

72 Torts (Interference with Goods) Act 1977 s 7.

having a right to claim to such extent as will avoid double liability'[73] and this claim is in turn designed to prevent a claimant from becoming 'unjustly enriched'.[74] Account may also be at the basis of contribution and indemnity (*cf* Ch 13 § 6). Under statute 'any person liable in respect of any damage suffered by another person may recover contribution from any other person liable in respect of the same damage'[75] and such contribution is based on what is found 'to be just and equitable having regard to the extent of that person's responsibility for the damage in question'.[76] Thus, if V suffers damage as a result of breach of legal obligations by D1 and D2 and D1 pays full compensation to V a statutory claim in debt based on equitable principles of apportionment will be available to D1 against D2.

(e) Subrogation

Another important equitable remedy used to prevent unjust enrichment is subrogation (Ch 5 § 5). It is said to be a remedy rather than a cause of action and it is available in a wide variety of situations in order to reverse a defendant's unjust enrichment.[77] Accordingly, where O recovers the value of his house first from P, his insurance company, and, secondly, from D, a tortfeasor responsible for its destruction by fire, P will be subrogated to the damages received from D and, indeed, will have an equitable lien on such money.[78] Furthermore, if O had not sued D for damages, P would have that right having been subrogated to the rights of O on the payment to O of the insurance money. Subrogation can also be valuable in allowing one person who discharges another's debt to be subrogated to any security upon which the original debt was secured.[79]

4 RESTITUTION AND PROPERTY RIGHTS

A more developed equitable 'quasi' monetary remedy central to restitution is the remedy of tracing (*cf* Ch 4 § 5(d)). This, seemingly, is a remedy founded not on an obligation right as such (*ius in personam*) but on a right *in rem*; the plaintiff entitled to trace is held to be the owner of the money claimed from the defendant's patrimony. An equitable tracing action is thus an *actio in rem*. In truth the exact status of tracing is, today, not easy to discern since it has been asserted recently that tracing 'is neither a claim nor a remedy but a process' which 'is not confined to the case where the plaintiff seeks a proprietary remedy; it is equally necessary where he seeks a personal remedy against the knowing recipient or knowing assistant.'[80] In addition to the equitable remedy of tracing, common law also recognises the notion of tracing. However, once

73 *Ibid*, s 7(3).

74 *Ibid*, s 7(4).

75 Civil Liability (Contribution) Act 1978 s 1(1).

76 *Ibid*, s 2(1).

77 *Boscawen v Bajwa* [1996] 1 WLR 328, 335.

78 *Lord Napier v Hunter* [1993] AC 713.

79 See Tettenborn, *Restitution*, paras 12-04, 12-07.

80 *Boscawen v Bajwa* [1996] 1 WLR 328, 334 *per* Millett LJ.

again, it is by no means so clear whether this action is a claim *in rem* in the full Roman sense of the term.

(a) Equitable tracing

A claim in equitable tracing is associated with the trust. Indeed it started out as a means of protection accorded by the Court of Chancery to the beneficiary of a trust and this helps explain its proprietary nature.[81] The remedy depends upon the continued existence of the trust property in the patrimony of the defendant, but the latter will have a complete defence if he can show that he is a *bona fide* purchaser for value without notice or that he has innocently changed his position.[82] One great advantage of tracing in equity over its counterpart in common law is that money can be traced into a mixed fund. However, if the defendant has parted with the trust property he will not be liable to an action for account in equity unless it can be shown that he disposed of the money knowing of the existence of the trust. Moreover, there must at some point have existed a fiduciary relationship (Ch 4 § 5(e)) which gives rise to the equitable jurisdiction to intervene.[83]

(b) Common law tracing

Tracing at common law is a much more difficult concept for several reasons. First, there is no actual *in rem* remedy at common law which itself gives expression to the property right; the actions are all *in personam* claims in damages or debt. Thus, tracing goods is achieved through the tort of conversion, which is an action for damages based upon the interference with a right of property.[84] Now there is no doubt that such a property right is, at a substantive level, independent from the obligation relationship just as bailment is independent of contract.[85] But at the level of remedies the actions which give expression to the property right are all classed as torts with the result that there is confusion between the law of obligations and the law of actions. Equally, tracing of money is effected through an action for money had and received which, again, is a personal rather than a real remedy.

A second reason why tracing at common law is difficult is because it does not appear to be a remedy in itself. According to Millet LJ:

> Equity lawyers habitually use the expressions 'the tracing claim' and 'the tracing remedy' to describe the proprietary claim and the proprietary remedy which equity makes available to the beneficial owner who seeks to recover his property *in specie* from those into whose hands it has come. Tracing properly so-called, however, is neither a claim nor a remedy but a process. Moreover it is not confined to the case where the plaintiff

81 Lawson, *Remedies*, pp 147–60.

82 *Boscawen v Bajwa* [1996] 1 WLR 328, 334.

83 See generally *Agip (Africa) Ltd v Jackson* [1991] Ch 547, 566; *Boscawen v Bajwa* [1996] 1 WLR 328, 335; *Westdeutsche Landesbank v Islington LBC* [1996] 2 WLR 802.

84 See generally Torts (Interference with Goods) Act 1977.

85 *Bowmakers Ltd v Barnet Instruments Ltd* [1945] KB 65.

> seeks a proprietary remedy; it is equally necessary where he seeks a personal remedy against the knowing recipient or knowing assistant. It is the process by which the plaintiff traces what has happened to his property, identifies the persons who have handled or received it, and justifies his claim that the money which they handled or received (and, if necessary, which they still retain) can properly be regarded as representing his property ... [86]

Admittedly Millett LJ is here discussing tracing in equity, but he has made a similar observation with respect to tracing at common law.[87] Now this lack of remedial status means that the proprietary nature of the claim must be inherent in the thing claimed since the legal notion of a 'process' is rather meaningless; and thus a debt, at one and the same time, can be both owed and owned. Or, put another way, one proceeds along two relationships, one between person and person (personal claim) and one between person and thing (proprietary claim). In terms of problem-solving this may be most flexible, but it is confusing when it comes to thinking in terms of a law of obligations in that obligations, in the civilian tradition at least, are concerned only with *in personam* rights. If tracing is to be seen as a restitutionary claim it must follow that the English law of unjust enrichment is as much a part of the law of property as the law of obligations.

5 UNJUST ENRICHMENT

In civil law systems, however, the law of unjust enrichment is very much part of the law of obligations. The idea of an obligations category beyond those of contract and delict (tort) was first developed in Roman law, although it has to be emphasised that neither the Romans themselves nor their medieval successors saw unjust enrichment in terms of a general action.[88] In Roman law unjust enrichment remained part of the law of actions and remedies were provided only in a number of defined situations. What the Romans did recognise was that these defined situations – *Negotiorum gestio* (management of another's affairs) and *Condictio indebiti* (recovery of money) being the most important[89] – were all based on a common denominator that found expression as a general principle: *Iure naturae aequum est neminem cum alterius detrimento et iniuria fieri locupletiorem* (by natural law it is equitable that no one should be enriched by the loss or injury of another).[90] In addition, late Roman law developed the separate obligations category *quasi ex contractu* and this category, and the general principle, have survived as twin ideas right up to the *Code civil*.[91] Later civil law induced out of these different quasi-contractual actions a general enrichment claim based on the general principle and thus German law recognises in paragraph 812(1) of its code that a 'person who acquires

86 *Boscawen v Bajwa* [1996] 1 WLR 328, 334.

87 *Agip (Africa) Ltd v Jackson* [1990] Ch 265, 285.

88 DH Van Zyl, The General Enrichment Action is Alive and Well [1992] *Acta Juridica* 115.

89 A Borkowski, *Textbook on Roman Law* (Blackstone, 1994), pp 297–301.

90 D.50.17.206. See also D.12.6.14.

91 Zimmermann, pp 837–38; CC arts 1371–81.

something without any legal ground through an act performed by another or at the expense of another in any other manner, is bound to render restitution'.[92] Equally, the New Dutch Code in Book 6 article 212 lays down that a 'person who has been unjustly enriched at the expense of another must, to the extent that it is reasonable, repair the damage suffered by that other person up to the amount of his enrichment.'

When one turns to English law, given all the different quasi-contractual and equitable remedies which appear to be designed to prevent unjust enrichment, it is tempting to hold that there exists in England the general principle of unjust enrichment. This temptation becomes even stronger when one looks at the historical basis of the common law which for many centuries thought in terms of debt and trespass (damages) rather than in terms of a strict dichotomy between contract and tort. Debt, as Lord Atkin pointed out, 'was not necessarily based upon the existence of a contract.' [93] And even with the adoption of the civilian categories of contract and tort (*cf* Ch 3 § 4(f)) the need for an independent law of restitution founded on the principle of unjust enrichment did, as Lord Wright subsequently pointed out, not diminish:

> It is clear that any civilised system of law is bound to provide remedies for cases of what has been called unjust enrichment or unjust benefit, that is to prevent a man from retaining the money of or some benefit derived from another which it is against conscience that he should keep. Such remedies in English law are generically different from remedies in contract or in tort, and are now recognised to fall within a third category of the common law which has been called quasi-contract or restitution.[94]

However, the problem became one of looking for a conceptual basis upon which one could found a duty to repay a debt in situations where there was no wrong as such. Such a conceptual basis was found in the existing law of contract: 'For there was no action possible other than debt or *assumpsit* on the one side and action for damages for tort on the other'; and the 'action ... for money had and received ... was therefore supported by the imputation by the Court to the defendant of a promise to repay'.[95] This notion of an implied contract no doubt worked well enough in a range of cases, but it could create logical difficulties in certain situations. For example, if an enriched defendant was, as a matter of law, incapable of making contracts through a lack of capacity, it logically followed that no contract could be implied and thus no quasi-contractual action allowed.[96] This implied contract theory has now been abandoned, but its replacement with a theory based upon a property right in the debt owed is just as much a fiction and may well cause problems for the future.[97] Consequently, the idea of a general action based directly upon the Roman unjust enrichment principle has, for some, become attractive.

92 *Ibid*, p 891.

93 *United Australia Ltd v Barclays Bank Ltd* [1941] AC 1, 26.

94 *Fibrosa Spolka Akcyjna v Fairbairn Lawson Combe Barbour Ltd* [1943] AC 32, 61.

95 Lord Atkin in *United Australia Ltd v Barclays Bank Ltd* [1941] AC 1, 27.

96 *Sinclair v Brougham* [1914] AC 398; *cf Westdeutsche Landesbank v Islington LBC* [1996] 2 WLR 802.

97 *Lipkin Gorman v Karpnale Ltd* [1991] 2 AC 548.

None of this is to deny that the principle exists in English law as a general maxim. Indeed the principle seems to have been used as the basis for decision in a few cases and it even appears in a modern statute.[98] Yet it would be wrong to say that the principle exists in England as an independent source of obligations.[99] What does exist are a number of *in personam* and *in rem* remedies which can be used, *inter alia*, to prevent unjust enrichment.[100] In other words, if there is a principle of unjust enrichment, it is a principle that operates only through the existing categories of substantive law – through contract, tort, equity or bailment – or through certain 'empirical' remedies belonging to the law of actions (action for money had and received, tracing, subrogation and the like). To go further than this would be to introduce a general enrichment action similar to the one found in German and Dutch law, and this would run counter to the traditional *mentalité* of English method and reasoning.[100a] Merely because enrichment is something of a mirror image of damage it does not follow that the two are in a symmetrical relationship: causing damage, for example, is not a goal of society even if it is a by-product, whereas personal and corporate enrichment is a specific goal. Those that cut corners and cause damage are not necessarily in the same class as those that cut corners to enrich themselves, particularly where the enrichment causes no specific loss to a specific legal person.[101]

What is valuable about unjust enrichment is that it provides a substantive idea to underpin non-contractual debt actions in much the same way as 'tort' provides a basis for non-contractual damages actions. Tort, however, is not a normative idea in itself; it is simply a general category or common denominator containing, or underpinning, a range of independent causes of action (trespass, negligence, nuisance, defamation and so on). Unjust enrichment should be viewed in a similar way. Consequently, what is important from a normative position is the remedy or cause of action (or even 'process') that is relevant to the factual situation and this means that, from a law of obligations position, it continues to be important to think both in abstract (unjust enrichment) and in concrete (remedy, cause of action) terms. But this, of course, is typical of English law.

---

98 Torts (Interference With Goods) Act 1977 s 7(4).

99 Orakpo, *op cit*, p 104; but see now *Lipkin Gorman v Karpnale Ltd* [1991] 2 AC 548 where Lord Goff states (p 578): 'The recovery of money in restitution is ... made as a matter of right; and ... the underlying principle of recovery is the principle of unjust enrichment.'

100 *Lipkin Gorman v Karpnale Ltd* [1991] 2 AC 548, 578.

100a *Westdeutsche Landesbank v Islington LBC* [1996] 2 WLR 802, 810.

101 See eg *Surrey CC v Bredero Homes Ltd* [1993] 1 WLR 1361.

CHAPTER TWELVE

NON-CONTRACTUAL OBLIGATIONS: DAMAGES ACTIONS (1)

We have seen that non-contractual obligations are, broadly speaking, empirically founded upon damage and enrichment and that monetary claims for unjustified enrichment can often be regarded as non-contractual debt actions (Ch 11). When it comes to damage the main remedy is damages since this is a remedy designed to compensate a plaintiff who has suffered harm at the hands of the defendant (*cf* Ch 6). Damages are, of course, available when the defendant has caused damage through his breach of contract, but in situations where there is no contractual *iuris vinculum* between the parties a plaintiff will have to rely upon a non-contractual damages claim. Such claims in civil law are called delict (together with quasi-delict) and in the common law torts or tort (*cf* Ch 8 § 3(d)).[1] One must add that while the majority of claims in tort involve the remedy of damages, the equitable remedy of injunction (*cf* Ch 5 § 4) can be of importance in the development of certain areas of the law of tort, for example torts involving property or interference with business relations. And so, strictly speaking, tort itself will embrace more than just claims for compensatory damages.

1 GENERAL AND COMPARATIVE REMARKS

Roman law distinguished *crimina publica* and *delicta privata*. From *delicta privata* originated an *obligatio ex delicto*, mostly with a penal character (*actiones poenales*), but in Roman law itself no general provisions for the effects of unlawful (delictual) responsibility ever really developed.[2] The most important remedies were based on specific delicts, for example the *actio furti* (theft), the *actio legis Aquiliae* (wrongful damage) and the *actio iniuriarum* (insult).[3] Apart from delicts, Roman law recognised quasi-delicts, not being delicts leading to a genuine *obligatio* (in the normative sense of the term), but nevertheless giving similar remedies, possibly on the basis of a *ius publicum* (administrative liability) relationship.[4] In French law, the distinction between *délits* and *quasi-délits* (both belonging to the category *responsabilité du fait personnel*, as opposed to *responsabilité du fait des choses* and *responsabilité du fait d'autrui*)[5] still exists, but in most other civilian systems this distinction is irrelevant.[6] The subsequent history of delict in the civil law is in some ways analogous to the civilian history of unjust enrichment: the

1 Zimmermann, pp 19–20, 907–08. The Roman law notion of quasi-delict still exists in French law (see eg CC art 1310 and 1370), although with a different meaning than in Roman law. And the Netherlands Civil Code does not distinguish delict and quasi-delict. *Onrechtmatige daad* (delict) is dealt with in NBW Bk 6 arts 162–97.

2 Zimmermann, pp 913–14.

3 See generally CF Kolbert, *Justinian: The Digest of Roman Law: Theft, Rapine, Damage and Insult* (Penguin, 1979).

4 Zimmermann, pp 1126–30.

5 See CC arts 1382–84.

6 Zimmermann, pp 1128–30.

development has been towards a general action for wrongful harm[7] and such an action was to find its most abstract expression in the *Code civil* which states in article 1382 that: 'Any act whatsoever by a person which causes damage to another obliges the person by whose fault it has occurred to repair it.'

Such a general principle can be traced back to the Roman action for wrongful damage based on a statute called the *lex aquilia.* This action dealt with harm caused through fault (*culpa*) and thus became the foundation for a liability for individual acts motivated by intention or negligence. And in such actions even the slightest negligence was enough to found liability.[8] However, the Romans also recognised that the public interest required that control itself of property could on occasions give rise to an action on behalf of someone injured by the *res.* Accordingly, an occupier of a building adjacent to a public highway could find himself liable for damage caused to a passer-by from anything thrown or poured from the building.[9] Such an action, according to the jurist Ulpian, was beneficial in that it was in the public interest that people should be able to move about without fear or danger.[10] This, and other claims *quasi ex delicto,* provided the material from which the later civilians induced a general principle of liability without fault.[11] And thus alongside the articles dealing with *culpa,* liability for individual acts, the French Civil Code lays down in article 1384 that: 'One is liable not only for damage caused by one's own act, but also for that caused by the acts of persons for which one must answer or for things under one's control (*sous sa garde*).'

Despite these broad general statements of liability, it is still held that – in principle – everyone has to bear the risk of his own damage. In order to transfer one's loss, so to speak, a reason for the transfer has to be found and it is in the provision of such reasons that the law of obligations finds its role. Yet in fulfilling its role the law of obligations ends up by making significant inroads into the principle that the loss lies where it falls and thus the law of obligations has to perform a balancing act between freedom to perform acts which carry a (statistical) risk of injury and the compensation of those victims who make up the statistics. In Roman law the balancing act was achieved by focusing on activities themselves and posing questions about the manner in which such activities were performed. Thus, 'to do a certain act at a certain time and place was *culpa,* but at another time or place it was not.'[12] In modern civil law the inroads into the loss lies where it falls principle are made by the legislator via a substantial set of statutes which impose liability for damage caused by one person to another, of which the paradigm examples are articles 1382 and 1384 of the *Code civil.* However, these articles are particularly abstract in that they do not specify particular interests that need to be invaded before a non-contractual damages claim can succeed. Accordingly, they can be contrasted with the German approach which lays down that there is no obligation to pay damages if the standard or duty that is violated was not ordained to

7 *Ibid,* pp 1031–49.

8 D.9.2.44pr.

9 Zimmermann, pp 1121–22.

10 D.9.3.1.1.

11 Zimmermann, pp 1141–42.

12 FH Lawson, *Negligence in the Civil Law* (Oxford, 1955), p 38.

protect the person who suffers damage against the specific type of loss suffered (*Normzweck* theory). Thus, paragraph 823(1) of the BGB states that a 'person who wilfully or negligently injures the life, body, health, freedom, property, or other right of another contrary to law is bound to compensate him for any damage arising therefrom.'[13] Merely to cause damage through *culpa* is not then enough; the plaintiff must also show that the defendant's act has invaded a protected interest or 'other right'.

The law of non-contractual obligations is, then, highly individualistic in its approach to liability. It tends to start out from individuals (careless acts) and work towards more social ideas through the use of contract (vicarious liability and contract) and liability without fault (liability for things). However, one very interesting development in Netherlands law is the liability for *onrechtmatige daad in groepsverband*, (collective, or 'group' liability),[14] codified in Book 6 article 166 of the New Dutch Code. The members of a group of persons are collectively liable for damage illicitly caused by the behaviour of the group if the risk of such behaviour should have prevented them from acting as a group, and this behaviour can be attributed to them.[15] Between the members of the group, the compensation paid should be shared proportionally, unless the rules of fairness require a different distribution, given the circumstances of the case.[16] Usually legal systems deal with this kind of problem through joint liability, although it is worth recalling that in Roman law where a group of persons stole something that was too heavy for any individual to carry the whole group was deemed guilty of theft and each was liable in delict to the owner. In strictly individualistic terms, as the Roman jurist recognised, this was *contra rationem* because it could be logically argued (*subtili ratione dici*) that no one should be liable since no individual could carry the thing.[17] However, one might say that in such a situation public policy took precedence over logic, for it would be more absurd (*longe absurdius*) if no one was liable.

When one turns to English law one finds a situation that is, if comparison is to be made with the civil law, closer to classical Roman law than to any modern system in that English law still tends to think in terms of particular torts (*cf* Ch 8 § 3(d)). In other words, there is no such cause of action as a 'breach of tort'.[18] Contract, of course, is different inasmuch as a breach of contract is a cause of action itself; but there is no general theory of tort in English law. A plaintiff must always establish a specific cause of action such as negligence, nuisance or defamation[19] and new liabilities are established often at the cost of deforming established heads of claim.[20]

13 *Ibid*, p 203.

14 NBW Bk 6 art 166-1: 'If a member of a group of persons unlawfully causes damage and if the risk of causing this damage should have prevented these persons from their collective conduct, they are solidarily liable if the conduct can be imputed to them' (translation Haanappel & Mackaay).

15 *Cf* English law: *Gulf Oil (GB) Ltd v Page* [1987] Ch 327.

16 *Cf* English law: Civil Liability (Contribution) Act 1978.

17 D.9.2.51.2.

18 *Bradford Corporation v Pickles* [1895] AC 587.

19 See eg Denning LJ in *Southport Corporation v Esso Petroleum Co Ltd* [1954] 2 QB 182. And see *Kingdom of Spain v Christie, Mason & Woods Ltd* [1986] 1 WLR 1120.

20 See eg *Khorasandijian v Bush* [1993] QB 727.

In fact it might seem ironical that tort (trespass), having once been the father of contract (*assumpsit*), should find itself in the twentieth century being the offspring of contract (*cf* Ch 3 § 4). Yet such historical developments help explain why a strict comparison between English and continental private law will always be difficult. The categories of contract and tort (delict), so well established in the civil law,[21] are in truth a relatively modern phenomenon when it comes to English law and this can mask the fact that in its formative days the common law tended to think, not in terms of 'a coherent body of rules based on general principles and abstract concepts',[22] but in terms of separate compartments of factual situations, each compartment being founded on a particular writ. This forms of action approach gave rise to a system of liability attached to categories of fact situation and types of injury.[23] Even today non-contractual damages cases can still be determined as much, for example, by the place where an accident happened[24] – or as much by the species of animal which causes damage[25] – as by any general principle of fault or risk (*cf* Ch 1 § 1(d)). The development of a general liability based on promise meant that a large section of the law of obligations was transferred from a law of debt and damages to a category of 'contract' (*cf* Ch 8 § 5), but the apparent architectural perfection of this contract category did not of itself mean that the non-contractual debt and damages actions would also find themselves in categories unified by a common denominator. Indeed English law has still not fully accepted that non-contractual debt claims are founded upon a general source principle of unjust enrichment (*cf* Ch 11 § 5). And with regard to non-contractual damages actions there is still a debate as to whether they belong to the category of torts or tort (*cf* Ch 8 § 3(d)).

2 STRICT LIABILITY

The debate over the question whether the non-contractual damages actions in English law belong to the category of tort or torts becomes particularly acute when one focuses on the difference between fault and strict liability. For although there have been major attempts to underpin certain kinds of damage and injury cases with a single principle, the existence of the so-called strict liability torts serves to remind English lawyers not only that 'the law of torts has grown up historically in separate compartments',[26] but that until recent times 'the facts [were] nearly always hidden behind formal pleadings'.[27] Strict liability thus finds itself as much a product of the law of procedure as of any rational debate amongst English jurists and this procedural aspect is still evident in some strict liability torts.[28] Moreover, tort's role in protecting real and personal

21 See Zimmermann, pp 1–33.

22 *Ibid*, p 907.

23 Milsom, pp 398–99.

24 See eg *Jacobs v LCC* [1950] AC 361.

25 Animals Act 1971.

26 Lord Simonds in *Read v J Lyons & Co* [1947] AC 156, 182.

27 Milsom, p 291.

28 For example, defamation: many of the cases involve pleading technicalities intermixed with substantive ideas. And see also Denning LJ in *Southport Corporation v Esso Petroleum Co Ltd* [1954] 2 QB 182.

property interests (*cf* Ch 13 § 8) has resulted in a number of remedies where strict proprietary entitlement rather than fault is the motivating factor.[29]

(a) Liability for the escape of dangerous things

All the same, in the middle of the 19th century in the famous case of *Rylands v Fletcher* Blackburn J laid down a general principle which seemed to be quite close to the spirit of article 1384 of the *Code civil.* He said that where a 'person who for his own purposes brings on his lands and collects and keeps there anything likely to do mischief if it escapes, must keep it in at his peril, and, if he does not do so, is *prima facie* answerable for all the damage which is the natural consequence of its escape.'[30] His decision was supported in the House of Lords, although Lord Cairns replaced Blackburn's subsequent comment 'who has brought something on his property which was not naturally there'[31] with the words 'non-natural use'.[32] This case clearly could have acted as the starting point for a non-contractual liability in respect of dangerous things that do damage. However, subsequent cases, instead of developing the principle, restricted it to such an extent that it was scarcely able to rise above its own particular facts. In 1947 the House of Lords specifically refused to use it as the basis for a general liability for damage done by a dangerous thing[33] – some speeches stipulated *obiter* that liability for personal injury was based only on fault (except for some strictly defined exceptions) and also suggested that a munitions factory was not a non-natural use – and more recently Lord Goff has endorsed this attitude.[34] The courts should not proceed in developing such a general theory of liability for damage caused by ultra-hazardous operations since 'it is more appropriate' for such liability 'in respect of operations of high risk to be imposed by Parliament'. Parliament can identify the 'relevant activities' and 'statute can where appropriate lay down precise criteria establishing the incidence and scope of such liability'.[35] Lord Goff did dismiss the 'non-natural use' restriction as belonging to a bygone age,[36] but he replaced this restriction with 'the view that foreseeability of damage of the relevant type should be regarded as a prerequisite of liability in damages under the rule'.[37]

(b) Legal rationality and the forms of action

Occasionally, strict liability has been justified on the basis of risk and insurance,[38] but on the whole it is treated with a certain suspicion by judges who seem unsure either of

29 Milsom, p 379.

30 (1866) LR 1 Ex 265, 279.

31 *Ibid,* at p 280.

32 (1868) LR 3 HL 330, 339.

33 *Read v J Lyons & Co* [1947] AC 156.

34 *Cambridge Water Co v Eastern Leather Plc* [1994] 2 AC 264.

35 [1994] 2 AC at p 305.

36 *Ibid,* at p 309.

37 *Ibid,* at p 306.

38 *Willis & Son v British Car Auctions* [1978] 2 All ER 392, 395–96.

the relationship between fault and risk in a modern industrial society[39] or of their own role in the litigation process.[40] Indeed in the very case that rejected a doctrine of strict liability for dangerous things, the House of Lords, through the voice of Lord Macmillan, claimed that the task of the courts, including their own task, was nothing more than that of deciding particular cases between particular litigants,[41] there being no duty to rationalise the law of England or to produce a code of principles founded upon legal consistency.[42] Such a duty is for Parliament. Now the problem with this attitude is twofold. First, even when Parliament does intervene with a strict liability statute there is a danger that such legislation will be narrowly construed[43] with the result that any inherent or underlying idea such as risk or equality[44] has little chance of emerging from the jurisprudence (*cf* Ch 13 § 3).

Secondly, the law of tort itself is never able to rise above the logical contradictions caused by excessive compartmentalisation. Thus, for example, a defendant who carelessly causes financial harm through a misstatement will be liable only in exceptional circumstances even if the victim can prove his loss;[45] yet a defendant who without negligence causes no financial loss through a misstatement might nevertheless be liable for high damages, without the proof of any actual loss by the plaintiff, if the statement is critical of the plaintiff. All that such a plaintiff need prove in this latter situation is publication to just one other person.[46] Or take some other examples. If a person is injured by a dog it may depend upon the characteristics of the animal itself whether the victim can obtain damages without having to prove fault;[47] if it was in the character of this kind of dog to bite this might deprive the victim of his strict liability claim under statute.[48] If a bus conductor carelessly injures a passenger the bus company will be strictly liable; but if he deliberately injures the passenger – that is to say, if his behaviour is worse than careless – this could deprive the passenger of any claim against the bus company and thus, in all probability, against the insurer.[49] If an employee steals a customer's car sent for repairs to his employer's garage the employer (and no doubt the insurer) will be liable;[50] yet if the same employee fails to save the car from fire as a result of industrial action such as a go-slow the employer might not be liable.[51]

---

39 *Cf Cambridge Water Co v Eastern Leather Plc* [1994] 2 AC 264.

40 For a modern example see *In re Workvale Ltd* [1991] 1 WLR 294, 300.

41 Lord Macmillan in *Read v J Lyons & Co* [1947] AC 156, 175; and see Lord Wilberforce in *Air Canada v Secretary of State for Trade* [1983] 2 AC 394, 438.

42 Lord Macmillan in *Read v J Lyons & Co* [1947] AC 156, 175; *Westdeutsche Bank v Islington LBC* [1996] 2 WLR 802, 810.

43 See eg *Merlin v British Nuclear Fuels* [1990] 2 QB 557.

44 On the equality principle see L Neville Brown & J Bell, *French Administrative Law* (Oxford, 4th edn, 1993), pp 183–91.

45 *Caparo Industries v Dickman* [1990] 2 AC 605.

46 *Morgan v Odhams Press* [1971] 1 WLR 1239 (HL).

47 This may involve the court – even the Court of Appeal – in an animal character studies exercise: *Curtis v Betts* [1990] 1 WLR 459.

48 Animals Act 1971 s 2(2)(b).

49 *Keppel Bus Co v Sa'ad bin Ahmad* [1974] 2 All ER 700 (PC).

50 *Morris v C W Martin & Sons* [1966] 1 QB 716.

51 *General Engineering Services v Kingston & St Andrews Corp* [1989] 1 WLR 69.

It is easy to isolate instances of logical contradiction in almost any system of law and some of the above situations may be familiar to jurists outside of the common law. All the same these examples go some way in indicating that in certain areas of non-contractual damages actions the forms of thought from a previous age have not yet been discarded. One reason for this conservatism is to be found in the fact that the old forms of action did protect particular, but diverse, kinds of interests. And, in order for new general forms of liability to emerge from the case law, movement will be required not just within the category of tort, but in other areas of the law so that these interests can be redistributed amongst more systematic classifications. If defamation and false imprisonment (trespass) cases were, for example, to be seen as part of public rather than tort law then the constitutional questions that lie behind many of these cases might be exposed for all to see. Equally, if the torts of conversion and trespass to goods could be separated from the law of obligations,[52] then this might help distinguish between entitlement rights and obligational duties.

(c) Strict liability and the fault principle

The differences of fact situation, and the co-habitation of rights and wrongs, within a single category certainly endows tort with an apparent flexibility, but this flexibility is misleading because in truth tort plays host to two quite different kinds of reasoning processes, each from a different stage of development. On the one hand there are the strict liability cases whose reasoning is located in a descriptive stage – that is to say, liability is determined by the descriptive form of the facts.[53] On the other hand there are the fault cases founded not on the pattern of facts as such (although such a pattern might in truth be relevant when it comes to establishing duty of care),[54] but upon a cause of action (*culpa*) which can be seen either as inductive or deductive. As Von Jhering put it, '[i]t is not the occurrence of harm which obliges one to make compensation, but fault' and he deemed this 'as simple as the chemical fact that what burns is not the light but the oxygen in the air'.[55] The existence of the descriptive and the inductive/deductive stages of reasoning within a single category (*cf* Ch 14) has created an imbalance in that the fault principle always appears more progressive than the strict liability patterns.[56] In some situations this may be a good thing, but in others the fault principle itself belongs, perhaps, to a bygone age. Thus, in Dutch civil law, a very flexible approach towards the categorisation of liability allows one to transcend the principles of fault and strict liability by adopting the concept of reasonableness when it comes to the choice of the legislation imposing no fault liability. The specific fact situation, taking into account all interests concerned (and, especially, insurance), plays

52 *Cf* Zweigert & Kötz, p 648.

53 See eg *England v Cowley* (1873) LR 8 Exch 126; *Esso Petroleum v Southport Corporation* [1953] 3 WLR 773; [1954] 2 QB 182 (CA); [1956] AC 218 (HL).

54 *Caparo Industries v Dickman* [1990] 2 AC 605, 617–18.

55 This comment by von Jhering is quoted in Zweigert & Kötz, p 671.

56 Private nuisance now seems to be being subsumed by the fault principle rather than by any idea of a liability for things: *Leakey v National Trust* [1980] QB 485.

an important role in determining whether liability exists. In English law this movement towards social reasonableness is happening only in a very negative sense. Some defendants are being isolated from liability even when they have caused harm through unlawful or careless acts on the basis that it is unreasonable to impose liability.[57]

This is not to claim that the Dutch system is more desirable or functional than the English approach. In fact 'reasonableness' plays a vital role in both systems. The point to be made is that in English law there is a real danger of confusion as the House of Lords attempts on the one hand to retreat from its decision in *Anns v Merton LBC*[58] (*cf* Ch 13 § 9) while on the other hand to take account of insurance and other 'policy' factors.[59] Such a balancing act cannot be achieved within the context of a strict adherence to fault as the nominal normative basis of liability since fault is related conceptually neither to insurance nor to the policy factors associated, for example, with public bodies. Strict liability, in contrast, is more adaptable to insurance and policy but, in the absence of legislation, lacks a normative basis.[60] What the English courts have done by failing to develop strict liability as an alternative to fault is to paint themselves into a corner where all they can do is to restrict fault liability for reasons of 'policy'. They cannot easily extend liability to those cases where there has not been negligence as such, but where the defendant, for reasons of policy or social principle, ought to bear the risk of the damage that has occurred. The New Dutch Code has gone some way, however imperfectly (from an English morality viewpoint), towards escaping from this corner, as has French law with its jurisprudential development of article 1384.

(d) European Union and developments in tort law

Strict liability raises questions about the scope and purpose of tort law. Now whether European developments in the area of tort will, in the future, enhance thinking in respect of this category, particularly in the context of harmonisation, is an open question. Nevertheless, EU law has already introduced strict liability into dangerous products,[61] and the case law of the European Court of Justice concerning no fault liability for failure to implement directives might act as the basis for further developments. Member States are strictly liable in damages to non-professionals when community law is infringed in a way attributable to the Member State and the national legislator has committed the infringement.[62] And the damages available under such actions should not be unduly restricted, for example just to *damnum emergens* (*cf* Ch 6). Europe might also influence developments with respect to mass torts and class actions,

57 See eg *X (Minors) v Bedfordshire County Council* [1995] 2 AC 633; *cf Marc Rich & Co v Bishop Rock Marine Co Ltd* [1996] 1 AC 211.

58 [1978] AC 728.

59 See eg *X (Minors) v Bedfordshire County Council* [1995] 2 AC 633; *Marc Rich & Co v Bishop Rock Marine Co Ltd* [1996] 1 AC 211.

60 *Cf* JA Jolowicz, 'Liability for Accidents' [1968] CLJ 50.

61 Council Directive of 25 July 1985 (85/374/EEC:L 210/29); Consumer Protection Act 1987 Part I.

62 *Francovich* [1991] ECR I-5357; *Brasserie du Pêcheur SA & Factortame Ltd* (C 46 & 48/93) [1996] 2 WLR 506.

particularly when dangerous products or the environment are in issue. Here the problem is as much one of procedure as of substantive law. Yet the real difficulty from the plaintiff's point of view with respect to fault liability (English law) is the actual proof of fault; changes in the burden of proof rules can thus be almost as effective as any change in substantive principle (see Ch 2 § 4). Accordingly, the main thrust of any change at the English level may well come through access-to-justice and procedural rules.

3 FAULT LIABILITY

Nevertheless, it is difficult to perceive change at present: for the whole concept of strict liability is coming under pressure in certain quarters of English law. In nuisance and in a claim under the rule of *Rylands v Fletcher* foreseeability is now the test of liability[63] and this means that, at common law, there is now no general principle of automatic liability for damage done by a thing under one's control. Equally, in a number of areas, strict liability for damage arising as a result of a breach of statute is giving way to liability founded upon negligence.[64] At the factual level the common denominator in many of the physical damage cases is fault. No doubt the degree of fault required will vary depending on the factual situation as presented through the causes of action – pollution, car accidents, medical mishaps and various other well-defined factual situations all attracting their own standards in terms of proof, pleadings and procedures. But the trend is unmistakable: control, escape and (or) damage are not enough in themselves to trigger a transfer of loss from the individual suffering it to another whose activity has caused it.

(a) Negligence

All the same, whatever one thinks about the role of fault in non-contractual damages actions in English law it should be evident that the old approach to liability through types of action has to some extent been broken down by the development of more general kinds of liability. The most important of these has been the emergence of negligence liability as an independent cause of action[65] whose rapid growth in this century has done much to turn the law of torts into a law of tort (*cf* Ch 8 § 3(d)). Today there is a general tort of negligence founded upon the idea of individual careless acts or statements and summed up in the general words of Lord Atkin in 1932: 'You must take reasonable care to avoid acts or omissions which you can reasonably foresee would be likely to injure your neighbour.'[66] Neighbour for this purpose does not have the connotation that it might have in the tort of nuisance. It means 'persons who are so closely and directly affected by my act that I ought reasonably to have them in

63 *Cambridge Water Co v Eastern Leather Plc* [1994] 2 AC 264.

64 See eg *X (Minors) v Bedfordshire County Council* [1995] 2 AC 633.

65 *Donoghue v Stevenson* [1932] AC 562.

66 *Donoghue v Stevenson* [1932] AC 562, 580.

contemplation as being so affected when I am directing my mind to the acts or omissions which are called in question.'[67]

The tort of negligence is, then, not dissimilar in principle to liability for fault in French law.[68] One difference, however, is that in England liability in negligence is not based upon fault, causation and damage alone; before a defendant can be held liable to an injured plaintiff the latter must prove that the former owed him a 'duty of care'. Traditionally, this duty was defined by particular kinds of factual relationships – manufacturers and consumers, occupiers and visitors, bailors and bailees (*cf* Ch 8 § 3(c)) and so on. And even now, especially in pure economic loss cases, the nature of the factual relationship can sometimes be of paramount legal relevance.[69] But the tendency today is to use the more general test of 'proximity' with the duty of care question more openly being recognised as a policy device. Indeed before liability can be imposed it must be 'fair and reasonable' to impose it;[70] and thus the general rule now is that where one person causes, through his negligence, physical injury to another person the former will in principle be liable unless he can show some very compelling policy reason as to why liability should be excluded.[71] In cases of pure economic injury, on the other hand, the reverse situation remains the rule: liability will be excluded unless the plaintiff can show very compelling policy reasons as to why liability should be imposed.[72]

These two general rules imply certain other qualifications. First, the distinction between physical and economic loss is indicative of the important role that the nature of the plaintiff's damage plays in the tort of negligence: the weaker the damage the more intense must be either the relationship between the parties – and here the notion of interest (*cf* Ch 3 § 3(c); Ch 4 § 2) is playing an increasingly important role in defining this relationship[73] – or the actual behaviour of the defendant.[74] And, secondly, the notion of causation is reflected not only at its own separate level (*cf* Ch 7 §§ 3-4), but at the level of duty of care as well. Thus, in order for a plaintiff to recover either for nervous shock damage or for an injury caused by a failure to act – factual situations involving three rather than two parties (leaving aside insurance companies) – it is important to establish some kind of relationship (family, employment, property) between shocked or injured plaintiff and immediate victim[75] or between plaintiff and defendant accused of *culpa in omittendo*.[76] Moreover, nervous shock has to be

---

67 *Ibid.*

68 CC art 1382; Zweigert & Kötz, pp 662–68.

69 *Caparo Industries v Dickman* [1990] 2 AC 605, 617–18.

70 *X (Minors) v Bedfordshire County Council* [1995] 2 AC 633.

71 *Murphy v Brentwood DC* [1991] 1 AC 398; but *cf X (Minors) v Bedfordshire County Council* [1995] 2 AC 633; *Marc Rich & Co v Bishop Rock Marine Co Ltd* [1996] 1 AC 211.

72 *Caparo Industries v Dickman* [1990] 2 AC 605; but *cf White v Jones* [1995] 2 AC 207.

73 *Pacific Associates Inc v Baxter* [1990] 1 QB 993, 1029; *Caparo*, above, at pp 626, 652.

74 It must be stressed, however, that English law does not think in terms of degrees of negligence. Nevertheless, it is perfectly possible for an English court to reflect the actual behaviour of the defendant via the existence or non-existence of a duty of care: see eg *Smith v Littlewoods Organisation* [1987] AC 241.

75 *McLoughlin v O'Brien* [1983] 1 AC 410; *Alcock v Chief Constable of S Yorks* [1992] 1 AC 310.

76 *Smith v Littlewoods Organisation* [1987] AC 241; *Marc Rich & Co v Bishop Rock Marine Co Ltd* [1996] 1 AC 211; *cf* Zimmermann, pp 1029–30.

distinguished from, in the eyes of the law at least, lesser forms of mental anguish such as bereavement[77] and distress,[78] while even a close relationship between plaintiff and defendant might still not be enough to ground liability in omission cases if the damage is only economic.[79]

In addition to establishing a duty of care the plaintiff must also show that it was a breach of this duty which caused his, her or its damage. Breach of duty is a question of fact once in the province of the jury (Ch 2 § 3(b)) – did the defendant behave reasonably or not?[80] – while causation is both a factual question (factual causation) and a legal question (remoteness of damage) (Ch 7). Damage itself is, obviously, a vital ingredient of the tort of negligence and, as we have seen, the nature of the damage can directly affect the duty question (and see Ch 13 § 9). Nevertheless, what amounts to 'damage' can on occasions give rise to difficult questions (*cf* Ch 6 § 1). Is impairment of a person's personal and intellectual development, for example, a form of damage recognised by the law?[81] The English law of tort is thus much closer to German than to French law.

In German and English law, the law of tort(s) is limited formally by the concept of *Tatbestand*[82] and duty of care respectively. It is not enough that the defendant wrongfully caused harm; he must also have invaded a specifically protected interest. In the French and Netherlands system, on the other hand, the concept of tort (delict) is open-ended.[83] Despite this difference in the conceptual background of the notion of tort, one can still find the existence of a common denominator, namely careful risk avoiding behaviour. Four elements constitute this rule: the nature and extent of the damage, the probability and foreseeability of the damage, the nature of the act causing the damage and the question whether precautionary measures could have been taken. In applying this general concept, judges differentiate according to the person committing the act ('the reasonable man test', taking into account specific circumstances or professions) and the objectives of a specific liability rule. Such objectives are risk-prevention, compensation of damage and reallocation of risks. Furthermore, the demands of society, the influence of insurance and the 'law and economics' school are other possible approaches. On the continent the importance of 'fault' seems to be diminishing in the field of 'tort' law,[84] but, as has been suggested, this is not true of English law. Nevertheless, there is a growing realisation that in both public and commercial law fault is an inadequate normative criterion in itself. The difficulty for English law, as has already been mentioned, is to find an alternative within a model that envisages society as a collection of individual persons and individual things.

---

77 Fatal Accidents Act 1976 s 1A.

78 *Best v Samuel Fox & Co Ltd* [1952] AC 716.

79 *Yuen Kun Yeu v AG of Hong Kong* [1988] AC 175.

80 See eg *Bolton v Stone* [1951] AC 850.

81 *X (Minors) v Bedfordshire County Council* [1995] 2 AC 633.

82 See § 823 BGB. See also § 826, which is complementary to the limited description of the grounds for delictual liability in §§ 823 and 824.

83 Zweigert & Kötz, pp 656–62.

84 *Ibid*, pp 686–723.

(b) Intentional injury

Negligence, of course, is not synonymous with *culpa*. There is also the question of damage caused intentionally. At first sight it might seem that all damage intentionally caused should be actionable, but economic loss deliberately caused will, in a competitive society, obviously attract a different set of principles from physical injury deliberately caused.[85] With regard to physical injury there is now a general principle that all such injuries arising from *culpa* are *prima facie* actionable in tort[86] and although such an action is founded in the tort of trespass rather than negligence it is based on a general principle. A defendant who wilfully does an act calculated to cause physical harm to another – to infringe another's legal right to personal safety – will, in the absence of justification, be liable to that person if damage is suffered.[87] And damage for this purpose will include both nervous shock[88] and mental distress.[89] Moreover, the principle will extend to infringements of liberty made without legal justification.[90] However, it will not automatically cover other kinds of damage such as interference with water[91] or the causing of economic harm. In order to be able to recover damages for economic loss the plaintiff will have to establish that the defendant has committed a legal wrong that has invaded a protected economic right.

(c) Abuse of rights

Malicious behaviour can, in civil law, bring into play the general principle of an abuse of a right. This is, seemingly, to be found in Roman law where Gaius claims *male enim nostro jure uti non debemus* (we ought not to use improperly our legal right),[92] but in truth it is a relatively modern idea because the Roman jurist, like the modern common lawyer, did not think in terms of rights.[93] It is only with the development of the idea of a right as a subjective power that the notion of an abuse of right – that is to say, an unreasonable exercise of a right – assumes much meaning. In France the unreasonable exercise of a right can give rise to an action in tort on the basis that any damage caused by the unreasonable exercise is damage flowing from the fault of another;[94] and in Belgian law, the link between good faith in contractual relationships and the theory of abuse of rights is strong. In Netherlands law, a special category of abuse of rights is unnecessary when dealing with delictual or contractual obligations because, in the general part of the Netherlands Civil Code (Book 3, patrimonial law in general), article

---

85 *Mogul SS Co v McGregor, Gow & Co* [1892] AC 25.

86 *Letang v Cooper* [1965] 1 QB 232.

87 *Wilkinson v Downton* [1897] 2 QB 57.

88 *Ibid.*

89 *Read v Coker* (1853) 138 ER 1437.

90 See eg Weir, *Casebook*, p 518.

91 *Bradford Corporation v Pickles* [1895] AC 587.

92 G.1.53; *cf* D.50.17.55.

93 G Samuel, '"*Le Droit Subjectif*" and English Law' [1987] CLJ 264.

94 Zweigert & Kötz, pp 659–61.

13 lays down that nobody is allowed to exercise any power abusively. In other words, abuse of power transcends the law of obligations as such in Dutch law.

In English law, by way of contrast, not only has it been held that the existence of an intention to injure cannot in itself turn a lawful act into a tort,[95] but it has also been said that a person who has a right under a contract is entitled to exercise it 'for a good reason or a bad reason or no reason at all'.[96] All the same, as with unjust enrichment (*cf* Ch 11 § 5), the position is not quite as simple as it first appears. In English administrative law abuse of power is now the central principle that motivates the judicial review remedies and this principle has recently been extended to cover abuse of ownership by public bodies.[97] It is probably true to say, then, that any act by a public official or public body maliciously aimed at damaging another will attract the attention of the courts. In fact it is possible that even a negligent exercise of a right by a public authority will occasionally be a tort if it causes damage to a foreseeable person,[98] although this is a difficult area now (*cf* Ch 13 § 3). In French law the doctrine of abuse of rights has been used to some extent to deal with problems of *culpa in contrahendo* (*cf* Ch 9 § 4; Ch 10 § 2) and it can now be said that a similar principle is in operation with respect to many public law contracts in English law; any considerations other than commercial ones will, by statute, be treated as abuses of contractual rights.[99] Accordingly, where there is an overlap between the law of obligations and public law there is a role for the notion of abusive behaviour acting as the basis for a remedy.

Equity also provides a number of remedies that can be used to prevent certain abuses of power and of rights and it may be that there is even a general equitable principle that a contractor will be prevented from exercising a right under a contract if the sole purpose of the exercise is maliciously to injure the other party. For if a party has no legitimate interest in enforcing a stipulation he cannot in general enforce it.[100] In addition to any equitable intervention, the law of tort can make use of the concept of abuse as a constituent part of one of its actions. Thus, the tort of nuisance is available against the unreasonable user of land and malice can, in this context, amount in itself to unreasonable use – at least if the act complained of is noise or some other form of pollution.[101] A majority of the Court of Appeal has also extended the tort of nuisance, via the interlocutory injunction (Ch 5 § 4(b); *cf* Ch 6 § 3(e)), to cover abusive phone calls: 'it is ridiculous if in this present age the law is that the making of deliberately harassing and pestering telephone calls to a person is only actionable in the civil courts if the recipient of the calls happens to have the freehold or a leasehold proprietary interest in the premises in which he or she has received the calls.'[102] Malice can also be

95 *Bradford Corporation v Pickles* [1895] AC 587.

96 *Chapman v Honig* [1963] 2 QB 502, 520.

97 *Wheeler v Leicester City Council* [1985] AC 1054.

98 *Ben Stansfield (Carlisle) Ltd v Carlisle City Council* (1982) 265 EG 475.

99 Local Government Act 1988 s 17. See also *Blackpool & Fylde Aero Club Ltd v Blackpool BC* [1990] 1 WLR 1195.

100 *White & Carter (Councils) Ltd v McGregor* [1962] AC 413.

101 *Hollywood Silver Fox Farm v Emmett* [1936] 2 KB 468.

102 Dillon LJ in *Khorasandijian v Bush* [1993] QB 727, 734.

used to undermine certain defences in the tort of defamation[103] and it may prevent a person from raising the defence of equitable estoppel.[104]

The truth seems to be, then, that although English law does not recognise a general principle of abuse of rights it nevertheless has a number of actions and torts designed to remedy certain kinds of abuses. However, perhaps the real difficulty with regard to recognising a general principle of abuse of rights is that English law does not really think in terms of the subjective right;[105] it thinks only in terms of particular rules and remedies arising out of the circumstances of the case (*cf* Ch 3 § 3(d)). In order to have a theory of abuse of rights it is necessary first of all to have a theory of rights and in order to have a theory of rights it is probably necessary to have a theory of ownership and of obligation. These theories are often missing from English law.

4 LIABILITY FOR UNLAWFUL ACTS

Negligence liability in English law has expanded so fast in this century that it sometimes gives the impression of having swallowed up most of the other forms of liability.[106] In fact this is by no means the case. The torts of conversion, deceit, defamation, trespass, malicious prosecution and nuisance, for example, remain quite separate forms of liability from negligence, even if negligence is encroaching upon them. And a distinction continues to be made between an injury arising out of a negligent act and an injury resulting from an unlawful (criminal) act.[107] There are two main torts dealing with unlawful acts: they are breach of statutory duty and public nuisance.

(a) Breach of statutory duty

The action for breach of statutory duty has experienced its most extensive growth this century in the area of industrial accidents where breach of certain types of legislation might give rise to a private action for damages in tort on behalf of any person belonging to the class of persons the statute was designed to protect.[108] But such liability is only rarely extended outside situations where the relationship between the parties is close (employer and employee being the paradigm example) and the damage personal injury.[109] The basic principle, then, is that in the ordinary case a breach of a statute does not, by itself, give rise to any private action in tort.[110] As Lord-Browne-Wilkinson has put it:

> The basic proposition is that in the ordinary case a breach of statutory duty does not, by itself, give rise to any private law cause of action. However, a private law cause of action

103 But see *Horrocks v Lowe* [1975] AC 135.

104 *D & C Builders Ltd v Rees* [1966] 2 QB 617.

105 Samuel, *Droit Subjectif, op cit.*

106 *China & South Sea Bank Ltd v Tan* [1990] 1 AC 536, 543.

107 *X (Minors) v Bedfordshire County Council* [1995] 2 AC 633.

108 PA Buckley, 'Liability in Tort for Breach of Statutory Duty' (1984) 100 LQR 204.

109 For an unsuccessful attempt to use the tort see *Lonrho v Shell Petroleum* [1982] AC 173; *cf Lonrho v Fayed* [1992] 1 AC 448.

110 *X (Minors) v Bedfordshire County Council* [1995] 2 AC 633.

> will arise if it can be shown, as a matter of construction of the statute, that the statutory duty was imposed for the protection of a limited class of the public and that Parliament intended to confer on members of that class a private right of action for breach of the duty. There is no general rule by reference to which it can be decided whether a statute does create such a right of action but there are a number of indicators. If the statute provides no other remedy for its breach and the Parliamentary intention to protect a limited class is shown, that indicates that there may be a private right of action since otherwise there is no method of securing the protection the statute was intended to confer. If the statute does provide some other means of enforcing the duty that will normally indicate that the statutory right was intended to be enforceable by those means and not by private right of action: *Cutler v Wandsworth Stadium Ltd* [1949] AC 398; *Lonrho Ltd v Shell Petroleum Co Ltd (No 2)* [1982] AC 173. However, the mere existence of some other statutory remedy is not necessarily decisive. It is still possible to show that on the true construction of the statute the protected class was intended by Parliament to have a private remedy. Thus, the specific duties imposed on employers in relation to factory premises are enforceable by an action for damages, notwithstanding the imposition by the statutes of criminal penalties for any breach: see *Groves v Wimborne (Lord)* [1898] 2 QB 402 ...[111]

This intention of Parliament test is, evidently, a fictional one, save where the statute itself provides a tort action, and thus each case turns on the provisions of each statute in question.

Breach of statutory duty has proved particularly useful in one of the great factual sources of personal injury actions, namely accidents at work. But it was rejected as a means of importing strict liability into the other great source of personal injury, traffic accidents.[112] Continental judges have, therefore, proved far more daring and imaginative in this area, as indeed have American judges.[113] In the field of consumer law the tort may have something of a future,[114] but in public law breach of statutory duty's scope has now been severely restricted by the House of Lords.[115] In order to claim damages from a public body for the careless exercise of a statutory power or duty, it usually has to be shown that the facts give rise to a duty of care at common law such as to found an action in negligence. And no such duty will arise in respect of anything done by a public authority within the ambit of statutory discretion (*cf* Ch 13 § 3(b)).

(b) Public nuisance

The crime of public nuisance also gives rise to a claim in private law for damages provided that the plaintiff has suffered special damage.[116] The basis of this action is an

---

111 *X (Minors) v Bedfordshire County Council* [1995] 2 AC 633, 731.

112 *Phillips v Britannia Hygienic Laundry Co* [1923] 2 KB 832.

113 Zweigert & Kötz, pp 708, 720–22.

114 Consumer Protection Act 1987 s 41 (1).

115 *X (Minors) v Bedfordshire County Council* [1995] 2 AC 633.

116 *Benjamin v Storr* (1874) LR 9 CP 400; G Kodilinye, 'Public Nuisance and Particular Damage in the Modern Law' (1986) 6 LS 182.

interference with 'the reasonable comfort and convenience of life of a class of Her Majesty's subjects' which 'is so widespread in its range or so indiscriminate in its effect that it would not be reasonable to expect one person to take proceedings on his own'.[117] It is, accordingly, close to a class tort whereby the Attorney General can seek an injunction on behalf of the community affected by the nuisance. The tort is useful as a means of tackling some kinds of pollution.[118]

The individual can seek redress provided he has sufficient interest, and such an interest will be secured the moment such an individual suffers damage over and above the rest of the community. It is a form of strict liability inasmuch as the plaintiff does not have to establish fault, but where the special damage is personal injury the tort does appear to have been partly subverted by negligence.[119] The plaintiff usually has to show some element of duty and foreseeability, although once this has been established it would appear that the great advantage of the tort is that it puts the burden of proof on the defendant.[120] Another advantage is that it is available for pure economic loss.[121] The tort has been used to extend the duties of an occupier to those outside the premises: thus, anyone who suffers injuries as a result of man-made structures which adjoin the highway will have an action against the occupier and (or) the owner.[122] In these highway accident cases arising from the control of things (*cf* below § 5), the tort of public nuisance has had the effect of introducing a form of strict liability by shifting the burden of proof on to the occupier.[123] Nevertheless, as we have seen with breach of statutory duty, the notion of liability arising from an unlawful act has not been extended to traffic accidents which remain governed by the tort of negligence.[124] Consequently, there are in English law different rules depending not only upon whether one is on public or private land,[125] but also upon whether one is hit by a car or a collapsing wall.

5 LIABILITY FOR THINGS

The tort of public nuisance provides examples of how common lawyers can, on occasions, attach liability to things rather than to people. Such liability, as we have seen, is common with regard to buildings which adjoin the highway[126] and a liability for the control of things is the approach that is adopted with regard to damage done by animals.[127] Motor vehicles can also attract liability where an owner has an interest in

117 *AG v PYA Quarries* [1957] 2 QB 169, 184, 191.

118 See eg *Halsey v Esso Petroleum Co Ltd* [1961] 2 All ER 145.

119 *Dymond v Pearce* [1972] 1 QB 496.

120 *Southport Corporation v Esso Petroleum Co Ltd* [1954] 2 QB 182, 197.

121 *Campbell v Paddington Corporation* [1911] 1 KB 869; *Tate & Lyle v GLC* [1983] 2 AC 509.

122 *Tarry v Ashton* (1876) 1 QBD 314.

123 *Mint v Good* [1951] 1 KB 517.

124 *Phillips v Britannia Hygienic Laundry Co* [1923] 2 KB 832; *Dymond v Pearce* [1972] 1 QB 496.

125 *Jacobs v London County Council* [1950] AC 361.

126 *Wringe v Cohen* [1940] 1 KB 229; *Mint v Good* [1951] 1 KB 517.

127 Animals Act 1971.

the journey undertaken by the negligent driver of the owner's car.[128] In addition, since the 19th century, there has, as we have seen, been a general principle of liability with regard to dangerous things brought on to property which escape and do injury.[129]

(a) Moveable things

The difficulty, however, with the liability that attaches to these different things is that the level of duty varies depending upon the thing in question. For example, with regard to damage done by a dangerous animal the liability is strict[130] and there is a similar duty with respect to damage caused by things falling from an aircraft.[131] However, the employee injured by a defective tool supplied by his employer must prove fault,[132] as must the employee injured by an unexplained explosion in the workplace.[133] The principle of strict liability has not been developed in English law into a general principle of 'risk' liability based upon dangerous activities. In fact the rapid growth of negligence during this century encouraged the courts to see all personal injury accident actions only in terms of individual acts.[134] Consequently, as we have seen, the two main sources of personal injury claims, namely road and factory accidents, remain largely governed by the torts of negligence and breach of statutory duty, the latter tort increasingly being subverted by negligence. Nevertheless, the idea of liability arising out of the control of things has found expression within negligence itself; and so those who put unsafe lorries on to the road,[135] or who are in control of unsafe supermarkets,[136] may find themselves in practice having to pay damages simply because they cannot disprove negligence. In the area of consumer law this burden of proof principle of *res ipsa loquitur* has been useful on occasions to those who have suffered injury as a result of unsafe products;[137] and statutory intervention has now made the liability of manufacturers even stricter.[138]

This strict liability with regard to products results from the EC directive on product liability.[139] The principle of this European product liability law is that the producer is liable for damage caused by a defect in his product; but this liability rule is not 'strict' in the juridical sense of the word because the producer can defend himself in specific

128 *Ormrod v Crossville Motor Services Ltd* [1953] 1 WLR 1120; *cf Morgans v Launchbury* [1973] AC 127.

129 *Rylands v Fletcher* (1866) LR 1 Ex 265; (1868) LR 3 HL 330.

130 Animals Act 1971 s 2(1).

131 Civil Aviation Act 1982 s 76(2).

132 Employer's Liability (Defective Equipment) Act 1969.

133 *Read v J Lyons & Co Ltd* [1947] AC 156.

134 *Read v J Lyons & Co* [1945] 1 KB 216; [1947] AC 156.

135 *Henderson v H Jenkins & Sons* [1970] AC 282.

136 *Ward v Tesco Stores Ltd* [1976] 1 WLR 810.

137 *Grant v Australian Knitting Mills Ltd* [1936] AC 85.

138 Consumer Protection Act 1987 s 2. But note s 4(1)(e) of the 1987 Act which does not appear to conform to the directive; *cf* s 1(1).

139 EC Directive of 25 July 1985 No 85/374/EEC.

circumstances. The harmonisation of product liability in the EU is complemented by a directive concerning general product safety[140] and the implications of these developments for English legal thinking on the theory of tort(s) are of importance. It may be, as has been suggested already, that a retreat from negligence will, in the longer term, be forced on the English law of obligations as a result of EU directives and the jurisprudence of the European Court.

(b) Land

Land can also attract liability for those who own or occupy it. Under statute an occupier of land owes a duty of care to all visitors[141] and the landlord (owner) owes, in certain circumstances, a duty to all persons who might suffer physical injury as a result of the defective state of any of his buildings.[142] Even the trespasser gets some protection against personal injury arising from negligence.[143] At common law any direct interference with another's property (or personal) rights attracts the tort of trespass,[144] while an indirect interference will give rise to a claim in private nuisance if it results from the unreasonable use of land.[145]

Liability in trespass[146] attaches more to possessory rights than to physical property as such – although it may often focus on land and chattels – but private nuisance is very much a property tort in that it arises either out of the use and condition of the land itself[147] or out of some activity upon, or associated with, land.[148] Private nuisance lies where a defendant has used his land in such a way as injuriously to affect the enjoyment of the plaintiff's land.[149] Behaviour can be of relevance here, particularly when a land user deliberately annoys his neighbour[150] (see above § 3(c)) or is guilty of *culpa in omittendo*;[151] but on the whole liability is measured more by looking at the nature of the locality (except where the damage is physical), the type and level of the interference and the wording of any legislation designed to authorise economically beneficial, but socially annoying and (or) environmentally damaging, activities.[152] One might add that

140 EC Directive of 29 June 1992 No 92/59/EEC.

141 Occupiers' Liability Act 1957.

142 Defective Premises Act 1972 s 4.

143 Occupiers' Liability Act 1984.

144 See eg *The Majfrid* [1942] P 43, 145 (CA).

145 *Cf Esso Petroleum v Southport Corporation* [1953] 3 WLR 773; [1954] 2 QB 182 (CA); [1956] AC 218 (HL).

146 For a discussion of the distinction between the torts of trespass and negligence see *Letang v Cooper* [1965] 1 QB 232. And see also Denning LJ's judgment in *Southport Corporation v Esso Petroleum Co Ltd* [1954] 2 QB 182.

147 *Leakey v National Trust* [1980] QB 485.

148 *Halsey v Esso Petroleum* [1961] 1 WLR 683; *Tetley v Chitty* [1986] 1 All ER 66.

149 *Southport Corporation v Esso Petroleum Co Ltd* [1954] 2 QB 182, 196.

150 *Hollywood Silver Fox Farm v Emmett* [1936] 2 KB 468.

151 *Leakey v National Trust* [1980] QB 485.

152 *Allen v Gulf Oil Refining Ltd* [1981] AC 1001; *Wheeler v JJ Saunders Ltd* [1995] 3 WLR 466.

the law of actions has a role here as well (*cf* Ch 5 § 4): the interlocutory injunction has been a useful vehicle for extending the tort of nuisance into areas beyond the enjoyment of land *per se*.[153] And this role has helped ease nuisance out of the law of property and into the law of obligations.[154]

6 LIABILITY FOR PEOPLE

The idea of imposing liability for individual negligent acts has, in the 20th century, acquired something of an unreal flavour in that a great many defendants are now organisations rather than humans. As a result a distinction has to be made at the level of legal personality between the acts of the legal person and the acts of a human person.[155] One way the law could have dealt with this issue was to treat any act by a member of an organisation as an act of the organisation itself; but the common law, like many other systems,[156] has only taken this approach in certain situations.[157] An employer will be strictly liable for the acts of his 'servants' (employees) acting in the course of their employment. In addition to this vicarious liability, one person can sometimes find himself directly liable to a plaintiff for an act committed by another person. In this situation one is not talking of vicarious liability as such; liability arises as a result of the breach of a direct duty between defendant and plaintiff.[158]

(a) Vicarious liability

The general principle with regard to the liability of organisations in tort is, as in French law,[159] that an employer will be vicariously liable for tortious acts committed by an employee acting in the course of his employment.[160] This general principle can be broken down into three specific rules: there must be a tort; committed by a servant; acting in the course of employment. Each of these rules can give, or has given, rise to its own problems. Thus, the tortious act must be distinguished from the non-tortious one;[161] the servant (employee) must be distinguished from the independent contractor;[162] and the organisational act must be distinguished from the individual

153 *Khorasandijian v Bush* [1993] QB 727.

154 See *Thomas v NUM* [1986] Ch 20.

155 See generally *Tesco Supermarkets v Nattrass* [1972] AC 153; *Photo Production v Securicor* [1980] AC 827, 848. See also *Meridian Global Funds Management Asia Ltd v Securities Commission* [1995] 2 AC 500.

156 See generally Zweigert & Kötz, pp 669–85.

157 In particular with regard to the law of contract: *Photo Production v Securicor* [1980] AC 827, 848.

158 See eg *Wong Mee Wan v Kwan Kin Travel Services Ltd* [1996] 1 WLR 38.

159 CC art 1384 para 5: '*Les maîtres et les commettants, du dommage causé par leurs domestiques et préposés dans les fonctions auxquelles ils les ont employés.*' And see NBW Bk 6 arts 170–71.

160 Roman law influence? See Zimmermann, pp 1135–36 and Zweigert & Kötz, pp 670–71: 'In the Germanic legal family, the liability of a superior for the harm caused by his staff always depends on whether any personal fault of his contributed to the harm ... It is an invention of the pandectists that there was no liability for others in Roman law unless the superior himself was at fault. In fact the Romans never considered the problem of liability for others as a whole at all; much less did they arrive at any general solution.'

161 *Staveley Iron & Chemical Co v Jones* [1956] AC 627.

162 *Ready Mixed Concrete v Minister of Pensions* [1968] 2 QB 497.

frolic.[163] None of the rules formulated to deal with each of these issues is always applied with logical consistency and the case law can on occasions give the impression of contradiction. Moreover, the nature of some activities and operations may be such that the law will impose liability on an employer even if the servant rule cannot be satisfied;[164] but in these 'independent contractor' situations, as we have just seen, the employer will be liable on the basis of a direct, 'non-delegable' duty between himself – or itself – and the plaintiff.[165]

The commission of a criminal act by an employee can (but will not always) free the employer from liability as a result of the course of employment rule of vicarious liability.[166] Yet sometimes an organisation can directly be liable on the basis that the criminal act either resulted from a breach of duty of care on its part[167] or gave rise to personal injury in circumstances where public law (Criminal Injuries Compensation Scheme) has undertaken to give compensation on a no fault basis.[168] In some situations, then, the case law may involve policy questions as to the allocation of risks given the damage in issue.[169] Curiously, however, the courts still refuse to take account of the existence of insurance,[170] and this means that if an organisation is found vicariously liable it can – or, under the principle of subrogation, its insurance company can – in strict law sue the employee at fault for breach of an implied term of the contract of employment (*cf* Ch 5 § 5) so as to recover in debt any damages paid to the victim.[171]

(b) Non-delegable duty

Where a defendant is found liable under the principle of a direct duty between defendant and plaintiff the liability can on occasions look like a form of vicarious liability. Take, for example, the following situation. C ships goods on O's ship and the goods are damaged owing to the unseaworthiness of the vessel; the ship is unseaworthy because it had been negligently repaired by R, a firm of independent contractors employed by O. If O is held liable to C for the damage to the goods this can at first sight look like a form of vicarious liability. O is being held responsible for the

163 *Morris v CW Martin & Sons Ltd* [1966] 1 QB 716; *cf General Engineering Services v Kingston & St Andrews Corp* [1989] 1 WLR 69.

164 *Honeywill & Stein v Larkin Brothers* [1934] 1 KB 191; but *cf Salsbury v Woodland* [1970] 1 QB 324.

165 See eg *McDermid v Nash Dredging and Reclamation Co* [1987] AC 906. Sometimes the non-delegable duty might be founded in a contractual or bailment relationship: *Riverstone Meat Co v Lancashire Shipping Co* [1961] AC 807; *Photo Production v Securicor* [1980] AC 827, 848; *Wong Mee Wan v Kwan Kin Travel Services Ltd* [1996] 1 WLR 38 (PC).

166 But see *Morris v C W Martin & Sons Ltd* [1966] 1 QB 716; *cf General Engineering Services v Kingston & St Andrews Corp* [1989] 1 WLR 69.

167 *Home Office v Dorset Yacht Co* [1970] AC 1004.

168 Criminal Justice Act 1988 ss 108–15; *cf Hill v Chief Constable of West Yorkshire* [1988] QB 60, 72–74, 76; [1989] AC 53.

169 *Smith v Littlewoods Organisation Ltd* [1987] AC 241.

170 *Launchbury v Morgans* [1973] AC 127.

171 *Lister v Romford Ice & Cold Storage Co* [1957] AC 555.

carelessness of R. In truth such liability would be based on a non-delegable duty: O has not only a contractual relationship with C but also a proprietary relationship arising out of the bailment (*cf* Ch 8 § 3(c)). It is these relationships which are 'non-delegable'.[172] A similar situation can arise with regard to real property. O employs C, a firm of independent contractors, to build a swimming pool on his land and C does the work carelessly with the result that water escapes and damages P's neighbouring property. If O is held liable to P for the damage caused, this will not be because O is vicariously liable for C's careless behaviour; O will be liable as a result of a non-delegable direct duty founded either on the rule of *Rylands v Fletcher* (above § 2(a)) or on the tort of nuisance.

The non-delegable duty can become particularly important in situations where one person contracts with another to provide a service which will actually be carried out by a third party. In this situation:

> The fact that the supplier of services may under the contract arrange for some or all of them to be performed by others does not absolve the supplier from his contractual obligation. He may be liable if the service is performed without the exercise of due care and skill on the part of the sub-contractor just as he would be liable if the sub-contractor failed to provide the service or failed to provide it in accordance with the terms of the contract. The obligation undertaken is thus, if the person undertaking to supply the services performs them himself, that he will do so with reasonable skill and care, and that if, where the contract permits him to do so, he arranges for others to supply the services, that they will be supplied with reasonable skill and care ... [173]

Consequently, the employer of an independent contractor may remain liable for the breach of the implied term to perform a contractual service with due care and skill[174] even though the actual unreasonable act was committed by a third party. There is here an important distinction between the contractual and the tortious obligations.

Sometimes it is not obvious whether liability is primary or vicarious. In *Esso Petroleum v Southport Corporation* (Ch 1 § 7(a)) it is by no means clear on the facts if the duty in question ought to be seen as a direct duty between defendant and plaintiff or if it is simply a question of whether the defendant was vicariously liable for the act of the captain. In the House of Lords it seems that the pleadings alleged only a vicarious liability which the defendants had successfully rebutted at the trial in showing that the captain had committed no tort. When the plaintiffs tried to argue that the defendants were in breach of a non-delegable duty in putting to sea an unseaworthy ship, the House of Lords responded by holding that they were not entitled to change the pleadings at such a late stage. Similar difficulties can arise in public law liability cases (*cf* Ch 13 § 3). A private property owner sues central government for damage done to his property by escaping borstal boys: is this a question of a direct duty between government and citizen or a matter of the government, as employer, being vicariously

172 *Riverstone Meat Co Pty Ltd v Lancashire Shipping Co Ltd* [1961] AC 807.

173 *Wong Mee Wan v Kwan Kin Travel Services Ltd* [1996] 1 WLR 38, 42.

174 Supply of Goods and Services Act 1982 s 13.

responsible for the careless act of a prison warder in allowing the escape?[175] A parent and child bring an action for damages for breach of statutory duty and negligence against a local authority in respect of the negligent act of a psychiatrist in not investigating properly an allegation of child abuse. Is this a claim based on a direct duty owed by the authority to local citizens or is it a vicarious duty arising out of the employee psychiatrist's careless act? According to the House of Lords the failure to allege and identify the correct duty 'is not a mere pleading technicality' since 'until the basis on which the servants are alleged to be under a separate individual duty of care is identified it is impossible to assess whether, in law, such duty of care can exist.'[176]

7 ACTS AND ACTIVITIES

It may be, then, that the English law of tort is more concerned with acts rather than activities as a judge once pointed out.[177] Nevertheless, the notion of an act can be extended to cover the acts of others if there is in existence an obligation to procure some minimal results. In these situations one can talk of a liability of one person for acts of another. But the basis of this liability is not one that traditionally functions within the principle of vicarious liability since this principle is in theory a discrete set of rules applying only in situations of employment (master and servant). It is a tort rule mitigating the rigours of an individualist obligation structure. However, the moment that one or more of these rules spills over into another area of the law of obligations the two separate notions of non-delegable duty and vicarious liability can become confused. Vicarious liability can appear to be extending beyond the boundary of the employment (master and servant) contract. This can sometimes be dangerous since it might allow a contractor to escape his obligation by arguing that a third party was acting outside the course of his employment. Thus, it has been held that the employer of a bus conductor was not liable for the conductor's assault upon a passenger who was travelling on a bus under a contract with the employer.[178] Equally, in *Photo Production*, although the argument that the arsonist employee was acting outside the course of his employment was rejected by the House of Lords, the House still seemed to assume that the vicarious liability course of employment rule was relevant to the contractual situation.[179] One advantage, then, of a law of obligations, as opposed to a law of contract and tort, is that it might provide a context for a re-alignment of the structures dealing with three-party situations. But this should, probably, only be done alongside a rethinking of the structures dealing with liability for things (see Ch 5 § 5).

---

175 *Cf Home Office v Dorset Yacht Co Ltd* [1970] AC 1004.

176 *X (Minors) v Bedfordshire CC* [1995] 2 AC 633, 770.

177 Scott LJ in *Read v J Lyons & Co* [1945] 1 KB 216, 228.

178 *Keppel Bus Co v Sa'ad bin Ahmad* [1974] 2 All ER 700.

179 *Photo Production Ltd v Securicor* [1980] AC 827.

CHAPTER THIRTEEN

NON-CONTRACTUAL OBLIGA7 DAMAGES ACTIONS (2)

Knowledge of the English law of tort cannot fully be encapsulated under the general headings used by the continental systems since liability for individual acts (fault) and liability for people and things (strict liability) are not in themselves adequate ideas to express the full complexity of factual and remedial distinctions that find expression in the English law of non-contractual obligations. This second chapter on non-contractual damages actions will, accordingly, look at some of the more general issues behind the law of tort and, like the last two chapters, its main focus of attention will be on obligations arising out of fact rather than out of promissory transaction. However, as we have seen (*cf* Ch 8 § 3), the distinction between legal acts and legal facts is unrealistic when it comes to the common law and so the chapter will also include some material relevant to contractual obligations. It is a chapter that looks, on occasions, more generally at damages actions in the common law.

1 LIABILITY FOR STATEMENTS

One area where contractual and non-contractual obligations are closely intertwined is liability for misstatement. The reason for this is that statements are capable of being categorised in a number of ways. They can be interpreted as promises which, if supported by consideration, might well give rise to liability in contract (Chs 9–10); or they might simply be regarded as lies, threats or insults. Equally, they may be seen as something upon which the recipient of the statement might act. Where a statement causes loss or damage to another the question arises as to whether such a statement can act as the basis of a damages claim; however, the forms of action continue to play an important role in the determination of this question in that a number of quite different causes of action have come to govern the outcome of the liability question.

(a) Deceit and negligence

Until quite recently a damages action was, in the absence of a contractual or a fiduciary relationship, generally available only in cases of fraudulent misstatement (the tort of deceit) or defamation (the torts of libel and slander). However, the problem with deceit was, and remains (except with regard to misrepresentations inducing contracts),[1] that fraud, by no means easy to prove, was essential.[2] Up until 1964 if one could not establish that a misrepresentation was either fraudulent or contractual (*cf* Ch 9 § 7), then there was no basis for an action for damages at common law. However, in 1964 all of this changed with the recognition in *Hedley Byrne & Co Ltd v Heller & Partners Ltd*[3] that

1 On which see Misrepresentation Act 1967 s 2(1).

2 *Derry v Peek* (1889) 14 App Cas 337.

3 [1964] AC 465.

: tort of negligence might be available for misstatement in situations where there had been a 'special relationship' between the parties at the time the statement was made. This special relationship is certainly less intense than a fiduciary relationship (*cf* Ch 4 § 5(e)), but it nevertheless seems to be a development from this equitable bond in that the reasoning moves outwards from a fiduciary duty to one of fiduciary care.[4] In order for an action to lie under the *Hedley Byrne* principle the reliance connection must be close or equivalent to a contractual relationship.[5] No doubt the House of Lords were coming close to re-establishing the old 19th century idea of equitable 'fraud' (or negligent 'deceit')[6] and statute was to confirm this development with respect to misrepresentations made to induce contracts (*cf* Ch 9 § 7(a)).[7] From a law of obligations position, one very important effect of this new duty of care is that it can turn certain negligent breaches of contract into torts with implications for third parties in business and commercial transactions.[8] Thus, if A contracts with B to produce a valuation report on a house to be purchased by C and the report turns out to be carelessly inaccurate causing loss to C, then C may have an action against B in tort.[9]

(b) Defamation

Defamation, compared with the tort of negligence, is a tort of quite a different character and complexity – although some factual situations may *prima facie* attract both torts[10] – in that it is based on the plaintiff's right rather than the defendant's wrong. Accordingly, fault on behalf of the speaker (slander) or writer (libel) is largely irrelevant; all that need be shown is that words capable of being defamatory – in effect, critical of the plaintiff[11] – were spoken or published to a third party, however obscure the three party situation.[12] Not surprisingly, there is a considerable body of case law devoted both to the meaning of words – was the actual statement capable of bearing the meaning alleged by the plaintiff?[13] – and to publication.[14] The position is made more complex by the fact that innuendo is a form of defamation.[15]

Given the strictness of liability, the defences in defamation play a central constitutional role. To escape liability the defendant must successfully plead truth, fair comment or privilege, but this is not easy as these defences are not as wide as they

4 *Cf Nocton v Lord Ashburton* [1914] AC 932, 947.

5 *Hedley Byrne & Co Ltd v Heller & Partners Ltd* [1964] AC 465, 486, 528–29; *Smith v Bush* [1990] 1 AC 831; G Samuel, Equity and the Legal Divisions – Part I (1986) 37 NILQ 211, 223–26.

6 *Peek v Derry* (1887) 37 Ch D 541.

7 Misrepresentation Act 1967 s 2(1).

8 *Henderson v Merrett Syndicates Ltd* [1995] 2 AC 145.

9 *Smith v Bush* [1990] 1 AC 831.

10 *Lawton v BOC Transhield Ltd* [1987] 2 All ER 608; *Spring v Guardian Assurance plc* [1995] 2 AC 296.

11 See eg *Cornwell v Myskow* [1987] 2 All ER 504.

12 *Morgan v Odhams Press* [1971] 1 WLR 1239 HL.

13 See eg *Lewis v Daily Telegraph* [1964] AC 234.

14 See eg *Morgan v Odhams Press Ltd* [1971] 1 WLR 1239.

15 *Tolley v Fry* [1931] AC 333.

might first appear.[16] On balance the law seems more interested in protecting the private rather than the public interest[17] and thus one finds that criticising public figures, filing complaints about public officials, or even attempting to debate in the press issues such as blood sports,[18] can be an expensive exercise given that the damages awarded by juries bear no relation to those awarded by judges for serious personal injury.[19] Admittedly, this damages problem has been alleviated to some extent now that the Court of Appeal has power to intervene in the *quantum* question.[20] Yet part of the problem here is that there is no constitutional principle upholding freedom of speech,[21] and so one can often find the private law of defamation acting as a forum for what are in truth issues of public law.[22] However, it may be that things are now changing with respect to the criticism of public bodies. Not only is there a statutory proposal for reform,[23] but the House of Lords has recently held that it 'is of the highest public importance that a democratically elected governmental body, or indeed any governmental body, should be open to uninhibited public criticism' and the 'threat of a civil action for defamation must inevitably have an inhibiting effect on freedom of speech'.[24] Individual politicians and civil servants will, no doubt, continue to be able to sue in their private capacity backed, perhaps, by public funds.

(c) Intimidation

Liability can also attach to threats. If a person threatens to commit a wrongful act and this causes loss to the plaintiff the latter may have an action in tort unless the person issuing the threat can show legal justification.[25] For intimidation over and above normal commercial pressure is something that can attract, if not always the law of tort,[26] then the law of restitution (*cf* Ch 11 § 3(c)).[27] Some threats are legal,[28] others may lose their legality if issued by a group rather than an individual.[29] And threats to go on strike cause many private law problems because English law does not recognise a

16 See eg *Blackshaw v Lord* [1984] 1 QB 1; *Brent Walker Group Plc v Time Out Ltd* [1991] 2 QB 33; *cf* Defamation Act 1952 which introduced some very limited protections for the press. And see now Defamation Bill 1995.

17 See Weir, *Casebook*, p 528.

18 *The Guardian* 15 January 1990, p 2.

19 *Blackshaw v Lord* [1984] QB 1; *Sutcliffe v Pressdram Ltd* [1991] 1 QB 153.

20 Courts and Legal Services Act 1990 s 8; RSC Ord 59 r 11(4). See *Rantzen v Mirror Group Newspapers Ltd* [1994] QB 670; *John v MGN Ltd* [1996] 2 All ER 35.

21 *Cf Hector v A G of Antigua & Barbuda* [1990] 2 AC 312 PC.

22 See eg John Pilger, Letter, *The Guardian* 9 July 1991; but see now *Derbyshire CC v Times Newspapers* [1993] AC 534.

23 Defamation Bill 1995; P Milmo (1995) 145 NLJ 1340; (1996) 146 NLJ 222.

24 Lord Keith in *Derbyshire CC v Times Newspapers* [1993] AC 534, 547.

25 *Rookes v Barnard* [1964] AC 1129.

26 *The Evia Luck* [1992] 2 AC 152.

27 *D & C Builder Ltd v Rees* [1966] 2 QB 617.

28 *Thorne v Motor Trade Association* [1937] AC 797.

29 *Gulf Oil (GB) Ltd v Page* [1987] Ch 327.

right to strike, only certain immunities under statute. Such a threat to strike can give rise not only to a breach of contract between employer and employee but to the tort of interference with contractual rights allowing the employer, or some other contractual party, to seek damages or an injunction.[30] Thus, if D encourages C not to perform his contract with P, then P may have an action in tort for damages and (or) an injunction against D. This tort of interference with contractual relations is, accordingly, of particular importance to labour and industrial law. If violence is directly threatened this may be enough for a trespass action even if the plaintiff suffers only mental anguish from fear of imminent attack by the defendant.[31]

(d) Intellectual property rights

The torts of passing off and trade libel are further forms of liability attaching to statements. These torts are primarily designed to protect intellectual property rights and business interests, but the emphasis is rather different depending upon whether the complaint is 'misappropriation' of the plaintiff's words[32] or damage incurred as a result of the statement.[33] A defendant does no wrong by entering a market created by another (an area dealt with by national and EU law on fair trading and competition), but he must not attempt to deceive the public – an area where public law also has an important role – or maliciously to injure the plaintiff's products or business reputation. Thus, a person may be prohibited by injunction (*cf* Ch 5 § 4) from marketing goods in a container the distinctive shape of which has become a form of (intellectual) property in itself.[34] If the defendant wrongfully uses the plaintiff's property (including confidential information) in order to make a profit for himself by, say, publishing a book he might well find that he has to disgorge such a profit through the remedy of account (*cf* Ch 4 § 5(g)) on the basis of unjust enrichment (*cf* Ch 11 § 3(d)). Indeed if a constructive trust is declared the defendant may find himself faced with an *in rem* remedy (*cf* Ch 11 § 4).

2 PROFESSIONAL LIABILITY

Liability for misstatement is, then, an area that now straddles both contract and tort in that the 'implied duty to take care' now extends beyond the contract itself. Thus, the professional valuer, the accountant and the solicitor may find themselves owing duties not just to the person who commissioned them for a report, but to other proximate persons who might foreseeably rely upon the report.[35] No doubt the duty test will remain very strict indeed in the economic loss cases.[36] Accordingly, in one of the most

30 *Torquay Hotel Co v Cousins* [1969] 2 Ch 106.

31 *Read v Coker* (1853) 138 ER 1437.

32 *Cadbury Schweppes v Pub Squash Co* [1981] 1 All ER 213, 223.

33 Defamation Act 1952 s 3.

34 *Reckitt & Colman Properties Ltd v Borden Inc* [1990] 1 WLR 491 HL. See also EU Draft Directive (as amended) on comparative advertisements, adopted 9 November 1995.

35 *Morgan Crucible Co Plc v Hill Samuel & Co Ltd* [1991] Ch 295.

36 *Cf White v Jones* [1995] 2 AC 207.

important negligence cases to be decided by the House of Lords in recent years it was held that a firm of accountants acting as auditors of one company owed no duty of care to another company considering a potential take-over.[37] Indeed even in physical damage cases the courts will be reluctant to impose liability in situations where it would unfairly affect the balance of contractual and insurance relations between commercial parties.[38] But in both contractual and non-contractual situations negligence has an important role to play in compensation claims against doctors, lawyers, architects and the like.

The liability is in form no different from any other liability under the fault principle. However, in substance there are two special characteristics. First, where a professional skill is concerned, the test for a breach of duty is not governed by the reasonable man test as such; it is governed by the standard of the reasonable person exercising that professional skill.[39] The test is the standard of the ordinary skilled man exercising and professing to have that professional skill. An accountant, architect, lawyer or doctor need not possess the highest expert skill; all he or she needs to exercise is 'the ordinary skill of an ordinary competent man exercising that particular art'.[40] Thus, when a medical operation goes wrong, although it may raise a presumption of fault under the *res ipsa loquitur* maxim, liability is by no means automatic because the risk of medical accident is, in the absence of carelessness, very much on the patient.[41] The law might impose a duty of care on doctors as a question of law, but the standard of care, a question of fact, is always a matter of medical judgment.[42] Risk also implies informed consent and so the medical profession must take care to give any necessary information, provided such information is in the 'best interests' of the patient.[43] Yet the courts are not overready to hold doctors and surgeons liable when things go wrong in the surgery or on the operating table.

This reluctance also results from a second characteristic of professional liability, the role of policy and the public interest.[44] No doubt all duty, breach and causation decisions contain an important policy element, but in certain areas this policy factor, sometimes under the guise of the public interest, can play a more direct role. Thus, the incompetent barrister cannot be sued for the way he or she handles litigation,[45] nor can the detective who fails to catch the murderer.[46] This is not to say that lawyers and public bodies cannot be sued – indeed they are both a regular source of litigation. The point to be made is that institutions like the National Health Service, the constabulary

37 *Caparo Industries plc v Dickman* [1990] 2 AC 605.

38 *Marc Rich & Co v Bishop Rock Marine Co Ltd* [1996] 1 AC 211.

39 *Bolam v Friern Hospital Management Committee* [1957] 1 WLR 582.

40 *Ibid* at p 586 *per* McNair J (to the jury).

41 *Roe v Minister of Health* [1954] 2 QB 66.

42 *Sidaway v Bethlem Royal Hospital* [1985] AC 871, 881.

43 *Sidaway v Bethlem Royal Hospital* [1985] AC 871.

44 See eg *Marc Rich & Co v Bishop Rock Marine Co Ltd* [1996] 1 AC 211, 240–41.

45 *Rondel v Worlsey* [1969] 1 AC 191.

46 *Hill v Chief Constable of West Yorkshire* [1989] AC 53.

and the courts are public law institutions and actions in the law of tort can raise issues of an administrative law nature (*cf* Ch 2 § 2; Ch 8 § 4(c)).

3 TORT AND PUBLIC LAW

We have seen that the tort of negligence has gone far in taking the law of torts towards a law of tort (*cf* Ch 8 § 3(d); Ch 12 § 3(a)) with the result that fault liability has assumed something of a central role in what a civil lawyer would see as civil liability (*la responsabilité civile*). Yet the tort of negligence, together with some of the other torts, has important implications for public law (*la responsabilité administrative*) as well. This is because various organs of the state can find themselves liable to those whom they carelessly, abusively or unlawfully injure; and this liability has, potentially, increased in scope with the recognition that pure economic loss flowing from a careless statement can give rise to a claim for damages (see below § 9). In theory, there is no difference between public and private liability in tort (*cf* Ch 2 § 2; Ch 8 § 4(c)), but in recent years the courts have increasingly recognised that public bodies can present special problems and that not all decisions by government officials can be allowed to be the basis of an action merely because they involve some negligence[47] or the breach of a statute.[48] There are issues of public law that must be taken into account.

(a) Judicial review and private damages claims

In the absence of carelessness the public law rule is that an *ultra vires* decision will not give rise to an action for damages unless the decision amounted to an abuse of public office.[49] Breach of a public law right to the performance of a public law duty is protected only by an action for judicial review and such an action does not encompass damages. In order to obtain compensation the victim must show a cause of action in contract or in tort.[50] The dichotomy, therefore, would seem at first sight to be one of abuse (using the term in a wide administrative law sense) of decision-making power (public law) on the one hand, and fault (private law) on the other.[51] Where the abuse is such that it amounts to the deliberate inflicting of damage, this may be a tort in itself; but anything less will be governed by ordinary principles of private law. Nevertheless, in interpreting abuse it must not be forgotten that since the early days of the common law one of the functions of the law of torts has been to protect constitutional rights; the torts of trespass and malicious prosecution have traditionally had a central role to play in guarding the citizen against governmental interference with his or her person or property not justified by lawful authority.[52] And in trespass situations it is the

47 *Fellowes v Rother DC* [1983] 1 All ER 513, 518.

48 *Bourgoin SA v Ministry of Agriculture* [1986] QB 716.

49 *Dunlop v Woollahra Municipal Council* [1982] AC 158.

50 *X (Minors) v Bedfordshire CC* [1995] 2 AC 633, 730.

51 *Rowling v Takaro Properties Ltd* [1988] AC 473; see also *Glinski v McIver* [1962] AC 726.

52 *Hill v Chief Constable of West Yorkshire* [1989] AC 53, 59. See eg *Cooper v Wandsworth Board of Works* (1863) 143 ER 414; *Christie v Leachinsky* [1947] AC 573; *cf* Police and Criminal Evidence Act 1984 s 28.

interference, not fault, which has been the basis of the action. Consequently, the task for the future, perhaps as the law of torts increasingly becomes a law of tort (*cf* Ch 8 § 3(d)), is to work out a rational role for private law damages actions in the field of public law;[53] and this task is now beginning to be worked out at the level of the law of actions by the recognition that there is a procedural, if not substantive, distinction to be made between public and private law.[54] Nevertheless, this step is only a procedural beginning. The main task will be to work out a substantive interrelationship between the various causes of action in tort (negligence, breach of statutory duty, trespass and so on) and the causing of harm by administrative decision or even inaction. Will the administrative (public law) relationship be capable in itself of giving rise to a compensation claim or will new or existing causes of action need to be developed within the law of tort?

(b) Tort and the exercise of discretion

Just where this distinction between public and private rights will lead to in relation to actions in tort against public bodies is difficult to predict as yet, save to say that in the short term it will result in a restriction in liability where the risk is one that belongs more to the private than to the public sector. Thus, the trend now is not to make public bodies responsible for investment[55] and property speculations.[56] Indeed in one of its most important decisions in respect of actions against local authorities, the House of Lords in *X (Minors) v Bedfordshire CC*[57] has decreed that '[w]here Parliament has conferred a statutory discretion on a public authority, it is for that authority, not for the courts, to exercise the discretion: nothing which the authority does within the ambit of the discretion can be actionable at common law.'[58] And even if the decision of the authority falls outside the statutory discretion, the court cannot intervene if the discretion involves matters of policy: 'a common law duty of care in relation to the taking of decisions involving policy matters cannot exist'.[59] In fact where personal injury is concerned the English courts have tended to put the risk on individuals rather than on the community at large[60] and this emphasis on fault means that in any case where the courts do wish to spread the burden of loss more widely they have to be somewhat imaginative in interpreting the facts to fit the private law principles.[61]

---

53 T Weir, 'Government Liability' [1989] PL 40; G Samuel, 'Government Liability in Tort and the Public and Private Division' (1988) 8 LS 277.

54 *O'Reilly v Mackman* [1983] 2 AC 237; *Roy v Kensington & Chelsea & Westminster Practitioner Committee* [1992] 1 AC 624.

55 *Yuen Kun Yeu v AG of Hong Kong* [1988] AC 175.

56 *Investors in Industry Ltd v South Bedfordshire DC* [1986] QB 1034.

57 [1995] 2 AC 633.

58 *Ibid* at p 738 *per* Lord Browne-Wilkinson.

59 *Ibid.*

60 *Watt v Hertfordshire CC* [1954] 1 WLR 835; *Dunne v NW Gas Board* [1964] 2 QB 806.

61 *Rigby v Chief Constable of Northamptonshire* [1985] 1 WLR 1242; Jolowicz [1985] CLJ 370.

(c) Public and private interests

Part of the problem facing the common law when it comes to the public and private division is that public bodies have traditionally been treated on the legal stage as private people having not just the same rights as real people – for example, with respect to reputation[62] – but the same responsibilities as well. This is sometimes healthy. Yet it can also be unfortunate because the public interest is often different from the commercial interest – as the courts have recently been reminded[63] – and so if English lawyers are now keen to distinguish between 'public rights' and 'private rights' they will need to do more than just distinguish between judicial review, injunction and declaration on the one hand and claims for damages on the other.[64] There will need to be a greater appreciation of the institutional differences between public and private legal subjects and this will require a more sophisticated approach towards constitutional theory and the 'public interest' than at present is to be found in the English courts.[65]

Accordingly, simply to distinguish between acts, discretion and policy is to confuse legal concepts at the level of tortious causes of action (breach of statutory duty, duty of care). Doctors, for example, may well have a policy of not giving patients full information if they judge it in a patient's best interest, but such a policy does not and cannot exclude the law of tort. It may well be that the task of a local authority in dealing with, for example, child abuse problems is 'extraordinarily delicate',[66] yet that does not mean that the professionals involved should be isolated from liability when things go wrong. For such isolation simply creates an area of 'non-law' where administrative discretion rather than legal principle governs. The whole point of public law is to fill the vacuum of 'non-law'. Or, put another way, public law is, or should be, concerned with individuals as social citizens; it should be concerned with human personality in terms of the social group and the ensuring of social rights, including the distribution of burdens when governing bodies fail in their duties. Private law is about protecting economic interests – economic being construed widely in this context[67] – and is thus about the protection of patrimonial rights within an economic law. No doubt the factual situations involved in a case like *X (Minors) v Bedfordshire CC*[68] are not strictly patrimonial as such; but if the response of the English court is simply to bar legal recourse, then the category of public law is failing in its purpose of ensuring that those who exercise power should be accountable to individual citizens damaged by

---

62 *Bognor Regis UDC v Campion* [1972] 2 QB 169. However, this case has now been overruled by the House of Lords *Derbyshire CC v Times Newspapers* [1993] AC 534, where it was held that to allow a local government authority to sue for libel would impose a substantial restriction on freedom of expression.

63 *R v Licensing Authority, Ex p Smith Kline & French Laboratories Ltd* [1990] 1 AC 64.

64 *Cf X (Minors) v Bedforshire CC* [1995] 2 AC 633, 730–31.

65 G Samuel, '*Le rôle de l'action en justice en droit anglais*', in Legrand (ed), pp 381–421. AIDS infections from contaminated blood transfusions raise urgent questions: *Le Monde* 3 July 1991, p 10; *The Observer* 16 June 1991, p 9. France now has a fund (Loi 91-1406 art 47).

66 *X (Minors) v Bedforshire CC* [1995] 2 AC 633, 750.

67 P Cane, *Tort Law and Economic Interests* (Oxford, 1991), pp 3–17.

68 [1995] 2 AC 633.

such an exercise. The absence of such accountability means that the interests of the public body or officials are given preference over the interests of individuals and this gives rise to a situation where the individual becomes a subject rather than a citizen. Perhaps United Kingdom public law is happy with such a situation, but the legal system of the European Union has a different vision.[69]

(d) Inequality in the face of public burdens

Instead of isolating public officials from the law, the courts should be rethinking the whole question of administrative liability itself. To argue that 'if a liability in damages were to be imposed, it might well be that local authorities would adopt a more cautious and defensive approach to their duties'[70] is not an argument that logically leads to non-liability of a public institution. It is simply an argument for putting the risk on the citizen when things go wrong and it is not obvious that the placing of such burdens on the individual is in the public interest. If a tenderer is entitled as of right to expect a local authority to give proper and non-negligent consideration to a commercial tender,[71] why is a parent not entitled as of right to expect proper consideration when it comes to more sensitive expectations? In many civil law countries the constitutionality of acts and statutes is beyond control of the courts and lies with Parliament, but organs of state can, nevertheless, be liable either *ex delicto* or in administrative law when acting in the public interest.

All this may seem far too extreme for English tastes (and procedures). Yet, instead of using the tort of negligence in delicate cases, it might be more sensible, and sensitive, to develop a tort such as breach of statutory duty – or indeed trespass[72] – to deal with cases where citizens find themselves damaged as a result of governmental action. It is statute that governs the *imperium* (power) relationship between the individual and the state and thus it makes sense that it should be this statutory relationship which should act as the basis for any damages claim. To deny the citizen a claim against governmental bodies when they act carelessly, or make careless decisions, is simply to concentrate power in the hands of government. Is not one important role for the law of tort to protect the individual against the unlawful exercise of power? The effect of the decision in *X (Minors) v Bedfordshire CC* is to deprive the individual of rights and effective remedies in the face of government incompetence and one might reflect whether this, as has been suggested, puts the United Kingdom out of line with developments in the public law systems of many of Britain's EU partners whose 'Roman law' systems were, originally, seen as more authoritarian and state-orientated.

4 CAUSATION

One fundamental principle that the English law of obligations does share with all of its Romanist EU partners is that before a claim in damages can succeed against a private or

69 See eg *Brasserie du Pêcheur SA v Federal Republic of Germany* [1996] 2 WLR 506 (ECJ).

70 *X (Minors) v Bedforshire CC* [1995] 2 AC 633, 750.

71 *Blackpool & Fylde Aero Club Ltd v Blackpool BC* [1990] 1 WLR 1195.

72 *Cf Cooper v Wandsworth Board of Works* (1863) 143 ER 414.

a public defendant it must be shown that the damage suffered by the plaintiff was caused by the defendant's act or a thing under his control. If there is no causal link there is no liability. This whole topic has already been discussed in relation to the law of actions (Ch 7), but it is worth stressing, once again, that it is not always easy to distinguish between duty of care, damage and causation problems in a number of factual situations. Moreover, unlike many other systems, English law tends to disperse the problem of causation across a range of legal devices and so, instead of asking directly whether the defendant has caused all of the damage or loss claimed, the common lawyer tends to ask whether the damage was 'too remote' (Ch 7 § 4) or whether the plaintiff has been guilty of 'contributory negligence' or a 'failure to mitigate' (Ch 7 § 5) his loss. There are cases where the courts directly have to decide causal issues (Ch 7 § 3), but on the whole, both in contract and tort, a great many causal problems are to be found operating at different levels of liability (see generally Ch 7).

It must be remembered, also, that the form of action can influence the causal question even in strict liability cases because the actionability and the remoteness questions tend to merge. Accordingly, the bailee who deviates from the terms of the bailment will find himself in a situation where unforeseeability is irrelevant simply because liability and damage become one and the same issue.[73] The same can be said for certain kinds of breaches of contract.[74] Where damage arises from an unlawful act (*cf* Ch 12 § 4) actionability and causation find themselves merged at the level of risk in that such damage has to be of a kind envisaged in the statute[75] or, in the case of public nuisance, at least within the realm of an objective state of affairs calling upon the defendant to justify the risk created.[76] In cases of interference with goods (see below § 8(a)) the amount of compensation recoverable is not dealt with as a liability issue because, as with bailment, liability itself is strict.[77] The question of 'consequential damages' in these interference cases[78] is either a damages problem to be decided as a question of damages or an issue that belongs more properly to the law of restitution.[79]

5 GENERAL DEFENCES

Contributory negligence and mitigation, because they do not normally affect liability itself,[80] tend to be seen as defences more than essential issues going to the primary obligation. Yet because they are legal devices dealing with causation they can on occasions be used to solve some of the more difficult questions of *culpa* and cause. They are legal devices that focus on the behaviour of the plaintiff.

73 *Mitchell v Ealing LBC* [1979] QB 1.

74 See eg *Vacwell Engineering v BDH Chemicals* [1971] 1 QB 88.

75 *Gorris v Scott* (1874) LR 9 Ex 125.

76 *Dymond v Pearce* [1972] 1 QB 496.

77 *The Winkfield* [1902] P 42.

78 Torts (Interference with Goods Act 1977 s 3(2)(a).

79 *Strand Electric Co Ltd v Brisford Entertainments Ltd* [1952] 2 QB 246.

80 But *cf The Solholt* [1983] 1 Ll Rep 605.

(a) Consent

To argue that contributory negligence is a form of consent is often to do injustice to the notion of consent itself. Failure to take proper care of one's safety is not the same as consenting to damage. Nevertheless, where a plaintiff has sustained his injuries in the course of an anti-social activity the court might have recourse to contributory negligence or mitigation in order to deprive him of part or all of his damages.[81] Alternatively, the court might refuse a damages action on the basis that the plaintiff actually consented to his injuries (*volenti non fit injuria*)[82] or was involved in an activity so anti-social that the illegality prevents any action arising (*ex turpi causa non oritur actio*).[83] It should be stressed, however, that the courts are not overready to resort to the *volenti* defence and statute has intervened in the case of a motor vehicle – but not aircraft[84] – passenger who freely embarks on a journey with an obviously drunk driver. Such a passenger cannot be deprived of compensation on the ground of antecedent agreement or acceptance of risk.[85] In road accident cases the primary emphasis is, then, on the compensation of (passenger) victims. All the same this policy of compensation can be overriden in cases of serious criminal behaviour,[86] and in situations where there is no accident insurance the courts might use the defence of *volenti* to protect the patrimonies of innocent third parties.[87]

(b) Limitation

Contributory negligence, consent and illegality are all defences of substance in as much as they require the courts to assess them in the context of a detailed examination of the circumstances of each case. By way of contrast, the defence of limitation is one that functions only at the level of form in that it goes to the remedy not the right[88] – although in the case of property rights the effect of limitation is in reality to extinguish title.[89] At common law limitation is entirely a creature of statute and in order to be effective it has to be specifically pleaded;[90] payment of a statute barred debt cannot therefore be recovered on the grounds of lack of an obligation to pay. With regard to equitable remedies there is no actual statutory limitation as such,[91] but time limits will be applied by way of analogy.[92]

---

81 *Murphy v Culhane* [1977] QB 94; but *cf Pitts v Hunt* [1990] QB 302.

82 *ICI v Shatwell* [1965] AC 656; AJE Jaffey, '*Volenti Non Fit Injuria*' [1985] CLJ 87.

83 *Murphy v Culhane* [1977] QB 94; *Pitts v Hunt* [1990] QB 302.

84 *Morris v Murray* [1991] 2 QB 6.

85 Road Traffic Act 1988 s 149.

86 *Pitts v Hunt* [1990] QB 302.

87 *Morris v Murray* [1991] 2 QB 6.

88 *Ronex Properties v John Laing* [1983] QB 398, 404.

89 *Buckinghamshire CC v Moran* [1990] Ch 623.

90 *Ronex Properties v John Laing* [1983] QB 398, 404.

91 Limitation Act 1980 s 36.

92 See eg *Leaf v International Galleries* [1950] 2 KB 85.

The standard time limit in a breach of contract and a tort action is six years from the accrual of the cause of action[93] and this means that there may be a difference of limitation between contractual and non-contractual damages claims. A cause of action in contract accrues from the date of the breach whereas a claim in tort arises only from the suffering of the damage.[94] However, there are a range of exceptions to this period depending on the nature of the action or on the nature of the damage. Thus, in the case of personal injury the time limit is three years from either the suffering of or the knowledge of the damage[95] – although the court does have a certain discretion to override this three year period where it 'would be equitable to allow an action to proceed'[96] – and there are special time limits for defamation, defective products, recovery of land and a number of other types of action.[97] Very complex problems have arisen as a result of latent damage and this has required special treatment both with regard to personal injury[98] and property damage.[99] There are now special rules about knowledge of damage in those cases where injuries or damage are not easily discoverable by the plaintiff.

(c) Necessity

A more controversial defence is that of necessity (*cf* Ch 7 § 6(d)). That there exists such a defence is not in doubt,[100] but the defence is controversial not just because it can on occasions result in delicate social problems – can a hospital administer emergency medical treatment without the consent of the plaintiff?[101] – but also because, when used by public authorities, it raises a problem of public law. If the police have to destroy a person's private property in order to recapture a dangerous prisoner, is it right that the state should be able to avoid compensating the owner of the private property on the ground of necessity?[102] In French law this public law necessity problem is avoided by the equality principle which ordains that a citizen ought not to carry the burden of an administrative act carried out in the public interest and for the public benefit – automatic compensation by the state will spread the loss amongst the community. But in English law, as we have seen, there is no such automatic liability. Indeed quite the opposite.[103] Consequently, the injured plaintiff must prove fault in order to escape the defence of necessity.[104]

---

93 Limitation Act 1980 ss 2, 5.

94 *Midland Bank Trust Co v Hett, Stubbs & Kemp* [1979] Ch 384.

95 Section 11.

96 Section 33.

97 See eg ss 4A, 11A, 15.

98 Section 14.

99 Latent Damage Act 1986.

100 *In re F* [1990] 2 AC 1, 74.

101 *In re F* [1990] 2 AC 1.

102 *Cf Rigby v Chief Constable of Northamptonshire* [1985] 1 WLR 1242.

103 *Dunne v NW Gas Board* [1964] 2 QB 806.

104 *Rigby v Chief Constable of Northamptonshire* [1985] 1 WLR 1242.

Necessity stretches beyond a mere defence to a claim in damages. It can also be important in certain circumstances for grounding an action for debt (see Ch 11 § 2) and damages (Ch 7 § 6(d)). P intervenes in an emergency situation to save D's life or property and suffers damage as a result: will the necessity of itself allow P to claim damages? Now officious intervention, even in emergency situations, cannot of itself give rise to any common law claim. However, the rescuer who intervenes to save life and limb will not only have a defence to any action brought against him by the person to whom he gives, for example, emergency medical treatment;[105] he will also have a claim in negligence against anyone – including the person rescued – whose carelessness caused the dangerous situation in the first place.[106] Public policy will prevent the defence of *volenti* from being raised against the rescuer, save perhaps where the intervention is not to save life and is unreasonable given the circumstances.[107]

6 TORT AND DEBT

One aspect of the legislation giving the court power to reduce damages in tort for contributory negligence is that it in effect allows the court to apportion losses between two parties who have both been guilty of wrongs.[108] Where there is more than one person potentially liable to a victim another piece of legislation allows the defendant who has had to pay full compensation to the victim – for a plaintiff injured by several tortfeasors can sue any one of them for full damages – to recover contribution from any other person liable or potentially liable in respect of the same damage.[109] And this contribution – or indeed complete indemnity[110] – will be recoverable 'whatever the legal basis of ... liability, whether tort, breach of contract, breach of trust or otherwise.'[111] The point to notice here, however, is that liability to pay contribution is not actually part of the law of tort even though it may well be influenced by some of its policies; it is a statutory debt claim based on the principle of unjust enrichment (*cf* Ch 11 § 2). Accordingly, the 'just and equitable' basis upon which the court decides the contribution question, while obviously based upon the defendant's share of the 'responsibility for the damage in question',[112] ought also, in principle at least, to be judged in the context of loss spreading and insurance generally.[113] Whether it will be is another question.[114]

---

105 *In re F* [1990] 2 AC 1, 76.

106 See eg *Chadwick v British Railways Board* [1967] 1 WLR 912. *Cf* French law: Cass civ 1.12.1969; DS. 1970.422 (Rudden, p 314).

107 See eg *Cutler v United Dairies (London) Ltd* [1933] 2 KB 297.

108 *Fitzgerald v Lane* [1989] AC 328.

109 Civil Liability (Contribution) Act 1978 s 1. See also *Birse Construction Ltd v Haiste Ltd* [1996] 2 All ER 1.

110 Section 2(2).

111 Section 6(1).

112 Section 2(1).

113 Presumably the court has the discretionary power 'to exempt any person from liability to make contribution' if it considers it to be 'just and equitable': s 2(1) and (2).

114 The court might feel that its discretionary power is governed by 'responsibility for the damage in question' in s 2(1).

T AND ACCIDENT COMPENSATION

tion for accidents is dependent upon fault and causation is one cial policy questions where personal injury and death are or a start there is the general question: how can severe personal injury, ccompanied by pain and mental suffering, ever adequately be compensated by money? Yet, if compensation is to be the guiding principle in damages awards, ought causation rules strictly to be applied? Should, for example, private personal injury insurance, or a generous donation from a relative or the public, be taken into account in assessing the damages? And what about social security benefits[115] and the National Health Service? These kinds of question give rise to much litigation whose complexity of detail is outside the scope of this general survey (but *cf* Ch 6).[116] However, two general points must be made.

The first concerns the family. Serious personal injury and death is as much a tragedy for the immediate family of the victim as it is for the victim him or herself and, in addition to their grief, dependants may well find themselves faced with severe economic hardship. Statute and case law now recognise that an award of damages to the victim may well contain a compensation element for the family. Accordingly, the cause of action of a dead victim survives his or her death for the benefit of the estate[117] and the interests of the family will now be taken into account in assessing damages payable by the tortfeasor.[118] Moreover, the death of the victim will also give rise to an independent cause of action on behalf of the victim's dependants;[119] here the measure of damages is the actual economic loss of each dependant entitled to sue, although a statutory sum for bereavement is also available to a spouse or parent in the case of the death of a wife, husband or child.[120]

The second general point concerns insurance. Most personal injury claims arise out of road and factory accidents and these are two areas where liability insurance is compulsory.[121] Accordingly, in most tort actions an insurance company will be a hidden party and this raises questions both about the role such companies ought to have in the apportionment of liability and about the aims and objectives of the law of tort itself.[122] Should the courts now recognise that the plaintiff's claim is in reality often against an insurance company rather than against the actual wrongdoer? And, if so, should the fault principle itself be modified or abandoned? Sometimes the courts are

---

115 See now Social Security Administration Act 1992 s 82.

116 See generally on this subject P Cane, *Atiyah's Accidents, Compensation and the Law* (Butterworths, 5th edn, 1993). For France: *Loi No 85-677 du 5 juillet 1985* (*Loi Badinter*)

117 Law Reform (Miscellaneous Provisions) Act 1934 s 1.

118 *Pickett v British Rail Engineering Ltd* [1980] AC 136.

119 Fatal Accidents Act 1976.

120 Section 1A.

121 But *cf Reid v Rush & Tompkins Plc* [1990] 1 WLR 212.

122 For cases raising these kinds of issues see: *Lister v Romford Ice & Cold Storage Co* [1957] AC 555; *Morris v Ford Motor Co* [1983] 1 QB 792.

prepared at least to recognise the role of insurance in risk allocation,[123] t whole they continue to see a tort claim as lying only between plaintiff and tortfeasor and thus, if the latter disappears, the victim, as far as the common law is concerned, will be left without compensation despite the existence of an insurance policy.[124] This continued reliance upon the fault system to determine accident compensation is, perhaps, an unfortunate situation which puts English law out of line with developments in other legal systems. Yet the answer to such compensation problems is not to be found only within the law of tort: for accident compensation is an area where tort interrelates both with the social policy issues of public law and the public interest and with the differing roles of damages and debt remedies within complex liability factual situations (*cf* Ch 5 § 5). Law reform, if and when it comes, will need to be comprehensive in scope.

8 PROPERTY RIGHTS AND THE LAW OF TORT

Accident compensation is not, however, the only function of the law of tort. In addition to such loss spreading – and the protection of constitutional rights – the law of tort has a central role in protecting property rights. Now just because English law does not have a theory either of ownership or of rights as such (Ch 3 § 3(d)) this does not mean that it has no remedies capable of protecting what the layman would see as property rights. English law, like Roman law, recognises ownership of things even if (again like Roman law) it has no definition of *dominium*.[125] In fact were English law to adopt a general definition of ownership along the lines of article 544 of the *Code civil* – a definition which sees ownership as an absolute right to enjoy and to dispose of property (*le droit de jouir et disposer des choses de la manière la plus absolue*) – it would result in the instant abolition of the trust, or at least its relegation to the law of obligations.[126] Consequently, property problems need to be handled without recourse to a legal definition of ownership.

(a) Interference with chattels

The common law achieves such protection of property rights without a definition of ownership by using, on the one hand, remedies in the law of tort in place of an *actio in rem*[127] and, on the other hand, *possessio* in place of *dominium*.[128] An action for damages is available in conversion, trespass or negligence for any interference with a person's possessory title to moveable property; and the proprietary nature of these remedies is

123 See eg *Smith v Eric Bush* [1990] 1 AC 831.

124 *Bradley v Eagle Star Insurance* [1989] AC 957. The position has now been remedied to some extent by statute: Companies Act 1989 s 141(5) (amending Companies Act 1985 s 651); *In re Workvale Ltd* [1991] 1 WLR 294.

125 Sale of Goods Act 1979 ss 17, 21.

126 F H Lawson, *Selected Essays,* Volume II (North-Holland, 1977), p 288; GH Jones, Jolowicz, para 366.

127 Torts (Interference with Goods) Act 1977 s 1.

128 Section 7(1)(a).

reflected in the damages rule that, *prima facie*, the plaintiff is entitled to the value of the goods converted[129] plus, where appropriate, consequential damages.[130] Under statute a court can also order a wrongful possessor of goods to redeliver them to the plaintiff.[131]

These kind of rules often go further than the law of tort as such in that the ability to be able to order consequential damages in addition to the value of the goods provides the court with a means of preventing unjust enrichment (*cf* Ch 11 § 5). If one person wrongfully detains a profit-earning chattel belonging to another the latter might well be able to reclaim any lost profits from the former on the basis that the former has acquired an unjust benefit.[132] However, this appears to be a rule of commercial law and so if the plaintiff is a public body the same principle might not apply.[133] Furthermore, if the court is convinced that the plaintiff has suffered no loss and the defendant has gained no benefit it is possible that a conversion claim will result only in nominal damages.[134]

One of the problems with using remedies and possession as the basis of an action for the full value of the goods is that a wrongdoer might be faced with a double liability. And so, for example, 'if a converter of goods pays damages first to a finder of the goods, and then to the true owner'[135] this might result in the true owner getting the goods or their value from the defendant and the finder getting the value of the goods from the defendant. Statute has now intervened using the remedy of account and the principle of unjust enrichment (*cf* Ch 4 § 5(g)); one claimant can be made liable to account over to the other person having a right to claim to such extent as will avoid double liability[136] and '[w]here, as the result of enforcement of a double liability, any claimant is unjustly enriched to any extent, he shall be liable to reimburse the wrongdoer to that extent'.[137] The value of this section is that it provides an excellent insight into how English law, via the law of actions, attempts to deal with complex liability problems involving three or more parties (*cf* Ch 5 § 5(a)). However, the end result is that the restitutionary remedies cannot easily be classified within any obligations structure (*cf* Ch 1 § 1). In theory, the damages claim for conversion is one in tort and so, logically, must belong to the law of obligations. Yet in substance the action is often much closer to an *actio in rem* in that it is not based on fault[138] and consists of a claim for the goods themselves or their value.[139]

---

129 *The Winkfield* [1902] P 42.

130 Torts (Interference with Goods) Act 1977 s 3.

131 *Ibid.*

132 *Strand Electric & Engineering Co Ltd v Brisford Entertainments Ltd* [1952] 2 QB 246.

133 *Stoke-on-Trent CC v W & J Wass Ltd* [1988] 1 WLR 1406.

134 *The Albazero* [1977] AC 774; *Brandeis Goldschmidt v Western Transport* [1981] QB 864

135 Torts (Interference with Goods) Act 1977 s 7.

136 Section 7(3).

137 Section 7(4).

138 Section 11(1).

139 Section 3(2).

This property flavour to the torts of conversion and trespass to goods is t in the location of liability in the relationship between person and thing.[140] They are torts of strict liability based on interference rather than actions for damages based on fault and as a result persons such as an auctioneer can be held liable if they innocently sell stolen goods.[141] Now, as we have mentioned, it is the (quasi) factual relationship of possession rather than the legal relation of ownership which acts as the focal point of liability; yet this must be treated with a certain amount of care since the real starting point for conversion is not the fact of possession but the right to possess.[142] In truth one is thus dealing with a rational rather than empirical concept and this means that conversion is, in substance, often more a question of *dominium* than strict *possessio*.[143] Damage, even serious damage, to the property itself is not conversion and will be a trespass only if it is done intentionally.[144] Careless damage to goods is a matter for the law of contract[145] or the tort of negligence[146] and in these situations the measure of damages is subject to the rules of causation (*cf* Ch 7).

But what if the defendant carelessly loses the plaintiff's goods: is this a question of damage or interference? Or, put another way, is it a matter for the law of obligations or the law of property? It has been said that the form of action is not important in situations where the defendant causes the loss of the plaintiff's ship by sinking it;[147]and in those cases where a bailee (*cf* Ch 8 § 3(c)) carelessly loses the bailor's goods it has been implied[148] that an action might be available either in detinue (now conversion) or in negligence under the *res ipsa loquitur* principle (*cf* Ch 2 § 4(b)). Yet the situation is not so simple because not only does the bailment relationship itself give rise to proprietary rights and duties, but the tort of negligence, as we shall see (below § 9), does still appear to distinguish between economic loss and physical damage.[149] Moveable property in truth gives rise to a range of conceptual problems because it acts as a focal point for a range of different legal remedies (conversion, trespass, damages) and a range of different categories (contract, tort, bailment).

Trespass can also play a negative role, as we have seen with respect to the case of *Waverley BC v Fletcher* (Ch 2 § 8).[150] F, using a metal detector on O's land, finds a valuable brooch: is it F or O who is entitled to this find? If F had found a brooch while he was lawfully on the land and the brooch had been lost by some untraceable previous person, then it would seem that he would have a better title than O.[151] Yet the

140 *Fowler v Hollins* (1872) LR 7 QB 616; (1875) LR 7 HL 757.

141 *RH Willis & Son v British Car Auctions* [1978] 1 WLR 438.

142 Weir, *Casebook*, pp 473–78.

143 *England v Cowley* (1873) LR 8 Exch 126.

144 *Letang v Cooper* [1965] 1 QB 232.

145 See eg *Photo Production Ltd v Securicor* [1980] AC 827.

146 See eg *Home Office v Dorset Yacht Co* [1970] AC 1004.

147 *The Mediana* [1900] AC 113.

148 *Houghland v RR Low (Luxury Coaches) Ltd* [1962] 1 QB 694.

149 But *cf* Torts (Interference with Goods) Act 1977 s 1(c).

150 [1995] 3 WLR 772.

151 *Parker v British Airways Board* [1982] QB 1004.

moment he becomes a trespasser the position seems to change. The owner of land appears to have *vis-à-vis* the trespasser a better title to the lost chattel. This situation is likely to appear strange to a civil lawyer since possession of a chattel is a question for the law of property rather than for the law of obligations (trespass) or the law of persons (status of trespasser).[152] However, in a system which does not distinguish between obligation and property rights there is no conceptual barrier by which the intentional act of trespass can be distinguished from the intentional act of taking possession; both acts become merged into a law of persons issue through which entitlement is resolved by reference to the standing of each party in relation not just to the *res* but also to each other. In fact the case of *Waverley* can also be understood as belonging just as much to the law of actions: the status of the finder 'estopped' him from asserting a possessory title (*ius possessionis*) to the brooch just as the behaviour of the owner in *Crabb v Arun DC*[153] estopped him (or it) from asserting his full property rights against his neighbour. One can see here the seamless nature of English law. Certainly, possession is a question for the law of property, but possession is often a matter to be decided in relation to the law of actions (trespass, conversion) which in turn may depend upon status or an *in personam* relationship. If the finder in *Waverley* had been allowed to keep the brooch, would this not have been to have allowed a member of the public to enrich him or herself at the expense of an owner who was holding the land on behalf of the public?[154] The problem with the case is that the finder was, in good faith, unaware of the council's prohibition on the use of metal detectors which is possibly one reason why the Court of Appeal chose to see the finder as a trespasser rather than a park-user.

(b) Interference with land

Land does not present quite the same property problems in that it cannot be stolen as such. The owner or rightful possessor can only be dispossessed and the main tort remedy here – trespass – is one of the oldest in English law.[155] Trespass deals with a direct invasion of possessory title to land and, as a result, it may be available to a possessor against the actual owner of the property.[156] All the same what actually constitutes an act of trespass can give rise to delicate problems not only in private law[157] but also in public law. Trespass to land is the main remedy used against government officials who abusively enter or destroy a person's property.[158] Indirect

152 M-F Papandréou-Deterville, *Fondement du droit anglais des biens* (*Thèse pour le doctorat en droit*, Université de Strasbourg III, 1996), p 125.

153 [1976] Ch 179.

154 See Auld LJ at p 785.

155 The dispossessed owner of land also has a real remedy at common law which is quite separate from an action in trespass: A Burrows, *Remedies for Torts and Breach of Contract* (Butterworths, 2nd edn, 1994), p 458.

156 *McPhail v Persons Unknown* [1973] Ch 447; *cf Delaney v TP Smith Ltd* [1946] KB 393.

157 See eg *Bernstein v Skyviews & General Ltd* [1978] QB 497.

158 *Cooper v Wandsworth Board of Works* (1863) 143 ER 414; *Robson v Hallett* [1967] 2 QB 939; *cf* Police and Criminal Evidence Act 1984 ss 15–19; Security Service Act 1989 s 3; Intelligence Services Act 1994 s 5.

invasions which interfere with the possessor's enjoyment of the l
a claim in private nuisance (*cf* Ch 12 § 5(b)) and here agai
defendant's unreasonable use of land is objective rather than fault-bas
public interest question can often arise via the defence of locality or as a resu
attaching to a remedy such as an injunction (*cf* Ch 4 § 1(b)).[159] Moreover, when a
person sues for physical damage to property fault of some kind is usually necessary.[160]

Private nuisance actions are usually available only for and against those with an interest in land[161] and this means that private nuisance is not a particularly suitable tort for general protection of the environment.[162] Pollution and environmental problems have usually to be tackled in public law through the use of statutory nuisance,[163] public nuisance (*cf* Ch 12 § 4(b)) or other statutory provisions and the remedies here might well depend upon the willingness of the local authority or some other public body to pursue the matter.[164] Landowners damaged by escaping things might be able to sue under the fault principle;[165] however, if the escaping thing is foreseeably dangerous in itself they might have an action under the (so-called) strict liability rule of *Rylands v Fletcher* (*cf* Ch 12 § 2(a)) or under certain strict liability statutory provisions.[166] In cases of undue noise or smell the remedy of injunction is probably the most appropriate[167] since there is a danger that damages in private nuisance for intangible harm might be somewhat modest.[168]

9 ECONOMIC LOSS

The nature of the damage can be of relevance in another way when it comes to the escape of a dangerous thing. Under statute a person suffering 'injury or damage' as a result of the escape of nuclear radiation is entitled to compensation without proving fault.[169] Does this cover the economic loss arising from the fall in the price of a house situated in the neighbourhood of a nuclear processing plant from which radiation has been leaking? The answer would appear to be that compensation is not available under statute because 'injury or damage' is to be interpreted as excluding pure economic loss.[170] Compensation is payable only in cases of physical injury.

This dichotomy between physical damage and financial loss is, as we have seen (*cf* Ch 6 § 3(a)), a characteristic of the tort of negligence and this characteristic was

159 See eg *Miller v Jackson* [1977] QB 966.

160 *Cambridge Water Co v Eastern Counties Leather Plc* [1994] 2 AC 264.

161 But *cf Khorasandijian v Bush* [1993] QB 727.

162 See eg *Esso Petroleum Co Ltd v Southport Corporation* [1953] 3 WLR 773; [1954] 2 QB 182; [1956] AC 218.

163 Environmental Protection Act 1990 ss 79–82.

164 Note the defence of 'best practicable means' in the 1990 Act: s 80(7).

165 *Leakey v National Trust* [1980] QB 485.

166 See eg Civil Aviation Act 1982 s 76(2).

167 *Kennaway v Thompson* [1981] QB 88.

168 *Bone v Seale* [1975] 1 All ER 787.

169 Nuclear Installations Act 1965 s 12.

170 *Merlin v British Nuclear Fuels Plc* [1990] 2 QB 557.

pecifically referred to by the court in its interpretation of 'injury or damage' in the escaping radiation case.[171] English law would, accordingly, appear to distinguish between loss, injury and damage[172] and in order to be able to obtain compensation for pure economic loss the relevant legal action must be one designed to compensate for this kind of harm.[173] Now an action in contract, and certain tort actions, will undoubtedly compensate for financial loss, in addition to compensating damage or injury, in that these actions are clearly designed to protect, *inter alia*, economic interests.[174] Accordingly 'special damage' resulting from a public nuisance will include financial loss[175] and injury to commercial patrimonies caused by certain kinds of wrongful acts or misleading statements (above § 1) may well be actionable via the so-called 'economic torts'.[176] However, when it comes to the tort of negligence, together with certain other torts such as breach of statutory duty, the duty of the defendant traditionally extended no further than 'damage or injury'. In other words, there was no duty in respect of pure economic loss.[177] This principle can be expressed another way: the tort of negligence was designed to protect physical interests in the person and in property and consequently those who do not suffer damage have no legitimate interest in the negligence *actio*.[178] Moreover, this position regarding interests also extended to the law of damages in that, in a negligence action, the court would distinguish between *damnum emergens* and *lucrum cessans* (*cf* Ch 6) in those cases where the substance of the action was a claim for the loss of a profit-earning chattel.[179]

The distinction between loss and damage has important consequences in both commercial and consumer law. In commercial law physical damage to a profit-earning chattel or other asset amounts to damage only for those having an actual proprietary interest in the chattel; those with a contractual right to the thing damaged are deemed to suffer loss and, prima facie, are owed no duty of care.[180] In consumer law the tort of negligence is traditionally available only to those who suffer physical damage to their person or property; compensation for the damaged product itself – loss arising from a bad bargain – has to be obtained through the law of contract.[181] Before 1972 these rules were fairly well established and seen as part of the general principle that

171 *Ibid* at p 572.

172 On the whole topic of 'damage' in English civil liability see T Weir, '*La notion de dommage en responsabilité civile*,' in: Legrand (ed), pp 1–55.

173 See eg Consumer Protection Act 1987 s 5(1), (2).

174 Note in this respect the language of statutes designed to protect economic interests: Air Travel Reserve Fund Act 1975 s 2; Financial Services Act 1986 ss 62(1), 150(1), 166(1); Courts and Legal Services Act 1990 s 44(1); and compare with statutes designed to protect other interests: State Immunity Act 1978 s 5; Civil Aviation Act 1982 s 76(2); Consumer Protection Act 1987 s 5; Housing Act 1988 s 27(3).

175 *Benjamin v Storr* (1874) LR 9 CP 400; *Tate & Lyle v GLC* [1983] 2 AC 509.

176 Weir, *Casebook*, pp 545–48.

177 See eg *Weller & Co v Foot & Mouth Disease Research Institute* [1966] 1 QB 569.

8 *Cf* NCPC art 31; NBW Bk 3 art 303.

partan Steel & Alloys Ltd v Martin & Co [1973] 1 QB 27.

181 *Aliakmon* [1986] AC 785; but *cf* Carriage of Goods by Sea Act 1992 s 2(1).

Marten Ltd v McManus Childs Ltd [1969] 1 AC 454, 469.

compensation was not available in the tort of negligence for pure economic loss. However, there were some areas of uncertainty. Loss arising from a negligent misstatement has been recoverable in tort since 1964 (above § 1(a)), but this could, and still can,[182] be seen as arising out of a special relationship which has more in common with contract and fiduciary relationships than with traditional damage cases.[183] In addition to these special relationship problems, a number of factual situations could give rise to problems of distinguishing between damage and loss.

In 1972 both of these uncertainties came together when a purchaser of a house, which subsequently turned out to be physically defective because it was built on insecure foundations, successfully sued a local authority for negligence on the basis of it having carelessly approved, pursuant to a statutory power, the foundations.[184] Was the harm suffered by the house purchaser physical damage (the walls were badly cracked) or was it only economic loss (she had purchased a bad bargain)? In 1978 the House of Lords decided that it was physical damage.[185] A year or so later another court decided that the loss of an expectation could be recoverable beyond the special relationship structure (above § 1) normally associated with negligent misstatement.[186] The way was now open to extend the duty of care beyond physical damage and into the area of economic loss.

This step was seemingly taken by the House of Lords some short time after,[187] but almost immediately there was a counter-revolution resulting in the re-establishment of the special relationship based on a near-to-contract structure.[188] The extension of the tort of negligence into the area of loss proved, it seems, to have been out of tune with the enterprise culture of the Thatcher years.[189] Twelve years after its decision holding the local authority liable for what was, subsequently, seen as a loss rather than damage, the House of Lords changed its mind and overruled its decision which had made local authorities liable in such circumstances.[190] The position now seems to be not only that investors and property speculators must carry their own losses rather than try to blame others,[191] but that consumers,[192] employees[193] and even schoolboys[194] may be caught by the re-emphasis of dichotomy between loss and damage. According to the House of

182 *Smith v Bush* [1990] 1 AC 831.

183 G Samuel 'Equity and the Legal Divisions – Part I' (1986) 37 NILQ 211, 223–26.

184 *Dutton v Bognor Regis UDC* [1972] 1 QB 372.

185 *Anns v Merton LBC* [1978] AC 728.

186 *Ross v Caunters* [1980] Ch 297; affirmed in *White v Jones* [1995] 2 AC 207.

187 *Junior Books v Veitchi Co Ltd* [1983] AC 520.

188 *Murphy v Brentwood DC* [1991] 1 AC 398, 481.

189 BA Hepple & MH Matthews, *Tort: Cases and Materials* (Butterworths, 4th edn, 1991), p 151.

190 *Murphy v Brentwood DC* [1991] 1 AC 398. However, this change of viewpoint applies only to the UK common law: *Invercargill City Council v Hamlin* [1996] 2 WLR 367 (PC).

191 *Caparo Industries Plc v Dickman* [1990] 2 AC 605; *Davis v Radcliffe* [1990] 1 WLR 821

192 Consumer Protection Act 1987 s 5(2).

193 *Reid v Rush & Tomkins Plc* [1990] 1 WLR 212.

194 *Van Oppen v Bedford Charity Trustees* [1990] 1 WLR 235.

Lords the causing of physical damage has universally to be justified, but the infliction of economic loss does not; in order to recover in the tort of negligence for such loss something more is required than the mere foreseeability of such loss.[195] The defendant must be under a duty to protect the specific financial interest of the particular plaintiff in question. For the notion of duty does not attach to abstract notions of person and injury but to actual individual legal subjects and to actual kinds of harm;[196] liability is descriptive and analogical rather than institutional and deductive.[197]

10 CONCLUDING REMARKS

The distinction between loss and damage serves to remind the obligations lawyer that the common law often starts out from empirical rather than scientific notions. The forms of action responded to types of harm rather than to species of obligation and this historical characteristic is still to be found in the various causes of action. And even contract continues to differentiate between a claim for a price for goods sold, or service provided, and an action in compensation. Nevertheless, this emphasis on the nature of the harm raises a more general question. What are the concepts which provoke decisions in contract, tort and restitution cases and how do they relate, if at all, to a normative system of obligations? The question is important in the context of the EU since, for better or for worse, there is a desire to harmonise private law. In this context the economic loss debate in English negligence law is not just an issue concerning the scope of the law of obligations; it raises more fundamental questions about technique and methods in law. For as Pierre Legrand has observed with regard to the economic loss case of *White v Jones*,[198] the reasoning used by Lord Goff to arrive at his solution was of a kind that a civil lawyer could never have employed.[199] Xavier Blanc-Jouvan expresses similar fears with regard to the *mentalités* of common lawyers and French lawyers.[200] If there exists, therefore, such a conceptual gap when it comes to science and technique there must be a more general problem about whether the notion of a law of obligations can ever have the status and meaning that it has in the civil law.

---

195 *Murphy v Brentwood DC* [1991] 1 AC 398, 487; *Caparo Industries Plc v Dickman* [1990] 2 AC 605, 643.

196 *Caparo Industries Plc v Dickman* [1990] 2 AC 605, 651.

197 See eg *X (Minors) v Bedfordshire CC* [1995] 2 AC 633, 751, 762–63.

198 [1995] 2 AC 207.

199 P Legrand, 'Legal Traditions in Western Europe: The Limits of Commonality', in R Jagtenberg, E Örücü & AJ de Roo (eds), *Transfrontier Mobility of Law* (Kluwer, 1995), p 72.

200 R David & X Blanc-Jouvan, *Le droit anglais* (PUF, 7th edn, 1994), p 125.

CHAPTER FOURTEEN

HARMONISATION AND THE LAW OF OBLIGATIONS

The adoption by common lawyers of the civilian generic category of the law of obligations goes far in suggesting, if not actually implying, the possibility of European harmonisation of private law. This possibility has been given added impetus by the European Parliament's calls in 1989 and 1994 for the elaboration of a European civil code.[1] In addition, there seems to be considerable doctrinal support, in continental Europe if not in the United Kingdom, for increasing harmonisation and, accordingly, in 1994 a collaborative work *Towards a European Civil Code* was published in English by a Dutch academic press.[2] This collaborative work, while accepting that harmonisation of private law was not yet a realistic project, nevertheless viewed with 'enthusiasm' the possibility of a European code capable of acting as a framework and a 'source of inspiration' for convergence.[3] It is the purpose of this concluding chapter to reflect upon English law in the context of a European law of obligations.

1 THE POSSIBILITY OF HARMONISATION

Similarity and difference is often a question of degree and it would thus be idle to suggest that between all the legal systems of Europe there is an absence of much that is common. Contract in France and in England might well be based upon different starting points (*cf* Ch 8 § 5), but the idea of a *vinculum iuris* between two persons acting as a form of private legislation is a notion that, more or less, is probably shared by many French and English lawyers. Or, put another way, a law of enforceable agreements is something that the common law would be happy to accept even if promise and consideration turn out to be quite different ideas than *conventio* and *causa*. In addition, the principles of wrongfully caused harm and unjustly acquired benefits act, at varying degrees of abstraction (even within the civilian systems), as direct or indirect normative motivators of damages and debt claims throughout the EU.

(a) The *ius commune*

From an historical position it has to be said that at first sight there appears to be little in common between the civil and the common law (*cf* Ch 3 § 4). Yet according to Reinhard Zimmermann 'a common European legal culture, centred around a common legal science and informed by the same sources, did once exist'.[4] Up until the 17th

1 Resolution of 26 May 1989 *OJEC* No C 158/401 of June 26 1989; EP 207 670/13 [1994] *OJ* C 205/518.

2 Hartkamp *et al*. See also B De Witte & C Forder (eds), *The common law of Europe and the future of legal education* (Kluwer, 1992).

3 E Hondius, in Hartkamp *et al*, p 13.

4 R Zimmermann, 'Roman Law and European Legal Unity', in Hartkamp *et al*, at p 67.

century there was the tradition of the *ius commune* which gave Europe a common legal grammar and this common grammar informed not only all the systems of the civilian tradition, but also endowed English law with a certain European character.[5] Indeed Zimmermann castigates Baker's statement, reprinted in 1990, that 'English law flourished in noble isolation from Europe'[6] as a complete myth.[7] In reality, says Zimmermann, English legal thought was never cut off from the continental culture in that Roman law, canon law and the *lex mercatoria* all influenced aspects of English and Scottish legal literature. Moreover, in the 18th and 19th centuries the links between civil and common law were particularly strong.[8] Accordingly, the possibility that Roman law could act as a means for achieving European legal unity is 'a programmatic topic'. Legal historians can contribute to harmonisation by 'fostering an awareness that a common legal tradition (which has indelibly been imprinted by Roman law) still informs our modern national legal systems'. A new *ius commune* can be carved out of a common systematic, conceptual, dogmatic and ideological foundation which has been buried under the debris of legal particularisation over the past 200 years; and a renewed intellectual contact can be made between positive law, comparative law and doctrinal legal scholarship – 'a contact which has largely been disrupted by the modern codifications'.[9]

Arguably, one of the most positive aspects of this Zimmermann thesis is its insistence that a knowledge of Roman law remains vital to any harmonisation project. Even if one is sceptical about a new *ius commune*, or about any meeting of minds between English and continental jurists, there remains an important role for Roman law in that, in its original form, it was a system which had as little in common with the modern codes as it supposedly has with the common law.[10] Roman law might, then, have the ability to act as a mediating system between English law and continental law. Indeed for Franz Pringsheim classical Roman law actually has more in common with modern English law than it has with modern civil law.[11]

(b) The inner relationship between English and Roman law

Given Zimmermann's emphasis on the role of Roman law in the movement towards harmonisation, the Pringsheim thesis is worth developing in a little more depth. According to Pringsheim classical Roman law and common law were connected by an 'inner relationship'. This inner relationship was based on the idea that both systems had

5 *Ibid*, at pp 69, 75 ff.

6 Baker, p 35.

7 Zimmermann, *op cit*, p 75.

8 On this point see also P Stein, 'Continental Influences on English Legal Thought 1600–1900', in P Stein, *The Character and Influence of the Roman Civil Law* (Hambledon, 1988), 224.

9 Zimmermann, *op cit*, p 80. See also G van den Bergh, '*Ius commune*, a History with a Future?', in De Witte & Forder, *op cit*, 593

10 M Villey, *La formation de la pensée juridique moderne* (Montchrestien, 4e ed, 1975), pp 526–28, 548–51.

11 F Pringsheim, 'The Inner Relationship Between English and Roman Law' [1935] CLJ 347

a 'taste for the particular, for the characteristic, for reality and reasonableness apart from all abstract ideas';[12] and, in turn, these similar tastes were based upon a similarity of 'spirit'. This *Volksgeist* was not, according to Pringsheim. amenable to rational explanation since it was an aspect of 'the fundamental character of a nation' which 'will always remain a secret'. Indeed 'it is not at all desirable to attack' such national characteristics 'with rational considerations'.[13] Roman law and common law were, accordingly, bound together, not by a history of causal events, but by a spiritual bond that lay deep in the national characters of two peoples. It was a connection that transcended history.

Evidently, such a thesis is open to ridicule. Nevertheless, weak concepts like the *Volksgeist* can prove extremely fertile in facilitating a re-orientation in theoretical thinking and it has to be observed that Pringsheim was not alone in his view that Roman and common lawyers appear to exhibit similar mentalities. Michel Villey and Zweigert and Kötz also comment upon the similarity of methods between English and Roman lawyers.[14] More importantly, perhaps, when one examines the texts from the two legal systems there are some striking similarities. For example, the classical Roman jurist, like the traditional common lawyer, thought in terms of remedies rather than rights; that is to say, both sets of jurists started out from the form of an action and worked from there towards a solution (*cf* Ch 1 § 3). *Ubi remedium ibi ius* (where there is a remedy there is a right). Furthermore, Roman lawyers and common lawyers tend to reason at the level of facts rather than at the level of a structured set of interrelating and abstract principles. Now this is not to suggest that within these facts there are not conceptual models of institutions and institutional relationships in play. It has already been noted that there are key elements and relations operating within the facts (*cf* Ch 1 § 1(c)). The point to be made is that legal development is largely a matter of pushing outwards from the facts: it is a matter of jurists hypothetically varying the facts and considering, on a 'what-if?' basis what the legal effect of such hypothetical variations would be.[15] It is a matter of pushing outwards from the facts: *ex facto ius oritur* (law arises out of fact).

(c) The history of science

These similarities do not of course depend upon any common *Volksgeist* as such. They can be explained quite rationally by the history of science which shows that it is a common feature of scientific development that a science passes through four stages of development. According to Robert Blanché, one should not think in terms of a binary division between the concrete and the abstract sciences; rather, one should see all sciences following the same development, although at different times, from an initial to

12 *Ibid*, at p 358.

13 *Ibid*, at p 365.

14 Villey, *op cit*, p 700; Zweigert & Kötz, pp 193–94.

15 T Weir, 'Contracts in Rome and England' (1992) 66 *Tulane LR* 1615, 1617; M Salter, 'Towards a Phenomenology of Legal Thinking' (1992) 23 *Journal of the British Society for Phenomenology* 167, 172; Samuel, *Foundations*, pp 191–96.

a final stage. The initial stage is the descriptive and the final stage the axiomatic; in between these two stages there is an inductive and a deductive stage respectively.[16] When this scheme is applied to legal science the inner relationship between classical Roman and common law becomes evident: both systems functioned within the inductive stage of scientific development with the result that they appear at odds with the modern codified civilian systems which in the 16th to 18th centuries passed from the inductive to the deductive stages to arrive, in the era of the codes, at an axiomatic stage.[17] This axiomatic stage is characterised by a model of rules functioning as a closed system – a pyramid – where all concepts are rigorously defined and completely divorced from the world of fact.[18]

The methodology associated with the deductive and axiomatic stages of legal science is quite different from that used in the descriptive and inductive stages. For a start, the axiomatic approach is one that sees legal knowledge as being completely divorced from the facts of society and social disputes. Legal rules are analogous to numbers and thus function according to their own conceptual symmetries and systematics. The result, in terms of the methodology associated with such an approach, is that the application of the law aspires to be simply a matter of formal logic. The abstract rule as found in a code provision forms the major premise and the set of litigation facts the minor premise; the conclusion – that is to say, the solution to the legal problem – automatically follows from the juxtaposition of the two premises. As one French writer has put it:

> The courts are entrusted with the duty of establishing the facts from which flow the legal consequences to apply having regard to the legal system in force. Once the facts are established, a legal syllogism is enough, whereby the rule of law constitutes the major premise, the established facts as envisaged by the conditions of the rule the minor premise and the court decision the conclusion. ... This implies that for each situation submitted to the judge there would be a legal rule applicable, that there would be only one and that this rule would be devoid of any ambiguity ... The legal system is, at the end of the day, assimilated to a deductive system constructed on the model of axiomatic systems existing in geometry or arithmetic.[19]

In terms of 'spirit', one can talk of a *mos geometricus* where 'the articles of the Code are no more than the number of theorems required to demonstrate the connection and to draw out the consequences: the pure jurist is a mathematician'.[20] In other words, an essential part of legal knowledge is to be found in the symmetrical architecture of the reasoning (deductive) model itself.

The methodology to be found in the inductive stage of legal science is, in contrast, very different even if it does on occasions make use of the syllogism (*cf* Ch 3 § 2). As

16 R Blanché, *L'épistémologie* (PUF, 3e éd, 1983), p 65.

17 Samuel, *Foundations*, pp 83–84.

18 Zweigert & Kötz, p 146.

19 G Timsit, *Thèmes et systèmes de droit* (PUF, 1986), pp 106–07.

20 L Liard, *L'enseignement supérieur* (1894), p 397 quoted in P Dubouchet, *La pensée juridique avant et après le Code civil* (L'Hermès, 2nd edn, 1991), p 127.

we have seen with Roman law (Ch 1 § 1(c)), one searches for the legal solution within the facts themselves rather than within some abstract conceptual model. Definition of various notions such as 'possession' or 'consent' might vary according to the circumstances in play. Moreover, there is no clear distinction between substantive and procedural ideas as the *Esso* case so clearly demonstrates (*cf* Ch 1 § 7(a)); and success or failure can depend upon whether electricity is analogous to water or an explosive shell is analogous to a dangerous animal (*cf* Ch 3 § 2(c)). The role of the court in an inductive system is simply to do justice between the parties, for there is no duty on the judges to rationalise the law since facts themselves have a tendency to baffle even the most intelligent human mind.[21] In an inductive legal science the art of deciding (*ars judicandi*) is still to be distinguished from the abstract organisation of law (*scientia iuris*) since the practitioner, unlike the professor, is little interested in constructing universal theories of knowledge.[22] The practitioner is content with a patchwork of concepts operating at a low level of abstraction.

(d) The retreat from science

The difference of mentality seemingly so clearly evident in any comparison of an English law report with its French counterpart (*cf* Ch 1 § 7) is, then, a difference not of spirit but of science and technique. In the civil law tradition *scientia iuris* and *ars judicandi* became merged in a *jurisprudentia rationalis*,[23] but in the common law there is little sympathy for the view that 'a judicial decision should be arrived at solely by an abstract juridical dialectic, without regard to those reasons of the heart for which the reason has at best but an indifferent understanding'.[24] Reasoning in the common law stretches beyond the juridical dialectic. Now there is no doubt that when Pringsheim gave his lecture the gap between the inductive and axiomatic approaches was real enough in the minds of jurists, however much of a myth the language of mathematics was proving to be in the reality of case law problem-solving. But it has to be asked if today this dichotomy between the inductive and the axiomatic is still valid. Do French and German judges still believe that the solutions to all legal problems are to be found in some abstract model constructed along the lines of mathematical logic? The answer is that while no culture can ever escape its own cultural history – and in France and Germany the influence of Wolff, Descartes, Leibniz and Savigny remains distinctive – there is no doubting that legal science has moved beyond the axiomatic stage.[25]

(e) Post-axiomatic stage of legal science

This movement beyond the axiomatic is evidenced, at the level of methodology, by the increasing movement away from logic towards argumentation. Civil law writers no

21 D.22.6.2.

22 Samuel, *Foundations*, pp 103–16.

23 P Dubouchet, *op cit*, p 78.

24 Lord Simon in *AG v Times Newspapers Ltd* [1974] AC 273, 315.

25 CM Stamatis, *Argumenter en droit: Une théorie critique de l'argumentation juridique* (Publisud, 1995), pp 34–50.

longer think that legal method consists of formal logic and hard conceptual models. Instead the focus is on dialectical reasoning and the methods of rhetoric;[26] for it is now recognised that law cannot be limited just to exercises in thinking since it has to allow for the satisfaction of the concrete requirements of everyday social life.[27] There is an increasing acceptance that behind the formality of the structured syllogism there is an interpretative process at work which cannot be explained just in terms of *scientia iuris*.[28] It is the lawyer and judge and not abstract propositions which act as the true source of law when it comes to actual problem-solving.

Théodore Ivainer in France for example argues that the *ars judicandi* is not in truth a matter of propositional knowledge founded on a logical application of the code.[29] It is a matter of interpretation of the facts. The approach, he claims, is still interpretative (hermeneutic) in method in that one is teasing out 'hidden facts' (*les faits inconnus*) from known facts (*les faits connus*).[30] But the point he emphasises is that the *ars judicandi* – the art of judging – is to be found in the movement from structuring the facts to choosing and inventing the normative principle, a process which involves the use of fuzzy concepts (*les concepts flous*). These concepts – for example, fault, damage, interests, good faith – act not only as the bridge between the facts and the text but also as the means by which the judges can inject into the act of interpretation their system, or systems, of values. 'If the starting point (fuzzy) is to be found in the legislative text', writes Ivainer, 'the evaluation of the context will be in the system of values chosen by the judge.' And so 'although the legal information is abstract and rigid, the legislative text never having its feet on the ground since it sets its sights only on categories, the distinctive feature of axiology is to operate *in concreto* in getting into the innermost recesses of life as it actually unfolds.'[31]

Instead of continuing to talk, then, of a clash between the inductive (common law) and the axiomatic (codes) it might be more desirable for those legal scientists keen on harmonisation in Europe to think in terms of a new epistemological stage beyond that of the axiomatic. This new stage would be forward-looking in that it would invite the epistemologist to think not in terms of a backward step to the inductive and descriptive, but towards a dialectical creation arising out of the tensions between descriptive and inductive methodology on the one hand and deductive and axiomatic techniques on the other. The post-axiomatic stage might be one where the dichotomy between science (law) and object of science (legal facts) is seen in terms of a single model; the 'geometry', in other words, becomes more concrete and the concrete more abstract. For 'the concrete is simply the abstract rendered familiar by usage'.[32]

26 See eg Ch Perelman, *Logique juridique: Nouvelle rhétorique* (Dalloz, 2e ed, 1979).

27 J-L Bergel, *Théorie générale du droit* (Dalloz, 2nd edn, 1989), para 249.

28 *Ibid*, paras 252–53.

29 T Ivainer, *L'interprétation des faits en droit* (LGDJ, 1988).

30 *Ibid*, pp 84–86.

31 *Ibid*, p 337.

32 P Langevin, quoted in R Blanché, *La science actuelle et le rationalisme* (PUF, 2nd edn, 1973), p 54.

(f) The inner relationship between English and French law

A post-axiomatic stage might also act as a contextual category in which some of the tensions between conceptualism and realism are finally rethought. The civilians have provided Europe with the idea of a system of rules logically and coherently arranged and this notion of system will continue to play an important role in understanding a law of obligations.[33] Yet law is also about values.[34] And these values might be said to be something which, in a post-axiomatic world, help endow the legal model with a 'plurality of images by which today's science can be represented, because of the presence here of different epistemological conceptions' forcing one to accept 'the full legitimacy of the existence of several methodologies'.[35] This plurality of images can be found even within the class of lawyers themselves: for example, the legal historian and the legal theorist may well have quite different conceptions of contract than the legal practitioner.[36] On the other hand, whatever the conceptual differences between the common law and the civil law (or between sub-groups within the legal class), all systems recognise, for example, that people are more valuable than things. And, more technically, all member states, together with the EU as an institution, accept, say, that consumers need more protection than *commerçants* and *professionnels* (Ch 8 § 4).

John Bell uses this focal point of values as a means, if not of harmonising English and French law, at least of establishing a fundamental relationship between the two traditions.[37] According to Bell the criticism that is often levelled at continental lawyers that they are lovers of concepts for their own elegance is misleading since 'there is ample evidence that, in fact, the French are as pragmatic and instrumentalist as the English, not only in public law areas such as public service, but in private law as well'.[38] French judges, in contrast to academic writers, make use of many of the same techniques as their English counterparts in arriving at their solutions, the conceptual and logical approach having been simply a creation of the law faculties trying to gain respectability much in the same way as English faculties were to do 50 years later. Bell's thesis, mirroring the conclusions of Ivainer,[39] seems to be that a distinction between *ars judicandi* and *scientia iuris* was always to be found in French law. The former exists in the conclusions of the *Ministère public*, the reports of the *juge rapporteur* and even in the notes accompanying the publication of cases; the latter informs the style of the actual written decision and much of the academic writing.

John Bell is of the view that the comparatist should be looking beyond legal concepts. The 'important driving force for legal thinking is not the self-perpetuating

33 *Cf* M van de Kerchove & F Ost, *Legal System Between Order and Disorder* (Oxford, 1994; trans I Stewart).

34 P Stein & J Shand, *Legal Values in Western Society* (Edinburgh, 1974).

35 V Villa, *La science du droit* (LGDJ/Story-Scientia, 1990; French trans O Nerhot & P Nerhot), p 29.

36 C Atias, *Épistémologie du droit* (PUF, 1994), pp 119–20.

37 J Bell, 'English Law and French Law – Not So Different?' (1995) 48 CLP 63.

38 *Ibid*, at p 98.

39 See also M Lasser, Judicial (Self-)Portraits: Judicial Discourse in the French Legal System (1995) 104 Yale LJ 1325.

logic of the legal concepts', he writes, 'but the values which the law is trying to enforce and lawyers to implement'.[40] Legal concepts are just building blocks to present arguments and it is values which actually determine the kind of building to be constructed. It is a matter of form rather than substance and, accordingly, the work of those comparatists who emphasise a difference of mentality between English and French law are in danger of finding that their work does not stand up to scrutiny. It is a myth based on the form of academic writing rather than the substance of judicial decision. Accordingly, the comparatist, using comparative law as a tool for getting over the initial disorientation caused by the way different legal systems present themselves, should be building upon these 'fundamentally common ways of thinking as lawyers' so as to facilitate common work on a future European agenda.[41]

2 THE OBSTACLES TO HARMONISATION

The Zimmermann and Bell view of European legal culture does not go unchallenged. In contrast to these writers who see only *rapprochement* there are others who continue to perceive only *la différence*. Just as the European languages cannot be reduced to a harmonised common discourse, so language-dependent legal systems remain closed cultural traditions.[42]

(a) Non-convergence of civil and common law

One of the most articulate and sustained criticisms of the whole *corpus iuris Europaeum* movement comes from Pierre Legrand. According to this author 'there exist in Europe irreducibly distinctive modes of legal perception and thinking, that the ambition of a European *concordantia* is (and must be) a chimera, that European legal systems are not converging'.[43] Legrand is adamant that the common law *mentalité* is irreducibly different from the civil law's for a number of reasons. The common law neither thinks in terms of rules nor cares for systematics – two features essential to the continental tradition – and, in addition, it has little understanding of the notion of a 'right' in the French sense of *un droit subjectif.* The English lawyer works primarily at the level of fact and uses on occasions reasoning arguments that no self-respecting civilian judge could ever find acceptable at the cognitive level.[44] Rather than harmonising these differences, the present interrelationship between the civil and common law within the European Union serves only to exacerbate them.

Legrand does not deny that, say, French law and English law can arrive at similar conclusions with respect to a similar fact situation. What he says is that to argue that such similarity of conclusion is evidence of similarity of mentality is to miss the point.[45]

40 Bell, *op cit*, p 98.

41 *Ibid*, p 101.

42 T Weir, '*Die Sprachen des europäischen Rechts*' [3/1995] ZEuP 368.

43 P Legrand, 'European Legal Systems are not Converging' (1996) 45 ICLQ 52, 81.

44 P Legrand, 'Legal Traditions in Western Europe: The Limits of Commonality', in R Jagtenberg, E Örücü & AJ de Roo (eds), *Transfrontier Mobility of Law* (Kluwer, 1995), p 72.

45 *Ibid*, p 74.

Each system arrives at its conclusion using a particular legal 'frame of mind' and these frames of mind are as different as those behind two linguistic propositions expressed in two quite different European languages.[46] The legal frame of mind involves acts of cognitive internalisation which cannot be reduced to a common denominator and, furthermore, the 'existence of a common historical reservoir, such as the *jus commune*, will not help to dispel the lack of appreciation by common law lawyers of the notions of "system" or "rule", as understood by civilians, nor will it serve to efface the lack of understanding by civilians of the importance of facts or the significance of the past at common law'.[47] Legal integration is doomed to failure unless it takes these differences of *mentalité* and culture into account.[48]

(b) The weakness of comparative law

A critic might respond that Pierre Legrand is focusing too much on the empty form of legal architecture rather than upon the solid substance of the social values which determine the actual shape and design of the building to be constructed. After all, as both Zimmermann and Bell make clear, the role of the comparatist is to facilitate a 'working together in building a common system'[49] at the level of legal education (Bell) or legal science (Zimmermann) and that 'the best comparisons focus on concrete issues, rather than on grand distinctions between legal systems'.[50] These no doubt are valid points. Yet two aspects of Legrand's thesis need to be emphasised here.

First, Legrand's theory must be viewed in the wider context of his own pessimistic analysis of the state of comparative law in Europe today. Comparative legal studies is 'the work of indifferent intellectuals' which, when not banal and vacuous, betrays 'an almost complete absence of theoretical insight'.[51] Thus, when German authors talk of harmonisation through dogmatisation (*Dogmatisierung*) and legal science (*Rechtswissenschaft*), it in effect amounts to a form of intellectual imperialism since any sophisticated comparatist should know that the whole tradition of the common law is distinctly *Unwissenschaftlichkeit*.[52] The inability of comparative law to engage seriously with theory has, according to Legrand, become what Bachelard would have called an 'epistemological barrier'[53] and what is needed is a programme that functions 'as an act of defiance or rebellion' which will dislodge 'the comforting certainties of conventional knowledge thereby affording a means of liberation' from 'ineffectual research agendas' that suppose the existence of law as some kind of non-ideological construction which

46 *Ibid*, p 73.

47 *Ibid*, p 74.

48 *Ibid*, p 83.

49 Bell, *op cit*, p 101.

50 *Ibid*, p 63.

51 P Legrand, *Comparatists-at-Law and the Contrarian Challenge* (Inaugural Lecture, Tilburg University, 1995), p 3.

52 *Ibid*, pp 3–4.

53 *Ibid*, p 18.

exists as a perfect isomorphy of the world such-as-it-is.[54] The good comparatist should be 'continually making small erosions to the established order'.[55]

(c) Comparative law and legal epistemology

Secondly, Legrand is particularly concerned by the apparent lack of commitment on the part of any comparatist to engage with theory. He argues that the comparatist 'must engage in epistemological investigations, that is, ask how knowledge is constituted and how rationalities are shaped'; he or she 'must consider the historical background that defines the conditions of possibility of particular forms of knowledge'.[56] In other words, a central task of comparative law is to investigate the question of what it is to have knowledge of law.

This epistemological claim for comparative law is what underpins Legrand's insistence that European legal systems are not converging. If one sees, like John Bell, legal concepts simply as instrumental building blocks for a grand structure designed by social, political, economic and moral values, then harmonisation of an area like the law of obligations is only a matter of adjusting the instruments or re-arranging the building blocks so as create a common edifice. Comparative law, according to Bell, does not focus on rules, norms, systems and concepts as such; it draws attention 'to the cultural, social, religious, and economic setting of a legal system' and to the specific legal tradition 'which has a significant effect on the way functions are performed'.[57] Yet such a 'realist' view is founded on the epistemological assumption that to have knowledge of law is basically to have knowledge of cultural tradition and the problem with this theory is that it tells us almost nothing about what it is to have legal knowledge. Lawyers for Bell are social problem-solvers always in search of the 'pragmatic solution'. Thus, even though the conceptual approach in France and in England to a claim by the victim of a railway or supermarket accident may well be different in the two legal systems, there is 'a presumption of similarity at least in terms of the general range of outcomes achieved by each system'.[58] As far as Bell is concerned, the conceptual architecture is a superficial aspect of legal knowledge hardly, it would seem, worthy of attention from the epistemologist. Legrand, in contrast, is of the view that differences of conceptual framework go to the heart of legal knowledge itself and so, for example, the differences to be found in the way that a French court and an English court handle a legal problem such as that of damage caused by a thing (*cf* Ch 1 § 7) is not just a matter of legal form. It is very much part of the deep structure of legal knowledge.

54 *Ibid*, p 20.

55 *Ibid*.

56 *Ibid*, p 23.

57 J Bell, 'Comparative Law and Legal Theory', in Krawietz, MacCormick & Henrik von Wright (eds), *Prescriptive Formality and Normative Rationality in Modern Legal Systems* (Duncker & Humblot, 1995) 19, 31.

58 Bell, 'English Law and French Law', *op cit*, p 71.

3 HARMONISATION AND EPISTEMOLOGY

It may appear, at first sight, that Pierre Legrand's contribution to the question of harmonisation of private law in Europe is, in contrast to the contributions in *Towards a European Civil Code*, at best a negative one. To take such a view would be to commit a fundamental error. For Legrand is raising the level of a debate which has on the whole been characterised by false epistemological assumptions, if not triviality. Before a comparatist can talk of harmonising legal knowledge he or she ought to have some sophisticated appreciation of what it is to have such knowledge. And writers such as Christian Atias and Pierre Legrand are showing that jurists not only lack this knowledge, but seem little interested, these days, in acquiring it.[59]

(a) The failure of legal theory

Atias suggests that one reason why lawyers are little interested in the grand questions of legal theory is that law as a subject has become increasingly specialised. The vast growth in legislative rules and regulations has led to a decline of the generalist with the result that there is a confusion between law and knowledge of law.[60] This, as Atias goes on to stress, is a rather simplistic explanation since the real question is why such increasing specialisation should make knowledge of general principles less useful. Yet the observation remains an interesting one from a legal theory point of view since the vast increase in rules and regulations helps confirm the view that to have knowledge of law is to have knowledge of rules. Perhaps, then, one should not be surprised that much legal theory in this century is premised on the assumption that to have knowledge of law is to have knowledge of linguistic propositions (rules and principles).[61] Admittedly, there are propositions and propositions. To the empiricist such rules may be commands or something more sophisticated like primary and secondary rules; to the metaphysician it may be a question of norms, that is to say 'ought' (rather than 'is') propositions existing entirely detached from social reality and legal commands. Yet legal theorists, including comparatists, ought now to be aware that legal theory itself is in a state of crisis in that it has proved impossible to construct an expert system on the basis of the rule-thesis that actually functions like a living lawyer. 'There do not exist any true expert systems', as one writer interested in Artificial Intelligence (AI) observes, that is to say, 'systems which reason by themselves or which ... come to surprise'.[62]

This failure of legal theory in the face of AI has profound implications for legal harmonisation in that, as Legrand says, there are 'serious difficulties with an approach which focuses on posited law in order to draw conclusions regarding the convergence of legal systems'.[63] Together with concepts, rules reveal little about the deep structures

---

59 Atias, *op cit*, p 106.

60 *Ibid*, p 92.

61 R Susskind, *Expert Systems in Law* (Oxford, 1987), pp 78–79.

62 J Goulet, '*Quelques variations sur le modèle thermodynamique et le droit artificiel*', in D Bourcier & P Mackay *(sous la direction de)*, *Lire le droit: Langue, texte, cognition* (LGDJ, 1992), at p 38. See also H Dreyfus, *What Computers Still Can't Do* (MIT Press, 1992).

63 Legrand, European Legal Systems, *op cit*, p 55.

of legal systems. Now this does not mean that one is forced towards the Bell solution of abandoning the architectural form in search for value substance. Rather it suggests that the location of formal legal knowledge is to be found beyond the rules and this is where traditional legal theory is wanting. As Richard Susskind has noticed, AI has had to rely upon the rule-model because legal theory has provided no alternatives.[64] Accordingly, the question to be faced is whether there exist any models that go beyond the rules and into the depths of legal knowledge to act as the foundation for a deep structure. If such a structure can be found, and it is one that is equally valuable for both the common law and civilian tradition, then it is arguable that a more profound basis for legal harmonisation in Europe exists. But such a (post-axiomatic?) model must concern itself with all aspects of legal knowledge. It must cater at one and the same time for *rapprochement* and *différence*. It must provide an epistemological thesis that accounts for the outlooks of Zimmermann, of Bell, and of Legrand.

(b) Legal epistemology

The starting point is epistemology itself. What is it to have knowledge of law? The term 'epistemology' is derived from the Greek words *épistémé* and *logos* which meant the critical study of (*logos*) science (*épistémê*). In its most precise modern sense it means 'the critical study of the principles, the hypotheses and the results of the various sciences, with the purpose of determining their logical (not psychological) origin, their value and their objective scope'.[65] With regard to law it concerns the forms or modes by which legal assertions are produced and grounded.[66] These definitions are far from uncontroversial since not only is there ambiguity about the word itself – in the English speaking world, for example, 'epistemology' has a wider meaning than its French counterpart *épistémologie* – but there are problems with regard to approaches. Some see the subject as necessarily bound up with the history and evolution of the sciences, while others reject the diachronic (historical and evolutionary) approach in favour of the synchronic (direct and timeless).[67] Knowledge structures, in particular logic, are intellectually independent of the history of logic just as modern language or numeracy is independent of the history of a language or the history of mathematics. Translated into the world of the law of obligations, one might say that it is possible to have knowledge of such an area without having a knowledge of its history or histories.

Piaget has offered a compromise in suggesting that knowledge is not predetermined as such, either in the mind of the subject or in the object of study.[68] It is the result of a continuous and mediating structural development which forms through an interplay between the developing mind and object of study. The aim is to disengage the roots of the various types of knowledge from their most elementary form right up to their most

64 Susskind, *op cit*, p 154.

65 A Virieux-Reymond, *Introduction à l'épistémologie* (PUF, 2nd edn, 1972), p 7.

66 Atias, *op cit*, p 4.

67 Blanché, *op cit*, pp 29–45.

68 J Piaget, *L'épistémologie génétique* (PUF, 4th edn, 1988); Blanché, *op cit*, pp 39–45.

developed level.[69] Now whatever the value of Piaget's theory in the natural sciences,[70] his approach has certain attractions for legal knowledge in the way it suggests that both *ars judicandi* and *scientia iuris* result gradually from the interplay of rational structures and social fact. In the descriptive and inductive stages of legal development law functions within the facts: *ex facto ius oritur*. This does not mean, as we have seen with Roman legal reasoning (Ch 1 § 1(c)), that there are not conceptual and interrelating structures working within these facts; but they are not hardened models dictating the normative solutions. They are highly flexible structures operating within their own local 'blocks'.[71] They respond to local rather than universal models.[72] The art of judging is the art of fashioning and manipulating the right local model, perhaps using arguments from outside the model itself (as has been seen with Denning LJ in *Esso*: Ch 1 § 7(a)). However, when law moves from the inductive to the deductive and axiomatic stages this flexibility is to some extent sacrificed on the alter of scientific certainty in that what drives legal knowledge is the now interrelated, and thus 'knowable', structure which not only becomes divorced from social fact but goes far in determining it. *Ex iure factum oritur* (out of law fact arises).[73] What drives this knowledge is the hardened model with its logical distinctions – between rights *in rem* and *in personam*, for example – and its fixed symmetries between legal subjects and legal objects.[74]

Yet even within these hardened models the interplay between abstract structure and social fact does not disappear. As Ivainer and Bell show, *ars judicandi* still functions behind the façade of *scientia iuris*; and the reason for this continuing element of flexibility is to be found in the notion of fact rather than law. The model may have become hardened and relatively inflexible in terms of its symmetry (Ch 1 § 7(b)), but facts themselves remain chaotic with the result that the emphasis shifts on to the categorisation and re-categorisation of factual situations. An accident in a supermarket can be re-categorised from what seem at first sight 'tort' (delict) facts into a contractual situation in order to help the injured consumer obtain her compensation;[75] similarly 'quasi-contract' facts can be hardened into contractual ones to help the rescuer.[76] All facts are viewed through a pre-categorisation since facts are never evident in themselves. There is no such thing as raw fact in that all facts have sense only in relation to a pre-existing model or theory.[77] Nevertheless, there is a constant coming-and-going from legal model to perceived fact with the result that no legal proposition can ever account for the state of the law; at the level of the rule all is both true and false.[78]

69 *Ibid*, p 6.

70 For a criticism see eg H Barreau, *L'épistémologie* (PUF, 2nd edn, 1992), pp 12, 14.

71 A Watson, *The Making of the Civil Law* (Harvard, 1981), pp 14–22.

72 Samuel, *Foundations*, pp 212–15, 232–34.

73 Michel Villey located this development in the work of the Humanists and Grotius: see Villey, *op cit*, pp 507–51, 597–634.

74 See eg Zweigert & Kötz, p 146.

75 Cass civ 20.10.1964; DS.1965.62; Samuel, *Foundations*, pp 138–40; Rudden, pp 311–12.

76 Cass civ 1.12.1969; DS.1970.422; Rudden, p 314.

77 J-P Astolfi & M Develay, *La didactique des sciences* (PUF, 3rd edn, 1994), pp 25–27.

78 Atias, *op cit*, p 122.

What matters in the deductive and axiomatic stages is the symmetry; in a post-axiomatic world this symmetry leaves the world of concept to govern the world of fact.

(c) The epistemological assumption

This symmetry has not, as we have seen, been the primary object of legal knowledge. Attention, instead, has been on the linguistic proposition, on the notion of a rule. One can understand why this assumption has become so persuasive: the notion of a legal rule not only seems to transcend all legal systems, acting not just as the object of a general legal science which, in turn, is capable of acting as an epistemological device for explaining the various sources of legal knowledge, but also seems, empirically and historically, to have been the only object of legal theory since the Humanists. Indeed, despite the rejection of the rule model by the Roman classical jurists,[79] the student textbooks (*institutiones)*, legislative commands (*leges*) and general principles of law (*regulae iuris*) all went far in establishing the written proposition as the epistemological basis of legal science. This thesis received added confirmation by the location of the source of all law in the will of the emperor.[80]

Perhaps another, equally important, reason for the dominance of the rule model is to be found in the fact that both the science and the object of legal science can seemingly be reduced to propositional knowledge. Thus, the symmetry of the civil codes, a symmetry inherited from Justinian's *Institutes* (in turn based on Gaius' *Institutes*) (see Ch 1 § 1), is capable of being expressed, if only imperfectly, through a number of propositions which in turn act as the pillars of private law. The fundamental relationship between subject (*persona*) and object (*res*), although it seems not defined by the Romans themselves, is elegantly expressed as a proposition in article 544 of the *Code civil*: 'Ownership is the right to enjoy and dispose of things in the most absolute manner'. And even the Romans attempted to reduce the other key relationship, that is, the bond between two legal subjects, to a proposition; accordingly, in Justinian's *Institutes* an obligation is defined as 'a legal bond whereby we are constrained to do something according to the law of our state' (*iuris vinculum, quo necessitate adstringimur alicuius solvendae rei secundum nostrae civitatis iura*).[81]

These statements can, evidently, be seen as rules. And in addition they can be seen as organising propositions since they orientate legal thinking around two fundamental and symmetrical relationships. These relationships are the one between legal subject and legal object, relationships *in rem*, and the one between legal subject and legal subject, relationships *in personam*. Yet neither statement can in itself act as a complete form of legal knowledge since not only do these propositions depend, with respect to the information they are supposed to contain, upon each other – indeed upon other propositions within the legal system as well – but their very brevity as symbols means that they suffer from an acute loss of information. Thus, article 544 cannot function

79 D.50.17.1.

80 D.1.4.1.

81 J.3.13pr.

within a knowledge system that has no appreciation of the notion of 'a right' (*un droit*) and the definition of an obligation is dependent upon the metaphor of a *iuris vinculum*. Moreover, the notion of an obligation, that is to say a relationship *in personam*, has no meaning whatsoever outside of the system of relations which also contains relations *in rem*. The idea of a *ius in rem* or a *ius in personam* is dependent, then, not just on the symbolic representation in terms of a linguistic proposition, but also on the notion of a system and on the idea of relationships between elements. The system is as much a part of legal knowledge as is the proposition.

Now from an historical perspective, that is to say from the perspective of the history of legal science, the rule theorist might well argue that the notions of a right and of a system and its symmetry are contained, if not in the rule of ownership or obligation itself, in other linguistic propositions that interrelate with this rule. Legal knowledge is thus a question of knowing the propositions and of developing the skill of interpretation, that is to say, of teasing out of the symbolic knowledge representation structure, which acts as the object of legal knowledge, all the hidden propositional knowledge. It is a matter of *scientia iuris* and *ars hermeneutica*. And the great advantage of reducing the whole of legal knowledge to a symbolic representation, that is to say, to propositional knowledge (rules and principles), is that harmonisation between legal systems becomes only a question of time. It is, at worse, a matter of encouraging a system like that of the common law or classical Roman law to move, no doubt gradually, from an inductive stage of legal science to a deductive, if not axiomatic stage. Indeed one might see the whole textbook tradition of Anglo-American law as furthering this project since 'if they are good they are more than mere guides, for they seek not only to arrange the cases systematically but to extract from them the general principles of the law and to show how those principles may be developed'.[82] Viewed from a methodological standpoint, legal knowledge is a question of induction and deduction, where one moves from proposition to decision by means of what one English judge has called the complex syllogism (*cf* Ch 3 § 2). Such an approach would appear to be more or less in harmony with the approach of civilian judges in that, as we have seen, they too have abandoned the formal syllogism in favour of reasoning structures that are less simplistic.[83] The post-axiomatic is, the rule theorist might argue, little more than merging the inductive with the axiomatic.

(d) Symbolic and non-symbolic knowledge

The question, of course, is whether structures that are primarily visual can be reduced to linguistic propositions without a significant loss of information. Can a hierarchical pattern be adequately captured by the words genus and species, or categories and sub-categories, or can the full knowledge value of a structure only be appreciated in terms of non-symbolic imagery? Does one need, in other words, the mental image of a hierarchical structure before one can have knowledge of its knowledge possibilities?

82 HF Jolowicz, *Lectures on Jurisprudence* (Athlone, 1963), pp 314–15.

83 Atias, *op cit*, p 119.

Equally, can the symmetry between property rights and obligation rights be encapsulated by propositional definition, or can the full knowledge essence only be captured by the image of a bond (*vinculum iuris*) between person and thing and between person and person? Indeed is not the whole normative idea of a right founded on the image of a bond between right holder (subject) and right (thing)? In short, can patterns be captured by language?

The point of asking these questions is that while symmetry has a pleasing simplicity, it can also act as a forceful and complex obstacle to harmonisation of patterns of legal thought in that incompatibility of pattern within the analysis of a factual situation will give rise to an incompatibility at the level of analysis itself. For example, in the codes, the idea of a law of obligations is, as we have seen, defined in part through its opposition, in terms of a pattern of relationships, to a law of property; contract and possession are different because they involve two quite different relationships. In turn this difference of pattern gives rise to the fundamental dichotomy between real and personal rights which, in its turn, acts as the foundation for the normative differences between the law of property and the law of obligations.

(e) Transgressing the symmetry

But what if a legal system refuses to conform to this symmetry?[84] What if, as in English law, one can have a personal action (*actio in personam*) based upon a real right (*ius in rem*) (*cf* Ch 4 § 5(d))? In *Lipkin Gorman v Karpnale Ltd*[85] a firm of solicitors brought an action against a gambling casino for the return of money embezzled from their client account by one of their partners and gambled away at the defendants' club. According to Lord Goff, 'the solicitors seek to show that the money in question was their property at common law.' However, 'their claim in the present case for money had and received is nevertheless a personal claim; it is not a proprietary claim, advanced on the basis that money remaining in the hands of the respondents is their property.'[86] Turning briefly to equity, the Law Lord made the point that even if legal title to the money did vest in the fraudulent partner immediately on receipt, nevertheless he would have held it on trust for his partners, who would accordingly have been entitled to trace it in equity into the hands of the respondents. However, no such equitable tracing claim was advanced by the solicitors; they were, it seems, content to proceed at common law by a personal action, that is to say an action for money had and received. Returning to the facts of the case before him Lord Goff observed that before the partner drew upon the solicitors' client account at the bank, there was no question of the solicitors having any legal property in cash lying at the bank since the relationship of the bank with the solicitors was essentially that of debtor and creditor. But such 'a debt constitutes a chose

84 This section (together with one or two other parts of this present chapter) is based on a conference paper: G Samuel, 'Confronting the Historical and Epistemological Obstacles to Harmonisation' (*Geschichte und europäisches Privatrecht: Entwicklung gemeinsamer Methoden und Prinzipien*, Olin Foundation for Legal History, Florence, May/June 1995).

85 [1991] 2 AC 548.

86 At p 572.

in action, which is a species of property; and since the debt was enforceable at common law, the chose in action was legal property belonging to the solicitors at common law.'[87] Lord Goff accordingly concluded that in his opinion there was 'no reason why the solicitors should not be able to trace their property at common law in that chose in action, or in any part of it, into its product' since such 'a claim is consistent with their assertion that the money so obtained by [the fraudulent partner] was their property at common law.'[88]

There is in fact no institutional reason why a debt cannot be a form of property since it is easy enough to turn it into a *res* which one can then claim as one's own. Yet, to a civil lawyer, the whole purpose of the symmetry behind the relations *in rem* and *in personam* is to reflect the difference between owning and owing. To rearrange the symmetry, as indeed the English law of restitution is quite happy to do, raises a major obstacle to harmonisation in that there is actually little point in talking about a law of obligations since, as *Lipkin Gorman* illustrates, an *actio* such as a debt claim is neither a purely personal action in the Romanist sense of the term nor a purely *in rem* claim. It is, quite simply, a mixture of both.

In fact this intermixing of owning and owing is a general difficulty facing those who would like to develop a law of tort from a law of torts in that tort as a category acts as the home not just to non-contractual personal claims but also to what many would see as remedies belonging to the law of moveable property (*cf* Ch 1 § 2; Ch 13 § 8). If one person interferes with the property rights – with the possession – of another person this will give rise to a claim for damages in tort on the basis of trespass or, perhaps, conversion (Ch 13 § 8(a)).[89] Yet the law of tort, in a harmonised European private law, would have to form part of the law of obligations since it is concerned with personal actions for damages; the fact that some of these personal claims would arise as a result of rights founded upon the relationship between person and thing cuts across the symmetry of the codes. From an historical position trespass, nuisance, debt and detinue simply do not conform to the symmetry of real and personal rights.[90]

Indeed there is also a problem with regard to the Romanist distinction between public and private law (*cf* Ch 8 § 4(c)).[91] In *Roy v Kensington & Chelsea Family Practitioner Committee*[92] a doctor brought an action in debt against his family practitioner committee for work done; he based the debt claim on a breach of contract. The family practitioner committee (FPC) sought to have the claim struck out as an abuse of process on the basis that the relationship between a doctor and the FPC was a matter only of public law and that the sole remedy available to the doctor was an action for judicial review. The House of Lords refused to strike out the claim even although,

87 At p 574.

88 *Ibid.*

89 See now Torts (Interference with Goods) Act 1977.

90 Milsom, p 6.

91 On which see G Samuel, 'What is it to Have Knowledge of a European Public Law?' in de Witte & Forder (eds), *op cit*, 171.

92 [1992] 1 AC 624.

according to Lord Bridge, the relationship between the doctor and the FPC was probably not contractual. 'Nevertheless,' he continued, 'the terms which govern the obligations of the doctor on the one hand, as to the services he is to provide, and of the family practitioner committee on the other hand, as to the payments which it is required to make to the doctor, are all prescribed in the relevant legislation and it seems to me that the statutory terms are just as effective as they would be if they were contractual to confer upon the doctor an enforceable right in private law to receive the remuneration to which the terms entitle him.'[93] According to Lord Lowry the court clearly had jurisdiction to entertain the doctor's action because it was concerned with a private law right. This was a claim for an ascertained or ascertainable sum of money and the existence of any dispute as to entitlement meant that the doctor was alleging a breach of his private law rights through a failure by the committee to perform their public duty. 'Although he seeks to enforce performance of a public law duty', concluded Lord Lowry, 'his private law rights dominate the proceedings.'[94] In other words, the right to sue in debt is a private right at the level of the *actio*, but a public right at the level of *ius*.

4 HARMONISING SYMMETRIES

Admittedly, this decision in *Roy* is likely to be much less of an obstacle to harmonisation than *Lipkin Gorman* since not all the civilian systems go quite as far as France in separating public and private rights. Nevertheless, it does illustrate the two-dimensional structure of the codes. Factual disputes involve the relationship either between legal subject and legal object (rights *in rem* or, more abstractly, rights *in re*) or between legal subject and legal subject (rights *in personam*); and the idea that there might be a further dimension involving a relationship between legal subject and legal remedy (*actio*) – or, indeed, between legal object (*res*) and legal remedy – has become lost in the rigid symmetry of axiomatic propositions.

(a) Comparing symmetries

When both the law and its science are reduced to the same symbolic model there is the great danger that the model will be incapable of giving full expression to the complexity of actual social life. Indeed this may be one reason why at the end of the Middle Ages practitioners were not as keen as students to adopt the Humanist legal model.[95] The *Digest* and its glosses might be disorganised and inelegant, but the Institutes, for all its harmonised structure, lacked the detail of everyday life. The inability of legal language to represent complexity is fully recognised by the civil lawyer. Problems giving rise to *bona fides* or abuse of rights cannot adequately be captured by propositions as such and knowledge thus becomes a matter of assimilating the jurisprudence and the art of judging. Nevertheless, the great historical weight of a

93 At p 630.

94 At p 654.

95 JW Jones, *Historical Introduction to the Theory of Law* (Oxford, 1940), pp 31–32.

positivistic rule-model must never be underestimated since the notion of a code is founded upon this epistemological and ideological thesis. Every time, then, that a court resolves a litigation problem using an article of the code it is subscribing to this epistemological and ideological model which in turn reinforces the model itself. All the same, this reinforcement is, as we have seen, now being brought into question by some of the judges themselves. Law is a matter of interpreting facts via the fuzzy concepts of the code.

The lack of a completely rigorous set of symbols by which law can be dogmatically represented means that the loss of information and dimension leads directly to a loss of complexity when it comes to the interpretation of natural objects. Damage done by any 'thing' (*chose*) in the possession (*sous sa garde*) of any person will theoretically give rise to a liability to pay damages under article 1384 of the *Code civil*. Such a mentality contrasts strongly with that of the common law which refuses on the whole, as we have said, to leave the world of actual objects. One will only be liable for damage done by an escaping thing under the rule in *Rylands v Fletcher*[96] if the thing itself is analogous, directly or indirectly, to water, the object that escaped in the original precedent itself (*cf* Ch 12 § 2(a)). And even if the thing is analogous to water, the notion of 'anything likely to do mischief if it escapes' has now to be considered in the context of the real world of political, economic and social considerations. Similarly, in the tort of negligence, it is a matter of an 'incremental approach by way of analogy'.[97] Such an approach may well limit, perhaps unreasonably, the scope of both strict and fault liability in English law; but it does illustrate just how the complexity of legal knowledge is by no means reducible to a dogmatic set of symbolic propositions. No rule or proposition can adequately represent the variety of categories of factual situation that go to make up the English law of civil liability.

(b) Fuzzy and quasi-normative concepts

In a codified system the legal situation is to be found in its own abstract world.[98] The texts of the codes are, or were thought to be, like axiomatic propositions existing simply as a rigorous and interrelating system of symbolic representations.[99] In the common law, on the other hand, the rules are rarely abstract. Indeed the whole notion of precedent is as much bound up with the material facts of a case as it is with any rule or principle and consequently the role of the jurist is to reason from these facts towards a normative situation using the tools of quasi-normative concepts. These quasi-normative concepts are those which function at one and the same time in the worlds of descriptive fact and normative law.

Accordingly, to say that one person has suffered 'damage' as a result of the 'fault' of another person is a descriptive sentence in that it can be viewed as a simple statement of

96 (1866) LR 1 Ex 265; (1868) LR 3 HL 330.

97 Lord Brown-Wilkinson in *White v Jones* [1995] 2 AC 207 at 270.

98 Dubouchet, *op cit*, pp 117–30.

99 R Blanché, *Le raisonnement* (Presses Universitaires de France, 1973), pp 219–20.

fact. It is also capable of generating a legal claim in that the juxtaposition of 'fault', 'damage' and 'causation' goes far in most Western legal systems in acting as the basis for a damages claim by the victim against the person who was at fault.[100] The notion of an 'interest' is more subtle since to say that a person's interest has been invaded is quite different from saying that his rights have been interfered with (*cf* Ch 3 § 3). Nevertheless, in Western systems, an interest acts as a half-way house between the descriptive and the normative and so, for example, where one person deliberately invades the interest of another person, just as when one person intentionally causes damage to another, the law will usually think quite carefully before refusing a remedy. Equally, where one person has a right to a legal remedy he may be refused access to the court unless he also has an interest in its enforcement.[101] *Pas d'intérêt, pas d'action.* Quasi-normative concepts act, therefore, as focal points within factual situations of all legal disputes and not only in respect of the qualification and analysis of the situations (*cf* Ch 3 § 3(c)). When they are related to the institutions of legal subject (*persona*), legal object (*res*) and legal remedy (*actio*) they become the means by which one moves from the factual situation to the legal situation (*cf* Ch 2 § 5).

Similar notions can of course be found in the codes and thus quasi-normative concepts might well act as an important focal point for harmonisation. In addition there are the fuzzy concepts which Ivainer has mentioned; and these *concepts flous* could also prove an invaluable focal point for approaching the question of harmonisation. However, the symmetry of the codes imposes itself on persons and things in a way that both disciplines and simplifies the object of legal knowledge, that is to say the 'real' world as constituted by the institutions of persons (*personae*) and things (*res*) together with the quasi-normative concepts of damage, fault, control, interests and the like. No doubt common lawyers construct their 'real' worlds using the same institutions and concepts.[102] Yet in refusing to see the normative force of law in the dogmatic normativism of symbolic language, and in the power of textual interpretation (*ars hermeneutica*), they can construct the source of law beyond that of language, forcing indeed the legislature to function often at the level of images (*cf* Ch 3). In place of the concise proposition to be found in article 1384,[103] the English lawyer has statutes devoted to animals (often at the level of particular species), dwelling houses, factory equipment, aeroplanes, trains, pickets, water, gas, waste, highways and so on.[104] These categories of things are more fundamental to English law than almost any category which relates exclusively to concepts functioning as part of an abstract and hierarchical symbolic structure of relations.

Of course there are exceptions, or at least apparent exceptions; and thus one might point to the trust, to contract and to the general duty of care. Yet the cases themselves

100 See eg *Khorasandijian v Bush* [1993] QB 727.

101 *Ibid*, p 29. And see eg NCPC art 31.

102 Samuel, *Foundations*, pp 191–207.

103 '*On est responsable non seulement du dommage que l'on cause par son propre fait, mais encore de celui qui est causé par le fait des personnes dont on doit répondre, ou des choses que l'on a sous sa garde.*'

104 See generally F Rose (ed), *Statutes on Contract, Tort & Restitution* (Blackstone, 6th edn, 1995).

tell a different story. There is in truth no general duty of care, simply a list of specific duties involving specific people (accountants, solicitors, employers, manufacturers, road users) and specific things (products, references, wills, trees, walls and the like); and even the apparent certainty of contract rules may not stand the test of the specific relationship between, say, local authority and business entrepreneur.[105] The facts of 'contract' cases continually exceed the province of the law of contract and have to be re-categorised as estoppel or tort cases (*cf* Ch 8 § 6).[106]

This may look, at first sight, like the inductive method of reasoning since the mental process is, seemingly, one that goes from the particular to the general (*cf* Ch 3 § 2). But this is just to apply the rule-model to a process that is not exclusively based on symbolic knowledge.[107] Indeed this aspect of legal reasoning is incorporated into the common law notion of *ratio decidendi* itself. In order to be binding the material facts of a precedent must be analogous to the facts of a litigation problem in hand; and so to arrive at the conclusion that 'for the purpose of the rule in *Rylands v Fletcher* electricity is analogous to water' or 'electricity is within the rule in *Rylands v Fletcher*'[108] one is reaching a conclusion by a reasoning process that involves the use of non-symbolic knowledge. For there is no rule as such that forces a judge to conclude that electricity is analogous to water. It is simply dictated by considerations outside the rule of *Rylands v Fletcher* itself and while some, perhaps many, of these considerations might be reducible to the symbolic language of propositional rules (*cf* Ch 12 § 2(a)), the actual process itself of comparing the image of water and electricity is not one that is reached through the manipulation of propositional symbols. It is a form of reasoning consisting 'not of symbols but of images, of emotional states, of conceptual structures, of prototype models often untranslatable by a linguistic expression'.[109] And when a translation into rules is possible, 'it is accompanied by a considerable loss of information, of dimension.'[110]

(c) The limits of two-dimensional symmetry

English law, in contrast, can construct at one and the same time various symmetries within a single factual situation, as both *Lipkin Gorman* and *Roy* illustrate. This, in turn, gives rise to a much richer reasoning structure since one can move from legal object (*res*) to legal action (*actio*) in order to construct an *in re* legal relation, while at the same time establishing, in another dimension so to speak, a quite separate legal relation between legal subject, or between the State, and another legal subject (*cf* Ch 3 § 2). Thus, in *Roy* the judges were able, at one and the same time, to talk about a *ius*

105 See generally Samuel, *Sourcebook*.

106 See eg *Crabb v Arun* [1976] Ch 179.

107 See generally G Samuel, '*Entre les mots et les choses: les raisonnements et les méthodes en tant que sources du droit*' [1995] RIDC 509.

108 Lord Simon in *FA & AB Ltd v Lupton* [1972] AC 634, 659.

109 J Delacour, *Le cerveau et l'esprit* (PUF, 1995), p 35.

110 *Ibid*, pp 35–36.

publicum relationship between plaintiff and defendant and a *ius privatum* bond between plaintiff and debt action. Equally, this third dimension allows one to comprehend the tracing action (*cf* Ch 4 § 5(d)). The relationship between *actio* and *res* (enrichment in defendant's patrimony) is proprietary in that it is founded upon a relationship in a thing or an abstract conception of it; the relationship between plaintiff and defendant is personal as between themselves. Not all judges see this and thus there is now a tendency to deny that tracing is an *actio in rem*. Tracing is a 'process' rather than a remedy or a substantive right.[111] Now the civilian jurist may not approve of Lord Goff's legal science. Yet from a constructivist reasoning and epistemological point of view it is perfectly rational: Lord Goff could move from the notion of a wrong (law of obligations) to a notion of a right (law of property) which, in turn, allowed him to escape from the logic of the implied contract theory of unjust enrichment debt claims.

(d) Three-dimensional symmetry

In itself the difference of symmetries between the common law and civil law models may seem relatively minor. Indeed the possibility of a model of legal relations between *persona*, *res* and *actio* may appear as a hopeful epistemological structure in that it can be used to make sense, within (or at least close to) the facts, of both the codes and the common law (*cf* Chs 1, 3).[112] Yet the construction of solutions from within the facts themselves through the manipulation of the three institutions (*persona*, *res* and *actio*) is a process that turns out to be rather different from the application of a symmetrical structure fixed relatively rigidly to institutions that form part of a symbolic, rather than non-symbolic, epistemological language. The range of combinational possibilities can turn out to be much greater when one is not constrained by a symbolic language itself constrained by a system whose fixed symmetry between elements – *persona* and *res* (legal subject and legal object) – has itself been reduced to dogmatic linguistic propositions (even accepting that this language contains many fuzzy concepts such as good faith).

The key to cases such as *Lipkin Gorman*, *Roy* and even *Esso* (Ch 1 § 7(a)) is, arguably, to be found in the idea that they involve a translation of the facts into a three- rather than a two-dimensional world.[113] That is to say, they transgress the two-dimensional symmetry by constructing at one and the same time relations between person and person, person and thing and person and action. A claim to trace money, for example, is founded upon a *vinculum iuris* both between *persona* and *persona* and between *persona* and *res*; it is a personal and a proprietary action. This should not surprise given that the real social world functions in three dimensions: facts are too complex by definition to be reduced to a two-dimensional dogmatic proposition. Accordingly, the moment one moves from the idea of a two-dimensional model to one that functions in three dimensions, one is entering a world where the complexities

111 *Boscawen v Bajwa* [1995] 4 All ER 769, 776 *per* Millett LJ.

112 See generally Samuel, *Foundations*, pp 155–294.

113 G Samuel, 'Epistemology and Legal Institutions' [1991] IJSL 309.

of the social facts can be represented with a much greater degree of precision. There is less of a loss of information than is the case with a two-dimensional model. Moreover, a three-dimensional model allows for the incorporation of the legal action, an institution removed from the civilian two-dimensional model when the law of actions was relegated to codes of procedure during the deductive stage of legal science, into the legal plan. This third institution was the means by which quasi-normative concepts such as 'interest' were introduced into the analysis in cases like *Miller v Jackson* (Ch 4 § 1(b)) and the Court of Appeal decision in *Beswick* (Ch 3 § 3(c)). Needless to say, these concepts were instrumental to the solutions arrived at. In a two-dimensional world the various connections flowing between institutions can easily eclipse each other with the result that rights become confused with interests and interests with rights. In a three-dimensional model the structural basis of certain concepts becomes very much clearer.

The problem with the linguistic proposition is that it is not in itself a cognitive medium capable of envisaging the three-dimensional structural possibilities that can exist at one and the same time between all the legal institution possibilities in a single set of facts. Language can, *ex post facto*, describe certain normative possibilities arising out of the institutional image, but it cannot determine the shape of the image. Thus, even when a proposition uses *un concept flou* such as good faith it cannot capture the full complexity of facts since such a term is nothing more than a 'fuzzy' concept blurring rather than capturing complexity. Complex facts require structural models of elements and relations to capture and to explain their patterns and it is these patterns – these symmetries – which determine the normative situation. *Esso* (Ch 1 § 7(a)) is not about rules; it is about structural relations between persons (oil company, captain, crew, local government body), things (ship, oil, sandbank, beach) and actions (trespass, nuisance, pleadings) which determine what ought to be the solution. Put another way, the epistemologist must distinguish between a rule-governed and a rule-described cognitive model of legal reasoning.[114]

(e) Symmetry and mental image

Does this institutional flexibility mean that there is little science in the common law? Certainly, from a dogmatic point of view the common law does not function with a model where certain possibilities are, as a matter of rationality, closed off from consideration. Thus, if the law of contract is unsuitable, the English lawyer can always turn to tort; if property rules prove too uncompromising, one can always try equity (see eg Ch 4 § 1(b)). If rights prove too rigid, there is the law of remedies (*cf* Ch 4).[115] The endless series of combinational possibilities between persons, things and actions is what makes the grasping of English law as a set of scientifically rationalised norms almost impossible. It is a seamless web which is deliberately elusive in that the moment one tries to construct a scientific image around, say, person and person, equity or the

114 W Bechtel & A Abrahamsen, *Connections and the Human Mind: An Introduction to Parallel Processing in Networks* (Blackwell, 1991), pp 227–28.

115 See eg *Miller v Jackson* [1977] QB 966.

law of actions intervenes with an alternative institutional image framed around the relationship between person and thing or between person and remedy.

Take once again the case of *Esso v Southport* (Ch 1 § 7(a)). As far as the trial judge was concerned this was a problem involving an obligational relationship between one person (local authority) and another person (captain of ship). In order for there to be liability it was thus essential, in the absence of a contract, to establish fault. The image was analogous to a traffic accident. In the Court of Appeal, however, a quite different image was constructed out of the relationship between person (Esso) and thing (ship); the image was closer to the one which underpins article 1384 of the *Code civil*. A similar change of image is to be found in *Miller v Jackson* (Ch 4 § 1(b)) where the majority of the Court of Appeal, in contrast to the dissenting judge, focused upon the relationship between person and *actio* (injunction) rather than upon the unreasonable use of land by the defendant. Equity invited the observer to view the problem from the position of a remedy. In *Beswick v Beswick* (Ch 5 § 4(f)) Mrs Beswick gave no consideration for the nephew's promise to pay her a weekly annuity after the death of her husband; yet the nephew's image of his common law rights and duties overlooked the institutional possibilities surrounding the equitable remedy of specific performance, an institution capable of attracting its own particular rules.[116] Indeed, in the Court of Appeal,[117] the promise to pay a debt was transformed, by institutional rearrangement, from a personal obligation into a real right, thus allowing, according to the majority of the court (who were overturned on this point by the House of Lords), Mrs Beswick to sue the nephew in her own personal capacity. At one level the jurist is referring to rules, that is to say, to propositional knowledge which can be seen as part of a symbolic system of representation (the rules dealing with privity of contract and its exceptions). But at another level these rules have grown out of an institutional image created, and rearranged, by the interrelation of these elements. The symbolic (rules) can be produced from the non-symbolic (institutional image).[118]

The common law, then, functions by constructing its solutions within the factual situation itself and not outside it. It rarely thinks in terms of models of rules, each bound one with another via the symmetry of the institutional system of relations between the abstracted elements of *persona*, *ręs* and *actio*. Instead it uses a model of institutions which functions within the facts and attaches to subjects and objects as individualised persons and things so as to organise a structure to conform with particular legal possibilities. Of course there is abstraction. But the level of abstraction becomes in itself part of legal knowledge (*cf* Ch 3 § 1). Thus, in 1936 it was not yet clear if the rule in *Donoghue v Stevenson*,[119] concerning injury done by a defective bottle of ginger-beer, would apply to a defective pair of underpants and thus counsel for the defendants in *Grant v Australian Knitting Mills Ltd*[120] argued, admittedly, it

116 *Beswick v Beswick* [1968] AC 58.

117 [1966] Ch 538. And see Samuel, *Foundations*, pp 234–35.

118 Delacour, *op cit*, p 121.

119 [1932] AC 562.

120 [1936] AC 58.

would seem rather weakly, that a rule fashioned for an article of drink should not apply to an article of clothing since they were quite different objects. In holding that the rule was applicable, the Privy Council was confirming that, as far as the facts of *Donoghue* and *Grant* were concerned, the *res* to which the rule attached was a 'product'. Other examples could be given. In fact, in the recent decision of *White v Jones*[121] the difference of opinion in the House of Lords between the majority and dissenting minority focused on the question of whether a duty was something that fixed to a particular factual class of persons (solicitors) or to an abstract structure of relations which transcended the facts.[122]

(f) Harmonising legal science and the object of legal science

Yet the point that needs to be stressed for the purposes of harmonisation is that the difference between law as symbolic knowledge and law as non-symbolic knowledge, the difference between *les mots et les choses*, raises a question not just about the mentality and methodology of reasoning but also about legal communication and legal education. How is complexity to be communicated? Can it be communicated with ease only at the cost of a significant loss of complexity?

The codes, it must be said, are easily assimilated by the mind and thus are easily communicated. Indeed one might say that the history of the civil law, from an epistemological viewpoint, is one of 'the invention of symbols as particularly efficient means of communication through their qualities of "simplicity" and "constructibility".'[123] And this is an aspect of the history of legal science that must never be underestimated. As Sir Henry Maine and others urged during the reforming era of English law, a code 'would give the law what it most lacked – simplicity, symmetry, intelligibility, and logical coherence'.[124] But the price of this symbolic (propositional knowledge) dogmatism is that the object of legal science 'is simultaneously and indissolubly created and expressed, posed and known; the same movement which delivers law to society to regulate it, gives law to its own science to be the means by which it is to be known'.[125] The result is that law and legal knowledge become one and the same. Or, from the position of a *scientia iuris*, the law becomes the object of its own science with the result that the institutional system of the codes (persons, things and obligations, actions having been relegated to codes of

121 [1995] 2 AC 207.

122 'If the claim in the present case is sound ... it must be sound in every instance of the general situation which I have already identified, namely, where A promises B for reward to perform a service for B, in circumstances where it is foreseeable that performance of the service with care will cause C to receive a benefit, and that failure to perform it may cause C not to receive that benefit' *per* Lord Mustill in *White v Jones* [1995] 2 AC 207 at 291. Compare this view with that of Lord Brown-Wilkinson at p 270: 'although the present case is not directly covered by the decided cases, it is legitimate to extend the law to the limited extent proposed using the incremental approach by way of analogy.'

123 Delacour, *op cit*, pp 61–62.

124 Jones, *op cit*, p 59.

125 Atias, *op cit*, p 116.

procedure) becomes both a part of the law (real and personal rights) and a scheme by which one analyses (legal science) and has knowledge (legal epistemology) of law.

Yet this may be the key to harmonisation. For if there is an institutional 'deep structure', consisting of elements (persons, things and actions) and relationships (ownership, possession, obligation), beyond the simplicity of rules and the complexity of facts, then there is an epistemological possibility for the post-axiomatic stage. One can, following Zimmermann, return to Roman law in order to discover within the *Institutes* and the *Digest* the construction of a legal world at one and the same time within and without the facts (*cf* Ch 1 § 1(c)). The institutions of *persona* (legal subjects), *res* (legal objects) and *actiones* (legal remedies) are both factual structures within a social world of physical persons, physical objects and physical courts and conceptual elements within an abstract science of law (Institutes, codes).[126] One can also avoid the *décalage* that Legrand has observed between law and fact, although this is not to guarantee that the legal model will not continue to be its own 'reality' more 'real' than the social facts themselves.[127] The institutional model becomes both the science (law) and the object of science (fact); it is the ontological (what exists) assumption upon which all legal discourse is founded. Perhaps, in addition, such an institutional model will be capable of expressing the value images so important to Bell: certainly, the class interests of consumers and the Republican values of France are capable of being expressed in terms of institutional structures (the personality and standing of consumer groups, the equality of relationships between citizen and state), just as the individualist ideology of the United Kingdom is given equal expression by the same, if differently constituted, institutional model.[128] Persons, things and actions are institutions because they act as a structure capable of envisaging at one and the same time a system of legal and a system of social relations.[129] Indeed so powerful is the structure that it has a relevance beyond law.[130]

5 CONCLUDING REMARKS

Despite the elegant and powerful analysis of a writer like Pierre Legrand, it would probably be unrealistic to insist that the harmonisation of private law in Europe will ultimately prove an impossible task, if only because one legal tradition will, in the end, come to dominate the other. It is evident from the preceding chapters that the English law of contract, tort and restitution can, at one level, be forced into a code-like framework even if whole sections remain squeezed out beyond the perimeters. And Millett LJ's re-interpretation of tracing (Ch 11 § 4(b)), aided and abetted by a range of academics, shows how the process is underway.

Nevertheless, the whole programme of harmonisation raises a central question about what it is to have legal knowledge – what, in other words, is being harmonised?

126 Samuel, *Foundations*, pp 171–90.

127 Legrand, *Comparatists-at-Law*, *op cit*, p 28; *cf* Samuel, *Foundations*, p 171.

128 See Samuel, *Foundations*, pp 76–79.

129 *Ibid*, p 173.

130 *Ibid*, pp 173–75.

– and this question, in turn, leads to questions about how such knowledge is represented and how it is used to achieve practical results. These questions, it must be said, are now becoming the focus of the attention of a number of writers[131] and, indeed, comparative lawyers have long struggled with the apparently fundamental differences of 'spirit' or 'style' between the civil law and common law traditions.[132] All the same, the great majority of jurists have never disputed the epistemological thesis that the object of legal science is a body of propositional knowledge (rules, principles or norms) and this rule-model has so dominated legal thought that not only are there few alternatives models but many comparative lawyers have assumed that harmonisation of law must be possible since legal science dictates that all legal systems share the same object of science. Legal harmonisation is simply a matter of the convergence of propositional knowledge.[133]

This view of legal knowledge is now being seriously challenged by AI and cognitive science research. There is today a body of opinion that the rule-model is incapable of adequately acting as a means of representing legal knowledge in its full complexity since rules and principles cannot, by themselves, solve actual cases in anything but a rather brittle and simplistic way. Or, put another way, between the rule and the solution resulting from its application there is always a hiatus.[134] Like all reductionist models, the rule thesis fails to encapsulate legal knowledge in all its dimensions[135] since the translation of *ars judicandi*, including its institutional context, into linguistic propositions results in a significant loss of information.[136] Accordingly, if harmonisation of the law of obligations takes place on the basis of the rule-model (law as propositional knowledge), what is being harmonised are symbolic representations that do not actually represent the object of the representation. Indeed a system like the common law tradition that thinks in images[137] is a mental process that, almost by definition, is one that does not think in terms of linguistic rules.[138] Consequently, those who try to redefine the common law by means of the rule-model are simply undertaking an ideological as opposed to epistemological exercise.[139] It may well be, then, that the rule-model is a major obstacle to harmonisation in that it implies that *ars judicandi* and *ars hermeneutica*, at least when bound together by a *scientia iuris*, are largely the same mental processes.

From the point of view of Europe, the question that now needs to be asked is how this epistemological crisis impacts upon ideas such as a new *ius commune*. Such a

131 See eg Atias, *op cit*; Legrand, *Comparatists-at-Law*, *op cit*.

132 See eg F Pringsheim, *op cit*, Zweigert & Kötz, pp 63–75.

133 See eg W Mincke, 'Practical and propositional knowledge as the basis of European legal education', in de Witte & Forder, *op cit*, 285.

134 M van de Kerchove & F Ost, *Le droit ou les paradoxes du jeu* (PUF, 1992), p 242, quoting P Ricoeur, *Philosophie de la volonté*, *tome* 1 (Aubier, 1949), p 165.

135 See eg Atias, *op cit*, pp 5–13.

136 Delacour, *op cit*, pp 34–35.

137 Samuel, *Foundations*, pp 147–49; Zweigert & Kötz, p 70.

138 Delacour, *op cit*, pp 34–42.

139 See on this point Legrand, *Comparatists-at-Law*, *op cit*, pp 3–4.

question requires, perhaps, not just a reappraisal of the history of legal thought itself – including a history of techniques and reasoning methods – but a reassessment of the methodological issues in the light of contemporary epistemological models (*cf* Chs 1, 3). The present book has attempted to tackle, in the context of a comparative-orientated analysis, all of these aspects. Thus, although it has impliedly insisted that a law of obligations is at least a working hypothesis, it has not attempted to suggest that the law of remedies can somehow be squeezed into the framework of the codes, even if it has on occasions used the language and structures of the *Institutes* of Gaius.

In addition it has attempted to connect with theory.[140] In this respect the aim has been to raise the level of comparison out of a 'mundane existence and to confront the enigmatical ... in other legal cultures'.[141] Epistemology might well be an alien discourse to the practitioner and law student. Yet arguably it is the key to any harmonisation project with respect to the law of obligations and thus 'the comparatist must engage in the interpretative act that will allow her, through her intrusion into alien forms of discourse, to decipher and explicate a range of phenomena that appear inhospitable to interpretation'.[142] An important aim of this work has, therefore, been to connect an introductory survey of the English law of remedies and obligations with aspects of legal method, legal history, legal theory and comparative law in order to take the investigator of these aspects of positive law into areas 'beyond the petrified and tyrannical form'.[143]

However, this present work does not wish to end on a (European) pessimistic note. Harmonisation of the law of obligations, together with the law of remedies, might be a possibility within the context of a new scientific stage provided that such a stage is one where all traditions accept that an epistemological obstacle needs to be overcome. Imperialism by one kind of (axiomatic-orientated) legal science or one kind of empirical (descriptive and inductive) methodology would, as Legrand has suggested, be unfortunate if not disastrous. Perhaps the starting point for a (scientific) revolution to overcome this obstacle will be found in the notion of a model as suggested in this chapter. Not an axiomatic or even argumentation model divorced from the construction and qualification of facts. But a (three-dimensional) model which functions at one and the same time in the science (law) and object of science (fact). But such a proposed model is not a theory as such since a theory is all-embracing in the way it fits both fact and law into a system of concepts.[144] A model is a half-way house between fact and theory. It is a means by which one can begin to think about complex phenomena in a manner that reveals hidden internal relationships and their connections with exterior values. European legal systems may not be converging, but that is all the more reason why one has need of a model.

140 Although building on existing published work: see generally Samuel, *Foundations*.

141 Legrand, *Comparatists-at-Law*, *op cit*, p 47.

142 *Ibid*.

143 *Ibid*.

144 G-G Granger, *La science et les sciences* (PUF, 2nd edn, 1995), p 111.

INDEX